MOON

D0924248

VIETNAM

DANA FILEK-GIBSON

Contents

DISCOVER
Vietnam

Vietnam grabs hold of you from the moment you step off the plane. Your senses are assaulted by the blare of bus horns and revving motorbikes, the scent of grilled meat wafting from street carts, and the influx of people, always moving, always with purpose. This is a country on the rise.

More than 40 years after a devastating war, Vietnam is in the midst of a comeback, rising in a cacophonous clash of old and new, traditional and modern. You're just as likely to see a luxury car roll past a rusty one-speed bike as you are to find the upper echelon of society eating from plastic tables on the street. Amid the bustling street stalls and frenzied markets, you'll find a thriving country.

Beyond its cities, another Vietnam awaits. Venture to the countryside or along the coast and find tranquil beaches and sleepy farming towns, never-ending rice paddies, and the eerie labyrinth of limestone islands.

Vietnam grasps your full attention. With open arms, an open mind, and a sense of adventure, you'll find yourself embracing it right back.

Clockwise from top left: a watchful four-headed statue; fishing boat; woman paddling a wooden sampan; terraced rice paddies of Vietnam's northwest; masks at Hanoi's Temple of Literature; view from Sam Mountain's Cave Pagoda.

12 TOP EXPERIENCES

1 **Cruising Ha Long Bay:** Take an **overnight cruise** (page 110) of the renowned bay to see soaring limestone karsts and impressive grottoes. Also consider **Bai Tu Long** (page 116) and **Lan Ha Bays** (page 122), which give their more famous counterpart a run for its money.

2 **Saigon's Nightlife:** The sun may go down, but Saigon stays up until the wee hours. Whether you want to hang out at bars, hit the clubs, or catch a live show, the southern hub has something for everyone (page 319).

3 **Visiting Vietnam's Ethnic Minority Villages:** Vietnam is home to 54 different ethnic groups, each with its own traditions, language, and culture. Learn more about these communities by heading inland to destinations like **Mai Chau** (page 86) and **Sapa** (page 93).

4 **Vietnamese Cuisine:** Explore Vietnam's culinary offerings, from ubiquitous, renowned standards like **pho** and **banh mi** to **regional specialties** (pages 170, 220, and 403) and **stellar street food** (page 336).

<<<

5 **Motorbiking:** Whether you're zipping around town on the back of a motorbike or heading out on a road trip like the **Northwest Loop** (page 100), travel on two wheels is an integral part of life in Vietnam. Rent your own or enlist the services of an **Easy Rider guide** (page 275).

>>>

6 **Hoi An:** A microcosm of **history, culture,** and **cuisine,** this charming former port town seduces scores of travelers every year with its traditional architecture, unique local dishes, and nearby **beach,** not to mention the best **shopping** in the country (page 201).

>>>

7 **Hanoi's Fresh Beer Scene:** On any given night, you can pull up a plastic chair streetside and enjoy the short shelf life of *bia hoi*—beer made without preservatives (page 56).

8 **Beaches:** With over 2,000 miles of coastline, Vietnam has some glorious beach getaways, from the island shores of **Con Dao** and **Phu Quoc** to mainland spots like popular **Nha Trang** and **Mui Ne** and up-and-coming **Quy Nhon** (page 26).

>>>

9 **Caving in Phong Nha-Ke Bang National Park:** If you can only visit one of Vietnam's national parks, make it this one (page 176). Its subterranean wonders are unique.

10 **Touring the Mekong Delta:** Tap into southwestern Vietnam's easygoing riverine culture by exploring **floating markets, flooded forests,** and **fruit orchards** (page 31).

11 **Imperial History in Hue:** The legacy of Vietnam's last imperial dynasty lives on in its former capital, where you can wander the **Imperial City** (page 156), pay your respects at the **royal tombs** of the Nguyen emperors (page 159), and explore the forgotten grounds of **Ho Quyen Royal Arena** (page 163).

>>>

12 **Excursion to Angkor Wat:** Hop over the border to explore one of the most famous religious sites in the world and its magnificent temples (page 372).

Planning Your Trip

Where to Go

Hanoi

Regal and refined, Vietnam's 1,000-year-old capital offers a hodgepodge of historical sights from across centuries, not to mention top-notch shopping in the vibrant **Old Quarter,** where you'll find plenty of mouthwatering cuisine alongside some of the city's best local color. Circle by **Hoan Kiem Lake,** the elegant, aging **Temple of Literature,** and somber **Ho Chi Minh Mausoleum** for the city's best sights, and get an introduction to Vietnam's diverse local cultures at the excellent **Vietnam Museum of Ethnology.**

Ha Long Bay and the Northern Coast

The mysterious, mesmerizing waters of the north coast form a seascape like no other, draped in lush mist-covered rainforest and dotted with gravity-defying limestone islands. Kick back on an **overnight cruise** around Ha Long, cycle your way across **Cat Ba Island,** climb the jagged cliffs of **Lan Ha Bay,** or admire these labyrinthine landscapes from a **kayak.** Even inland, the karsts of **Ninh Binh** provide the perfect backdrop for a peaceful rowboat ride through rice paddies and beautiful northern countryside.

The Central Provinces

Replete with crumbling imperial tombs, trendy modern shops, sleek contemporary skyscrapers, and the riotous colors of ancient pagodas, the central provinces are a jam-packed juxtaposition of old and new. **Hue,** former capital of the Nguyen dynasty, boasts impressive royal relics, while everything from winding, picturesque **Hai Van Pass** to the jaw-dropping **Phong Nha-Ke Bang**

mosaic mural in Hanoi

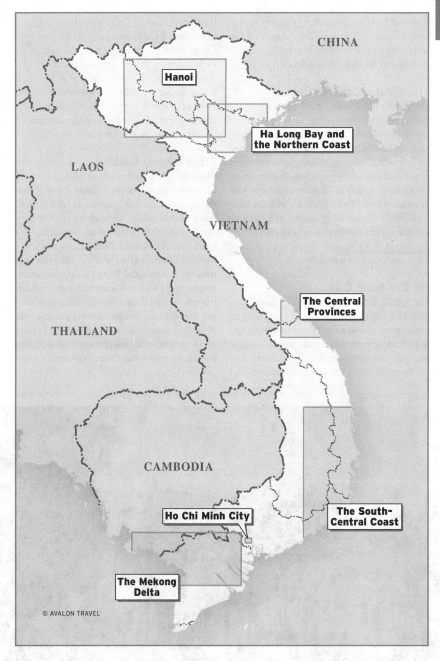

CHINA

Hanoi

Ha Long Bay and
the Northern Coast

LAOS

VIETNAM

The Central
Provinces

THAILAND

CAMBODIA

Ho Chi Minh City

The South-
Central Coast

The Mekong
Delta

© AVALON TRAVEL

National Park is within striking distance. Farther south is **Danang,** Vietnam's latest ultracool urban center, and the charming town of **Hoi An,** an oasis for shoppers, shutterbugs, and foodies.

The South-Central Coast

The south-central coast has all but cornered the market on beach destinations in Vietnam. From hip and happening **Nha Trang Beach,** brimming with nonstop energy and aquatic activities, to the tranquil shores of **Mui Ne,** a resort enclave to the south, the belly of the *S* is where travelers flock for a few days of R&R between more hectic destinations. Water sports are popular here, with plenty of snorkeling, diving, and kitesurfing. **Dalat,** the anomaly of the region, boasts a mixture of cool mountain air, rural charm, and off-the-beaten-path adventure.

Ho Chi Minh City

The high-octane commercial hub of the country, Ho Chi Minh City (known to locals as Saigon) buzzes from morning until night, caught up in a whirlwind of motorbikes, street vendors, megamarkets, and miniature local shops. The colossal **Reunification Palace** and **Notre Dame Cathedral** break up the chaotic clutter of downtown District 1. **Chinatown** kicks the pace up a notch, its 21st-century residents careening past hazy, incense-filled ancient pagodas and ramshackle houses. Hop on the back of a *xe om* and breeze through local traffic, enjoy an ice-cold *ca phe bet* (sidewalk coffee) in 30-4 Park, or dine at any one of the city's thousands of **street stalls** for the best cuisine the country has to offer.

The Mekong Delta

The nine spidery veins of the mighty Mekong branch out across western Vietnam, creating a bizarre fusion of water and land where markets float, boats become houses, and narrow winding tributaries wend through lush **fruit orchards.** The area's leisurely laid-back attitude captivates many travelers seeking a glimpse of local life. Navigate the early-morning **Cai Rang Floating Market,** overnight with a local family on lush **An Binh Island,** tour the Khmer pagodas of sleepy, seductive **Tra Vinh,** or step into the storybook setting of **Sa Dec.** Angkor-bound travelers can explore the riverine sights of **Chau Doc,** while beachgoers should cast off for **Phu Quoc,** Vietnam's fastest-growing island destination.

Notre Dame Cathedral

bicycle in Hoi An's old town

incense drying roadside near Hue

Know Before You Go

High and Low Seasons

Vietnam's weather changes considerably from north to south. The best months for exploring Vietnam are **September** and **October,** just as rainy season comes to a close in the south but before winter has settled over northern Vietnam, or **April** and **May,** when the country's northern destinations have thawed and rain has yet to reach the south. **High season** runs outside both these times, with visitor numbers peaking **November-March.** Things get especially busy over Christmas in December and **Tet** (Vietnamese Lunar New Year) in January or February. While this is a holiday of fascinating local traditions, it makes for a poor visit, as the entire country shuts down for weeks before and after. Those businesses that remain open often hike their prices double or triple, and transportation is unreliable. While fewer foreigners travel during the summer months, **July** and **August** see droves of domestic holidaymakers, who flock to hot spots like Ha Long Bay and Nha Trang.

If you're sticking to the north, the best months are **September-October** or **April-June,** when you'll encounter warm temperatures and plenty of sunshine, while high season tends to be chilly and perpetually plagued by mist. The light fog that sits atop everything north of Hue can be beautiful, provided you don't arrive expecting sunny days. Down south, cooler temperatures prevail **November-March,** but the build-up to rainy season begins shortly thereafter, bringing temperatures up to 38°C with high humidity before the downpours start in mid- to late May. Though travelers have to plan around the afternoon showers, rainfall between May and September is predictable, only becoming unpredictable at the end of the season in October.

on the Mekong Delta

Passports and Visas

Visitors are required to secure a **tourist visa** prior to arrival in Vietnam. This can be arranged up to six months before your trip. For most international travelers, visas are available in one- and three-month increments with both single-and multiple-entry options. U.S. travelers have additional six-month and yearlong tourist visa options.

Travelers entering Vietnam over land must visit an embassy or consulate to prepare their visa ahead of time. Air travelers have the additional option of applying for an e-visa, a significantly more cost-effective route, though this is only available to those arriving at one of Vietnam's three major airports: **Tan Son Nhat** in Ho Chi Minh City, **Noi Bai** in Hanoi, or **Danang International Airport.** Although e-visa services are not advertised by the Vietnamese government, it is a legitimate option, provided you arrange your documents through a reliable company. International air travelers must have a passport with at least six months' validity at time of travel.

Vaccinations

While there are **no required vaccinations** for Vietnam, the Centers for Disease Control recommend that travelers vaccinate against **hepatitis A** and **typhoid** prior to visiting in order to prevent food-borne illness. Additional preventative measures, such as the **rabies vaccine,** are suggested for cyclists and those who may come into contact with animals.

Though **malaria** does exist in Vietnam, its prevalence is low, with only rare incidences in the Mekong Delta. Most travelers opt to use insect repellent and cover up at dawn and dusk.

Transportation

Most travelers arrive at either **Tan Son Nhat International Airport** in Ho Chi Minh City or **Noi Bai International Airport** in Hanoi and set off from there. **Public transportation** is easily accessible, from planes and trains to buses and boats. For shorter journeys, hitting the road is the cheapest option; for long-distance trips—from Hanoi to the central provinces, for example, or the central provinces down to Nha Trang—you're better off in the air or on the rails. **Budget** airlines like Jetstar and VietJet fly to a number of domestic destinations, while **overnight trains** run the spectrum from cheap hard-seat cars to air-conditioned sleeper berths.

Vietnam often convinces long-term travelers to buy a **motorbike,** driving the length of the country and then selling it at the end of their journey. This is the **most independent** option and affords you the freedom to explore. Outside of major coastal cities you'll be hard-pressed to find any English speakers or Western amenities, so a **phrasebook** and a good **map** will come in handy. **Cars** can be rented here, but, due to driving regulations, it is required that you have a **Vietnamese driver.**

What to Pack

Most Western amenities are available in Vietnam, though some are more affordable and accessible than others. **Sunscreen,** for instance, is available in many coastal destinations, though it can be tricky to find and is always more expensive. It's best to bring your own from home. Other items, like **contact lens solution** and **tampons,** can be difficult to come by.

Vietnam tends to be **more formal** than the United States. In rural areas and outside of major hubs like Ho Chi Minh City and Hanoi, local women often dress more conservatively than their Western counterparts, opting for long pants and covered shoulders. Many Vietnamese women in the city have adopted a Western approach to fashion. You can get away with shorts, T-shirts, and tank tops in most tourist destinations. When visiting pagodas or sights of national importance, it's important for both men and women to opt for **conservative clothing,** wearing **long pants** and **shoulders covered,** as this is considered a sign of respect.

a girl bicycling in Hue

The Best of Vietnam: Down the Dragon's Spine

While Vietnam is, at points, no wider than 48 kilometers across, the distance from the northern border down to the deep south is on par with a drive from Boston to Miami, and on roads far more congested and much less well maintained. This itinerary describes a brisk two-week trip, covering the full length of Vietnam's coast, with a few detours to the interior. For a more relaxed pace, extend your trip to three weeks and linger in the places you like best.

Those with less than two weeks to spare will be hard-pressed to cover the entire country in such a short span of time. Focusing on a specific region, however, can allow you to make the most of your trip to Vietnam. Areas like Hanoi and surrounding regions, like the northern coast or central provinces, are your best bet as you'll be able to pack in a plethora of history, culture, food, and outdoor activities. Travelers with only a handful of days to spare should focus on Hanoi and

nearby destinations like Sapa and Ha Long Bay, while those with a week can probably tack on a trip to Hoi An as well; you might follow along the lines of this itinerary up to Day 7.

Hanoi

Spend a weekend in the capital city, focusing on the hectic, narrow alleys of the Old Quarter.

DAY 1

Touch down at **Hanoi's** Noi Bai International Airport and head toward the city. Dive right into the action with a cyclo ride around the **Old Quarter,** taking in its frenetic pace from the safety of your seat. Stroll around the placid **Hoan Kiem Lake** to see where locals hang out and catch a glimpse of **Turtle Tower** and the ornate **Ngoc Son Temple.** You can grab lunch in the Old Quarter or head to the clutch of cafés and restaurants around **St. Joseph's Cathedral**

A tourist cycles past Hoi An's vibrant Hainan Assembly Hall.

before charting a course south to **Hoa Lo Prison** and the **Vietnamese Women's Museum.**

Wind down the day on the streets of the chic **French Quarter,** either atop the **Press Club** terrace or at the roadside **Tadioto.** In the evening, grab dinner at **Ngon** before catching a **water puppet** or *ca tru* (ancient chamber music) show.

DAY 2

Rise early for a morning bowl of *pho,* Hanoi's favorite breakfast food, before heading off to Ba Dinh Square to line up for a visit at **Ho Chi Minh Mausoleum.** Once you've paid your respects, swing by Uncle Ho's famed **stilt house** or head to the nearby **One Pillar Pagoda** for a different era of Hanoian history. From there, the **Military History Museum,** flanked by the **Flag Tower** and **Lenin Park,** is just a short walk away.

In keeping with the Communist spirit, stop for coffee at **Cong Caphe** or head straight down to **KOTO** for lunch. Spend the afternoon getting to know Hanoi's **Temple of Literature** before wandering back toward the Old Quarter. Once traffic picks up and rush hour is in full swing, head for some *bia hoi* (freshly brewed light beer) and a night on the town.

Ha Long Bay Cruise
DAYS 3-4

Set off early for **Ha Long Bay** on a two-day, one-night cruise. It's a four-hour drive to the docks; you'll have a chance to stop for lunch before leaving shore. While itineraries vary from company to company, you can kick back, take in the scenery from your sun deck, and explore a cave or two.

Provided the skies are clear, a sunrise on Ha Long Bay is worth waking up for. Enjoy breakfast on the boat and another day of guided activity, which usually includes a cruise by some of the bay's more famous landscapes, like **Incense Burner** and **Ga Choi,** as well as kayaking.

Your boat will dock back at Ha Long City around noon and from there it's a four-hour drive back to Hanoi. After you return, either hop on an overnight train to **Danang** or fly there via one of

the country's budget airlines. Both are roughly the same cost. The train departs in the evening, while flyers have the choice of going straight to the airport or spending another night in Hanoi and heading out first thing the following day.

Alternate Option: North to Mountainous Sapa

If you're not one for the water, leave Hanoi for Sapa, where you can opt to trek through Vietnam's **northern mountains,** visiting **remote villages.**

DAYS 3-4

Catch an overnight train from Hanoi and head to **Sapa.** You'll arrive in Lao Cai in the morning and take a quick minibus ride to the small mountain town. Take the rest of the morning to explore the town, passing by its **museum** and shopping along **Cau May** street. In the afternoon, head to **Cat Cat Village** or hire a motorbike to visit the nearby **waterfalls** and **Tram Ton Pass.** You'll also want to arrange a **trek** for the following day, either through a local guide or one of the tour outfits in town.

Rise early and set off with your local guide to one of the nearby **ethnic minority villages** and get a more intimate look at the varied cultures of Vietnam. The trek takes a few hours, including lunch. In the afternoon, return to Sapa for a bit of R&R and last-minute shopping before heading back to Hanoi via overnight train or bus. Plan for a flight to Danang the following morning.

Hoi An

Hoi An draws visitors with its photogenic **wooden houses,** nearby **beaches,** and **tailor-made clothing.**

DAY 5

Train travelers from Hanoi will arrive in **Danang** by late morning; those traveling via air will arrive around noon. Hop in a cab bound for **Hoi An,** your base for the next three days. Spend an easy day exploring the **old town,** from its charming local market to the famous **Japanese Covered**

Best Beaches

With kilometers of stunning coastline, it's no surprise that Vietnam offers something for everyone in the realm of beach destinations. From mainstays on the tourist trail to remote near-deserted islands, this country's pristine shores afford a healthy mix of active, fast-paced water sport hubs and easygoing seaside venues.

- **Quy Nhon:** Though it's long been a Vietnamese resort town, the sleepy shores of Quy Nhon have only attracted international attention in recent years. Set up a towel on the city's **downtown beach** or head south to **Bai Xep** for a laid-back lounge and a wander around its nearby fishing village (page 236).

- **Nha Trang:** This **bustling beach hotspot** (page 248) welcomes sunbathers, snorkelers, and divers to explore its shores. After dark, the party moves on land, where all-night celebrations go late. **Doc Let** (page 260) to the north offers a quieter, more exclusive shoreline.

- **Mui Ne:** A well-traveled spot on the south-central coast, this ever-expanding **resort town** delivers low-key shores and **Western comforts.** It's also known as the country's **kitesurfing capital** (page 291).

- **Con Dao Islands:** This island oasis has dense rainforest, soaring seaside cliffs, and sun-bleached shores, with some of the country's most alluring and difficult-to-reach beaches. Enjoy the turquoise waters and partake in some of Vietnam's **best diving** (page 368).

Long Beach on Phu Quoc Island

- **Phu Quoc Island:** Vietnam's go-to resort destination, popular with couples and families, Phu Quoc Island houses several good options. **Long Beach** is lively, happening, but not claustrophobic. **Sao Beach** to the south is pristine. **Ganh Dau** to the north is a perfect place to commune with nature and escape the more touristed parts of the island (page 457).

Bridge and a clutch of **Chinese Assembly Halls.** Browse the wares of tailors, jewelers, and dressmakers that have set up shop downtown. Dive into mouthwatering local dishes unique to Hoi An, including *cao lau* (local noodles), **fried wontons,** and **white rose dumplings.** Around mid-afternoon, visit the *banh beo* (steamed rice flour cake) vendor that sets up shop in front of the Ngu Bang Assembly Hall.

Place your order for custom-made clothes as soon as possible, allowing time for alterations

later on. Sip wine on the waterfront at sundown at **White Marble Wine Bar.**

DAY 6

For your second day in Hoi An, rent a bicycle and set off, pedaling to the photogenic **Tra Que vegetable village** north of town. Wander through the rows of veggies, then grab a meal on the breezy veranda of **Baby Mustard.**

Carry on north to hit **An Bang Beach.** Spend the afternoon catching rays before you cycle back to town. Some top-notch dinner spots include **Ba Le Well, Miss Ly's,** and **Morning Glory.** For dessert, swing by the **Cargo Club** for decadent cakes and pastries, then grab a beer at **Dive Bar.**

DAY 7

Your last day in Hoi An can be spent a few different ways. Venture up the coast to the limestone **Marble Mountains** before carrying on to cosmopolitan **Danang** for a visit to the **Museum of Cham Sculpture** or over to nearby Son Tra peninsula, where the statue of Quan Am at **Linh Ung Pagoda** dominates the landscape.

If you'd rather stay put, Hoi An has plenty of tours and courses, including the **Taste of Hoi An** food tour, as well as a slew of **cooking classes** and a **photo tour** for aspiring shutterbugs.

At the end of the day, board a night bus or make your way back to Danang and hop on a train bound for Nha Trang.

Nha Trang

Spend a few days taking in the energy of Nha Trang, Vietnam's **beach capital** and nonstop **party hub.**

DAY 8

Roll into **Nha Trang** in the early hours of the morning. From there, you'll have the option to hit the beach or head to the local **mud baths** for a restorative spa day. For some local culture, make for **Long Son Pagoda** and its giant Buddha on a hill, or go over the river to the ancient Hindu **Po Nagar Towers.**

Rest up for the evening, as Nha Trang comes alive after dark, with all-night beach parties at the **Sailing Club** and plenty of cheap drinks and busy dance floors throughout the backpacker neighborhood.

DAY 9

Leave the planning to the professionals on your second day in Nha Trang and book a full-day tour on the water. Travelers can choose from **snorkeling** or **diving** excursions, exploring **local marinelife** or simply kicking back on a

sun deck. When you return to shore, hop on an overnight train bound for Ho Chi Minh City, or head to the airport to fly there.

Ho Chi Minh City

DAY 10

Spend your first morning in Ho Chi Minh City taking it easy with a coffee in the shadow of **Notre Dame Cathedral.** From here, both the **Central Post Office** and the **Reunification Palace** are within walking distance. Wander north toward **Turtle Lake** for lunch and then carry on to the city's **War Remnants Museum** for the afternoon.

Head to the backpacker area later in the day for a happy-hour drink or dress up and spring for a cocktail at **Chill Skybar** or the sky-high **Saigon Skydeck** to appreciate the city from a different angle.

For dinner, grab a cab to District 1's Tan Dinh neighborhood, where local favorites like **Banh Xeo 46A** and upmarket eateries like **Cuc Gach Quan** await. For live music, check out **Yoko** in the evening or hit the dance floor at **Apocalypse Now.**

DAY 11

Today, visit bustling **Chinatown,** where the mammoth **Binh Tay Market** sprawls over several blocks and a tasty array of Chinese meals can be found. Back toward downtown, **Thien Hau Pagoda** is an incense-filled haze of reds and golds, lacquered woodwork, and ornate effigies, with neighboring **Chaozhou Congregation Hall** and **Cho Lon Mosque** adding an extra level of diversity.

Return to District 1 for some retail therapy at **Ben Thanh Market** and along posh **Le Loi,** passing by the colonial-era **Hotel de Ville** and local **Opera House.** Pop into the historic **Rex Hotel** for a sunset drink on its rooftop bar or head back to the backpacker district for a laidback evening.

Mekong Delta

This **whirlwind tour** of the delta hits the

carved stone faces at the Bayon at Angkor Thom

highlights. To spend more time exploring, follow the *Touring the Mekong Delta* itinerary (page 31).

DAY 12

From Ho Chi Minh City, board a bus to **Can Tho,** the largest city in the **Mekong Delta.** You'll arrive in the late morning, leaving the rest of the day to explore the **riverfront.** Around sundown, turn up at **Ninh Kieu Park,** the liveliest spot in the city after dark, with plenty of shopping and street stalls.

DAY 13

Get up early to visit **Cai Rang Floating Market.** This will take up most of your morning and some of the afternoon.

Get back on the bus to Ho Chi Minh City by mid- to late afternoon. Enjoy the city's best jazz musicians at **Sax N Art Jazz Club,** venture out for a classy drink at **Layla,** or sample Saigon's craft beer at **Pasteur Street Brewing Company.**

Excursion: Angkor Wat

If you have more time, consider crossing the border to visit epic **Angkor Wat,** easily accessible from HCMC.

DAY 14

From Saigon, take the hour-long flight to **Siem Reap.** Once you've settled in to your accommodations, grab a bite at the charming **Sister Srey Café** before spending an afternoon on the town. Swing by **King's Road Angkor** for some shopping or head to the **Angkor National Museum** to brush up on your history before seeing the temples. Take it easy the rest of the day but be sure to secure your transportation or hired guide for the following day. Take a trip out to the Apsara ticketing office around 5pm to purchase your Angkor access pass for tomorrow. Grab dinner either in town at **Amok** near the melee of the **Angkor Night Market,** or book a table at **Cuisine Wat Damnak** for a more fine dining experience. Make it an early night.

DAY 15

Start your day by catching sunrise over the placid waters of **Srah Srang,** a far less touristed sunrise venue than Angkor Wat. If you're feeling peckish, you could head back to town for breakfast or grab a snack at one of the refreshment stalls in the park and beat the crowds by visiting tree-covered **Ta Prohm** as soon as it opens. Once you've finished here, move on to **Angkor Wat,** the most famous of all Angkorian temples. By the time you've finished exploring its many nooks and crannies, you'll be ready for lunch at the **Blue Pumpkin Angkor Café** across the road.

Take a quick break before carrying on to **Angkor Thom,** yet another sprawling temple complex whose sights include the many-faced towers of **Bayon** as well as the **Terrace of the Elephants** and other structures like **Baphuon** and **Phimeanakas.** End your day of temple-hopping by taking in the sunset from atop **Pre Rup,** arriving by 4pm to get a spot. Head back to town for a relaxed dinner and prepare to head home the next day.

Hanoi and Ha Long Bay

While the 1,000-year-old city holds plenty of history, the most captivating moment in Hanoi is the present. Follow this five-day itinerary to explore the capital as well as discover the breathtaking natural landscapes of Ha Long Bay.

Hanoi

DAY 1

Follow the locals and start your day early with breakfast at the hotel or a piping hot bowl of pho on the street. Any good Hanoian adventure begins with a trip to **Hoan Kiem Lake,** the epicenter of town, followed by nearby **Ngoc Son Temple.** From the northern edge of the water, you should be able to enlist the services of a cyclo driver, who will ferry you around the narrow chaotic streets of the **Old Quarter** in order to witness the city in full swing. If you're up for it, walking is also an option, though the uninitiated will find downtown Hanoi's streets hectic. There are ample opportunities for shopping along **Hang Gai** and around the web of streets north of the lake.

Around lunchtime, you'll want to head toward **St. Joseph's Cathedral** on the western flank of the lake. Swing by the **Le Thai To Monument** and **Nam Huong Temple,** overlooking Hoan Kiem on the way, before cutting in toward the church. If you're hungry, tuck into a savory bowl of *chao suon* (rice porridge), served daily in the alley near the cathedral, or visit the clutch of chic international restaurants sitting in the shadow of

its towers. Nearby, **Hanoi Social Club** offers a tasty alternative. Finish off your midday meal in true Vietnamese form at one of the cafés around St. Joseph's. Several cheap local **street cafés** offer affordable coffee and tea and plastic stools to perch on.

In the afternoon, make your way toward **Hoa Lo Prison** for a bit of history before turning east toward the top-notch **Vietnamese Women's Museum.** As the day winds down, stroll and shop along trendy **Trang Tien** street or pay a visit to the **Opera House** nearby. Enjoy a sunset drink from the terrace bar of the **Press Club** or grab a seat street-side in the artsy front room of **Tadioto.**

Dinner is left up to you, as you'll probably want to hop on a *xe om* or grab a cab to reach one of Hanoi's more authentic local meals. **Ngon** makes a great choice, as does **Cha Ca Thang Long** just north of the lake. If you're up for some live entertainment in the evening, the band at **Minh's Jazz Club** puts on a nightly show, as do a rotating list of acts at **Swing.**

DAY 2

Get an early jump on your second day, as the sights west of Hoan Kiem Lake require time and patience. In the morning, hop on a bus from the northern edge of the lake to Ba Dinh Square, where you can queue up for a visit to the **Ho Chi Minh Mausoleum.** Dress respectfully; the rules are strict here. After you've made your way through the procession, you can snap photos of the square or head back toward Uncle Ho's famous **stilt house** and the **One Pillar Pagoda.** From here, those interested in learning more about Vietnam's war-related history should chart a course for the **Military History Museum,** while travelers who'd rather explore a local neighborhood can wander down the maze of alleys that precede **B-52 Lake.**

Around noon, head south toward the **Temple of Literature.** Just across the street, **KOTO** is a busy lunchtime destination and great spot for a meal. Wander back to the Old Quarter via Nguyen Thai Hoc, shopping as you go, or spend an hour at the nearby **Museum of Fine Arts** nearby. Take the rest of the afternoon to relax and then set off again in the early evening for any one of Hanoi's local *bia hoi* (freshly brewed light beer) shops. The area around *bia hoi corner* in the Old Quarter offers a host of affordable streetside dining options as well as a collection of lively dance floors and laid-back hangouts.

Ha Long Bay Cruise
DAYS 3-4
Rise early on your third day to set off for the remarkable landscapes of Ha Long Bay. In order to make the most of your time on the water, you'll want a two-day, one-night cruise. Most tour outfits arrange pickup and drop-off in Hanoi, meeting you at your hotel in the capital and arriving in Ha Long around lunchtime. Shoestring travelers would do well to look into **Halong Fantasea Cruises,** while those with a mid-range budget ought to spring for a trip with **Indochina Junk** and luxury travelers will appreciate **Bhaya Cruises.** Most cruises involve a visit to at least one of the bay's caves as well as a beach and perhaps a fishing village in addition to famous landmarks such as **Dog Rock** and **Ga Choi.** Activities

like swimming and kayaking are usually available as well, depending on the cruise.

Weather permitting, be sure to catch sunrise over the bay on the morning of day four. Spend the rest of your morning enjoying the scenery before returning to shore and back to Hanoi. Most two-day tours roll into the capital by around 5pm. Check into your hotel and grab a relaxing dinner in the city. For high-end fare, head over to **La Badiane,** or dig in to some tasty local *bun bo nam bo.* Once you've eaten, grab a nightcap at the cozy **Polite Pub** or turn in for the night.

Hanoi
DAY 5
Spend the morning at the **Vietnam Museum of Ethnology** west of downtown. Because it's a trek (take the bus or a taxi) and the museum itself is extensive, you'll want to allow ample time to explore the grounds, which include several outdoor replicas of traditional ethnic minority houses. Head back toward West Lake around noon for a roadside bowl of *bun cha* (grilled meat and rice noodles in fish sauce) on Hang Than street.

After lunch, walk over to **Quan Thanh Temple** before taking a leisurely stroll along **West Lake.** If you're up for it, you can follow the edge of **Truc Bach** lake or simply head straight to **Tran Quoc Pagoda.** Grab a coffee from one of the street vendors near here and admire the lake view from this vantage point, or visit the bar at the **Pan Pacific Hanoi** for a more upscale environment. Have dinner in the charming historical villa at **Green Tangerine** in the Old Quarter before catching a cultural performance in the evening. Both the **water puppet theater** near Hoan Kiem Lake and a pair of *ca tru* (ancient chamber music) troupes hold regular shows throughout the week.

Touring the Mekong Delta

Down in the far reaches of the south, the Mekong Delta is a more authentic, off-the-beaten-track part of Vietnam. Things move a bit slower, with less infrastructure than other parts of the country and fewer English speakers. Spend as little as a single day from Saigon out to My Tho or Vinh Long, or keep busy for as long as a week, following the Tien River toward the border before hopping over to Chau Doc and onward into Cambodia.

The Delta via Ho Chi Minh City

Bookend a trip to Ho Chi Minh City with a long weekend in the delta. It's an easy bus ride from HCMC to Vinh Long, one of the delta's northern towns.

DAY 1

From downtown Ho Chi Minh City, hop on a **Phuong Trang bus** bound for **Vinh Long.** Once you arrive, you'll want to arrange a **homestay,** either by visiting one of the local travel outfits,

stopping by the ferry to **An Binh Island**—where you should be able to recruit a willing local to put you up for the night—or simply heading across to the island on your own and scoping out potential accommodations.

Spend some time with your local family, but don't forget to hop on a **bicycle** and explore the rest of the island, too. You'll find a charming church and plenty of fruit orchards down An Binh's narrow concrete paths. Make a point of catching sunset over the river, and eat dinner with your host family.

DAY 2

In the morning, travelers have two choices. The first is to enlist the services of your homestay family or an island boat to head out to **Cai Be floating market.** Do this early, as much of the vibrancy of the market is lost by late morning. The second option is to linger a little longer on An Binh, enjoying your breakfast and a final goodbye

fishers reeling in the day's catch

produce for sale at the Cai Rang Floating Market

to your host family before you head to **Can Tho,** where another, larger floating market awaits.

Once you arrive, you'll have the rest of the day to explore the city's charming waterfront, including the colorful **Ong Pagoda,** swing by a **Khmer wat,** or visit the local **museum.** At some point, you'll need to arrange your floating market tour for the following day, either with an independent boat at Ninh Kieu Pier or via a hotel or tour outfit.

In the early evening, grab a seat along the river and take in Can Tho's bustling nighttime activity. If you're interested in local cuisine, you can hit the town with **Open Tour CT,** which runs nightlife tours in addition to its daytime offerings. You'll probably want to get to bed at a reasonable hour, as Can Tho's floating market is an early-morning affair.

DAY 3

Rise before the sun to visit **Cai Rang Floating Market,** the Delta's largest on-the-water trading post. Depending on your tour, travelers can spend most of the morning and even part of the afternoon plying the waters of the Can Tho River.

Get back to the downtown docks by mid-afternoon at the latest and either spend the rest of the day taking it easy or hop straight on a bus bound for **Tra Vinh.**

DAY 4

Enjoy an early breakfast at one of the shops overlooking the town's main traffic circle. From here, you can rent a **bicycle** and set off for **Ba Om Pond** and **Ang Pagoda.**

Head back to town for lunch. Spend the afternoon exploring the shaded lanes of Tra Vinh, swinging by **Ong Pagoda** and **Ong Met Pagoda** on the way. If you're up for another Buddhist hall of worship, **Hang Pagoda** is a cycle or taxi ride away, but you can just as easily relax at one of the local cafés in town. Grab dinner at the local market or stop in to **La Trau Xanh** for a fancier meal.

The Delta to the Cambodian Border

This itinerary works well as a bookend to your Vietnam trip, especially if you're continuing onward to Cambodia.

DAY 1

Starting from Ho Chi Minh City, make your way to the delta, specifically Vinh Long. See Day 1 of *The Delta via Ho Chi Minh City* (page 31) for a suggested itinerary for today.

DAY 2

In the morning, take a boat to **Cai Be floating market.** Head there early, as much of its vibrancy is lost by late morning. Relax while your vessel meanders down narrow canals and back up the river to An Binh. From here, catch a ferry back to Vinh Long and take the bus to **Sa Dec.** Perhaps the most photogenic town in the Delta, Sa Dec is worth a visit to see the **house of Huynh Thuy Le,** the richly decorated **Kien An Cung Pagoda,** and Sa Dec's famous **flower gardens.**

Hop on a bus headed for **Cao Lanh** (or hire a car to drive there) and find accommodations for the night. Those pressed for time can also take a direct bus from Vinh Long to Cao Lanh.

DAY 3

Plan for an early start, as you'll want plenty of time to reach **Tram Chim National Park** before late morning for the best bird-watching. Keep an eye out for red-headed sarus cranes, the world's tallest flying bird, along with the 230 other bird species found here. After your tour, head back to Cao Lanh to check out the local **Nguyen Sinh Sac Memorial Park** and **Do Cong Tuong Temple.**

DAY 4

In the morning, depart for **Chau Doc.** You'll arrive around noon, leaving the rest of the day for relaxing and exploring this small border town. Grab lunch near Chau Doc's local market before making the trip out to **Sam Mountain.** Scale the altar to Lady Xu, protector of Chau Doc's Sam Mountain

many steps to the top by passing through **Tay An Pagoda** or hitch a *xe om* ride to its summit.

On your way back down, swing by **Cave Pagoda** and the **Temple of Lady Xu.** In the afternoon, book a boat trip for the following morning through one of the local hotels. Evenings in Chau Doc are a tame affair, so you'll have plenty of opportunity for rest and relaxation as the sun goes down.

DAY 5

Take a guided ride on the **Bassac River (Hau River),** passing **fish farms** and **floating houses,** as well as Chau Doc's **floating market.** Upon returning to shore, wander around Chau Giang District, home to the town's **Cham community** and the green-and-white minaret of **Mubarak Mosque** or kick back near the waterfront. **Victoria Chau Doc** is a great place to unwind, with a top-notch bar and restaurant, as well as a riverside pool.

DAY 6

For your last day in Vietnam, motor out to **Tra Su Bird Sanctuary,** awash with flooded forests of cajuput trees and feathered residents. Enjoy a peaceful rowboat ride and the views from its soaring watchtower. Avid history buffs and nature enthusiasts can carry on to **Ba Chuc** or explore the surrounding countryside. Enjoy the rest of your afternoon; cross into Cambodia the following day.

Phong Nha-Ke Bang National Park

Vietnam counts 30 national parks. Several stand out from the bunch for their impressive landscapes, diverse wildlife, and unique outdoor adventures.

IF YOU'RE LOOKING FOR . . .

- **Active Adventures:** Offering the same stunning scenery as Ha Long but with greater access to its lush rainforest-covered karsts and tranquil bay, **Cat Ba National Park** (page 119) boasts a combination of hiking trails, soaring seaside cliffs, and a handful of caves, all of which serve as an idyllic backdrop for trekking, swimming, climbing, and cycling adventures. Though they're not easily spotted, the island is also home to the Cat Ba langur, one of the world's most endangered primates.

- **Untouched Caves:** Far and away a highlight among Vietnam's already-captivating array of natural sights, **Phong Nha-Ke Bang National Park** (page 176) boasts a maze of subterranean chambers beneath its soaring limestone karsts. Down rivers and buried under mountains, these gargantuan caverns harbor a host of ethereal, mind-bending vistas that remain largely untouched by local tourism—at least for now. While not all adventures in Phong Nha are easy on the wallet—a foray into Son Doong, the largest cave on earth, costs around US$3,000—affordable, adventurous caving tours are now accessible to the average traveler, and tourism in the park is set to take off.

- **Mountain Hiking:** North of Dalat, the rolling slopes of **Lang Biang Mountain** are but one part of the primitive **Bidoup-Nui Ba National Park** (page 285). The best hiking trails are on this mountain, as well as beautiful panoramic vistas of Dalat and the Central Highlands. Climb the challenging path up to the summit or take it easy at Rada Lookout below. Local guides lead visitors deeper into the forest for more off-the-beaten-track adventures.

- **History and Nature Intertwined:** Set on an island with dual reputations for its heartbreaking colonial past and unparalleled natural beauty, **Con Dao National Park** (page 368) is one of the country's least visited and therefore best preserved green spaces. Devouring nearly all of Con Son, the largest island in the Con Dao archipelago, this park is home to 160 species of land animals as well as over 1,000 varieties of aquatic creatures, making it a worthy spot for hiking, swimming, diving, and snorkeling for travelers who make the time to reach this remote island.

- **Bird-Watching:** The waterlogged fields of **Tram Chim National Park** (page 421) are home to over 230 bird species, including the 1.8-meter-tall sarus crane, the world's tallest flying bird. Navigate its calm waters by motorboat, winding through a series of narrow canals that burrow deep into the park's flooded forests for a glimpse of Vietnam's diverse bird life.

Hanoi

Look for ★ to find recommended
sights, activities, dining, and lodging.

Highlights

★ **Hoan Kiem Lake:** Take in the bustle and noise of downtown Hanoi from the shores of this legendary lake, where history and mythology meet (page 39).

★ **Ho Chi Minh Mausoleum:** Pay a visit to Vietnam's most revered national hero, embalmed and at peace under glass in a blocky, Soviet-style mausoleum (page 46).

★ **Temple of Literature:** A long series of lacquered pavilions, lotus ponds, and stone stelae, this Confucian temple marks the site of Vietnam's first university (page 50).

★ **Vietnam Museum of Ethnology:** Learn all there is to know about Vietnam's 54 ethnic groups (page 53).

★ **Sapa's Ethnic Minority Villages:** Whether perched on the steep cliffs of the Hoang Lien mountain range or sheltered by lush green river valleys, these communities are a world apart from the rest of the country (page 93).

★ **Mount Fansipan:** Reach the "Roof of Indochina" via an action-packed ascent that winds through clouds and over limestone ridges. (page 99).

The fertile, low-lying Red River Delta that surrounds Hanoi has been inhabited since prehistoric times.

Well before it became the capital of Vietnam, the region was used as an administrative and political center by the Chinese, who colonized Vietnam for a millennium-long stretch beginning in 208 BC. The city's official history began in AD 1010, when emperor Ly Thai To moved the capital from Hoa Lu north to a bend on the western bank of the Red River. Originally known as Thang Long ("ascending dragon"), the imperial citadel remained in this spot for centuries.

At the turn of the 19th century, emperor Gia Long, the first of the Nguyen Dynasty, moved his capital to Hue, in the center of the country. During much of the Nguyen Dynasty's reign, Hanoi served as a regional capital. It received its current moniker in 1831, courtesy of emperor Minh Mang, Gia Long's son and successor. The city later reclaimed its capital status in 1902, when the colonial French government chose it as the capital of French Indochina. It continued to serve as the seat of power after Ho Chi Minh declared Vietnamese independence in 1945. Nine years later, the Geneva Accords of 1954 granted northern Vietnam to the Viet Minh, who carried out their political operations in the grand colonial buildings left behind by the French.

The American War ushered in darker days, with heavy bombing reducing large parts of the city to rubble. Long Bien Bridge saw routine bombardments, while Bach Mai Hospital was almost completely destroyed during the Christmas bombings of 1972. The damage to the city would take years to rebuild. After the war, Hanoi struggled to regain its footing, through Vietnam's 1979 border war with China and the poor economic policies that followed reunification. When the country's *doi moi* reforms were enacted, allowing for greater economic freedom, Vietnam began to blossom into the country that it is today, bringing Hanoi out of its misery and back on the path to prosperity.

PLANNING YOUR TIME

Hanoi is no more than a three-day affair, thanks to its compact size, allowing visitors to cover plenty of ground in a short time. For additional adventures, such as Perfume Pagoda or Tam Coc, set aside an extra day. Trips to Sapa or Mai Chau require as few as 2-3 days or as many as 5, if you have time to spare.

Previous: Song Da Lake near Mai Chau; Hanoi's Hang Ma street. **Above:** fruit vendor walking a narrow alley.

Hanoi

SEE "WEST LAKE AREA" MAP

CHULA/ HANOI BICYCLE COLLECTIVE

UPS

VIETNAM MUSEUM OF ETHNOLOGY

West Lake

LONG BIEN BRIDGE

HO CHI MINH MAUSOLEUM

GIA LAM BUS STATION

SEE "OLD QUARTER" MAP

CAU GIAY

MY DINH BUS STATION

SEE "BA DINH DISTRICT" MAP

HOAN KIEM LAKE

CHAU VAN LIEM

FAMILY MEDICAL PRACTICE

TEMPLE OF LITERATURE

VINH TUY

DAI LO THANG LONG

US EMBASSY CONSULAR SERVICES

US EMBASSY

SEE "FRENCH QUARTER" MAP

THAN NHAN

DAI LA

PHUC LOI

NGUYEN TRAI

VAN PHUC VILLAGE

NGUYEN TRAI

NGUYEN XIEN

GIAP BAT BUS STATION

KIM NGUU

BAT TRANG VILLAGE

0   1 mi

0   1 km

© AVALON TRAVEL

Most museums are closed on Monday, and many pagodas close for at least two hours for lunch. Sightsee in the morning, when more of the city's attractions are open.

Weather conditions in Hanoi are different from the tropical temperatures of the lower half of the country. November-February, Hanoi gets cold, with steady mist and temperatures 10-15°C. Conditions are more pleasant March-May, when temperatures start to rise. The heat becomes unbearable and sweltering in August, before another brief period of mild weather in September and October.

ORIENTATION

Hanoi is divided into 12 districts, 17 communes, and one hamlet, though most travelers stick to the downtown districts and the areas just beyond.

Hoan Kiem District is home to the eponymous Hoan Kiem Lake, Hanoi's most famous landmark and a useful point of reference. Hoan Kiem comprises the bustling **Old Quarter**, where much of the city's commercial activity takes place, the posh **French Quarter,** and, along its western side, the **Cathedral District.** Along with picturesque St. Joseph's Cathedral, the Cathedral District houses cheap backpacker accommodations and trendy boutiques.

Northwest of Hoan Kiem, **Ba Dinh District** is where many of the capital's 20th-century historical sights are situated. North of these downtown districts, **Tay Ho (West Lake)** is more upscale, with a residential feel and plenty of high-end shops and restaurants.

Hanoi's streets are winding and narrow, with names that change several times over the course of a kilometer. There are plenty of English-speaking residents downtown who can help point you in the right direction. The city's public bus system is well-organized and affordable, with wide coverage and frequent service downtown and in other tourist-driven areas. *Xe om* and taxis are abundant and businesses are well-marked with street addresses.

Sights

Hanoi's attractions span the entirety of its illustrious history, covering everything from imperial relics to colonial grandeur, the Communist revolution, and beyond. Scores of age-old pagodas dot the downtown neighborhoods, rubbing shoulders with crumbling art deco architecture, a pair of legendary lakes, a few blocky Soviet-style buildings, and several museums that showcase the best of Hanoi's art, history, and culture.

This is the kind of place where the journey rivals the destination. Rather than hop in a cab to the Temple of Literature, enlist the services of a cyclo driver or head for Ba Dinh District on foot. Even if it takes an extra hour and a few wrong turns, exploring the city this way brings it to life.

OLD QUARTER

A teeming, tight-knit neighborhood barely contained by the tiny streets north of Hoan Kiem Lake, the historic Old Quarter is bright, chaotic, and fun. Hanoi's most visited commercial district, it has been in business for centuries and holds its own amid the recent crop of shopping malls and high-end stores that have sprung up elsewhere in town. Throngs of shoppers, street vendors, motorbikes, and storefronts crowd the narrow one-way streets and bustling alleys of this dense neighborhood, which functions like a large central market.

★ Hoan Kiem Lake

The focal point of the Old Quarter, **Hoan Kiem Lake** (corner of Dinh Tien Hoang and Le Thai To) is tranquility surrounded by chaos, its placid water ringed by traffic. Legend has it that emperor Le Thai To received a magical sword from the heavens, which he used to drive the Ming Chinese out of Vietnam in the early 15th century. After his victory, the king was rowing on the lake when a massive turtle appeared, took the sword from his belt, and sank back into the depths below. Le Thai To realized that the blade had been returned to its original owner, thus the lake became known as Hoan Kiem ("Lake of the Returned Sword"). On a small island near the southern end of the water is **Turtle Tower**, a structure built in 1886 to honor Le Thai To. During the French occupation, the tower held a small version of the Statue of Liberty, but it was destroyed when the city was wrested from French rule.

The lake and its surrounding park are a meeting place for locals. On weekends, the city government closes the roads around Hoan Kiem to traffic, transforming the area into a lively pedestrian street full of kids zipping around on inline skates, vendors selling snacks, and impromptu dance and musical performances.

Ngoc Son Temple

On a small islet near the northern end of Hoan Kiem Lake, the grounds of **Ngoc Son Temple** (Dinh Tien Hoang, 7am-6pm Mon.-Fri., VND30,000 adults, free under age 15) originally served as a fishing dock for emperor Le Thanh Tong during the 15th century. Though the structure you see wasn't built until 1865, this small patch of land once housed a palace and later a pagoda. Ngoc Son Temple combines its Buddhist past with Confucian and Taoist influences.

The temple's front half is dedicated to Quan Cong, a loyal and courageous Chinese general of the Shu Han Dynasty. A flurry of red, black, and gold lacquerwork encircles his three-tiered altar, laden with fruit offerings. Alongside Quan Cong's beloved red horse is La To, a practitioner of traditional medicine and Taoist spirit.

Vietnamese general Tran Hung Dao presides over the latter portion of the temple, tucked behind a high altar. Tran Hung Dao is credited with the defeat of two Mongol

Old Quarter

QUÂN THÀNH

Hang DauPark/
Hang Dau Flower Garden

PHAN ĐÌNH PHÙNG

HÀNG ĐẬU

MOSAIC
MURAL

NGUYỄN THIẾP

HÀNG KHOAI

CAO THẮNG

HOANG LONG
BUS

0   100 yds
0   100 m

DONG XUAN
MARKET

ĐỒNG XUÂN

CẦU ĐÔNG

SINH
TOURIST

NGUYỄN THIỆN THUẬT

TRẦN NHẬT DUẬT

HÀNG CHIẾU

HÀNG LƯỢC

HÀNG MÃ

NGUYỄN SIÊU

HANOI
OLD TOWN
HOTEL

HANOI
BACKPACKERS
DOWNTOWN

PHÙNG HƯNG

HÀNG CÓT

HÀNG ĐƯỜNG

LÃN ÔNG

ADVENTURE
INDOCHINA

ĐÀO DUY TỪ

HANOI
HOSTEL

BACH MA
TEMPLE

DRAGONFLY

THE MOOSE & ROO
PUB AND GRILL

HÀNG VẢI

HÀNG GA

BÁT SỨ

HÀNG THIẾC

CỬA ĐÔNG

SF SPA

DONG XUAN
NIGHT MARKET

HÀNG CÁ

SINH
TOURIST

NEW DAY
RESTAURANT

HANOI
HERITAGE HOUSE

COM GA

HÀNG NGANG

ESSENCE
HOTEL HANOI

BIA HOI
CORNER

HANOI
GUESTHOUSE

CONG
CAPHE

HANOI CITY
HOSTEL

HÀNG BỒ

HÀNG BẠC

HANOI
CA TRU CLUB

CHA CA
THANG
LONG

HÀNG ĐIỂU

OLD
QUARTER

HÀNG ĐÀO

ORIENTAL
CENTRAL HOTEL

MEKONG
QUILTS

HÀNG BÈ

CHA CA
THANG LONG

HÀNG NÓN

ĐỊNH LIỆT

TIRANT
HOTEL

CALYPSO
SUITES HOTEL

GIANG
CAFE

HÀNG TRE

BUN BO
NAM BO

BUN CHA
DAK KIM

HÀNG QUẬT

GIA NGƯ

GINKGO

GREEN
TANGERINE

NGUYỄN HỮU HUÂN

LITTLE
INDIA

HÀNG THÙNG

HÀNG GAI

CẦU GỖ

THANG LONG
WATER PUPPET
THEATRE

HÀNG BÔNG

ĐINH TIÊN HOÀNG

BUS 9,
BUS 14

ELECTRIC
CAR SERVICES

LÒ SŨ

LA SIESTA DIAMOND
HOTEL & SPA

NGÕ BẢO KHÁNH

NGOC SON
TEMPLE

CATHEDRAL
DISTRICT

SEE
"CATHEDRAL
DISTRICT"
MAP

HOAN KIEM
LAKE

Hoan Kiem
Lake

ĐINH TIÊN HOÀNG

TRẦN NGUYÊN HÃN

QUANG TRUNG

LÊ THÁI TỔ

ST. JOSEPH'S
CATHEDRAL

TURTLE
TOWER

Ly Thai To Park

LÊ LAI

TRÁNG THI

CENTRAL
POST OFFICE

© AVALON TRAVEL

invasions, most famously in 1288, when he drove off Kublai Khan and his army after impaling their ships with wooden spikes. He is worshipped as one of the country's collective ancestors.

Ngoc Son houses a small exhibit on the turtles of Hoan Kiem Lake. The lake's last living turtle died in 2016. Leading to Ngoc Son's entrance gate is a bright red footbridge, a popular photo spot. On the far side of the path, look for a relief of a tortoise on the left, carrying Le Thai To's famous sword. The area before Ngoc Son boasts nice views of Turtle Tower and the lake.

Hanoi Heritage House

Acting as both a tourist information center and an example of traditional Hanoian architecture, the **Hanoi Heritage House** (87 Ma May, 8am-5pm daily, VND10,000) is a long and narrow building stocked with a variety of Vietnamese handicrafts and helpful English explanations of each item's origin. The house hails from the late 19th century and is punctuated by a small roofless courtyard, which provides ventilation.

Both levels are stocked with souvenirs, including Dong Ho folk paintings and ceramics, stone carvings, and other traditional wares.

While it can feel like a shop, there's no pressure to purchase. At the front desk are a few books outlining the history of the neighborhood and its many small streets, as well as their former purposes. Curious travelers can ask questions about the city.

Bach Ma Temple

The oldest temple in Hanoi, 11th-century **Bach Ma Temple** (76 Hang Buom, 8am-11am and 2pm-5pm Tues.-Sun., free) may be modest in size, but through its humble gates are inner walls drenched in red and gold, floor-to-ceiling lacquerwork, intricate paintings, and masterful woodwork. This tranquil hall honors deity Long Do, the chief of Hanoi's first settlement, who lived during the 4th century and is believed to have reappeared several times throughout Vietnamese history, particularly during conflicts with the Chinese, as a protector of the city and its people. Since he would sometimes appear in the form of a white horse, it is fitting that the temple's name translates to "white horse." In its current incarnation, built in the 1700s, a large statue of a bright white stallion stands at the center of the building, surrounded by offerings and massive gilded ironwood columns. Overhead, Bach Ma's collection of lintels (large lacquered

Turtle Tower on Hoan Kiem Lake

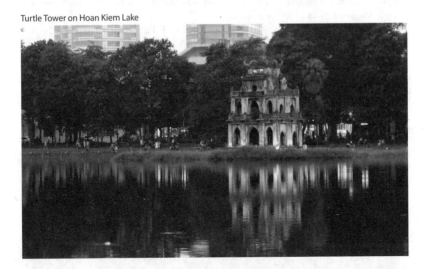

wooden panels) featuring Chinese inscriptions, bear phrases such as "Thang Long's Guardian to the East" and "Indomitable Spirit of Heaven and Earth."

Temple caretakers typically break for lunch at midday. Visitors who turn up on the 1st or 15th of a lunar month are free to visit from morning to night, as these are special days in Vietnamese culture.

Long Bien Bridge

Long Bien Bridge (east of Tran Nhat Duat), a weathered iron structure, holds a special place in Hanoi's history. Completed in 1902 by French architects, the bridge was originally named after Indochina's governor general Paul Doumer. It played a key role in both the Franco-Vietnam and American Wars. During the Viet Minh's fight against colonialism, rice and other supplies traveled across Long Bien to the troops at Dien Bien Phu, who defeated their French enemies in 1954. Through the 1960s and 1970s the bridge served as a crucial link between Hanoi and the port city of Haiphong. As the only route across the Red River, Long Bien was bombed heavily during the American War and had to be rebuilt in 1973.

Only pedestrians and two-wheeled vehicles are permitted on the bridge. Nearby Chuong Duong Bridge serves as a link for trucks and other large vehicles.

Mosaic Mural

Running beneath Long Bien Bridge along Tran Nhat Duat, Hanoi's **mosaic mural** began as a project to commemorate the city's 1,000-year anniversary. It spans almost four kilometers along the western bank of the Red River, making it the longest ceramic wall in the world. Both local and foreign artists took part in the mosaic's creation, combining abstract pieces from international artists with several prominent Vietnamese symbols, such as a mosaic version of a Dong Son drum head and the ever-popular giant turtle of Hoan Kiem Lake carrying a sword on its back.

CATHEDRAL DISTRICT
St. Joseph's Cathedral

An imposing structure amid the narrow houses and one-room shops of downtown Hanoi, **St. Joseph's Cathedral** (40 Nha Chung, tel. 024/3825-4424, 8am-11am and 2pm-5pm Mon.-Sat., 7am-11:30am and 3pm-9pm Sun., free) is one of the city's more recognizable landmarks, its pair of faded Gothic bell towers presiding over a small clearing just west of Hoan Kiem Lake. Originally the site of Bao Thien Pagoda, a Buddhist hall of worship dating as far back as the city itself, the church, built to resemble Paris's Notre Dame Cathedral, opened in 1886 to a devout French parish. St. Joseph's remained open until the end of the American War, when the Communist government forbade religious gatherings. The cathedral reopened its doors in the early 1990s.

The modest square before the church, ringed by cafés and boutiques, boasts a statue of Mother Mary and is often busy in the late afternoons with students and locals. Though the front doors are usually closed, there is a side door where visitors can enter to glimpse the brilliant red, white, and gold interior. Most prefer to just take in the building from outside. Visitors can drop by the cathedral's English-language mass at 11:30am on Sunday.

Le Thai To Monument and Nam Huong Temple

Overlooking Hoan Kiem Lake, the towering **Le Thai To Monument** (Le Thai To, 7:30am-7pm daily, free) commemorates Le Thai To, the emperor who played a pivotal role in Vietnam's history and mythology. Also known as Le Loi, this 15th-century king defeated Chinese invaders with the help of a magical sword. Topped by a small statue of the emperor, the 1896 monument is well-preserved and vibrant, bordered by an array of blooms and large shade trees. A sturdy pavilion obscures the base of the memorial where incense and other offerings are laid.

Behind the statue, **Nam Huong Temple** honors the emperor and a handful of other

Cathedral District

deified citizens. It once served as a popular gathering place for writers, poets, and scholars, moving to its present location at the turn of the 20th century. While the temple is small (the width of the room is about five paces), the emperor's altar holds a riot of colorful offerings, decorative statues, and a few lacquered wooden tablets.

FRENCH QUARTER
Opera House

The grand old **Opera House** (1 Trang Tien, tel. 024/3933-0113, www.hanoioperahouse.org.vn) is a stately structure overlooking the frenzied August Revolution Square. The theater, a yellow-and-white behemoth built in the colonial style, took a decade to complete, first opening its doors in 1911. Back then, only European performers were invited onto the stage, and French colonists made up most of the audience. By 1940, Vietnamese citizens were able to rent out the massive hall, modeled after Paris's own opera house. When politics took center stage in 1945 and Vietnam declared its independence from the French, Hanoi's Opera House served as a meeting venue for gatherings of the new government.

Performances take place year-round. The opulent theater seats 598 spectators on three levels. Though visitors aren't permitted to wander indoors, the exterior is worth a look while you're in the French Quarter.

National Museum of History and Revolutionary Museum

Housed in the former Louis Finot Museum,

the **National Museum of History** (1 Pham Ngu Lao, tel. 024/3824-1384, www.bao tanglichsu.vn, 8am-noon and 1:30pm-5pm daily, VND40,000) showcases over 200,000 artifacts, documents, and historic relics. The main building is devoted to ancient civilizations such as the Sa Huynh, Oc Eo, and Champa, along with northern Vietnam's Dong Son, a culture that existed roughly 1000 BC to AD 100 and whose large bronze drums are a symbol of Vietnam. Scores of artifacts (stone implements, pottery, and jewelry) occupy the downstairs level, while the museum's upper floor packs in several centuries of dynastic rule, from the Dinh and Le eras of the AD 900s to Vietnam's last emperors, the Nguyen dynasty, whose ornate everyday items, from mother-of-pearl inlaid dressers to enamel jars, detailed ceramics, and vibrant lacquerware take up a display to themselves.

Despite a fair amount of English signage throughout the building, a lack of general historical information can leave non-Vietnamese speakers adrift.

Where the National Museum of History leaves off—with the text of Uncle Ho's famous declaration of independence, given at Ba Dinh Square on September 2, 1945—the **Revolutionary Museum** across the street picks up, with a smaller range of documents, artifacts, and propaganda from the Franco-Vietnam and American Wars.

Entry to both museums is included in the ticket price, and visitors can spread out their visits over more than one day. There is a camera fee (VND15,000) to take photos within the museums. Both museums are closed the first Monday of the month.

Vietnamese Women's Museum

One of Hanoi's better offerings, the **Vietnamese Women's Museum** (36 Ly Thuong Kiet, tel. 024/3825-9936, www. baotangphunu.org.vn, 8am-5pm daily, VND30,000) takes a comprehensive look at the country's female citizens. Permanent exhibits cover everything from marriage and birth customs to family life, the crucial role of women in Vietnamese history, and the traditions practiced by various ethnic groups, all with ample English signage. A handful of temporary displays also appear in the modern three-story building. The museum's clear organization places it a cut above many others in the city.

Hoa Lo Prison

In the heart of the French Quarter is a small

Opera House and August Revolution Square

French Quarter

portion of **Hoa Lo Prison** (Hoa Lo and Hai Ba Trung, tel. 024/3934-2253, www.hoalo.vn, 8am-5pm daily, VND30,000, free for children under 15), the infamous jail that once housed thousands of Vietnamese revolutionaries during the colonial period and, later, American prisoners of war. While most of the original complex has been demolished, the remainder of Hoa Lo serves as a museum, documenting its history and the struggles of its inmates.

Built by the French at the end of the 19th century, the facility then known as the Maison Centrale quickly surpassed its original 450-prisoner capacity, overflowing with nationalist Vietnamese who had rebelled against colonial rule. As many as 2,000 inmates were crammed in at one time, making for dismal conditions on top of the torture

doled out by French prison guards. The museum holds ample evidence of these transgressions, including life-size mannequins of Vietnamese prisoners, lined up and shackled at the feet, as well as a guillotine used by the colonial government during the early 20th century. Following the Franco-Vietnam and American Wars, several of Hoa Lo's inmates went on to serve as high-ranking officials in the Vietnamese Communist Party.

From the 1960s onward, the prison was dubbed "Hanoi Hilton" by American soldiers. The complex was repurposed by North Vietnamese forces for prisoners of war. Here, the story fractures into two separate accounts: that of its captives—including U.S. Senator John McCain, who spent over five years at Hoa Lo—who recall torture and brutality, and that of the Vietnamese government, which paints a rosy portrait of life on the inside, complete with Christmas dinners and organized sports.

The museum has a small memorial to its Vietnamese prisoners at the back of the complex. Visitors are free to wander the exhibits at their leisure. Skip the information booklets on sale at the ticket booth, as much of their text is featured on signs throughout the museum.

Hanoi Police Museum

For a glimpse into the lives of the capital's law enforcement officials, pay a visit to the **Hanoi Police Museum** (67 Ly Thuong Kiet, tel. 024/3939-6941, www.baotangcongan. hanoi.gov.vn, 8am-5pm daily, free). Though the museum originally opened in 2008, entry was previously limited to police and government officials. In 2015, to commemorate the 70th anniversary of the Vietnam People's Police, city officials decided to open the museum to the public free of charge. Visitors can now stop by to learn about the evolution of the capital's law enforcement agencies as well as the development of the police across Vietnam. You'll find a catalog of the force's many uniforms as well as a record of its operations since 1945.

Quan Su Pagoda

Just around the corner from the Hanoi Police Museum, the wide yellow **Quan Su Pagoda** (Chua Quan Su, 73 Quan Su, 8am-11am and 1pm-4pm daily, free) is one of Hanoi's most popular centers of worship and home to the Buddhist Association of Vietnam. Though it's not the city's oldest or even most decorated pagoda, Quan Su, also known as the Ambassador's Pagoda, began in the 15th century as a guesthouse for visiting emissaries from Buddhist countries and has only grown since then. The current building was constructed in 1942 and features a dimly lit congregation of Buddha effigies on the main altar, a many-armed Quan Am, and a small section dedicated to local martyrs. Despite its downtown location, the pagoda courtyard is a peaceful place most days, though dozens

gather here during religious festivals and holidays. For anything and everything Buddhism-related, check out the surrounding shops, where scores of religious books, relics, and other goods are sold.

BA DINH DISTRICT

You could easily pass a day in Ba Dinh District, where many of Hanoi's most prominent historical monuments cluster together south of West Lake. Though these sights focus on Vietnam's 20th-century history, much of it war-related or steeped in Communism, there are a few other worthy attractions in the area, such as the city's Museum of Fine Arts and the centuries-old Temple of Literature.

★ Ho Chi Minh Mausoleum

A stark stone cube occupying the western edge of massive Ba Dinh Square, the **Ho Chi Minh Mausoleum** (Ba Dinh Square, tel. 024/3845-5128, www.bqllang.gov.vn, 7:30am-10:30am Tues.-Thurs., 7:30am-11am Sat.-Sun. summer, 8am-11am Tues.-Thurs., 8am-11:30am Sat.-Sun. winter, free) bears only the words "President Ho Chi Minh" on its exterior. Guarded day and night by police in crisp white uniforms, this is perhaps one of Hanoi's most bizarre sights. On most mornings, dozens of local visitors line up to catch a glimpse of their leader's embalmed body. The swift, two-line procession moves indoors past one of Uncle Ho's most famous quotations—"Nothing is more precious than independence and freedom"—before gliding in a semicircle around the body and back outside. Upon his death in 1969, Uncle Ho requested to be cremated and his ashes scattered in three parts throughout the north, south, and central regions of Vietnam, a wish that was obviously ignored.

Respectful dress is a must. Strict silence is observed indoors and no photography or camera equipment is permitted beyond the security checkpoint at the southern end of Ba Dinh Square, nor is the use of cell phones. Once you enter the line, it moves quickly, letting out on the opposite side of the building, where you can collect your electronics and carry on, either back out to the street or to any one of the Uncle Ho-related sights nearby.

Presidential Palace and Ho Chi Minh's Stilt House

Behind Ho Chi Minh's mausoleum, the **Presidential Palace** (1 Bach Thao, tel. 024/0804-4287, 7:30am-11am Mon. and Fri., 7:30am-11am and 1:30pm-4pm Tues.-Thurs. and Sat.-Sun. summer, 8am-11am Mon. and Fri., 8am-11am and 1:30pm-4pm Tues.-Thurs. and Sat.-Sun. winter, VND40,000) and his famous **stilt house** are remnants of both the French colonial government and its Communist successors. The bright sunflower-hued palace, once home to the governor general of Indochina, served as both a private residence and administrative building for the colonial powers. Following Vietnam's independence, it was expected that Uncle Ho, as president, would move into the massive house. Instead, he converted the building into a solely political and administrative structure and made his home in a smaller structure nearby, now known as the 54 House, named after the year in which he moved in. This residence was short-lived.

At the same time, Ho Chi Minh commissioned a wooden stilt house, built in the style of Vietnam's ethnic minorities, where he lived for most of his remaining days. The modest two-story building features an open ground floor, used for business, and sparsely furnished living quarters upstairs. The nearby fish pond and mango trees occupied much of the president's downtime. A third and equally humble residence sits on the far side of the stilt house, completed in 1967 out of concern for Uncle Ho's well-being, as American bombs began to rain down on Hanoi in greater numbers. Ho Chi Minh died here in September 1969.

The interior of the Presidential Palace is open only for visiting heads of state. At the stilt house, you can only observe the upper floor of the building on an adjacent platform. A handful of artifacts are on display, including a few gifts presented to Ho Chi Minh by world leaders, as well as three gleaming antique cars used by the late president for travel, two of which were donated by the Soviet Union.

For more insight into this area, request a free English-speaking guide at the ticket booth. Guides are primarily university students who have taken the job to practice their language skills, so don't be surprised if the tour isn't terribly thorough.

Ho Chi Minh Mausoleum

Ba Dinh District

BOTANICAL GARDEN

PRESIDENTIAL PALACE

UNCLE HO'S STILT HOUSE

B-52 LAKE

NGO 158 NGOC HA

HO CHI MINH MAUSOLEUM

BA DINH SQUARE

HO CHI MINH MUSEUM

ONE PILLAR PAGODA

CHUA MOT COT

BA DINH DISTRICT

DOI CAN

190 DOI CAN

LE HONG PHONG

CONG CAPHE

SON TAY

FLAG TOWER

KIM MA

NGUYEN THAI HOC

TRAN PHU

MILITARY HISTORY MUSEUM

STATUE OF LENIN   Lenin Park

BARBECUE CHICKEN

FINE ARTS MUSEUM

GOETHE INSTITUTE

CAT LINH

BICH CAU

Temple of Literature

INDIGO STORE

TEMPLE OF LITERATURE

QUOC TU GIAM

KOTO

NGUYEN KHUYEN

0   200 yds
0   200 m

© AVALON TRAVEL

Ho Chi Minh Museum

The gargantuan, lotus-shaped **Ho Chi Minh Museum** (19 Ngoc Ha, tel. 024/3846-3757, 8am-noon and 2pm-4:30pm Tues.-Thurs. and Sat.-Sun., 8am-noon Mon. and Fri., VND40,000) is not the only Ho Chi Minh-related museum in Vietnam, but it is hands-down the biggest, packed with thousands of historical documents and artifacts, photographs, and exhibits on the life and achievements of the revolutionary leader. Over two floors, the museum's displays cover much of Uncle Ho's time abroad and his involvement in politics in France, China, and the United States, before his return to take up arms against the French. While the heavy-handed Communist glorification and English signage fail to offer big-picture synopses of Ho Chi Minh's life, it's a worthwhile attraction for history buffs. Before visiting, read even just a few paragraphs about Ho Chi Minh for a better appreciation of the exhibits.

One Pillar Pagoda

The short, squat **One Pillar Pagoda (Chua Mot Cot)** (8am-5pm daily, free) is dwarfed by the grand Communist monuments nearby, but it bears an interesting origin story. Standing four meters high, the modest shrine, dedicated to Quan Am, is believed to date back to AD 1049 and the reign of emperor Ly Thai Tong. The legend goes that the inspiration for the pagoda came to the emperor in a dream, but there are conflicting versions of what the vision contained. Some say that the emperor dreamed of Quan Am sitting on a lotus blossom, holding a baby boy in her arms. The emperor, who wished for a son, became a father shortly thereafter and erected the monument as a thank-you to Quan Am. Given that Ly Thai Tong's son was born a few years before he ascended the throne in 1028, it doesn't seem likely that this version is correct.

The second version says that the emperor dreamed of Quan Am bringing him to a lotus lamp. Ly Thai Tong's mandarins worried that it was a bad omen. In an effort to counteract this negativity, the emperor commissioned the pagoda, paying homage to Quan Am.

The pagoda has undergone countless restorations and was rebuilt in 1249 and again in 1954, after the French destroyed it. Opposite the small shrine, **Dien Huu Pagoda** is a newer, more colorful building filled with a collection of statues and shrines that pairs nicely with a stroll up the steps of One Pillar. The pagoda's proximity to Ho Chi Minh Museum and Ho Chi Minh Mausoleum makes it a frequent stop for visitors in Ba Dinh.

B-52 Lake

B-52 Lake (Ho Huu Tiep) (Ngo 158 Ngoc Ha or Ngo 55 Hoang Hoa Tham) sits amid a sleepy residential neighborhood, all but forgotten. Faded into Hanoi's everyday bustle, its tepid green waters serve as the backdrop for morning commutes, daily garbage collection, and the comings and goings of street vendors. Stretching up from the lake's surface is the mangled husk of a B-52 military airplane, shot down during the 1972 Christmas bombings that rocked northern Vietnam. While much of the nearby landscape has changed, the lake remains frozen in time, a modest but powerful visual.

B-52 Lake elicits mixed reactions. For history and war buffs, it's a worthwhile stop paired with a visit to Ho Chi Minh Mausoleum and other surrounding sights. There is a simple plaque that stands at the near

altar outside of Dien Huu Pagoda

end of the water, and the plane's wreckage is surprisingly small.

To reach B-52 Lake you'll have to navigate several small alleys. Keep an eye out for signs that read "Ho B-52" or "Ho Huu Tiep" (the original name of the lake), as there are no English signs.

Military History Museum

The national **Military History Museum** (28A Dien Bien Phu, tel. 024/6253-1367, www.btlsqsvn.org.vn, 8am-11:30am and 1pm-4:30pm Tues.-Thurs. and Sat.-Sun., VND40,000) gathers various artifacts from Vietnam's two most prominent 20th-century wars, against French and American forces, within a bright white building. The indoor displays feature photos of the destruction that occurred.

The museum's outdoor exhibits provide more intrigue, with a sizable collection of military aircraft and ammunition, including one of the famous tanks that crashed through the gates of Saigon's Independence Palace on April 30, 1975, ending the American War. The museum highlights the cunning and resilience of a nation that, equipped with few resources, took on one of the world's most powerful armies and prevailed.

The grounds of the Military History Museum house Hanoi's redbrick **Flag Tower,** a remnant of the imperial era built by emperor Gia Long in 1812. While it is possible to enter the tower and take the steps up to the highest of its platforms, those who pass on the museum can still see the monument from the street, and the photos are just as good, if not better, from here. The museum charges a camera fee (VND30,000), which includes the outdoor exhibits.

★ Temple of Literature

Hanoi's **Temple of Literature** (58 Quoc Tu Giam, tel. 024/3845-2917, 7:30am-6pm Sun.-Fri., 8am-9pm Sat. Apr. 16-Oct. 14, 8am-6pm Sun.-Fri., 8am-9pm Sat. Oct. 15-Apr. 15, VND30,000) harks back to AD 1070, when emperor Ly Thanh Tong ordered

the construction of this temple complex. In 1076, emperor Ly Nhan Tong inaugurated Vietnam's first university, Quoc Tu Giam, on the long, rectangular grounds. The professors were court-appointed mandarins who taught lessons on Confucianism, administration, literature, and poetry.

While the university no longer stands, its grounds still hold an attractive garden, several lotus ponds, and the temple itself. Outside the main gate, a pair of stone engravings (in traditional Vietnamese characters) commands visitors to dismount from their horses. Through the imposing front door is a pleasant garden, filled with bright red flowers and frangipani trees. Lanterns line the central walkway that leads to the Khue Van pavilion, built in 1805, a tall, ornamental structure topped with bright red lacquered wood.

The temple's most famous attractions rest on 82 giant stone tortoises, meant to symbolize wisdom and longevity. The 82 stelae honor Quoc Tu Giam's 1,304 doctoral graduates. While you can't wander through the rows of stelae, you can see the stone tablets up close.

The courtyard before the Temple of Literature once held altars for 72 of the most respected students to study under Confucius and, later, Chu Van An, a 13th-century scholar considered the father of Vietnamese education. The altar has been replaced with souvenir vendors hawking incense and a few interesting handicrafts.

The temple itself is divided into two sections. Under the first roof, a high altar sits in the open air, flanked by tortoise and crane statues. Everything from the ironwood columns to the gold Chinese inscriptions shines with heavy lacquer, and incense fills the air. Beyond the high door—used to ensure entrants bow their heads in respect—is a large statue of Confucius and his disciples, dressed in lavish robes. A gold-plated ceramic tortoise sits to the left, while several smaller altars line the outskirts of the room.

Behind the temple are the original university grounds, now known as Thai Hoc courtyard. This area is dedicated to three

Vietnamese emperors: Ly Thanh Tong, responsible for the original temple's construction; Ly Nhan Tong, founder of the national university; and Le Thanh Tong, the ruler who commissioned the first of the stelae.

While signage within the temple complex is fairly sparse, visitors can hire a guide (VND100,000) at the ticket booth or buy the information booklet (VND8,000). Though nothing beats a knowledgeable and enthusiastic guide, the booklet provides insight and historical background for a fraction of the cost.

WEST LAKE AREA
West Lake

North of the Old Quarter, **West Lake (Ho Tay)** is Hanoi's largest body of water and a center for the city's wealthier residents. Ringed with luxury hotels and high-end restaurants, the lake once served as the northern frontier for Thang Long citadel. Of the legends related to the lake's origin, the most popular one goes that the area was once a forest, terrorized by a nine-tailed demon, which Lac Long Quan, original leader of the Vietnamese people, drowned in the waters of West Lake. Another story goes that an 11th-century monk by the name of Khong Lo traveled to China to aid the emperor and, as a reward for his services,

carried home large amounts of bronze. He used that bronze to make a bell with a sound so powerful that it confused a golden calf, who mistook the noise for its mother calling and, in his hurry to find her, created the deep rut that would form West Lake.

A narrow strip of land runs between West Lake and its smaller neighbor, **Truc Bach.** Though these two bodies of water were originally one, the southern lake received its own name after the completion of the Co Ngu causeway, upon which Tran Quoc Pagoda now sits. Truc Bach is remembered in Vietnam's war history as the site where, on October 26, 1967, American pilot John McCain parachuted into the water after his plane was shot down. Vietnamese civilians rescued the pilot before turning him in to Hoa Lo, where he spent over five years as a prisoner of war. A plaque near the lakeshore commemorates the event.

A trip to West Lake provides plenty of peace and quiet, and the lake boasts a 16-kilometer road around its shoreline, making for a scenic stroll or bike ride.

Tran Quoc Pagoda

One of Hanoi's oldest houses of worship, the **Tran Quoc Pagoda** (Thanh Nien/Co Ngu

the tranquil gardens of Hanoi's Temple of Literature

West Lake Area

HANOI
ROCK CITY

NGÕ TÔ NGOC VAN

ZED'S ● JOMA
THREADS

VEGGY'S

QUANG BA

TAY HÔ JUST
MASSAGE

DANG THAI MAI

DANG THAI MAI

ANNAM GOURMET/
RAFFLES MEDICAL

NGÕ 200 ÂU CƠ

XUÂN DIÊU

QUANG AN CLOM'S
CLOSET 88 LOUNGE

NGÕ 124 ÂU CƠ

CHUA CÁ CÔNG CHUA

SAINT
HONORE

SHERATON
HANOI

ÂU CƠ

INTERCONTINENTAL
WEST LAKE

NGHI TÂM

0   200 yds

0   200 m

HIDDEN
HANOI

LANG YÊN PHU

YÊN PHU

West Lake

TRAN QUOC
PAGODA

SOFITEL
PLAZA HANOI

AN DUONG

Truc Bach
Lake

THANH NIÊN

CỬA BAC

QUAN THANH
TEMPLE

HANOI COOKING
CENTRE/BOOKWORM

NGÕ XÃ

TRAN VU

TỬ LACH

DANG TAT

QUÁN THÁNH

PHAN DINH PHUNG Nguyen Bieu

HÀNG DÂU

YÊN PHU

HONG NGOC
HOSPITAL

54
TRADITIONS

MANZI

HÀNG THAN

BUN CHA

NGHÊ NHAI

HÒNG PHÚC

HOÀNG DIÊU

© AVALON TRAVEL

causeway, 7:30am-11:30am and 1:30pm-6:30pm daily, free) dates back to the 6th century, when its first incarnation was built on the banks of the Red River during the reign of emperor Ly Nam De. Its current home looks out over the gentle waters of West Lake and provides lovely views of the surrounding area.

Through a large yellow gate, the front half of Tran Quoc houses a collection of colorful stupas dwarfed by the 11-tiered tower at their center, which houses a ring of white Buddha statues on all sides. From this courtyard, visitors are able to peek in on the pagoda's ancestral altars, which line the wall of a shallow room off to the right. Farther back, a larger clearing houses a broad, leafy bodhi tree, gifted to the pagoda in 1959 by Indian president Rajendra Prasad. The bodhi tree carries religious significance as the type of tree under which the Sakyamuni Buddha attained enlightenment in India. Another altar sits indoors, dedicated to Buddha and piled high with fruit offerings and lacquered ornamentation.

Quan Thanh Temple

As old as Hanoi itself, **Quan Thanh Temple** (corner of Quan Thanh and Thanh Nien, 7:30am-5pm daily, VND10,000) was built in the 11th century under the reign of emperor Ly Thai To. Sitting just below West Lake, the temple honors Huyen Thien Tran Vu, protector of the city's northern gate, one of four directional deities who were believed to guard the Thang Long citadel in Hanoi's earliest days. The existing temple dates back to the 19th century and houses several precious antiques, including a 3.5-meter, four-ton statue of Tran Vu, cast in 1677, that takes up the back wall, as well as an oddly shaped gong from the 17th or 18th century. Through the temple's high white gate, a pair of stone elephants guard the courtyard leading up to Tran Vu's altar, lined with benches and large shade trees. Inside, lacquered woodwork decorates much of the shrine, while a photocopied map hangs on one of the building's columns, illustrating the parameters of Thang Long citadel and Quan Thanh Temple around 1490.

★ Vietnam Museum of Ethnology

Though it's removed from the rest of Hanoi's attractions, the **Vietnam Museum of Ethnology** (Nguyen Van Huyen, tel. 024/3756-2193, www.vme.org.vn, 8:30am-5:30pm Tues.-Sun., VND40,000), about seven kilometers from downtown Hanoi, is worth the jaunt out to the western suburbs. The large round building, modeled after a Dong Son bronze drum, features exhibits on all 54 of Vietnam's ethnic groups, from the Kinh, or ethnic Vietnamese, who make up roughly 86 percent of the country's population, to the Cham, H'mong, Muong, Jarai, and Ede, many of whom live in the mountainous regions of northwestern and central Vietnam. Ample signage guides visitors through the museum's vivid and educational exhibits, which cover customs, traditional dress, religion, architecture, farming techniques, handicrafts, and rituals practiced by each ethnicity. A small section on the 2nd floor organizes interactive activities for younger visitors, including traditional games and crafts.

Behind the building, several examples of traditional architecture are on display, including a stilted Ede longhouse and the soaring pitched roof of a Bahnar communal house, standing 19 meters tall. **Water puppet performances** (10am, 11:30am, 2:30pm, and 4pm) take place daily in the pond nearby.

The museum is home to a small bookshop and souvenir store, as well as a café, run by the Hoa Sua School, an organization that trains disadvantaged Vietnamese youth. Book **guided tours** (VND100,000) ahead of time by calling the museum. There is also a camera fee (VND50,000) to take photos within the museum grounds.

To the right of the museum entrance is a building that curates a collection of cultural items from across Southeast Asia. Though still in its infancy, the Southeast Asian arm of the ethnology museum will feature the same in-depth displays on customs, styles of dress, handicrafts, religions, and other facets of culture within Vietnam and its neighboring nations. It's worth a look while you're here.

SIGHTSEEING TOURS

In a city as accessible as Hanoi, city tours aren't necessary as most travelers are able to hit their preferred points of interest alone.

the courtyard at Quan Thanh Temple

Skip the standard, generic city tours in plentiful supply around town—they don't enhance your Hanoian experience. But a handful of outfits excel at providing urban excursions with a more personal touch.

Hanoi Kids (tel. 09/4370-0689, www.hanoikids.org, 9am-5pm daily) is a free student-run tour service that pairs curious travelers with young Vietnamese hoping to practice their English. Guides participate in regular training sessions before hitting the town with their new foreign friends, and your only costs as a traveler are admission fees and transportation for you and your guide. These young Hanoians are enthusiastic and outgoing, making the experience feel more like a friendly outing than a run-of-the-mill tour. Reserving a spot ahead of time is a must. The booking department at Hanoi Kids sometimes needs a reminder; confirm your tour in advance and, if response seems slow, give the office a call and check in.

A popular and reliable operator for tours both in town and around northern Vietnam, **Adventure Indochina** (6 Ma May, tel. 024/6683-5539, www.adventureindochina. com, 8am-9pm daily) arranges trips to Ha Long Bay and Sapa in addition to running city tours of Hanoi, cyclo excursions, a one-day journey around the city's pagodas, and a tasty street food tour. Staff are knowledgeable and efficient, and prices tend to be affordable.

About 3.5 kilometers north of the Old Quarter, **Hidden Hanoi** (147 Nghi Tam, tel. 09/1225-4045, www.hiddenhanoi.com. vn, 9am-8pm daily, VND450,000-1,245,000) introduces travelers to the finer points of Vietnamese culture through food, language, and walking adventures around the city. Its popular cooking classes take place at the center's charming location on the eastern edge of West Lake, as do a handful of language courses. Several walking tours, along with a much-touted street food tour, take place around the Old and French Quarters. Prices vary depending upon the activity, but all guides are enthusiastic and knowledgeable.

Vietnam Museum of Ethnology

Entertainment and Events

NIGHTLIFE

As the sun sets over the capital, Hanoi's nightlife festivities take place in fast-forward, unraveling in a few short hours between sundown and midnight. By 6pm or 7pm, work has barely let out but locals line the streets, gathering on clusters of low plastic stools to enjoy fresh beer and *do nhau* (drinking food), as they rehash the day's events. An hour later, nightlife is in full swing, with droves of foreigners and Vietnamese packed onto the makeshift furniture of so many independent beer vendors, noshing on grilled meat or local favorite snails, washed down with a local brew. The streets of the Old Quarter are especially lively, drawing people from all walks of life.

Across town, the well-heeled pay a visit to swanky cocktail lounges and upmarket watering holes around West Lake and throughout the French Quarter, where top-shelf spirits, terrace seating, and mellow mood music speak to a more refined ambience, while the catch-all bar-and-restaurants near St. Joseph's Cathedral sling cheap beer in a laid-back environment. Wherever you are, the night reaches its peak between 9pm and midnight, when a fairly strict curfew is enforced and most businesses close their doors for the evening. A handful of bars quietly remain open for another hour or so.

There is hope for late-night revelers. As a city that prides itself on traditional values, Hanoi has been resistant to progress on the nightlife front, but city officials are beginning to come around in the interest of developing tourism. Beyond the weekend street closures around Hoan Kiem Lake, a growing number of bars and clubs are keeping their doors open past midnight.

Bars

True to its name, the **Polite Pub** (5B Bao Khanh, tel. 09/6894-9606, 8am-midnight daily, VND35,000-150,000) serves as a slightly more upscale watering hole than some of its Old Quarter competition farther north, without getting too pretentious. Tucked down a quiet street off Hoan Kiem Lake, the cozy venue functions as a café from 8am until 4pm, the start of happy hour, when it serves beer, wine, spirits, and cocktails. Ample seating is available up front, while a pool table occupies the back room.

Lounges

A cozy street-side lounge not far from the Opera House, **Tadioto** (24B Tong Dan, tel. 024/6680-9124, 9am-midnight daily, VND35,000-270,000) exudes a laid-back vibe with plush couches, leather bar stools, and bright red French doors in a prime people-watching neighborhood. Prices are reasonable, and a happy hour drink looking out onto Tong Dan is worthwhile. The bar boasts an assortment of beer, wine, and cocktails.

From a rooftop in the French Quarter, Hanoi's chic and sophisticated **Press Club** (59A Ly Thai To, tel. 024/3934-0888, www.hanoi-pressclub.com, 8am-midnight daily, VND100,000-700,000) affords pleasant views of one of the city's most upscale neighborhoods as well as a range of signature cocktails, top-shelf spirits, wine, and beer. Seating is available indoors at the Press Club's elegant bar or outside on a breezy, palm-fringed terrace. Live music acts occasionally pop up here, while regular drink specials run throughout the week.

The swanky and sophisticated **88 Lounge** (88 Xuan Dieu, tel. 024/3718-8029, www.88group.vn, 11am-1am Sun.-Wed., 11am-2am Thurs.-Sat., VND50,000-400,000) overlooks West Lake, with three floors of open-air seating that afford top-notch views of the water from an array of antique upholstered chairs. Pair this with dim lighting, a well-stocked downstairs bar, and an impressive collection of fine wines on display, and

Hanoi's Fresh Beer Scene

As the workday comes to a close and an army of motor-bikes floods the city streets, the place to be in the capital is a plastic chair by the roadside with an ice-cold glass of *bia hoi* in hand. This light, refreshing lager is a staple of northern nightlife, drawing crowds to the bustling sidewalks of downtown Hanoi daily. What sets this brew apart is its makeup: Local breweries concoct the amber liquid using basic beer ingredients like hops, yeast, and rice. Without any preservatives or additional chemicals, the beer's shelf life becomes especially brief, with most *bia hoi* unfit to drink by the end of the night. Local establishments must plan ahead, ordering just enough to last a single day. In the wee hours of the morning, a representative goes to the brewery to pick up an order of *bia hoi*. From the time it reaches the premises, shopkeepers work to unload as much of their stock as possible, slinging drinks throughout the day, but the rush comes in the evening, when Hanoi's sidewalks come alive and a healthy drinking culture helps push sales. *Bia hoi* is often enjoyed with street-side snacks, known as *do nhau* in

tourists and locals enjoying *bia hoi*

Vietnamese. The brew comes in at roughly 4 percent alcohol by volume, making it highly drinkable, if a little watery. Best of all, its price tag runs no higher than VND10,000 in the big city, making it the most affordable beverage by far. You can also look for the slightly more expensive *bia tuoi*, a similar recipe with a bit more flavor. Both varieties are commonly translated as "fresh beer."

There are many *bia hoi* shops in downtown Hanoi. The most popular is often referred to as **bia hoi corner** (corner of Ta Hien and Luong Ngoc Quyen, 10am-midnight daily). While not all of the corner shops serve genuine *bia hoi*, you'll find plenty of the brew on the southeast edge of the junction. Beyond this swarm of nighttime activity, a clutch of more locally frequented *bia hoi* are situated around Bat Dan and Duong Thanh near the western side of the Old Quarter, though you won't find any English speakers here.

the place is a hit, one of the neighborhood's best stand-alone lounges. Prices are steep, but these folks know their wines, not to mention everything else, from whiskey and scotch to soju, sake, and tequila.

Nightclubs

Loud, lively, and filled with nonstop energy, **Dragonfly** (15 Hang Buom, tel. 09/7970-0666, 9pm-1am daily, VND40,000-150,000) is a small Hanoian version of a nightclub, slipped between the shops along Hang Buom. Those looking for a spot to let loose on the dance floor will appreciate the up-tempo beats and cheap drinks. For a slightly quieter

atmosphere, head to the second floor, though don't expect to leave here without at least a little hearing damage. If you're looking for a drink earlier in the evening, Dragonfly functions as a café and restaurant during the day; it turns into a nightspot after 9pm.

Live Music

Every evening from 9pm, the loud and lively **Minh's Jazz Club** (1A Trang Tien, tel. 024/3933-6555, www.minhjazzvietnam. com, 8am-4pm daily, live music 9pm-11:30pm daily, VND60,000-200,000) showcases the best of Hanoi's jazz talent. Self-taught saxophonist and accomplished musician Quyen

Van Minh, the club's owner, has cultivated an appreciation of jazz in the city, drawing nightly crowds into the intimate café for an impressive live performance. No cover charge is required, though prices double at showtime to accommodate for the musicians.

Bright and eye-catching, the main entrance of **Swing** (21 Trang Tien, tel. 024/3824-5395, www.swinglounge.com.vn, 8am-midnight daily, VND35,000-190,000) is decked out in bright lights, announcing this chic musical venue from a block away. Though it moonlights as an upscale café for the business crowd during the day, the lounge is at its best after dark, when the entire black-and-white space is transformed by nightly performances. The usual beer, wine, and cocktails are on offer, as well as nonalcoholic café beverages, and cozy sofa seating is scattered throughout. Music begins at 9pm and runs until closing time.

Buried down an alley north of West Lake, **Hanoi Rock City** (27/52 To Ngoc Van, tel. 018/8748-7426, www.hanoirockcity.com, 4pm-midnight Sun.-Thurs., 4pm-3am Fri.-Sat., VND50,000-200,000) continues to make its mark on Hanoi's live music scene as one of the premier venues for both local and international artists to showcase their talent. Boasting a spacious interior as well as a sprawling garden area, the funky West Lake venue also hosts the occasional DJ or film screening and keeps a regular list of upcoming acts on its website and Facebook page. Events often include a cover charge, usually less than VND150,000.

THE ARTS

Hanoi boasts a glut of Vietnam's most talented artists, from musicians and photographers to lacquer painters, sculptors, and masters of traditional theater and puppetry. Scores of small independent galleries and cultural centers exist alongside institutions like the national Museum of Fine Arts and the imposing Opera House. Even cafés have gotten in on the city's arts and culture scene with small film screenings, ongoing exhibitions, artist talks, and other events. For the

most up-to-date information, keep an eye on *The Word* (www.wordhanoi.com), with on-line and print editions that include an events calendar with upcoming shows, concerts, exhibitions, and other performances, as well as **Hanoi Grapevine** (www.hanoigrapevine.com), another reliable event-listing site.

Performing Arts

For everything from ballet to orchestral music, jazz concerts, piano recitals, operas, and traditional Vietnamese theater, Hanoi's historic **Opera House** (1 Trang Tien, tel. 024/3933-0113, www.hanoioperahouse.org.vn, box office 8am-5pm daily) is the go-to venue.

The talented musicians of the **Hanoi Ca Tru Club** (42-44 Hang Bac, tel. 016/6604-3688, www.catru.vn, 8pm Wed., Fri., and Sun., VND320,000) put on daily performances in the heart of the Old Quarter. In an intimate space, the hour-long show celebrates *ca tru,* a centuries-old form of northern Vietnamese poetry set to music, typically featuring one female singer, a male instrumentalist, and a drummer. While the traditional music is well-known, *ca tru* is a dying art, as most of its musicians are older. Today, accomplished musicians keep the tradition alive through regular shows, usually for foreign visitors. The audience is small, and participation by audience members is often required. Tickets can be purchased 8am-5pm daily; aim for one day in advance. It's sometimes possible to snag a seat on the evening of a performance.

The vivacious characters of **Thang Long Water Puppet Theater** (57B Dinh Tien Hoang, tel. 024/3824-9494, www.thanglongwaterpuppet.org, shows 3pm-8pm daily, box office 8:30am-8:30pm daily, VND100,000) know how to make a splash, zipping across their watery stage several times a day at Hanoi's best-known *mua roi nuoc* (water puppet) venue. As early as the 11th century, rice paddies and other shallow waters in the Red River Delta served as performance spaces for these lacquered wooden puppets and their masters, who maneuver the characters from behind a bamboo screen. Nowadays, the performances, combined with lively voice actors and traditional Vietnamese music, are a popular cultural attraction for visitors. Each show runs around 50 minutes, featuring a handful of individual vignettes. While the performance takes place in Vietnamese, the watery antics of these puppets provide enough information that no translation is necessary.

Galleries and Museums

Spread over three floors, exhibits at the **Museum of Fine Arts** (66 Nguyen Thai Hoc, tel. 024/3733-2131, www.vnfam.vn, 8:30am-5pm daily, VND40,000) cover the creative achievements of Vietnamese painters, sculptors, and other craftspeople from the 11th century onward. Beginning with the stone and wood carvings of several of Vietnam's early dynasties, displays proceed chronologically through the country's artistic development, showcasing beautiful functional pieces and religious relics from the earliest days of the empire before carrying on to the 19th- and 20th-century fusion of Western ideas and materials with Vietnamese aesthetics. The resulting artwork, which includes vivid lacquer paintings alongside other mediums, like oil and acrylic, remains straightforward,

depicting everyday Vietnamese scenes, portraits, and still life renderings. The most recent paintings hail from the 1980s and 1990s. Its sole showroom of conceptual art is a letdown. The museum overall is a rewarding stop and remains intriguing for both its artwork and the visible evolution of ideas over the years. Visitors are free to explore the many rooms of this 1930s colonial building on their own; a handy map is provided that helps guide you through the museum's many numbered exhibits.

One part art space, one part café, the hip and happening **Manzi** (14 Phan Huy Ich, tel. 024/3716-3397, 8am-10:30pm daily) sits a few blocks beyond the Old Quarter and hosts regular art exhibitions, talks, film screenings, and music and dance performances within its updated French colonial digs. White walls and minimal furniture give the place a gallery feel. Visitors are invited to sit and enjoy the café, either downstairs amid the calm of alley life or upstairs with the art. Both international and Vietnamese artists have been featured in Manzi's two-story space, and its rotating schedule of cultural performances and events is updated regularly on Facebook.

Located just behind the Temple of Literature and a short walk from the Museum

Hanoi's historic Opera House

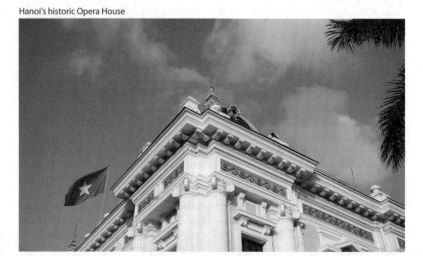

of Fine Arts, Hanoi's **Goethe Institute** (56-58 Nguyen Thai Hoc, tel. 024/3734-2251, www.goethe.de/hanoi, 9am-noon and 1pm-5:30pm Mon.-Fri., 9am-noon and 1pm-5pm Sat.) remains an active part of the local art scene, holding regular exhibits, workshops, and film screenings. Many of these events are free and open to the public. Check out the institute's website or Facebook page for a list of upcoming exhibitions.

The pristine white walls of **Green Palm Gallery** (15 Trang Tien, tel. 09/7762-7722, www.greenpalmgallery.com, 8am-8pm daily) display some of Hanoi's top contemporary talents, such as Nguyen Thanh Binh, Nguyen The Dung, and Nguyen Manh Hung. With a layout that pays homage to traditional Vietnamese architecture, paintings and sculptures are spread out over three rooms, separated at the center by a small courtyard. Each piece is given its due space, and knowledgeable employees are on hand to answer questions. The gallery also has a second location (39 Hang Gai, tel. 09/1321-8496, 8am-8pm daily) closer to downtown, but the Trang Tien branch offers more peace and quiet.

With a laundry list of featured artists, the **Apricot Gallery** (40B Hang Bong, tel. 024/3828-8965, www.apricotgallery.com.vn, 8am-8pm daily) is one of Hanoi's most established showrooms, bringing together a variety of materials and aesthetic styles under one roof. Paintings tend to be oil or acrylic, though there are a few lacquer works here, too, and the long, narrow exhibit space, which extends a few floors up above, offers plenty to admire as you wander from room to room.

FESTIVALS AND EVENTS

While the **Mid-Autumn Festival** (early-mid Sept.) sweeps across the whole country, Hanoi's festivities are especially lively. The holiday, which falls on the 15th day of the eighth lunar month, typically takes place during the first half of September and features scores of colorful decorations. Brightly hued paper lanterns hang from every shop and house in the city, many of them originating from **Hang Ma,** which becomes the city's very own *pho long den* (lantern street) in the weeks leading up to the celebration. Running the gamut from traditional red-and-yellow lanterns to cartoon-shaped paper torches, shops along this narrow Old Quarter road do big business for the holiday, as local families, many of them with young children, partake in the festivities with paper lanterns and moon cake (*banh trung thu*), a dense round pastry with a reputation not unlike fruitcake: pretty, ornamental, and not nearly as delicious as it looks.

Shopping

Hanoi's compact and chaotic Old Quarter is a microcosm of dressmakers and tailors, craftspeople, carpenters, souvenir vendors, and galleries. Independent designers and skilled artisans display their finest wares, often at a price, while mass-produced items like T-shirts, buttons, and hats fill the narrow crevices between buildings. The Old Quarter, particularly around Hang Gai and Hang Bong, is chock-full of high-quality brands. For budget shoppers, the long road (known as Hang Dao, Hang Ngang, or Hang Duong at different points) leading from Hoan Kiem Lake to Dong Xuan Market holds a host of clothing and souvenir shops, as does the intersection where Hang Dao and Hang Gai connect. Retail outfits along the Old Quarter's Ma May and Ngo Huyen in the Cathedral District also carry the standard array of souvenirs, T-shirts, casual pants, and sundresses. The streets south of Hoan Kiem Lake toward Hom Market have a handful of more exciting men's options.

One-stop convenience may elude the city's

busy streets, but avid shoppers will appreciate the Hanoian retail experience, stumbling on charming boutiques and modest out-of-the-way shops, each bringing its own unique personality to the multifaceted neighborhood. While most of the city's downtown businesses use price tags, the cost of common souvenirs is negotiable wherever you are.

MARKETS
Dong Xuan Market

The sprawling **Dong Xuan Market** (Dong Xuan and Cau Dong, tel. 024/3828-2170, 6am-6pm daily), just west of Long Bien Bridge, packs everything under the sun into its two-story shelter. The French-built trading center is a Hanoian institution, famous for its array of products and so popular that it has spilled out onto the streets, turning the road in front of the building into a lively shopping area that becomes the city's night market after dark. Expect to find cheap souvenirs, along with countless bolts of fabric, T-shirts, and many other items.

Hom Market

For fabric shopping, **Hom Market** (Pho Hue, 5am-7pm daily) just south of Hoan Kiem Lake is the go-to venue, lined with stall upon stall of materials at bargain prices. The usual market items are sold here, from food and household products to shoes, clothing, and other goods, but the real reason to venture into its maze of vendors is the innumerable bolts of fabric. Be sure to haggle, as Hom Market's shrewd businesswomen can drive a hard bargain.

Night Market

Hanoi's regular **night market** (Hang Dao north to Dong Xuan Market, 7pm-midnight Fri.-Sun.) runs from the end of Hang Dao north all the way to Dong Xuan Market, turning the road into a pedestrian-only affair flush with shops selling clothing, dry goods, and souvenirs. Be sure to haggle on this road, as prices tend to start high. Purchasing multiple items can usually get you a discount. While the bazaar only takes place on weekends, many vendors still set up smaller versions of their street stalls on the other days of the week.

SHOPPING DISTRICTS
Trang Tien

Wedged between the southern end of Hoan Kiem Lake and the Red River a few blocks to the east, Trang Tien is Hanoi's luxury shopping neighborhood, replete with high-end

Dong Xuan Market

The Streets of the Old Quarter

In centuries past, each narrow road in the Old Quarter carried a specific product. Hang Quat, for instance, sold fans, or *quat*, while Hang Giay made its money from paper, or *giay*. Cha Ca was where you went to buy grilled fish, silver was on Hang Bac, and Hang Duong held much of the city's sugar supply. Today, many of these streets have changed trades, but the traditional names have stuck. Hang Dau, the former oil street, now specializes in shoes, for instance.

fashion, international brands, and familiar designer labels. Ply the narrow streets that spider off August Revolution Square, and you'll discover droves of art galleries, swanky boutiques, and posh cafés.

Running the length of a city block, **Trang Tien Plaza** (corner of Dinh Tien Hoang and Trang Tien, tel. 024/3937-8599, www.trangtienplaza.vn, 9:30am-9:30pm Mon.-Thurs., 9:30am-10pm Fri.-Sun.) houses international luxury brands and designer labels, such as Bulgari, Louis Vuitton, and Dior, over six floors. The center was first built in 1901 to accommodate the city's French colonial shoppers. Its current incarnation opened to the public in 2013 as Hanoi's first luxury shopping center.

You can find English-language reading material at **Thang Long Books** (53-55 Trang Tien, tel. 024/3825-7043, 8am-9pm daily), just down the road from Trang Tien Plaza. To the right of the entrance, the shop's foreign book section includes Vietnam-related reading material as well as the usual government-approved collection of English-language classics, a cache of souvenir items, and road and city maps.

Old Quarter

Squeezed into an impossibly small neighborhood north of the lake, Hanoi's historic Old Quarter offers some of the best and most diverse shopping in the city, with stores to fit every budget and taste. From sleek, well-crafted furniture to eye-catching independent boutiques, traditional handicrafts, and the odd art gallery, **Hang Gai** and its nearby lanes represent the bulk of the area's offerings. There is also the occasional shop slipped between restaurants and hotels around Ma May, as well as a few of the more affordable souvenir shops buried within the backpacker alley off Ly Quoc Su near the cathedral. Head down sleepy Au Trieu on either side of St. Joseph's, and the hip clothing stores and independent labels reappear.

For fun, colorful, Vietnam-inspired T-shirts, **Ginkgo** (79 Hang Gai, tel. 024/3938-2265, www.ginkgo-vietnam.com, 8:30am-10pm daily) offers well-made, affordable men's and women's threads with more originality than the stock souvenir items around town. Ginkgo also has a second location (44 Hang Be, tel. 024/3926-4769, 8:30am-10pm daily) removed from the frenzy of Hang Gai.

The smart, understated clothing at **Indigo Store** (33A Van Mieu, tel. 024/3719-3090, 8am-7pm daily) may not jump out at you, but the beauty of these items lies in their simplicity. Using traditional methods, the shop sticks to indigo-dyed clothing for both men and women, using all-natural fabrics and embroidery courtesy of Vietnam's ethnic minorities, whose colorful, intricate needlework jumps out from the plain blue background.

One of a few skilled tailors on the block, **Ha Dong Silk** (102 Hang Gai, tel. 024/3928-5056, hadongsilks@gmail.com, 8am-8pm daily) fashions high-quality custom items. The shop also boasts a range of ready-made women's clothing along with accessories and jewelry. The ground floor of the building houses off-the-rack options; the fabric selection is upstairs.

The two floors of local favorite **Tan My Design** (61 Hang Gai, tel. 024/3938-1154, www.tanmydesign.com, 8am-8pm daily) are a catchall of jewelry, accessories, women's clothing, and housewares, run by three generations of a Hanoian family. From dresses to necklaces, bags, and bedding, Tan My pairs bright, bold colors with a distinctly Vietnamese flair, drawing upon the best of the old and the new. There is a small black-and-white café in the back of the narrow all-white store. Across the street is Tan My's original location (66 Hang Gai), which specializes in beautiful hand-embroidered silks and other fabrics.

Perhaps the most affordable tailor on the block, **Tagilis** (12 Hang Bong, tel. 09/3440-2974, www.tagilis.wordpress.com, 9am-9pm daily) specializes in well-made women's dresses in a range of materials and styles. The cheerful folks who run the shop are willing to copy designs or come up with new ones, and the average knee-length dress should set you back around VND670,000, give or take a few dollars depending upon the cut and fabric. Ready-made items are also available in bright colors and prints.

Cathedral District

A less hectic extension of the Old Quarter, Hanoi's Cathedral District is home to a handful of unique creative boutiques selling women's clothing, ceramics, and other knick-knacks. Prices are a little more reasonable here, away from the main shopping drag. This area is still well within the bounds of Hanoi's touristy area, so expect to find plenty of foreign shoppers and souvenirs.

Hidden amid a street full of European restaurants and dwarfed by the nearby St. Joseph's Cathedral, Japanese brand **Nagu** (20 Nha Tho, tel. 024/3928-8020, www.zantoc.com, 8am-9pm daily) offers a combination of simple, understated women's clothing, accessories, homewares, and kids' toys with a local touch.

The vision of a French-Vietnamese designer **Marie-linh** (74 Hang Trong, tel. 024/3928-6304, www.marie-linh.com, 9am-6pm daily) creates smart and affordable women's clothing. Combining high-quality fabrics with Eastern and Western influences, the shop's shirts, pants, shorts, and dresses offer casual comfort without sacrificing style. A more upscale version of Marie-linh is open a few doors down, as is another location (11 Nha Tho, tel. 024/3928-8773, www.marie-linh.com, 9am-6pm daily) nearby.

Packed with plush quilts and bright home furnishings, **Mekong Quilts** (13 Hang Bac, tel. 024/3926-4831, www.mekong-plus.com, 9am-9pm daily) offers well-made products for a good cause. Aimed at providing women in southern Vietnam and Cambodia with a sustainable income, this nonprofit organization has been assisting local communities since 2001. An array of quilts, bamboo products, and other housewares feature in this tiny shop, with half of the proceeds from each sale going back to the village from which the product came.

Ba Dinh District

Though this district is reserved more for historical sights than retail outlets, the one or two shops you'll find in Ba Dinh District are well worth your time.

54 Traditions (30 Hang Bun, tel. 024/3715-1569, www.54traditions.com.vn, 8:30am-6pm daily) celebrates the diverse cultures of Vietnam's 54 ethnicities, particularly its northern minority groups. Founded in 2004, the shop not only sells ancient artifacts, shamanic artwork, textiles, jewelry, and everyday objects from minority communities, it also educates its customers about these items. Each purchase comes with at least 1,000 words on the object. Some stock dates all the way back to the Dong Son culture, and many items are museum-grade. Items range from a few dollars to a few thousand dollars.

Avid readers will be at home among the stacks of **Bookworm** (44 Chau Long, tel. 024/3715-3711, www.bookwormhanoi.com, 9am-7pm daily), an independent English-language bookstore. The shop boasts over 15,000 new and used titles in its two-story collection. A smaller room dedicated to Southeast Asia and Vietnam touches on topics such as history, culture, and local issues.

Tailor Made

Along Hang Gai and throughout the Old Quarter, tailors are easy to come by, but quality and affordability together can be hard to find. A handful of standouts offer reliable service and skill at reasonable prices. To have tailoring done in Hanoi, plan ahead, as tailors in the capital tend to require more time than the speedy seamstresses of Hoi An. The average purchase can take anywhere from a few days to a week to complete, not including extra fittings or alterations. Most Hanoian tailors stock their own fabrics, saving you the trouble of visiting the market, though be prepared to pay a premium for this service. Whether you opt for the materials in-store or choose to purchase your own, it's best to swing by your preferred shop ahead of time to ensure that you buy enough of the required fabric and to get an idea of how much you should be paying for it.

Tagilis (12 Hang Bong, tel. 09/3440-2974, www.tagilis.wordpress.com, 9am-9pm daily) in the Old Quarter is your best bet for reasonably priced women's clothing. For a bit more quality try **Ha Dong Silk** (102 Hang Gai, tel. 024/3928-5056, hadongsilks@gmail.com, 8am-8pm daily), located on the same Old Quarter street, which provides a more upmarket range of fabrics and services. If it's more sophisticated tailoring you seek, West Lake shops like **Clom's Closet** (31A Xuan Dieu, tel. 024/3718-8233, www.clomscloset.com, 9am-7pm Thurs.-Tues.) and the high-fashion **Chula** (18 Nha Chung, tel. 09/0425-8960, www.chulafashion.com, 9am-6pm daily) come at a price, but their quality is unmatched. Men looking for affordable, well-made dress shirts and pants would do well to check out **Zed's Threads** (36 To Ngoc Van, tel. 024/6258-0208, www.zedsthreads. com, 8:30am-5:30pm Mon.-Sat.), a men's-only tailoring shop also located in West Lake.

Each of these shops also sells quality off-the-rack clothing.

West Lake

For a calmer shopping experience, the West Lake neighborhood is home to more upmarket shopping, falling somewhere between the Old Quarter and Trang Tien. Though it's less accessible than its southern counterparts, with fewer shops, the neighborhood includes a unique set of tailors for both men and women, not to mention a greater chance of finding Western sizes than Hanoi's downtown shops.

Full of vivid colors and daring designs, the handmade dresses at **Chula** (18 Nha Chung, tel. 09/0425-8960, www.chulafashion.com, 9am-9pm daily) are sure to get you noticed. The brainchild of a Spanish duo, this independent design house specializes in formal wear, creating vibrant original pieces and tailor-made items for women. A wide array of ready-made outfits is available for purchase. You can also commission the skilled Diego to fashion something custom. Prices are similar to American department stores, but the quality is unparalleled. For the full experience, you can also find Chula's dresses, skirts, jackets and tops at its original location (43 Nhat Chieu, tel. 09/0425-8960, www.chulafashion. com, 9am-6pm daily) in West Lake.

Stepping into **Clom's Closet** (31A Xuan Dieu, tel. 024/3718-8233, www.clomscloset. com, 9am-7pm daily) feels like entering a very fashionable wardrobe. Tastefully decorated and featuring men's and women's clothing, handbags, and accessories, this upmarket tailor produces truly beautiful formal wear using high-quality materials from around the world. Western prices apply here, but the quality and skill of Clom's tailors is worth the cost.

While its fashion may not be as bold as other shops, **Zed's Threads** (36 To Ngoc Van, tel. 024/6258-0208, www.zedsthreads.com, 8am-5:30pm Mon.-Sat.) is one of the only menswear stores in Hanoi that offers strictly men's clothing in sizes that fit Westerners. A range of quality shirts, pants, and suits take up the shop's racks. Made-to-measure services (8am-noon and 1pm-5pm Mon.-Sat.) are available, free of charge, but you'll have to make an appointment beforehand, either by phone or online.

Sports and Recreation

There are a few activities for recreation once you've exhausted your sightseeing and shopping options. You'll find charming green spaces around the city. Spas are a growing industry, as are cooking classes for those keen to master the art of Vietnamese cuisine.

PARKS

Scattered throughout Ba Dinh, Hoan Kiem, and Hai Ba Trung districts are Hanoi's array of small but well-loved parks, which serve as exercise tracks for early-risers, meeting spots for midday revelers, and communal areas for friends and family once the workday adjourns. While few of these green spaces are large, Hanoi's dozens of miniature clearings are a pleasant break from the madness of its usual hustle and bustle. The ring around **Hoan Kiem Lake** is the most popular, drawing hundreds of locals and visitors each day, including a small but devoted collection of young Vietnamese students hoping to strike up a conversation with a passing foreigner to practice their English.

Opposite Hoan Kiem Lake sits **Ly Thai To Park** (Dinh Tien Hoang between Le Lai and Le Thach), a modest square dominated by its imposing statue of the emperor of the same name. As the founder of Thang Long (what's now known as Hanoi), Ly Thai To features heavily on street signs, businesses, and monuments throughout Hanoi. The open concrete square is packed with early-morning exercisers or rollerblading school kids later in the day.

A small wedge of green opposite the Military History Museum, **Lenin Park** (Dien Bien Phu between Hoang Dieu and Nguyen Tri Phuong) bears a domineering stone statue of its namesake at the far end of the clearing overlooking the city's famous Flag Tower. Trees line the edge of the concrete space, acting as a buffer between the downtown traffic and the relative peace of the square.

For a genuine escape from the Old Quarter chaos, Hanoi's **Botanical Garden** (Vuon Bach Thao, Hoang Hoa Tham, tel. 024/3845-5114, 6am-10pm daily, VND2,000) offers silence in a city with a lot of noise pollution. In truth, this peaceful green space is pretty average, but thanks to its location and size, the pleasant grounds, equipped with two fish ponds, plenty of seating, and a collection of blocky abstract sculptures, take the edge off Hanoi's frantic traffic. Animal-lovers would do well to bypass the cage near the entrance, as the birds inside are not particularly well looked after. While the park is a lovely place during the day, it's wise to stay away after dark.

CYCLING

On the bicycle front, Hanoi has come a long way in recent years, cultivating a healthy crop of both local and expat cyclists who have taken to its streets in style, pedaling everything from flashy fixies to sleek ultra-light road bikes to vintage, basket-toting city vehicles. Several small cycling groups exist throughout the city, meeting up for a jaunt down one of the larger roads or around West Lake. The capital has encountered some growing pains recently, as it attempts to make Hanoi more bicycle-friendly without altering the breakneck chaotic traffic that congests its downtown streets. Bicycle rentals are possible, and guided tours can be found through the city's best-known foreign cycling group, the Hanoi Bicycle Collective.

For cycling enthusiasts, a visit to **The Hanoi Bicycle Collective** (33 Nhat Chieu, tel. 024/3718-3156, www.thbc.vn, 9am-7pm Mon.-Sat.) is a must. Founded in 2009 by Spaniard Guim Valls Tereul and his Vietnamese wife, Thuy Anh Nguyen, the shop has served as a base for Hanoi's foreign cyclists, offering bicycles and cycling gear for sale, city tours for curious travelers, and a regular "bike doctor" (Mon.-Sat.) to assist with repairs. The shop offers a complimentary maintenance check to those cycling through Hanoi on a longer trip. The shop also runs regular cycling tours (VND865,000) of downtown Hanoi and the West Lake area and provides a variety of bike rentals (VND120,000-400,000 per day), including city bikes, touring vehicles, and mountain bikes.

MASSAGES AND SPAS

While Hanoi boasts its fair share of quality massage parlors, spa services in the capital are more expensive than other destinations in the country. Tipping 15-20 percent is a standard practice in most massage parlors.

Aimed at training disadvantaged local youth for a career in massage therapy, **Just Massage** (237 Au Co, tel. 024/3718-2737, www.justmassage.org.vn, 9am-9pm daily, VND250,000-500,000) offers everything from Swedish and shiatsu massages to hot stones and aromatherapy treatments. Staff are friendly and speak English, allowing you to communicate with your massage therapist, and prices won't break the bank.

The tranquil **SF Spa** (30 Cua Dong, tel. 024/3747-5301, www.sfintercare.com, 9am-11pm daily, VND420,000-2,300,000), located on the western edge of the Old Quarter, is among Hanoi's more ambient retreats. Featuring a variety of foot and full-body massages, body treatments, facials, waxing, and all-encompassing spa packages, this charming day spa boasts a chic modern decor with experienced English-speaking massage therapists. The last booking of the day is at 10:30pm.

Located within the La Siesta Diamond Hotel on the eastern edge of the Old Quarter is

La Siesta Spa (32 Lo Su, tel. 024/3935-1632, www.elegancehospitality.com, 9am-9pm daily, VND380,000-1,250,000). Boasting the same range of high-quality spa services, massages, facials, and body scrubs, the company's downtown facility provides a tranquil escape from the chaos outdoors, as well as several package treatments inspired by the principle of the five elements: earth, water, fire, metal, and wood.

COOKING CLASSES

Boasting a range of courses designed by Australian chef Tracey Lister, coauthor of three books on Vietnamese cuisine, the **Hanoi Cooking Center** (44 Chau Long, tel. 024/3715-3277, www.hanoicookingcentre. com, 8:30am-5:30pm daily, VND1,350,000) may offer the most expensive cooking classes in the city, but its experienced staff provide a clean environment, top-of-the-line cookware, and plenty of hands-on instruction about Vietnamese cuisine. Choose from several themed courses, including a vegan tofu option, a session on barbecue and salads, and a half-day class devoted to spring rolls. Each course runs around four hours, with three in the kitchen and one to enjoy your sumptuous creations, and class sizes average 8-10 people. The center also offers street eats and market tours (Mon.-Sat., VND1,320,000), which take visitors on a four-hour trip around town, enjoying several varieties of local fare. Their children's cooking classes (VND1,320,000) allow young chefs to partake in some basic supervised cooking. Hanoi Cooking Center runs a small **café** (9am-5:30pm daily, VND20,000-200,000) on the ground floor, serving mostly Western meals as well as European and Vietnamese coffee.

Food

Holding the distinction of best pho in Vietnam, the capital city collectively enjoys thousands of helpings each morning. Other Hanoian specialties earn equal notoriety for their flavors and textures. The unsung hero—made famous by Barack Obama and Anthony Bourdain, who tucked into the dish on a 2016 episode of *Parts Unknown*—is *bun cha,* a delicious northern version of grilled meat and rice noodles doused in *nuoc cham,* a diluted fish sauce that comes with pickled veggies, fresh greens, and the occasional fried spring roll. You'll find this mouthwatering specialty on every street corner and likely smell it from a few blocks away, as the scent of barbecue floats up from street stalls. What Hanoi does, it does well: Mouthwatering, square-shaped seafood spring rolls, also known as *nem cua be,* are a must-eat in the capital. Several *cha ca* (pan-fried fish) restaurants round out the best Vietnamese offerings.

Hanoi's non-Vietnamese fare offers plenty of variety, from Indian and Malaysian meals to Thai, French, and American. Upscale eateries make a greater effort in the service department, opting for a Western approach, and there are more than a few foreign chefs and owners behind some of the city's well-known Western restaurants. The need for reservations is greater here, as the limited space of the Old Quarter means that dining rooms can fill up fast.

The streets of Hanoi are a good place to experience roadside dining in Vietnam. Crammed onto already-busy sidewalks and hidden down narrow alleys, chefs serve everything from tasty Vietnamese sandwiches to piping hot soups, rice porridge, barbecue, and local specialties, often at VND40,000 or less per meal.

Safe street food is easy to find, provided you stick to clean outdoor kitchens. When in doubt, look for hot meals, such as soups or grilled meats. High cooking temperatures eliminate some of the risk.

OLD QUARTER
Vietnamese

Even amid scores of backpacker eateries and shops catering to Western tourists, **New Day** (72 Ma May, tel. 024/3828-0315, www.new-dayrestaurant.com, 10am-10:30pm daily, VND40,000-260,000) retains a strong local following. With a well-rounded menu that covers everything from pork, chicken, and beef to frog, duck, oysters, and vegetarian fare, New Day has reasonable prices.

You'll find one of Hanoi's specialties, *cha ca la vong,* at the aptly titled ★ **Cha Ca Thang Long** (21-31 Duong Thanh, tel. 024/3824-5115, www.chacathanglong.com, 10am-9pm daily, VND120,000). The restaurant serves only its namesake: sizzling pans of *cha ca* (pan-fried fish) accompanied by rice noodles and peanuts. A small beverage selection rounds out the offerings, and the staff is notably quick on their feet and helpful.

Com Ga (1 Cua Dong, tel. 024/3923-3728, comgacafe@gmail.com, 8am-11pm daily, VND55,000-180,000) sits on a busy corner along the western edge of the Old Quarter. The restaurant prides itself on its hearty helpings of the namesake *com ga* (Hoi An-style chicken and rice). The second-floor balcony makes an ideal spot for a drink and late-afternoon people-watching.

French-Vietnamese Fusion

One of Hanoi's best-known venues, **Green Tangerine** (48 Hang Be, tel. 024/3825-1286, www.greentangerinehanoi.com, 11am-11pm daily, VND175,000-600,000) specializes in French and Vietnamese fusion, pairing unlikely ingredients to create unique and memorable dishes. The restaurant's 1928 colonial villa makes a worthy setting for a fancy meal. Prices run high, but the set menus offer decent

Hanoi's Best Meals

bun cha

- **Cha Ca Thang Long:** Experience Vietnam's communal dining at its finest with this beloved Hanoian meal of sizzling pan-fried fish, heaps of dill, and fresh rice noodles.

- ***bun cha:*** Try the unsung hero of Hanoian street food—an unbeatable combination of rice noodles, grilled pork, fresh greens, and pickled veggies—at this spot on Hang Than.

- ***chao suon:*** A perfect breakfast or midday snack, this piping hot rice porridge topped with tasty fried dough and pork floss is doled out by no-nonsense women at the top of Ngo Huyen in the Cathedral District.

- **Hanoi Social Club:** For an eclectic menu of both Vietnamese and Western contemporary cuisine, head to Hanoi's unofficial hipster hangout.

- **KOTO:** One delicious meal at the flagship restaurant of this nonprofit, which aims to uplift disadvantaged Vietnamese youth, and you'll understand why half the kitchens in Hanoi are staffed by KOTO grads.

value, with two-course lunches beginning at VND275,000. Given its popularity (it has been featured in a handful of high-profile publications, as well as on CNN's Travel website), reservations are advised.

Street Food

Directly opposite Hang Da Market is a small, open-front shop that doles out tasty *mien luon* (87 Hang Dieu, tel. 024/3826-7943, 6:30am-11pm daily, VND20,000-60,000). The bowls of piping hot soup feature glass noodles and fried eel. Order the rice porridge or any of the other eel dishes from a large picture menu mounted on the wall. The metal-and-plastic furniture fit right in with the street-food vibe.

Fresh, flavorful, and good enough for seconds, the ***bun bo nam bo*** (67 Hang Dieu, 7:30am-10:30pm daily, VND60,000) at the skinny storefront near Hang Da Market is a popular choice among locals. Metal tables line the long, narrow dining area and a dexterous assembly line prepares heaping portions of the tasty rice noodle and beef dish, complete with fresh greens, pickled carrots, peanuts, and sauce.

While there are hundreds of street stalls serving this classic Hanoian dish, the ★ *bun cha* (34 Hang Than, tel. 024/3927-0879, 8am-4pm or until sold out daily, VND35,000) on Hang Than is the best of its kind. Hearty helpings of grilled pork and ground meat come swimming in *nuoc cham,* a lighter cousin of fish sauce, accompanied by pickled carrots and daikon. Add rice noodles and as many fresh greens as you'd like, stir, and enjoy. This spot is best visited at lunch, and its product is well known among locals. If you're short on time or prefer to stay closer to the Old Quarter, **Bun Cha Dac Kim** (1 Hang Manh, tel. 024/3828-5022, www.bunchahangmanh.vn, 10am-9pm daily, VND40,000-60,000) is another well-known local spot for *bun cha.*

Cafés and Bakeries

Modest and unassuming, **Giang Cafe** (39 Nguyen Huu Huan, tel. 09/8989-2298, www.cafegiang.vn, 7am-10:30pm daily, VND15,000-40,000), in business since 1946, is hidden from the street by a narrow passageway between two larger storefronts. Try a cup of Hanoi's famous *ca phe trung* (egg yolks, condensed milk, and Vietnamese coffee). This may not sound appetizing, but the thick, decadent concoction is a treat on a cold day. The modest shop serves regular coffee, tea, and other refreshments at local prices. Its founder, Nguyen Giang, worked as a bartender at the legendary Metropole hotel before opening Giang Cafe.

Indian

The best of Hanoi's clutch of Indian restaurants, **Little India** (32 Hang Tre, tel. 024/3926-1859, www.littleindiahanoi.com, 11am-10:30pm daily, VND50,000-200,000) boasts not only an impressive range of Indian cuisine but also a list of Malaysian dishes, including *nasi goreng* and beef *rendang,* as well as a few Chinese meals. Portions are generous, prices are right, and the staff aims to please. As a 100-percent halal establishment, you won't find alcohol here, but you're no more than a few blocks from nightlife venues should you require a nightcap afterward.

Gastropubs

A classy pub and grill, **The Moose & Roo** (42B Ma May, tel. 024/3266-8081, www.mooseandroo.com, 11am-midnight Mon.-Fri., 10am-midnight Sat., 10am-11pm Sun., VND125,000-300,000) serves hearty pub

egg coffee, Hanoi's signature beverage

a bowl of *chao suon*, or pork rice porridge

Cafés and Bakeries

A large, comfy, Western-style shop, **Joma Bakery & Cafe** (22 Ly Quoc Su, tel. 024/3747-3388, www.joma.biz, 7am-9pm daily, VND30,000-180,000) offers delicious breakfasts, sandwiches, bagels, European coffee, and mouthwatering pastries. Relax in the small seating area up front near the main counter, or head out back to the larger café, where cozy couches and quiet tables await. You'll also find another location at **Joma To Ngoc Van** (43 To Ngoc Van, tel. 024/3718-6071, www.joma.biz, 7am-9pm daily, VND30,000-180,000). Both outlets have delivery services. A portion of their sales go to local charitable organizations.

Just off the main drag, the storefront of **Loft Stop Cafe** (11B Bao Khanh, tel. 024/3928-9433, www.loft-stop-cafe.com, 8am-11pm daily, VND25,000-200,000) is lit up by two well-stocked display cases laden with decadent treats. Pastries, cakes, and other goodies attract more than a few visitors. Its cool, quiet, street-side digs offer some respite, and with a range of coffee, tea, and other beverages populating the menu, it's a good place to pop in for dessert or a snack. The Loft Stop also makes a solid pizza.

International

The ★ **Hanoi Social Club** (6 Hoi Vu, tel. 024/3938-2117, 8am-11pm daily, VND95,000-170,000) dishes out an eclectic array of international fare, including burgers and breakfast foods alongside goulash, roti wraps, mango curry, and Moroccan chicken. Its chefs are able to adjust dishes for vegetarian, vegan, and gluten-free diners. The beverage menu is equally varied, including European coffees and teas as well as a few Vietnamese favorites, such as egg coffee and *ca phe sua da* (iced coffee with milk). Comfy chairs, whimsical decor, and indie music round out the Social Club's offerings. You can often find live music here on evenings and weekends.

It's hard not to be charmed by the laid-back ambience and breezy second-floor balcony at classy **Buon Dua Le Cafe** (20 Hang Hanh,

dishes, from burgers, steaks, and savory pies to full Western breakfasts. Beer, wine, and cocktails are on offer, including hard-to-find top-shelf scotches and whiskeys. Dining in this cozy narrow space is well worth the price, and it makes for an excellent spot to unwind after a day of shopping and sightseeing.

CATHEDRAL DISTRICT
Street Food

After one bowl of rice porridge, called ★ *chao suon* (Ly Quoc Su and Ngo Huyen, 7am-9pm daily, bowl VND25,000), from the small street-side outfit near St. Joseph's Cathedral, you'll be coming back for seconds. A smooth, stew-like consistency, this particular vendor's porridge is served with savory pork and *quay,* essentially a fried breadstick, on top. On the miniature plastic stools that line the road, sit and enjoy the bustle of the city while tucking into your piping hot *chao.* For extra flavor, toss in some black pepper. Portions are just right, making this a great breakfast or midday snack.

tel. 024/3825-7388, 6:30am-10:30pm daily, VND45,000-275,000). Down a quiet side street but close to Hoan Kiem Lake, the place is outfitted with polished wooden furniture and the artwork of local painter Duc Loi. The menu is mainly Vietnamese, with a few Western dishes. The open-air hangout makes a perfect place to start your day or kick back with a happy hour beverage as the sun goes down.

FRENCH QUARTER
Vietnamese
Ngon (18 Phan Boi Chau, tel. 09/0212-6963, www.quananngon.com.vn, 6:30am-10:30pm daily, VND45,000-360,000) and its extensive menu provide solid guidance on what to eat and how to eat it. Thanks to the place's market-style setup, diners are able to peruse everything before choosing. Set within a large courtyard, the bustling street food-style eatery is packed during lunch and evenings. Delve into soups, sautés, spring rolls, and sauces.

French
La Badiane (10 Nam Ngu, tel. 024/3942-4509, www.labadiane-hanoi.com, 11:30am-2pm and 6pm-9:45pm Mon.-Sat., VND520,000-1,590,000) is the city's finest French restaurant. Venture through the restaurant's arching, vine-covered white corridor and you'll find a host of gourmet dishes, from lamb shank and duck breast, steak tartare and carpaccio to pan-fried foie gras, homemade pasta, and sumptuous desserts. Each meal is a work of art, carefully plated. Chef Benjamin Rascalou, a veteran of the Parisian restaurant circuit, keeps things interesting with a regularly changing menu.

Vegetarian
Hidden down an alley, **Nang Tam Com Chay** (79A Tran Hung Dao, tel. 024/3942-4140, www.nangtam.com.vn, 9am-9pm daily, VND25,000-100,000) is a popular Vietnamese vegetarian joint that features scores of meatless dishes, from standard tofu-and-tomato-sauce to mock-meat re-creations of traditional

local fare. Tasty, filling set lunches go for as little as VND60,000. The small, air-conditioned dining area is usually full of locals at lunch and dinner.

BA DINH DISTRICT
Street Food
If you are near the Temple of Literature in the afternoon, swing by Ly Van Phuc, where you'll find finger-licking **barbecue chicken** (end of Ly Van Phuc, 4pm-late daily, VND6,000-15,000 per piece) starting around 3pm-4pm. Snacks are pay-as-you-go, with varying prices for legs and wings. These tasty treats make the perfect *do nhau* (drinking food) to pair with a beer. Though there are several shops along this street, the ones at the far end are the best.

Cafés and Bakeries
The folks at **Cong Caphe** (32 Dien Bien Phu, tel. 09/1181-1141, www.congcaphe.com, 7am-11:30pm daily, VND30,000-80,000) have taken the aesthetics of Vietnamese Communism and applied it to an urban coffee shop, with a decor featuring weathered wood, peeling paint, exposed brick, and stark concrete. The brown-paper menus list coffee, tea, and smoothies alongside coffee-coconut shakes and coffee with yogurt. There are other locations around town, including a spot on Nguyen Huu Huan (35A Nguyen Huu Huan, tel. 09/1181-1130, 7am-11:30pm daily, VND30,000-80,000). Cong occasionally hosts live music, during which time it serves a few alcoholic beverages.

International
A training restaurant and one of the most popular spots in town, ★ **KOTO** (59 Van Mieu, tel. 024/3747-0337, www.koto.com.au, 8am-10pm daily, VND85,000-500,000) has made an impact on the restaurant scene as well as the lives of its many graduates. Started in 1999, KOTO (Know One, Teach One) admits young disadvantaged Vietnamese into its two-year training program, which provides job training in the hospitality industry. The restaurant acts as a training ground for

Know One, Teach One

When Vietnamese-Australian Jimmy Pham first opened the KOTO hospitality training center in Hanoi over a decade ago, it was his goal to provide a small number of Vietnam's disadvantaged youth with a better future. Years on, KOTO has not only given young people without resources a steady income and hope for the future but the necessary skills and training to succeed in the hospitality industry at an international level. KOTO, which stands for Know One, Teach One, has two training centers, in Hanoi (59 Van Mieu, tel. 024/3747-0337, www.koto.com.au, 8am-10pm daily, VND85,000-500,000) and Ho Chi Minh City (19 Nguyen Dinh Chieu, D1, tel. 028/3822-9357, www.koto.com.au, 11am-10pm daily, VND65,000-500,000) and recruits roughly 30 young people between the ages of 16 and 22 to the program every six months.

students while serving delicious renditions of both Vietnamese and international favorites. The eatery's location makes it conducive to a lunchtime visit, though things can get hectic around this time. Seating is spread out over four floors.

WEST LAKE AREA
Cafés and Bakeries
Saint Honore (5 Xuan Dieu, tel. 024/3933-2355, www.sainthonore.com.vn, 6:30am-10pm daily, VND35,000-200,000) is a charming little Parisian-style bistro, replete with flaky, decadent pastries, fresh bread, and a deli counter that wraps around the end of the building. Delicious sandwiches and crepes feature on the menu alongside a range of coffee and tea options; while there are a handful of more sophisticated meals on offer, stick to simpler fare, as this is where the café excels. Saint Honore also has a second location (24 Trang Tien, tel. 024/6027-8591, 6:30am-10pm daily) closer to downtown.

SELF-CATERING
Hanoian cuisine is as varied as it is delicious. Those with dietary issues, or those who simply prefer more control in the preparation of their meals, will appreciate shops like **Veggy's** (99 Xuan Dieu, tel. 024/3719-4630, 8am-8pm daily), a small but well-stocked grocery store near the northern end of West Lake that's packed with familiar Western brands like Kraft, Campbell's, and Betty Crocker. For even more selection, **Annam Gourmet** (51 Xuan Dieu, tel. 024/6673-9661, www.annamgourmet.com, 7am-9pm daily), located in the Syrena Shopping Center, offers a range of useful cooking items and canned goods as well as a small bakery and deli counter, where you'll find several different types of cheese and cold cuts. Prices at both of these shops run on the high side, but you'll find a much larger selection than local supermarkets.

If you're simply looking for basic groceries and other essentials, there are several **Circle K** convenience stores located throughout the Old Quarter and beyond. These shops sell snacks, drinks, and basic care items such as soap, shampoo, and toothpaste.

Accommodations

The bustling streets and narrow, snaking alleys of Hanoi's downtown districts hold accommodations to fit every budget, from basic dorm beds to palatial five-star suites. Base yourself within reach of Hoan Kiem Lake, as this will ensure a reasonable proximity to most of Hanoi's sights, restaurants, and shopping. With a reputation as one of the country's most walkable metropolises and a surplus of quality budget, mid-range, and high-end accommodations, there is no reason not to stay in the downtown area.

As travelers to the city will quickly learn, the Old Quarter is not a place for light sleepers. While there is no shortage of accommodations in Hanoi, several factors come into play when booking a room, not the least of which is noise level. Those with a tolerance for white noise or, at the very least, a set of earplugs will find no fault in the many rooms north of the lake; those who prefer more quiet may find peace down the web of alleys beside St. Joseph's Cathedral, where many of the cheaper budget accommodations have set up shop. A clutch of luxury hotels populates the French Quarter, many of them bearing unique historical significance in addition to high-end amenities and five-star service.

OLD QUARTER

This small but incredibly dense neighborhood manages to squeeze plenty of top-notch accommodations into a few blocks north of Hoan Kiem Lake, right in the center of the action. Prices run higher here while rooms can be small. Noise levels are higher than elsewhere in the city.

Under VND210,000

Away from the spirited backpacker haunts, **Hanoi Hostel** (91C Hang Ma, tel. 024/6270-0006, www.vietnam-hostel.com, VND125,000 dorm, VND340,000-570,000 double) offers a peaceful place for weary budget travelers to lay their heads. The mixed and female dorms have clean, comfy beds and en suite baths, personal lockers, daily breakfast, and a free happy-hour beer. The outfit in charge runs a tour service downstairs. While there's not really much of a common area, this hostel's location and laid-back vibe make up for that.

Hanoi Backpackers' Downtown (9 Ma May, tel. 024/3935-1891, www.vietnambackpackerhostels.com, VND185,000-340,000 dorm, VND1,150,000 double) is a good option for those in search of travel buddies, though if it's quiet you seek, then this is not the place to crash. Single mixed dorms, female-only rooms, and double bed dorms are available, all with personal lockers, air-conditioning, Wi-Fi, and communal baths. Breakfast is served in the restaurant each morning. Though a few private rooms are available, you're better off going elsewhere if you'd prefer your own space.

VND210,000-525,000

Rooms at **Hanoi City Hostel** (95B Hang Ga, tel. 024/3828-1379, www.hanoicityhostel.com, VND455,000-570,000, breakfast included) are spacious and a bit worn but right for the rates, counting hot water, air-conditioning, TV, Wi-Fi, a fridge, and tea- and coffee-making facilities among its standard amenities. Front-facing rooms boast large windows and lots of light, and back-facing rooms offer more quiet away from the traffic noise of the downtown area. The staff can help arrange onward travel and transportation.

VND525,000-1,050,000

In a big and hectic city, the ★ **Hanoi Guesthouse** (85 Ma May, tel. 024/3935-2572, www.hanoiguesthouse.com, VND610,000-885,000, breakfast included) truly feels like a homier stay than most, with free refreshments on tap in the lobby and a notably attentive staff. Rooms are a great value, outfitted

Hanoi's Best Hotels

- **Hanoi Guesthouse:** This charming home away from home welcomes guests with a cozy common area, friendly staff, and well-appointed rooms.

- **Oriental Central Hotel:** This chic Old Quarter hotel combines modern comforts and sophisticated design with a perfect location.

- **Hanoi La Siesta Diamond Hotel:** For high-end service at a mid-range price, this hotel sets a high bar for Hanoian hospitality and boasts, among other things, an on-site spa and a penthouse restaurant.

- **Hanoi Backpackers':** Find clean beds and ample opportunities to make friends with other like-minded travelers at this lively hostel.

- **Sofitel Legend Metropole:** The capital's most famous luxury hotel has welcomed everyone from Charlie Chaplin to Jane Fonda during its many years of operation.

with TV, Wi-Fi, hot water, air-conditioning, a minibar, an in-room safe, and tea- and coffee-making facilities. Add-ons include airport transfer, travel bookings, laundry, and luggage storage.

Cozy, well-appointed, and right in the heart of the Old Quarter, rooms at the **Hanoi Old Town** (95 Hang Chieu, tel. 024/3929-0783, www.hanoioldtown.com, VND550,000-650,000) feature sizable beds, hot water, TV, air-conditioning, and Wi-Fi access. Facilities are older than other hotels in the area, but the staff at Old Town is a cheerful bunch and assists with travel services and tours around northern Vietnam. For lots of light and a street view, front-facing rooms are a solid choice; but for quiet, opt for a spot at the back, where noise levels aren't so high. Breakfast can be included, if desired.

VND1,050,000-2,100,000

The ★ **Oriental Central Hotel** (39 Hang Bac, tel. 024/3935-1117, www.orientalcentral-hotel.com, VND1,130,000-1,585,000, breakfast included) stands out thanks to top-notch staff and a modern look. Well-appointed rooms come with standard amenities as well as complimentary daily water. The antique-style bronze showerheads and framed photographs of everyday Vietnamese scenes add to the ambience. The superior, deluxe, and suite rooms have varying degrees of natural light. Opt for a junior if you prefer external windows, as these afford a better view. Additional services like travel bookings and airport pickup can be arranged.

Calypso Suites Hotel (11E Trung Yen, Dinh Liet, tel. 024/3935-2753, www.calypso-suiteshotel.com, VND1,090,000-1,250,000, breakfast included) bears a charming red, black, and white design scheme and equally conscientious service. Expect standard amenities as well as Wi-Fi, DVD players, and in-room safes. The hotel's alley location minimizes the noise of the Old Quarter.

Essence Hanoi Hotel (22 Ta Hien, tel. 024/3935-2485, www.essencehanoihotel.com, VND1,365,000-1,585,000, breakfast included) provides quality service and 66 plush mid-range boutique rooms that feature in-room computers, in-room safes, and daily complimentary water on top of the standard amenities. The hotel's à la carte restaurant operates throughout the day. Services such as laundry, luggage storage, and tour bookings can be arranged at reception. Spa services are available as well. Rooms vary in size and access to natural light; take a step up from the most basic option for a room with a view.

The grand **Tirant Hotel** (36-38 Gia Ngu, tel. 024/6265-5999, www.tiranthotel.com, VND1,575,000-3,045,000) boasts a larger property than much of its Old Quarter competition, no easy feat in this packed neighborhood. Above the lavish reception area, 80 well-appointed rooms are outfitted in regal furnishings and come with an in-room computer, minibar, and tea- and coffee-making facilities in addition to standard amenities. Breakfast is served each morning in the hotel's top-floor restaurant, overlooking the nearby lake. You'll find a fitness center and swimming pool here, as well as a ground-floor spa. A travel desk can assist you with transportation and tour bookings.

Over VND2,100,000

Part of the Elegance chain, ★ **Hanoi La Siesta Diamond Hotel** (32 Lo Su, tel. 024/3935-1632, www.hanoielegancehotel. com, VND1,585,000-3,500,000) is one of the company's best properties. Perched on the edge of the Old Quarter, the Diamond houses boutique rooms and the Gourmet Corner, a much-touted top-floor restaurant with pleasant lake views, as well as an outdoor terrace bar. Rooms feature simple but elegant decor, plush beds, an in-room safe, a computer, and complimentary water alongside the usual amenities.

CATHEDRAL DISTRICT

Situated just north of St. Joseph's Cathedral is a tiny backpacker enclave on Ngo Huyen that provides decent rooms at lower prices than in the Old Quarter.

Under VND210,000

The original ★ **Hanoi Backpackers'** (48 Ngo Huyen, tel. 024/3828-5372, www.vietnambackpackerhostels.com, VND115,000-140,000 dorm, VND575,000-690,000 d, breakfast included) sits about halfway down narrow Ngo Huyen, a stone's throw from the Cathedral and Hoan Kiem Lake. Both mixed and all-female dorms are available, with hot water, Wi-Fi, air-conditioning, and personal lockers. While there are a handful of private rooms, it's better to look elsewhere for quiet, because the crowd here likes to party.

The staff can help arrange onward travel and transportation.

VND210,000-525,000

Espacen Hotel (28 Tho Xuong, tel. 024/3824-4401, www.especen.vn, VND350,000-550,000) offers clean, spacious rooms in the heart of the Cathedral District. Tucked down an alley, the hotel is a five-minute walk from Hoan Kiem Lake. Rooms offer single or queen beds and come equipped with TV, air-conditioning, Wi-Fi, and hot water. Long-term stays can be arranged for a discounted rate, and the friendly hotel staff can assist with travel plans around the city as well as throughout the north. There are a number of copycats in the area that have duplicated the hotel's sign. Go to this exact address to avoid impostors.

VND525,000-1,050,000

Tucked tightly down an alley off the road circling Hoan Kiem Lake, **Little Hanoi Hostel 2** (32 Le Thai To, tel. 024/3928-9897, www. littlehanoihostel.com, VND550,000 d) is a pleasant surprise. Quaint, quiet, and incredibly close to the water, this mini-hotel's location eliminates much of the noise problem that comes with being downtown. It boasts cozy well-kept accommodations that count air-conditioning, hot water, Wi-Fi access, TV, and natural light among their amenities. The staff is cheerful, willing to help with transportation and travel arrangements, as well as city recommendations.

The most affordable in a chain of well-run, family-owned accommodations, **Splendid Star Grand Hotel** (14 Tho Xuong, tel. 024/3938-1435, www.splendidstarhotel.com, VND800,000-1,025,000, breakfast included) features bright, comfortable rooms with hot water, air-conditioning, TV, Wi-Fi access, complimentary water, an in-room safe, minibar, tea- and coffee-making facilities, and a DVD player. The staff can help arrange onward travel and transportation.

VND1,050,000-2,100,000

Decked out in miniature chandeliers, plush

carpet, and snakeskin wallpaper, the **Angel Palace Hotel** (173 Hang Bong, tel. 024/6299-8666, www.angelpalacehotel.com.vn, VND910,000-1,590,000, breakfast included) makes a statement with its style as well as its service. All accommodations are modern and well-appointed, counting hot water, air-conditioning, TV, Wi-Fi access, complimentary water, a writing desk, and tea- and coffee-making facilities in the standard list of amenities. Additional services, such as laundry and tour arrangements, can be made with the friendly and professional folks at the front desk.

FRENCH QUARTER

The chic French Quarter is home to the city's most historic and high-end hotels. From the world-famous Metropole to elegant modern hotels like Hotel de l'Opera, and Hilton Hanoi Opera, this is a neighborhood for the affluent traveler.

Over VND2,100,000

The spectacular, stately ★ **Sofitel Legend Metropole** (15 Ngo Quyen, tel. 024/3826-6919, www.sofitel.com, VND7,900,000-63,585,000) opened in 1901. Its historic white building, with black shutters and stocky balustrades, earned a reputation as the finest hotel in Indochina, catering to famous visitors and well-to-do residents. The five-star opulence of the Metropole is evident in its plush, sophisticated rooms, which come with a television and complimentary bottled water. The hotel boasts a pair of luxurious restaurants, spa, swimming pool, gift shop, sauna, and fitness center.

The five-star **Hilton Hanoi Opera** (1 Le Thanh Tong, tel. 024/3933-0500, www.hanoi.hilton.com, VND2,500,000-22,400,000) stands just south of the city's historic theater and exudes class from its regal vaulted reception hall to the elegant well-appointed guest rooms. Accommodations feature standard hotel amenities alongside a minibar, in-room safe, Internet access, and tea- and coffee-making facilities. A fitness center, outdoor pool,

sports bar, two restaurants, and a swanky café round out the hotel's offerings.

A cross between cozy guesthouse and high-end hotel, the **Hilton Garden Inn** (20 Phan Chu Trinh, tel. 024/3944-9396, www.hilton-gardeninn3.hilton.com, VND2,000,000-4,200,000) provides a more casual approach to luxury accommodations, with B&B-style lodgings and five-star service. Room amenities include TV, Wi-Fi access, an in-room safe, desk, fridge, and tea- and coffee-making facilities, as well as use of the business center and gym. A bar, restaurant, and 24-hour pantry market round out the inn's additional services.

The **Hotel de l'Opera** (29 Trang Tien, tel. 024/6282-5555, www.hoteldelopera.com, VND3,480,000-8,100,000) is not the first five-star hotel to grace this spot. At the turn of the 20th century, an elegant building known as the Hanoi Hotel served as a popular meeting place for local socialites. That building was eventually torn down in 2004 and rebuilt. Now outfitted with bold decor and first-class facilities, including flat-screen television and Wi-Fi access, the hotel stands out for its unique design, furnished in vivid, eye-catching colors. The chic, ground-floor **Cafe Lautrec** is a posh and popular French Quarter dining spot.

WEST LAKE

West Lake, with a handful of secluded high-end hotels, is the quietest neighborhood in the capital city. Xuan Dieu, the street bordering the eastern edge of the water, features several nice restaurants and bars, though options are limited.

Over VND2,100,000

Well removed from the chaos of downtown, the **Sheraton Hanoi** (K5 Nghi Tam, 11 Xuan Dieu, tel. 024/3719-9000, www.sheraton-hanoi.com, VND2,725,000-34,000,000) sits about 3.5 kilometers from the Old Quarter and has a pool, spa, garden, opulent lobby, and several restaurants on its sprawling lake shore property. Guest rooms feature the standard hotel amenities as well as a minibar, fridge, in-room safe, complimentary water, and tea- and coffee-making facilities.

Off the eastern shore of the lake, **InterContinental Hanoi Westlake** (5 Tu Hoa, tel. 024/6270-8888, www.hanoi.intercontinental.com, VND4,068,000-34,000,000) boasts over 300 guest rooms, including stunning over-water guest rooms connected to shore by a maze of floating walkways. Plush rooms are outfitted with a fusion of traditional Asian-inspired elements and modern decor, and include Wi-Fi access and a private balcony. The hotel's three restaurants serve a range of international and Vietnamese cuisine. The outdoor pool and a state-of-the-art fitness center are free for guests to use.

Nestled between West Lake and Truc Bach, the **Pan Pacific Hanoi** (1 Thanh Nien, tel. 024/3823-8888, www.panpacific.com, VND2,725,000-9,500,000) is blessed with attractive natural surroundings. Its location brings travelers closer to the heart of the city while still providing peace and quiet. The five-star hotel boasts 273 guest rooms outfitted with plush modern decor, an in-room safe, Wi-Fi access, and a flat-screen TV. A pair of posh restaurants showcase Chinese, Western, and Vietnamese cuisine, while the Summit Lounge overlooks the lake. A swimming pool, spa, and fitness center are part of the hotel's offerings.

Information and Services

VISITOR INFORMATION

You'll find scores of travel agencies boasting "free tourist information" around the Old Quarter, but this local wisdom extends no farther than a brochure of the company's tour packages. Your hotel is usually the best place to seek out unbiased travel tips, not to mention other extras like free maps.

BANKS AND CURRENCY EXCHANGE

You'll find ATMs on nearly every street corner in Hanoi, particularly in the downtown area.

Most hotels and tour agencies offer to exchange currency, as do the majority of banks in the downtown area. Look up the actual exchange rate to ensure that you receive a fair conversion. If you're pressed for time, the bank is your best bet.

Most banks in the capital are open 8am-5pm Monday-Friday. Vietnamese institutions like **Vietcombank** (www.vietcombank.com.vn) and **Sacombank** (www.sacombank.com.vn) tend to take a lunch break during the day, shutting their doors 11:30am-1pm; foreign companies like **HSBC** (www.hsbc.com.

vn), **Citibank** (www.citibank.com.vn), and **ANZ** (www.anz.com) stay open all day. Some Vietnamese banks are open on Saturday mornings.

While much of the country remains cash-only, a growing number of places in Hanoi, including high-end hotels and upscale restaurants, accept credit cards as a form of payment. This is the exception rather than the rule, so check ahead of time. Many businesses tack on a small additional charge for using cards over paper money.

POSTAL SERVICES AND INTERNET

Hanoi's **international post office** (6 Dinh Le, tel. 024/3825-4503, www.vnpost.vn, 7am-7pm Mon.-Sat., 8am-7pm Sun.) has English-speaking employees. For additional services, visit the **central post office** (75 Dinh Tien Hoang, tel. 024/3825-5948, www.vnpost.vn, 7:30am-8pm Mon.-Fri., 8:30am-5:30pm Sat.-Sun.) just next door. You are less likely to find an English speaker, but employees will usually point you in the right direction.

When shipping packages, Hanoi offers

three options: the local post, often slow and less reliable, though affordable; **UPS** (26 Pham Van Dong, tel. 024/3514-2888, www.ups.com, 7:30am-6pm Mon.-Fri.); and **DHL** (1 Ba Trieu, tel. 01/800-1530, www.dhl.com, 8am-6pm Mon. and Wed., 9:30am-2:15pm and 3pm-6pm Tues. and Thurs.-Fri.). Unless absolutely necessary, avoid international shipping, as costs are high.

You'd be hard-pressed to find a hotel in town that does not have a desktop computer in the hotel lobby or, at the very least, a Wi-Fi connection. Indeed, most cafés and restaurants offer free wireless Internet for paying customers.

PHONE SERVICE

Many travelers buy a local cell phone. SIM cards and basic reliable Nokia phones are widely available, both new and second-hand, from electronics shops around the Old Quarter as well as at **The Gioi Di Dong** (24-26 Ly Quoc Su, tel. 1/800-1060, www.thegioididong.com, 8am-10pm daily), with the cheapest options beginning around VND350,000. Once you obtain a phone and SIM card, you'll have to purchase mobile credit, which is found at most local *tap hoa* (convenience stores). The three main cell carriers in Vietnam are Vinaphone, Mobifone, and Viettel, all of whom operate on a pay-as-you-go basis. Credit comes in increments of VND20,000, VND50,000, VND100,000, and VND200,000.

EMERGENCY AND MEDICAL SERVICES

Vietnam employs three separate phone numbers for emergency response services: 113 is for police assistance in the event of robberies, traffic accidents, and crime-related incidents; 114 is for firefighters; and 115 is for medical emergencies. None of these hotlines are likely to have an English speaker on the other end, and the city's emergency response teams are sluggish at best.

In the event of a medical emergency, the best thing you can do is contact a foreign medical center directly for help. Local facilities like **Hong Ngoc Hospital** (55 Yen Ninh, tel. 024/3927-5568, www.hongngochospital.vn, 8am-5pm daily) are reliable for simple issues. International hospitals such as **Family Medical Practice** (298 Kim Ma, Van Phuc Compound, tel. 024/3843-0748, www.vietnammedicalpractice.com), which staffs experienced English-speaking foreign and Vietnamese doctors, stay open 24 hours and assist with more serious problems. **Raffles Medical** (51 Xuan Dieu, tel. 024/3934-0666, www.rafflesmedicalgroup.com, 8am-8pm daily) provides a similar level of quality.

PHARMACIES

Scores of pharmacies, also known as *nha thuoc tay,* are scattered throughout the Old Quarter and across town. These facilities stock prescription and over-the-counter remedies, as well as products like tampons and contact lens solution. Most downtown pharmacies also employ at least one English-speaking staff member. The **pharmacy** (119 Hang Gai, tel. 024/3828-6782, 7:30am-10pm daily) located on Hang Gai is a reliable option, as are the several businesses that run along Phu Doan near the cathedral.

DIPLOMATIC SERVICES

While there is a **U.S. Embassy** (7 Lang Ha, tel. 024/3850-5000, www.vn.usembassy.gov), all inquiries regarding U.S. citizens must be directed to the Rose Garden Building, where **consular services** (Rose Garden Bldg., 170 Ngoc Khanh, 2nd Fl., tel. 024/3850-5000, www.vietnam.usembassy.gov, by appointment only 8:30am-11:30am and 1pm-3:30pm Mon.-Thurs.) are carried out, around the corner from the embassy. Due to the fact that all visitors must have a scheduled appointment on the books, look at the embassy's website ahead of time in order to discern what you'll need before venturing to this area. Appointments can also be made online. For emergencies, American citizens are advised to contact the embassy and consular services (tel. 024/3850-5000).

LAUNDRY

The majority of Hanoi's accommodations provide laundry services at an additional cost, and there is usually a markup for going this route. Standard pricing on the street is around VND25,000 per kilo, while you'll pay upward of VND35,000 for the convenience of going through your hotel. The turnaround is usually about a day; in lousy winter weather be prepared to wait a little longer, as dryers are seldom used and the cold, humid winter months tend to leave everything damp.

Getting There

AIR

Flights from around the country and across the globe arrive at Hanoi's **Noi Bai International Airport** (HAN, Phu Minh ward, Soc Son district, tel. 024/3886-5047, www.noibaiairport.vn), 32 kilometers north of the city. Several budget airlines, including Jetstar, Air Asia, and VietJet, pass through here in addition to a host of other international carriers. Flights from Ho Chi Minh City take roughly 2 hours and Danang about 1.25 hours. Customs and immigration procedures move quickly; those completing pre-approved visa processing should expect to wait in line for a short while before passing through customs inspections. Those traveling domestically from other in-country destinations will be spared this waiting.

Once you've exited the airport, it's about a 45-minute ride into the city by taxi, minibus, or public bus. Many hotels can arrange airport pickup for an additional fee (starting around VND350,000), so long as you contact them in advance.

Taxi from the Airport

The airport is notorious for a host of taxi troubles: drivers quote flat rates that border on extortion or insist that the destination you've presented is closed, full, or for some other reason unavailable in hopes of steering you to another hotel, where they usually receive a kickback. When metered vehicles are available, it is not uncommon for meters to run up the fare at lightning speed. Your best bet is to write down the name and exact address of your hotel before leaving the airport. This way, you have a clear destination to show your driver and, should he or she attempt to take you elsewhere, you are able to politely refuse and point to the place on the paper.

The easiest way to procure a cab from the airport is to walk to the taxi stand (easily visible when leaving the arrivals area), where a flat rate (to downtown) will be posted on the sign out front. Once you have a taxi, confirm again with your driver the exact price as some drivers will still attempt to overcharge. Stick to trusted companies like **Mailinh Airport** (tel. 024/3822-2666). From the airport to the downtown area should cost no more than VND300,000.

Airport Minibus

An airport **minibus** (tel. 024/3884-0496, www.nasco.vn, 5am-7:30pm daily, VND40,000), courtesy of Vietnam Airlines, leaves from Noi Bai when it has enough passengers to make the journey worthwhile, usually every 30 minutes or so. The minibus drops passengers off in front of the Vietnam Airlines office downtown, one block south of Hoan Kiem Lake. While you may have to wait a few minutes at the airport, this is by far the cheapest and most hassle-free option if you are traveling light. Even if your hotel is not within walking distance of the minibus stop, the combined cost of the minibus fare and a cab from downtown Hanoi to your final destination will be less expensive and reduce the risk of being overcharged by a taxi. The same minibuses also travel the reverse route back to the airport, leaving from the Vietnam Airlines office (corner of Quang Trung and

Hai Ba Trung). There's no need to buy a ticket in advance; just hop on.

Public Bus from the Airport

A **public bus** (VND30,000) also makes a trip into town from the airport. **Bus number 86** travels via the Nhat Tan Bridge and lets off in downtown Hanoi, not far from Hoan Kiem Lake, opposite a stretch of the city's ceramic wall. **Bus number 7** also departs from Noi Bai, traveling to the western suburbs of the city. For more specific directions to your destination, it's possible to double-check your route with Google Maps, as its representation of the Hanoi public bus system is accurate and far easier than attempting to decipher the route listings on the Hanoi Bus website.

TRAIN

Hanoi's mammoth **train station** (120 Le Duan, tel. 024/3942-3949, www.gahanoi. com.vn) serves southern cities like Danang (17 hours), Nha Trang (28 hours), and Ho Chi Minh City (33 hours), in addition to offering an overnight service north to Sapa. Tickets can be purchased through the station directly as well as from the rail company's website (www.dsvn.vn), and they are offered at travel agencies across town. Ask around when booking through a travel agency, as some outfits charge excessive commission.

Taxi from the Train Station

The train station attracts plenty of cab drivers eager to catch a fare from an unsuspecting or weary traveler, often at several times the actual price. Opt for one of the **Mailinh** (tel. 024/3833-3333) cabs waiting out front. Expect to pay around VND70,000 for a trip from the train station to Hoan Kiem Lake (a 10-minute ride).

BUS

Hanoi has three separate bus stations scattered around the outskirts. **Giap Bat** (Giai Phong, tel. 024/3864-1467) handles all routes heading south to destinations such as Ninh Binh and Hue, while vehicles at **Gia Lam** (9

Ngo Gia Kham, tel. 024/3827-1529) depart for Ha Long and Haiphong on a regular basis. To the west, **My Dinh** (20 Pham Hung, tel. 024/3768-5549) offers the occasional fare to Lao Cai and other northwestern towns.

You can eliminate the hassle of getting out to the station and navigating Vietnamese bus timetables and fare collectors by taking one of the comfy, air-conditioned coach buses that leave from the offices of **Sinh Tourist** (52 Luong Ngoc Quyen, tel. 024/3926-1568, www.thesinhtourist.vn, 8am-10pm daily) as well as several other local companies, all of which are located in the downtown area. Sinh Tourist has only the Luong Ngoc Quyen location and another on Tran Nhat Duat (64 Tran Nhat Duat, tel. 024/3929-0394, 6am-8:30pm daily). All other signs advertising "Sinh Cafe," "The Sinh Cafe," or "Sinh Cafe Tourist" are impostors. Go to the correct address and look for the blue-and-white logo.

Hoang Long (28 Tran Nhat Duat, tel. 024/3928-2828, www.hoanglongasia.com, 7:30am-7pm daily) also offers good-value tickets. The company has satellite offices at the Giap Bat and My Dinh bus stations as well as its Old Quarter office.

While buses can be a convenient way to get around northern Vietnam and perhaps even into the central region, traveling to Ho Chi Minh City on two wheels is a long haul. You won't find any buses running nonstop between Hanoi and the southern hub; the total travel time between the two cities is around 42 hours. For this reason, you're better off flying, booking a train ticket, or making at least one stop somewhere along the way.

Taxi from the Bus Station

If taxis from the airport come with a bad reputation, the cabs loitering outside of bus stations across the city are in an equally poor standing. Before you even step off the bus, there will be a swarm of drivers crowding the vehicle's entrance, just waiting for a tired, confused, or unsuspecting tourist to wander their way. The best thing you can do when stepping off a bus is grab your luggage and make a beeline for the exit. Ignore the touts, cab drivers, *xe om*, and anyone else who insists upon giving you a ride and walk to the street. From there, you needn't head more than a block before you find that cab drivers have backed off the hard sell, and it's much easier to pick out a reputable vehicle and set off.

MOTORBIKE

As it rolls into the capital, Vietnam's famous Highway 1 goes by a few different names before splitting in two directions to avoid the city altogether; from here, Ngoc Hoi transitions into Giai Phong and eventually Le Duan, landing you squarely in the heart of town just a few kilometers from Hoan Kiem Lake. For those arriving from the east, a pair of equally hectic national roads, Highway 14 and Highway 1, come together 13 kilometers outside of the city and head across the Chuong Duong Bridge into town. Travelers from the west will follow Highway 6 directly to the city center, while those coming from the north have a few options. Thang Long Boulevard reaches Hanoi from the northwest, heading in toward Hoan Kiem Lake; there is also an airport road that passes by West Lake before approaching the city from the north. Being an obvious center of activity, no one highway is less crowded than the others. If possible, arrive before or after the evening rush hour.

Getting Around

Hanoi's traffic is hectic. Only confident, experienced drivers should brave Hanoian traffic. Much of the Old Quarter lacks streetlights or stop signs. Narrow roads combined with fast-paced driving can easily result in accidents. Many streets in downtown Hanoi are one way, and turning right on red is forbidden in the capital city.

TAXI

Taxis in the capital have a less-than-stellar reputation for overcharging tourists, either

rush hour traffic

through hyperactive meters or by making a few extra turns to run up the fare. Companies like **Mailinh** (tel. 024/3833-3333) and the red-and-blue **Taxi Group** (tel. 024/3853-5353) are reputable. When hailing a cab downtown, move away from the heavily touristed areas like Ma May or Ly Quoc Su and hop in a taxi near the main road instead, as this will decrease your chances of encountering an opportunistic cabbie. Taxis should always be metered; while some drivers attempt to quote a flat rate, these are almost never in your favor so it's best to stick to the machine. If possible, try to pay with exact change or something close to it, as cab drivers often insist that they don't have small bills in hopes of gleaning a few extra thousand dong from you. Should you find yourself in a situation where you feel as though you're being taken advantage of—the meter is running too high, for example—stop the cab where you are, pay the fare, and exit the vehicle. Protesting or waiting to negotiate a price may result in more trouble.

RIDE-HAILING APPS

Regional ride-hailing app **Grab** (www.grab.com) has made its mark on Hanoi's traffic, much to the ire of traditional *xe om* drivers and cabbies alike. It offer riders dirt-cheap rates in two- and four-wheeled vehicles. While Grab drivers can be a mixed bag—your driver might be a knowledgeable local, a whiz with GPS, or someone who just moved to the city yesterday—the service is generally safe and prices are unbeatable. You can also opt to pay by card or in cash in Hanoi.

XE OM

Walking around the Old Quarter, you will soon become accustomed to the waving hands and calls of "Hello! Motorbike!" that follow travelers around the city. *Xe om* drivers perch on most corners in the downtown area and can be relentless in their sales pitch. Agree upon a fare before hopping on board. From the Old Quarter to most tourist destinations in the area (barring faraway sights like the Museum of Ethnology and West Lake), your

fare should not exceed VND50,000. If a particular driver is not willing to budge on the price, find another driver.

Hanoi's *xe om* drivers are daredevils, weaving through a hectic web of traffic that hurtles haphazardly down the narrow streets of downtown Hanoi. For safety's sake, insist upon wearing a helmet. Even if most Vietnamese helmets are not up to Western standards, better to have a little protection in the event of an accident than none at all.

CYCLO

Slow-moving and seemingly less dangerous than their motorized compatriots, cyclos are the vehicle of choice for many travelers, as they give you the opportunity to sit back as you ply the streets of downtown Hanoi without fear of being run over by a motorbike. These sluggish, human-powered trikes ferry tourists all over the Old Quarter with occasional jaunts out to the French Quarter or Ba Dinh Square and beyond, depending on the passenger's needs. A standard cyclo trip lasts about an hour, weaving through the narrow downtown streets and allowing you to get a genuine feel of the city without tackling Hanoi traffic on your own. You'll have to bargain for your fare; most hour-long journeys begin around VND200,000. Your driver will be cycling you around with his own two legs, and so you should expect to pay more than you would for a motorized trip.

BUS

Hanoi's **public bus** (tel. 04/3843-6393, www.transerco.vn, 5am-9pm daily, VND7,000) lines run all over town and are the most cost-effective way to navigate its narrow streets. While maps of the entire system are not readily available, Google Maps accurately plots the city's bus routes, which makes finding the right bus line as easy as plugging your start and end destinations into the app. On the street, all stops are clearly marked with a blue sign bearing the bus number and its route, and fares are posted on the outside of each vehicle. Most rides around the city cost

VND7,000. From the northern edge of Hoan Kiem Lake, buses 9 and 14 are especially useful, as these stop either directly in front of or not far from several popular sights, including Ho Chi Minh Mausoleum, the Temple of Literature, the Hanoi Flag Tower, and the Museum of Ethnology. While many of the more common downtown bus routes stop service at 9pm, some stop around 8pm. Both Google Maps and the Hanoi Bus website have accurate information regarding bus run times.

ELECTRIC CAR

Dong Xuan Market runs an **electric car service** (north side of Hoan Kiem Lake, tel. 024/3929-0509, dongxuantours@gmail.com, 8am-10pm daily, VND200,000 for 35 minutes, VND300,000 for 1 hour) that ferries tourists around Hoan Kiem Lake and the Old Quarter area. A handful of standard routes are available, stopping at some of the city's more noteworthy landmarks and shopping areas. Electric cars seat a maximum of seven people and, while it is possible to travel with less than seven to a car, you'll have to cover the cost for the entire vehicle regardless of how many are on board.

MOTORBIKE

Motorbike rentals are widely available in the downtown area, especially around Ngo Huyen near St. Joseph's Cathedral and along Dinh Liet to the north of Hoan Kiem Lake. Some of the foreign-owned rental outfits charge as much as VND210,000 per day, but you can easily rent a bike of reasonable quality for VND100,000 from one of the Vietnamese shops nearby. There are a handful of outfits on Dinh Liet that rent out vehicles at reasonable prices. Some shops may request collateral for the vehicle, in the form of either an ID or a cash deposit. Do a lap around the block and check for any issues before setting off for the day and insist upon a helmet for the trip. Though you'll see plenty of locals flaunting this rule, Vietnamese law requires that all drivers wear a helmet when driving.

cyclos

Vicinity of Hanoi

Beyond the city limits, Hanoi's suburbs and surrounding countryside offer a few easygoing day trips. At the heart of the Red River Delta, a pair of booming traditional handicraft villages complement the urban chaos, while a serene pagoda complex southwest of the city affords an altogether different view of northern Vietnam. Jaunts to Tam Coc and Hoa Lu, Ninh Binh's main attractions, are possible, with plenty of tour providers offering day trips to the area.

PERFUME PAGODA

One of over 30 pagodas dotting the mountains of Ha Tay province, the beautifully austere **Perfume Pagoda (Chua Huong)** (8am-5pm daily, VND80,000, plus boat fare) is Hanoi's most popular day-trip destination. Perfume Pagoda, named for the clouds of incense permeating the cave's interior, is located inside a cave at the top of a mountain. Sixty-four kilometers west of the capital, the pagoda complex sprawls across a series of hills overlooking the Yen River and is considered northern Vietnam's most important Buddhist

center of worship. Though it's become increasingly more commercial, with the usual roving vendors and boat drivers, the scenery and famous incense-filled grotto are worth a visit for those looking to escape the city.

Most trips to Perfume Pagoda are done via all-inclusive tour, as this is the most hassle-free way to visit. Tour outfitters transport passengers to Yen Vy, a boat station in the town of Huong Son. From here, travelers board a small wooden **rowboat** (VND50,000 pp). The boat glides on a small river past craggy limestone mountains and dense forest, taking about an hour. When your vessel reaches the pagoda complex, venture through the impressive three-door gate, a stark, towering structure whose black Chinese characters stand out against a bright white background. Past the gates, the temple Chua Thien Tru, also known as Heaven's Kitchen, houses a statue of Quan Am. It's one of the more atmospheric pagodas in the north.

The highlight of the pagoda complex is Huong Tich Cave, which is 50 meters above the water's edge atop a mountain. Though

Perfume Pagoda

Vicinity of Hanoi

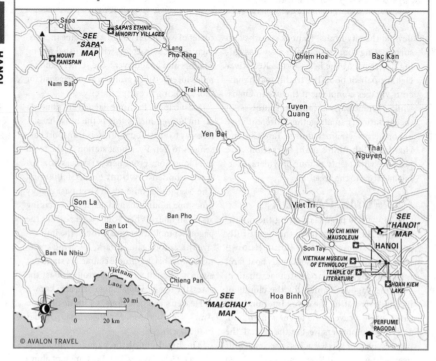

Sapa

SEE "SAPA" MAP

SAPA'S ETHNIC MINORITY VILLAGES

MOUNT FANISPAN

Lang Pho Rang

Chiem Hoa

Bac Kan

Nam Bai

Trai Hut

Tuyen Quang

Thai Nguyen

Yen Bai

Son La

Viet Tri

HO CHI MINH MAUSOLEUM

Ban Pho

SEE "HANOI" MAP

Ban Lot

Son Tay

HANOI

VIETNAM MUSEUM OF ETHNOLOGY

Ban Na Nhiu

TEMPLE OF LITERATURE

Vietnam

Laos

Chieng Pan

SEE "MAI CHAU" MAP

Hoa Binh

HOAN KIEM LAKE

0   20 mi

0   20 km

PERFUME PAGODA

© AVALON TRAVEL

you have the option of reaching Huong Tich on foot, following a winding path up the mountain, most visitors prefer to jump in a brightly colored cable car (VND100,000 one-way, VND160,000 round-trip) to the mouth of the cave, where a set of stone steps descends into the darkened grotto. The cave interior is filled with small altars, obscured by an incense haze, and lacquer effigies. Once you've wandered through, walk back down toward the river. The steps become treacherous in foul weather; you can also hop on the cable car for the return trip. Respectful dress is a must at the complex.

While it's possible to reach the complex on your own via motorbike, the hassle of urban traffic is not really worth the few dollars you might save. Moreover, the journey to Perfume Pagoda is not nearly as picturesque as the site itself. Dozens of tour companies in Hanoi offer full-day excursions that include transportation, entry fees, lunch, and a guide for as little as VND550,000.

HANDICRAFT VILLAGES

Across Vietnam, dozens of villages lay claim to culinary specialties or unique traditional crafts. These small, tight-knit communities have produced marble statues, fine silk, traditional Vietnamese lacquerware, or handmade pottery for centuries. Just outside of Hanoi, Bat Trang to the south and Van Phuc to the west each boast a long tradition of producing top-quality items and are known throughout Vietnam for their skilled craftspeople.

Bat Trang

Sixteen kilometers south and across the Red River, the small village of **Bat Trang** has been making high-quality ceramics since the 15th century and is a popular stop for shoppers in search of ceramics. Today, its pottery is nationally famous and exported around the world, with modern-day potters crafting both the traditional blue-and-white ceramics of the past as well as more colorful contemporary designs. Price tags in some of the larger outlets tend not to vary much from those in the city, but you'll find that there is more room for bargaining here and seemingly endless variety.

Most shops (which are also people's houses) are open from around 7am to 5pm or 6pm daily, and vendors sell similar objects. Visiting Bat Trang is like perusing a large pottery market.

Often, shops will have someone working on pottery, giving a glimpse of the pottery-making process. Ask permission before taking photos, though most shops will likely give permission. If a vendor invites you to try out the pottery wheel or help you make something, there will almost always be an expectation that you buy something in return.

Travelers can reach Bat Trang independently by taxi, bus, or hired vehicle. Bus 47A departs every half-hour from the large bus stop near Long Bien Bridge just north of the Old Quarter off Hang Dau street. Cyclists and motorbikes can reach the area by way of Provincial Road 378 on the eastern bank of the river. When crossing, cyclists should use Long Bien Bridge, while other vehicles should use Chuong Duong Bridge directly south.

Van Phuc

West out of town en route to Perfume Pagoda, the whirring looms of **Van Phuc** silk village draw droves of curious shoppers exploring the countryside for the day. As early as the 9th century, local residents raised mulberry trees and silkworms here, spinning their fragile cocoons into fabric for sale both in the village and across the country. During the days of the Nguyen dynasty, Van Phuc was required to produce bolts of silk to clothe the royal family. Today, the village houses over 1,000 looms and its goods are often exported beyond Vietnam's borders. While shoppers will find the cost of raw material about the same as in the city, ready-made items like scarves, ties, and shirts are notably less expensive here.

Shops generally open at 8am or 9am and close at 5pm daily. Most of the shops in Van Phuc are also workshops. The silk is made there, so you can watch as local proprietors weave different fabrics with a loom. Shop owners are often happy to let you try out the loom, but you will be strongly encouraged to buy something in return.

While most visitors to Van Phuc get here by way of a day tour to Perfume Pagoda, it is also possible to reach Van Phuc independently. Bus 2 travels out to the village by way of Highway 6, departing from the French Quarter and the lower part of Hoan Kiem district near the train station. Drivers can access Van Phuc via the same route.

Mai Chau

A rustic escape from Vietnam's chaotic capital, Mai Chau has soaring emerald mountains and paddy fields dotted with the traditional wooden stilt houses of the region's ethnic Thai people. This little corner of the country is an up-and-coming spot for more adventurous travelers thanks to its beautiful scenery, friendly local communities, and blissfully disconnected status.

While the town of Mai Chau is nothing more than a whistle-stop light on attractions and organized activities, its landscape has seduced many travelers. Those with a go-with-the-flow attitude easily find things to do, from checking out nearby caves and waterfalls to exploring the countryside on a bicycle or motorbike to visiting some of Vietnam's ethnic minority communities in nearby villages.

Mai Chau's weather is best September-May, when temperatures are pleasant and the skies relatively clear. It can get chilly December-January, but you're better off packing a few extra layers than braving Mai Chau's sweltering summer months. As a small destination, travelers shouldn't need more than 2-3 days to cover Mai Chau and its surrounding area, though you could easily stay for an extra day or two.

SIGHTS

TOP EXPERIENCE

Ethnic Minority Villages

West of Mai Chau's main road, Route 15, and slightly south of Mai Chau, some of Vietnam's ethnic minority communities make their homes, primarily the White Thai and Muong. These small villages are where you'll find most of the area's tourist infrastructure: Ban Lac 1, Ban Lac 2, and Poom Coong. Visitors typically stay in or near one of these villages.

Ban Lacs 1 and **2** are more retail-oriented than their neighbors, with a handful of shops that produce traditional White Thai textiles featuring incredibly detailed embroidery and batik dyeing. **Poom Coong** is nearby and easily walkable. The surrounding villages of **Na** **Phon,** a few kilometers northwest of the Ban Lacs and Poom Coong, and **Chieng Chau,** a few kilometers south, are best explored on a bicycle or in an electric vehicle. Either way, the lush hills, charming stilt houses, and green fields make for excellent scenery, and you're likely to get at least a hello or two as you wander around.

Since the appeal of this area is its landscapes, most travelers just wander the narrow, concrete roads off the main highway. You won't find many maps to guide you, but homestay owners can provide some guidance regarding the Ban Lacs/Poom Coong area, which is very small and easy to navigate. Even with the surrounding villages, this is not a very big place, so travelers can't really get too lost.

Hang Chieu

Sometimes referred to as the 1,000-Step Cave, **Hang Chieu** (Route 15, sunrise-sunset, free) is not for the faint of heart. As you might have guessed, a staggering 1,000—some say 1,200—steps lead up the mountainside to a modest cavern overlooking the valley, its stilt houses, rice paddies, rolling mountains, and green forest spread out below as far as the eye can see. You'll be more than happy to explore

view of Mai Chau Valley from Hang Chieu

Mai Chau

the cave, enjoying its cool interior, after the long journey to the top. It's a one- to two-kilometer walk north from Ban Lacs 1 and 2 and Poom Coong to the cave. You'll notice a blue-and-white sign along Route 15 announcing the turn in for Hang Chieu's entrance. Bring water with you for the ascent, and make sure to wear sunscreen as there's little to no shade on the path.

Mo Luong Cave

Mo Luong Cave (Route 15, sunrise-sunset, free) is a pleasant spot to poke around and a far less strenuous alternative to neighboring

Hang Chieu. The steps up to this subterranean chamber are low, well shaded, and decorated with European-style balustrades. Though its interior is sometimes padlocked—the Mai Chau Lodge directly across the road has exclusive use of the place—visitors can access it if they're guests of the lodge or if they book a tour through its partner, Asia Outdoors. One intriguing way to gain access is to sign up for regular yoga class (VND200,000) held inside the cave through **Asia Outdoors** (Mai Chau Lodge, tel. 0218/386-8859, www.asiaoutdoors.com.vn).

Scenic Drive to Ba Khan

Experiencing the stunning road to **Ba Khan,** overlooking **Song Da Lake,** is a must. Without stops, the 45-kilometer loop takes 2-2.5 hours, but the road conditions along this stretch—not to mention the scenic photo ops—make this a daylong affair. The scenic drive takes you through lush, green forest and offers panoramas overlooking the turquoise Song Da Lake, which has a series of Ha Long Bay-esque limestone islands covered in foliage. You'll also follow a series of mountains whose higher vantage points provide nice views of the surrounding rice paddies, rolling hills, and open land. A handful of rest stops are along the loop, including a clutch of food and drink stops, but offerings are basic, so you may want to bring some snacks with you.

The loop begins on Route 15, where **Mai Chau Lodge** is located. From here, you'll head north. Route 15 becomes Route 6 and hits a small junction bearing a sign for **Go Lao Waterfall.** Follow the sign for the turnoff onto a narrow, concrete road, and you'll reach a small house where some local folks have set up a parking lot for the waterfall. You'll keep right from here, with the lake to your left. Continuing on this road, drivers will veer south away from the lake, past sleepy Ba Khan, a small, nondescript town, and back toward Route 6. Once you hit Route 6, you'll turn right and pass the **Mai Chau Flagpole,** a stop that offers nice views of the sprawling Mai Chau Valley. Back on the road, you'll hit Route 15 again, taking a left for Mai Chau to complete the loop.

Since the road to Ba Khan is rural and not well maintained (some cracks, potholes, downed trees), it's recommended only for experienced motorbike drivers. Be careful, go slow, and be prepared to turn back if it looks like the weather's going to take a turn for the worst. Bring a smartphone if you can; even without service, the phone's GPS will often display your location in Google Maps, making it easy to ensure you're on the right track. Others can hop into a taxi (around VND750,000) to experience the loop.

Go Lao Waterfall

About 12 kilometers north of town, **Go Lao Waterfall** (Route 15, sunrise-sunset, VND10,000) makes for a pleasant adventure. Standing 20 meters tall, it's a beautiful sight during rainy season but even in the drier months still makes an impression. Follow Route 15 as it becomes Route 6 then Route 15 again, then follow the handful of signs directing you from this main road to the falls. You'll find an impromptu parking spot in front of a local house, where you can make your way down to the bottom of the cascade via a five-minute walk. Be careful here, as the descent is steep and can be slippery in wet weather.

Tours

Travelers can easily explore Mai Chau and its surrounding villages independently on foot or by bicycle, motorbike, or electric car. Many people opt for a homestay in Mai Chau, and hosts are often keen to assist with visits to sights that require transportation. Many homestays offer bicycles to guests free of charge.

Active travelers will appreciate the growing number of opportunities for rock climbing, rappelling, trekking, caving, cycling, and kayaking in Mai Chau. At the moment, the only game in town is **Asia Outdoors** (Mai Chau Lodge, tel. 0218/386-8859, www.asiaoutdoors.com.vn, 8am-8pm daily, VND200,000-1,600,000).

SHOPPING

Mai Chau's White Thai ethnic minority is known for its hand-embroidered quilts and batik-dyed fabrics. You'll find these on offer throughout Ban Lac 1 and Poom Coong villages. Some bargaining is acceptable, but with Mai Chau yet to become a tourist trap, even the sticker price is usually reasonable. While some of Ban Lac 1's shops have begun to stock cheaper mass-produced versions of the area's local fabrics, products from **Mai Chau Handmade** (Ban Lac 1, tel.

016/8427-9656, maichauhandmadeshop@ gmail.com, 6am-9pm daily) are the real deal. Authentic handmade Thai textiles are used to create everything from scarves and table runners to bags and pillow covers. Prices run a bit higher than other places but the quality of the handiwork makes these products worth it. **Hoa Ban Plus** (Ban Lac 2, tel. 09/4315-7000, 7am-9pm daily) is a social enterprise that employs local women with physical disabilities to create souvenirs such as bags, shoes, stuffed animals, and scarves for sale. Prices are reasonable and the staff is always keen to strike up a conversation.

FOOD

Mai Chau may not have any famous specialties of its own, but the area's grilled chicken and *ruou can*, a type of rice wine, are popular. When it comes to dining, most homestays include at least one meal, usually dinner, and sometimes breakfast as well. This is almost always your best bet.

Get your barbecue fix at the restaurant below Homestay 39, **Ha Cong Khui** (Ban Lac 1, tel. 016/4897-4350, 10am-8pm daily, VND100,000-150,000). You'll likely find a solid meal at any one of the eateries surrounding this corner, but Homestay 39 offers a modest menu of grilled chicken, buffalo, fish, skewers, and a few other eats. Look for the smoking grill as you approach.

Modest **Mai Chau Countryside** (Poom Coong, tel. 016/4423-5140, toanlatmchb@ gmail.com, 9am-8pm daily, VND30,000-180,000) serves up mostly Vietnamese cuisine along with a bit of Western fare such as pizza and burgers. Vegetarians will also find options, and there are especially nice views from the café and bar area.

At the end of a day of adventure, grab a drink at **Sunset Bar** (Poom Coong, tel. 09/6282-6233, www.maichausunset.com, 7am-11pm daily, VND25,000-150,000), one of the only watering holes in town. This small rooftop spot boasts a pleasant view of the town below and its greenery, and the staff is easygoing.

ACCOMMODATIONS

Most accommodations in Mai Chau are homestays, though this is a broad term used to describe several different types of lodgings. Still, most are bare-bones, featuring thin mattresses, no air-conditioning, and mosquito nets on the top floor of a traditional wooden stilt house. For genuine one-on-one family homestays, seek out a place in Poom Coong,

traditional textiles of Mai Chau's White Thai people

which is the quietest of the towns. Things get a little livelier in Ban Lacs 1 and 2, where guesthouse-style homestays—essentially dormitories—can be found, while a handful of actual guesthouses in the area also provide private rooms. Nearly all of these places, homestays included, offer Wi-Fi as well as a meal or two.

Under VND210,000

The amiable family at Poom Coong's **Guesthouse 14—Ha Cong Thanh** (Poom Coong, tel. 09/8953-1820, VND100,000 bed, VND200,000 with breakfast and dinner) offers the top floor of their home to homestay guests. Though the family doesn't speak much English, Thanh, the head of the house, is a cheerful guy who knows his way around Mai Chau's most popular sights and can assist with motorbike rentals and Mai Chau area navigation. Beds are modest but comfortable and the property has Wi-Fi as well as fans. Add on breakfast and dinner if you can, as meals are top-notch.

The vibe at **Mai Chau Hostel** (Ban Lac 1, tel. 012/3585-8688, namsppt@yahoo.com, VND130,000 bed) is a little more in line with a backpacker dorm than a homestay, but the staff is friendly and the hostel runs a small restaurant downstairs. Shared baths are notably clean, and beds come with Wi-Fi and a fan.

VND1,050,000-2,100,000

The charming **Mai Chau Valley View** (Route 15, Mai Chau, tel. 0218/386-7080, www.maichauvalleyview.com, VND900,000-1,135,000, breakfast included) sits directly on Route 15 overlooking the fields that lead onto Poom Coong village. Rooms are bright and clean, if a little worn, and bicycle rental is included. A small dining area downstairs also stays open throughout the day, and the staff can assist with tour bookings. The hotel's roadside location increases the possibility of traffic noise.

One of Mai Chau's oldest accommodations, the rustic **Mai Chau Lodge** (Route 15, Mai Chau, tel. 0218/386-8959, www.maichaulodge.com, VND1,500,000-4,100,000) offers a touch more luxury in its 16 well-appointed rooms, with air-conditioning, satellite TV, room service, an on-site swimming pool, a jetted pool, and a spa. Guests also have complimentary use of the lodge's bicycles and kayaks, which can be used on a neighboring pond. Mai Chau Lodge also arranges transfers from Hanoi for those who prefer to travel in style.

Mai Chau Lodge

Over VND2,100,000

The beautiful, secluded bungalows of **Mai Chau Ecolodge** (Na Phon, tel. 0218/381-9888, www.maichau.ecolodge.asia, VND2,900,000-6,165,000) blend seamlessly into the surrounding countryside. Situated on a hill overlooking a sea of paddy fields, two kilometers west of Mai Chau off of Route 15, each boasts a view of the area's stunning scenery as well as an in-room safe, a mini-bar, and complimentary rice wine, fruit, and mineral water. Bright, spacious rooms are outfitted with Thai handicrafts and bamboo furnishings, outdoor showers, and in some cases, large wooden bathtubs. Atop the ecolodge's hill, guests are free to visit the swimming pool, restaurant, and bar. The friendly staff can set you up with extra activities like cooking classes, guided tours, and spa services.

INFORMATION AND SERVICES

The town **post office** (Route 15, Mai Chau, tel. 0218/386-7091, 7am-11am and 1:30pm-5:30pm daily) is located along the main road and can handle basic postal needs.

The basic **Mai Chau General Hospital** (Route 15, Mai Chau, tel. 0218/386-7397) is located along Route 15 and can handle minor bumps and bruises, but for anything more serious, it's best to head to Hanoi.

GETTING THERE
Bus

Local minibuses to Mai Chau depart daily from Hanoi's **My Dinh bus station** (20 Pham Hung, tel. 024/3768-5549) and cost around VND80,000. Several bus companies run trips twice a day, typically departing between 6:30am-7:50am and 1:30pm-2pm. The ride is about 3.5-4 hours long. These buses can be a bit cramped but include air-conditioning. Be sure to ask the price before you climb on board as many companies forego the ticket booth and instead collect rider fares on the bus. These vehicles will drop you somewhere along the main road rather than the bus station as they carry on with their journey westward.

To depart from Mai Chau, your best bet is to ask your homestay or hotel, as Mai Chau's official bus station sits empty most of the time. Instead, minibuses bound for Hanoi make a slow drive through town every morning and early afternoon to pick up passengers. One reliable option is **Ha Loan** (tel. 09/1249-0679, 8am and 1:30pm daily, VND80,000), which runs two trips daily between Mai Chau and Hanoi. If you're planning to hop on board, it's not a bad idea to call ahead and secure a specific pick-up spot, but you'll need a Vietnamese speaker to help. Alternatively, you can head to Route 15 next to the Mai Chau Lodge around departure time and flag down a bus.

Motorbike

If you're traveling by motorbike, the road into Mai Chau is an introduction to northwestern Vietnam's ups and downs, with sweeping valleys and a handful of mountain passes along the way. Getting out of Hanoi can be a bit hairy, but drivers will take Route 13 to what becomes picturesque Route 6, staying on this highway until just past the Mai Chau Flagpole, where there's a left turn onto Route 15, the main road running through Mai Chau town and just east of the area's ethnic minority villages. Mai Chau is about 140 kilometers southwest of Mai Chau, and the drive takes about 3.5-4 hours.

GETTING AROUND

If you're staying in either Ban Lac 1 or 2, or Poom Coong, it's easy to get around the immediate vicinity on foot. For slightly longer trips around the valley, **bicycles** are available free of charge at most homestays.

For a break, travelers can also hire **electric vehicles.** Most drivers charge around VND200,000 per vehicle for an eight-village tour. These golf cart-esque vehicles seat up to six people and can usually be found at the southern edge of Ban Lac 1. For greater distances, hop in a **Mai Chau** taxi (tel. 0218/386-8788). You can also hire a motorbike; while most homestays are able to find you a rental, the folks at **Dan Thu** (Poom Coong, tel. 016/7937-6046), a guesthouse, offer rates around VND200,000 per day. Pickup and drop-off times are flexible. Novice drivers ought to be careful, as driving around Mai Chau involves more varied road conditions as well as a few more ups and downs than you might find near the coast; roads are a mixture of sealed roads, sections of highway that have fallen into disrepair, and smaller roads made of concrete (particularly slippery in wet weather), and the mountains mean lots of hairpin turns and winding roads.

Sapa

Perched high above Muong Hoa Valley, the sleepy little town of Sapa is fast becoming one of Vietnam's most popular destinations thanks to its magnificent scenery and diversity. A world apart from its urban contemporaries, Sapa is known for its rolling hills and verdant, many-tiered rice terraces, as well as its local minority cultures, whose traditional dress, rituals, religious ceremonies, and ways of life continue to exist in much the same fashion as they have for centuries.

Though its tourism industry has seen a major boom in recent years, this hilltop town has long captivated visitors, attracting French attention in the early 20th century. Some ethnic Vietnamese moved into the area in the 1960s, but it wasn't until well after the war's end in the 1990s that Sapa saw major growth.

The fresh air, ample hiking trails, and opportunity for cultural exchange with some of Vietnam's lesser-known communities draw luxury travelers and adventure seekers with the prospect of visiting the area's ethnic minority villages or scaling the colossal Mount Fansipan, Vietnam's tallest peak.

Inclement weather can ruin a visit to Sapa. The best months are September and October, just before the rice harvests take away much of its visual appeal, or at the start of spring, for better views of the valley. From November to February, temperatures plummet, earning Sapa a reputation as one of the only towns in Vietnam that sees snow. In winter, heavy fog makes for poor visibility, spoiling much of the point of a visit to Sapa.

SIGHTS

In a few short years, Sapa town has transformed into a place buzzing with domestic and foreign visitors, large tour groups, and independent travelers. Construction seems to be everywhere these days, as new hotels and attractions go up left and right. The town's sights are easily accessed on foot, though you'll get a workout traipsing up and down some of the nearby inclines. It's the views farther outside of Sapa town, however, that captivate most visitors. For nearby attractions, a small downtown park dominated by a monument to Ho Chi Minh leads onto the large local square, a popular gathering place in the mornings and evenings. Farther north near the main highway, **Sapa Lake** makes for a pleasant stroll, surrounded by manicured gardens and plenty of park benches.

Sapa Market

Sapa's newer, bigger, and slightly emptier **central market** (corner of Route 4D and Luong Dinh Cua street, 6am-6pm daily) is open from dawn to dusk and focuses more on handicrafts and tourist souvenirs than practical items, though you will find a few necessities in the stalls on its ground floor. For genuine handmade textiles produced by local ethnic minority women, head upstairs to the very back of the market, where you'll find a group of mostly H'mong and Red Dao women hawking their wares. Vendors can get a bit pushy but keep your cool and feel free to haggle a bit when making a purchase.

Sapa Museum

Located in a traditional wooden stilt house behind the Tourist Information Center, **Sapa Museum** (2 Fansipan, tel. 0214/387-1975, 7:30am-11:30am and 1:30pm-5pm daily, free) gives a solid introduction to the town and the area, telling the story of Sapa's history under the French and its growth as a town during the 20th century. While a handful of the traditions and customs of Sapa's ethnic minorities are touched upon, there's far less background on the H'mong, Dao, Tay, Phu La, and Giay people who inhabit the region. For this, link up with a local guide to learn more about life in the village.

Our Lady of Rosary Church

The diminutive stone **Our Lady of Rosary Church** (Sapa Town Square, tel. 0214/387-3014, www.sapachurch.org) was first built in 1926 to accommodate Sapa's European parishioners. It is a pretty landmark in town, its gray exterior rounding out the eastern edge of the town square. While the doors are closed except during mass, its steps are often used as a gathering place along with the square nearby.

Cat Cat Village

Cat Cat Village (6:30am-5:30pm daily, VND70,000 adults, VND30,000 children) is home to the Black H'mong. The trip to the village is one of the more accessible walks in the Sapa area. This particular jaunt falls somewhere between a hike and a trek (just over five kilometers round-trip), with paved, well-trodden paths winding through what is now more of a tourist attraction than an actual village. The walk down to Cat Cat from Sapa affords stunning panoramas of Muong Hoa Valley. En route to Cat Cat's ticket booth, you'll pass by small clapboard houses, which remain the most authentic part of the village. Once you've paid and passed through the entry gate, the line of handicraft stalls runs almost unbroken from the top of the steps all the way down to Tien Sa Falls, showcasing skirts and scarves, T-shirts, hats, jewelry, and heavily detailed indigo-dyed blankets. Across a suspension bridge that teeters above a rushing waterfall, Black H'mong cultural performances (9am-4pm daily with a break for lunch, additional fee), featuring songs and traditional dances, take place nearly every hour.

Complete the Cat Cat loop by continuing along the stone path and back up. *Xe om* drivers wait just beyond the second bridge and are happy to ferry passengers back to Sapa town for no more than VND50,000.

For shoppers, it pays to visit when Cat Cat is in full swing (10am-2pm), but travelers who simply want to explore the village and get a glimpse of local life should start by 9am. This early in the day, fewer vendors have set up along the path and you're more likely to elude the roving groups of Black H'mong saleswomen along Fansipan Road. For particularly good views, a bit of local art, and a refreshment, the back veranda of **Gem Valley Art Gallery** (Cat Cat, tel. 09/1284-9753, 7am-10pm daily, VND25,000-100,000) is a fine spot to rest your legs.

Allow 45-60 minutes to complete the trip there and back.

TOP EXPERIENCE

★ Ethnic Minority Villages

Beyond Sapa's borders, the surrounding hills and valleys are studded with **ethnic minority villages** (VND30,000-75,000), particularly those of the Black H'mong and Red Dao. Most of these remote areas bear a resemblance to each other, partly because many groups have coexisted for many years. Visiting any of the villages affords visitors a window into the daily lives of Sapa's minority communities, as well as the pleasure of trekking through the verdant landscape. Wander past rows of modest wooden houses, where women dye indigo cloth or embroider intricate designs. Share a meal with a local family, or even spend the night. Here, several hundred meters above sea level, Sapa's nearby residents are a world apart from the rest of the country.

You'll find sound advice and useful maps

Sapa

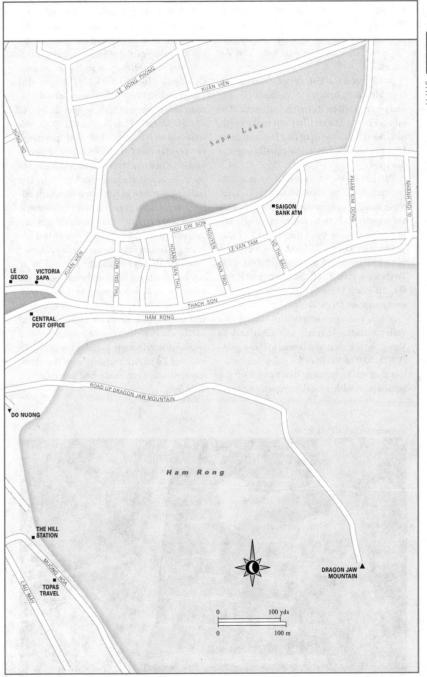

of Sapa's vicinity at the **local tourism office** (2 Fansipan, tel. 0214/387-1975, www.sapa-tourism.com, 7:30am-11:30am and 1:30pm-5:30pm daily), which can help you get oriented.

Just beyond Cat Cat, the next-nearest village, **Sin Chai,** belongs to the Black H'mong and prides itself on its traditional music. The villages of **Ma Tra** and **Ta Phin** to the north, patchwork settlements of Red Dao and Black H'mong households, make equally popular day trips.

Farther south, **Ta Van** is home to a Giay community not far from **Lao Chai** village, another Black H'mong settlement, both of which are popular and can be visited in a single day. Just beyond these two villages is a Red Dao community, **Giang Ta Chai,** which can also be tacked onto a trek if you're up for the walk. To the east, **Hau Thao, Sa Seng,** and **Hang Da,** all Black H'mong villages, are another worthy option for trekkers.

While you can navigate the Muong Hoa valley villages—namely Lao Chai and Ta Van—on your own, you'll need to hire a guide (VND200,000-300,000) for any other excursions, as you're far more likely to get off the beaten path with a local on hand, and these individuals will have answers for your questions regarding the ins and outs of Sapa's minority cultures. Depending on where you go, a good guide can also help dissuade villagers from pummeling you with sales pitches. Companies like **ETHOS** (79 Nguyen Chi Thanh, tel. 016/6689-2536, www.ethosspirit.com, 8am-11am and 1:30pm-6pm daily) and **Sapa O'Chau** (8 Thac Bac, tel. 0214/377-1166, www.sapaochau.org, 7:30am-6:30pm daily) run regular tours to various ethnic minority villages. On a tour, travelers often hike out to the villages and are bused back to Sapa. The walking distance varies based on which villages are visited, ranging 4-16 kilometers. Tours cover no more than three villages in a day, with most going to only one or two (allowing travelers more time in each village).

Many villages can also be accessed by *xe om,* but this takes most of the fun out of the experience, as Sapa's more secluded landscapes are best explored on foot. Homestays and overnight excursions covering several nearby communities can be arranged with a tour outfitter. In more popular towns like Ta Van and Lao Chai, travelers with their own transportation can easily find homestays on their own.

H'mong children in Cat Cat Village

Silver Falls and Love Falls

About 10 kilometers out of town, a pair of waterfalls lines the highway up to Tram Ton Pass. The nearest and most popular is **Silver Falls (Thac Bac)** (6am-6pm daily, VND20,000), a charming natural sight. It's not worth the walk up to the top, as you can get the gist from the ground. The walk up is a steep set of stairs, but the going is easy.

Farther up the road, **Love Falls (Thac Tinh Yeu)** (6am-6pm daily, VND70,000) makes more of an impression. Though it's hidden off the highway about a 800 meters into the forest, the trek to the falls makes a nice nature walk, strolling through the trees beside Golden Stream (Suoi Vang). You'll need a good pair of shoes and reasonable mobility to reach the end; the stone walkway later deteriorates into a dirt track in some spots, and a few downed trees cross the path. The finale, a pretty moss-covered cascade more than 100 meters tall, makes the journey worthwhile.

Tram Ton Pass

The towering **Tram Ton Pass,** also known as O Quy Ho, is the highest road in Vietnam, coming in at 2,012 meters above sea level. This never-ending maze of switchbacks teeters on the edge of the Hoang Lien mountains, winding its way from Tam Duong, a small town about 50 kilometers west of Sapa, up along a narrow, cliff-hugging road before plunging back down to Sapa and, later, Lao Cai. While its highest point, perpetually obscured by dense forest, does not afford the kind of awe-inspiring views you might expect, with time and a motorbike (or, for the very fit, a bicycle) you can venture down the serpentine highway, admiring the view from some of its lower sections. Stop at established pullouts to admire the view and take photos. Drivers on this particular road should exercise great caution, as conditions are risky even in good weather and downright treacherous in foul weather. Take extra care when rounding corners and keep a safe distance from the outside shoulder of the road, as it's a straight drop down.

Dragon Jaw Mountain

Rising above Sapa in the southeast, **Dragon Jaw Mountain** (Ham Rong, 6am-6pm daily, VND70,000 adults, VND30,000 children) affords some pleasant views of town as well as a standard helping of Vietnamese kitsch. The most developed peak in the area, Dragon Jaw bears a spidery network of paths crisscrossing its northern side that look out over the sleepy

view of Sapa from Dragon Jaw Mountain

settlement below as well as toward Fansipan. While it's not exactly a genuine commune with nature, the stone steps that ramble up to the **Cloud Yard,** the platform with the best views of Sapa, are a nice way to pass time on your first day or as you wander around town. Thanks to its paths, solid footwear is not so essential here. You'll want to allow an hour or so to fully explore the winding routes up top. Visitors receive a map of the mountain from the ticket booth; this does little to orient you once you've started on the long stairway up. Regardless, you'll find yourself passing by a restaurant, a rather tired orchid garden, several covered lookouts, a park dotted with statues of the 12 Vietnamese zodiac animals, and, inexplicably, Mickey Mouse.

SIGHTSEEING TOURS

In order to get the most out of exploring Sapa, many travelers sign up for a guided tour to one of the nearby villages, to a bustling local market, or simply deep into the mountains for a homestay. Because so much of Sapa's tourism relies on connecting with other cultures, it is particularly important to be discerning when choosing a tour company, as you want your experience to be authentic and worthwhile not only on your part but also for the local people with whom you interact. There are a handful of trekking and tour outfits in town that focus heavily upon ensuring that the benefits of this region's tourism go directly to its local residents. If trekking to one of the nearby ethnic minority villages is on your itinerary, have a local guide bring you along, as that person will be able to explain the ins and outs of his or her culture better than anyone else. While linking up with an independent local guide was once a common thing for travelers to do, Sapa's tourism officials now discourage travelers from hiring guides off the street.

More than just a trekking outfit, the incredible **Sapa O'Chau** (8 Thac Bac, tel. 0214/377-1166, www.sapaochau.org, 6:30am-6:30pm daily) does as much for the local community as it does for its customers, providing authentic, adventurous treks off the beaten path as well as changing the lives of Sapa's young people. In a region where many minority children do not attend school beyond adolescence, Shu Tan, a young H'mong woman, has made it her mission to afford local students the skills, education, and opportunities that have long eluded this part of the country. Beginning in 2009 as a single homestay in Lao Chai, Sapa O'Chau operates a school for local students as well as its tour outfit. Training programs assist aspiring tour guides in gaining experience in the field. Sapa O'Chau is a two-way cultural exchange, in which both travelers and community members benefit. The outfit arranges single-day treks (VND450,000-910,000) and multiday treks (VND910,000-2,850,000) to various villages in the surrounding area, as well as homestays, market visits, and other adventures.

ETHOS (79 Nguyen Chi Thanh, tel. 016/6689-2536, www.ethosspirit.com, 8am-11am and 1:30pm-6pm daily, VND910,000-2,800,000) goes to great lengths to ensure that its tours are not only authentic and far-removed for the tourist crowds but that each of its excursions benefits the local community. From treks into the nearby hillside and village visits that don't appear on any other tour company's itinerary, ETHOS focuses on genuine human interactions with activities like sharing a meal or visiting someone's home that lend themselves more to one-on-one interaction. The tour agency also assists with train bookings and longer trips, including a guided tour of the Northwest Loop.

SHOPPING

As the only major tourist town in the northwest, shopping is a popular activity in Sapa, particularly when the fog rolls in to obscure its panoramic views. The main handicraft of the H'mong and Red Dao is textiles; both groups are equally skilled in colorful and detailed embroidery, which often features on skirts, jackets, blankets, bags, and other accessories. Silver jewelry and indigo-dyed items are another specialty of the H'mong. Along Cau May and Muong Hoa streets, plenty of retailers hawk knockoff North Face items for the Fansipan-bound, while handicrafts are virtually everywhere, including on the arms of roving vendors, whose sales pitches range from friendly to downright aggressive.

Hidden beneath the Cat Cat View Hotel, **Indigo Cat** (46 Fansipan, tel. 09/8240-3647, 9am-7pm Sun.-Fri.) is a small shop that specializes in Fair Trade products made by H'mong women, namely bracelets, bags, skirts, jewelry, and a few other odds and ends. Look out for the small handouts scattered throughout the store, which explain the significance of many of the intricate patterns you see on the clothing of local minority women. Indigo Cat also organizes occasional workshops on various activities like sewing and batik-making. Swing by the shop to find out more about the week's events.

SPORTS AND RECREATION

With plenty of green space, rolling hills, and incredible scenery, Sapa is an active destination and a base for trekking day trips to surrounding villages and overnight homestays with local families. These journeys range from leisurely to challenging, with Mount Fansipan being the mother of all treks, but there's also room for cycling and, when the weather takes a turn, a massage.

Trekking

With dozens of small communities peppering the mountains and valleys of northwestern Vietnam, gaining access to the more authentic villages of the area requires at least some travel on foot up the steep inclines of the surrounding hills and along the muddy dirt paths that lead to Sapa's more remote residences. In town, easier walks to **Cat Cat Village** and around **Dragon Jaw Mountain** are blessed with paved roads and stone steps. Once you leave town the highway branches off into smaller, rockier trails that bring you away from the buzz of Sapa's tourist center and out to peaceful paddies and stunning mountain vistas. For standard day-long treks and one-night homestays, bring along water and a sturdy pair of shoes. For longer excursions, especially to Fansipan, you'll need to stock up on proper trekking gear. Scores of shops in the area sell North Face goods, most of them knockoffs but some genuine, as well as a host of hiking boots, first-aid essentials, and the like.

Two companies that provide guided treks are **Sapa O'Chau** (8 Thac Bac, tel. 0214/377-1166, www.sapaochau.org, 6:30am-6:30pm daily) and **ETHOS** (79 Nguyen Chi Thanh, tel. 016/6689-2536, www.ethosspirit.com, 8am-11am and 1:30pm-6pm daily).

★ MOUNT FANSIPAN

Towering above its surroundings, **Mount Fansipan** is often referred to as the "Roof of Indochina," standing well above any other peak in neighboring Laos or Cambodia. Looming over the opposite flank of the Muong Hoa Valley, its silhouette can be seen from the town's hillside windows on a clear day.

Fansipan's trails are a little worse for wear these days, cluttered with rubbish and beginning to get too well-worn, but the enigmatic mountain remains a point of interest among many adventure-seeking travelers.

Guided excursions to the top can be attempted in as little as a day or as long as five days, depending upon your level of fitness and willingness to sleep in the rather damp and dingy camps that hover around 2,100-2,700 meters elevation. One-day treks up to the summit are not for the faint of heart: It's a 10-hour hike at best and the gently rolling trails at the start of the journey soon give way to steeper climbs before a final push to the summit. Instead, reasonably fit travelers may want to opt for a two-day trip, while those who'd prefer to take their time can venture out into the wild for longer. Shrouded in a bluish haze, the view from 3,143 meters can be fickle even during the summer months due to wind and rain. Standing next to the pyramidal marker that signals the end of your uphill climb is well worth the wet shoes and chilly temperatures.

Exploring the Northwest Loop

Venture into Vietnam's far north and you'll discover another world altogether, awash with rich green paddy fields and wide, flowing rivers that wind around the region's oversize landscapes. Those who strike out on Vietnam's **Northwest Loop** will be handsomely rewarded with soaring mountains, plunging valleys, isolated villages, and unfathomable vistas. This is an independent adventure on which you'll find few to no English speakers, no high-end hotels, and not a Western meal to speak of. The views from the northwest's serpentine roads make it well worth the journey.

Starting from Hanoi, this 1,160-kilometer circuit runs west toward Dien Bien Phu, the city where Vietnam defeated its French enemies once and for all, turning north past Muong Lay and Lai Chau, before scaling the death-defying cliffs of Tram Ton Pass, rolling into Sapa town, and coasting back down to the capital.

Most travelers make the trip on a motorbike in about a week; cyclists can complete the Northwest Loop in two weeks. Invest in a quality vehicle for the journey, as there aren't many repair shops in the area. What shops do exist have far more experience with motorbikes than with bicycles. Cyclists should stock up on tools, tubes, and other necessities before leaving Hanoi. Before you set off, commit the Vietnamese words for hotel (*khach san,* pronounced "cack san"), guesthouse (*nha nghi,* pronounced "nyah ngee"), and restaurant (*nha hang,* pronounced "nyah hang") to memory, as these will be essential when you're looking for a place to stop.

Road conditions throughout this region are good, with smooth, sleek asphalt most of the way. Opt for heavy-duty tires on both bicycles and motorbikes. Guardrails and barriers are nonexistent. Even though there's little traffic on the roads of the northwest, serious accidents can happen, and adequate medical care is a long way away.

A handful of tour outfits in Sapa arrange guided motorbike tours that follow this route, though the cost will be astronomically greater than doing it on your own. You can usually arrange these tours in Hanoi or Sapa and expect to take at least six days to complete the full circuit.

Climbers who sign up for a trip to the top should invest in a sturdy pair of hiking boots and some warm clothes. A decent jacket is still recommended in summer, as the air cools down significantly at this height. Most guided tours begin around VND1,050,000 pp for a one-day excursion, including transportation, entry fees, a guide, and, for overnight trips, a porter or two. When booking your Fansipan trek, it's important to be clear about what's included in the tour, as you'll want to know whether things like water and snacks are provided or you should be packing your own.

It's strongly advised that you pay for the necessary guide for this trek. Going it alone is not only forbidden but could easily become dangerous. In 2016 a young British hiker went missing during an unguided Fansipan trek and was later found dead. There is little to direct you once you set out for the summit and, particularly in foul weather, the trail becomes treacherous.

If you're not up for the physical challenge, you can hop on a **cable car** (tel. 0214/381-8888, www.fansipanlegend.com.vn, 7:30am-5:30pm daily, round-trip VND600,000 adults, VND400,000 children) that drops passengers within a few hundred steps of the summit. While the system managed to break two Guinness World Records (longest nonstop three-rope cable car and greatest elevation difference by a nonstop three-rope cable car), its presence has taken a bit of the magic out of scaling the Roof of Indochina, with the summit now a frequent stop for tour groups. Cable cars depart from a station located between Cat Cat and Sin Chai villages, and all tickets are sold as a round-trip package.

Cycling

There are a small number of local companies that arrange cycling tours. These excursions are expensive, justified by the quality of the equipment, but then take all the challenge out of the trip by driving travelers uphill before allowing them to roll down to the bottom. Some companies offer customized tours, however, allowing you to cater the journey to your fitness level.

To combine cycling with a bit of sightseeing, rent a mountain bike and blaze your own trail up to Silver Falls and Tram Ton Pass. For more in-depth excursions, book a tour, as the area is remote and finding your way can be difficult without someone to guide you.

For bike tours of the area, pay a visit to **Topas Travel** (21 Muong Hoa, tel. 0214/387-1331, www.topastravel.vn, 8am-5pm daily), an adventurous and enthusiastic bunch with ample experience. Half- and full-day cycling tours into the Sapa countryside cost around VND1,485,000-2,050,000 per person.

Massages and Spas

When the fog rolls into Sapa and obscures its views, a popular activity among weary travelers is a trip to the spa. The several outfits that advertise spa services, including a traditional Red Dao herbal bath, are hit or miss. For assured quality at a higher price, the spa at **Victoria Sapa** (Xuan Vien, tel. 0214/387-1522, www.victoriahotels.asia, 7am-10pm daily, VND630,000-1,260,000) provides massage services and other treatments. Nonguests are welcome at Victoria's sauna or pool (VND250,000 pp). For a more affordable option, the **Beauty Salon Spa** (43 Fansipan, tel. 09/7789-3566, 9am-10:30pm daily, VND120,000-500,000) does a decent job with quality spa services.

Cooking Classes

The Hill Station Signature restaurant (37 Fansipan, tel. 0214/388-7111, www.thehill-station.com) runs a **H'mong cooking class** (VND660,000) for culinary-minded travelers. During the class, you'll visit a local market to pick out ingredients, work with an English-speaking chef, and learn how to create a menu of five H'mong dishes. Students also visit a farm in nearby Hau Thao village, run by a local family, where the restaurant gets all of its ingredients.

FOOD

You won't find too many regional dishes in this foggy northern town, but local favorites include miniature barbecue skewers, which make for an excellent afternoon snack, as well as roast suckling pig, which you'll find on a spit in front of a few eateries in town. Though it's not native to the area, trout has become a popular local commodity. Sapa's minority groups also have some dishes of their own. Most restaurants in town seem to hold to the notion that Western travelers would prefer Western food, and so it can be tricky to find more authentic Vietnamese fare, though one or two restaurants in Sapa town excel at providing genuine homemade meals.

Clustered around the foot of Dragon Jaw Mountain beneath a maze of tarpaulins are several *do nuong* (barbecue) vendors (mid-morning-late afternoon daily, VND5,000-10,000 per skewer). These tiny stalls are no more than a single miniature grill and a few tables. The colorful displays of skewers, packed with everything from pork and veggies to chicken wings, dumplings, and tofu, are enticing after a long walk up the mountain. Often accompanied by bamboo tubes of sticky rice, these tasty morsels are enjoyed as a snack or alongside a few drinks and hit the spot during cold, rainy weather.

A local restaurant, **Co Lich** (1 Fansipan, tel. 09/1282-8260, 8am-midnight daily, VND40,000-300,000), at the top of Fansipan street, does a tasty suckling pig, which appears on the rotating spit out front. Beyond pork, you'll find a slew of Vietnamese meat and vegetable dishes on its extensive menu, all at reasonable prices, as well as an enticing spread of skewers out front, featuring everything from meat to taro cakes to sticky rice in bamboo tubes.

The charming **Little Sapa** (18 Cau May, tel. 0214/387-1222, 11am-3pm and 5pm-10pm daily, VND45,000-150,000) may well be one of the most affordable eateries in a town of tourist-heavy restaurants. Its well-rounded menu of dishes showcases a more genuine version of Vietnamese cuisine and, while Little Sapa's clientele is largely foreign, the prices and tastes are more local than its competition. Indoors, embroidered tablecloths and plenty of festive lighting add some cheer, and the staff is an industrious and friendly bunch.

A cozy little spot, **Good Morning View** (47 Muong Hoa, tel. 09/1292-7810, 8am-10pm daily, VND50,000-250,000) serves up tasty Vietnamese meals prepared with fresh local ingredients. A handful of tables line the walls of the small one-room dining area and a cheerful staff is always ready to make recommendations. For something fancier, spring for one of the hotpots (VND300,000-550,000), which come with your choice of pork, veggies, or Sapa's homegrown trout. For a break from local cuisine, the centrally located **Le Gecko Café** (33 Xuan Vien, tel. 0214/387-1898, www.legeckosapa.com, 7am-10pm daily, VND65,000-220,000) offers European fare as well as pastries, coffee, and a full bar. Sit outside and people-watch on the patio or keep warm in the restaurant's cozy dining room. Vegetarian meals are also available here, and the café does a decent set breakfast (VND80,000-100,000).

The chic and omnipresent **Hill Station** (7 Muong Hoa, tel. 0214/388-7114, www.thehillstation.com, 7:30am-10:30pm daily, VND75,000-275,000) is clearly doing well for itself, as the trendy eatery now counts a deli and a signature Vietnamese restaurant in its offerings around town. At its main venue, an exposed brick building just near the foot of Cau May, you'll find deli-style sandwiches, pastries, cheese, and charcuterie on the menu.

For an upscale and authentic meal, the ★ **Hill Station Signature** (37 Fansipan, tel. 0214/388-7111, www.thehillstation.com, 7:30am-10:30pm daily, VND70,000-185,000) showcases a host of dishes unique to Sapa's minority cultures, particularly H'mong cuisine, from banana flower salad to fried chicken with wild ginger and smoked pork belly. Vegetarian options are available, taking advantage of several mountain greens you won't find elsewhere in Vietnam, along with homemade tofu. Throw in a bit of rustic chic, with low tables and mounds of hemp as seat cushions, simple porcelain, and a killer view of the valley, and Hill Station Signature is

Hill Station Signature

easily one of the best eateries in town. Higher tables are also available.

ACCOMMODATIONS

You'll find plenty of excellent mid-range and luxury accommodations lining the two main tourist streets of town, Cau May and Fansipan, not to mention a scattering of other hotels that ramble up the nearby hillside, affording incredible views of Muong Hoa Valley. Thanks to some fierce competition in the area, travelers can look forward to well-appointed rooms, plush furnishings, and a higher level of service in most hotels above the VND525,000 mark. Solo travelers and those on a shoestring are not spoiled for choice. A handful of quality budget hotels offer well-kept rooms at good prices; dorm beds are few and far between, especially if your requirements include clean bedding and baths.

VND210,000-525,000

Rooms at **Sapa Stunning View** (63 Muong Hoa, tel. 0214/387-1163, VND205,000-460,000) are large and relatively basic, but the accommodations up front come with small balconies and, when the weather's nice, excellent views. Though the hotel is a short walk from the main part of town, its location allows for easy access to the Muong Hoa Valley villages, and light meals are available downstairs along with tour booking and transportation assistance.

Though its exterior blends in well with the surrounding neighborhood, the **Sapa Capsule Hotel** (1A So Than, tel. 024/6292-2262, www.sapacapsule.com, 230,000-250,000 s, VND450,000 d) features some ultramodern miniature digs. High-tech sleeping compartments feature a variety of lights, mirrors, and charging facilities for all your gadgets. Take your pick between mountain and garden views as well as single- and double-bed capsules. Lockers are also provided, and the friendly staff downstairs can assist with everything from motorbike rentals to transportation and light meals.

VND525,000-1,050,000

While the **Sapa Unique Hotel** (39 Fansipan, tel. 0214/387-2008, www.sapauniquehotel.com, VND1,480,000-1,925,000) is as good as any on the block, its staff sets the place apart with top-notch service and a genuine effort to ensure that travelers enjoy their stay. Rooms are cozy and well-appointed, featuring hot water, air-conditioning, Wi-Fi, TV, and modern furnishings.

Tucked off the town's main square, **Sapa Elegance Hotel** (3 Hoang Dieu, tel. 0214/388-8668, www.sapaelegancehotel.com, VND700,000-1,900,000, breakfast included) earns top marks for its location, overlooking the valley but just far enough removed to lie beyond the reach of Sapa's touristy streets. Outfitted in cozy, modern furnishings, each guest room features hot water, Wi-Fi, TV, air-conditioning and heating, a minibar, an in-room safe, and tea- and coffee-making facilities. The hotel's pleasant staff assists with tours and travel arrangements.

Over VND2,100,000

Perched on the hillside above Cau May, the **Sapa Horizon** (18 Pham Xuan Huan, tel. 0214/387-2683, www.sapahorizonhotel.com, VND2,160,000-3,860,000, breakfast included) has undergone a rebrand but retains its great service. Rooms are plush and well-appointed, with an in-room safe, TV, Wi-Fi, hot water, and an in-room computer. The upper floors afford pleasant views, while certain rooms also include a private balcony. The hotel assists with booking tours and other travel arrangements.

INFORMATION AND SERVICES

Sapa's **Tourist Information Center** (2 Fansipan, tel. 0214/387-1975, www.sapa-tourism.com, 7:30am-11:30am and 1:30pm-5:30pm daily) is one of the more helpful of its kind, dispensing free advice and maps with a smile. Tours can be arranged without the hard sell you might find elsewhere.

In the more touristy part of town, the local

Agribank (Cau May, tel. 0214/387-1107, www. agribank.com.vn, 8am-11am and 1pm-4pm Mon.-Fri.) offers both ATM and foreign exchange services. Should you run into any trouble with this machine, you can find a **Vietcombank ATM** farther into town.

Sapa's **central post office** (6 Thach Son, tel. 0214/387-1689, 7am-11:30am and 1:30pm-5:30pm daily Apr. 16-Oct. 15, 7:30am-noon and 1:30pm-5pm daily Oct. 16-Apr. 15) can handle mail and postal services for travelers.

The local **hospital** (Dien Bien Phu, tel. 0214/390-0119) sits on the northern edge of town, but medical care in the remote northern mountains is poor compared to Vietnamese cities. In the event of an emergency and for any serious issues, head back to Hanoi.

GETTING THERE
Bus

Buses from Hanoi to Sapa take about six hours and cost around VND250,000 one-way. You'll find several buses depart from Hanoi throughout the day and night; these same vehicles also make the return trip from Sapa's **bus station** (in front of Sapa Market, 5am-10:30pm daily).

While there are several bus companies operating trips back to Hanoi at various hours of the day and night, it's wise to travel while it's still light out, as the mountain road leading to Sapa is winding and narrow; safe, experienced drivers are an absolute must.

Train

When heading to Sapa, the preferred method of travel is by sleeper train, and in recent years Vietnam Railways has managed to make its Hanoi-Lao Cai route one of the nicest. Bare-bones hard sleeper cabins feature a single thin palette accompanied by a worn blanket and pillow, but even the most basic soft sleepers are cozy enough to sleep on an overnight journey. For additional comfort, a number of private companies run plush train cars equipped with air-conditioning, comfier mattresses, and cleaner bedding. A lower berth ticket allows you to be closer to your belongings, which will inevitably be slid underneath the bottom bunk; while it's not especially common, theft occasionally occurs on sleeper trains.

Ticket prices among Hanoian travel agents vary drastically based on the agent's fee, but you'll find the best prices directly through Vietnam Railways, either at the train station or on the **Vietnam Railways website** (www.dsvn.vn). Fares from Hanoi to Sapa can run as low as VND400,000, and though the site isn't especially user-friendly, travelers are able to complete their booking in English and pay either via credit card or, in some cases, by cash at designated payment locations around the city. At the train station, lines and organization are not a major focus at the ticketing counter, but there are one or two agents who speak English and can help to arrange your trip.

The final stop for northbound trains is not Sapa (which does not have a train station), but the **Lao Cai train station,** roughly 37 kilometers northeast of town near the Chinese border. From Lao Cai, get to Sapa by taking a minibus. The standard fare for a trip from Lao Cai to Sapa city center is VND45,000. More than a few touts will try to scoop you up before you make it to the information counter at the train station, but you can find the official posted minibus rate here as well as a driver to ferry you to a vehicle. Be sure to verbally agree upon the fare before setting off; there are enough minibuses around that you can walk away from anyone who attempts to overcharge.

If you're really on a shoestring, you can also hop on the **public bus** (6:30am-6:30pm daily, VND30,000), which runs every 30 minutes between Lao Cai station and Sapa city center throughout the day. Both buses 1 and 2 pass by the Lao Cai train station and Sapa's stone church.

GETTING AROUND
Taxi and *Xe Om*

Plenty of *xe om* drivers hang out near the town square, waiting to offer a ride or rent a motorbike to you. For larger vehicles, call **Taxi Xanh** (tel. 0214/363-6363).

Motorbike

Walking around downtown Sapa, you'll see tons of hotels and independent enterprises renting motorbikes to travelers. Semi-automatic vehicles run around VND80,000 per day, while an automatic will set you back VND120,000 a day. Check the brakes and all other functions of the bike before taking off, as roads are steep and medical attention is far away. While traffic may move slower uphill, many a truck or motorbike will come racing down an incline at top speed, not always on the appropriate side of the road, and locals often walk along the shoulder of the highway.

Ha Long Bay and the Northern Coast

Boasting wild, uncharted rainforests and karst-studded seas, Vietnam's northern coast captivates travelers. Whether on water or land, these otherworldly landscapes provide a stunning backdrop for adventure.

Ha Long Bay (literally, Bay of the Descending Dragon) is the country's most famous attraction, entrancing the millions of visitors who tour its islands and caves each year. The placid waters of the bay are awash with luxury cruise liners and modest wooden junk boats that spill over into Ha Long's smaller and less crowded neighbors, Lan Ha Bay and Bai Tu Long Bay. Jagged, rocky islands pepper the seascape, along with hundreds of weather-worn grottoes, making this one of the most photogenic places in Vietnam.

Blanketed in dense green rainforest and razor-sharp limestone peaks, the majority of Cat Ba, Ha Long's largest island, remains untouched, rounding out the western edge of the bay. Here you can lounge on a quiet beach or trek through the rainforest in a national park, looking out for the island's varied wildlife.

Where Ha Long is often overrun with tourist junk boats and foreign travelers, the smaller, quieter Lan Ha Bay, located off Cat Ba Island's eastern shores, remains wonderfully unencumbered. The area's trademark limestone karsts rise dramatically out of the sea in sharp, striking ridges and rippled rock faces, their bases worn away by erosion. Lush foliage sprouts from the porous rocks, seemingly growing out of nothing, and if you're lucky you may catch a monkey or two swinging between the trees.

Farther south near Ninh Binh are the mesmerizing karsts of Tam Coc and Trang An, affectionately nicknamed "Ha Long Bay on Land." This region is growing more popular with tourists, and functions as a great base from which to explore northern Vietnam.

HISTORY

For thousands of years, the waters of the north coast played a crucial role in Vietnamese history, with significant military victories on the Bach Dang River just west of Ha Long Bay. In AD 938, emperor Ngo Quyen famously

---

Previous: Vung Vieng fishing village; a colorful dragon at Ninh Binh's Mua Cave. **Above:** cruise ship boat detail.

Highlights

© AVALON TRAVEL

★ **Ha Long Bay:** Relax amid the placid waters and craggy, mist-drenched islands of Vietnam's most storied natural wonder (page 110).

★ **Cat Ba National Park:** Kayak, climb, and hike through the tangle of dense green rainforest that extends across the island's northern half and into the bay beyond (page 119).

★ **Lan Ha Bay:** Take in stunning, mist-covered views among the limestone giants of this bay, a captivating miniature version of Ha Long (page 122).

★ **Trang An:** Explore limestone karsts, water-logged paddy fields, ancient temples, and tunnel-like caves in what's known as "Ha Long Bay on Land" (page 140).

★ **Cuc Phuong National Park:** With independent hiking options and a top-notch primate conservation center, this park offers adventure and an up-close look at endangered langurs (page 145).

Ha Long Bay and the Northern Coast

defeated the Chinese here by planting sharpened ironwood spikes beneath the water, which rendered his enemy's vessels immobile when the tide went out. This victory allowed Ngo Quyen to begin the first major Vietnamese dynasty.

By the 12th century, Ha Long Bay was a successful international trading port, drawing in merchants from near and far, though it was still occasionally used for military purposes. Vietnamese revolutionaries used the caves within the bay's limestone karsts during the Franco-Vietnam and American Wars. Hospitals and meeting halls were set up inside the dank confines of these underground chambers, many of which remained undetected by enemy forces.

Today, the bay has traded its duties as a military and commercial port for a starring role in the region's tourism, with dozens of white junk boats gliding across the water. Few of Vietnam's attractions have achieved the level of international recognition of Ha Long Bay, where even the off-season teems with domestic and foreign travelers.

PLANNING YOUR TIME

A visit to Ha Long Bay can take as little as two days or as long as four, depending upon your enthusiasm for on-the-water adventure. Most travelers—particularly those on a shorter schedule—opt for Ha Long Bay or Ninh Binh, as Ninh Binh also goes by the nickname "Ha Long Bay on Land."

In Ha Long Bay, how you travel plays a role in the amount of time you'll need. For a day cruise on the bay, devote two days of travel to arrive in Ha Long city, book a cruise, go on the cruise, and return to Hanoi. For an overnight cruise, set aside 2-3 days, depending on the boat's itinerary. For a stay on Cat Ba Island, give yourself a minimum of three days.

A visit to Ninh Binh requires just one or two nights, with an extra day if you're keen to see the langurs at Cuc Phuong National Park. Cuc Phuong can also be reached as a day trip from Hanoi.

The hottest months, June-August, are an absolute madhouse, as domestic holidaymakers flock here in droves and prices skyrocket. September-December, things quiet down considerably, while the weather holds steady. Traveling from late December to late February promises a slightly more peaceful atmosphere, though hundreds of Chinese tourists still cross the border for a quick visit and weekenders arrive from Hanoi. During this time, inclement weather can often sideline boat cruises in Ha Long. The best bet is to visit between September and early December, when the crowds are thinning out and the weather is calm enough to allow boats onto the bay.

Ha Long Bay and Vicinity

An enigmatic maze of blue-green waters and jagged limestone karsts, Ha Long Bay is the best-known attraction in the country. Millions of years in the making, this aquatic enclave off the northern coast boasts a staggering 1,969 islands, countless caves, and over 2,000 different species of plant and animal life. Particularly in the colder months, when a dreary mist hangs heavy over the craggy islands and creaking wooden boats of the bay, it's hard not to be drawn in by the mystery of Ha Long.

Beyond its worldwide reputation for captivating scenery—it was voted one of the New 7 Wonders of Nature in 2011—the bay holds great historical significance. Scholars believe Ha Long housed no less than three prehistoric cultures, stretching its history several thousand years into the past. During the 10th and 13th centuries, monumental battles were fought here, including revered general Tran Hung Dao's defeat of Mongol forces in 1288 and the demise of the Han Chinese under Ngo Quyen in 938.

While much of Ha Long's beauty remains, tourism has impacted the area. Many tourist boats are packed onto the same handful of sightseeing routes, and there's more than a little trash floating in the placid water. Local residents have borne the brunt of the bay's popularity as well. Ha Long maintains a few small fishing communities, whose floating houses populate the quieter corners of the bay. These families will soon be forced to move as the government attempts to clear the area for increased tourism.

TOP EXPERIENCE

★ HA LONG BAY

Ha Long Bay is home to caves, islands, a few small beaches, and sleepy fishing villages. Between the leisurely pace of the bay's cruise boats (a result of the high volume of traffic) and the sheer number of islands in the area, it's impossible to reach all of Ha Long's attractions on a single trip. Most overnight cruises do a nice job of hitting the more noteworthy spots. Because the bay is accessible only by boat tour, you have little to no control over which sights you see once you've booked your trip. Check cruise company itineraries for particular attractions before booking. The entry fee for the bay (VND200,000-750,000) is included in the price of most cruise packages.

Thien Cung Cave

Thien Cung Cave (6:30am-6:30pm daily), or Heaven Palace, sees droves of tourists each day shuffling along its 190-meter path, which winds around towering, distorted stalagmites and beneath spiky formations that dangle from above. Now one of the most popular attractions in the bay, not to mention the

Ha Long Bay in One Day

A day trip to Ha Long Bay is a rushed experience—if at all possible, try to book an overnight cruise. However, those strapped for time and intent on seeing the famous attraction, or wanting to save money by taking a day trip, have some options. Low-budget day cruises from Ha Long City are officially run through the **Tuan Chau Pier** (tel. 020/3384-2134, www.tuanchau-halong.com.vn, 6:30am-6:30pm daily), so you could head there directly, though the language barrier means it's usually better to book through your lodging ahead of time. Individual travelers can choose from one of the five set day **tour routes** (VND200,000-250,000). **Private boats** (VND250,000-600,000) are also available for hire, and these vessels must also follow one of the set tourism routes (VND100,000-300,000). Either way, all travelers have to factor in the additional cost of the bay's **entry fee** (VND120,000) per passenger. Such tours visit popular Ha Long spots—Titov Island or Dau Go, Thien Cung, or Sung Sot Caves, for example—making for particularly crowded sightseeing and taking away from the ambience of the bay, a less than ideal excursion. Communication challenges, too, can become an issue in the planning and preparation from Ha Long City. If possible, you're better off spending a little extra cash and springing for a more expensive day tour with a private tour operator.

A handful of Hanoi-based tour companies offer both group and private single-day trips, albeit at a price. Group day tours through these cruise companies range from VND980,000-2,050,000, while private day tours range from VND3,415,000-4,100,000. These services can be coordinated either from Hanoi or Ha Long City, but bear in mind that a day trip to Ha Long Bay from Hanoi involves a good deal of time on the road to and from the coast (four hours each way). In reality, you'll only spend about 3-4 hours on the water with this option—hardly worth the effort or money. Travelers who opt to overnight in Ha Long City and splurge on this day tour option don't do much better, as tour companies setting off from Hanoi simply pick up Ha Long City-based tourists and fold them into the same cruise as their Hanoi counterparts. Still, such companies provide set itineraries for one-day tours and typically include transportation to and from Hanoi in the tour price, as well as entry and route fees. Reputable outfits like **Glory Legend Cruises** (office 5/33B Pham Ngu Lao, Hanoi, tel. 024/3927-5797, www.glorylegendcruises.net, 9am-5pm Mon.-Fri., 9am-3pm Sat.-Sun.) offer both group and private tours, while **Gray Line Cruises** (office 125 Hong Ha, Hanoi, tel. 024/3717-3366, www.graylinehalong.com, 8am-5:30pm daily) and **Bhaya Cruises** (office 47 Phan Chu Trinh, Hanoi, tel. 024/3944-6777, www.bhayacruises.com, 9am-6pm daily) provide private one-day excursions.

closest to shore, Thien Cung has lost a bit of its natural luster as a network of neon fluorescent lights and the constant flashbulbs of cameras illuminate the interior, but it's still an impressive sight. Its 3,000-square-meter interior consists of two floors, both of which were formed 7,000-11,000 years ago. (Visitors are only permitted to wander the top level.) The sheer number of people packed into Thien Cung can feel like cattle being herded.

Dau Go Cave

Dau Go Cave (6:30am-6:30pm daily) remains obscure, often overlooked on boat tours. Where visitors step off the narrow path leading out of Thien Cung and back to the boating docks, hang a right into Dau Go, about 100 meters away from Thien Cung; you will find it far less crowded and devoid of artificial additions. Its wide entrance opens onto the first chamber, a bright and cavernous room. A narrow pathway passes over limestone and under slender, bizarre stalactites, traveling the perimeter of the cave's three chambers before looping back out to the front, where you'll find a small stele engraved with the words of emperor Khai Dinh, who visited Dau Go in 1918.

Dau Go, known in English as the Cave of the Wooden Stakes, gets its name from a famous historical event. Legendary Vietnamese general Tran Hung Dao prepared here the ironwood stakes that he and his men would use to defeat the last Mongol invasion on the Bach Dang River in 1288. They sharpened the spikes and planted them in the nearby river, just deep enough to be invisible during high tide. When the Mongol ships sailed down the Bach Dang and the tide ebbed, they became trapped and easily defeated by Vietnamese forces.

Sung Sot Cave

Also known as Surprise Cave or Amazing Cave, **Sung Sot Cave** (6:30am-6:30pm daily) is a regular stop on overnight cruises. From its large opening, several steps and 25 meters above sea level, to the picturesque landing just outside the exit, Sung Sot's vaulted chamber houses a variety of formations. One formation resembles the Buddha, while another, beside the cavern's entrance, resembles a horse with a sword. According to local legend, this is where Thanh Giong, a Vietnamese folk hero, came to rest after defeating his enemies. The legend goes that when he died, Thanh Giong left behind his horse and sword at the mouth of Sung Sot in order to protect the cavern against demons. This cave's expanse is impressive, though it can get crowded, and artificial lighting takes away from the natural appeal.

Other Caves

A few other spots feature on some tour itineraries and are equally as interesting, though not as popular as the most-visited caves. One of these is **Golden Tortoise Cave (Dong Kim Quy)**, teeming with stalactites. According to local legends, this cave is the final resting place of Hoan Kiem Lake's tortoise, a petrified stone formation deep inside the cave.

In the early 15th century, Vietnamese emperor Le Thai To used a magical sword to defeat Chinese invaders. Following his victory, the emperor was rowing on Hanoi's Hoan Kiem Lake when a giant tortoise swam up to his boat, took the sword in its mouth, and disappeared beneath the surface. This event earned Hoan Kiem Lake its name, which translates to Lake of the Returned Sword. The tortoise took the blade back to Ha Long Bay where it encountered evil spirits and was forced to defend itself. Though it defeated the assailants, the tortoise was so exhausted that it found a cave in which to rest and soon after turned to stone. Today, visitors rub its back for good luck. Follow the path through the stalactite and stalagmite formations, and you'll pass the tortoise toward the end of the path.

Another storied set of caves are **Virgin**

Ha Long Bay

Choosing a Ha Long Bay Tour

Not every cruise ship or tourist boat plying Ha Long Bay is worth the cost. Here are some tips for booking your overnight stay in the bay.

Expect to spend more money for a quality tour. The extra money spent on a cruise with a reputable company can make a monumental difference in the safety, quality, and value of your experience. Any cruise company that offers an overnight tour for under VND2,100,000 is probably using an aged fleet.

The brochures are too good to be true. Every booking office and travel agency in Hanoi (where most Ha Long trips are arranged) will show you glossy photos of beautiful wooden junk boats and plush beds sprinkled with rose petals. While mid-range and luxury cruise boats tend to match their promotional materials, don't be fooled: More than a few of the budget cruise brochures are either outdated or false. A clue: All boats in Ha Long Bay are painted white.

Choose safety first. A handful of fires and sinkings have occurred in the last decade, most recently in 2017, when a ship returning from an overnight cruise burst into flames. Though accidents and fatalities are rare, cheaper cruises tend to use poorly maintained boats, so there is a risk inherent in choosing a lower-priced option.

Know the cancellation policies. Make sure the tour provider clearly outlines its policies regarding weather-related cancellations. Authorities will sometimes shut down the bay (particularly Nov.-Jan.), ordering all boats off the water due to inclement weather. Ask exactly which costs are reimbursed and how the situation will be handled.

Cave (**Dong Trinh Nu**) and the adjacent **Drum Cave (Dong Trong),** named after a pair of unrequited lovers. The tale goes that a beautiful woman loved a young fisherman. The couple hoped to marry, and the young man set off to sea in order to catch fish for their wedding. While the young man was away, the girl's family, who was very poor, sent their daughter to live with a rich man. Devastated, the young woman refused to go, and her wealthy suitor exiled her to a small island in the bay, where she turned to stone. When the young man heard that she was in danger, he began searching for his lover. From his boat, he shouted as loud as possible but could not make himself heard over the weather, which had turned into a terrible storm. Wet and exhausted, he too turned to stone. In Virgin Cave, the formation is of a young woman lying down with her hair falling over her head, looking toward the sea. In Drum Cave, the formation is of a young man with his face turned toward Virgin Cave, as if calling to the woman. Cruise boats often stop outside the caves, as guides relate the story of

the lovers. Tours don't usually let passengers disembark to explore these caves.

The small **Me Cung Cave** often makes it onto tour itineraries. Its contents offer fascinating insight into the ancient history of the bay, with several fossilized animals inside the narrow chamber. Tour guides can point out where the fossils are.

Farther afield on Dau Be Island, **Ho Ba Ham,** or Three-Tunnel Lake, is another seldom-visited spot that is sometimes included on tours stopping at Cat Ba. As the name suggests, its peaceful, walled-in lagoons are accessed by a series of tunnels, usually in wooden boats at low tide.

Titov Island

Named after Soviet cosmonaut Gherman Titov, the second man to orbit the Earth, **Titov Island (Dao Ti Top)** (6:30am-6:30pm daily) was christened after a 1962 visit by the man himself, in which Titov and his host, Ho Chi Minh, admired Ha Long's scenery from this island's shores. The island's small stretch of white-sand beach, a rarity in the bay, is slightly grubby but manages to attract a fair number of visitors. The volleyball net and beach chairs for rent—not to mention the view—help, and swimming is a popular activity during the warmer months. Titov's best asset is its hilltop lookout, the reward at the end of a zigzag maze of 427 stone steps. While you may have to catch your breath once or twice en route to the summit, views at the top are the best in the bay, making it a highlight of Ha Long's more frequented attractions.

Other Sights

Stippled with miniature islands and solitary rock formations, some teetering upon no more than a meter of limestone at their base, Ha Long has a host of iconic locales. The **Incense Burner** is a miniature karst standing just off the western side of Dau Go Island. It resembles the incense urns that appear outside local pagodas. It's also featured on Vietnam's VND200,000 note. Farther along, **Dog Rock** and **Ga Choi,** also known as Fighting Cock Island, are equally notable landmarks. These formations are large enough to see from the boat, making for good photos. They are only pointed out in passing, so you'll need to pay attention to catch sight of them.

Cruises

Most travelers prefer to visit Ha Long Bay by two- or three-day cruise. These excursions can be regimented, packing many sights and activities into a short time. Spending a night on the water not only affords you more time to explore the bay but also makes the experience memorable. These all-inclusive cruises eliminate much of the hassle involved in traveling to Ha Long, arranging a boat, and setting fees with a local provider. Accommodations run the gamut from dilapidated wooden junks to lavish luxury liners.

Negotiating with budget tour providers is a must. Overnights on the lower end of the spectrum begin at around VND2,000,000 pp for a two-day, one-night cruise. These are often disappointing, and anything lower than that price is likely downright dangerous, as not all boats are properly maintained or inspected on

Ha Long cruise ship

a regular basis. The companies listed in this section have solid reputations for providing safe, affordable, and enjoyable cruises, but there are also dozens of other well-known operators in the area. All listed prices are quoted per person for a double-occupancy cabin; if you're traveling solo, you will likely be required to pay an additional single supplement.

While everything from entrance fees to meals and lodging is included in the package price, you will, in most instances, be expected to pay for your own beverages, which are usually marked up a few times the going rate on land. Occasionally tourists attempt to sneak beverages onto boats in an attempt to avoid these fees, but the boat crew does not take kindly to this practice. Some higher-end companies provide day trips to the bay, but with a four-hour drive to and from Hanoi, it's hardly worth the effort.

BUDGET

One of the more reliable budget providers, **Halong Fantasea Cruises** (office 78B

The Legend of Ha Long Bay

The name Ha Long Bay, also known as the "Bay of the Descending Dragon," has been around for centuries. The story goes that, in the early days of Vietnam, attacks by sea were a constant threat for the people of the north coast. Seeing their plight, the Jade Emperor, a godlike figure, dispatched Mother Dragon and her children to protect the Vietnamese people. As enemy ships sailed into the bay, preparing for attack, the dragons swooped down, spitting jade pearls into the water, which instantly turned to stone. The treacherous maze of limestone islands caught the enemy ships off guard and they crashed into the rocks. Once the invaders had been defeated, Mother Dragon chose to stay on earth, settling down in Ha Long Bay, while her children made their home nearby in Bai Tu Long.

Hang Non, Hanoi, tel. 024/3938-0529, www. halongfantaseacruise.com, 7:30am-8pm daily, 1-day VND980,000, 2-day VND2,385,000-2,500,000, 3-day VND3,180,000-4,090,000) executes well-run excursions to the bay that save money and are safe and organized. Both deluxe and superior rooms are available, though deluxe offerings tend to be closer to the engine and therefore more prone to noise and the scent of gasoline. A handful of complimentary drinks are included on the trip, though others come with a marked-up price tag. All of Ha Long's most popular sights make the itinerary, including Titov Island and Sung Sot Cave. Daily swimming opportunities and scheduled kayak outings are offered. Some three-day itineraries also stop on Cat Ba Island. Dietary exceptions can be made for vegetarians and those with other restrictions, provided you inform the company ahead of time. The company's booking agents tend to be more straightforward than some of their counterparts, offering honest information on the state of the boat, rooms, and other necessary details.

MID-RANGE

Glory Legend Cruises (office 5/33B Pham Ngu Lao, Hanoi, tel. 024/3927-5797, www. glorylegendcruises.net, 9am-5pm Mon.-Fri., 9am-3pm Sat.-Sun., 2-day VND5,725,000-6,405,000, 3-day VND9,835,000-11,200,000) provides a pleasant combination of friendly staff, knowledgeable tour guides, and staterooms for multiday cruises of the bay. Visit Sung Sot Cave, less-frequented spots like Soi Sim Beach and Lan Ha Bay, and a few fishing villages. Activities like swimming, kayaking, and squid fishing are available, as is evening entertainment like board games and playing cards.

The chic and well-appointed **Pelican Cruises** (office 5/33B Pham Ngu Lao, Hanoi, tel. 024/3759-3098, www.pelicancruise.com, 7:30am-5:30pm daily, 2-day VND5,400,000-10,315,000, 3-day VND9,245,000-18,515,000) operates a small fleet of plush high-end junk boats that ferry travelers to some of Ha Long's more famous attractions as well as a few less-frequented ones. Pelican's cabins are exceptionally well kept, with modern baths, enclosed showers, and large comfy beds. Three-day excursions make it out to Lan Ha Bay and its more peaceful surroundings, and activities like swimming and kayaking are included in several itineraries. Ground transportation is not part of the price, with the exception of the one-day trip, though a shuttle bus is available.

The local arm of a century-old American brand, **Gray Line Cruises** (office 125 Hong Ha, Hanoi, tel. 024/3717-3366, www.gray-linehalong.com, 8am-5:30pm daily, 1-day VND1,500,000, 2-day VND4,545,000-6,590,000, 3-day VND7,950,000-9,100,000) has been cruising Ha Long since 2013, with modern boats and experienced local guides. The outfit offers cruises to some of Ha Long's more famous sights as well as Lan Ha Bay, Cat Ba, and the outer edge of Bai Tu Long. Activities like kayaking, swimming, cycling on Cat Ba, and squid fishing are included in some itineraries, and additional snorkeling and diving excursions can be purchased.

Transportation to and from Hanoi is not included in the rates, though you can pay to hop on the company shuttle bus.

LUXURY

As the first cruise provider to receive full permission to venture into neighboring Bai Tu Long Bay, **Indochina Junk** (office 58 Au Trieu, Hanoi, tel. 024/3926-4085, www.indochina-junk.com, 8am-6pm daily, 1-day VND2,400,000, 2-day VND4,600,000, 3-day VND6,900,000) escapes the well-traveled routes of Ha Long. A series of two- and three-day tours ply the waters east of Vung Vieng floating village, trading the heavy traffic of Ha Long's caves for a quieter cruise to the equally stunning karsts of Bai Tu Long. Better still are the company's efforts to conserve the bay's natural beauty, spearheading a program known as "For a Green Ha Long Bay," which aims to spread the benefits of tourism to local fishers and communities, organizes clean-up efforts in the bay, and raises awareness about environmental protection. All of Indochina Junk's boats are built as traditional Chinese-style junks and include beautiful, well-appointed rooms with air-conditioning, making this a luxury option at mid-range prices.

One of the bay's more well-known operators, **Bhaya Cruises** (office 47 Phan Chu Trinh, Hanoi, tel. 024/3944-6777, www.bhayacruises.com, 9am-6pm daily, 1-day VND3,850,000, 2-day VND3,250,000-11,800,000, 3-day VND5,795,000-9,000,000) runs an eight-vessel fleet of high-end boats that are replicas of emperor Khai Dinh's famous wooden ship. Cruises ply the waters between Ha Long, Cat Ba Island, and the outer edge of Bai Tu Long, with stops at much-visited and off-the-beaten-path attractions. Swimming and kayaking at Vung Ha Beach and guided cycling tours of Cat Ba feature on some itineraries. Transportation to and from Hanoi is not included in the cost.

Also operated by Bhaya, **Au Co Cruises** (office 47 Phan Chu Trinh, Hanoi, tel. 024/3944-6777, www.aucocruises.com, 9:30am-6pm daily, 3-day VND10,200,000-16,900,000)

is the more luxurious offshoot of its parent company. Their vessel, the *Au Co*, has swanky cabins, with bamboo and sliding glass doors, enclosed showers, and chic design accents. They have a high-end restaurant on board. The one-day cruises are not as worthwhile as the three-day outings, which tour Ha Long, Bai Tu Long, and Cat Ba, and include leisurely activities, such as kayaking at Vung Ha Beach and cycling tours at Cat Ba.

Transportation

The majority of overnight tours include transportation to and from Hanoi in the rates. For those making their own way to Ha Long City, booking agents and travel outfits in Hanoi can arrange minibus transport to the city for around VND230,000 pp. The trip takes around four hours and usually includes a stop at an overpriced souvenir outlet somewhere along the way.

Many cruise operators provide a shuttle bus or private car option, but these are far more expensive, with shuttle buses running VND600,000-700,000 pp and private cars costing at least VND2,000,000 per vehicle.

Local buses travel from **Gia Lam** (9 Ngo Gia Kham, tel. 024/3827-1529) in Hanoi to **Bai Chay bus station** (near the corner of Le Huu Trac and QL18, tel. 0203/364-9230) in Ha Long City. At VND150,000 pp, you're better off arranging tourist transportation, as this saves you the additional cost of getting to and from these bus stations, not to mention navigating the bus system.

As of 2016, all tourist boats bound for Ha Long Bay and the surrounding area cast off from **Tuan Chau Island** (Tuan Chau Island, tel. 0203/384-2134, www.tuanchau-halong.com.vn), about 11 kilometers west of town.

BAI TU LONG BAY

Legend puts the home of Mother Dragon in Ha Long Bay; her children are just next door in Bai Tu Long, a cloudy aquamarine expanse dotted with the same limestone karsts, mysterious caves, and lush greenery. Separated by an invisible border a few kilometers east of the city, this nearby smaller bay has long played second fiddle to its more famous neighbor but is fast gaining favor among foreign visitors for its less-crowded waters away from the heavy traffic of Ha Long. Local residents live amid its gravity-defying islands and larger-than-life landscapes.

Vung Vieng Fishing Village

Easily Bai Tu Long's most-visited sight, **Vung Vieng** is one of the bay's fishing communities, a modest collection of floating houses. Residents live 24 kilometers offshore in the shadow of soaring limestone karsts, taking shelter in small buoyant dwellings that are clustered together on Bai Tu Long's placid waters. Local fishers row visitors to village sights, like the schoolhouse and a few residents' homes, for a taste of daily life in Vung Vieng.

Thien Canh Son Cave

Thien Canh Son Cave is the most impressive of Bai Tu Long's caverns, a vast chamber of sparkling stalactites and unusual formations that is lit by just a few standard light bulbs, retaining the cave's natural atmosphere and beauty. It takes 30-45 minutes to tour the expansive interior.

Quan Lan Island

Once an 11th-century trading port, **Quan Lan Island** is among a handful of islands in Bai Tu Long inhabited by locals that is now slowly beginning to reap the benefits of tourism. This long, narrow stretch of rock sits on the southern border of the bay, facing away from the mainland toward the stunning Gulf of Tonkin, an hour's ferry ride from shore, and boasts some of the most secluded beaches in Vietnam. Once you've reached the island, there isn't much to do beyond admire the scenery. Its sleepy village and unbeatable views are enough to attract at least a few visitors and to get local authorities to seriously consider how best to develop the area for foreign visitors.

Transportation

TOURS

Thanks to a fair amount of guidebook hype and growing tourist interest, more than a few tour providers list the bay in their travel programs. **Indochina Junk** (58 Au Trieu, tel. 024/3926-4085, www.indochina-junk.com, 8am-6pm daily, 2-day VND4,600,000, 3-day VND6,900,000) is the original outfitter approved by local authorities to enter Bai Tu Long's waters, but in recent years a handful of other tour operators have also received permission, including **Bhaya Cruises** (47 Phan Chu Trinh, Hanoi, tel. 024/3944-6777, www.bhayacruises.com, 9am-6pm daily, 3-day 10,200,000-16,900,000). These tours cover Bai Tu Long's best spots, including Thien Canh Son Cave. Many other agencies that include a trip to Bai Tu Long simply touch the border of the two bays, stopping over at Vung Vieng fishing village.

FERRIES TO QUAN LAN ISLAND

Independent travelers can overnight on largely undeveloped Quan Lan Island. Daily **high-speed ferries** (9:30am daily, VND180,000) depart from Hon Gai in downtown Ha Long as well as from Cai Rong Port (8:15am and 3:15pm daily, VND100,000), just over 50 kilometers east of Ha Long City. Hon Gai vessels return at 3:30pm, while those heading back to Cai Rong depart for the mainland at 7:15am and 2:15pm. Local buses from Hanoi make the trip to Cua Ong Market, not far from the port, and from there tourists hop on a boat to Quan Lan.

Once you arrive, there is little to do on the island other than wander and enjoy the view. A handful of guesthouses in the main town offer overnight accommodations. Expect little to no English and limited dining options. Nicer hotels run VND500,000-700,000, with cheaper guesthouses around VND150,000-200,000. Amenities will be no more than running water and a fan at the cheaper places, and perhaps air-conditioning in the nicer hotels, with the potential for hot water. Book ahead of time to ensure there's a room available,

Cat Ba Island

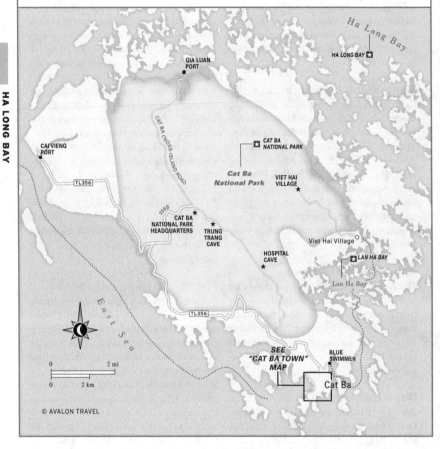

though you may need to enlist a Vietnamese speaker, or book through a local travel agency.

CAT BA ISLAND

You would never know how popular Ha Long Bay is from a visit to Cat Ba National Park, surrounded by nothing but nature, or while plying the placid waters of nearby Lan Ha Bay. From Cat Ba Island, you'll enjoy a quieter and more independent version of Ha Long, escaping the heavy traffic of the larger bay's tourist boats. Cat Ba's main town is an unattractive jumble of cookie-cutter hotels and travel agencies, but beyond the main drag is plenty

of hiking, cycling, kayaking, and climbing amid the incredible coastline of northern Vietnam.

Cat Ba's wild and wonderful national park is a real must-see, and includes hiking and trekking. Equally appealing are the waters of Lan Ha Bay, a smaller, quieter version of its northern cousin, Ha Long. Lan Ha can be enjoyed on a basic boat tour, scaling the limestone karsts of the bay on a rock-climbing outing, or kayaking through eroded tunnels to one of the bay's 100-plus beaches.

Though it can be gloomy in the off-season, particularly as the north's signature mist drifts in and obscures the island's beautiful views, the eerie winter fog is pleasant company compared to the droves of visitors the island receives June-August, when Vietnamese tourists are on holiday.

Getting to Cat Ba requires extra effort, but the rewards are worth the work. A growing number of tour companies include stopovers on Cat Ba during their three-day itineraries, but these will only give you at most an overnight on the island.

With the exception of Hospital Cave, Cannon Fort, and the Cat Co beaches, most sights in Cat Ba require a guide in order to visit. Much of the island is remote and is most safely enjoyed with a knowledgeable local.

★ Cat Ba National Park

Legend has it that the rugged limestone mountains and winding underground caverns of **Cat Ba National Park (Vuon Quoc Gia Cat Ba)** (tel. 0225/368-8981, www.vuonquocgia-catba.com.vn, 8am-5pm daily, VND40,000) came about after a dragon tumbled into the sea, denting the island's terrain with its tail. These rolling hills and rutted formations on the northeastern part of the island provide a habitat for civets, leopards, giant squirrels, dozens of stunning bird species, and over 1,500 varieties of plants, as well as the Cat Ba langur, among the most endangered primates in the world.

A handful of relatively untouched trails wind through the heart of Cat Ba. Most trails range from moderate to strenuous and meander deep into the rainforest. On the bay, activities like rock-climbing are available on a few islands, as is swimming, kayaking, and boating. On most adventures, a guide is necessary to show you the ropes.

TRUNG TRANG CAVE

One of the park's highlights is **Trung Trang Cave,** an underground passageway that lies just up the road from Hospital Cave before the park's head office. Discovered in 1938, this cavern winds 300 meters through the base of a limestone karst and was used in the early

1960s as a hideout for the Vietnamese navy. Inside the cave, the small meandering tunnel transitions from smooth, polished walls to spindly stalactites to barnacle-like growths wallpapered against its interior, which is home to scores of tiny bats that nap overhead.

Guides don't speak much English, but they'll point out several formations, some of which resemble elephants, birds, or Buddhas; one or two of these require some imagination. Be prepared to crouch down, as the cavern has low ceilings in some places. Before entering Trung Trang, head past the cave to the national park headquarters to buy an entry ticket and link up with one of the required guides (VND70,000).

KIM GIAO WATCHTOWER

On a clear day, the **Kim Giao Watchtower** boasts some of the best views on the island. To get here, it's a moderate hike up to the mountain's summit. The two-hour out-and-back journey (just over 800 meters each way) begins at the park's headquarters on a paved route that turns into a well-trodden dirt path, which then becomes stone steps on the ascent. The path zigzags up to a small lookout, where you can take in a panoramic view of the park.

Guides (VND100,000) can be arranged either directly from the park or through one of the tour operators in town as a half-day excursion.

TREK TO VIET HAI VILLAGE

The most challenging trek in the park is to **Viet Hai Village** (VND40,000, plus VND500,000 for a guide), a 15-kilometer, four- to five-hour journey. The hike rambles up massive limestone boulders and over five different forested peaks before sliding into a peaceful farming village on the eastern side of the island. This is one of the best excursions Cat Ba has to offer. If you're lucky, you might catch a rare glimpse of wild macaques and even the Cat Ba langur.

Though the route begins as a paved road from the national park headquarters, it soon deteriorates into limestone boulders to

Cat Ba Town

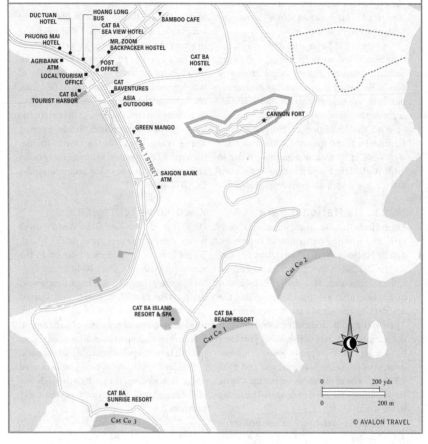

scramble over and, later, a narrow dirt path that winds its way through some of the island's most untouched areas. Three to five kilometers in, the hike passes Frog Lake, no more than an oversize puddle. On reaching Viet Hai Village, you will have an easy seaside walk to the port, where a slow boat floats you back to town.

Substantial footwear is a must, as are long pants. Mosquito protection is not a bad idea, and you'll probably want to bring a backpack or something that keeps your hands free, as the latter part of the descent into Viet Hai Village has you scrambling over rocks.

Tours still run on rainy days and can be just as fun, though the wetter the trail gets the more treacherous it becomes. Most guides are highly experienced and do a good job of keeping you safe, but some of the more challenging passes can still be dangerous for less-confident hikers. This is a difficult hike on a normal day; it's very difficult on a rainy day.

While the national park provides travelers with all the tools required to do this trek, it's more cost-effective to hop on a tour from town. To do the trek independently, it costs VND40,000 for park entry, VND500,000 for the required guide, and an additional

VND500,000 to hire a boat from Viet Hai back to Cat Ba Town. For a full-day excursion through one of the local tour providers, the going rate is around VND660,000 pp and includes both lunch and transportation to and from Cat Ba.

Hospital Cave

A popular stop en route to Cat Ba National Park, **Hospital Cave (Hang Quan Y)** (8am-5pm daily, VND40,000) was used as a medical facility, shelter, and strategy base for North Vietnamese forces during the American War. Alongside their Chinese allies, Communist soldiers constructed a three-story complex inside the massive cave from 1963 to 1965 with 17 rooms, including patient beds, an operating theater, a meeting hall, a cinema, and several other facilities. The first floor, made entirely of concrete, was where most operations took place and boasts incredible acoustics—one person's voice will reverberate throughout the entire floor. The second-floor space, where films were sometimes played, provides more natural surroundings, with vaulted limestone ceilings. The cave could house 200 people at any given time during the war. Though bombs were dropped around this site, nothing inside the cavern was damaged by American attacks, as this particular cave remained undetected throughout the war.

When visiting Hospital Cave, your only option is to park across the street at a small roadside café, where entry tickets are sold. It's not required, but you're better off hiring the onsite **guide** (VND30,000), who is knowledgeable and well versed in the history of the place, bringing to life the war within these bare concrete rooms. Afterward, the café across the street is a nice spot for a drink and the owners are a friendly crowd.

Cannon Fort

On a clear day, the view from **Cannon Fort** (Phao Dai Than Cong, tel. 0225/388-7988, 7am-7pm daily, VND40,000) is one of the best on the island. Built by the French in 1942, this 20th-century military lookout was used to protect the city of Haiphong from attack during the Franco-Vietnam War, and later used during the Japanese occupation and the American conflict. Three sides of the island are visible from the top of this 177-meter hill, including some stunning views of the fishing port and the bay, and you'll be able to catch a glimpse of the two hilltop cannons for which the place is named. There is a small exhibition room located in one of the bunkers, though it lacks signage. The main reason for a visit here is the view, so make this trip only on a clear day.

The road leading to Cannon Fort begins in Cat Ba Town. There is a sign at the bottom of the hill directing visitors to the fort.

Cat Co Beaches

A short walk from Cat Ba town, the trio of **Cat Co beaches,** snuggled into as many coves on the southeastern tip of the island, are worth a visit during warm weather. There are resorts located right on the water, which regulate access to the beaches, particularly Cat Co 2 and 3. In order to spend time on the beach, you're expected to purchase a drink or meal from the resort, but you don't need to be staying at a resort.

Cat Co 1 is a more local affair and the most easily accessible of the beaches. It's where **Cat Ba Island Resort and Spa** (Cat Co 1, tel. 0225/368-8686, www.catbaislandresort-spa.com) has set up a **water park** (6am-6pm daily, VND200,000) along the shore that is popular with Vietnamese tourists during the summer. The park is virtually a ghost town in the off-season. During November and December, it's often possible to access Cat Co 1 for free.

From the main road, hang a left and you'll come to the **Cat Ba Beach Resort** (Cat Co 2, tel. 0225/388-8686, www.catbabeachresort.com, 6am-10pm daily) on Cat Co 2.

A pretty cliffside path from Cat Co 1 leads around to the **Cat Ba Sunrise Resort** (Cat Co 3, tel. 0225/388-7360, www.catbasunriseresort.com, 7am-8pm daily) on Cat Co 3, a quieter stretch of sand where resort guests and outside visitors can come and soak up the sun. Of the three resorts, this is the only one worth staying at.

★ Lan Ha Bay

In the small, quiet **Lan Ha Bay,** located off Cat Ba's eastern shores, trademark limestone karsts rise sharply out of the sea. Dotted with roughly 400 islands, over 100 miniature white-sand beaches, and secluded fishing villages, the bay is a popular venue for kayaking, sailing, and deep-water soloing excursions, in addition to standard boat cruises. Lan Ha gets busy in the summer months, when domestic tourists hit the island, but with so many travelers opting for a trip to nearby Ha Long over the bay, this is a far more serene and authentic option.

Lan Ha is experienced via boat tour from Cat Ba Island. Prices for boat tours begin around VND590,000 for a full-day outing to Lan Ha Bay with a brief stop at one or two of Ha Long's most famous sights. These are a popular option, though read the itinerary before signing up; some outings are advertised as day tours of Ha Long when, in reality, boats tend to stick to Lan Ha and only make a quick jaunt into the larger bay.

One boat tour outfitter is **Cat Ba Ventures**

(223 1 Thang 4, tel. 09/1246-7016, www.cat-baventures.com, 7:30am-8pm daily). Another, **Asia Outdoors** (229 1 Thang 4, tel. 0225/368-8450, www.asiaoutdoors.com.vn, 8am-8pm daily), offers rock-climbing and kayaking trips. **Blue Swimmer** (Ben Beo, tel. 09/1506-3737, www.blueswimmersailing.com, 8am-6pm daily) also offers kayaking tours.

Tours

Nearly every hotel, restaurant, and guesthouse on 1 Thang 4 offers standard excursions to the national park and the island's surrounding bays.

Half- and full-day guided rainforest treks to the national park are available for as little as VND365,000 pp. For the best value, shop around along the harbor front. The folks at **Cat Ba Ventures** (223 1 Thang 4, tel. 09/1246-7016, www.catbaventures.com, 7:30am-8pm daily) are a good choice for both trekking and boat tours, though they only seem eager to offer a helping hand after you've forked over your cash.

Sports and Recreation

With the incredible outdoors so close to town, the wild and wonderful Cat Ba has fast developed into Vietnam's best-known adventure

Cat Co beach

Saving Cat Ba's Langurs

It's rare to spot a Cat Ba langur, one of the world's most endangered primates, swinging through the trees of the island's national park. These small, golden-headed creatures are native only to Cat Ba Island, and decades of poaching have reduced their numbers from approximately 2,500 in the 1960s to somewhere between 60 and 70 today. Hunted almost exclusively as an ingredient in traditional Chinese medicine, the langur's population reached rock-bottom in 2000, with only 53 animals remaining in the wild.

Thanks to the efforts of a number of German conservation groups, including the Muenster Zoo and the Frankfurt Zoological Society, the fate of the langur is looking up. The **Cat Ba Langur Conservation Project** (www.catbalangur.org) helps monitor preservation efforts, which protect the natural habitat of seven small subpopulations within Cat Ba National Park who use caves for shelter and survive mostly on flowers, shoots, and leaves. Only three of the seven groups are able to reproduce, further challenging the future of the species. Local communities have become involved in the protection endeavors and Cat Ba's langur is now considered a symbol of the island.

tourism hub. Activities like cycling, climbing, trekking, and kayaking are popular here and can be arranged through most tour companies in town. Sand flies are present at the beaches; insect repellent can be a big help with this. Most tour outfits have their own repellent for guest use, but check beforehand.

CYCLING

The only place to offer quality mountain bikes for exploring the island is **Blue Swimmer** (Ben Beo, tel. 09/1506-3737, www.blueswimmersailing.com, 8am-6pm daily, VND340,000 per day), located beside the harbor in Lan Ha Bay about five minutes from town. All bikes are imported Treks, which helps to justify the high price, and they can be brought to your hotel if requested. Guided day trips are available for an additional fee, and the company has a few sample itineraries listed on its website for those interested in blazing their own trails.

ROCK CLIMBING

Easily the best location for rock climbing in Vietnam, Cat Ba and its infinite limestone mountains are a perfect place to get started or flex your pro climbing muscles. The many rock faces can be found in places including beaches in Lan Ha Bay or deep within Butterfly Valley. For experienced climbers,

deep-water soloing is an option, affording those keen on seeing the bay with a more challenging way to climb. **Asia Outdoors** (229 1 Thang 4, tel. 0225/368-8450, www.asiaoutdoors.com.vn, 8am-8pm daily), Cat Ba's first certified climbing outfit, runs daily trips (VND1,070,000 pp) to its beachfront climbing space in Lan Ha Bay combined with a bit of kayaking. They can also tailor trips to a traveler's individual requests. Climbing staff is fun, friendly, and knowledgeable in both climbing and the area. For more information, stop by the office and chat with the staff or pick up a copy of Asia Outdoors' climbing guidebook for Vietnam.

KAYAKING

Lan Ha's soaring cliffs and peaceful waters are best explored by kayak. Paddle your way across open channels and into secluded lagoons; sidle up beside a towering rock face; or float your way through the eroded arches that sit beneath the bay's gravity-defying islands. Dozens of travel outfits in Cat Ba town offer kayaking excursions around Lan Ha at varying rates. When booking, clarify whether or not you'll have a guide paddling along with you and exactly how much time you'll have to explore. The folks at **Blue Swimmer** (Ben Beo, tel. 09/1506-3737, www.blueswimmersailing.com, 8am-6pm daily, VND989,000) offer full-day kayaking excursions, as does **Asia Outdoors** (229 1 Thang 4, tel. 0225/368-8450, www.asiaoutdoors.com.vn, 8am-8pm daily, VND590,000).

TREKKING

With the vast majority of Cat Ba covered in dense rainforest, trekking opportunities abound here, both in and around the national park. To venture farther off the beaten track, excursions in and around Lien Minh, one of the oldest villages on the island, offer more scrambling over rocks and up hills. Guides are required on all trips and can be hired via the national park or booked through a tour in town. To hike to Viet Hai via Frog Lake in Cat Ba National Park, jump on a tour from town to save some money. Standard tours to Viet Hai cost VND660,000 through **Cat Ba Ventures** (223 1 Thang 4, tel. 09/1246-7016, www.catbaventures.com, 7:30am-8pm daily). The outfitter also offers treks to Kim Giao watchtower (VND365,000), but **Asia Outdoors** (229 1 Thang 4, tel. 0225/368-8450, www.asiaoutdoors.com.vn, 8am-8pm daily) is one of the few to venture into Lien Minh (VND550,000-960,000).

Food

Most of the fare on the island is bland, with every harbor-front hotel offering a similar menu of standard but overpriced backpacker grub. For cheaper options, head inland up Nui Ngoc. Wherever you eat, this is not the place to revel in the tastes of Vietnamese cuisine. For snacks and other necessities, swing by the cache of convenience stores off the main road on Nui Ngoc south of the main harbor.

A short walk uphill from the waterfront, **Bamboo Cafe** (58 Nui Ngoc, tel. 09/4620-8870, 7am-10:30pm daily, VND30,000-150,000) offers a decent mix of Western and Vietnamese dishes at reasonable prices, not to mention some of the better service in town. Owned by a former tour guide, the restaurant serves average meals in addition to offering useful travel advice. The rest of the family,

who staff the eatery, are equally amiable and willing to help.

You'll find the fanciest dining on Cat Ba at **Green Mango** (1 Thang 4, tel. 0225/388-7151, 7am-10pm daily, VND70,000-350,000), a white-tablecloth place that is well-priced for its offerings, which include Western breakfasts, pizzas, and other dishes. Both indoor and outdoor seating is available, with the latter facing the harbor. The restaurant has inconsistent hours during the low season.

Accommodations

Hotels on Cat Ba are multiplying at a breakneck pace, with a new construction job starting every other day. You'll find tons of hotels along 1 Thang 4, with rooms that offer excellent views of the harbor at slightly higher but still reasonable prices. The hostels and guesthouses tucked down Nui Ngoc and farther from the water go for much less. In the off-season, private beds can be had for as little as VND80,000, though many hoteliers also work as tour guides or travel agents, so these accommodations are usually accompanied by a big push for tours and additional services. Few hotels on the island include a breakfast that's worth the cost. Don't expect much from your hotel's wireless connection, as there is usually a single router placed on the ground floor that is weak at best. Hoteliers on the island have taken to keeping the switch for the water heater downstairs at reception, so expect to ask for your hot shower beforehand.

The summer months are especially hectic on Cat Ba. If you're dying to grab a waterfront spot or have a particular hotel in mind, make your reservation 1-2 weeks ahead of time. The rest of the year, hotels have many vacancies, so you can book a room the same day. Listed rates are based on the high season for foreign travelers (Nov.-Dec.), rather than the Vietnamese high season (June-Aug.), when the island is at its busiest and prices are highest. Verify rates beforehand if you plan to visit June-August.

UNDER VND210,000

At the top of Nui Ngoc away from the harbor, **Cat Ba Hostel** (160 Nui Ngoc, tel. 09/7789-4883, www.catbahostel.com, VND80,000 dorm, VND130,000 d) is a worthy choice for budget travelers, with unbeatable prices and clean, well-kept accommodations to match. Hot water, air-conditioning, TV, and Wi-Fi are featured in all rooms, and you'll find personal lockers in the dorms, as well as en suite baths. Downstairs, the hostel runs a travel outfit and can offer advice on the surrounding area.

Dirt-cheap and clean, **Mr. Zoom Backpacker Hostel** (25 Nui Ngoc, tel. 0225/369-6230, VND140,000 dorm) is tucked just off the harbor-front road and offers no-frills accommodations for the backpacker crowd. Rooms include hot water, air-conditioning, and semi-hard beds. The owner speaks English well and can arrange tours and various excursions around the island.

VND210,000-525,000

Right in the middle of 1 Thang 4 street, the **Cat Ba Sea View** (220 1 Thang 4, tel. 0225/388-8201, www.catbaseaviewhotel.vn, VND250,000-300,000) is the nicest of the island's harbor-front accommodations and boasts a notably friendly staff to go with its tidy, well-kept rooms. Amenities include TV and Wi-Fi, hot water, air-conditioning, plush duvet covers, and a fridge. Beautiful views of the harbor are available on the street-facing side of the hotel, while rooms at the back provide equally good-value accommodations without the view. There is a small restaurant and café downstairs.

Right in the center of town, rooms at the **Phuong Mai** (193 1 Thang 4, tel. 09/1461-8308, VND210,000-250,000) are on par with most other accommodations on this street. The amiable owner, Mr. Khan, and his family go a long way to make the experience unique and can help with advice on the island. Rooms come with hot water, Wi-Fi, air-conditioning, and TV, not to mention some nice views of the harbor. The first two stories of the building serve as a hair salon.

The **Duc Tuan Hotel** (210 1 Thang 4, tel. 0225/388-8783, VND410,000-460,000) offers clean, well-appointed rooms, many of which come with a nice harbor-front view. Amenities include air-conditioning, hot water, touch-and-go Wi-Fi, TV, a minibar, an in-room safe, and tea- and coffee-making facilities. Mattresses are a little hard. Downstairs, the hotel operates a restaurant and a tour-booking agency out of the ground floor, in addition to renting out motorbikes and bicycles. Breakfast is included in the rates, but it is also possible to opt out. Prices dip as low as VND250,000 in winter.

VND1,050,000-2,100,000

The finest of the lot on Cat Ba, **Sunrise Resort** (Cat Co 3, tel. 0225/388-7360, www.catbasunriseresort.com, VND1,800,000-4,600,000) is nestled away in the peaceful cove of Cat Co 3 beach, far enough removed from town to avoid the tourist trail but still within walking distance. As the only property on the beach, its spacious, modern rooms feature the height of local luxury, including TV, Wi-Fi, a minibar, hot water, air-conditioning, tea- and coffee-making facilities, an in-room safe, and the best sea views on the island. Nicer rooms have a balcony, and all guests enjoy a complimentary breakfast as well as use of the beach out front. Restaurant and massage services are available on-site, though additional services tend to be overpriced.

Information and Services

VISITOR INFORMATION

With so many travel and tour agencies attached to hotels, it can be difficult to come across independent information on Cat Ba, as most of these booking offices are not interested in assisting travelers unless they can earn a cut in the process. **Asia Outdoors** (229 1 Thang 4, tel. 0225/368-8450, www.asiaoutdoors.com.vn, 8am-8pm daily) has plenty of useful information on its website and is more than willing to help in person, while a local **tourism office** (228 1 Thang 4, tel. 0225/368-8215, www.dulichcatba.com.vn, 7am-9pm daily) has also gone up next to the island's new boat dock and can assist with any minor queries. You can also ask your hotel for a map, which most are willing to at least loan to travelers.

BANKS

There is an **Agribank ATM** (1 Thang 4) located right on the main drag of Cat Ba town as well as a **Saigon Bank ATM** (1 Thang 4) down the farther end of the harbor. There aren't many ATMs on the island, so bring enough currency. Some hotels may be able to change currency, but make sure the rate isn't too high. If possible, change your money before arriving on the island.

POSTAL SERVICES AND INTERNET

The island's **post office** (1 Thang 4 and Nui Ngoc, tel. 0225/388-8569, 8am-noon and 2pm-6pm daily) is often closed during the winter months but sports a letter box outside the building, which is allegedly emptied twice a day. It's probably better to save your mail for your next destination to ensure that it arrives. Most wireless connections on the island are dismal; if Internet is a must, your best bet is to ask your hotel.

MEDICAL SERVICES

There are no medical facilities on Cat Ba with the exception of the island's sole hospital, a small and often empty clinic about 1.5 kilometers out of town that is poorly equipped. For anything that a first-aid kit can't fix, head back to the mainland.

Getting There
FROM HA LONG CITY

A rusted open-air local **ferry** (Tuan Chau Island, tel. 0203/247-3668; 7:30am, 11:30am, and 3pm daily Jan.-Apr. 29; 7:30am, 9am, 11:30am, 1:30pm, and 3pm daily Apr. 30-Sept., VND80,000) runs to Cat Ba Island from the city of Ha Long each day, arriving on the northern side of the island at Gia Luan port.

The ferry ride is 35-45 minutes. This point of entry can sometimes make a bad first impression—you may encounter some hassle from buses and *xe om* drivers on the Cat Ba side—but it is possible to get from Gia Luan port on the northern side of the island down to Cat Ba town without too much trouble. As you disembark at Gia Luan port, the usual group of touts will appear, demanding exorbitant rates (VND200,000-800,000) for motorbikes and taxis into Cat Ba town. However, there is a **local bus** (VND30,000), which runs directly into Cat Ba town.

FROM HAIPHONG

The fastest and most hassle-free way to reach Cat Ba is from Haiphong. Daily **hydrofoil boats** (45 minutes, VND180,000) depart at 7am, 9am, 1pm, and 3pm daily, dropping passengers directly in the heart of Cat Ba town. These aging vessels are operated by **Cat Ba Island Resort and Spa** (Cat Co 1, tel. 0225/358-8999, www.catbaislandresort-spa.com). Tickets are sold at the Haiphong dock (4 Ben Binh) as well as at the train station (tel. 0225/392-0026, 7:30am-6pm daily) and should be purchased ahead of time during summer. The rest of the year, tickets can be purchased at the time of departure. Ticket vendors roam the pier in Haiphong, but not all are honest; if you know you plan to go, you're better off purchasing your ticket at the train station ahead of time. The boats also run in the opposite direction, with boats departing from the **Cat Ba Tourist Harbor** (Ben Tau Du Lich Cat Ba) on 1 Thang 4 street in Cat Ba town at 8am, 10am, 2pm, and 4pm daily.

Bus-boat-bus tickets can be purchased from both Haiphong (2 hours, VND90,000-120,000) and Hanoi (5.5 hours, VND230,000). These tickets are also available at the Haiphong office of **Hoang Long** (5 Pham Ngu Lao, tel. 0225/392-0920, www.hoanglon-gasia.com, 7am-7pm daily). The bus hops on a series of ferries via Cat Hai Island before arriving on Cat Ba and bringing passengers directly into town. When booking your bus ticket, confirm where it lets off. To get back to

Haiphong from Cat Ba, the most reliable bus provider on the island is **Hoang Long** (217 1 Thang 4, tel. 0225/388-7224, www.hoanglongasia.com, 7:30am-6pm daily).

Getting Around

BUS

If you're not comfortable on a motorbike, the cheapest and easiest way to get to Cat Ba National Park and its many sights is by **local bus** (VND25,000). Minibuses depart from the town center starting around 8am and follow the road out to the park's headquarters, passing by Hospital Cave. For the return trip, it's just as easy to flag down a minibus heading in the opposite direction in order to get back to town.

TAXI AND *XE OM*

Motorbike drivers are easily found on the harbor-front street. Should you venture anywhere else (the national park, for example), arrange transportation back ahead of time. Larger vehicles can be hired through your hotel. Taxis are few and far between.

BIKE AND MOTORBIKE

Most hotels and guesthouses around town rent out motorbikes to travelers, starting around VND80,000 per day. Bicycles are also available, though it's recommended that you opt for the more expensive, high-quality rental if you're planning a cycling day, as the island's hills are not easily tackled on a basic bike. Check the quality of your vehicle before setting off: Cat Ba's less-than-stellar roads can be challenging enough even on a well-maintained vehicle.

HA LONG CITY

Despite the bay's majestic waters and forest-clad karsts, Ha Long City is a rather underwhelming place. It's best used as a base from which to do a day cruise of Ha Long Bay, as a substitute for the pricey overnight cruises. Few people stray beyond the droves of hotels and clutch of restaurants overlooking the bay from Ha Long City's western side.

Food

The strip along Ha Long Street offers enough culinary variety for a day or two. The city's one specialty is its seafood, which comes from the bay and is particularly fresh.

Come dinner time, the **Hong Hanh 3** (Ha Long, tel. 0203/381-2345, 10am-10pm daily, VND95,000-200,000) is often busy, doling out excellent local seafood in both its cozy interior and on the patio next door. Dishes are prepared family-style and therefore more expensive. Service is quick and the place is popular with locals, too.

A good lunch or dinner spot, the hotel restaurant at **Linh Dan** (104 Bai Chay, tel. 0203/384-6025, 8am-8pm daily, VND70,000-200,000) does a tasty turn in seafood, from shrimp and squid to snails and fish, as well as a handful of beef and chicken offerings. Seats are available indoors and out. The prices are right for these delicious meals.

Among the many boxy buildings lining the road, **Bamboo Bar** (Ha Long, tel. 0203/364-0899, baranhphong@vnn.vn, 7:30am-11pm daily, VND50,000-150,000) is a cheerful spot outfitted in bamboo and offering burgers, pasta, pizza, and a few Vietnamese options, as well as beer, wine, and cocktails. Western food prices are more reasonable than other nearby restaurants and the staff is a friendly bunch.

Artful renditions of famous landmarks cover the walls at **Wander Station** (32 Van Lang, tel. 09/3206-2186, www.wcoffee.vn, 6:30am-11pm daily, VND15,000-100,000), from the karsts of Ha Long Bay to the Eiffel Tower and Statue of Liberty. This travel-focused café serves both Vietnamese and European coffee in addition to tasty local lunches and a variety of other beverages. The owners are a cheerful pair who speak English well and can offer up sound travel advice for those passing through Ha Long.

At first glance, **Rock House Pizza** (12 Van Lang, tel. 012/7668-8844, 7:30am-10pm Tues.-Sun., VND60,000-310,000) may look like your run-of-the-mill tourist restaurant, but its laid-back atmosphere and friendly staff set the place apart. Tasty Western eats like burgers,

Ha Long City

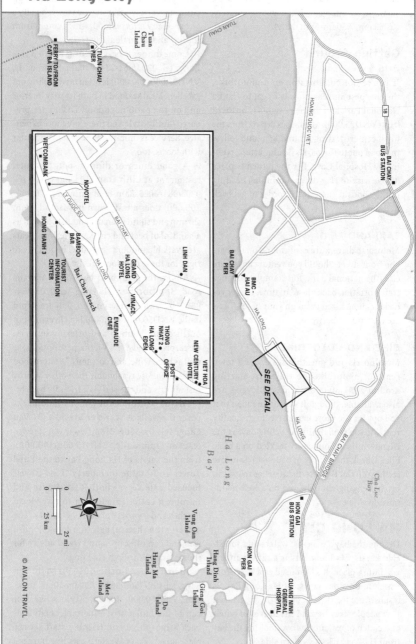

© AVALON TRAVEL

pasta, waffles, and ice cream all make it onto the menu at reasonable prices. As the name suggests, pizza is the standout here, especially Rock House's Hawaiian offering. Ice-cold beer is also available, and the restaurant occasionally offers live music in its cramped quarters.

Accommodations

Few travelers stay more than a night or two in Ha Long City. Budget visitors are best off staying close to Bai Chay, a few kilometers east of Tuan Chau port. Here, a string of cheap and cheerful mini-hotels line the left side of Vuon Dao street, just off the main road.

A few mid-range options dot the main road, but if you're looking to unwind in style, there are posh hotels gathered around Tuan Chau Pier, 11 kilometers west of the Bai Chay area. The majority of luxury cruise boats depart from Tuan Chau. The only upmarket hotel near Bai Chay is the Novotel.

It's easiest to wait to book a bay tour until you reach Ha Long City. From here, every hotel has its own travel service and it's all but assumed that you'll be using your hotel's tour outfitter for your bay tour. If you book with a different company from your hotel, expect your hotelier to be (at best) a little gruff. It's a good idea to consider the tour offerings and the hotel behind the tour as one unit.

June through August, room rates are highest, and reservations are imperative, as local tourists arrive in droves to visit the bay. Costs can be higher on weekends for the same reason.

VND210,000-525,000

The bright, spotless rooms at ★ **Viet Hoa Hotel** (35 Vuon Dao, tel. 0203/384-6035, VND300,000-450,000) are part of a string of budget hotels along Vuon Dao, but this one stands out due to its owners, who go out of their way to be helpful and are one of the only tour providers on the block who do not overcharge travelers with alarming rates. Hot water, air-conditioning, TV, Wi-Fi, and a minibar are included in the hotel's amenities, along with private balconies for street-facing rooms. Mattresses at Viet Hoa—and, indeed, most accommodations in this vicinity—are not plush, so don't bother if you can't handle a solid bed.

With the most impeccably clean baths in Ha Long City, **New Century Hotel (The Ky Moi)** (27 Vuon Dao, tel. 0203/384-4314, www. thekymoihotel.com, VND385,000-400,000) makes for a solid budget option. Rooms are basic but spacious and count Wi-Fi, TV, hot water, air-conditioning, and a fridge in their amenities, though beds are hard. Cheap boat trips can be arranged from here, as well as motorbike rentals, transportation, and a whole host of other add-ons.

Thong Nhat 2 (Ha Long, tel. 09/1716-8999, VND320,000-800,000) is a slightly older hotel whose view is somewhat obscured by its next-door neighbor. Rooms are well kept, featuring Wi-Fi, TV, air-conditioning, and hot water. Rooms at the back offer partial views of the bay. Should Thong Nhat 2 be full, check out the other Thong Nhats (1, 3, and 4) on either side.

A short uphill jaunt from the main drag, the rooms at **Linh Dan** (104 Bai Chay, tel. 0203/384-6025, VND410,000-500,000) are spacious and clean, featuring large windows, Wi-Fi, TV, hot water, air-conditioning, and a fridge. Baths are on the small side, but the hotel's location offers more peace and quiet than some of the other accommodations closer to the bay.

OVER VND2,100,000

While it's not a four-star place as advertised, the **Grand Ha Long** (Ha Long, tel. 0203/384-4041, www.grandhalonghotel.com. vn, VND1,900,000-5,300,000, breakfast included) is a worthy option for this price range. Rooms are well appointed, featuring standard amenities as well as Wi-Fi. Though the furniture is slightly small, beds are comfortable. Use of the swimming pool is included in the rates. Some rooms offer a nice view of the bay. Downstairs, the hotel operates a restaurant and bar within its retro lobby.

★ **Novotel Ha Long Bay** (Ha Long, tel.

0203/384-8108, www.novotelhalong.com, VND1,300,000-5,220,000) is a standout in the high-end price range. Of the four different room types, the bay-facing rooms are best, affording incredible views and large bathtubs, cozy beds, and a balcony. Downstairs are a swanky restaurant, café, and an outdoor seating area that overlooks the bay. Spa services and a fitness center are available to guests, as are cooking classes, kayaking, city tours, and bay cruises. Breakfast can be included for a few extra dollars.

Information and Services
VISITOR INFORMATION
Ha Long's local **tourist information center** (Ha Long, tel. 0203/362-8862, www.halong-tourism.com.vn, 8:30am-5pm daily) does a great job of cluing independent travelers in on all of the sights both in the bay and beyond, provided you ask the right questions. Feel free to inquire about the office's complimentary info booklet, a small paperback printed by the bay's management department that details the history of the area as well as gives a round-up of its most famous attractions. Maps of the bay are available free of charge.

BANKS
ATMs are all over Ha Long road. For currency exchange, the local **Vietcombank** (166 Ha Long, tel. 0203/381-1808, www.vietcombank.com.vn, 7:30am-11:30am and 1pm-4:30pm Mon.-Fri.) can help.

POSTAL SERVICES AND INTERNET
A large **post office** (To 1, Khu 2, Ha Long, tel. 0203/384-6203, 7:30am-11:30am and 1pm-5pm Mon.-Sat., 8:30am-10:30am and 2:30pm-4pm Sun.) sits on the corner of Ha Long and Vuon Dao streets and provides mail services. For Internet access, most hotel rooms come with Wi-Fi access.

MEDICAL SERVICES
Quang Ninh General Hospital (Tue Tinh, tel. 0203/382-5489, www.benhviendktin-hquangninh.vn) is the best medical facility

in the area. For any serious condition, head to Hanoi.

Getting There
BUS
From Hanoi (4 hours, VND200,000), minibuses most often drop off passengers along Vuon Dao or the main strip. The majority of budget and mid-range cruise outfitters include bus transportation from Hanoi in the cost. If you don't have a tour booked in advance, any travel agent or hotel in Hanoi can arrange a minibus to transport you to Ha Long City. This costs more than taking a local bus from Hanoi (VND80,000-150,000), but the tourist bus will pick you up from your hotel.

The **Bai Chay bus station** (near QL279 and QL18, tel. 0203/364-9230) sits about nine kilometers from the Tuan Chau Pier. From here, daily buses depart for Hanoi.

BOAT
From Gia Luan port on the northern side of Cat Ba Island, a **local ferry** (tel. 0203/247-3668, 7:30am, 11:30am, and 3pm daily Jan.-Apr. 29, 7:30am, 9am, 11:30am, 1:30pm, and 3pm daily Apr. 30-Sept., VND80,000) runs throughout the day (confirm ahead of time during the off-season). The ride across the bay takes about 1.5 hours. It lands 11 kilometers from Bai Chay at the southern end of **Tuan Chau Island** (Tuan Chau Island, tel. 0203/384-2134, www.tuanchau-halong.com.vn).

Make the trip back from Cat Ba into Ha Long City, or book a bus-boat-bus ticket (wherein the bus boards a ferry) from Cat Ba directly to your next destination. Those who arrive in Ha Long City via Tuan Chau Island will have to either snap up one of the few *xe om* (VND100,000) drivers loitering around the ferry dock or opt for a taxi (VND150,000) into town.

Getting Around
The *xe om* drivers of Ha Long are particularly eager to help you find your way: Expect to receive more than a few honks, shouts, and

catcalls walking down the main road. For taxis, the local **Mailinh** (tel. 0203/362-8628) cabs are one of a few companies in town.

Many of the hotels along Vuon Dao rent out **motorbikes** or **bicycles** to travelers. Those that provide this service tend to advertise it on the front door, so you shouldn't have too much trouble finding a vehicle.

HAIPHONG

The third-largest city in Vietnam, Haiphong is a hectic northern port seldom visited by foreign travelers but for a few who use the town as a transit point en route to Cat Ba Island. Haiphong's bustling streets function as a significant economic and political center up north as well as an important transportation hub for imports and exports within the country. You will find a few traces of colonial architecture in town, leftover from the days of the French, who aided in developing Haiphong's port during the 1870s, as well as a monument to revered local and national hero Le Chan, a gutsy female general who led the charge against Chinese colonists in the third century.

Given the fact that Haiphong's major draw is its daily hydrofoils to Cat Ba Island, a stopover in the city needn't last more than one night. In the downtown area, and specifically

along Dien Bien Phu, there are plenty of hotels, restaurants, and other necessities to tide you over until your boat comes. A stroll along the former Bonnal Canal or a quick visit to one of the local pagodas can keep you entertained.

Sights

There are a handful of sights around Haiphong that can be explored in an afternoon, most of them on foot. When visiting Haiphong's pagodas and temples, dress respectfully, as the local reception of foreign tourists is sometimes stony and any revealing clothes will likely not be well received.

HAIPHONG MUSEUM

The **Haiphong Museum** (66 Dien Bien Phu, tel. 0225/382-3451, 8am-10:30am and 2pm-4:30pm Tues.-Fri., 8am-10:30am Sat.-Sun., VND5,000) is a Gothic behemoth situated right in the center of town. Covering one hectare, the large colonial-style building was completed in 1919 and houses a nice collection of ancient ceramics and wood carvings from the Le and Tran dynasties, vintage photographs from the days of French colonialism, and a few other odds and ends, including a coin collection, an old-school Mobylette bike, and a

Haiphong Museum

Haiphong

BOATS TO
CAT BA

PHAN DINH PHUNG

TAM BAC

LE CHINH DAN

POST
OFFICE

NGUYEN TRI PHUONG

MINH KHAI

KY LU TRONG

VAN TUE

MAXIM'S
HOTEL

AVANI
HARBOR
VIEW

HAIPHONG
MUSEUM

MONACO
HOTEL

KIM THANH
HOTEL

HUNG DAO

BACH DANG

PHONO BOX

JETSTAR

DA HANH

MAXIM
BKK
BAO ANH HOTEL
TEXAS BBQ

DIEN BIEN PHU

TRAN PHU

TRAN QUANG KHAI

HOA
DAI

HA LY

HOANG VAN THU

LUONG KHANH THIEN

Haiphong
Park

SACOMBANK

OPERA HOUSE

HOANG
LONG BUS

TAM BAC

V VOI CHAU

VIETNAM
AIRLINES

TRAIN
STATION

QUANG TRUNG

Tam Bac Lake

NGUYEN DUC CANH

STATUE OF
LE CHAN

NGHE
TEMPLE

LE LOI

VIETJET

CAT CUT

CAT DAI

BAKERIES

CAU DAT

VIETNAM-CZECH
FRIENDSHIP HOSPITAL

TO HIEU

LOTUS LAKE
STADIUM

CHO CON

NAM CUONG
HOTEL

HANG KENH

NGO LY PHINH

LA CH TRAY

YON DUC THANG

CHUA HANG

DU HANG
PAGODA

DU HANG

Lotus
Lake

HO SEN

0   250 yds

0   250 m

To
Niem Nghia Bus Station

© AVALON TRAVEL

rickshaw. The standard exhibit on Vietnamese sovereignty in the Paracel and Spratly islands is also on display. English signage is available, but translations are only sometimes comprehensible. This is not a bad spot to pass the time if you're wandering around town.

HAIPHONG PARK

A sliver of land winding from Dien Bien Phu around to the Tam Bac River, Haiphong's local **park** lies in the center of town and boasts a charming esplanade, complete with flower stalls and manicured gardens. Once the Bonnal Canal during colonial days, parts

of this waterway have been filled in, but a small stretch remains, complementing some of Haiphong's other architectural sights, including the Opera House and a generous **statue of Le Chan** (intersection of Me Linh and Nguyen Duc Canh), local heroine and revered Vietnamese historical figure. The statue is over seven meters tall and weighs 19 tons.

OPERA HOUSE

If you're strolling along the parkway downtown, chances are you'll pass Haiphong's **Opera House** (65 Dinh Tien Hoang, tel. 0225/382-3084), a grand pale-yellow colonial incense urns and kumquat trees at Nghe Temple

hall completed in 1904. Built by the French, this 400-seat theater is shuttered most days, but its architecture complements the waterfront scene and the large open square before it.

NGHE TEMPLE

From the outside, **Nghe Temple (Den Nghe)** (sunrise-sunset daily) appears to be nothing special, its stark gray walls rubbing shoulders with a local schoolyard. But through the three-door entrance gate is a lavish homage to local hero Le Chan, a female general who aided in the 2nd-century uprising of the Trung sisters.

Born in An Bien, a small village northwest of Haiphong, Le Chan was from a well-to-do family. But, at the time, Chinese colonization meant that even the upper echelons of Vietnamese society were subject to oppression. When To Dinh, the leader of what was then known as Giao Chi, a Chinese territory, attempted to make Le Chan his wife, she refused, an act of dissent that caused To Dinh to harm her parents. For 10 years, Le

Chan bided her time until, in the spring of AD 40, the Trung sisters launched a rebellion against the Chinese occupation, driving To Dinh and his army out of Vietnam. Le Chan and her forces were instrumental in this takeover. Two years later, the Chinese returned in greater numbers, rekindling the battle. The Trung sisters, who had ruled Vietnam in the interim, committed suicide rather than risk capture by the Han Chinese. Upon their deaths, Le Chan continued to fight for another year, falling back to fiercely defend the village of Lat Son until, in AD 43, when defeat was inevitable, she threw herself off Giat Dau mountain. Vietnam's remaining generals buried her in secret, and she has been a revered hero ever since.

The original temple on this site was no more than a modest shrine. Today's two main halls, built in 1919 and renovated several times over the years, are ornate and intricate. Several stone animals, including elephants, horses, and lions, populate the courtyard, while Le Chan's altar is off to the right. Beautiful floral arrangements surround the legendary woman's statue, and lacquered woodwork hangs overhead.

Entertainment and Events
FESTIVALS AND EVENTS

Toward the start of September each year, the annual **Do Son Buffalo Fighting Festival,** a long-held tradition, takes place 19 kilometers south of the city center. Shortly after the Lunar New Year, local participants begin their search for a prize buffalo. Once a trainer has settled on a chosen animal, he or she prepares the buffalo to fight. Training can last up to eight months.

The preliminary stages of the competition take place around late June or early July, with the first showdown held on the eighth day of the sixth lunar month. These contests continue up until the ninth day of the eighth lunar month (early September), when the final competition is attended by scores of Vietnamese from near and far.

During the competition, buffaloes do not

harm one another; rather, the animals lock horns to assert their strength. The loser usually flees, chased by the winner, signaling the end of a fight. After the festival, all the buffaloes are slaughtered. Their blood is offered to the Jade Emperor, while the meat is sold at the market and its consumption is believed to be good luck.

Food

At **Hoa Dai** (39 Le Dai Hanh, tel. 0225/382-2098, 7am-11pm daily, VND40,000-100,000), the laminated menu is entirely in Vietnamese. Thankfully, the owner speaks a few words of English, and there are some handy ClipArt illustrations to guide you. You'll find beef, pork, and fish among the offerings. Prices are not on the menu, so ask beforehand.

Though its faded white exterior could use a renovation, the lively **Van Tue** (1A Hoang Dieu, tel. 0225/374-6338, www.vantue.com.vn, 8am-9pm Mon.-Thurs., 8am-11pm Fri.-Sun., VND45,000-400,000) is a popular local restaurant that serves all manner of Vietnamese cuisine, including scores of beef, chicken, pork, and vegetarian dishes, including more adventurous fare like frog and eel. Staff speak some English and the price tag makes Van Tue not only one of the more active spots in town but also one of the more affordable.

The chic and sophisticated **BKK** (22A Minh Khai, tel. 0225/382-3994, bkk_haiphong@hotmail.com, 10am-10pm daily, VND75,000-500,000) serves delicious Thai and pan-Asian cuisine, including coconut curries and spicy salads, in a posh colonial building just off the main drag. Its extensive wine collection, sleek wooden furniture, and collection of black-and-white vintage photographs add to the experience. Dine inside or alfresco on the equally classy front patio. Prices are more expensive but fit the style and service.

Down a street of international restaurants, **Texas BBQ** (27 Minh Khai, tel. 0225/365-3450, www.texasbbq.com.vn, 8:30am-10:30pm daily, VND100,000-600,000) is the only spot in town to offer Tex-Mex cuisine, including quesadillas, tacos, and enchiladas, as well as pizza, burgers, and steak, making for a hearty departure from local cuisine. Delivery service is available, but the bright, narrow dining room is equally inviting.

The chefs at **Indian Kitchen** (22D Minh Khai, tel. 022/5384-2558, 10am-11pm daily, VND40,000-200,000) serve an array of Indian cuisine, both vegetarian and non-vegetarian, alongside staples like naan and roti. Seating is cozy in a brightly colored dining room. Staff is friendly, the service is decent, and the restaurant provides a pleasant alternative for those seeking a break from local fare.

Accommodations

Rates tend to be higher in Haiphong than other Vietnamese cities. The best value options run no less than VND250,000 in most places. Conditions in the city's cheaper hotels are pretty abysmal and make it worth shelling out the extra couple bucks for a comfier bed and a room that's been properly cleaned. On the more expensive end, you can find plenty of well-appointed mid-range and top-tier accommodations thanks to Haiphong's regular business visitors.

VND210,000-525,000

One of the better mid-range options, **Kim Thanh Hotel** (67 Dien Bien Phu, tel. 0225/374-5264, VND400,000) is clean and well kept, though its beds are of the more solid variety. TV, air-conditioning, hot water, and Wi-Fi are in each room, and the staff assists with general queries regarding Haiphong.

The well-kept ★ **Maxims Hotel** (3K Ly Tu Trong, tel. 0225/374-6540, www.maximshotel.vn, VND405,000-910,000) is your best bet when it comes to mid-range accommodations in Haiphong. Rooms are clean and feature modern furnishings with comfy beds, air-conditioning, TV, and Wi-Fi. The downstairs restaurant serves food all day, and staff can assist with travel-related queries. Due to the limited number of mid-range options in town, this hotel is sometimes full; check availability before arriving.

VND525,000-1,050,000

A clear step above the less-expensive mid-range options in Haiphong, **Monaco Hotel** (103 Dien Bien Phu, tel. 0225/374-6468, www.haiphongmonacohotel.com, VND680,000-1,370,000) boasts a spacious reception area decked out in European decor and, inexplicably, a pair of sphinxes guarding the main staircase. The staff is hit-or-miss. Rooms are plush as far as mid-range accommodations go, featuring TV, Wi-Fi, hot water, air-conditioning, a minibar, and modern furnishings. Breakfast is included in the rates.

Though it's fairly basic, **Bao Anh Hotel** (20B Minh Khai, tel. 0225/382-3406, www.hotelbaoanh.com, VND400,000-1,000,000) boasts one of the better locations in town, alongside a street full of restaurants and close to the city center. Accommodations are clean, modern, and equipped with TV, Wi-Fi, a minibar, hot water, and air-conditioning. Breakfast is included in the rates, though you're better off skipping the rather limited selection and venturing out on your own.

OVER VND2,100,000

The rather posh **Nam Cuong Hotel** (47 Lach Tray, tel. 0225/382-8555, www.namcuonghaiphonghotel.com.vn,

VND2,200,000-4,530,000) sits a short way south of the park and boasts four varieties of high-end accommodations, all of which are outfitted with a host of amenities, including Wi-Fi access and daily fresh fruit and water. Guests are also invited to a welcome drink and can enjoy the daily complimentary buffet breakfast in the hotel restaurant. Use of the sauna, whirlpool tub, and swimming pool are all included.

Overlooking the water, **AVANI Harbor View** (12 Tran Phu, tel. 0225/382-7827, www.avanihotels.com, VND2,225,000-3,860,000) is Haiphong's best hotel. An updated grand colonial-style building, complete with arched windows and balustrades, this four-star hotel houses 122 guest rooms, two restaurants, two bars, a swimming pool, a spa, and a fitness center. Rooms come in varying levels of luxury, but each bright and well-appointed room features TV, Wi-Fi, a minibar, tea- and coffee-making facilities, a spacious sitting area, a work desk, and an in-room safe. Hotel eateries serve a range of Asian and Western cuisine, and additional activities like tai chi and cooking classes are available.

Information and Services

You should have no trouble locating an ATM

Maxims Hotel

downtown. The local **Sacombank** (119-121 Dinh Tien Hoang, tel. 0225/356-9345, www.sacombank.com.vn, 7:30am-11:30am and 1pm-5pm Mon.-Fri., 7:30am-11:30am Sat.) exchanges currency.

The city's central **post office** (5 Nguyen Tri Phuong, tel. 0225/384-2547, 7am-noon and 1pm-7pm Mon.-Sat., 7:30am 11:30am and 1:30pm-5pm Sun.) assists with mail.

The largest and best-equipped local hospital is the **Vietnam-Czech Friendship Hospital (Benh Vien Viet-Tiep)** (1 Nha Thuong, tel. 0225/370-0436, www.viettiephospital.vn), though any serious health issue should be brought to Hanoi.

Getting There
BOAT
Speedboats make daily trips to Haiphong from Cat Ba Island. Slightly tired but functional vessels are operated by **Cat Ba Island Resort and Spa** (4 Ben Binh, tel. 0225/358-8999, www.catbaislandresort-spa.com, VND180,000), with departures from Cat Ba to Haiphong at 8am, 10am, 2pm, and 4pm daily. Boats depart from Ben Binh, the town's main pier, just opposite 1 Thang 4 street. You can purchase your tickets at the pier itself or at the train station, where a small corner of the ticketing office sells both bus (2 hours, VND90,000-120,000) and speedboat (45 minutes, VND180,000) tickets to Cat Ba.

BUS
Shuttles depart every 10 minutes daily from Hanoi's Gia Lam bus station (2 hours, VND85,000) for Haiphong, arriving at **Niem Nghia bus station** (273 Tran Nguyen Han, tel. 0225/371-7824). From southern destinations like Ninh Binh (3 hours, VND160,000), buses stop at **Niem Nghia bus station** (273 Tran Nguyen Han, tel. 0225/371-7824), about three kilometers from the city center. **Hoang Long** (5 Pham Ngu Lao, tel. 0225/392-0920, www.hoanglongasia.com, 7am-7pm daily) receives two daily buses from Cat Ba

(VND90,000-120,000) via the bus-boat-bus route. Buses depart from Cat Ba's town center each afternoon.

TRAIN
Though it's not wired into the general north-south Reunification Line, Haiphong's **train station** (75 Luong Khanh Thien, tel. 0225/392-1333, 5am-6:30pm daily) is connected to Hanoi. Trains from Hanoi (2.5 hours, VND65,000) make daily runs to Haiphong.

AIR
Flying is the least popular and most expensive way of getting to Haiphong, but it's possible. **Cat Bi International Airport** (HPH, Le Hong Phong, tel. 0225/397-6408, www.catbiairport.vn) is eight kilometers southeast of downtown Haiphong and welcomes multiple daily flights from Danang and Saigon (2 hours, VND600,000-1,000,000) as well as a growing number of smaller destinations, including Dalat, Nha Trang, and Quy Nhon. **Vietnam Airlines** (ticketing office 166 Hoang Van Thu, Haiphong, tel. 0225/381-0890, www.vietnamairlines.com), **VietJet** (ticketing office 7 Tran Nguyen Han, Haiphong, tel. 0225/363-0032, www.vietjetair.com), and **Jetstar** (ticketing office 36 Hoang Van Thu, Haiphong, tel. 0225/355-9550, www.jetstar.com) serve Cat Bi airport.

Getting Around
For four-wheeled vehicles, try a local **Mailinh** (tel. 0225/383-3833) or **Hai Phong** (tel. 0225/373-7373) taxi. As usual, *xe om* are present on street corners across town.

Vehicles for hire can be arranged through several hotels. As a less touristed destination, you won't find many affordable motorbike rentals, so be prepared to jump on a *xe om* if necessary, or stick to exploring on foot. If you prefer a bicycle, most accommodations don't advertise the option but it is possible to procure a bike from some hotel receptionists.

Ninh Binh

One hundred kilometers south of Hanoi, the small provincial town of Ninh Binh may not come off as a worthy tourism destination, but venture west and you'll be greeted by the sharp and mysterious limestone peaks of Tam Coc and Trang An. Known as "Ha Long Bay on Land," Ninh Binh's serene flooded fields stand in stark contrast to its scores of karst formations, casually rising out of the pancake-flat landscape and shrouded in lush greenery. Throw in a handful of ancient temples and one of the earliest capitals in Vietnamese civilization, all of which fit nicely into the romantic, mist-obscured countryside, and you've got reason enough to spend at least a day in Ninh Binh.

Several Hanoian tour companies make day trips to the area, hitting Tam Coc, Bich Dong Pagoda, and the nearby rice fields, but it's just as easy to do the trip on your own. Given the modest costs of lodging and food, Ninh Binh is an excellent spot from which to explore northern Vietnam's stunning scenery, especially in the cold and misty winter. Summer brings plenty of sun and better visibility. Tam Coc is best enjoyed during April and May, before the rice harvest takes away its signature paddy fields. Trang An is at its best around October, when water levels are low and the area's caves are more accessible.

Trang An and Tam Coc are a short drive or cycle away from Ninh Binh. Blue-and-white road signs provide directions. Most hotels and guesthouses can arrange a tour on the spot or point you in the direction of one. Most sights around Ninh Binh will require a boat, as the best views in the area are from the water. Rowboat rides tend to take more time, with most trips lasting 2-3 hours, so plan your day accordingly.

TAM COC AND VICINITY
Tam Coc
Long touted as Ninh Binh's main event, **Tam**

Coc (tel. 0229/627-0373, 7am-5pm daily, entry VND120,000, boat VND150,000) is a meandering waterway that weaves through emerald-hued rice fields and under great limestone karsts. In the flooded country fields, farmers have worked around the soaring mountains that interrupt Tam Coc's otherwise flat terrain, creating an eye-catching array of greenery and rutted cliffs. Now an increasingly popular stop among travelers, some of the area's luster has been lost to concrete embankments along the canal and a healthy contingent of souvenir vendors and other touts, but the beauty of the area remains undeniable.

At the boating dock, a veritable army of rowers ferries passengers, usually no more than two to a boat, down the Ngo Dong River and back, often reclining to maneuver the oars with their feet, a trick which features in many tourist photo ops. The entire two-hour trip brings you through three tunnel-like caves beneath the mountains of Tam Coc before reaching the far end of the river journey.

This is where the magic begins to wear off: Thanks to the number of visitors, the area has become something of a tourist trap. At the turnaround point, a group of floating vendors lies in wait, eager to sell you a cold drink or some fruit. Should you refuse, they'll suggest that you buy a drink for your boat driver, though these are later sold back to the vendors at half-price, cutting both parties in on the profit. Some drivers even make a pit stop on the return trip to haul out their own cache of souvenirs for you to peruse. Tips are expected and freely requested at the end of the ride. This pressure to tip is higher than in other areas of Vietnam.

Thai Vi Temple
The humble **Thai Vi Temple** (sunrise-sunset daily, free) harks back to the 13th century, when rulers of the Tran dynasty thrice defeated Yuan-Mongol armies attempting to

Ninth Binh

© AVALON TRAVEL

★ CUC PHUONG NATIONAL PARK

0
2 km
0
2 mi

VANCOUVER HOTEL
NGOC ANH 2
NGOC ANH 1
NAM THANH
GAME SHOP
HONG PHONG
LY TU TRONG
TRUONG HAN SIEU
PHUONG DINH
TRAN PHU
KIM DONG
VIETIN BANK
POST OFFICE
TRAN HUNG DAO
VAN GIANG
PHAN DINH PHUNG
LE DAI HANH
NINH BINH BUS STATION
HOA THAM
VAN GIANG
QUEEN HOTEL
QUEEN MINH HOTEL
NGO TTT LE DAI HANH
TRUNG TUYET
NGO 88 LE DAI HANH
LE DAI HANH
HOANG LY THAI TO
LE VAN TAM

Van Long Nature Reserve

BAI DINH PAGODA

TAM COC GARDEN
BICH DONG PAGODA
★ TRANG AN
★ HOA LU
THAI VI TEMPLE
TAM COC BOAT STATION
MINH TOAN
MUA CAVE

Ninh Thang
Ninh Binh

SEE DETAIL

invade Vietnam. Within the small shrine, you'll find an effigy of Tran Thai Tong, a king who abdicated the throne to live as a monk after the Yuan-Mongol's first unsuccessful invasion in 1258, as well as Tran Quang Khai and Tran Hung Dao, Vietnam's most famous military general, who drove the invaders out of the country on two occasions. The countryside setting makes Thai Vi a nice tangent from the bustling main area of Tam Coc. The temple is about 800 meters from Tam Coc. Take a right just before the ticket booth on a small narrow road, which leads out to Thai Vi.

Bich Dong Pagoda

A three-tiered mountainside masterpiece, **Bich Dong Pagoda** (sunrise-sunset daily, free) rambles up a limestone rock. From the bottom, a long, souvenir-lined walkway leads you across a small stone bridge to the pagoda's entrance, where the first shrine, Chua Ha, pays homage to the ancestors. Farther uphill, Chua Trung is a larger building, housing statues of the Buddha. Beyond the middle altar, a small cave winds around in an S shape, leading up to the final structure, Chua Thuong, where Quan Am has a shrine to herself. There is a beautiful (though small) white stone statue of the goddess looking out over the cliff. The

views are pleasant from here. If you're keen to get all the way to the top, follow the path beyond the pagoda up to the very peak, where you can take in the surrounding fields. It's a fairly easy walk up to the top with stairs. The pagoda is 1.5 kilometers past Tam Coc, along the main road.

Mua Cave

While the actual **Mua Cave** (tel. 0229/361-8754, 7am-5pm daily, VND100,000)—a small cavern at the base of a limestone karst—may not be worth your time, the view from the top of the nearby mountain earns this sight a place among Ninh Binh's other wondrous natural landscapes. Now part of a slightly gaudy oversize tourism complex, the karsts bordering its far end are made accessible by a maze of 486 stone steps and zigzagging white battlements that give the place a medieval feel. Pause at each clearing and look back at the expanse of low-lying water-logged rice paddies below. On a clear day, the views from the top, beside Mua Cave's Quan Am statue, are stunning. In the fog, its series of Buddhist spires and misty forest-clad hills paint an eerie portrait. Once up on the mountaintop, some tourists will venture off the path and scramble over a few rocks to catch a glimpse of the boats at Tam Coc

roof of a pagoda

from above. Be careful on this section, as the rocks can be dangerous, especially after rain.

The cave is about six kilometers from Ninh Binh. Ask for directions in Tam Coc.

TRANG AN AND VICINITY
★ Trang An

Winding through a maze of rainforest-covered limestone karsts and picturesque countryside scenery, a ride in one of the modest wooden rowboats at **Trang An** (tel. 0229/627-9956, 7am-5pm daily, VND200,000 adults, VND100,000 children) is time well spent. Less frequented by foreign travelers than the waters of Tam Coc, this stunning river landscape, dotted with temples devoted to local heroes and meandering tunnels that burrow beneath the area's rustic cliffs, is hugely popular with the Vietnamese. Business is booming at Trang An, helped by the addition of a larger, updated tourism complex and its status as a UNESCO World Heritage Site. It's the first World Heritage Site in Vietnam to receive dual distinctions for natural and cultural properties.

It's hard to miss the brand-new boating docks, thanks to a massive billboard and the string of brightly colored flags swaying outside the main entrance. With a ticket, visitors can board one of the rowboats, which seat 4-6, and be on their way. Local boat operators are well versed in the complex's two main routes, sometimes even rowing with their feet. It's impressive to see a single person navigate the labyrinthine passageways that snake beneath these limestone mountains with such ease. Visitors are free to select from Trang An's two rowboat routes, the first of which leads through a series of nine caves, stopping at a few temples and pagodas along the way. The second route also takes you through some caves and manages to swing by a few temples, as well as a still-standing film set from the 2017 Hollywood flick *Kong: Skull Island*. Each ride lasts approximately three hours.

Be sure to tell your boat driver which route you prefer. While movie buffs might appreciate the latter, the first and original route provides a more worthwhile cultural experience. One cave in particular houses a well, roughly 13 meters deep, whose water was once used for distilling rice wine; nowadays you can see a tasteful display of ceramic jars meant to symbolize the process. There are three temple stops, described below, only on the original route, each featuring a shrine to a different local hero connected to Ninh Binh's ancient history.

It's best to arrive early in the morning to avoid the crowds, and steer clear on weekends, as Hanoians sometimes make day trips down to Ninh Binh, further adding to the madness. While you may be spared the request for a tip, it's possible that your boat driver will insist upon gratuity. You are not obligated to provide one; tip only where you feel inclined to do so.

TRINH TEMPLE
The first stop along Trang An's original route, **Trinh Temple** is dedicated to two of King Dinh Tien Hoang's generals, Ta Thanh Tru and Huu Thanh Tru, who are credited with rescuing the king's youngest son, Dinh Toan. After the king and his two older sons were assassinated, the two generals carried the young boy into hiding. Boats stop here for 15-20 minutes to give visitors time to look around.

TRAN TEMPLE
Up and over a high limestone karst, **Tran Temple** lies at the end of a rambling stone staircase that reaches the peak of the mountain. The temple is a small stone structure with dragons carved into the roof. Hemmed in by thick foliage, it offers no scenic vistas. Follow the stairs down the other side of the mountain and you'll discover a modest shrine to Quy Minh Dai Vuong, a general of the 18th King Hung, the last in a line of rulers who are believed to be the founding fathers of the Vietnamese people.

The original temple was constructed during the 10th century under Dinh Tien Hoang. It was rebuilt in 1258 by emperor Tran Thai

Tong, who came to Trang An and lived as a monk for a time. The altar out front is from the days of the Nguyen dynasty and is often busy with locals paying their respects. Boats stop at a dock on the far side of a karst from the temple; from there, a steep walk (about 10 minutes each way) is required to see the temple. It's possible to go inside the temple, but the more decorative aspects are seen from the outside.

PHU KHONG

The largest of the temple areas at Trang An, **Phu Khong** has a few low stone buildings, decorated with yin-yang tiles and dragon carvings. The most important structure is a shrine that houses eight figures. These represent a group of mandarins loyal to King Dinh Tien Hoang who, upon the assassination of their beloved leader, committed suicide to follow the emperor into the afterlife. Near the mandarins' temple is a Buddhist pagoda, built in the same style as its neighbors. Boats stop at Phu Khong to give visitors time to explore.

Hoa Lu

For the latter half of the 10th century, the ancient citadel at **Hoa Lu** (6am-6pm daily summer, 6:30am-6:30pm daily winter,

VND20,000) served as the political, cultural, and economic center of the Dai Co Viet, predecessors to modern-day Vietnamese. A pair of 17th-century temples in honor of the Dinh and Tien Le dynasties stands on the grounds of the former city.

Hoa Lu was originally founded in 968 by King Dinh Tien Hoang, who was later assassinated alongside two of his sons. Le Hoan, a high-ranking military official, ascended the throne to become Le Dai Hanh, first ruler of the Tien Le dynasty.

Today, the remaining Dinh and Le temples are almost identical, with large wooden effigies of each emperor in his respective building. Dinh Tien Hoang is flanked by the two sons who died with him, and his temple faces Ma Yen, the mountain atop which he was buried. In Le Dai Hanh's domain, his son sits to his right, while a memorial for his wife stands at his left. Both structures feature traditional Vietnamese architecture, including an entrance partitioned into three doors and high door frames, which force visitors to look down when entering the temple, thus showing respect to the deities inside. A stop at the Dinh and Le temples is really only worthwhile if combined with a visit to Trang An. Hoa Lu is 11 kilometers from downtown Ninh Binh and

rowboats at Trang An

about three kilometers north of the main gate at Trang An. If you're already visiting Trang An, continue on the main road to find the main entrance of Hoa Lu.

Bai Dinh Pagoda

The largest Buddhist complex in the country, **Bai Dinh Pagoda** (tel. 0229/627-0516, 5am-5pm daily) began construction in 2004, and was completed in 2015. This massive center of worship has set several records, including the longest pagoda corridors in Asia, which trail on for over 1.5 kilometers from the entrance all the way up to the main hall. At the far end of a long stone bridge, a three-door front gate ushers visitors inside, where two towering guardians supervise the comings and goings at the pagoda. From here, Bai Dinh's endless covered walkways begin, rambling up the hillside accompanied by a collection of 500 stone arhat statues, each weighing five tons and standing over 2.5 meters tall.

While there are several shrines dedicated to different statues of the Buddha and other prominent Buddhist figures, such as Quan Am, the centerpiece of this opus is the grand main hall, where a trio of enormous 50-ton, floor-to-ceiling gold-plated Buddhas sit in a row, representing the past, present, and future. Surrounded by 2,000 smaller sparkling Amitabha Buddhas set in alcoves in the walls, the sheer size of the room and its contents are enough to inspire awe. A wander around to the rest of the shrines, including a larger-than-life 1,000-arms-and-eyes sculpture of Quan Am, confirm that the rest of the sprawling complex is, indeed, just as lavish.

While Bai Dinh's volume does make for an interesting spectacle, the newness of the complex detracts from its wow factor. Visitors to the pagoda usually pull up to an **electric car station** (VND30,000 pp one-way) just under two kilometers from the main entrance. You're free to walk in on your own, though it's easier to just take the ride, as you'll be doing plenty of walking once you reach the pagoda grounds.

TOWARD CUC PHUONG NATIONAL PARK
Van Long Nature Reserve

About 32 kilometers northwest of Ninh Binh, the **Van Long Nature Reserve** (Gia Van, tel. 0229/386-8798, 7am-5pm daily, VND50,000) is a protected wetland home to hundreds of plant and animal species, including 72 varieties of birds and the largest wild population of Delacour's langurs, one of the most

a pond at Bai Dinh Pagoda

endangered primate species in the world. Limestone karsts dot the marsh, which is only accessible by rowboat.

If possible, it's best to time your visit during the summer, as this is when your chances of seeing wildlife are highest. Your driver will likely request a tip at the end; provide a tip at your discretion. At least half the entrance fee goes to the nature reserve, so without a tip, the boat drivers only take home a small amount for an hours' work.

TOURS

Single-day tours to Ninh Binh's main attractions can be arranged either from Ninh Binh or from Hanoi. Tours leaving from Ninh Binh tend to be more motorbike taxi services than guided excursions. While there are a few travel outfits based in the town, your best option when booking a tour in Ninh Binh is to talk to your hotel. Most accommodations can arrange a trip that includes Tam Coc, Bich Dong Pagoda, and a few other surrounding sights, though you can also pick and choose your own itinerary. You'll find a lot more variety and service in the day trips offered from Hanoi, but these excursions are more expensive, as they require transportation to and from town.

Chookie's Travel (tel. 09/4834-6026, www.chookiestravel.com, VND550,000-2,000,000) runs tours from Ninh Binh to Tam Coc, Trang An, and Cuc Phuong National Park. **A-Travel Mate** (39D Dinh Tien Hoang, tel. 024/3926-3370, www.atravelmate.com, 8am-9pm daily) operates out of Hanoi and offers group tours to Tam Coc for VND892,000. Private tours from Hanoi to Tam Coc are VND2,818,000-3,250,000.

FOOD

Don't expect to find much variety in Ninh Binh, as most eateries remain humble, front-of-the-house set-ups with a few plastic chairs and a selection of Vietnamese dishes. The town itself is known for its goat meat, which is often served in a hot pot or with *com cháy*, another local specialty made from rice that is sun-dried and later fried. This is usually served in the same way as steamed rice, with an accompanying meat or tofu dish. Vegetarians take care, as the name of the dish can be misleading: You'll see signs all over town for *com cháy*, the Ninh Binh specialty. Vegetarian food, or *com chay*, is spelled almost exactly the same.

One of a few modest, open-front shops clustered around the train station, **Trung Tuyet** (14 Hoang Hoa Tham, tel. 09/1285-9371, 8am-9:30pm daily, VND30,000-180,000) seems to be the friendliest and best-equipped of the bunch, with welcoming owners and a host of good, cheap meals. Standard Vietnamese meals and a few backpacker favorites, including banana pancakes, appear on the menu. It's also possible to order your food in different portion sizes, depending upon your level of hunger, and you'll likely get an orange slice or two at the end of the meal as a goodwill offering.

Near the bank of hotels on Luong Van Tuy, **Chookie's** (17 Luong Van Tuy, tel. 09/4834-6026, chookiesninhbinh@gmail.com, 11:30am-10pm Wed.-Mon., VND50,000-130,000) serves as both a restaurant and small travel outfit. Proudly boasting one of the only European coffee machines in town, this bright spot is decked out in vibrant artwork and run by friendly English-speaking staff. The menu includes a few Vietnamese options and the only Western food in Ninh Binh, with items like tuna melts and burgers. This is a great spot to visit for sound travel advice, as the staff is well-versed in Ninh Binh's tourism attractions and more than willing to help you navigate your way around town.

Just before the Tam Coc boat station, the cheerful folks at **Minh Toan Restaurant** (Tam Coc, tel. 09/4844-3268, 10am-10pm daily, VND35,000-230,000) offer your usual Vietnamese fare, including pork, chicken, beef, and tofu in addition to snails, goat, and *com chay*. Both indoor and outdoor tables are available and the family that runs the place is a little less pushy than some of the other local restaurants along the strip. This is a worthy lunch stop for those touring the area.

ACCOMMODATIONS

Ninh Binh doesn't yet have droves of quality accommodations, but there are a few well-priced guesthouses and smaller, family-run hotels that do the trick. These are fairly spread out over the city's modest downtown area. Some of the budget options are near the local train station. You can also find a string of hotels and guesthouses outside town around the Tam Coc boat station: the upside to this location is its easy access to nearby sights. But, with Tam Coc well on the tourist trail, it's also a little exhausting to stick around here for any longer than a few minutes, as vendors and restaurant owners are quick with sales pitches.

Under VND210,000

Queen Mini Hotel (21 Hoang Hoa Tham, tel. 0229/387-1874, VND100,000 dorm, VND180,000-340,000 d) sits on a cozy corner opposite the larger Queen Hotel and not far from another similarly named lodging. This is the most affordable of the lot and provides budget backpackers with unbelievably cheap dorm beds or private rooms that come with air-conditioning and hot showers. The staff is amiable, though expect a hard sell on things like bus tickets, vehicle rentals, and tours. Tour information is readily available and there are a handful of affordable eateries in the area.

VND210,000-525,000

Ngoc Anh Hotel (36 Luong Van Tuy, tel. 0229/388-3768, www.ngocanh-hotel.com, VND410,000-570,000, breakfast included) takes the prize for best-kept rooms in the city, with spotless tile baths, comfy beds, and all the usual amenities. Three room types are available; the cheapest run small but are perfectly adequate, while the middle- and top-tier choices are virtually the same, although the more expensive rooms come with more light. The staff is cheerful, informative, and will set you up with vehicle rentals and affordable tours of the area.

VND525,000-1,050,000

You can also check out **Ngoc Anh 2** (26 Luong Van Tuy, tel. 0229/388-3768, www.ngocanh-hotel.com, VND795,000-1,115,000), just down the road from Ngoc Anh Hotel, if you find that the original is full.

The smartest lodging on the block, **Queen Hotel** (20 Hoang Hoa Tham, tel. 0229/389-3535, www.queenhotel.vn, VND480,000-800,000) is well furnished and clean, with generous beds and enormous baths. All rooms feature hot water, air-conditioning, TV, and Wi-Fi access, as well as a minibar and complimentary breakfast included in the rates. Three types of accommodations are available, from good value standard rooms to spacious deluxe beds, which also come with a balcony and a bathtub. Downstairs, the hotel arranges tours and transportation to nearby sights.

VND1,050,000-2,100,000

The charming, family-run **Vancouver Hotel** (1/75 Luong Van Tuy, tel. 0229/389-3270, www.thevancouverhotel.com, VND1,480,000-2,050,000) sits down a quiet alley just off Luong Van Tuy and provides a rare mid-range option among mostly budget guesthouses. Its chic rooms feature Wi-Fi, TV, an in-room safe, tea- and coffee-making facilities, hot water, air-conditioning, and some heavenly mattresses, alongside more space and ambience than you'll find in other Ninh Binh's accommodations. Breakfast is included in the rates.

Over VND2,100,000

A tranquil boutique resort set amid rice fields, **Tam Coc Garden** (Hai Nham Hamlet, tel. 024/6273-3615, www.tamcocgarden.com, VND3,295,000-4,430,000) consists of 16 rustic countryside rooms. The retreat is close enough to Tam Coc to provide easy access to nearby sights while maintaining some distance from the tourist melee. Each room offers minimalist decor and modern amenities, with plush low beds, handcrafted wooden furniture, and the famous pottery of Bat Trang village. Wi-Fi is not provided in all rooms. The bamboo-outfitted restaurant offers pleasant views of the surrounding paddy fields. Bicycle use is free for guests. The friendly staff can offer local recommendations.

INFORMATION AND SERVICES
Visitor Information

Hotel owners are your best bet for things like maps, restaurant recommendations, and general advice. While you're not likely to find a detailed map of Ninh Binh anywhere, the rudimentary maps offered at most accommodations do the trick, and receptionists are willing to share their knowledge with travelers. For additional info, you can swing by **Chookie's** (17 Luong Van Tuy, tel. 09/4834-6026, chookiesninhbinh@gmail.com, 11:30am-10pm Wed.-Mon.).

Banks

You'll find ATMs handy along Tran Hung Dao and near many of Ninh Binh's hotels. The local **Vietin Bank** (951 Tran Hung Dao, tel. 0229/387-2614, www.vietinbank.vn, 7:30am-11:30am and 1:30pm-5pm Mon.-Fri., 7:30am-11am Sat.) can assist with currency exchange and has an ATM out front.

Postal Services and Internet

The **central post office** (1 Tran Hung Dao, tel. 0229/387-6666, 7am-11:30am and 1pm-5:30pm Mon.-Sat., 7:30am-11:30am and 1pm-5pm Sun.) is located near Lim Bridge.

Medical Services

The colossal **Ninh Binh General Hospital (Benh Vien Da Khoa Ninh Binh)** (Tue Tinh, tel. 0229/387-1030, www.benhvienninhbinh. vn) lies south of Lim Bridge and can deal with minor ailments, though don't expect to find an English-speaking doctor.

TRANSPORTATION

Local buses to Ninh Binh come in from Hanoi (1.5 hours, VND160,000) and the surrounding area on a daily basis and arrive at the **bus station** (207 Le Dai Hanh, tel. 0229/387-1069) just opposite Lim Bridge.

The **Ninh Binh train station** (Hoang Hoa Tham, tel. 0229/367-3619, 7am-11pm daily) has daily runs north and south, with regular arrivals from Hanoi (2.5 hours, from VND80,000) and a slew of southern destinations.

Xe om can be found outside of bus stations and on street corners around town. For larger vehicles, try **Mailinh** (tel. 0229/363-6363) or **Hoa Lu** (tel. 0229/221-1444) taxis.

Most hotels and guesthouses in Ninh Binh rent out motorbikes (from VND100,000 per day) and bicycles (around VND30,000). Around the backpacker enclave at Tam Coc, prices go up, sometimes as much as double.

★ CUC PHUONG NATIONAL PARK

The oldest national park in Vietnam, **Cuc Phuong National Park (Vuon Quoc Gia Cuc Phuong)** (tel. 0229/384-8006, www. cucphuongtourism.com.vn, 6am-5pm daily, VND60,000) has been protected since 1962. It's home to several species of langurs, a fast-disappearing monkey found throughout Asia. Its most famous resident, the black-and-white Delacour's langur, is among the most critically endangered primates in the world, with an estimated 200 remaining in Vietnam. Thanks to the park's conservation efforts, at least some of their diminishing numbers are protected, as are a host of other primates and turtles. Beyond these creatures, the 22,200-hectare park is also home to 336 species of birds, 76 species of reptiles, and a host of other insects, amphibians, and fish.

Cuc Phuong offers many do-it-yourself hikes. Visit a prehistoric cave dwelling or trek through the dense forest to see a towering 1,000-year-old tree. Local guides can bring you on bird-watching and wildlife-spotting tours, organize homestays with the park's Muong population, or arrange a camping excursion in the woods. While nature hikes can be a fun way to pass the day at any time of year, Cuc Phuong is at its best March-June, when the rain recedes and more of the park's animals are out and about. Cuc Phuong is an easy and accessible trip from either Ninh Binh or Hanoi, as either a daylong or overnight excursion.

Sights

Most day visitors to Cuc Phuong see the major highlights of the park on their own. Just before the main entrance, the visitors center provides useful maps and information. For daylong explorations, **bicycle rentals** (VND100,000) make for a fun and active way to explore the major attractions. Visitors to the primate conservation center can join a regular guided tour, which takes place every half-hour. Guides manage to provide interesting information on the various endangered species within each center and introduce each of the creatures in their care.

Farther along, it's possible to make an independent visit to Mac Lake, a pretty little spot just inside the entrance gate, as well as the prehistoric cave and the ancient tree. Park guides can be hired for lengthier excursions into Cuc Phuong's grounds, including a trek into the forest in search of ancient fossils, a stroll around the botanical garden, and a multiple day camping trip through the best of Cuc Phuong's foliage. All of these things can be arranged at the park's headquarters upon arrival.

Bring insect repellent, as Cuc Phuong's smallest residents can be pesky in the thick of the rainforest, and substantial footwear is advised, particularly during rainy times, as the park's limestone rocks can become pretty treacherous when wet.

ENDANGERED PRIMATE RESCUE CENTER

Founded in 1993 by the Frankfurt Zoological Society, Cuc Phuong's **Endangered Primate Rescue Center** (9am-11am and 1:15pm-4pm daily, VND30,000) rehabilitates primates that were once a part of the illegal wildlife trade, a black-market industry fueled by demand for traditional Chinese remedies, many of which contain animal parts. Specializing in endemic species like Cuc Phuong's signature Delacour's langur and the nearby Cat Ba langur, both of which are among the most endangered primates in the world, this center cares for and studies newly rescued creatures before releasing the rehabilitated animals into a seven-hectare semi-wild enclosure. From there, the monkeys learn to fend for themselves again before returning to their natural environment.

monkeys at Cuc Phuong's Endangered Primate Rescue Center

Visitors to the center are given a tour of the animals and a brief introduction into its rescue operation. Guides take visitors to the animals' cages, where some of the more curious monkeys will approach for a closer look.

After you've paid the park entry fee at the visitors center, head over to the rescue center, where guided tours—included in the center's additional VND30,000 entry fee—run every 30 minutes.

TURTLE CONSERVATION CENTER

The **Turtle Conservation Center** (9am-11am and 2pm-4pm daily, VND30,000) sits opposite the Endangered Primate Rescue Center and focuses on rescuing and protecting turtles from the illegal wildlife trade, in which they're used for food or traditional medicine. Visitors are able to roam the grounds and see a host of different species in the center's ponds and wooded areas. An informative display explains some of the challenges stemming from this illicit industry as well as the work of the center. Turtles wander freely, with only low barriers separating their living spaces from footpaths. Visitors are required to have guides—included with the additional VND30,000 entry fee—who can explain the different species.

PREHISTORIC CAVE

Discovered in 1966, the **Prehistoric Cave (Dong Nguoi Xua)** at Cuc Phuong National Park is believed to date back as far as 7,500 years. When it was first unearthed, locals came across stone implements and other ancient tools inside, as well as a few tombs, suggesting that its residents practiced their own customs and traditions.

From the road, rent a **flashlight** (VND10,000) or bring your own to explore the darkened recesses of the cavern. It's a 300-meter walk from the road up a few flights of stone steps to the entrance, where the wide, round space is filled with miniature shrines and small incense urns. This is a nice pit stop on the way to the 1,000-year-old tree and the larger Palace Cave.

The cave is five or six kilometers along the park road and easy to find as it's marked by a sign and a parking guard on the roadside.

PALACE CAVE AND THE 1,000-YEAR-OLD TREE

From the park's interior outpost (different from the office at the park entrance), it's about 30 minutes on the paved walkway to **Palace Cave.** Hemmed in by dense rainforest on either side, this path winds through lush, canopied grounds where you may be able to spot a few creatures en route. Palace Cave is a long tunnel that's virtually untouched; bring a flashlight.

After exploring the cave, continue on the path for about 10 minutes to the park's **1,000-year-old tree.** While this sight doesn't warrant a trip on its own, the cave is impressive and the moderate 1.5-kilometer stroll through the rainforest is a pleasant excursion. To make things more interesting, you can complete the full loop from the park's outpost along the paved trail to the ancient tree and then back around the long way, following a seven-kilometer dirt track back to the outpost, though be aware that this is a more challenging route. The path on this side of the loop is not maintained and is harder to follow.

Tours

Independent day tours from both Ninh Binh and Hanoi are available. Your best option is to hire a park-authorized guide, who will be able to lead you on anything from a daylong hike to a longer overnight excursion. For multiple-day trips, get in touch with the park beforehand, either via phone or email, to confirm a guide's availability. Cuc Phuong's website (www.cucphuongtourism.com.vn) is a useful resource in planning your visit.

Food

There are two **restaurants** (7am-8pm daily, VND20,000-150,000) within the park, one at the main headquarters and another at the park's outpost near Palace Cave and the 1,000-year-old tree. The menu features plenty of grilled meat and Vietnamese dishes, as well as a limited number of vegetarian choices, at reasonable prices. There is also a snack shop just outside the visitors center.

Accommodations

Cuc Phuong National Park runs a bare-bones **guesthouse** (VND105,000 pp, VND450,000-615,000 d) with two different room options. The cheaper accommodations include an outdoor bath and shower but lack most basic amenities, such as hot water and air-conditioning. For a few extra dollars you can have a standard double with an indoor bath, hot water, and air-conditioning. Neither option is upscale, but they do the job for a short stay.

To book a room at the guesthouse, get in touch with the park's tourism office (tel. 0229/384-8006, www.cucphuongtourism.com.vn). Availability depends on the day. Vietnamese tourists travel in large groups, so if a Vietnamese group comes through, the guesthouse could easily fill up. Otherwise, you shouldn't have a problem arranging a room at the guesthouse, but book ahead.

Transportation

Cuc Phuong National Park lies roughly 56 kilometers from Ninh Binh and 129 kilometers from Hanoi. Both single- and multiple-day trips to the park can be arranged from either city.

FROM NINH BINH

Travelers departing from Ninh Binh will have to arrange transportation to the park, either by hired car, taxi, or hired motorbike. While cars run on the expensive side, particularly for individual travelers, this is a good option for groups. Make your return arrangement with the same driver, as there are no cars to hire in the park area.

Travelers who feel comfortable on a motorbike can navigate the back roads of Ninh Binh on their own, though signage is limited and English speakers are nonexistent. Depending on the weather, roads leading out to the park can become treacherous, as certain sections are dirt track rather than paved highway.

From Ninh Binh, head south along 30 Thang 6 street, which turns into Highway 1 as you exit the city. The road will curve west and change names to Quang Trung. Turn right onto Dong Giao street and keep straight to Cuc Phuong in 39 kilometers. Jot down the name of the national park in case you need directions. Most locals will know the park and can point you in the right direction.

FROM HANOI

From Hanoi, the same hired vehicle options apply, though travelers hoping to make the trek solo are far better to depart from Ninh Binh, as an 129-kilometer journey on a motorbike will eat up more of your day than the actual visit. Instead, you're better off taking the **Cuc Phuong bus** (VND150,000) from Hanoi's Giap Bat station at 3pm and catching the return vehicle back from the park at 9am to save yourself time and hassle, although an overnight here will be necessary.

BIKE

Bicycles (VND100,000 per day) can be rented from Cuc Phuong's visitors center by the day to explore the park grounds.

The Central Provinces

Look for ★ to find recommended
sights, activities, dining, and lodging.

Highlights

★ **Imperial City:** Step into the bygone world of mighty emperors and opulent palaces in Hue (page 156).

★ **Phong Nha-Ke Bang National Park:** Explore a mind-blowing maze of ethereal subterranean chambers, never-ending rice paddies, and dense green rainforest (page 176).

★ **Linh Ung Pagoda:** Stand beside the towering white figure of Quan Am, Danang's 30-story-tall protector, while admiring panoramas of the metropolis (page 188).

★ **Hai Van Pass:** Take a ride on Vietnam's most breathtaking coastal road, complete with lush emerald mountains and picture-perfect panoramas of the East Sea (page 197).

★ **Hoi An's Old Town:** Discover the laid-back charm of Hoi An's vibrant meeting halls and centuries-old traditional houses (page 203).

With the stunning curves of a mountainous coastline and the heartbreaking scars of war, Vietnam's central provinces are a microcosm of captivating destinations.

The region boasts top-notch cuisine and natural, cultural, and historical attractions catering to both adventurous backpackers and luxury travelers. The central provinces are home to an imperial citadel, a sun-soaked port town, and an ultramodern city. Explore Hoi An, a shopper's paradise, where master tailors can put together a dress, shirt, or pair of pants in less than a day. Take to the shores of Danang, the central region's coolest contemporary city, powered by a fusion of hip cosmopolitan culture and Vietnam's laid-back local scene. Dive into the fascinating history of Hue, Vietnam's last imperial capital.

Beyond its urban hot spots, central Vietnam holds a host of wild landscapes, replete with rainforests, rice fields, and gargantuan limestone formations. Phong Nha-Ke Bang National Park and its jaw-dropping subterranean chambers, hollowed out by several million years of erosion, are a must-see. The eerie, overgrown ruins of My Son, former Cham holy land, and several crumbling relics of the American War, including the dividing line between North and South Vietnam, add to the awe and mystery of the region.

HISTORY

If Vietnamese culture hails from its northern region and the country's southern territory helped to shape its more recent history, then Vietnam's central provinces were instrumental through many of the events in between. As early as 1000 BC, the region was home to the Sa Huynh culture, an ancient people whose tenure overlapped with the Dong Son in the north.

The Sa Huynh culture was a precursor to the Hindu nation of Champa, responsible for three settlements that stretched from the port of Hoi An west to the temples of My Son around the 4th century AD. After several decades of conflict with the Vietnamese, at the end of the 10th century, the Cham were driven down the coast and out of the central region.

At that time, international trade had been a longstanding business in Hoi An. The thriving port welcomed ships from as near

The Central Provinces

SEE "VICINITY OF HUE" MAP

Hue

⊞ IMPERIAL CITY

Huong Thuy

PHU BAI INTERNATIONAL AIRPORT

To ⊞ PHONG NHA-KE BANG NATIONAL PARK

Thon Phu An

Chon Dong

SEE "LANG CO" MAP

NORTH CENTRAL COAST

Phu Loc

⊞ HAI VAN PASS

Thanh Khe Beach

SEE "DANANG" MAP

Nong Truong

Son Tra

Nam Dong

Ap Huong Phuoc

Danang

BA NA HILLS CABLE CAR

DANANG BUS STATION

⊞ LINH UNG PAGODA

Cham Island

BA NA HILL STATION

Ai Yin Young

SOUTH CENTRAL COAST

Thuong Duc

Ha Nong Trung

THE NAM HAI

An Bang Beach

SEE "HOI AN" MAP

⊞ HOI AN'S OLD TOWN

THANH HA POTTERY VILLAGE

0   10 mi
0   10 km

MY SON RUINS
★

Thuong Trung

Thanh Binh

Ben Giang

© AVALON TRAVEL

as Thailand and India and as far as France, Portugal, and England. In the 16th century, scores of Chinese and Japanese traders began setting up shop in what was then known as Faifo. The town was the most prosperous economic center in central Vietnam until the 19th century, when the waters of the Thu Bon River became too shallow for ships to dock at the port.

Beginning in 1802, when the newly crowned emperor Gia Long moved Vietnam's capital to Hue, the region began to play an influential role on the national level. The emperor was first in a 13-generation line of rulers that would make up Vietnam's last imperial dynasty. Moving the capital south afforded him influence over the northern and southern halves of the country, and ushered in an age of cultural fanfare in Hue that attracted poets, painters, scholars, and mandarins from across the country.

The French stormed Danang's port in 1858, imposing colonial rule. By the 20th century, growing dissent among the general population had many calling for an end to French colonialism. As World War II approached, public opinion, influenced by the ideals of the Viet Minh, favored a new form of political authority, headed by the Communist Party. Emperor Bao Dai, the final ruler of the Nguyen dynasty, turned over power to the Viet Minh in 1945, just days before Ho Chi Minh gave his independence speech at Ba Dinh Square.

Though this ended Hue's tenure as capital of Vietnam, the central region was not finished shaping national history. Several provinces became instrumental in conflicts throughout the American War. Home to the Ben Hai River, which served as the boundary between North and South Vietnam, Quang Tri, an area about 80 kilometers north of Hue, saw some of the heaviest fighting and bore thousands of tons of bombs, Agent Orange, and other toxins. Now-infamous places like Khe Sanh, Hamburger Hill, and the Rockpile dot the countryside in Quang Tri and its southern neighbor, Thua Thien-Hue, a stark reminder of Vietnam's recent military struggles.

PLANNING YOUR TIME

Hue and Hoi An are the main highlights of the region. On a cross-country road trip, allocate one week to cover the region. From each of these cities, shorter day-long excursions to nearby sights like My Son and the DMZ area are possible for visitors with a more relaxed schedule.

If you have more time, take a day to travel from Hue to Hoi An or vice versa and stop along the way to enjoy the beach at Lang Co or Danang's stunning Hai Van Pass. Remote Phong Nha-Ke Bang National Park, easily the country's best up-and-coming destination,

is worth a visit but requires more time and money than a visit to most coastal towns. It's a full day of travel to get there and back, and you should spend at least two days there, so budget 4-5 days.

The main route between Hue and Hoi An is Highway 1, which runs through Danang. This is the most popular route and is easy to navigate.

The central provinces are home to some of the country's most extreme weather. Its location on the belly of the S makes it more prone to storms. This area is rocked by flash floods, monsoon rains, and other storms every year, often sweeping away houses and affecting local crops. Hoi An is notorious for its November deluge in particular, when locals get around by canoe. While plying these temporary canals makes for a memorable shopping experience, the weather in central Vietnam is more of a hindrance than a novelty. Time your visit outside September-January, when rainfall is highest. August is a brutally hot month in the region. February-May are the best months in central Vietnam, with temperatures on the rise but not yet unbearable.

Hue

Boasting an intricate patchwork of imperial legacy and wartime history, French colonialism and ancient civilization, Hue is a city with an exceptional past. For 13 generations, this charming riverside town served as the Nguyen dynasty's political, cultural, and intellectual center, housing an impressive royal citadel along the northern bank of the Perfume River, not to mention scores of historical relics still scattered across town and throughout the southern countryside, evidence of Vietnam's last imperial rulers. As a result of its unique past and grand architecture, Hue's imperial sights gained UNESCO World Heritage status in 1993 and have since become a major

tourism draw for the city. Travelers keen on delving into the nation's earlier history will appreciate the storied Imperial City complex as well as Hue's surrounding royal tombs, each paying homage to the life and achievements of a different Vietnamese king. Foodies can dig into a plethora of bite-size local specialties, as this city boasts a well-deserved reputation as one of the country's top culinary destinations.

Many of Hue's riverine streets provide a picturesque setting for an afternoon cycle, passing the many-tiered bell tower at Thien Mu Pagoda or the sleepy streets bordering the smaller An Cuu River. Outside town, Hue's surroundings are an attractive sea of verdant

Hue

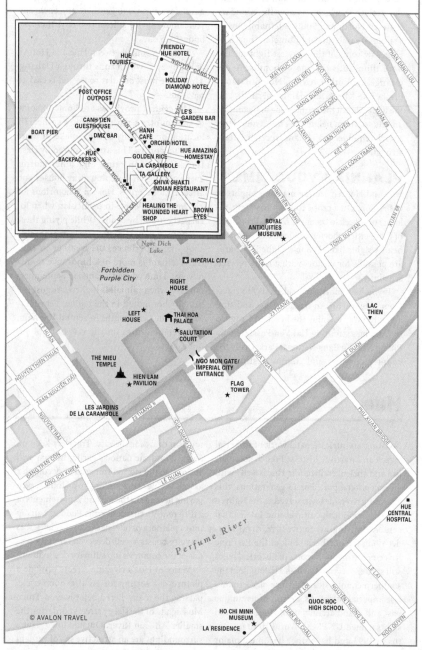

FRIENDLY
HUE HOTEL

HUE
TOURIST

HOLIDAY
DIAMOND HOTEL

POST OFFICE
OUTPOST

LE'S
GARDEN BAR

CANH TIEN
GUESTHOUSE

HANH
CAFE

BOAT PIER

DMZ BAR

ORCHID HOTEL

HUE AMAZING
HOMESTAY

HUE
BACKPACKER'S

GOLDEN RICE

LA CARAMBOLE

TA GALLERY

SHIVA SHAKTI
INDIAN RESTAURANT

HEALING THE
WOUNDED HEART
SHOP

BROWN
EYES

Ngoc Dich
Lake

IMPERIAL CITY

ROYAL
ANTIQUITIES
MUSEUM

Forbidden
Purple City

RIGHT
HOUSE

LAC
THIEN

LEFT
HOUSE

THAI HOA
PALACE

SALUTATION
COURT

THE MIEU
TEMPLE

NGO MON GATE/
IMPERIAL CITY
ENTRANCE

HIEN LAM
PAVILION

FLAG
TOWER

LES JARDINS
DE LA CARAMBOLE

HUE
CENTRAL
HOSPITAL

Perfume River

© AVALON TRAVEL

QUOC HOC
HIGH SCHOOL

HO CHI MINH
MUSEUM

LA RESIDENCE

paddy fields and coastal landscapes that were also the backdrop for some of the American War's most brutal battles. Regular trips to the demilitarized zone north of the city and along the coastal route south toward Danang add to Hue's appeal. The city experiences its best weather between March and June, when temperatures climb and the mist dissipates; during January and February, however, it's constant rain. While you could easily pass four days in the former capital, most travelers prefer to stick around for two or three and still manage to visit the Imperial City, one or two royal tombs, and a few other countryside attractions.

SIGHTS

The Imperial City, Hue's main attraction, lies directly at the center of town and is easily accessible from the backpacker area. You'll have to rely on a bicycle or motorbike to make it to sights like the royal tombs or Thanh Toan bridge. Bicycle rentals are an inexpensive and popular way to get around town, and you could easily pass an afternoon exploring Hue's riverside roads on two wheels. Dragon boats can ferry you to and from sights like Thien Mu Pagoda, the Imperial City, and Hue Nam Shrine.

The sheer number of historical sights in Hue can make it hard to decide which places to visit. Even though the high price can be discouraging, make a point to see the Imperial City and one or two of the royal tombs. There is a package ticket (VND280,000) that includes access to the Imperial City, the Royal Antiquities Museum, and the royal tombs of Khai Dinh and Minh Mang, as well as one that adds the tomb of Tu Duc (VND360,000). These tickets are available at Ngo Mon Gate, the main entrance into the Imperial City, as well as at the tomb entrances. Tickets are good for two days from the date of purchase, allowing you to visit each sight without breaking the bank.

★ Imperial City

From the early 19th century through the end of the Vietnamese monarchy in 1945, Hue's **Imperial City** (23 Thang 8, 7am-5pm daily winter, 6:30am-5:30pm daily summer, VND150,000) housed an impressive cache of temples, palaces, and administrative buildings belonging to the 13 kings of the Nguyen dynasty. On the northern side of the Perfume River, the walled Citadel complex reached a total of 148 buildings during its prime, most of which were constructed between 1802 and 1832. Today 20 remain, making for a captivating sight. Wide, opulent palaces and dimly lit temples pepper the now-overgrown grounds, boasting a mix of traditional Vietnamese architecture, vibrant lacquered woodwork, and ornate rooftops, not to mention 143 years' worth of imperial history.

Avoid heat and crowds by visiting early in the morning. Allot at least 1.5 hours to explore this sight at your own pace; there is a fair bit of ground to cover. Electric car services are available, as are **tour guides** (VND150,000). Guides hired at the Imperial City tend to lead only a "greatest hits" tour, skipping the mostly destroyed Forbidden Purple City and the Thai Binh Reading Pavilion to visit The Mieu Temple Complex, and can sometimes push hard for a tip. Hiring a guide is not a bad option for someone who has time constraints and a limited budget, but if you're looking to get the whole story, you're better off arranging a private guide or hopping on a public tour with a more knowledgeable leader.

NGO MON GATE AND THE SALUTATION COURT

Before you pass through the enormous **Ngo Mon Gate** (Noon Gate), take a moment to look toward the equally huge **flag tower** flying Vietnam's colors on the opposite side of the road. This tower is Hue's most recognizable icon. The massive three-tiered stone structure has been around since 1807 and is as much a symbol of the city and central

Vietnam as anything else within the Citadel complex.

To enter the Imperial City, visitors cross over a small moat and go through one of the five doors at Ngo Mon Gate. In addition to providing access to the administrative buildings and living quarters of the royal family, the top of this structure was once reserved for the king during special ceremonies and Lunar New Year celebrations. In the days of the monarchy, the pavilion was reserved strictly for men; no women were permitted to ascend its stone steps until near the end of the Nguyen dynasty, when emperor Bao Dai invited his queen, Nam Phuong, to stand beside him. Below, each of the gate's five doors granted access to a different group of individuals, with the central opening kept strictly for royalty, the two beside for civil and military mandarins, and the far doors used for elephants.

On the other side of Ngo Mon is the **Salutation Court,** a large open space often used for royal celebrations, such as birthdays, as well as the twice-monthly Grand Audience, an event in which the king and all high-ranking mandarins gathered within the Imperial City. Beyond a rectangular fishpond, the clearing's three levels were used to organize civil and military mandarins into their respective ranks, lining up single-file beside the miniature stelae bordering either side of the courtyard today. Lesser members of the royal family, relatives of the queen mother, for example, were relegated to the back, near the entrance; soldiers, horses, and elephants took up the pair of green lawns beside the stone courtyard.

THAI HOA PALACE AND THE RIGHT AND LEFT HOUSES

At the far end of the Salutation Court is **Thai Hoa Palace,** the Imperial City's largest and best-preserved structure. Wide and rectangular, this double-roofed building holds the original throne of the Nguyen dynasty. Its exterior, decorated with yin-yang tiles and vivid mosaic facades, captures the spirit of the Imperial City's heyday. Inside, the palace's pair of roofs are bolstered by 80 solid ironwood columns lacquered in red and gold. Up above, decoration alternates between a series of poems and picture characters just below the ceiling. The building, completed in 1805, has undergone major renovations twice, in 1833 and again in 1923, and now stands as the most intact structure in the complex.

At the center of Thai Hoa's main room, the royal throne might not be the grand seat of the empire you might expect, but this small chair made of red-and-gold lacquered wood was used from the reign of Gia Long, first emperor of the Nguyen dynasty, all the way through to Bao Dai, its last. The throne sits upon a platform with three levels, symbolizing the relationship between human beings, heaven, and earth, and is covered by a decorative canopy that hangs over the platform.

Beyond the royal throne, the second room of the palace offers an informational video about the history of the Imperial City that's worth a watch, as well as a model of what the Citadel looked like in its prime. This gives an idea of the grandeur of the complex before much of it was destroyed by the conflicts of the late 20th century.

After you've wandered through Thai Hoa Palace, you'll exit onto the sunny grounds bordered by the **Right and Left Houses.** While their functions have changed considerably—one is now an exhibition hall, the other a photo studio where guests can dress up in imperial garb for portraits on a replica of the throne—these buildings were once the offices of the Nguyen dynasty's civil and military mandarins.

FORBIDDEN PURPLE CITY

Past the Right and Left Houses is a deteriorating stone wall that once separated the Imperial City from the emperor's private residence. This structure is in good shape compared to the rest of the **Forbidden Purple City,** most of which now exists as an open field, its few ruins buried under a tangle of grass. During the height of the Nguyen dynasty, Can Chanh Palace served as the administrative building in which the emperor conducted his daily business, while Can Thanh Palace just behind housed his living quarters. Today, you would never know the two even existed but for a small plaque in the middle of the open space. Though its skeleton is still recognizable, the Kien Trung Palace, built in 1827 and once home to the empress, has met a similar fate, as it is now no more than a stone platform from which to look out over the empty inner complex. If you use your imagination, you can reconstruct not only the homes of the emperor and empress but the living quarters that housed his royal concubines to the left and the princes and princesses to the right. A covered walkway runs the width of the Forbidden Purple City, as do a pair of newly renovated paths leading from the front gate through to Kien Trung Palace.

THE MIEU TEMPLE COMPLEX

On the far left side of the grounds, **The Mieu Temple Complex** holds a trio of well-preserved buildings constructed under Minh Mang, second emperor of the Nguyen dynasty. Dedicated to the worship of Nguyen royalty, **The Mieu Temple** honors 10 of the 13 emperors in the dynasty, with the exceptions of Duc Duc, Hiep Hoa, and Bao Dai, all of whom abdicated. Lined up across the wide hall are identical shrines to the emperors, beginning with an incense altar and photograph at the front, followed by fruit offerings and each king's lacquered wooden tablet at the far end of the hall.

Opposite The Mieu is the **Hien Lam Pavilion,** an open-air structure that looks back at the temple and the nine bronze urns that stand between them. These, too, were placed here by Minh Mang, who chose nine as a lucky number and believed that his lineage would produce at least nine kings. In the days of the empire, The Mieu Temple Complex was limited to male members of the royal family and civil and military service; even the empress was not permitted to enter. Around the back of the complex, women honored emperors past at **Phung Tien Temple,** especially on the anniversary of their deaths. Today, the pockmarked gate to the temple is all that remains. The nearby **Chuong Duc Gate** is an impressive and colorful sight.

THAI BINH READING PAVILION

On the other side of Thai Hoa Palace and the Forbidden Purple City, the **Thai Binh Reading Pavilion,** built under Thieu Tri,

The Mieu Temple Complex

remains intact, though it can only be viewed from outside.

Not far from here is the slightly dusty **Royal Theater** (tel. 0234/351-4989, www.nhanhac.com.vn), another explosion of red and gold, where musical performances (10am and 3pm daily, VND200,000) are held. Farther back, the crumbling, moss-covered walls of **Ngoc Dich Lake** add to the scenery. From here, use the walkway heading east to reach the exit at Hien Nhon Gate, where electric shuttles make the short trip from the Imperial City to the Royal Antiquities Museum for free.

Royal Antiquities Museum

Gain free admission to the **Royal Antiquities Museum** (3 Le Truc, 7am-5pm daily winter, 6:30am-5:30pm daily summer, free with Imperial City ticket), a short walk from the Imperial City, by bringing along your Imperial City ticket. Housed inside Long An Palace, the collection features an array of artifacts from eras past, including carved wooden furniture inlaid with mother-of-pearl, dishware from the reign of several emperors, vivid enamel trinkets, and massive porcelain vases, not to mention items used in the sacrificial ceremonies held at Nam Giao. A few replicas of traditional royal dress are on display at the back; the garden outside is peppered with stone mandarin statues and antique cannons; and there is a small side room with a display on Ham Nghi, a Nguyen emperor and noted revolutionary.

Dieu De Pagoda

On the northeastern bank of the narrow Dong Ba River, **Dieu De Pagoda** (100B Bach Dang, sunrise-sunset daily, free) is on the site of emperor Thieu Tri's birth. First constructed in 1844, the long grounds of this pagoda are filled with drooping palms and well-tended flowers. The main hall is watched over by four guardians on either side, while indoors is the requisite Buddha statue as well as a few others nearby.

The Royal Tombs

Dotting the hillsides south of town is an impressive collection of tombs that belong to the deceased emperors of the Nguyen dynasty. These larger-than-life memorials, sometimes designed and even lived in by an emperor prior to his death, come in all shapes and sizes, showing off the individual personality of each ruler. In every complex, you'll find a handful of common elements, including a Salutation Court, where concrete statues of mandarins and horses usher the emperor into the afterlife, as well as a lengthy inscription detailing that particular ruler's biography and accomplishments. There are also areas for worship and for the grave itself.

The tombs vary in size and style, depending on both the ruler and the time period. Minh Mang, for instance, was one of the earlier Nguyen emperors and a staunch nationalist, living in the first half of the 19th century and refusing any and all connections with Europe and the outside world. His tomb is stark, employing traditional Vietnamese architecture. Khai Dinh, the second-to-last emperor, spent much of his life working alongside the colonial government and was something of a Francophile, evidenced by the ostentatious mosaics and life-size bronze statue within his tomb. The tombs of Gia Long, Dong Khanh, and Thieu Tri are close by but less interesting, and not as worthy of the time and money needed to view them.

TOMB OF TU DUC

The closest of Hue's imperial burial sites is the **Tomb of Tu Duc** (7am-5pm daily winter, 6:30am-5:30pm daily summer, VND100,000), about 6.5 kilometers from town. A sprawling complex of romantic landscapes and crumbling moss-covered stone, the tomb was built in 1864. Tu Duc, the longest-reigning emperor of the Nguyen dynasty, did not die until 1883, giving him over a decade to enjoy the peace and serenity of his own grave.

Luu Khiem Lake, surrounded by wistful

greenery and a fading stone border, is to the right of the main entrance. To the left on a raised platform is Chi Khiem Temple, which honors both Tu Duc and his empress Le Thien Anh, who died in 1902.

The tomb complex is occupied by structures that mimic the Imperial City, with mandarin houses, a palace, and other buildings. During the 16 years between the completion of the tomb and Tu Duc's death, these buildings functioned as a workspace for the emperor and his mandarins. The first structure, **Hoa Khiem Temple,** mirrors Thai Hoa Palace in many ways and once served as an administrative building, though after the emperor's death it was converted into a temple honoring the royal couple. Today, you can see lacquered wooden tablets dedicated to the emperor and empress on an altar at the end of the hall.

Behind Hoa Khiem is **Luong Khiem Temple,** originally Tu Duc's secondary residence, which has functioned as a temple for Tu Du, the queen mother, since her death in 1901. On both sides of these buildings are rooms known as On Khiem and Minh Khiem, which acted as royal theaters, used for performances by the king's concubines. On the left beside this group of palaces are the former residences of Tu Duc's concubines, whose numbers were believed to be over 100. Now buried under a tangle of grass and wildflowers, the area remains an attractive sight.

Three royal tombs lie beyond the worship area. Tu Duc's is the largest, preceded by a Salutation Court and a gargantuan structure housing the stele on which the emperor's autobiography was engraved. While it was typical in the Nguyen era for the son of each emperor to write his father's funereal stele, Tu Duc did not have any children and so penned his own life story.

Past the stele are a pond and a towering wall, which keeps the actual tomb from view. An ornamental entrance gate opens to a view of the understated concrete tomb, with a single tiny incense urn upon it. To the right, Queen Le Thien Anh's modest tomb is enshrouded by a high stone wall (in traditional temples, this wall is often lacquered wood). Just beside the queen is a small grave for emperor Kien Phuc, adoptive son of Tu Duc, who served as emperor for a mere eight months before dying in 1884 at age 15.

To get to the tomb, follow Huyen Tran Cong Chua south from Hue for six kilometers. The entrance to the tomb is on Doan Nhu Hai, a small side street.

TOMB OF KHAI DINH

A departure from the more traditional elements of his predecessors' mausoleums, the **tomb of Khai Dinh** (7am-5pm daily winter, 6:30am-5:30pm daily summer, VND100,000) rambles up a hillside in three separate sections, about eight kilometers south of Hue. The 12th emperor of the Nguyen dynasty, Khai Dinh ruled Vietnam for only nine years, from 1916 to his death in 1925. Construction of his intricate memorial lasted until 1931. Vietnam's second-to-last monarch, Khai Dinh became fond of European culture, as evidenced by the style and decoration of his tomb.

From the roadside, a soaring wrought-iron three-door gate opens onto the first set of stone steps. These lead up to a pair of ceremonial right and left houses honoring the civil and military mandarins who served under Khai Dinh. Nowadays, the buildings function as a souvenir shop and a place to hire tour guides. (The guides are seldom present, despite the sign posted out front.) More stone steps lead to the second level and the stelae of Khai Dinh, which easily surpass three meters in height. The stelae are housed in a black stone pavilion, surrounded by rows of mandarin statues as well as a pair of towering stupas, which represent the power of the Nguyen dynasty. From both this level and the one above, rolling green hills come into view.

On the top tier, decked out in all white, the exterior of Thien Dinh Palace contradicts the dour ambience of the lower levels. Its main hall explodes into a riot of green, blue, gold, and red. Inside the building is a small foyer featuring an informational video, a photo exhibit and a bronze statue of the emperor, and a modest collection of Khai Dinh's French porcelain. In the central room, a mind-blowing mosaic covers every inch of the walls and ceiling with wide-eyed dragons and sparkling patterns. An incense altar bears the emperor's photograph and is flanked by two tortoise and crane statues. Deeper into the tomb is a life-size bronze statue of Khai Dinh, cast in France in 1920, seated upon a replica of the throne, complete with three-tiered platform and a massive cement canopy. Flashy orange glass rises from the back of the platform, forming sun rays behind the emperor. At the back of the room is another altar and lacquered wooden tablets belonging to Khai Dinh and his empress.

TOMB OF MINH MANG

Set upon a sweeping natural landscape, the **tomb of Minh Mang** (7am-5pm daily winter, 6:30am-5:30pm daily summer, VND100,000) is a tribute to traditional Vietnamese architecture and bears a strong resemblance to buildings in the Imperial City. Completed in 1843, two years after emperor Minh Mang's death, this 28-hectare complex is one of the more lavish mausoleums from the Nguyen era.

Minh Mang spent over a decade searching for the perfect place to position his tomb. The emperor left behind 142 children—78 princes and 64 princesses—and had an estimated 500 concubines.

The entrance to the walled complex is on the left side of the main gate. At the center of the vast green landscape is the Salutation Court, where a small number of stone mandarin statues and elephants line the path up to the Stele House, guarding the emperor in the afterlife. Inside the stele house, a three-meter-tall stone tablet is etched with 2,500 characters describing the life and accomplishments of Minh Mang, as written by his son and successor, Thieu Tri.

Farther along, Hien Duc Gate leads the way to the tomb's worshipping area, where a pair of structures, called right and left houses, honor the civil and military mandarins who served under Minh Mang. The altar dedicated to the emperor and his first wife, Ta Thien Nhan Ho Thi Hoa, sits at the center of Sung An Temple, a barren building. Behind this, another set of houses served as the living quarters for Minh Mang's royal eunuchs and concubines after his death.

Just past these buildings is a section of Trung Minh Lake that breaks up the long path

Detailed carvings surround the entrance to the tomb of Khai Dinh.

toward the tomb. Beyond a trio of side-by-side bridges, the two-story Pavilion of Light, the tallest building in the complex, was built in 1841. It symbolizes the emperor's passing from one world to the next, as well as his contributions to his people. Across the pavilion, lush gardens and another lake, Tan Nguyet, lie before Minh Mang's actual tomb. While there is nothing to see at the end of this walkway, as the tomb has been sealed and does not open except for the anniversary of the emperor's death, it's worth the short walk if only to look back at the sight of the pavilion surrounded by natural beauty.

Nam Giao Esplanade

At first glance, **Nam Giao Esplanade** (Le Ngo Cat and Dien Bien Phu, 7am-5pm daily winter, 6:30am-5:30pm daily summer) may appear to be nothing more than a park, but its three-tiered terrace is the site where, from as early as 1806, emperors of the Nguyen dynasty came to offer sacrifices to a higher power. Because monarchs were considered to be the descendants of God, only an emperor could rightfully pay respects to his "parents," heaven and earth. Each spring, an annual tribute was offered by the emperor. The central platform represents the relationship between human beings at the lowest level, earth in the middle, and, within the circular terrace at the top, heaven. The ceremony would begin at 2am and last several hours, with offerings and burning incense. The emperor would arrive at Nam Giao a few days before to prepare. High-ranking mandarins and the emperor himself were responsible for tending to the pines surrounding the ceremonial area. The last offering ceremony was held in 1945 by emperor Bao Dai. The esplanade is about three kilometers south of Hue.

Tu Hieu Pagoda

Surrounded by nature, **Tu Hieu Pagoda** (Le Ngo Cat, sunrise-sunset daily, free) began as a small hut in 1843, built by a local monk. It grew into something larger a few years later, when the royal eunuchs of the Nguyen dynasty contributed to its renovation and Tu Hieu became a full-fledged pagoda. Tucked at the end of a narrow winding road off Le Ngo Cat, this secluded building sits amid a tangle of greenery, fronted by a half-moon pond that holds a collection of large fish as well as turtles. Within the main hall, altars to Buddha and the pagoda's monks can be found, as can a shrine for the royal eunuchs who backed the project. A few of the crumbling, moss-covered

the tomb of Emperor Minh Mang

tombs scattered around the pagoda belong to these individuals. The pagoda is about three kilometers south of Hue.

Ho Quyen Royal Arena

Though it's a little tricky to find, the **Ho Quyen Royal Arena** (Kiet 373 Bui Thi Xuan, sunrise-6pm daily) is worth a visit if you're en route to the royal tombs. From the mid-1800s to the turn of the 20th century, this large, circular clearing was used for elephant fights, which the king and his fellow spectators enjoyed from atop the solid stone border of the arena. Though it's no longer possible to scale the crumbling walls, the arena's caretaker can unlock the gates and let you inside for a different perspective. To the right of the arena is a large pond surrounded by trees and vines, where the elephants were raised. A small temple opposite the pond honors the creatures and their caretakers. Ho Quyen is particularly appealing for its lack of visitors and the peaceful, friendly neighborhood in which it now resides. For shutterbugs, this is a great spot to explore and get a taste of Hue's past history and local life today.

Getting to Ho Quyen can be tricky. The arena is located down an alley off Bui Thi Xuan, not far beyond the turnoff for the royal tombs, but the blue-and-white sign signaling the turnoff is small and only in Vietnamese. If you keep an eye out for "Ho Quyen," you'll find the signpost on your left, opposite a roadside market.

Hue Nam Shrine

Though it bears many of the same traces of Hue's bygone imperial era, the **Hue Nam Shrine** (end of Huyen Tran Cong Chua, 7am-5:30pm daily, VND40,000) is an unusual departure from much of the rest of the city's history. The current structure, built under Minh Mang, is a shallow wooden temple devoted to the goddess Thien Y A Na, a motherly deity who watches over Vietnam and its people. As far back as the 13th century, the Cham empire, a medieval kingdom that ruled large parts of central Vietnam and the south-central coast, used this land to worship Lady Po Nagar, their protector and most revered goddess. Her story served as the origin for her Vietnamese counterpart, Thien Y A Na.

Beyond the temple, which was last renovated in the late 1880s, a handful of shrines dot the nearby riverbank, including altars dedicated to the goddesses of the five elements (water, earth, fire, wood, and metal) and to the famous red and white horses of Chinese general Quan Cong. On the lower level leading up to Hue Nam Shrine, still another shelter houses an altar for the general. The view of the Perfume River from Hue Nam's vantage point is worth admiring.

To get to Hue Nam, follow Huyen Tran Cong Chua, the road leading out to most of the royal tombs, all the way to its end. Bearing right, you'll come to a dead end at the riverbank, where a boatman waits for passengers to ferry across. Bidding starts around VND50,000 pp. Once you're let off at the other side, chances are the ferry will leave you while it runs back to look for other passengers; stand at the docking area when you're ready to leave and he'll swing back around. Hue Nam isn't necessarily a must-see attraction, but the atmosphere and the pleasant ride through the countryside bolster its appeal.

Thien Mu Pagoda

Thien Mu Pagoda (Kim Long, sunrise-sunset daily, free), perched on a hill overlooking the Perfume River, is one of Hue's most famous religious buildings. Since its inception in 1601, the long and narrow grounds of the complex have acquired a few add-ons to make it the sight it is today. From the stone steps out front, the first thing to greet you is Phuoc Dien, the iconic, aging, seven-tiered tower, which was actually last to arrive at Thien Mu in 1844. Before that, the four small structures surrounding Phuoc Dien were built to house various artifacts, including a trio of stone stelae, the largest of which rests atop a massive white tortoise, meant to symbolize wisdom and longevity; it appeared in 1715. One of the houses also stores a massive bell, cast in 1710. You'll get the best views of the river from this area, as Kim Long street wraps around a curve in the riverbank.

Farther back, the guardians of the pagoda usher you through a three-door entrance gate, their glowering faces watching over each of the passageways that leads onto the main hall, where several golden Buddhas await. Around back, another piece of Vietnamese history sits parked to the left of the pagoda: a pale blue car in which the Venerable Thich Quang Duc, senior monk at Ho Chi Minh City's Xa Loi Pagoda, rode to the intersection of Cach Mang Thang Tam and Nguyen Dinh Chieu on the morning of June 11, 1963, before setting himself on fire in protest of the religious oppression of the southern government. As the first monk to do so, Thich Quang Duc's death generated a massive international outcry and an increasingly negative image of southern president Ngo Dinh Diem's administration. The monk's heart, which had failed to burn during the process, was preserved and regarded as a religious relic. Today, the car at Thien Mu is accompanied by a photograph of Thich Quang Duc's heart and the Pulitzer Prize-winning photograph by Malcolm Browne that captured his self-immolation on camera. At the end of the pagoda grounds, you'll pass the monks' quarters and a collection of decorative bonsai trees before reaching a small clearing with a gray stone stupa.

The pagoda is about five kilometers west of Hue, on the north side of Perfume River.

Ho Chi Minh Museum

Hue's **Ho Chi Minh Museum** (7 Le Loi, tel. 0234/382-2152, 7am-11am and 1:45pm-4:30pm Tues.-Sun., VND10,000) offers an interesting look into the life of Vietnam's most famous patriot, who lived in Hue twice in his younger days. An upstairs exhibition room features a sizable collection of old photographs, which capture places like Dong Ba Market and the Citadel area during the early 20th century. Clunky English signage and

revolutionary artifacts are on display alongside photos of Ho Chi Minh himself, charting his decades-long transformation from Nguyen Tat Thanh, a boy from Nghe An province, to young revolutionary Nguyen Ai Quoc, to the man with the trademark beard that went on to become president.

Quoc Hoc High School

Hue's **Quoc Hoc High School** (10 Le Loi) is the alma mater of many of Vietnam's most famous political figures from both the north and south. Lining the Perfume River, its dark red buildings were originally the site of a royal navy headquarters from the early 1800s. They were transformed into the country's National College in 1896. Students from the upper echelons of Vietnamese society were trained for government service under the emperor. A host of national leaders, from southern president Ngo Dinh Diem to heavy-hitting northern generals and politicians like Vo Nguyen Giap, Le Duan, and even Ho Chi Minh attended the school. Uncle Ho was later expelled for participating in demonstrations against the French government. Today, Quoc Hoc High School remains one of the most prestigious institutions in the country. It's sometimes possible to go inside (5pm-6:30pm daily) by getting the permission of the on-site security guard, but you can get the gist from just passing by.

Thanh Toan Covered Bridge

About six kilometers east of town, the **Thanh Toan Covered Bridge** (Thuy Thanh District) is a smaller version of Hoi An's Japanese Covered Bridge, bedecked with glazed yin-yang tiles and a colorful roof. The wooden structure was built in 1776 thanks to the financial contributions of Tran Thi Dao, a wealthy local woman and wife of a high-ranking mandarin. The bridge's frame is made of seven compartments, with the middle one housing an altar dedicated to the bridge's benefactor.

The bridge is only one part of the area's appeal: While it can be tough to find, the ride to Thanh Toan takes you into the countryside,

Thanh Toan Covered Bridge

last ones before you reach Thanh Toan is the **Tran Family Temple** (sunrise-sunset daily, free), where several generations of Ms. Tran Thi Dao's ancestors are worshipped alongside the patron herself, who has a small shrine in the courtyard. You'll recognize this particular building by the small sign posted out front. If you're lucky, the caretakers will be around and more than willing to let you in for a look.

TOURS

You'll find dozens of cheap city tours around the Pham Ngu Lao area; these trips tend to provide varying levels of information, exclude entrance fees, and often act more as a bus service. Visit sights like the Imperial City and the royal tombs on your own, and save that extra cash for tours farther beyond the city limits to places like Thanh Toan bridge, some of the less-visited tombs, or the DMZ area. Plenty of Easy Rider-style motorbike excursions are available around the countryside and onward to other destinations, as are more traditional trips to these same places.

If you're keen on learning about royal history, more in-depth tours of the imperial sights are available from outfits like **A-Travel Mate** (33 Vo Thi Sau, tel. 0234/393-4455, www.atravelmate.com, 8am-9pm daily), which does half- and full-day tours of the city's most famous attractions with smaller group sizes and more experienced guides.

The friendly folks at **Cafe on Thu Wheels** (3/34 Nguyen Tri Phuong, tel. 0234/383-2241, www.cafeonthuwheels.com, 6:30am-10:30pm daily) run local tours to the Imperial City, the royal tombs, and several nearby sights, as well as out to the DMZ area and farther afield. Both group and private tours are available, and custom arrangements can be made. The office runs a small café with cheap local food and drinks.

Hue to Go Tours (tel. 09/8595-9768, www.huetogotours.com, VND340,000-1,090,000) arranges a variety of motorbike excursions in and around the city. You can choose from single- or multiple-day trips to places like Phong Nha, Bach Ma National Park, the DMZ area,

surrounded by kilometers of green paddy fields and a surprising number of large, decorative temples amid the humble houses of rice farmers. Travelers seem to be catching on to this, as a tourist map of the area has gone up at a junction on the road to the bridge, pointing out a handful of nearby shrines and temples. Still, expect to get lost at least once or twice on the short trip to Thanh Toan. Follow Truong Chinh out of town until it turns into Hoang Quoc Viet and as you get farther into the fields, a couple of aging kilometer stones will be there to guide you; look for "Thanh Toan." In the paddy fields there are usually farmers who can help direct you. With a growing number of guided tours heading out to Thanh Toan, they'll probably be able to guess what you're looking for.

Once you get on the final stretch toward Thanh Toan, keep an eye on the buildings to your left: Between ramshackle wooden houses and concrete bungalows are jaw-dropping temples and pagodas, covered top to bottom in mosaics and vibrant murals. One of the and a whole host of sights in town, as well as adventures to Hoi An and farther afield. Guides are English-speaking and attentive. Hopping on the back of an Easy Rider motorbike is a more expensive option than the average backpacker choices, but it's worth the money if you're interested in getting off the beaten path and combining your transportation with sightseeing. Though the outfit doesn't have a physical office, you can arrange tours or ask questions by contacting Hue To Go via phone or email.

Boat Tours

If you're interested in plying the waters of the Perfume River, dragon boat tours are an option. The cheapest of these are available at the **boat pier** (51 Le Loi), where a gaggle of boat touts will be more than happy to take you along the river to several famous sights, such as the Citadel, Thien Mu Pagoda, Hue Nam Shrine, and a royal tomb or two. These trips begin around VND400,000 per boat, excluding entrance fees to the sights. A typical river outing can run as short as one hour or take the better part of a day, starting around 8am and wrapping up at about 3pm. If you're keen to catch a ride on the river, this can be a nice way to see the sights, though the trip is less a guided tour and more a water taxi service. Dragon boats generally include a driver in the fee rather than a certified guide. Similar trips booked through reputable tour outfits will be able to supply an English-speaking guide to properly introduce the places you visit.

ENTERTAINMENT AND EVENTS
Nightlife

Though it's not nearly as active as Hanoi or Ho Chi Minh City, Hue is probably the liveliest spot in central Vietnam, with several bars open late around the backpacker area. There is plenty of outdoor seating for happy hour, and several late-night watering holes offer regular drink specials, pool tables, and dance floors. Most of this is focused on Pham Ngu Lao and Chu Van An streets.

A regular fixture of Hue's nightlife scene, **DMZ Bar** (60 Le Loi, tel. 0234/382-3414, 7am-late daily, VND20,000-185,000) serves beer and cocktails both outside on their corner patio, a great spot for people-watching on a warm night, and inside next to the pool table and bar. Though there isn't a dedicated dance floor, loud music and a few drinks usually get people moving. Happy hour specials are often available, and the staff is a pleasant bunch.

The best place to start your evening is at **Hue Backpackers** (10 Pham Ngu Lao, tel. 0234/382-6567, www.vietnambackpacker-hostels.com, 8am-late daily, VND25,000-150,000). A cast of lively characters get the party going around happy hour and keep the masses entertained till the early morning with games like the "duck egg challenge" (in which one consumes a whole fertilized duck egg, along with a shot of rice wine and a local beer), beer pong, and a host of other alcohol-related activities. Regular drink specials are offered throughout the night as well as several local beers and every manner of cocktail imaginable. The place also makes its own infused vodkas, which range from strawberry to garlic to Fisherman's Friend. Plenty of seating is scattered throughout the open downstairs bar as well as along the sidewalk.

Both the laid-back garden seating and lively indoor areas at **Brown Eyes** (56 Chu Van An, tel. 0234/382-7494, browneyesbarcafe@yahoo.com, 5pm-late daily, VND30,000-260,000) are open until the wee hours of the morning, mixing affordable cocktails and strong bucket drinks. Lighter beverages like beer and wine are also available, and you'll find a pool table in the dark interior alongside a cartoonish rendition of Michael Jackson in full "Thriller" regalia. Later in the evening, the back corner of Brown Eyes often doubles as an impromptu dance floor.

A newer fixture on the Hue nightlife scene, **Le's Garden Bar** (28 Vo Thi Sau, tel. 0234/393-3955, 10am-11:30am daily, VND25,000-150,000) offers beer, cocktails, and just about every manner of drink imaginable. The indoor bar is equipped with a pool table, while the veranda out front has plenty of trees and tables to sit and watch the world go by. Food is available, though it's best to stick to drinks here.

Festivals and Events

Taking place over seven days in April, the **Hue Festival** (www.huefestival.com, mid-late Apr.) has been a huge draw for the city since its inception in 2000. Showcasing the traditional arts and culture of Vietnam through song, dance, and other performances, the festival brings in an international element, inviting musicians and dance troupes from Europe, Africa, South America, Australia, and elsewhere in Asia to share in its cultural exchange. The event ushers in large crowds with its activities, including fashion shows and banquet dinners. Tickets can be purchased on-site for individual events. As you might expect, travelers visiting Hue during this time will want to book ahead for accommodations.

SHOPPING

While Hue isn't necessarily a retail hot spot, it's possible to pick up many of the standard Vietnamese souvenirs you see throughout the country. If you're willing to bargain, Dong Ba Market is not a bad place to start; you can also visit a few shops scattered around Pham Ngu Lao street and the rest of the backpacker area that specialize in original artwork and locally made handicrafts.

Markets

The city's busiest trading center is **Dong Ba Market** (Tran Hung Dao, sunrise-sunset daily), which remains a flurry of activity from sunup to well after sundown. Just east of the Citadel, this market is frequented by both locals and foreign travelers; you'll find a plethora of household items alongside clothing, bags, shoes, souvenirs, and food products, from the grayish-purple *mam tom* (fermented shrimp paste) to local treats like peanut candies. Be sure to haggle, as prices start off steep. If all else fails, remember that there are often other market stalls offering the same product.

Art Galleries

Showcasing the work of both established and up-and-coming local artists, the **Ta Gallery** (44 Pham Ngu Lao, tel. 0234/382-4894, 7am-11pm daily) stocks mostly lacquer paintings but also dabbles in oil on canvas and other mediums in addition to stocking a handful of well-made souvenirs. Upstairs, the second floor of the building has transformed into a cozy café with a handful of beverages and sweet treats as well as pleasant views of the street below.

Housed in a grand white colonial building overlooking the river, the **Le Ba Dang Gallery** (15 Le Loi, tel. 0234/383-7411, lebadangarthue@gmail.com, 7:30am-11:30am and 1:30pm-5:30pm daily, VND30,000) displays the work of Le Ba Dang, a prolific artist born in Quang Tri province in 1921. The collection, which spans several rooms over two floors, is a fascinating range of media, with everything from wood and paper cutouts to oil and acrylic paintings, 3-D mixed-media pieces, silk, and a variety of unusual topographical paper creations. Vivid black, white, and red paintings mimic traditional Chinese calligraphy, while colorful graphic prints and detailed abstract paintings line the walls of other small rooms. At the back, a small souvenir shop sells postcards and smaller paintings.

Gifts and Souvenirs

Made entirely from recycled materials, the souvenirs at **Healing the Wounded Heart** (23 Vo Thi Sau, tel. 0234/381-7643, 8:30am-11am and 2pm-10pm daily) are for two worthy causes: creating eco-friendly products from materials that would otherwise be thrown away and providing housing, a steady income, and employment to residents with disabilities in Hue. The shop, which works in conjunction with California-based SPIRAL Foundation and the Hue College of Medicine and Pharmacy, began in 2009 and has since improved the lives of its artisans as well as funded over a dozen heart surgeries for young Vietnamese patients. Traditional baskets made from strips of aluminum instead of bamboo are sold here, along with bags fashioned out of colorful rice sacks and a variety of crafty creations using recycled telephone wire. Travelers can also visit the artisans at HWH's nearby **workshop** (69 Ba Trieu); ask at the shop for more details.

Bookstores

For reading material, the gargantuan **Phuong Nam** (131-133 Tran Hung Dao, tel. 0234/352-2000, www.pnc.com.vn, 7:30am-9:30pm daily), across the water at the end of Truong Tien Bridge, offers a decent variety of English-language books.

FOOD

Considered one of Vietnam's most famous culinary cities, Hue has no shortage of sumptuous dishes unique to the region. You'll find an abundance of street food on every corner, as well as outside the bustling Dong Ba Market. A few international options are available, featuring mostly standard backpacker meals like cheeseburgers and pancakes. With so many delectable local options, you should have no problem finding something to suit your palate.

Vietnamese

Not far from the backpacker area, **Hanh Restaurant** (11 Pho Duc Chinh, tel. 0234/383-3552, 10am-9:30pm daily, VND25,000-80,000) sees enough foreign visitors to have an English menu but stays true to its Vietnamese tastes, offering a selection of Hue specialties, including *banh beo* (steamed rice cakes) and *banh khoai* (the local version of a savory pancake), as well as rice noodles with grilled pork and a few other tasty dishes. Prices are reasonable, and dining is more authentic than at some of the eateries in the area that cater specifically to travelers.

Just outside the Citadel walls, **Lac Thien** (6 Dinh Tien Hoang, tel. 0234/352-7348, 8am-9pm daily, VND25,000-85,000) is a small, cheerful, family-run business that does tasty local food at local prices. Dishes include *bun thit nuong* (rice noodles and grilled pork),

banh beo (steamed rice cakes), and several other Hue specialties. Their signature plate is *banh khoai* (a local version of the Vietnamese savory pancake).

A lovely spot on the main backpacker drag, **Golden Rice** (40 Pham Ngu Lao, tel. 0234/362-6938, giangthinh.goldenrice@gmail.com, 11am-11pm daily, VND40,000-200,000) may cater to a tourist crowd but has excellent Vietnamese dishes of chicken, beef, seafood, pork, and vegetarian offerings and local specialties. Meals are well-priced, and there is a room upstairs for overflow.

The cheap and cheerful **Nina Cafe** (16/34 Nguyen Tri Phuong, tel. 0234/383-8636, 8:30am-10:30pm daily, VND35,000-95,000) is hidden from sight down the budget alley 34 off Nguyen Tri Phuong. It has covered outdoor seating and lanterns and faux greenery to add to its decor. The welcoming folks at Nina expertly prepare the usual Vietnamese dishes, all served with a smile.

While it's located in a tourist area and caters mostly to Western visitors, the few staff at **Family Home Restaurant** (11/34 Nguyen Tri Phuong, tel. 0234/382-0668, 7:30am-10pm daily, VND40,000-100,000) go out of their way to make you feel welcome and serve tasty renditions of several local meals, including signature Hue specialties of pork, chicken, and beef as well as vegetarian options. The exceptionally pleasant owners make this a place worth visiting. Breakfast is also available, as are a few backpacker favorites, like banana pancakes.

Street Food

To eat like a local, the central market is always a good place to start, but you can also venture down to the far end of Truong Dinh, where there are plenty of tasty street-side dining options, as well as a few backpacker-friendly joints closer to the center of town along Vo Thi Sau.

Deep within the maze of the bustling **Dong Ba Market** (Tran Hung Dao, sunrise-sunset daily) you'll find several food stalls surrounded by low tables and plastic stools.

Not all of these spots are the cleanest; peruse your options first and check for posted prices. Dishes include the signature *bun bo Hue* (soup with beef and rice noodles) and *bun thit nuong* (rice noodles and grilled pork). You can also find a few street vendors in front of the market, where things are a little cleaner and streetside dining is available.

There is a general consensus among the people of Hue that the city's best *com hen* (baby clams with rice) comes from **Ba Cam** (2 Truong Dinh, tel. 0234/625-0003, 6am-2pm daily, VND25,000 per bowl), a small street-side eatery with medium-size portions of *hen* (baby clams) with your choice of rice or noodles, a few veggies, and some broth on the side. Breakfast starts early and is usually finished by late morning, so make sure you get here before the pot is empty.

A narrow yard bounded by a pair of buildings in Phu Cat District serves some of the best ★ ***bun bo Hue*** (7 Nguyen Du, tel. 09/3481-7992, 2pm-7pm daily, VND25,000) around. This particular collection of low plastic tables is a popular choice among local residents and offers a nice opportunity to explore a less-visited part of town. Look for the sign out front that reads "Quan Bun Bo Hue O Phung Chu Vong."

Cafés and Bakeries

The brightly lit display of decadent cakes and flaky pastries should be enough to get you in the door of **La Boulangerie Francaise** (46 Nguyen Tri Phuong, tel. 0234/389-6469, www.laboulangeriefrancaise.org, 7am-8pm daily, VND15,000-90,000), but its charitable cause is another good reason to stop in for coffee and a bite to eat. In addition to providing excellent Western-style baked goods, the shop runs a training school for disadvantaged young Vietnamese, teaching them to become pastry chefs and bakers. Trainees work as café staff and often go on to work at high-end hotels. All proceeds from the shop go toward funding a local orphanage.

Opposite Dong Ba Market is the bustling **Bao Thanh Bakery** (265 Tran Hung Dao, tel. 0234/352-4160, 6:30am-9:30pm daily, VND5,000-20,000), complete with flashing neon lights and neatly arranged rows of Asian baked goods, both savory and sweet.

International

Hue offers an interesting handful of non-Vietnamese options, though it's nowhere near as varied as other cities. More than a few local restaurants are geared toward foreigners with even those specializing in Vietnamese cuisine

banh khoai, a local dish

Local Cuisine: Hue

Known nationwide, Hue cuisine is a point of pride among the Vietnamese, thanks to its varied and flavorful dishes. For an introduction into the city's food scene, sample some of the following.

- *banh beo:* Often served in a porcelain dish, these miniature steamed rice cakes are usually topped with dried shrimp and pork crackling. For best results, add liberal amounts of fish sauce.

- *banh loc:* Slightly different from other Hue snack foods, *banh loc* uses tapioca starch to make a small steamed dumpling with a whole prawn at the center alongside a hint of pork fat.

- *banh khoai:* A local version of *banh xeo*, this savory pancake includes the usual bean sprouts, pork and shrimp, though in a crunchier shell. Servings are usually individual and, while the meal includes fresh greens, the entire spread is often enjoyed with chopsticks rather than wrapped inside a whole salad leaf—an equally delicious meal with a little less mess.

- *banh nam:* Another variety steamed rice cake, *banh nam* comes wrapped in banana leaves and features a center of minced pork and shrimp. These, too, are best eaten with ample amounts of fish sauce.

- *banh ram it:* Another version of a steamed dumpling, *banh ram it* pairs a steamed sticky rice dumpling with a crunchy, fried base. You'll find pork and shrimp at the center, and fish sauce is the recommended condiment.

- *bun bo Hue:* One of the city's most popular meals, this rice noodle and beef soup features an orange-hued broth with a bit of a kick, as well as the standard helping of fresh greens. Add-ons include ham hock and congealed duck blood.

- *com hen* and *bun hen:* Whether with rice or rice noodles, Hue's *hen*, or baby clams, are a local favorite that often come topped with fresh veggies and a bit of broth on the side.

offering Western backpacker favorites like banana pancakes and hamburgers. Beyond the places listed here, you're better off sticking to local meals, as foreign cuisine is not Hue's strongest suit. For reasonably priced Western dishes, check out **Hue Backpackers** (10 Pham Ngu Lao, tel. 0234/382-6567, www.vietnambackpackerhostels.com, 8am-late daily, VND40,000-200,000).

The menu at **La Carambole** (19 Pham Ngu Lao, tel. 0234/381-0491, la_carambole@hotmail.com, 7am-11pm daily, VND80,000-280,000) is a blend of French and Vietnamese, featuring Hue specialties alongside duck l'orange and steak frites. Its bistro ambience adds luxury, with cozy indoor tables and a nice alfresco section. The cheese platter and wine are particularly exciting for travelers who have been away from home for a while. La Carambole is often full; it is possible to make

a reservation or, if you'd rather wing it, turn up earlier or later to escape the rush.

For a break from local fare, you can visit either **Shiva Shakti** (27 Vo Thi Sau, tel. 0234/393-5627, 9:30am-10pm daily, VND65,000-200,000) or **Ganesh** (34 Nguyen Tri Phuong, tel. 0234/382-1616, www.ganesh-hue.com, 10am-10pm daily, VND65,000-200,000). These two Indian places are pretty much identical, down to the menu, which is exactly the same, though the staff seems to be a bit more cheerful at Shiva Shakti. Prices are reasonable and portions are a decent size.

With a minimalist approach to decor and fake cherry blossoms peppering the restaurant, **Ta-ke** (34 Tran Cao Van, tel. 0234/384-8262, 10:30am-10pm daily, VND35,000-220,000) attempts to evoke Japanese culture while preparing its menu of sushi and other Japanese fare. Both à la carte items and large meals are available. It's a short walk from the main backpacker neighborhood.

ACCOMMODATIONS

The majority of accommodations cluster around the area southeast of Truong Tien Bridge, where a small backpacker enclave caters to the foreign crowd. The surrounding shops, restaurants, and travel agencies are set up with tourists in mind. For a slightly quieter option away from the hustle and bustle, look to alley 34 of Nguyen Tri Phuong, where a handful of budget options and cheap and cheerful restaurants are tucked off the main road.

Standard amenities for budget spots are hot water, air-conditioning, and Wi-Fi. Those amenities plus a fridge, minibar, and a coffeemaker are standard in mid-range hotels. At the budget hotels, the advertised hot water and Wi-Fi are likely to be unreliable.

Under VND210,000

The city's most famous budget spot, ★ Hue Backpackers (10 Pham Ngu Lao, tel. 0234/382-6567, www.vietnambackpacker-hostels.com, VND140,000-225,000 dorm, VND450,000 d, breakfast included) occupies some of the best real estate on Pham Ngu Lao. The mixed and all-female dorms come with air-conditioning, Wi-Fi, lockers, and a shared bath with hot water. Queen-size dorm beds are available for a few extra bucks. The upstairs verandas are great for relaxing. The lobby functions as a café and bar. Hue Backpackers is very social, so it is noisier than the average.

In the heart of town, the Hue Amazing Homestay (2/10 Vo Thi Sau, tel. 09/1263-0219, VND115,000 dorm, VND275,000 d, breakfast included) is a cross between a hostel and a homestay. Run by friendly Mr. Duyen and an amiable staff, facilities are basic but clean and include hot water, Wi-Fi, and air-conditioning. Quality tours are organized through this hostel as well, and the staff can

supply you with sound travel advice. This is a good spot to link up with other backpackers.

Sunny A Hotel (17/34 Nguyen Tri Phuong, tel. 0234/382-9990, VND90,000 dorm, VND230,000-340,000 d) is an updated budget hotel offering great value. Private rooms are basic but modern, and feature air-conditioning, hot water, TV, a fridge, and big, comfy beds. Dorm beds are the cheapest rate in town, though they don't include personal lockers. Spend a few extra dollars for the private rooms and you'll get more space.

VND210,000-525,000

A short walk from the riverside, the Canary Boutique Hotel (8/43 Nguyen Cong Tru, tel. 0234/393-6447, VND400,000-650,000, breakfast included) is down a small alley off the main road. It offers great value for its well-appointed rooms. Modern furnishings, comfy beds, and standard mid-range amenities are provided. The pleasant staff adds to its value. There is a Canary Hotel on the main stretch of Nguyen Cong Tru not far away, so make sure you're at the right place.

For a good value mid-range spot, the Friendly Hue Hotel (10 Nguyen Cong Tru, tel. 0234/383-4666, www.thanthienhotel.com.vn, VND400,000-500,000) does the job, pairing comfortable rooms with modern furnishings and staff to match its name. Amenities include TV, hot water, air-conditioning, Wi-Fi, and a fridge. Assistance with transportation and travel can be arranged, and there is a restaurant downstairs that serves breakfast for an additional fee.

The comfy Jade Hotel (43 Hung Vuong, tel. 0234/393-8849, www.jadehotelhue.com, VND365,000-600,000, breakfast included) provides decent rooms and friendly service at a reasonable price. Three double-occupancy options are available, with increasingly more space and better views. Amenities include the usual hot water, Wi-Fi, air-conditioning, in-room safes, and TV. Hotel staff can also assist with travel planning, transportation, and sound advice.

VND525,000-1,050,000

The charming, purple ★ **Orchid Hotel** (30A Chu Van An, tel. 0234/383-1177, www.orchid-hotel.com.vn, VND735,000-1,155,000, breakfast included) stands out for its top-notch staff, who are especially service-minded. Its rooms also exceed mid-range standards, with modern decor and furnishings, standard amenities, a minibar, TV, tea- and coffee-making facilities, and an in-room computer. The hotel is close to both the riverfront and the backpacker area.

Down a popular alley off Nguyen Cong Tru, the **Holiday Diamond Hotel** (6/14 Nguyen Cong Tru, tel. 0234/381-9844, www.hueholidaydiamondhotel.com, VND500,000-760,000, breakfast included) offers superior, deluxe, and city-view rooms close to both the river and Hue's backpacker area. The decor is a little uninspired, but each room comes with high-quality amenities, including hot water, air-conditioning, Wi-Fi, TV, a DVD player, a minibar, tea- and coffee-making facilities, and, in some cases, an in-room computer.

Despite the dusty alleyway leading to it, the **Serene Palace Hotel** (21/42 Nguyen Cong Tru, tel. 0234/394-8585, www.serenepalace-hotel.com, VND750,000-800,000) is modern, well appointed, and a short walk from the backpacker area. The usual mid-range amenities apply. The decor is splashy, with a busy wooden cutout framing the wall-mounted TV, and showers are especially good. The service-minded hotel staff assists with travel information, tours, and transportation.

VND1,050,000-2,100,000

The cozy **Cherish Hotel** (57-59 Ben Nghe, tel. 0234/394-3943, www.cherishhotel.com, VND1,020,000-2,520,000) is on the fancier end of mid-range options but its modern, well-appointed rooms represent good value and are centrally located. Amenities include air-conditioning, hot water, TV, Wi-Fi, a minibar, tea- and coffee-making facilities, an in-room safe, and a personal laptop with Internet. Some rooms offer nice balcony views, and the

swimming pool and fitness center are free for hotel guests.

Over VND2,100,000

The historic **Hotel Saigon Morin** (30 Le Loi, tel. 0234/382-3526, www.morinhotel.com.vn, VND2,250,000-6,300,000, breakfast included) is one of the oldest hotels in the city. Famous guests like Andre Malraux and Charlie Chaplin have spent the night here, and the restaurant and bar was popular with French colonials during the early 1900s. Rooms are chic and well appointed, combining old-world charm with modern amenities, such as cable TV, generous bathtubs, work desks, and an in-room safe. Guests have full access to the on-site swimming pool and fitness center. There is also a spa and souvenir shops.

Chic and sophisticated, ★ **La Residence** (5 Le Loi, tel. 0234/383-7475, www.la-residence-hue.com, VND4,980,000-19,550,000) sits at the far end of Le Loi, a sprawling white building overlooking the river. With art deco influences, rooms are furnished in tasteful, modern elegance, featuring bold colors against white walls. Amenities include hot water, air-conditioning, TV, Wi-Fi, an in-room safe, a coffeemaker, and, in some rooms, a private balcony. The hotel counts an upscale restaurant, a ritzy bar, a fitness center, a spa, a saltwater pool, and a tennis court among its offerings, not to mention complimentary bike rentals and a travel desk.

INFORMATION AND SERVICES
Visitor Information

There is a tourist information kiosk or travel agent on just about every corner in downtown Hue, though many are more interested in selling their own services than assisting travelers. For sound travel advice, your best bet is asking the receptionist at your hotel.

Banks and Currency Exchange

You'll find dozens of ATMs in and around the backpacker area, including a set of them on either side of the Century Riverside Hotel on Le Loi. For currency exchange or a proper bank, stop by the **Vietcombank** (2A Hung Vuong, tel. 0234/382-7337, www.vietcombank.com.vn, 7:30am-11:30am and 1:30pm-4:30pm Mon.-Fri.) just behind the Saigon Morin Hotel. There is also a **Sacombank** (2 Ben Nghe, tel. 0234/383-9002, www.sacombank.com.vn, 7:30am-11:30am and 1pm-5pm Mon.-Fri., 7:30am-11:30am Sat.) nearby.

Postal Services and Internet

For postal necessities, you can head to the central **post office** (8 Hoang Hoa Tham, tel. 0234/382-3496, 7am-7pm Mon.-Sat., 7am-6pm Sun.). For Internet, most hotels have a desktop computer for guests to use, but you can also pop into any one of the small Internet shops around town.

Medical Services

For illnesses and injuries, the **Hue Central Hospital** (16 Le Loi, tel. 0234/382-2325, www.bvtwhue.com.vn) is just past the Phu Xuan Bridge.

GETTING THERE

Air

Phu Bai International Airport (HUI, 14.5 kilometers southeast of Hue off Hwy. 1) receives daily flights from Ho Chi Minh City and Hanoi. **Vietnam Airlines** (23 Nguyen Van Cu, tel. 0234/382-4709, www.vietnamairlines.com, 7:30am-11:30am and 1:30pm-4:45pm Mon.-Fri.) flies to these destinations and has a ticketing office in Hue. There is a **VietJet** (www.vietjetair.com) counter inside the airport, while **Jetstar** (12 Hung Vuong, tel. 0234/395-5955, www.jetstar.com, 7:30am-11:30am and 1:30pm-5:30pm daily) has a ticketing office in town as well. To get from the airport into town, hop in a taxi or buy a bus ticket (tel. 0234/382-6826, VND50,000, 6am-12 midnight daily). Look for the ticket kiosk as you leave the airport.

Flights from Hanoi to Hue are just over an hour and cost VND500,000-2,000,000. Flights from HCMC to Hue are 1.5 hours long and cost VND299,000-900,000. There are multiple flights per day from both Hanoi and HCMC.

Bus

Hue has two bus stations on either side of the city. All local buses arriving from Hanoi to the north pull in to the **northern bus station** (132B Ly Thai To, tel. 0234/352-2716). The ride to Hue from Hanoi on a sleeper bus is 10-12 hours and costs VND280,000. Buses from southern destinations like Danang and Hoi An arrive at the **southern station** (97 An Duong Vuong, tel. 0234/382-5070). From Danang or Hoi An, buses leave twice daily (morning and afternoon). The ride to Hue is about three hours and costs around VND150,000. The northern station is 6.5 kilometers from the center of Hue, while the southern station is 5 kilometers away. Hail a cab to get to your hotel from either station.

Both **Sinh Tourist** (37 Nguyen Thai Hoc, tel. 0234/384-5022, www.thesinhtourist.vn, 6:30am-8:30pm daily) and **Hanh Cafe** (28 Chu Van An, tel. 0234/383-7279, 7am-9pm daily) have offices in downtown Hue and modern, air-conditioned buses.

Train

The **Hue train station** (2 Phan Chu Trinh, tel. 0234/382-2175, 7am-5pm daily) sits about 1.5 kilometers from the backpacker area at the end of Le Loi. Both slow and express trains arrive from all over the country, and daily departures bound for both northern and southern destinations are available. It's possible to walk to your hotel from the station, provided you're willing to carry your luggage.

From Danang, the train ride is about 2.5 hours and costs VND60,000-150,000. There are several daily departures. From Hanoi, the ride is about 12 hours and costs VND550,000-1,302,000, also with several daily departures.

GETTING AROUND

Mailinh (tel. 0234/389-8989) taxis are all over town, as are droves of *xe om* drivers.

One of the more popular ways to get around town is by bicycle. Most hotels and guesthouses rent out city bikes at about VND40,000 per day. You can also stop by an independent rental outfit, of which there are many around the backpacker area. For reliable bikes, try **Minh & Coco** (1 Hung Vuong, tel. 0234/382-1822, 7am-11pm daily, bicycle VND30,000, motorbike VND100,000). Expect to put down some collateral in exchange for the vehicle.

Vicinity of Hue

DMZ TOURS

A popular option for history buffs and those traveling between Hue and Phong Nha-Ke Bang National Park, **DMZ tours** showcase some of the most significant sites of the American War. Both single- and multiple-day trips around this region focus on central Quang Tri province, where the 17th parallel sliced northern and southern Vietnam in half for roughly two decades. Now filled with rice paddies and small villages once more, this is where some of the war's most brutal battles took place.

After the 1954 Geneva Accords ensured Vietnamese independence from the French, it was agreed that a temporary boundary along the banks of Quang Tri's Ben Hai River would divide the north and south until general elections were held to unify the country. Over the next decade, this area became a barren wasteland, rutted with bomb craters and leftover weapons. From the time the Americans arrived on the scene until the end of the conflict, thousands of tons of bombs and heavy napalm use plagued the province. In addition to suffering the constant threat of violence back in the 1960s and 1970s, the area today is also notably affected by things like Agent Orange and unexploded ordnance, carrying on the terrible legacy of war.

Most DMZ tours cover the highlights in a single day. It's a long journey, so it's possible to expand the tour over two or three days. Hop on an Easy Rider-style motorbike excursion, which guarantees one guide per person, or opt for the less-expensive (albeit less personal) bus tour. Travelers leaving Phong Nha can also sign up with local guide **Mr. Shi** (tel. 09/6991-7642, shi.homestays@gmail.com), who runs a combined tour-and-transport service to Hue that includes stops at the Vinh Moc Tunnels, the Hien Luong Bridge, Ben Hai River, and DMZ monument for VND500,000. This fee includes transportation, entry fees, and a local guide. Minibuses leave Phong Nha at 7am and arrive in Hue around 12:30pm.

Two other outfitters that offer DMZ tours are **Cafe on Thu Wheels** (3/34 Nguyen Tri Phuong, tel. 0234/383-2241, www.cafe-onthuwheels.com, 6:30am-10:30pm daily, VND460,000) and **Hue to Go Tours** (tel. 09/8595-9768, www.huetogotours.com, VND1,090,000). While each tour is different, most visit a handful of noteworthy spots within Quang Tri.

Vinh Moc Tunnels

Not far from the 17th parallel, the quiet village of Vinh Linh was hit by 7,000 tons of bombs between 1965 and 1972. Instead of fleeing, the residents of Vinh Linh, most of whom were poor farmers, chose to tunnel beneath a group of seaside hills, creating the **Vinh Moc Tunnels.** Where the Cu Chi tunnels near Ho Chi Minh City were used almost exclusively for fighting, the wider underground passageways of Vinh Moc became a subterranean village complete with a hospital, a school, a meeting hall, and plenty of residential housing (a narrow cubicle that could fit a family of five). The tunnels, completed in 1968, were made up of three levels: one at 12 meters, one at 15 meters, and one at 23 meters below ground. The deepest tunnels were used for weapon storage and bomb shelters, while the middle section provided housing for roughly

Vicinity of Hue

NORTHERN
BUS STATION

TL10

To
Tam Giang
Lagoon

TL10

BUN BO HUE
DIEU DE PAGODA

THANH TOAN
COVERED BRIDGE

SEE "HUE" MAP

TL3

IMPERIAL CITY

AN DINH
PALACE

THIEN MU
PAGODA

VAN MIEU

HUE TRAIN
STATION

TU CUNG
RESIDENCE

SOUTHERN
BUS STATION

TL3

HO QUYEN
ROYAL ARENA

TU HIEU PAGODA

NAM GIAO
ESPLANADE

TL3

TOMB OF
TU DUC

To PHONG NHA-KE BANG
NATIONAL PARK

HUE NAM
SHRINE

FERRY TO
HUE NAM
SHRINE

QL49

QL1A

TOMB OF
KHAI DINH

AH1

QL1

0   1 mi

QL49   TOMB OF
MINH MANG

0   1 km

© AVALON TRAVEL

300 villagers at a time. At its height, Vinh Moc was home to around 600 people. The success of the Vinh Moc Tunnels also came from their secrecy, as American officials knew nothing of this underground village during the war.

17th Parallel

From 1954 until the end of the American War, the Ben Hai River separated North and South Vietnam at the **17th parallel,** with only the modest wooden **Hien Luong Bridge** serving as a connector. On the southern side, not far from the riverbank, was Doc Mieu, a large American base that housed planes and was often used to survey the northern side. The bridge still stands, leading across the river to a large statue of a woman and child, both of whom are looking north, waiting for their

husbands and fathers to return. A massive flag tower, now decorated in colorful murals, marks the official DMZ line, and the exhibition hall across the road is filled with plenty of shrapnel, artifacts, and photographs, which give a chilling visual of the now-flat paddy fields surrounding Ben Hai, once pocked and cratered by bombs.

Truong Son Soldiers' Cemetery

Though soldiers' cemeteries are spread throughout the country, and even the smallest towns and villages are outfitted with their own cemeteries for fallen soldiers, the largest of Vietnam's military cemeteries is **Truong Son Soldiers' Cemetery.** It is located 100 kilometers north of Hue almost directly on the

17th parallel, where seemingly endless rows of headstones bear testament to the human cost of the war. Instead of the large cemetery, some tours pass by **Gio Linh Cemetery,** a smaller but no less heartbreaking memorial near the Ben Hai River, where the vast majority of graves are emblazoned with the words *"chua biet ten"* ("name unknown").

Long Hung Church

The site of a major 1972 battle that lasted 81 days and became one of the bloodiest in the entire war, **Long Hung Church** sits inconspicuously along Highway 1. Today, it stands completely gutted, with only the shell of the building still in place, its frame rife with bullet holes. In a country that has largely moved on and rebuilt, this site provides a very real visual of the scope of destruction that took place during the U.S. Army's 1972 Easter Offensive. Look above the doorframe for the tattered, faded star and banner of the North Vietnamese army.

TOP EXPERIENCE

★ PHONG NHA-KE BANG NATIONAL PARK

A labyrinth of subterranean tunnels and jaw-dropping, otherworldly landscapes, **Phong Nha-Ke Bang National Park** (TL20, Son Trach village, tel. 0232/367-7021, www.phongnhatourism.com.vn, 7am-5pm daily, entry fees charged per cave) may still be relatively quiet compared to Vietnam's coastal destinations, but its anonymity is fading fast. Ever since a team of British cavers turned up in 2009 to explore the vast interior of Son Doong, the world's largest cave, at nine kilometers long and tall enough to comfortably house a high-rise, tourism to the area has taken off. Add to this a few high-profile visitors, such as the cast and crew of 2017 blockbuster *Kong: Skull Island,* which was filmed here, and the word is out about Phong Nha's incredible scenery.

Just over 210 kilometers north of Hue, Phong Nha's major draw is its three sprawling cave systems, Phong Nha, Vom, and Nuoc Mooc, which add up to roughly 145 kilometers of darkened passageways and have earned the area UNESCO World Heritage Site status. Decked out in eerie alien rock formations and spindly stalactites, these tunnels are estimated at 3-5 million years old and, according to researchers, may be a mere handful of the caves in existence between here and the Laotian border.

It's possible to visit the park without a guided tour, but you'll be limited to certain caves. For many of the more impressive caves, visitors must be a part of a tour group. Phong Nha offers cave tours only through certified companies and limits the number of annual visitors to Son Doong, which can be explored for a cool US$3,000 a head.

Day trips from Hue are cheap, though these are hardly worth the effort, as the long drive to and from the park eats up most of your time. Staying closer to the park offers you the chance to experience Phong Nha in greater depth. On longer excursions, you may find yourself wading into a subterranean river, rappelling down a rock face, or camping out in a cave. While these adventures are a little more expensive than most, the quality of the park's conservation efforts and the expertise of local caving companies more than justify the price tag.

Visit Phong Nha between February and September, when the weather allows for full access to its underground attractions. Rainy season, particularly October and November, can be restrictive, as rivers rise and the area's rainfall renders some of the more adventurous options unavailable. Phong Nha is a budding tourism destination, so don't expect to find five-star hotels or fine dining. Travel to and from the area can require more time and money due to its remoteness, but those who do so will find this destination one of the most memorable in Vietnam.

Sights

This area is riddled with caves, both within the national park and beyond to the Laotian

The World's Largest Cave

You could fit a jumbo jet or a city block inside **Son Doong** and still have room left over. This massive grotto stretches about five kilometers into the earth, with a range of landscapes you'd seldom imagine inside a darkened cave. A river roars through Son Doong, tumbling over cliffs and around corners. Clouds pass through its many chambers each day. Thanks to a pair of large skylights, Son Doong is also home to a rainforest, complete with monkeys, snakes, flying foxes, and birds, not to mention a few new species discovered within its massive boundaries.

The discovery of this jaw-dropping subterranean world belongs to Ho Khanh, a local farmer who happened upon the entrance one day in 1991. At the time, the find was of little consequence, and so the man carried on but filed its location away in the back of his mind. Not until 2009 would Howard Limbert and the British Cave Research Association enlist Ho Khanh's assistance in tracking down the cavern once more. Cavers were able to measure the size and length of Son Doong, far larger than Malaysia's Deer Cave, the previous record holder. There is still plenty to be learned about Son Doong and the surrounding area—many believe there are even bigger underground chambers nearby.

An expert team of caving professionals at **Oxalis** (Son Trach village, tel. 0232/367-7678, www. oxalis.com.vn, 7:30am-noon and 1:30pm-5:30pm Mon.-Fri., 7:30am-noon Sat.) have begun running four-day excursions into Son Doong for US$3,000 pp. The outrageous cost makes at least some sense when you consider the number of porters required, not to mention the fact that you have to rappel down a cliff and trek through the rainforest just to reach Son Doong's entrance. In order to preserve the wildlife and landscapes of the cave, only 500 permits were issued in 2016. Oxalis is the only outfit with permission to enter the cave. All this is set to change, however, as local authorities have expressed support for a controversial cable car project that would carry thousands of visitors into the rainforest for a glimpse of Son Doong. Though specifics of the project have yet to be announced, it's possible the cable car could be in the works in the near future. If you're keen to see Son Doong in all its natural glory, now is the time to go.

border. The most famous and accessible of these is Phong Nha Cave, which, along with nearby Paradise Cave and the Nuoc Mooc Eco-Trail, are affordable and do not require a guide to visit. These are good options for those short on both money and time.

Single- and multiple-day guided excursions can be arranged to places like the Tu Lan cave system, a series of subterranean passages outside of the park, and Hang En, known for its resident swallows.

PHONG NHA CAVE

Though it's no longer the king of the park's underground attractions, **Phong Nha Cave** (6:30am-5:30pm daily, VND150,000 plus boat fee) remains the most visited spot in the area. Accessible only by boat, the echoing chambers of this cavern have been common knowledge for centuries. As early as the late 1800s, the missionary Leopold Cadiere ventured into the low opening just beyond Son Trach village with nothing more than a small wooden boat and a light. The Frenchman made it just over 400 meters into the darkness before turning back; while inside, he discovered a set of ancient Cham etchings, suggesting that the cave had been in use well before his discovery. It wasn't until 1924 that another adventurer, an English astronomer, ventured about 1.5 kilometers into its recesses.

Tourism to the site began in the colonial era, when a handful of wealthy French came, but this, too, met an abrupt end during the Franco-Vietnam and American Wars, when the cave was repurposed as a weapons cache and hideout for Viet Minh and North Vietnamese troops. The next expedition into Phong Nha didn't occur until 1990, when Howard Limbert and the British Cave Research Association wandered the full length of the cave.

Phong Nha reaches 83 meters from the riverbed to the ceiling. To get to the cave, hop on a boat from the dock near the **park ticket office** (tel. 0232/367-7021, www.phongnhatourism.com.vn, 7am-5pm daily), where you'll buy your ticket to the cave and pay for the boat ride. These small wooden vessels travel down a little river, going just over 400 meters into the cave before stopping on a sandy embankment inside. From here, wander through a maze of artificially lit and oddly shaped stalactites, stalagmites, and other formations. Hop back onto the boat to return to Son Trach village from here. Between the boat docks and the mouth of the cave, you can also swing by **Tien Son Cave** (VND80,000), a smaller grotto discovered in 1935 and newly outfitted with a wooden boardwalk and an extensive lighting system, though Phong Nha is the more worthwhile of the two. Let your boat driver know if you'll be visiting Tien Son so you're not left behind at the caves. Signing up for a tour through the national park lets visitors head over four kilometers inside in the cavern by kayak.

Boats cost VND360,000 for the entire 14-seat vessel; the more people ride, the lower the price per person. Link up with fellow travelers outside the ticket office in order to minimize costs. For those who wish to see Tien Son Cave in addition to Phong Nha, boat fees rise to VND400,000 per vessel. Try to visit either mid-morning or around 2pm or 3pm, as large tour groups come through just after lunch.

PARADISE CAVE

Twenty-one kilometers from the park's visitors center, **Paradise Cave (Dong Thien Duong)** (7am-5pm daily, VND250,000) is one of five entrances into the Vom cave system and an increasingly popular spot for travelers in the area, as it lacks the over-the-top lighting that takes away from some of Phong Nha's natural appeal. Though it was originally discovered in 1992 by members of the British Cave Research Association, researchers failed to map the cave entrance and later lost its location. Thankfully, locals were able to pinpoint the entrance once more in 2005 and, after further research, experts explored the entire subterranean chamber, which spans three kilometers.

Paradise Cave is one of the few sights in the park that can be visited independently. From Phong Nha village, take the Ho Chi Minh West highway, stopping at the ticket booth before carrying on to the entrance. A sign bears the cave's Vietnamese name where

Phong Nha-Ke Bang National Park

the road veers off onto a smaller concrete path. Past the entrance gate, there's a 15- to 20-minute walk before you reach the cave itself, following a paved route through the forest and up a mountainside; electric car services are also available along this road (VND60,000 pp), but the vehicles only go as far as the foot of the hill.

The effort is rewarded by the initial descent into Paradise Cave: from the very top, a long, winding wooden staircase, dimly lit, leads deeper into the cavern, whose soaring ceilings dwarf the large viewing platform below. While you'll be forced to take extra care on your way down, as the steps are often damp and slippery, this affords you plenty of time to glimpse the eerie ridged formations and towering stalagmites that line the wooden walkway. Independent visitors can wade just over 800 meters into the cave, while the national park's tours take you all the way to its end. Once you've reached the far end of the path, make the return trip back up to the entrance before shuffling down a total of 518 steps back to the rainforest path. Thanks to its rapidly growing popularity, trips to Paradise Cave are best timed during the week and either earlier or later in the day, avoiding lunch time, as this is when most tour groups come through.

NUOC MOOC ECO-TRAIL

The **Nuoc Mooc Eco-Trail** (7am-5pm daily, VND80,000, plus kayak hire) may offer a little less wow factor than some of Phong Nha's other sights, but it's believed that the rushing waters of its natural spring may signal an even bigger cave in the area, dwarfing the mammoth chambers of Son Doong. If experts are correct, this waterway could lead through a subterranean cavern that winds all the way to Laos. For the time being, Nuoc Mooc is a good spot to enjoy a leisurely walk among the trees. Visitors are allowed to swim in the blue waters of the spring. If you're keen to paddle around, kayaks (VND100,000 per hour) can be rented from the park. The trail is en route to Paradise Cave, just off the main road.

DARK CAVE

Branching off of the Chay River, **Dark Cave** (7am-5pm daily, VND80,000) is without the lighting system of its sister caves at Phong Nha and Paradise, making for a more authentic experience as you wade into the pitch-black cavern's large underground lake. Visitors have two options for accessing the cave, either by kayak (VND10,000 pp) or zip line. The first option isn't really worth it, as this only affords travelers limited access to the cave. To get to the full experience, you're better off opting to zip-line to the entrance, swim inside, and gain access to Dark Cave's natural mud baths for VND270,000; this fee includes cave entry, zip-line use, a kayak on the return trip, safety equipment, and a local guide. For even more on-the-river fun, opt for the VND450,000 ticket, which grants you the same zip-line access to the cave as well as use of a kayak and a few other activities along the Chay River.

From the mouth of the passage, hop out to wander through its soaring 80 meters chamber, which carries on for nearly 2.5 kilometers in the darkness. While it is possible to go it alone, the cave can be tricky to find, and most people prefer to take a guided tour, either through the national park headquarters or on Phong Nha Farmstay's caving day trip.

HANG EN

The sky-high cavern of **Hang En** was first explored in May 2011 and opened to visitors only a few months later. The 1.5-kilometer-long cave is home to scores of swallows, which nest in the far reaches of the subterranean chamber, and leads onto the river valley that holds the mouth of Son Doong. Its entrance, a staggering 140 meters across, and the sheer size of Hang En's interior make it among the largest caverns in the world. Hang En can only be reached by guided tour, but those who do will have the opportunity to trek through thick, untouched rainforest, stop by some of the most remote villages in Vietnam, spend the night inside a cave, and reach the river valley that leads onto Son Doong. **Oxalis** (Son Trach village, tel. 0232/367-7678, www.oxalis.com.

vn, 7:30am-noon and 1:30pm-5:30pm Mon.-Fri., 7:30am-noon Sat., VND7,500,000) runs two-day, one-night excursions to Hang En.

TU LAN CAVE SYSTEM

The **Tu Lan cave system** is a 200-hectare karst center just outside of Phong Nha-Ke Bang National Park near the Laotian border. Discovered in 2009 by a group of fishermen, recent expeditions into the caves have led to the discovery of several underground chambers over the last few years, expanding the system even more. Tu Lan gained worldwide attention when *National Geographic* photographer Carsten Peter captured a prize-winning shot of Hang Ken, one of Tu Lan's caverns, on film for the magazine. **Oxalis** (Son Trach village, tel. 0232/367-7678, www.oxalis.com.vn, 7:30am-noon and 1:30pm-5:30pm Mon.-Fri., 7:30am-noon Sat., VND1,800,000-15,000,000) exclusively runs one- to four-day trips to Tu Lan, which offer trekking, overnights in the rainforest, and plenty of time to explore the caves as well as a host of other impressive aboveground sights.

Tours

Only three outfits operate tours to the area's caves. The most affordable of these options are the **Phong Nha-Ke Bang National Park Tours** (Son Trach village, tel. 0232/367-7021, www.phongnhatourism.com.vn, 7am-5pm daily, VND1,350,000-9,055,000). The folks at **Phong Nha Farmstay** (1 kilometer east of Ho Chi Minh Hwy. E., tel. 0232/367-5135, www.phong-nha-cave.com, 7am-8pm daily, VND1,450,000-8,000,000) arrange slightly pricier one-, two-, and three-day trips that are well worth the extra cash, including the service of guides with stronger English skills.

For the crème de la crème of cave tours, book with **Oxalis** (Son Trach village, tel. 0232/367-7678, www.oxalis.com.vn, 7:30am-noon and 1:30pm-5:30pm Mon.-Fri., 7:30am-noon Sat., VND1,800,000-68,700,000), the specialized caving and trekking outfit that has exclusive rights to both Son Doong and the Tu Lan cave system. Though these excursions

are expensive, the company spares no cost on expert guides, safety equipment, and transportation, and its sustainable tourism philosophy ensures the incredible landscapes that draw people to Phong Nha-Ke Bang remain well preserved.

Food

There is little in the way of dining variety in Phong Nha. Those who opt for a homestay or lodging farther from the main road upon which the park's visitors center is located will likely be bound to that same place for meals. If you stay closer to town, there are one or two independent options. **Easy Tiger** (TL20, tel. 0232/367-7844, easytigerphongnha@gmail.com, 6am-10:30pm daily, VND100,000-250,000) is a popular spot for reasonably priced Western food, cold beer, and making new travel buddies.

Accommodations

Most accommodations in Son Trach village are basic but do the job. Rooms are limited, as overnights are becoming the preferred way to visit Phong Nha and the number of hotels hasn't caught up with the demand. Book a bed in advance, particularly during high season.

A handful of small local hotels are clustered along the road not far from the Phong Nha-Ke Bang visitors center, offering private rooms on the cheap; more social hostel beds are also available, both in town and at a few nearby homestays. Because this area is on the verge of a tourism boom, lodging options are rapidly changing, and new homestays are opening regularly.

A five-minute walk from the Phong Nha-Ke Bang visitors center, **Easy Tiger** (TL20, tel. 0232/367-7844, easytigerphongnha@gmail.com, VND180,000 dorm) provides clean, cozy four- and six-bed dorms outfitted with mosquito nets and personal lockers as well as en suite baths with hot water. Downstairs, the lively common area makes a good place to unwind on the patio, grab a beer at the bar, or play a game of pool. Occasional live music and regular happy hour specials take place at night. The hostel rents out bicycles and books quality tours from its reception desk. Staff can help arrange onward travel.

One of the first places in the area to cater to foreign travelers, **Phong Nha Farmstay** (1 kilometer east of Ho Chi Minh Hwy. E., tel. 0232/367-5135, www.phong-nha-cave. com, VND750,000-1,170,000, breakfast included) opened in 2010 and has since grown into the area's best-known lodging. In addition to its private double rooms, the French colonial-inspired building boasts breezy verandas overlooking the surrounding rice paddies, a garden, a swimming pool, a restaurant, and a top-notch travel outfit. Rooms include mosquito nets, air-conditioning, Wi-Fi, and hot showers.

From the moment you arrive, the phenomenal folks at **Ho Khanh's Homestay** (Son Trach, tel. 09/1679-4506, www.phong-nha-homestay.com, VND780,000-900,000, breakfast included) will go out of their way to make you feel at home. Owned by Ho Khanh, credited with the discovery of Son Doong, this charming little spot overlooks the river and features a combination of private bungalows and cozy rooms in a traditional wooden house. All accommodations come with Wi-Fi as well as a fan, air-conditioning, and mosquito nets for each bed. Generous breakfasts are served every morning in the small garden café, which operates downstairs next to a stunning view of the Con River, and the staff is keen to assist with logistics, including transportation.

Information and Services

For local travel information, the **Phong Nha-Ke Bang National Park visitors center and ticket office** (tel. 0232/367-7021, www.phongnhatourism.com.vn, 7am-5pm daily) displays a list of the most affordably priced caving tours and assists with booking its own tours, though English speakers are harder to come by at this office. For more in-depth information, make a stop at **Easy Tiger** (TL20, tel. 0232/367-7844, easytigerphongnha@gmail.com), whose staff can introduce you to a number of tour options as well as one or two free activities. Or ask around at your homestay or hotel, as most accommodations in this area also assist with travel-related queries.

The only **ATM** in town is located opposite the national park visitors center and can be temperamental. Bring enough currency to cover all your expenses before arriving in Phong Nha to prevent any problems. If you're interested in taking a caving tour, look into the expected costs beforehand, as these add up quickly. You'll find Internet access at most hotels, but other basics like mail service will have to wait for a larger destination.

There is no reliable medical service available in Phong Nha; the closest hospital of any quality lies in Dong Hoi, 64 kilometers away. For minor injuries, some of the town's lodgings will likely have a first-aid kit and be able to assist. Any serious illness or injury will require a 30-minute car trip to the coast.

Getting There

Transportation to and from Phong Nha requires extra planning and cash. Book your bus or train tickets ahead of time. Most vehicles arrive in Dong Hoi, the nearest major city, about 65 kilometers from the actual park. From there, you can attempt to flag down a taxi or *xe om* driver who is willing to make the trip to Phong Nha (45 minutes, VND600,000), or hop on the local bus from Dong Hoi station. Buses depart from Nam Ly station in Dong Hoi throughout the day, with the final vehicle leaving around 5pm; look for bus B4 with the words "Phong Nha" across its front. It is also possible to arrange a place on the shuttle car organized by **Easy Tiger** (TL20, tel. 0232/367-7844, easytigerphongnha@gmail. com, VND125,000-500,000), as long as you book ahead of time. The cost varies depending on the number of passengers.

BUS

Travelers coming from Hue can arrange bus transportation straight to the park by hopping on one of the day tour minibuses, run by various companies and departing daily in the morning, bound for Phong Nha and getting off in town. Most travel agencies in Hue can organize this for you, and the cost usually runs VND220,000-250,000; clarify that you'd like a ride only and not the full day tour. The ride is 3.5-4 hours. It's also possible to hop on the **DMZ minibus** (VND150,000), which departs from Hue around 2pm and travels directly to Phong Nha; you must book this transportation in advance through the enterprising **Mr. Shi** (tel. 09/6991-7642, shi.home-stays@gmail.com).

Another great option combines your trip with sightseeing en route: For VND500,000, the same **DMZ minibus** has a longer option to visit several major sights in the DMZ area on the way from Phong Nha to Hue, including the Vinh Moc tunnels and the Ben Hai River. This is the best and most cost-effective option for exploring both Phong Nha and the DMZ. The trip departs from Phong Nha at 7am and arrives in Hue at 12:30pm. The cost covers transportation and a guided tour to some of the less-accessible sights in the area, but this join-in service only runs from Phong Nha to Hue and not in the opposite direction. It's possible to arrange a similar transportation-and-tour package from Hue to Phong Nha but via private vehicle—leaving Hue at 2pm and arriving at Phong Nha around 6:30pm—so the cost will be slightly higher; you'll likely have to tack on between VND150,000-300,000 extra per person, but this depends heavily upon the number of passengers. Either way, book ahead with **Mr. Shi** (tel. 09/6991-7642, shi.homestays@gmail.com).

TRAIN

The nearest **train station** (Thuan Ly, tel. 0232/383-6789, 24 hours daily) to Phong Nha-Ke Bang National Park is in Dong Hoi. Trains from Hue (3 hours, VND100,000-170,000) run several times daily. From the train station, take the local bus or a taxi to the park, or arrange private transportation through your lodging ahead of time.

Getting Around

Son Trach village is about a 10-minute walk from end to end, but for exploring, you'll need a **bicycle** or **motorbike.** Many accommodations offer free bicycles with your stay, or at least are willing to rent out push-bikes to guests. With limited options in the area, prices for a daily rental are exponentially greater than in other destinations, with the going rate around VND20,000 per hour or VND120,000 per day. Motorbikes, too, are overpriced at around VND200,000 per day, and you can also find them through some local hotels; the small guesthouses along the main drag typically hire out motorbikes. Travelers can also ask their accommodations for more information on rentals.

BACH MA NATIONAL PARK

With fickle weather patterns and a slow pace of development, **Bach Ma National Park** (tel. 0234/387-1330, www.bachmapark.com. vn, 7am-5:30pm daily, VND60,000) sees fewer visitors than some of its more famous counterparts, but the views from atop Bach Ma mountain, overlooking Lang Co and the sparkling East Sea, are worth the extra effort for birders and nature enthusiasts. Twenty-three kilometers from the coast, the park sits between Danang and Hue, crisscrossed with a half-dozen hiking trails through its heavily forested lowlands and up to the summit of Bach Ma, 1,448 meters above sea level. Though it didn't become an official member of Vietnam's national parks until 1991, the 22,000-hectare park has welcomed visitors since the early 1930s, when the French built a hill station (mountain retreat town) halfway up its namesake mountain, complete with a resort, a swimming pool, and tennis courts. Vietnam's tumultuous struggle for independence cut short the holiday in the mid-1940s, and Bach Ma spent the next few decades as a strategic military outpost, working for both U.S. and Vietnamese forces before the end of the American War in 1975.

Today, Bach Ma's flora and fauna serve a

small but growing number of avid ornithologists and wildlife watchers. Nearly 250 bird species nest in the park's forests, several endemic species among them, including the Annam partridge and the Edwards' pheasant, previously thought to be extinct until its rediscovery just outside the park boundaries in 1996. Bach Ma also qualifies as an area of great importance for plant life, with well over 1,000 different species of flora packed into its diverse landscapes, which range from coastal lagoons to mountainous forests dotted with a series of rushing waterfalls. A few dozen mammals and other creatures roam the area, including several varieties of monkey.

While most travelers prefer to visit the park from Hue, 68 kilometers north—most tours to the park set off from here—there's no reason you can't make Danang your point of departure, as it's equidistant from Bach Ma's headquarters. The best time to visit is March-September, before the leeches come out. Being in one of the wettest regions of the country, rain is a year-round affair here, so it's best to keep a close eye on the weather, as the forecast can change suddenly. Warm clothes and water-resistant garments are always a wise choice. Birders will appreciate the park's overnight facilities since you'll have to rise early to make the most out of your wildlife-watching time here.

Sights and Recreation

The main activity on most trips to Bach Ma is hiking. A collection of six short footpaths lead off the main road up to the summit, taking adventurers deep into the forest, where dozens of streams and waterfalls add to the secluded beauty of the park. The most popular of these routes is **Rhododendron Trail,** a 1.5-kilometer-long path that leads to the rushing Do Quyen Waterfall. Visitors can admire the view from above or brave the 689 steps down to the bottom of the 300-meter drop, though you will have to climb back up. Other pathways, such as the **Five Lakes** trail, meander past a series of freshwater pools where visitors can jump in and have a swim, while

the route up to Hai Vong Dai summit affords stunning views of the coast on a clear day. Not far from the peak, you'll find the deserted remains of Bach Ma's modest hill station, including a now-empty post office and several rundown villas, as well as a small network of tunnels used by the North Vietnamese army from 1973 until the war's end.

While none of these hikes require a guide, it's wise to use one, as getting lost is easy in the dense forest. You'll also want to stay on the marked trails since this park is still in the early stages of its development and, with a past that includes heavy military involvement, unexploded ordnance may still be around. The **visitors center** (7am-5:30pm daily) at the park entrance arranges English-speaking guides for travelers, provided you call ahead of time; they also stock a few English-language brochures and other helpful handouts.

Food

Bach Ma's sole on-site restaurant, near the visitors center, prepares just about any Vietnamese dish you request, catering to vegetarians and other dietary restrictions, though you'll have to order your meals in advance (through your tour guide). With a limited number of patrons, the kitchen only opens upon request, and often shuts down for the day by 7pm.

Accommodations

Visitors who wish to overnight in the park and get an early start on the following day can use a conventional campsite or two barebones **guesthouses** (VND750,000-1,150,000 d), one at the base of the mountain near the visitors center and another near the summit. Rooms are damp, given the constant rainfall in the area, but they come with hot water. Advanced bookings are a good idea, and it's easiest to book through a tour company in Hue for language reasons.

Getting There

Bach Ma National Park can easily be visited from Hue in a single day, whether by bus, car, motorbike, or guided tour. Finding the park entrance is straightforward, with no more than a single turn off Highway 1. Motorbikes and other vehicles are forbidden from driving up the steep road to Bach Ma's summit. Arrange transportation to the top from the visitors center (via a park-approved vehicle) or make your way on foot.

BUS

While it's possible to reach the park via local bus, this option requires more time and patience. Travelers can hop on a bus from either Hue (48 kilometers) or Danang (80 kilometers), disembarking in Phu Loc town. From there, you'll have to commission a xe om driver for the remaining three-kilometer drive to the park (around VND40,000-50,000).

VEHICLES FOR HIRE

For private transportation, travelers can hire both cars and motorbikes in Hue.

From the city it's a straight shot down Highway 1 before turning off the main road in Phu Loc town (20-30 minutes). It's another three kilometers to the park from here. Bring a map as you'll likely need to ask for directions. You'll see signs for the park on the side of the highway. A vehicle for hire costs around VND600,000 for a day.

It's also possible to hire a xe om driver directly from Hue, though the fare is steep (starting at VND400,000), and you'll have to negotiate a rate for the driver to wait while you're in the park.

TOURS

The simplest option, particularly for solo travelers, is to hire a guide directly from Hue and sign up for a day tour. Due to the relative anonymity of Bach Ma, only private tours are offered. Reliable companies like **Hue To Go** (tel. 09/8595-9768, www.huetogotours.com, VND1,070,000) provide motorbike transportation and amiable, experienced guides to ferry you to and from the site. Most other independent companies also arrange private excursions on request.

Danang

While it's often overlooked by travelers zipping from Hue to Hoi An or vice versa, Danang's sleek, sky-high towers and cosmopolitan riverfront offer an optimistic glimpse into the country's future. Surrounded by rolling mountains and a pristine coastline, this sophisticated city retains the telltale markers of urban Vietnamese life—street food stalls and bustling markets, droves of motorbikes, and modest, family-run shops alongside trendy new buildings—but trades the frenzy of Hanoi's narrow streets and Saigon's overcrowded neighborhoods for a more organized and efficient version of chaos.

The Danang Museum and the Museum of Cham Sculpture can fill an afternoon, while nearby My Khe Beach and the haunting white figure of Quan Am across the sea at Linh Ung Pagoda provide a stunning shoreline to relax on. The city may not boast many historical sights or much in the way of local cuisine, but its casual atmosphere and natural landscapes make the mellow spot an easy place to love, worth at least a day of your time.

Western Danang boasts the majority of the city's museums, dining, and nightlife. While this neighborhood is farther from the beach, its central location offers more services and amenities. Far quieter and more spread out, the eastern side of the city sits directly on the beach and offers accommodations that live up to the prices, unlike some of the city's downtown hotels. Stick to the streets south of Pham Van Dong for a more concentrated area where you won't need to walk so much in order to find restaurants or other services.

While some prefer to just make a day trip from Hoi An, travelers can also stay a night

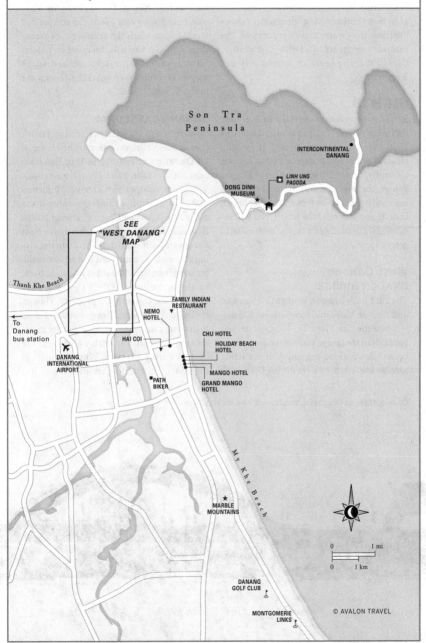

Danang

Son Tra Peninsula

INTERCONTINENTAL DANANG

LINH UNG PAGODA

DONG DINH MUSEUM

SEE "WEST DANANG" MAP

Thanh Khe Beach

To Danang bus station

FAMILY INDIAN RESTAURANT

NEMO HOTEL

HAI COI

CHU HOTEL

HOLIDAY BEACH HOTEL

DANANG INTERNATIONAL AIRPORT

PATH BIKER

MANGO HOTEL

GRAND MANGO HOTEL

My Khe Beach

MARBLE MOUNTAINS

0   1 mi

0   1 km

DANANG GOLF CLUB

© AVALON TRAVEL

MONTGOMERIE LINKS

or two to fully appreciate the nearby beach. Danang experiences heavy rainfall and severe storms September-December. The city is at its best February-May, when temperatures are reasonably warm and skies are clear. The summer months are filled with good weather, though it really heats up around July and August.

SIGHTS

Spread out over the downtown area, the coast, and nearby Son Tra peninsula, Danang's sights are mostly ornamental, providing pleasant photo ops alongside a bit of history. Centrally located attractions like the Dragon Bridge, the museum, and the local cathedral are easily reached on foot in the downtown area. If you stay near the beach, you will require the assistance of a taxi or motorbike to get into town.

West Danang
DRAGON BRIDGE

The 2013-built **Dragon Bridge** (Vo Van Kiet and Nguyen Van Linh) spans nearly 800 meters over the Han River. The long, slender yellow body of the bridge's namesake dragon arcs up and down along the length of the structure, an eye-catching sight during the day. At

night, the dragon's 15,000 LED lights come to life, turning an array of colors throughout the evening. Weekend visitors can see a pyrotechnic display every Saturday and Sunday around 9pm, when the creature's sea-facing head spits out fireballs, followed by powerful water cannons spraying from the dragon's mouth. Look for the crowd that gathers at the bridge to watch the show.

DANANG CATHEDRAL

Constructed in 1923 and designed by French priest Louis Vallet, the pale pink bell tower of the **Danang Cathedral** (156 Tran Phu; mass 5pm Sat., 5:15am, 8am, 10am (in English), 3pm, 5pm, 6:30pm Sun.) stands 70 meters high, topped with a rooster, earning it the nickname "Chicken Church" among locals. Its grand Gothic exterior matches that of most European-built cathedrals in Vietnam, rising above a large courtyard that separates the building from Tran Phu street while, out back, an alcove dedicated to the Virgin Mary sits hidden at the corner of the property. Though the church is not actually open outside of mass hours, you can get the gist by admiring its exterior architecture, or catch a glimpse of the indoors during a service. While the gates at the front of the building are often closed, it is

Danang's famous Dragon Bridge slithers across the Han River.

West Danang

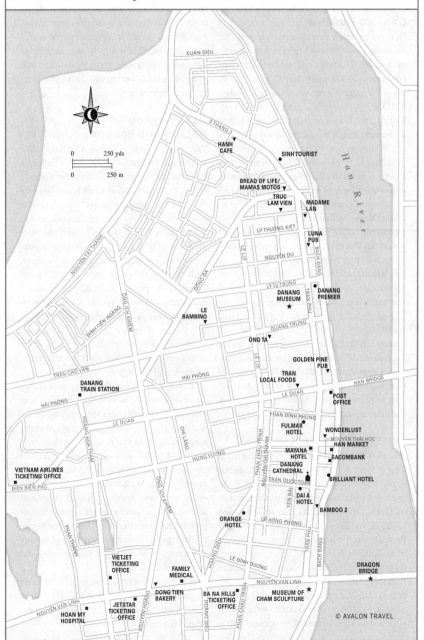

XUÂN DIỆU

3 THÁNG 2

HANH CAFE

SINH TOURIST

Han River

0   250 yds
0   250 m

BREAD OF LIFE/ MAMAS MOTOS

TRUC LAM VIEN

MADAME LÂN

LÝ THƯỜNG KIỆT

LUNA PUB

NGUYỄN DU

BÁCH ĐẰNG

LÝ TỰ TRỌNG

DANANG MUSEUM

DANANG PREMIER

TRẦN PHÚ

LE BAMBINO

QUANG TRUNG

ÔNG TA

GOLDEN PINE PUB

TRAN LOCAL FOODS

HAN BRIDGE

LE DUAN

POST OFFICE

NGUYỄN TẤT THÀNH

ÔNG ÍCH KHIÊM

ĐINH TIÊN HOÀNG

ĐỐNG ĐA

LÊ LỢI

LÊ LỢI

TRẦN CAO VÂN

HẢI PHÒNG

DANANG TRAIN STATION

HẢI PHÒNG

LE DUAN

CHI LĂNG

HOÀNG HOA THÁM

HÙNG VƯƠNG

PHAN ĐÌNH PHÙNG

FULMAR HOTEL

WONDERLUST

NGUYỄN THÁI HỌC

HAN MARKET

MAYANA HOTEL

SACOMBANK

DANANG CATHEDRAL

BRILLIANT HOTEL

PHAN CHÂU TRINH

NGUYỄN CHÍ THANH

TRẦN QUỐC TOẢN

DAI A HOTEL

YÊN BÁI

BAMBOO 2

VIETNAM AIRLINES TICKETING OFFICE

ĐIỆN BIÊN PHỦ

ÔNG ÍCH KHIÊM

ORANGE HOTEL

LÊ HỒNG PHONG

PHAN THÀNH

HOÀNG DIỆU

LÊ ĐÌNH DƯƠNG

TRẦN PHÚ

BÁCH ĐẰNG

DRAGON BRIDGE

VIETJET TICKETING OFFICE

FAMILY MEDICAL

DONG TIEN BAKERY

BA NA HILLS TICKETING OFFICE

NGUYỄN VĂN LINH

MUSEUM OF CHAM SCULPTURE

NGUYỄN HOÀNG

HOÀNG DIỆU

PHAN CHÂU TRINH

NGUYỄN VĂN LINH

JETSTAR TICKETING OFFICE

HOAN MY HOSPITAL

© AVALON TRAVEL

possible to enter from the office of the Danang Diocese next door.

DANANG MUSEUM

In every province there is a government-run museum that offers a brief flash of the region's past. The large and modern **Danang Museum** (24 Tran Phu, tel. 0236/388-6236, www.baotangdanang.vn, 8am-5pm daily, VND20,000) is truly a cut above the rest. With three floors of informative exhibits and ample English signage, this museum is one of the city's more interesting sights. The first floor features everything from Sa Huynh jewelry and ceramics dating back 1,000 years or more to displays on fishing practices and local burial rituals associated with whales, while the second and third levels showcase a collection of artifacts from the French and American Wars that is more extensive and informative than others in the region. Customs and traditions of the area's ethnic minorities are included, providing insight into some of Vietnam's lesser-known cultures.

The museum is the historical site of Dien Hai Rampart, a military fort originally constructed in 1813 near the Danang port, which was moved 10 years later to its current location. The building itself is a modern construction, but you can still see the stone walls that once bordered the original rampart encircling the museum grounds.

MUSEUM OF CHAM SCULPTURE

Danang's **Museum of Cham Sculpture** (2 2 Thang 9, tel. 0236/357-4801, www.chammuseum.vn, 7am-5pm daily, VND60,000) is the most complete and well-preserved collection of Cham artifacts in the country. Founded in 1919 by French archaeologist Henri Parmentier, the museum showcases dozens of sculptures, friezes, and other engravings from as far back as the 7th century alongside valuable information on Cham history and Hinduism. The sprawling ground-floor displays are collections separated by the site at which it was discovered. The museum does an impressive job of organizing the sculptures, blending columns and pieces of sandstone and terra-cotta frieze into the building itself. Particularly for those who plan to visit the Cham ruins at My Son or along the south-central coast, this is a must-see, as it helps patrons to appreciate just how detailed and impressive the towering structures were during the Cham empire.

East Danang

★ LINH UNG PAGODA

Visible from Danang's My Khe Beach, the awe-inspiring figure of Quan Am, a Buddhist bodhisattva and the most important female figure in Buddhism, at **Linh Ung Pagoda** (Hoang Sa, sunrise-sunset daily, free) is enough to make you do a double-take as you lounge on shore. Rising up from the lush greenery of Son Tra peninsula, this imposing statue, the tallest of its kind in Vietnam, looks out over the gentle curve of My Khe and is believed to protect the coast and its fisher-folk from harm. At 30 stories tall, this version forms a trio of Quan Am statues together with two statues at two other Linh Ung Pagodas (on Marble Mountain and atop Ba Na Hill) outside of Danang. They are thought to act as protectors of the region.

Though you'll pass the large and colorful main entrance to Linh Ung first, visitors enter the pagoda complex through a side road just past the gate. From here, a set of stone steps leads up to the main hall of worship, a vibrant and decorative building flanked by nine statues on either side. But the main event is Quan Am herself, standing at the far end of a massive clearing. This area is packed on holidays and weekends with droves of visitors, both foreign and local, who come to pay their respects to the bodhisattva and to take in stunning views of the My Khe shoreline and downtown Danang.

Make your visit to the pagoda in the early morning or late afternoon to avoid the worst of the heat. Dress respectfully—this is a revered religious site.

BEACHES
My Khe Beach

Danang's most accessible stretch of sand, **My Khe Beach** (Pham Van Dong and Vo Nguyen Giap) is barely out of town, with only a short distance separating it from the city center, but its 6.5 kilometers of unbroken coast provide a pleasant escape from the urban landscapes farther inland. Bordered by the East Sea Park, a small, shadeless patch of concrete and trees, My Khe is notably clean for a city beach and boasts plenty of room to sunbathe. There are beach chairs for rent (VND20,000-40,000), though you should bargain, as they are sometimes overpriced. Several restaurants and bars are also set up around the shoreline to accommodate hungry and thirsty beach-goers.

You'll spot a few "no swimming" flags in the area: these do not prohibit you from wading into the ocean a short way, but local lifeguards will call you back should you venture too far out. My Khe and the surrounding coast experience strong undertows and can be dangerous.

Thanh Khe Beach

Hugging the bay just north of the city, **Thanh Khe Beach** (Nguyen Tat Thanh) is a much quieter area than its counterpart on the other side of Son Tra peninsula, with only a few fishermen reeling in the day's catch, but it is more frequented by Vietnamese tourists during the summertime. Its shores are notably clean and a sea wall separates the area from Nguyen Tat Thanh's racing traffic. Thanks to the peninsula and its protection, Thanh Khe sees calmer waters for swimming and wading than My Khe. There are few amenities available here—just a few restaurants across the road.

ENTERTAINMENT AND EVENTS
Nightlife

Danang's riverfront lights up after dark, making it the go-to spot for locals and foreigners, with plenty of bars and cafés overlooking the water. On the weekends, festivities can run into the early hours of the morning, but most venues wrap up around midnight. Out toward the beach, a more laid-back atmosphere exists, with a few casual hangouts scattered among the local hotels and restaurants.

Equal parts Italian restaurant and hipster garage bar, **Luna Pub** (9A Tran Phu, tel. 0236/389-8939, 11am-midnight daily, VND25,000-270,000) offers an endless pricey list of foreign and domestic beer along with

Incense burns before a Buddha at Danang's Linh Ung Pagoda.

serious cocktails. There are occasional live music events and DJ-ing from the hollowed-out truck parked at the back of the restaurant.

A lively hole-in-the-wall whose low ceilings are patterned in old beer labels, **Bamboo 2** (216 Bach Dang, tel. 09/0554-4769, www.bamboo2bar.com, 10am-midnight daily, VND25,000-85,000) offers cramped indoor seating downstairs, sidewalk tables, a pool bar on the open-air second floor, and plenty of beer and cocktails to keep you going.

Festivals and Events

On weekends, the mouth of Danang's iconic Dragon Bridge **breathes fire** (9pm Sat.-Sun.). Though it's a short display (15-20 minutes)—two sets of fireballs, followed by the dragon spraying water—locals and visitors alike gather at the east end of the bridge to watch the show.

Two nights a year, the annual **Danang International Fireworks Competition** (Apr. 29-30) brings together the world's most skilled pyrotechnic experts to create a spectacular display over the Han River. National teams are judged on their respective displays, which light up the skies above Danang with an array of reds, greens, blues, and yellows. Cultural performances take place on the waterfront. April 30 is also Reunification Day, a public holiday in Vietnam, and combined with the firework festivities, it's wise to book ahead if you plan to come for the festival.

SPORTS AND RECREATION

Recreational activities are mostly limited to sunbathing, golf, and wandering the downtown area. A handful of high-end hotels and resorts offer access to their swimming pools or fitness centers, though these come at a price, usually upward of VND200,000.

Cycling

The folks at **Path Biker** (141 Chuong Duong, tel. 09/1349-0718, www.pathbiker.com, 7am-5pm daily, VND795,000-2,520,000) can set you up with knowledgeable tour guides, high-quality bikes, and a cycling route that caters to your level of fitness, ranging from leisurely rides through the countryside to a full-on adventure south to My Son or north to Hue. Chan Nguyen, the man in charge, tailors each trip to travelers' wishes and also arranges excursions departing from Hoi An or Hue. Fees vary depending upon the number of people and the specifics of each route; get in touch with the company ahead of time.

Golf

Perched just a short way from My Khe Beach is **BRG Danang Golf Club** (My Khe Beach, tel. 0236/395-8111, www.dananggolfclub.com, 6am-8pm daily, VND2,650,000-3,850,000), a picturesque 18-hole course overlooking the ocean. Complete with several restaurants, locker rooms, and a well-stocked pro shop, the course offers a challenging game complemented by natural scenery. Lessons are available for golfers of all levels of experience.

Right beside the Danang Golf Club, **Montgomerie Links** (near My Khe Beach, tel. 0235/394-1942, www.montgomerielinks.com, tee times 6am-3pm daily, VND2,700,000-3,950,000) is one of the country's most exclusive and challenging courses, boasting top-notch facilities that include a clubhouse as well as a driving range. Designed by famed golfer Colin Montgomerie, this course regularly makes the number-one spot on lists of the best courses in Vietnam and sits just beside My Khe Beach en route to Hoi An. You may want to steer clear on weekends, as it gets crowded.

FOOD

Danang boasts an interesting combination of local and international cuisine. Homegrown dishes like *mi quang* (rice noodle soup with shrimp and pork) and *bun cha ca* (rice noodle soups with fish cakes) make up the city's best local offerings, while one or two European eateries provide authentic fare.

Vietnamese

With both garden and indoor seating, the

popular **Tran Local Foods** (4 Le Duan, tel. 0236/384-9022, 7am-11pm daily, VND16,000-99,000) dishes up a variety of Danang specialties in a kitsch atmosphere with more lime green than your eyes can handle. From do-it-yourself pork spring rolls, the restaurant's bestselling item, to *mi quang* (rice noodle soup with shrimp and pork), *banh beo* (a steamed rice flour cake), and the incredibly strong *bun mam* (Vietnamese seafood gumbo), Tran's is a popular spot for many Danang residents.

A local favorite, **Truc Lam Vien** (8-10 Tran Quy Cap, tel. 0236/358-2428, www.truclamvien.com.vn, 6:30am-10pm daily, VND50,000-350,000) pairs Vietnamese cuisine with a peaceful garden setting, its open-air pavilions modeled in traditional Hue-style architecture. A range of chicken, beef, seafood, and vegetable dishes are served, as well as a few cheaper breakfast options. Truc Lam Vien is most active at night but also functions as a café during the day and is open for breakfast and lunch.

An inviting yellow building at the end of Bach Dang, **Madame Lan** (4 Bach Dang, tel. 0236/361-6226, www.madamelan.vn, 6:30am-9:30pm daily, VND45,000-250,000) serves an extensive list of local dishes, including *mi quang* (rice noodle soup with shrimp and pork), and plenty of fresh seafood, with an English menu to boot. Its simple wooden furniture and open-air seating are an upmarket take on local street-dining.

Street Food

You'll find plenty of street food along **Nguyen Chi Thanh.** Down the southern end are a few nice *banh cuon* shops, which serve steamed rice-flour crepes with mushrooms, Vietnamese cold cuts, fish sauce, and fresh greens. Farther north you'll find some of the city's best *bun cha ca* (rice noodle soup with fish and fish cake).

The humble storefront of **Ong Ta** (113 Nguyen Chi Thanh, tel. 0236/389-8700, 6am-10pm daily, VND25,000) is a well-known vendor of Danang's signature version of *bun cha ca*, featuring assorted greens, and, in this city,

tomato and even pumpkin. Portions are generous, so bring your appetite. This particular street is lined with a range of good options in case your meal doesn't fill you up.

The dining area at **Hai Coi** (2 Nguyen Van Thoai, 3pm-1am daily, VND15,000 per wing) is nothing more than an outdoor collection of low plastic chairs and metal tables, but this lends itself well to a beer-and-chicken restaurant. Sizzling open-flame barbecues line the sidewalk out front, where you watch as your Hanoian-style chicken wings are grilled to perfection. These finger-licking wings are too good to pass up. With dirt-cheap prices and a lively crowd in the evenings, this is an excellent spot to take in the local atmosphere.

French

A genuine French eatery hidden down one of the city's alleys, **Le Bambino** (122/11 Quang Trung, tel. 0236/389-6386, www.lebambino.com, 4pm-10pm daily, VND120,000-475,000) has a menu that lists sumptuous European fare, like lamb shank and foie gras, not to mention a long list of wines. The cozy dining room looks into a small open courtyard.

Cafés and Bakeries

For some excellent Asian-style pastries, try the **Dong Tien Bakery** (93 Nguyen Van Linh, tel. 0236/362-1645, www.dongtienbakery.com.vn, 5:30am-10:30pm daily, VND5,000-20,000). These tasty treats are more than worth the trek from the riverfront, particularly the mung bean pastries. Dong Tien has another location (15 Dong Da, tel. 0236/389-9191, www.dongtienbakery.com.vn, 5:30am-10:30pm daily, VND5,000-20,000) near the town center, as well as several farther from the downtown area.

The chic black-and-white storefront of **Wonderlust** (96 Tran Phu, tel. 0236/399-0123, 7am-11pm daily, VND15,000-50,000) would not be out of place in North America, with its windowed facade and bright minimalist interior. Serving both Vietnamese and Western coffee as well as pastries and cupcakes, the café offers plenty of space downstairs as well as a small sitting area upstairs. The café also shares its space with a few local brands so you can shop while you get your caffeine fix.

Indian

The tasty **Family Indian Restaurant** (231 Ho Nghinh, tel. 09/4260-5254, www.indianres.com, 10am-10pm daily, VND55,000-150,000) rounds out the end of a string of budget hotels with delicious Indian fare and friendly service. The menu features a nice range of dishes, including vegetarian cuisine as well as traditional Indian desserts and drinks. The chef prepares each dish with your preferred level of spice. Both indoor and outdoor seating is available. A handful of Vietnamese dishes make it onto the menu, though Indian cuisine is the main event.

International

Helping to improve the lives of deaf Vietnamese for nearly 10 years, **Bread of Life** (4 Dong Da, tel. 0236/356-5185, www.breadoflifedanang.com, 9:30am-2:30pm and 5:30pm-9:30pm daily, VND40,000-200,000) is popular not only for its do-good reputation but for the top-notch pastries, Western breakfasts, vegetarian meals, and Mexican fare. Founded in 2005 by Bob and Kathleen Huff, an expat couple with a long history in Vietnam, the organization has provided hearing-impaired locals with sign language and vocational training as well as English classes, housing, and other services.

Italian and Pizza

Luna Pub (9A Tran Phu, tel. 0236/389-8939, 11am-midnight daily, VND110,000-400,000) comes off like an upscale mechanic's garage, though far more chic. With exposed brick and copper piping, a hollowed-out truck-turned-DJ-station, and waitstaff in blue coveralls, this Italian joint serves mouthwatering classics with a quirky bent, such as beef tenderloin with gorgonzola sauce, Nordic pizza, and green lasagna. Homemade pastas, pizza, and hearty fish and meat entrées come out of the large open kitchen. The pub's lengthy menu includes a host of foreign and local beer. A top-notch selection of Italian gelato takes up space on the blackboards behind the bar.

ACCOMMODATIONS

Visitors who prefer to take advantage of the beach are better off finding a spot on the eastern side of the river closest to the water, while foodies and city slickers may want to stick to downtown Danang in the west. Wherever you stay, both sides of the Han River are easily reached; without a motorbike, you may find yourself hopping into cabs or onto the back of a *xe om* fairly often, as there are a few kilometers between the downtown area and the beach.

West Danang

VND210,000-525,000

In a decidedly mid-range city, **Fulmar Hotel** (11 Yen Bai, tel. 0236/381-0809, www.fulmarhotel.com, VND330,000-440,000) is one of the most affordable accommodations on the western side of town. While the rooms are well-kept and stocked with the usual amenities—air-conditioning, hot water, TV, and a fridge—they are also closet-size. If all you're planning to do in your hotel is sleep, this shouldn't be an issue, but if you require more space, look elsewhere.

The charming **Mayana Hotel** (40 Nguyen Thai Hoc, tel. 0236/386-6777, www.mayanahotel.com, VND400,000-700,000, breakfast included) sits just west of the riverfront and provides cozy, well-appointed rooms with ambience. From the gilded handles on the front door to the ornate tiled floors and plush beds, Mayana's decor adds to its character. Amenities include hot water, air-conditioning, TV, a minibar, coffee- and tea-making facilities, and a work desk.

VND525,000-1,050,000

Dai A Hotel (51 Yen Bai, tel. 0236/382-7532, www.daiahotel.com.vn, VND615,000-730,000, breakfast included), a large and inviting property near Danang Cathedral, offers spacious rooms with uninspired decor, but the hotel staff are friendly and the rooms clean. All feature air-conditioning, hot water, TV, and a minibar.

VND1,050,000-2,100,000

Tucked away in a skinny building just off Thai Phien, the exceptionally welcoming staff and bright corridors of **Orange Hotel** (29 Hoang Dieu, tel. 0236/356-6176, www.danangorangehotel.com, VND1,155,000-3,115,000, breakfast included) are a pleasant introduction to this boutique hotel. Rooms offer more space than other lodgings in the area and feature hot water, air-conditioning, a minibar, and TV.

Luxurious and elegant, the **Brilliant Hotel** (162 Bach Dang, tel. 0236/322-2999, www.brillianthotel.vn, VND1,790,000-6,490,000, breakfast included) lives up to its name. With unobstructed views of Dragon Bridge and the Han River, each beautifully furnished room includes plush beds and floor-to-ceiling windows, hot water, air-conditioning, a minibar, TV, and access to the hotel's swimming pool and fitness center. A spa and several restaurants are attached to this four-star hotel.

OVER VND2,100,000

An emblem of the city's fast-paced development and growing business community, every room in the **Novotel Danang Premier** (36 Bach Dang, tel. 0236/392-9999, www.novotel-danang-premier.com, VND3,625,000-6,385,000) offers beautiful views of the Han River from its waterfront location. Rooms are outfitted with large plush beds, hot water, air-conditioning, TV, Wi-Fi, tea- and coffee-making facilities, a balcony, and a minibar. In-room espresso machines and iPod docking stations are included in the more upscale offerings. The Novotel runs several bars and restaurants, including a panoramic bar on the building's 35th floor, as well as a swimming pool for guests.

East Danang
VND210,000-525,000

Named after a beloved movie character, **Nemo Hotel** (100/2 Nguyen Van Thoai, tel. 0236/395-1951, levy@danangnemohotel. com, VND350,000-500,000) features modern rooms with large windows and plenty of light. Each room's separate all-glass toilet and shower cubicles make for an odd bath configuration, but lodgings are clean and well-kept, and you'll find the usual amenities: air-conditioning, hot water, TV, Wi-Fi, and comfy duvets. The hotel is a short walk from the beach, and its location off the main road minimizes traffic noise.

Located amid popular budget and midrange lodgings, **Mango Hotel** (50 An Thuong 1, tel. 0236/395-4345, mangohoteldanang@gmail.com, VND350,000-750,000, breakfast included) provides friendly service at a more affordable price than most in the neighborhood. TV, hot water, Wi-Fi, and air-conditioning are included in the rates. While not as lavish as its sister hotel on the corner, Mango's excellent location near the beach makes this a worthy spot for budget travelers.

VND525,000-1,050,000

Perched at the end of a string of near-beachfront accommodations, ★ **Grand Mango Hotel** (60 An Thuong, tel. 0236/398-5888, www.grandmangohotel.com, VND800,000-1,300,000, breakfast included) offers well-appointed rooms and friendly service at one of the best rates around. Its rooms run the gamut from comfortable, city-facing standards to bright ocean-view rooms. TV, Wi-Fi, hot water, air-conditioning, and coffee- and tea-making facilities are included in each room, and the hotel can assist with other services, including transportation and travel.

Chu Hotel (2-4 An Thuong 1, tel. 0236/395-5123, www.chuhotel.com, VND950,000-1,500,000, breakfast included) sits just behind the mammoth Holiday Beach Hotel and pulls off well-appointed lodgings and a pleasant eatery all in one, with the shaded outdoor patio acting as a café and restaurant while the upper floors house comfortable modern rooms with an antique feel, featuring brass accents and dark wood furniture. Your choice of standard, superior, and deluxe rooms are available, and the usual amenities apply: air-conditioning, Wi-Fi, hot water, TV, and a minibar. Chu Hotel now has spa and massage services.

OVER VND2,100,000

The opulent **Holiday Beach Hotel** (Vo Nguyen Giap, tel. 0236/396-7777, www. holidaybeachdanang.com, VND2,065,000-8,320,000) is a smaller, more central version of the resorts down the road. From the sparkling high-ceilinged reception area to plush guest rooms, which feature marble baths, Japanese-imported bathtubs, and NASA-certified mattresses (in addition to the standard amenities), Holiday Beach lives up to its price tag, with extras like complimentary spa services. The hotel boasts several bars and restaurants, a fitness center, daily shuttles to Hoi An, and a rooftop swimming pool with stunning views of the shoreline below.

Son Tra's five-star **Intercontinental Danang** (Son Tra Peninsula, tel. 0236/393-8888, www.danang.intercontinental.com, VND9,200,000-31,000,000) is the peak of luxury. The views are reason enough to spend time here—the property rolls gently down the side of Son Tra Mountain and onto the beach. It features spacious rooms and lavish suites, along with a spa, a fitness center, two swimming pools, several restaurants, and activity centers for kids and teens. Rooms come with a balcony, a rainforest shower, vanity sinks, flat-screen TVs, and the standard amenities. Top-tier lodgings include butler service and afternoon tea. Additional activities such as trekking, snorkeling, yoga, tai chi, and kayaking can be arranged.

INFORMATION AND SERVICES
Visitor Information

For a friendly chat and a wealth of useful information, stop by the **Danang Visitor Center** (108 Bach Dang, tel. 0236/355-0111, www.tourism.danang.vn, 7am-10pm daily), whose receptionists have personal recommendations on restaurants, sights, and the rest. Free maps featuring the city's bus routes and important phone numbers are available. You can also hop on Danang's citywide complimentary Wi-Fi and visit sites like **indanang. com** for more helpful tips or sign up for the visitor center's app, Danang FantastiCity.

Danang also runs an **assistance hotline** (tel. 0236/355-0111) for foreign visitors that fields general questions and complaints of overcharging and other unbecoming behavior that might tarnish the city's image. This feedback is usually taken seriously, so report any issues.

Banks and Currency Exchange

As one of the country's larger cities, you'll find no shortage of banks downtown. Many financial institutions staff English-speaking employees. For currency exchange and an ATM, visit the local **Sacombank** (130-132 Bach Dang, tel. 0236/358-2612, www.sacombank. com.vn, 7:30am-11:30am and 1pm-5pm Mon.-Fri., 7:30am-11:30am Sat.) or other nearby facilities.

Postal Services and Internet

You'll find a **post office** (64 Bach Dang, tel. 0236/384-9054, 6:30am-7pm daily) on the riverfront that can assist with your needs. Danang is one of the only cities in Vietnam to provide complimentary Wi-Fi throughout town.

Medical Services

Danang's medical facilities are notably better than most in the area. **Family Medical Practice Danang** (96-98 Nguyen Van Linh, tel. 0236/358-2699, www.vietnammedical-practice.com, 24 hours daily) has Western doctors and receives patients at its clinic in addition to a **24-hour emergency hotline** (tel. 09/1391-7303). **Hoan My Hospital** (161 Nguyen Van Linh, tel. 0236/365-0950, www. hoanmydanang.com, 7am-11:30am and

1:30pm-5pm Mon.-Sat.) is the only quality Vietnamese hospital that doesn't overcharge foreigners for its medical services.

GETTING THERE
Air
Danang International Airport (DAD, www.danangairportonline.com), five kilometers from downtown, is one of the country's nicer facilities, with domestic and international flights daily from **Jetstar** (137 Nguyen Van Linh, tel. 0236/358-3583, www.jetstar.com, 7:30am-noon and 1:30pm-5:30pm Mon.-Sat.), **VietJet** (157-159 Ham Nghi, tel. 0236/369-2665, www.vietjetair.com, 7am-8pm daily), and **Vietnam Airlines** (27 Dien Bien Phu, tel. 0236/382-1130, www.vietnamairlines.com, 7:30am-11:30am and 1:30pm-5pm daily).

Flights from Ho Chi Minh City to Danang (1 hour, VND350,000-900,000) depart every two hours or so. Flights from Hanoi to Danang (1 hour, VND780,000-1,300,000) leave with the same frequency.

Bus
Local buses from Hoi An and Hue arrive at the gargantuan **Danang Bus Station** (159 Ton Duc Thang, tel. 0236/376-7679), where there are connections to the rest of the country at any hour of the day or night.

From Hoi An, hop off downtown rather than at the bus station. Public vehicles travel the length of Bach Dang, the riverfront street, before turning and heading to the station, which is actually 6.5 kilometers from the city center. Buses from Hoi An (1 hour, VND30,000) run 5:30am-6pm daily. From Hue (2.5 hours, VND100,000-200,000), it's a 100-kilometer trip.

Private bus companies **Sinh Tourist** (16 3 Thang 2, tel. 0236/384-3259, www.thesinhtourist.vn, 7am-8pm daily) and **Hanh Cafe** (118 3 Thang 2, tel. 0236/352-5052, www.hanhcafe.vn, 6:30am-9pm daily) have offices in Danang. Buses let off at their office locations. Both outfits book onward transportation to Hue and other cities. There is also a

Mailinh Express (tel. 0236/379-2929, www.mailinhexpress.vn, 7:30am-6pm daily) counter at the bus station that does daily runs to less-visited interior cities like Buon Ma Thuot, Kon Tum, and Quy Nhon. **Phuong Trang** (tel. 0236/378-6786, www.futabuslines.com.vn, 6am-9pm daily) also does trips down to Quy Nhon and Nha Trang.

Train
The major stop for the central region on the country's Reunification Line, Danang's **train station** (200 Hai Phong, tel. 0236/382-3810, 7am-5pm daily) links the city with the rest of the coast. There is no train service connecting Danang with Hoi An, making Danang a popular transit hub for train travelers.

There are multiple daily trains from Hue to Danang (3 hours, VND80,000-150,000). The ride from Nha Trang to Danang (12 hours, VND120,000-560,000) is a long one, so consider buying a higher-priced ticket for a more comfortable seat. There are multiple daily departures.

GETTING AROUND
Taxi and *Xe Om*
You'll find *xe om* drivers near the local market and on every other street corner. For taxis, you can flag down a cab from **Mailinh** (tel. 0236/356-5656) or **Vinasun** (tel. 0236/368-6868).

Bus
Danang's **public bus system** (tel. 0236/371-1468, www.danangbus.vn, 5am-9pm daily) has five separate routes that crisscross the city and its surroundings. A shuttle to My Son runs 5:30am-5pm daily. Look out for the posted price on the side or back of the bus. When traveling around the city, fares run around VND5,000. While the city's central bus station is far from the downtown area, you'll find that most buses pass by the riverfront, so you may want to catch a bus from there rather than making the trek to the station. Check the bus system's website for route details.

Motorbike

Renting a motorbike in Danang is easy, but not always at a reasonable price. Many rental outfits charge upward of VND120,000 per day, and not all vehicles come in great shape. Your best bet is to ask your hotel for information on rental vehicles. In many cases, you'll be asked to provide some kind of collateral, such as a passport or a security deposit.

MARBLE MOUNTAINS

A collection of limestone karsts sprouting up from amid the modest houses and paddy fields beyond Non Nuoc Beach, the famous **Marble Mountains** (11 kilometers southeast of Danang, 7am-5:30pm daily, VND40,000) are each named after an element—earth, water, fire, metal, and wood—and house a popular array of religious sites. Thuy Son (Water Mountain) is the largest of the five and offers the most impressive assortment of Buddhist relics.

a cave pagoda inside the Marble Mountains

From the foot of Thuy Son, visitors scale a set of stone steps up to **Linh Ung Pagoda,** one of the oldest religious venues in Danang. Built sometime in the 15th century, this colorful, mosaic-clad structure was rebuilt in 1825 by emperor Minh Mang, a staunch Buddhist who spent several prayer stints in these mountains during his reign.

Around the back of the pagoda is a set of caves, which house several statues of the Buddha in different positions, as well as the mountain's oldest relic, a 7th-century Cham Hindu altar, complete with sandstone gate and a small linga-yoni statue. Off to the right is a clearing known as Chess Cave, where the emperor used to play board games during his free time in the mountains.

Up another level of stairs, you'll come to the seven-tiered Xa Loi tower, which houses yet another altar as well as affording some pleasant views of the surrounding area. This is where the elevator (VND15,000) lets off if you prefer not to walk up the first half of the stone staircase. From here, follow the path past the tower to Van Thong Cave, a larger grotto from which you can access the mountain's

highest point. Though the path is treacherous—its smooth stones make for limited traction when climbing up the dark passageway to the top, and there are plenty of low-hanging outcroppings on which to hit your head—clamber through the passageway and you'll be rewarded with the Marble Mountains' best views of Non Nuoc Beach and the beautiful landscapes of the coast.

The way back down from Van Thong is more forgiving, with a proper staircase built into the mountainside that leads to the last and largest of the caves, a vaulted room in the heart of the mountain decorated with altars to Buddha and Quan Am, and populated by unusual natural rock formations. During the American War, this grotto served as a hospital and administrative office for the North Vietnamese army.

Opposite the grotto is Linh Ung's counterpart, Tam Thai Pagoda, an equally intricate structure, as well as a west-facing lookout from which to see the nearby town and the remaining Marble Mountains.

Time your visit for the early morning or late afternoon to avoid the heat of the day. As a popular place for local visitors, the mountains are busier on weekends and holidays, in part because of their religious significance but also thanks to the booming trade in marble statues that takes place at the base of the mountain. Once a humble stone-sculpting village, the area around Water Mountain is now teeming with vendors selling genuine marble statues and cheaper versions. You may face some aggressive sales pitches, but the scenery and the countless caves make up for the unwanted attention. For more in-depth information, English-speaking guides (VND100,000) can be hired at the ticket office (beside the steps leading up to the mountain). The Marble Mountains are between Hoi An and Danang and can be reached by taxi, *xe om*, or public bus.

★ HAI VAN PASS

Rising above the pristine white-sand beaches north of Danang, **Hai Van Pass** is one of central Vietnam's most touted natural attractions. Over 21 kilometers, this stunning cliffside road traces the edge of the Truong Son Mountains, overlooking verdant sloping hills that sink into the turquoise waters of Lang Co Bay. Up top, the pass is nothing special, though a few old military bunkers are left from Vietnamese, French, and American forces. The drive itself and the unbelievable scenery are what make Hai Van Pass a must-see.

Visitors can visit the pass by hiring a *xe om* in Danang. It's also possible to do the drive yourself by motorbike, but with the narrow roads and the beautiful scenery, it's much more enjoyable to let an experienced driver take the wheel. The drive to the top takes about an hour and costs more than the average *xe om* ride (around VND600,000-800,000 for the round-trip from Danang). Easy Rider-style guides can be hired to take travelers on the drive, though costs for a day trip usually run north of VND1,000,000 and include other sights, such as Lang Co Beach or the Marble Mountains south of Danang.

The same things that account for Hai Van's incredible scenery also make the road a dangerous one. A small guardrail lines the far side of the asphalt; beyond lies a sheer drop. Caution and focus are musts on this road, as the occasional bus or motorbike can come around a corner at breakneck speed. It's best to stop for photos only on stretches where the shoulder has been widened to accommodate

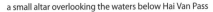

a small altar overlooking the waters below Hai Van Pass

vehicles. You can always walk back to your desired photo spot, if necessary. Factoring in photo stops, budget around three hours to get to the pass, do the drive, and return to Danang.

BA NA HILL STATION

West of Danang and 1,487 meters above sea level, **Ba Na Hill Station** (37 kilometers west of Danang, tel. 0236/374-9888, www.banahills.sunworld.vn, 7:30am-9pm daily, cable car VND650,000) is the central provinces' answer to Dalat. Since the early 1900s, this French-established resort has served as a rustic getaway for the well-to-do of Danang and Hue, complete with beautiful mountain vistas and a much cooler climate than the coast. In its heyday, Ba Na was on the verge of becoming a proper town, outfitted with schools, post offices, hotels, and restaurants. While its long-term residents have dwindled to almost zero, this mountaintop retreat remains a popular domestic tourist destination best known for its scenic cable car ascent, one of the world's longest (and a Guinness World Record holder), as well as Linh Ung Pagoda, one of a trio of Buddhist worship halls of the same name in the region. In recent years, the cable car operator, Sun Group, has also added theme park-like attractions such as an arcade, amusement rides, and a wine cave—all free with the cable car ticket—as well as some other attractions that cost extra, like a wax museum (VND90,000).

In addition to its record-breaking Toc Tien-L'Indochine line, Ba Na now boasts a network of five cable car routes, which lead visitors to different attractions on the hillside. Be mindful of departure times, as different routes have different hours of operation, and there are breaks in service throughout the day. Those heading to Ba Na for the scenery would do best to take the Toc Tien-L'Indochine line, but other routes also lead up to the summit, albeit with stopovers at some of Ba Na Hills' other attractions. Once at the summit, the principal attraction is the scenery. There's also a resort for overnight guests, but day trips are

recommended, as the actual hill station does not provide much in the way of activities.

If you've got your own wheels, it's possible to drive to the Ba Na cable car, though it can be tricky to find. You can also hire a taxi at a fixed rate, usually VND500,000-900,000; the driver will have to wait for you at the bottom. The base of the cable car is roughly 27 kilometers west of town. Tickets can be purchased in both Danang and Hoi An. The **Ba Na tour company** (93 Nguyen Van Linh, Danang, tel. 09/0576-6777, www.banahills.sunworld.vn, 8am-5pm daily) can assist with queries.

LANG CO

Wedged between a freshwater lagoon on one side and the East Sea on the other, Lang Co is a sleepy fishing village built around a 10-kilometer stretch of Highway 1 and hidden from view by the Truong Son Mountains. Its beautiful combination of saltwater and freshwater, lush green hills, and sandy beaches make this an increasingly popular spot for budget travelers and resort-goers alike to enjoy a more unassuming destination, where things are still quiet and the main attraction is the beach. Most visitors stick around just for the day or overnight, long enough to get in some sunbathing before continuing on to other destinations like the tourist-heavy Hoi An or bustling Hue.

Thanks to its proximity to Danang, a visit to Lang Co can be done as a day trip. The drive to and from the city is just over an hour. With the awe-inspiring Hai Van Pass in between, the journey itself is part of the fun. If possible, try to time your visit in March-August, the warmer, drier months. Rainy season, September-February, can be cold and gray, with temperatures as low as the mid-60s and high winds. July and August see sweltering temperatures.

Beaches

The one and only reason travelers stop in Lang Co is for its beach. While the shores of this small fishing village are not unlike those of My Khe in Danang, Lang Co offers a cheaper, more local option that some prefer over its busier southern neighbors. The 10 kilometers of sand along the eastern edge of **Lang Co Beach** are pleasantly deserted, though not without some rubbish. A handful of restaurants are accessible from the beach. From the main road, it's easy to find Lang Co Beach.

Food

Beyond the eateries attached to various beach resorts, a slew of cookie-cutter rice and noodle stalls line either side of Lac Long Quan, along with a few local truck-stop restaurants. To enjoy the view, take a stroll down the road along the lagoon, where you'll find several small coffee stands from which to admire the lagoon and the surrounding mountains.

A collection of stalls along the town's main road sell **rice and noodle dishes** (Lac Long Quan between Minh Nguyet Guesthouse and Lang Co Beach Resort, VND15,000-80,000), from the spicy *bun bo Hue* (soup with beef and rice noodles) to *bun thit nuong* (a dry noodle dish accompanied by grilled pork and the occasional fried spring roll) to your standard pick-and-point rice offerings. These are the most inexpensive options; shop around at a variety of stalls before settling upon your preferred dish. These stalls usually open and close earlier than restaurants.

For a solid meal, the folks at **Minh Tam** (Lac Long Quan, tel. 012/8272-9203, 6:30am-10pm daily, VND50,000-80,000) serve well-executed rice and noodle staples alongside chicken, pork, beef, or seafood. The jovial owner can also help with travel-related questions, as English speakers are few and far between in this town.

Accommodations

For the most part, lodgings in Lang Co are significantly less expensive than Danang. Be prepared for a little less luxury than you might find in a larger place. Budget accommodations are basic and acceptable for a day or two while you're out enjoying the sun. Not all hotels and guesthouses have English-speaking staff.

Lang Co

UNDER VND210,000

Just opposite Lang Co Beach Resort, **Chi Na Guesthouse** (396 Lac Long Quan, tel. 0234/387-4597, VND160,000-200,000) is run by an inviting family and offers decent rooms close to both the lagoon and the beach. The accommodations, with basic furnishings, hot water, air-conditioning, and TV, are right for the price. The proprietors are more than willing to help with onward bus transportation and local recommendations.

A few doors down from the mammoth Thanh Tam Resort is **Minh Nguyet Guesthouse** (Lac Long Quan, tel. 09/8511-5690, VND200,000), another basic place with friendly owners and a clean bath, comfortable beds, hot water, air-conditioning, and TV. Beach access is about 100 meters from the front steps and, depending upon the season and the length of your stay, you may be able to talk down the price; though even at VND200,000, the rooms are agreeable.

VND210,000-525,000

The **Quynh Lien Hotel** (Loan Ly, Lac Long Quan, tel. 0234/387-3429, VND350,000-550,000) may be flashier than the droves of guesthouses along Lac Long Quan, but its proprietors are slightly less inviting. Rooms are spacious and feature air-conditioning, hot water, and TV. While some lodgings are without windows, the reception area has great views of the nearby lagoon and the beach is within walking distance of the hotel.

VND1,050,000-2,100,000

A collection of nice semidetached villa accommodations, the **Lang Co Beach Resort** (463 Lac Long Quan, tel. 0234/387-3555, www.langcobeachresort.com.vn, VND800,000-3,975,000, breakfast included) sits directly on the beach and features spacious rooms with floor-to-ceiling windows, air-conditioning, hot water, TV, mosquito nets, and an in-room safe. Accommodations vary in price with proximity to the ocean, with both garden and beach views available. The resort also counts a restaurant and a swimming pool for guests in its offerings.

Information and Services

The small community of Lang Co takes up no more than a few kilometers along the coast, so ATMs are less common. Bring enough cash to last you through to your next destination rather than fuss with money machines in this area, though there are a handful of machines along the highway.

While several places in town advertise Wi-Fi Internet, connections are weak at best. Be prepared to have technical difficulties getting online. Your hotel may be able to help, but if you require a connection, your best bet is to head into town near the southern end of the isthmus.

There are no medical care facilities equipped to deal with even minor illnesses or injuries. For any emergencies, the nearest hospital is in Danang.

Getting There

Lang Co may be a short distance from Danang, but the two places are separated by the steep and spiraling Hai Van Pass. Travelers can scale the winding road and incorporate this stunning section of the coast into their trip, or opt for a ride through the Hai Van Tunnel. Buses and other large vehicles will almost always take the tunnel; the pass, while beautiful, is decidedly less safe for large vehicles. If you're on a motorbike and driving during the day, you should take Hai Van Pass, as this is one of the most beautiful coastal roads in Vietnam.

Driving through the tunnel via motorbike is not permitted due to its size. Instead, drivers must buy a **motorbike ticket** (VND30,000) and a **bus ticket** (VND10,000), which ensures the passage of both you and your vehicle through to the other side. Vehicles are strapped onto a truck that makes the journey through the narrow passageway, while you hop on a bus to get to the other side. This service runs 5:30am-9pm daily with vehicles departing every 15-30 minutes.

If you're not up for driving on your own, it is possible to hire one of the Easy Rider-style *xe om* drivers from the city to take you over the pass. It costs more than your average ride (VND600,000-800,000 from Danang) since the distance is greater and requires trickier driving.

BUS

From the Danang bus station (159 Ton Duc Thang, tel. 0236/376-7679), local buses to Hue depart regularly (6am-6pm daily). Jump on one of these buses and notify the fee collector that you'd like to get off at **Lang Co** (20-30 minutes, VND70,000). The collector will alert you when you arrive at Lang Co's main strip. Check the fare board at the Danang bus station to verify the cost.

TRAIN

Lang Co's **train station** (south of Lang Co Bridge, tel. 0234/387-4423, 7am-5pm daily) is about 1.5 kilometers from the beach and only a few stops from the Danang station (200 Hai Phong, tel. 0236/382-3810, 7am-5pm daily). Its route around Hai Van is especially beautiful, hugging the base of the mountain as it brushes the shore. Trips to and from Danang run about 1.5 hours and cost VND30,000-40,000. There's just one train to Lang Co each morning at 6:40am. From Hue, travelers can reach Lang Co on the 6:50am train. Tickets range from VND31,000-80,000 and the trip takes about 1.5 hours. When it comes to purchasing tickets for onward travel, try to do this online or at another train station, as the Lang Co station's ticket counter is not consistently open.

Getting Around

Most accommodations are within walking distance of the beach, and you'll find restaurants and other services along Lac Long Quan, the main road, or at your resort. If you're heading somewhere farther afield, your only real option is to jump in a **Thanh Cong Taxi** (tel. 0234/357-5757). It's doubtful that you'll catch *xe om* drivers loitering on this route; if you pop into a restaurant or shop and ask, they may be able to connect you with a driver. There are no official rental shops in Lang Co. Ask your hotel if they have bicycles or motorbikes to rent out.

Hoi An

TOP EXPERIENCE

Crisscrossing the riverfront and drenched in a vibrant saffron yellow, Hoi An is easily the most photogenic town in the country. Now a major stop on the tourist trail, its charming wooden houses and colorful lanterns remain a few centuries in the past, stuck in Hoi An's heyday as a famous trading port. While business has changed—the town makes its living off a thriving tourism industry and an army of skilled tailors, who can turn around a silk dress or three-piece suit in a matter of hours—locals hold steadfastly to their traditions, and there is a great sense of pride in the cultural preservation of Hoi An. For visitors, the picturesque old town, a nearby beach, and the best shopping in the country are major draws.

The area's first inhabitants, the Sa Huynh, existed a few thousand years ago. They were followed by the Champa kingdom, a powerful empire that set up religious, political, and economic centers in and around Hoi An. From the 2nd century up through the 14th, the Thu Bon River was used to facilitate trade with nearby kingdoms. In the early 1300s, a Cham king married a Vietnamese princess, gifting the province of Quang Nam to the Vietnamese. Shortly thereafter, the king died and his successor refused to honor the arrangement, angering the Dai Viet, who promptly entered into a war with their southern neighbors that continued for much of the next century.

By the time the 16th century rolled around, trading in Hoi An was back in full swing, with Chinese and Japanese merchants setting up shop on the shores of what was then known as Faifo. This golden age lasted until the 19th century, when the Thu Bon River became too shallow for large trading ships to enter the port. Throughout the next few centuries, Hoi An's original buildings endured, later serving as an administrative center for the French during colonial rule.

Officially recognized as a UNESCO World Heritage site, downtown Hoi An sees over a million tourists each year, sending its modest population through the roof during high season (mid-Nov.-Feb.). While the best time to visit is March-June, when the rains have dried up, this town sees a constant stream of visitors year-round, even in August, its hottest month, and during rainy season, when typhoons and flooding are not uncommon. In November especially, you'll find parts of the old town underwater and locals in rain ponchos plying the roads in wooden canoes.

Once you've had your fill of the colorful old town, there is a host of attractions waiting in the countryside beyond downtown Hoi An, from the crumbling temples of My Son to the sunny shores of An Bang. Many travelers

Hoi An

Cam Kim Island

CAM PHO COMMUNAL HOUSE

TICKET BOOTH

BUS TO DANANG

HOI AN SILK VILLAGE

PHUOC LAM PAGODA

HUNG VUONG

HAI BA TRUNG

LE HONG PHONG

SEE DETAIL

TRAN PHU

BACH DANG

SEE "OLD TOWN HOI AN" MAP

HOI AN'S OLD TOWN

TRAN HUNG DAO

LY THUONG KIET

LY THAI TO

BABY MUSTARD RESTAURANT

HAI BA TRUNG

TRA QUE VEGETABLE VILLAGE

TOMB OF TANI YAJIROBEI

HAI AU HOTEL

VAIA BOUTIQUE HOTEL

TRAN PHU

CUA DAI

SUNFLOWER HOTEL

THE EARTH VILLA

HOI AN

DINGO DELI

LOTUS HOTEL

HOI AN CHIC

LAC LONG QUAN

TRAN NHAN TONG

TON VAN SUONG

CUA DAI

GREEN BAMBOO

CUA DAI

LY THUONG KIET

Cua Dai Beach

CHAM ISLAND FERRY

0   25 km
0   25 mi

© AVALON TRAVEL

THIEN THANH HOTEL

PHAT TIRE VENTURES

THIEN NGA

BA TRIEU

HAI BA TRUNG

TRAN CAO VAN

LY THUONG KIET

MINH HIEN VEGETARIAN

CAFE 43

HOA MY HOTEL

TRAN PHU

SINH TOURIST

TASTE OF HOI AN

rent bicycles, getting lost down countryside alleys and amid stunning rice fields. Danang lies only 29 kilometers north of Hoi An, making all of the attractions between these two destinations easily reached on a day trip from town.

SIGHTS

The majority of Hoi An's most famous sights are packed into a few blocks north of the riverfront, making this one of the most walkable destinations in the country. From Bach Dang to Tran Phu, this neighborhood can easily be covered in an afternoon, and thanks to a local traffic ordinance, these streets are **pedestrian-only** (9am-11am and 3pm-9:30pm daily) at certain times. Outside of these hours, drivers race kamikaze-style through the narrow roads, which are often still filled with pedestrians.

In the old town area, respectful dress is a must, as Hoi An is big on tradition. Local temples and pagodas enforce this requirement more than most. No matter the temperature, stick to long pants and covered shoulders when exploring the town's sights.

As you reach the outskirts of the old town area, you'll notice that the barriers that prohibit motor vehicles from entering often read "ticket requested area." Expect to show a ticket when visiting one of the museums, meeting halls, or other sights covered by the UNESCO ticket. Your ticket is technically valid for 24 hours, but enforcement of this time frame is pretty lax; you should be able to use your ticket over two days without any trouble.

★ Old Town

The small riverfront **old town** (Bach Dang north to Tran Phu) remains frozen in its heyday, lined with vivid centuries-old wooden houses, zigzagging Chinese lanterns, and a menagerie of decorative animals perched atop the roofs of local pagodas and meeting halls.

Several common architectural traits appear in most houses and traditional buildings. Above the front door of a building, you'll often find a pair of intricately carved wooden dials: These are the eyes of the house, meant to watch over its residents and protect the building from evil. Along the ceiling, particularly at the front of a structure, five vertical wooden beams are meant to signify the elements: earth, water, fire, metal, and wood. These intersect with another trio of beams that run horizontally and mirror the three lines in the palm of your hand, which stand for heaven, earth, and human beings. Each building is long and narrow, extending from the reception area back into an open-roofed central courtyard, which is instrumental in cooling the house during Hoi An's sweltering summer months. Still deeper, the living quarters of the family sit at the back of the building, sheltered by a small second-floor storage space, which gets put to good use in October and November, when floods swallow the ground floor of houses along the riverfront and all of the family's possessions are moved upstairs.

While locals are accustomed to the rising waters, occasionally the wear and tear necessitates renovations, which can be an ordeal when your home is 200 years old. In order to maintain the identity of the neighborhood, old town houses must be repaired using the same 18th-century materials and construction methods by which they were built. In some cases, the wooden framework within a house is completely disassembled in order to repair just one column. Finding skilled craftspeople and traditional materials can be a tough and costly chore, but this is precisely what your ticket fee goes to. Families in need of building renovation are expected to front a percentage of the costs, usually about half, while the rest is funded by the local government and profits from ticket sales.

Nearly all of the historical monuments within Hoi An's old town are accessible with a **UNESCO ticket** (VND120,000), whose proceeds go to the preservation and maintenance of the neighborhood's sights. Travelers can purchase an entry ticket, which grants access to a total of five monuments within the neighborhood, at any of the ticket booths

Old Town Hoi An

BÀ TRIỆU

HAI BÀ TRƯNG

HOA BINH HOTEL

VINH HUNG LIBRARY HOTEL

TRẦN CAO VÂN

NGUYỄN TRƯỜNG TỘ

MADAME KHANH BANH MI

TRẦN HƯNG ĐẠO

BLUE CORAL DIVING

LÊ LỢI

VIETIN BANK

BA LE WELL

BA LE WELL RESTAURANT

HAI BÀ TRƯNG

TRAN FAMILY CHAPEL

PHAN CHÂU TRINH

LIFESTART FOUNDATION WORKSHOP

TRẦN PHÚ

CANTONESE ASSEMBLY HALL

TICKET BOOTH 5

DAM VEGETARIAN

71 ĐƯỜNG PHAN CHÂU TRINH

FUJIAN ASSEMBLY HALL

MUSEUM OF SA HUYNH CULTURE

HAI BÀ TRƯNG

REACHING OUT TEA HOUSE

KAZIK SQUARE

NGU BANG ASSEMBLY HALL

JAPANESE COVERED BRIDGE

TICKET BOOTH/ATM

MUSEUM OF TRADE CERAMICS

TICKET BOOTH

TRẦN PHÚ

DUC AN ANCIENT HOUSE

HOI AN ROASTERY

BANH BEO

YALY COUTURE

VINH HUNG HERITAGE HOTEL

MORNING GLORY TASTE OF HOI AN

DIVE BAR

LÊ LỢI

BEFORE 'N NOW

HOI AN'S OLD TOWN

Q BAR

DIEP DONG NGUYEN ANCIENT HOUSE

NGUYỄN THÁI HỌC

GEMSTONES ART MUSEUM

NGUYỄN THÁI HỌC

HOANG KIM TAILOR

AN HỘI BRIDGE

CARGO CLUB

SILK ROAD

YALY COUTURE

MEMORY

WHITE MARBLE WINE BAR

BẠCH ĐẰNG

HOI AN TRADITIONAL PERFORMANCE HOUSE

MANGO MANGO

TAN KY ANCIENT HOUSE

NGUYỄN PHÚC CHU

REACHING OUT WORKSHOP

THE O COLLECTIVE

NGUYỄN HOÀNG

NGUYỄN PHÚC TẤN

LƯU QUÝ KỲ

NGÔ QUYỀN

HEAVEN & EARTH BICYCLE TOURS HEAD OFFICE

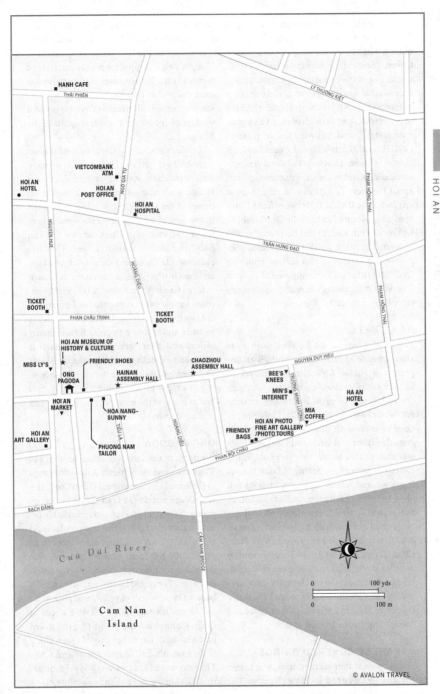

HANH CAFE

THÁI PHIÊN

LY THƯỜNG KIỆT

PHẠM HÔNG THÁI

HOI AN
HOTEL

VIETCOMBANK
ATM

HOI AN
POST OFFICE

NGÔ GIA TỰ

HOI AN
HOSPITAL

NGUYỄN HUỆ

HOÀNG DIỆU

TRÂN HƯNG ĐẠO

PHẠM HÔNG THÁI

TICKET
BOOTH

PHAN CHÂU TRINH

TICKET
BOOTH

MISS LY'S

HOI AN MUSEUM OF
HISTORY & CULTURE

FRIENDLY SHOES

ONG
PAGODA

HAINAN
ASSEMBLY HALL

CHAOZHOU
ASSEMBLY HALL

NGUYỄN DUY HIỆU

BEE'S
KNEES

MIN'S
INTERNET

HA AN
HOTEL

HOI AN
MARKET

HOA NANG-
SUNNY

TIÊU LA

PHƯƠNG MINH LƯỢNG

MIA
COFFEE

HOI AN
ART GALLERY

PHUONG NAM
TAILOR

FRIENDLY
BAGS

HOI AN PHOTO
FINE ART GALLERY
/PHOTO TOURS

PHAN BỘI CHÂU

HOÀNG DIỆU

BẠCH ĐẰNG

CAM NAM BRIDGE

Cua Dai River

Cam Nam
Island

0   100 yds
0   100 m

© AVALON TRAVEL

around the old town. Visitors create their own itinerary. In order to get the gist of what the old town has to offer, swing by the Japanese Covered Bridge (Hoi An's most famous landmark), one of the Chinese congregation halls, a traditional house, a museum, and one other monument of your choosing. If you're looking to get the full story on each of Hoi An's sights, enthusiastic and knowledgeable **guides** (VND125,000) can be hired from the ticket booths. Guides provide additional recommendations and other informational tidbits about the area. Tickets can be purchased at any one of the **UNESCO ticket offices** (7am-6pm daily), located at 12 Phan Chu Trinh, 78 Le Loi, 37 Tran Phu, 19 Hai Ba Trung, and 52 Nguyen Thi Minh Khai. Unless stated otherwise, the listings in this section require a UNESCO ticket and are supposed to be open 7am-9pm daily, though in reality some sights close earlier, around 5:30pm-6pm.

BA LE WELL

The locally famous **Ba Le Well** (down the alley opposite 35 Phan Chau Trinh) is an important part of Hoi An's culinary history: This ancient water source—dug by the Cham in the 10th century—provides the key ingredient in *cao lau*, a local specialty. Only *cao lau* noodles made with this particular water are considered the real deal, and local residents take their *cao lau* recipes very seriously. Water collectors gather here during the day, throwing down and retrieving plastic buckets full of Ba Le water to sell to restaurants and other businesses. To find the modest well, nothing more than a stone opening behind a house, head down the narrow alley opposite 35 Phan Chau Trinh, past Ba Le Well restaurant, a popular street food spot, and make a right. It's easy to miss, as the well is pretty unassuming, but you should be able to spot the water collectors first. Ba Le Well is a free sight, and doesn't require the UNESCO ticket.

JAPANESE COVERED BRIDGE

Hoi An's most famous landmark, the iconic **Japanese Covered Bridge** (Nguyen Thi Minh Khai) is among the oldest structures in town, dating back to the early 17th century, when the Chinese and Japanese quarters of Hoi An's thriving port were separated by a narrow inlet. Its beautiful exterior and age have made this wooden footbridge a popular photo spot. Shutterbugs vie for a good vantage point on the street just south of the bridge.

Inside, a pair of dog statues guard the entrance. These statues, along with the monkey statues watching over the western side of the bridge, are historical markers: Construction began in the year of the monkey and ended in the year of the dog. From the open side of the bridge, visitors can look out over the Thu Bon River and the western edge of Hoi An's old town. On the other side, you'll find a later addition by the Chinese community. Known as Chua Cau in Vietnamese, this modest, one-room temple pays homage to the Emperor of the North, Tran Vo Bac De, who controls the weather and is thus a popular figure among sailors and fisherfolk. The bridge itself is short, and a quick glimpse into the temple reveals much of its ornamentation. Those hoping to snap a photo should visit early; this bridge is one of the most documented corners of the old town.

ONG PAGODA

While there are dozens of other buildings in Vietnam—and throughout Asia—dedicated to the famed Chinese general Quan Cong, Hoi An's **Ong Pagoda** (24 Tran Phu), directly opposite the central market, is a remarkably ornate version that still welcomes regular local visitors. Hoi An residents often stop in to pray to the red-faced bearded general, who is known for his courage and strong moral character. The pagoda's exterior, built in 1653, boasts a vivid splash of yellow and pink.

The main altar holds a massive statue of Quan Cong, his long beard trailing down past his waist. On either side of Quan Cong is Quan Binh, his adoptive son, and Chau Thuong, one of Quan Cong's loyal mandarins. His horses, one red and one white, flank the three men, making for a crowded and colorful scene.

HOI AN'S ANCIENT HOUSES

The long-and-narrow yellow-hued buildings of the old town exist as they did in centuries past. Thanks to local preservation efforts and the town's UNESCO status, these houses are required to maintain their original architecture, which accounts in large part for the neighborhood's charm. While visitors can see the telltale signs of 18th- and 19th-century architecture in every tailor and souvenir shop around the old town, a handful of its more storied ancient residences are open for UNESCO ticket-holders to explore. These family-owned houses have been maintained by generations of Hoi An residents and carry a great deal of history alongside their traditional design and building methods.

With over 90 percent of its original structure still intact, **Tan Ky House** (101 Nguyen Thai Hoc) is a prime example of traditional Hoi An architecture. Thick, wooden columns and sunbaked tile floors appear throughout the house, punctuated by its central courtyard, a natural ventilator and a feature of the house's feng shui. Up front, the seventh-generation owners greet their daily visitors with a cup of tea and a brief rundown of the house's history. Beyond the courtyard, walk to the far end of the 30-meter-long house to the place where Tan Ky opens onto the river, once allowing for easy transportation of the former merchant family's goods. When floods overtake much of the old town during October and November, everything goes upstairs by way of a pulley system, hidden in the attic. Along the far wall you can see where the family has documented the level of these floodwaters in years past.

Another relic of centuries past, the most recent incarnation of **Duc An House** (129 Tran Phu) was built in 1850. The land on which it stands has been in the family for roughly 400 years. Once a well-known bookstore in Hoi An, the former shop stocked a host of Vietnamese and Chinese books and served as an important base for Communist activity during the French resistance, in which former resident Cao Hong Lanh was an important local player. Another revolutionary great, Phan Chau Trinh, also regularly dropped by the house. Duc An was later converted into a Chinese pharmacy in the 20th century.

With a blend of Japanese, Chinese, and Vietnamese influences, the **Diep Dong Nguyen House** (80 Nguyen Thai Hoc) sits a block north of the river and houses a generous collection of coins and ceramics, some of which date back generations. The building, constructed in the late 19th century, once served as a pharmacy for traditional medicine and is easy to spot for the large Buddha emblazoned on the front facade.

TRAN FAMILY CHAPEL

Unlike Hoi An's other traditional houses, none of the residents at the **Tran Family Chapel** (21 Le Loi) are among the living. Rather, this small, dimly lit structure honors several generations of a wealthy local family, whose 19th-century relative commissioned the building over 200 years ago. From the entrance gate, a sparse garden takes up the first half of the property, lined with a few ornamental trees and other greenery. The front of the house bears a Chinese-style trio of doors with one large central entryway flanked by two smaller ones. According to custom, the left door is meant for men, the right for women, and the middle for spirits. The middle door is only opened for the Lunar New Year and the death anniversaries of relatives, during which time the ancestors are able to pass in and out of the building.

Inside, you'll be invited to sit in the reception area, where a family member gives you a quick tour of the building and its many features. The reception room boasts the most noteworthy architecture, with Chinese, Japanese, and Vietnamese influences present in the wooden beams running along the ceiling and the house's front facade. Throughout the building, great emphasis is placed upon yin and yang. Beyond the front room lies the familial altar, a large high table bearing a series of simple painted wooden boxes. These contain the ashes of generations of the Tran family. Because Vietnamese culture celebrates a person's date of death, the boxes are opened on each ancestor's death anniversary for prayers and offerings. To the right of the altar, you'll find still more members of the Tran family in the photographs that line the wall, as well as the family tree book, penned in Chinese script, on a table in the corner. Keep an eye out for the yin-yang coins as well, which sit in a bowl near the ancestral shrine.

CHINESE ASSEMBLY HALLS

Spread throughout the old town are Hoi An's five bright and colorful assembly halls, each built by a different community of Chinese settlers. Hailing from Fujian, Canton, Hainan, and Guangdong provinces in China, each individual group has its own dialect and local traditions, all of which were preserved during Hoi An's heyday through regular gatherings at these ornate halls, where trade and business arrangements were often discussed within the community and deities from each respective province were worshipped. In addition to these four provincial assembly halls, a fifth building held gatherings for all Chinese residents, whose numbers swelled in the 17th century as refugees from southern China fled the country's civil war, settling in Vietnam by the thousands.

Separated from the street by a generous walkway, the **Fujian Assembly Hall (Hoi Quan Phuoc Kien)** (46 Tran Phu) is a swirl of vivid colors, mosaic animals, lavish altars, and grand facades. Originally built in 1697 as the Vietnamese Kim Son Pagoda, its current incarnation was completed in 1757 and, while no longer used as a meeting hall, continues to attract plenty of visitors thanks to its design. Inside, three main altars take up the far end of the building, the middle of which features a group of six Fujianese mandarins who were loyal to the Ming dynasty. As civil war broke out in China in the mid-17th century, these

the detailed roof of the Hainan Assembly Hall

men attempted to avenge the fall of their beloved emperor but failed; they are now honored on the 16th day of the second lunar month each year. To the left, you'll find the god of prosperity, a popular fixture in most Chinese halls, and on your right are the three goddesses of fertility and 12 midwives, all of whom are visited by couples hoping to conceive. Behind each of the three altars is a mosaic animal: the phoenix for female beauty, the unicorn for male strength, and the dragon for royal power. A large wooden replica of a merchant boat is featured in the building, which sailors and fishermen often visited before heading out to sea.

Not far from the Japanese bridge, Hoi An's **Cantonese Assembly Hall (Hoi Quan Quang Trieu)** (176 Tran Phu) is a riot of color packed into a small space. From its busy rooftop decorations to the vivid murals along its wall or the enormous, slow-burn incense coils winding down from the ceiling, this is one of the old town's most eye-catching assembly halls. Built in 1885, the main altars pay homage to Chinese general Quan Cong, flanked by a pair of horses, as well as Thien Hau, goddess of the sea.

Ngu Bang Assembly Hall (64 Tran Phu) once united all of the local Chinese communities under one intricate, brightly hued roof. Built in 1741, the hall worships Thien Hau, goddess of the sea and a vital deity for those who do business on the water. Ngu Bang features ample decoration as well as several smaller altars to Confucius, Chinese revolutionary Sun Yat-Sen, and a group of Chinese soldiers killed by the Japanese during World War II conflicts in Vietnam.

HAINAN ASSEMBLY HALL

Though it's not as big or ornamental as some of its old-town counterparts, the **Hainan Assembly Hall** (Hai Nam, 10 Tran Phu, sunrise-sunset daily) comes with an interesting story. Constructed by members of the local Hainan community, the altar at this assembly hall honors 108 Chinese sailors who suffered at the hands of sea captain Ton That Thieu. On July 16, 1851, Captain Thieu's naval ship happened on three merchant vessels, belonging to local Hainan immigrants, off the coast of Quang Ngai province. The captain attacked, firing shots and later boarding the vessels to loot and kill. Though it would eventually become clear that the sailors were innocent, Captain Ton That Thieu ordered his men to kill them all; only one of the 108 survived. In order to cover up his actions, the captain painted the fishing boats black and reported to Emperor Tu Duc that he had found and captured a group of pirate ships. The emperor later uncovered the truth, and the families of the Hainan sailors received reparations and permission to construct the hall, which now houses a set of large lacquered wooden tablets in honor of the deceased.

The front of the property has been converted into a miniature souvenir shop. The building's architecture, from its brightly hued wooden columns to the intricate rooftop designs, is worth a look.

MUSEUM OF FOLK CULTURE

Housed in the largest wooden building in the old town, Hoi An's **Museum of Folk Culture** (33 Nguyen Thai Hoc) runs a full 57 meters from Nguyen Thai Hoc to the waterfront Bach Dang and displays the artifacts and everyday items of the town's traditional occupations as well as its vibrant performing arts scene.

MUSEUM OF SA HUYNH CULTURE

Essentially a one-room exhibition, the **Museum of Sa Huynh Culture** (149 Tran Phu) provides interesting insight into central Vietnam's first documented culture. Displays include ancient pottery, burial jars, primitive tools, and jewelry, most of which dates back to the Iron Age. There's not a great deal of signage to orient visitors.

MUSEUM OF TRADE CERAMICS

The **Museum of Trade Ceramics** (80 Tran Phu) revisits Hoi An's glory days as a successful port by displaying the array of pottery and ceramics that passed through the town during its busiest years. Artifacts date back as early as the 13th century and hail from all over Asia, including Thailand, China, and Japan. Each exhibit includes information on the pieces displayed, and visitors are free to wander through the spacious old building.

Beyond Old Town
PHUOC LAM PAGODA

Anyone armed with a bicycle and some spare time will appreciate a wander around **Phuoc Lam Pagoda** (Thon 2, Cam Ha, sunrise-sunset daily, free). Now a few centuries old, this elaborate building, all colorful mosaics and detailed paintings, enjoys relative obscurity, with most visitors sticking to the old town rather than venturing farther afield. Locals, too, seem to have forgotten the place, but that doesn't take away from its impressive decoration and aging beauty. Nestled among the foliage of Phuoc Lam is a collection of gravestones—some old, some new—bearing the names of former monks. The interior of the pagoda is not often open, but the few monks who still live here are a welcoming bunch. Dress respectfully, as this is a more traditional pagoda than most.

CAM KIM ISLAND

When you tire of the heckling and cries of street vendors around Hoi An's old town, the large and beautiful **Cam Kim Island** is a perfect escape from the tourist trail. Just a 15-minute ferry ride away, this peaceful farming community trades the bustle of the old town for verdant rice paddies and gracefully aging pagodas. The best thing to do on Cam Kim is bring a bicycle and get lost down the many narrow concrete roads of the island. The locals are an inviting bunch and quick to offer a "hello" or a smile, and some of the younger residents speak English well. With pretty scenery and a pleasant atmosphere, this is a great place for a morning cycle or a late afternoon wander.

To get to the island, hop on a **ferry** (near corner of Bach Dang and Hoang Van Thu, sunrise-sunset daily, VND20,000-50,000) from the riverfront. There is no fixed fee for a ride across the Thu Bon so you may be forced to haggle. Expect to pay up to VND 50,000 pp. The best thing you can do is ask the fee before boarding and, should your driver attempt to overcharge you, politely state the price you're willing to pay. If this price is met with any resistance, keep your cool, appear disinterested and say you'll wait. In most cases, the boat drivers fold quickly. Once you've agreed upon a fee, jump on board with your bicycle and enjoy the ride.

Traditional Villages

A traditional village is a small community that has a long history of trading in one particular skill or handicraft. There are traditional villages all over Vietnam, some of which date back centuries. Typically, traditional villages focus on handicrafts like lacquer, silk, and ceramics, but there are occasionally outliers like Tra Que, which is known for its fresh produce.

TRA QUE VEGETABLE VILLAGE

A longtime farming community, the sleepy **Tra Que vegetable village** (4 kilometers north of Hoi An on Hai Ba Trung, 8am-5pm daily, VND20,000) has been cultivating its fresh green produce for the better part of a century. Organized into neat plots of lettuce and basil, cabbage and coriander, Tra Que's gardens use a special kind of algae found in the nearby river, which fertilizes the soil and, according to locals, accounts for the area's

the ornate roof of Phuoc Lam Pagoda

superior vegetables. Nowadays, in addition to moving heaps of green goods at the market, the farmers of Tra Que have taken advantage of their photogenic fields and famed veggies by inviting outsiders in for a visit. Fee collectors are pretty lax about enforcing ticket purchases, so don't worry if no one stops you on your way in. Tour groups regularly make the trip, often by bicycle, to wander the narrow brick lanes that run through Tra Que's fields and enjoy a meal.

Veering off Hai Ba Trung, the entrance into Tra Que has a few local restaurants, but the best, located on the other side of Hai Ba Trung, is **Baby Mustard (Nha Hang Cai Con)** (Tra Que, tel. 09/3572-5740, babymustard.restaurant@gmail.com, 11am-9pm daily, VND35,000-120,000). With a modest set of bamboo tables and chairs, this tiny spot cooks up stellar local food, namely its mouthwatering *banh xeo* (savory Vietnamese pancakes). A variety of fish and shrimp dishes make it onto the small menu, along with some vegetarian options. The friendly proprietor is happy to recommend a dish or explain its ingredients. The greens come straight from the fields surrounding the restaurant, and a nice breeze moves through its open-air

seating area, making this the perfect spot to sit and enjoy a local lunch or an afternoon drink. Personalized **cooking classes** (VND455,000-500,000) are also offered.

Most travelers prefer to take the scenic route to Tra Que, opting for a leisurely cycle along Hai Ba Trung past paddy fields and lazy rivers, an easy ride to do without the aid of a guide. On this road is the **tomb of Tani Yajirobei,** a Japanese merchant who lived in Hoi An during the 17th century and allegedly took a Vietnamese lover. Though it's easy to miss, look for a placard and small stone marker on the roadside that directs you to the gravesite in the middle of a vast low-lying paddy field. The tomb is an interesting piece of local history and offers some particularly nice views of the surrounding area.

Taxis and *xe om* can also easily make the trip to Tra Que for VND60,000 and VND40,000, respectively. You should be able to find transportation back into town, so there's no need to ask the driver to wait for you. The village charges a VND20,000 entry fee via the ticket booth just before the village's small roads, though enforcement is very lax. If no one is there on your way in, feel free to wander around anyway.

Tra Que vegetable village

THANH HA POTTERY VILLAGE

A centuries-old vocational community, the expert craftspeople of **Thanh Ha pottery village** (5 kilometers west of Hoi An, 8am-6pm daily, VND25,000) continue to fashion many of the same pots, jars, and dishes as in the Nguyen dynasty, along with a few updated items, like piggy banks, whistles, and other small trinkets. With no more than a pottery wheel and a bit of clay, local potters can produce up to 300 jars in a single day, which then sit in the sun to dry before being placed in front of a wood fire. These items are shelved and sold within the village or shipped outside to other locations throughout Vietnam.

The best way to visit Thanh Ha is by bicycle, as you get to enjoy the countryside landscapes en route, and it's easiest to navigate the narrow brick lanes of the area either on two wheels or on foot. Before you reach the end of the road leading to Thanh Ha, you'll pass a small ticket booth out front. Depending on when you arrive, you may not find anyone on duty and may not be able to pay the ticket price. (If this happens, go ahead and enter, but be sure to buy something from one of the vendors during your visit.) If you continue past the booth, this wider asphalt road turns into a concrete alley. Hang a left when you spot a brick lane, otherwise you'll pass the village entirely and wind up next to a nearby river.

Inside, visitors are free to roam around, peeking in on the small workshops of Thanh Ha. Some of the potters speak a bit of English, though don't expect a lengthy conversation. You may also get a chance to try your hand at the pottery wheel for free; when this happens you are usually expected to buy something from that shop.

HOI AN SILK VILLAGE

While this isn't technically a village so much as a tourist attraction, the **Hoi An silk village** (28 Nguyen Tat Thanh, tel. 0235/392-1144, www.hoiansilkvillage.com, 8am-4pm daily, short tour VND100,000, long tour VND400,000) continues the region's traditional methods of silk-making. For a fee, you can have a guide steer you through the complex's many buildings, where you'll learn about the silk-making process from start to finish, meet a few dozen silkworms, check out the 100-year-old collection of *ao dai* (traditional garment of Vietnam) on display, witness the dizzying speed of a Vietnamese loom, and learn how to tell genuine silk from its impostors.

The short tour runs around 45 minutes. The longer version takes over an hour, including lunch and the opportunity to try your hand at feeding the silkworms and, later, spinning their cocoons into thread. At the end, you'll have an opportunity to peruse the silk shop, which features handmade items using traditional silk-making methods. This is a fun opportunity to learn about garment-making and Hoi An history.

Tours

While only the original half-day trip offered by **Hoi An Free Tours** (tel. 012/0603-0551, www.hoianfreetour.com) is free of charge, this outfit provides pleasant half- and full-day excursions at better rates than most. Guided by local university students, tourists can visit nearby Tra Que village (VND250,000) or, for a higher fee, dig in to some of the city's best street food. The original, free-of-charge excursion to Cam Kim Island takes place on Tuesday, Saturday, and Sunday only, and participants are expected to cover their own bicycle rental and ferry fare across the river. This group does not have a booking office; make reservations through the website.

Whether you're an avid or amateur shutterbug, the **Hoi An Photo Tour** (42 Phan Boi Chau, tel. 09/0567-1898, www.hoianphototour.com, VND1,020,000) combines stunning countryside scenery and the Thu Bon River with helpful tips and tricks straight from a professional photographer. Founded by French photographer Etienne Bossot, a long-time Hoi An resident, these early morning or late afternoon excursions take travelers to a photogenic fishing village, where the local harbor makes for a frenzied but beautiful scene, or into verdant paddy fields just before sunset. The tour caters to all levels of experience, as well as varying levels of equipment, from a simple point-and-shoot camera to the souped-up, high-quality machines used by the pros. Once you're done for the day, you can swing by Bossot's **Hoi An Photo Gallery** (42 Phan Boi Chau, tel. 09/0567-1898, 9am-8pm daily), where beautiful prints of Hoi An and the nearby countryside are on display.

In a place with cuisine as rich and varied as its history, the **Taste of Hoi An** (58B Tran Cao Van, tel. 09/0538-2783, www.tasteofhoian.com, VND1,600,000) street food tour provides a solid rundown of all the town's best culinary offerings. This five-hour morning excursion begins with a walking tour of the old town and a trip to the market and several local street food stalls before guests turn back to Family Restaurant, where you'll sit and enjoy your purchases in a quiet and comfortable setting.

BEACHES

Just north of Hoi An is **An Bang Beach** (end of Hai Ba Trung). All sun, sand, and wooden lounge chairs, this lazy stretch of coast presents a completely different side of Hoi An, shaking off the old-world ambience that decorates the downtown area in exchange for good old-fashioned beach time. You'll find a cluster of no-frills restaurants lining the waterfront as well as plenty of wide open space. Due to strong undertow, swimming is not always allowed at this beach, but there are lifeguards present most days, and the beach is pleasant even without swimming. Travelers can easily reach the beach on their own by bicycle, taxi, or *xe om*. Plenty of parking is available near the waterfront.

Cua Dai Beach is right next to An Bang Beach, northeast of Hoi An, and while it used to be the go-to tourist spot, serious erosion means it's now more a collection of sandbags than a beach.

ENTERTAINMENT AND EVENTS
Nightlife

Nightlife isn't especially raucous in Hoi An, though there are a few places across the river that are beginning to resemble the wilder establishments of other Vietnamese towns. Most places shut down by midnight, but a few spots stay open around the old town as well as over the bridge on Nguyen Phuc Chu. Many restaurants and cafés offer happy hour

An Bang Beach

specials, making sundown the best time for a laid-back drink on the river.

Despite the name, **Dive Bar** (88 Nguyen Thai Hoc, tel. 0235/391-0782, www.vietnamscubadiving.com, 10am-midnight daily, VND25,000-200,000) is anything but. This cool, casual bar in the middle of the old town has a laid-back vibe and accompanying reggae tunes. Colorful cushions and bamboo furniture litter the deceptively large building, which extends all the way back to a small open-roof courtyard, passing a pool table and plenty of comfy couches on the way. In addition to beer, wine, and cocktails, the bar serves a variety of Vietnamese food and a few Western snacks (VND50,000-150,000). The bar is named for its dive outfit, which does trips to nearby Cham Island.

Q Bar (94 Nguyen Thai Hoc, tel. 0235/391-1964, 11am-midnight daily, VND45,000-500,000) is Hoi An's resident swanky cocktail lounge hidden among the shops along Nguyen Thai Hoc. Mood music, plush couches, dim lighting, and a massive dye-cut wooden screen create a trendy vibe that extends all the way from its open storefront back to the intimate seating beyond the bar. In addition to beer, wine, and cocktails, Q Bar offers food after 6pm, including a tapas menu

(from VND60,000) and several full meals (VND100,000-200,000).

White Marble Wine Bar (98 Le Loi, tel. 0235/391-1862, www.visithoian.com, 10am-11pm daily, VND130,000-200,000) transforms one of the neighborhood's many heritage buildings into the self-proclaimed first and only wine bar in Hoi An. Featuring a long list of vintages alongside sumptuous Vietnamese cuisine, this beautiful corner building makes for a perfect place to enjoy a drink at sunset or a nice meal, though food prices are steep. Wines are imported from all over the world, and the downstairs seating area is a prime people-watching location.

Festivals and Events

Every night, as the sun sets over Hoi An, the scores of brightly hued lanterns floating overhead get put to good use, acting as street lights throughout the old town. Head down to the riverfront, where young girls in traditional dress sell **lanterns** (from sunset) to passing travelers; the lanterns are then placed upon the water. Though it takes a few hours, as more and more lanterns are set free, the effect of so many tiny lights flickering along Thu Bon River is an impressive sight.

Lanterns brighten up the night sky in Hoi An's Old Town.

SHOPPING

Famed for its tailors, Hoi An is an easy place for travelers to fill their suitcases and lighten their wallets. Hundreds of shops hawk shoes, clothing, souvenirs, handicrafts, and other knickknacks. Thanks to its history of silk production and a handful of traditional handicraft villages nearby, you'll find almost every storefront downtown packed with Vietnam's best shopping. While the sales pitches can wear over time, this is the best destination for custom-made clothes.

Hoi An and its surrounding localities are well-known for their lanterns and pottery. You'll find these in shops throughout the old town. For pottery, it's also possible to go straight to the source and pay a visit to nearby Thanh Ha village, where you can watch your souvenirs being made and pick up a few items at a much lower cost. For original artwork, you'll find a few galleries around town with oil and lacquer paintings on display, many of which are concentrated along Nguyen Thi Minh Khai, past the Japanese bridge.

Prices in Hoi An tend to be higher than elsewhere, but you're also more likely to find original handmade items here. Bargaining is a necessity: Many stores around the old town do not put price tags on their goods, and where one vendor might ask for VND100,000, another could go as high as VND500,000. Shop around first, peruse all your options—and ask for prices—before deciding upon a particular shop. Remember that patience in these negotiations makes a vendor more likely to agree on your asking price. If all else fails, the item you want is probably available in another shop around town.

Souvenirs

The unique, handcrafted ceramics, jewelry, and accessories at **Reaching Out** (103 Nguyen Thai Hoc, tel. 0235/391-0168, www. reachingoutvietnam.com, 8:30am-9:30pm Mon.-Fri., 9:30am-8:30pm Sat.-Sun.) are worth a look. Founded in 2000 by resident Le Nguyen Binh, this nonprofit enterprise trains, employs, and supports Vietnamese citizens with disabilities, with the aim of providing opportunities and raising local awareness. In-house craftspeople, most of whom have physical impairments, create greeting cards, handbags, home wares, and other knickknacks in the workshop out back, where visitors are invited to say hello and meet the people behind the products. The innovative take on traditional Vietnamese items like tea sets and lanterns makes it hard to leave without a purchase. Reaching Out also runs a peaceful tea shop on Tran Phu staffed entirely by employees with hearing impairments.

Another socially conscious business, the **Lifestart Foundation Workshop** (14 Nguyen Thai Hoc, tel. 016/7355-9447, www. lifestartfoundation.org.au, 9am-7pm daily) sells a range of handicrafts and other souvenirs, including jewelry, home wares, and handbags, along with offering a traditional Vietnamese painting course as well as a lantern-making workshop for visitors. The center, founded by Australian Karen Leonard, trains and employs locals with disabilities (many of whom would otherwise be unable to work), in addition to providing disadvantaged youth with educational scholarships. Courses run on a daily basis. Both the lantern-making workshop and the painting class are VND720,000, and participants keep their creations at the end.

A more trendy and colorful take on local souvenirs, **The O Collective** (85 Nguyen Thai Hoc, tel. 09/0589-3740, the.o.collective@ gmail.com, 9am-9:30pm daily) houses the work of several different Vietnamese brands that produce everything from fun, modern women's clothing to home wares, accessories, and more, including a monster-making workshop for kids. While prices can be steep on some of the larger items, particularly the clothing, this unique array of souvenirs is worth a look.

Right beside the local market, **Hoi An Art Gallery** (6 Nguyen Thai Hoc, tel. 09/0591-1428, 10am-5pm daily) showcases the artwork of local painters within the serene, vibrant setting of Hy Hoa Temple. A variety of oil and

Tips for Buying Custom Clothing

Packed into the old town and running wild along the surrounding streets, the tailors and shoemakers of Hoi An offer custom shoes, bags, and clothing with a quick turn-around (usually no more than a day) and at a fraction of what tailor-made items cost in the United States. This is the best destination for high-quality custom-made clothing, but the hundreds of options can make it hard to distinguish between good value and too good to be true. When ordering tailored clothes, here are a few things to keep in mind:

Allow yourself enough time. While every tailor in town will claim to make your items in 24 hours or less, you'll want to budget in time for alterations. Tackle your shopping as soon as you arrive in town, so you can allow your tailor plenty of time to perfect your items.

Agree on a price beforehand, and then pay later. With so many tourists milling around town, it's understandable that a shop would require some sort of deposit when taking an order, and it's not uncommon for customers to put down half of the agreed-upon cost up front (always in exchange for a receipt). Unless you've chosen one of the few shops that offers a money-back guarantee, do not pay the full amount for your purchases before they have been made. While there are plenty of good tailors in Hoi An, there are some who produce lower-quality items. If you've paid your entire bill beforehand, you have no negotiating power in alterations or improvements. Prices at most tailors are negotiable, and customers who order multiple garments from a shop can usually arrange a discount.

Pay attention to detail. Once you've chosen a tailor, discussed your options, and placed an order, you'll return the following day for a fitting, at which time you have the opportunity to request adjustments or voice any dissatisfaction you might have. Due to the high volume of orders most tailors receive, not every item comes out perfect, but the mark of a good tailor is in his or her willingness to correct a mistake. Scrutinize each of your purchases and, if something displeases you, speak up before settling up.

---

silk paintings, lacquer work, and even a few handicrafts are on hand to peruse.

Tailors

One of the most affordable tailors in town, **Hoa Nang—Sunny** (9 Tran Phu, tel. 012/9765-6275, duongchungmy@hotmail.com, 9am-9pm daily) churns out loads of pleasing dresses and suits in a variety of different styles. Off-the-rack clothing is available for purchase, or you can peruse the dozens of dresses around the shop for ideas on your tailored items. Prices are notably cheaper than most places in town, though the quality of the fabric may not live up to other tailors. The skilled Sunny knows her way around a sewing machine and completes one-day orders with quality and ease.

Run by second-generation tailor Thu Thao, **Phuong Nam** (15 Tran Phu, tel. 0235/386-1475, www.hoian-tailors-phuongnam.vn, 9am-7pm daily) boasts quality and efficiency while being easier on the wallet than some of Hoi An's other tailors. The small shop offers tasteful ready-made clothing and custom orders. Its fabric selection hints at a slightly more male clientele. Phuong Nam has women's dresses off-the-rack. Items are well-made and well-priced.

Though **Silk Road** (91 Nguyen Thai Hoc, tel. 0235/391-1058, 9am-9pm daily) is only a small shop opposite Hai Cafe, don't let its size fool you. Backed by a team of knowledgeable tailors and an array of fabric options, the tiny shop produces men's and women's clothing and offers helpful tips and recommendations to those who wish to tailor an item but haven't yet decided exactly what they want. Prices are reasonable and reflect the quality of both the fabric and the craftsmanship.

One of the old town's most reputable tailors, **Hoang Kim** (57 Nguyen Thai Hoc, tel. 0235/386-2794, yenlekim2003@yahoo.com, 9am-9pm daily) boasts an endless array of fabrics and a team of skilled craftspeople who can turn around a suit and tie in only a day or two. Salespeople are helpful and attentive. You should have an idea of what you'd like beforehand, as there are fewer options on hand, but Hoang Kim's tailors are masters at copying a garment. Prices are reasonable for the quality and the shop's impeccable attention to detail is part of the reason behind its popularity.

A bit of an assembly line rather than a family-run tailor, **Yaly Couture** (47 Nguyen Thai Hoc, tel. 0235/221-2474, www.yalycouture.com, 8am-9:30pm daily) is a successful local business that boasts three shops in town (358 Nguyen Duy Hieu; 47 Tran Phu). From the moment you step in the door, an army of sales associates and tailors assist shoppers in selecting designs, picking out a fabric, and taking measurements. Though it all feels a bit more cookie-cutter than in other shops, there is an obvious reason for Yaly's success. The group's fabrics, skill, and range account for the extra cost.

Accessories

Memory (96A Bach Dang, tel. 0235/391-1483, memoryvietnam@gmail.com, 9am-9pm daily) produces beautiful, if pricey, original jewelry in a variety of different colors, styles, and materials.

The small display room at the **Gemstones Art Museum** (130 Nguyen Thai Hoc, tel. 0235/393-8468, www.gam-hoian.com, 8am-10:30pm daily) is well worth a visit for its bizarre but beautiful raw materials, a collection of sparkling gemstones mined from throughout Vietnam. Founded by the talented Vietnamese designer behind the adjoining **Duong shop**, the cool and unusual exhibition shows shoppers how these precious stones go from raw material to beautiful, original jewelry. The finished products are available for purchase and, given the quality and design, their higher prices are understandable.

An offshoot of the well-known shoemaker Friendly Shoes, **Friendly Bags** (44 Phan Boi Chau, tel. 09/3521-1382, www.friendlybaghoian.com, 9am-9pm daily) is fast gaining ground among those in the market for handmade leather goods. Tucked down a quiet street east of the market, this mini-factory produces high-quality bags in a range of designs with a friendly, professional staff to boot. The owner places a strong emphasis on attention to detail, and a full refund is provided to customers who are not satisfied with their order.

One of the most popular shoemakers in town, **Friendly Shoes** (18 Tran Phu, tel. 09/3521-1382, www.friendlyshophoian.com, 9am-8pm daily) has a reputation for quick, professional service and well-made men's and women's footwear in a variety of materials. Whether it's loafers, heels, flats, sandals, or sneakers, the shop can complete a pair of tailor-made shoes in less than a day and offers a full refund to those not completely satisfied with their order. Peruse the hundreds of shoes that line the store walls in addition to a catalog of previous designs. The expert shoemakers can also copy items from the Internet.

SPORTS AND RECREATION

Hoi An is an R&R destination. Aside from shopping—which, in this town, could be categorized as an Olympic event—you won't find too much in the way of active options, but there are plenty of cooking classes and a few cycling opportunities to keep you entertained.

Diving

With the sun-soaked Cham Island nearby, Hoi An has a small but active diving scene, with two major outfits touring the waters nearby. A variety of options are available for certified and noncertified divers as well as a few snorkeling trips. Visibility is best in the area between July and September, but divers still get in underwater exploration as early as February. October-January, however, you won't find much information on local diving, as most outfits close up shop for the off-season. Hoi An isn't the diving capital of Vietnam, but those who have left Nha Trang or Phu Quoc out of their plans should consider this as their next best bet.

Operating out of Dive Bar, the **Cham Island Diving Center** (88 Nguyen Thai Hoc, tel. 0235/391-0782, www.vietnamscubadiving.com, 9am-9:30pm daily, VND990,000-1,900,000) has been in town for over a decade and offers one-day and multiple-day trips with experienced dive masters. PADI courses are available, as is a wealth of free information regarding the islands, the beach, and the town in general. While the diving center is only open until 5pm, stop by later if you have questions, as Dive Bar stays open late.

The combined efforts of an English expat and a Hoi An native, **Blue Coral Diving** (33 Tran Hung Dao, tel. 0235/627-9297, www.divehoian.com, 9am-9pm daily, VND1,000,000-2,000,000) employs a team of experienced PADI-certified dive masters alongside a local crew with vast knowledge of the seas around Cham Island. Trips for both certified and non-certified divers are available, as is a snorkeling package and a few PADI courses.

Cycling

Flyers advertising **Heaven and Earth Bicycle Tours** (61 Ngo Quyen, tel. 0235/386-4362, www.vietnam-bicycle.com, 7:30am-9:30pm daily, VND385,000-2,050,000) can be found on almost every bulletin board and reception desk across town, and with good reason. Hoi An's most popular cycling tour provider, this locally run outfit takes travelers on a leisurely ride into the nearby countryside, opting for a more off-the-beaten-path experience. Both half- and full-day excursions are available, including trips to My Son and local fishing villages as well as the group's original countryside tour, where you can watch local artisans crafting bricks, straw mats, and wooden ships, among other things. Multiple-day homestay trips can be arranged, where travelers have more opportunity to gain one-on-one contact with local people.

The Hoi An arm of popular Dalat-based adventure outfit **Phat Tire Ventures** (80 Le Hong Phong, tel. 0235/653-9839, www.

ptv-vietnam.com, 7:30am-8pm daily, VND885,000-2,156,000) offers half- and full-day cycles to places like Tra Que vegetable village, the Marble Mountains, and the My Son ruins, as well as multiple-day excursions between Hue, Dalat, Nha Trang, Hoi An, and several other destinations. High-quality equipment and experienced guides take visitors into Hoi An's surrounding countryside for a day of leisurely cycling. For thrill-seekers, the company provides rock-climbing and rappelling adventures at nearby Marble Mountain.

Cooking Classes

It seems every restaurant in town has set up a cooking class for visitors to try their hand at local fare. You'll find half-day courses as cheap as VND400,000, most of which cut right to the chase and roll out a host of prepared ingredients for you to combine as instructed. Others include a market visit, while still more courses go a step beyond and offer hands-on preparation, taking students from start to finish with several local dishes. The classes at **Baby Mustard (Nha Hang Cai Con)** (Tra Que, tel. 09/3572-5740, babymustard.restaurant@gmail.com), a modest little spot near Tra Que vegetable village, are a solid option.

Combine your cooking with a little sightseeing on the half-day **Thuan Tinh Island Cooking Tour** (Thon 1, Cam Thanh, tel. 09/0647-7770, www.cooking-tour.com, 8:30am-5:30pm daily, VND775,000). Guests visit the local market, exploring the many ingredients that go into Vietnamese cooking before taking a 30-minute boat ride to the picturesque Thuan Tinh Island. From there, you'll prepare a set menu of four tried-and-true local dishes, including beef pho and fresh spring rolls. Each participant leaves with a recipe booklet of some of Vietnam's most popular dishes. The booking fee includes both pickup and drop-off, and vegetarian options are available.

Green Bamboo Cooking School (21 Truong Minh Hung, tel. 09/0581-5600, www.

greenbamboo-hoian.com, 8am-3:30pm daily, VND1,135,000) is run by the patient and experienced Ms. Van, a top-notch chef and teacher who provides day-long cooking classes with thorough instruction from start to finish. A market visit is included in the day's outing, and each student is tasked with making one dish. Both carnivorous and vegetarian options are available, and Ms. Van caps her class at 12 students, allowing each participant to gain some hands-on experience. All levels are welcome, and the course fee includes a recipe book as well as complimentary pickup and drop-off from your hotel.

FOOD

Hoi An is a foodie's paradise, blessed with an incredible set of local specialties, most of which cannot be found elsewhere in Vietnam. The tastes and traditions of this town's unique cuisine are a must-try. From hearty *cao lau* (a local noodle specialty) to the dim sum-style "white rose" (steamed shrimp dumplings), there are plenty of local meals to keep your taste buds interested. Hoi An's masterful chefs boast the skills to execute excellent Vietnamese meals and sumptuous Western creations. Peruse the menus of several old town eateries and in upmarket spots you'll find fusion cuisine, sesame-crusted tuna, and Moroccan couscous.

Vietnamese

A short walk from the old town brings you to **Cafe 43** (43 Tran Cao Van, tel. 0235/386-2587, tranquangcaocuong90@gmail.com, 8:30am-10pm daily, VND25,000-140,000), where the shaded open-air dining area is often packed with foreigners and you'll find tasty Vietnamese food at a fraction of the downtown price. This quiet, friendly spot sees hungry backpackers throughout the day, and its fresh beer keeps the place open well into the night.

Miss Ly's (22 Nguyen Hue, tel. 0235/386-1603, lycafe22@yahoo.com, 11am-9pm daily, VND50,000-150,000) cozy, welcoming little restaurant sits a short walk north of the central market and has been serving customers for decades. Hoi An specialties like *cao lau* and Chinese-style wonton soup as well as hearty home-cooked Vietnamese meals are on the menu. Paintings line the wall, and each sturdy wooden table is set with a single rose. Large windows open onto the street, affording diners a pleasant vantage point from which to take in the passing scene. Miss Ly has expanded to a second venue next door.

Learn how to cook like a local at Baby Mustard's cooking classes.

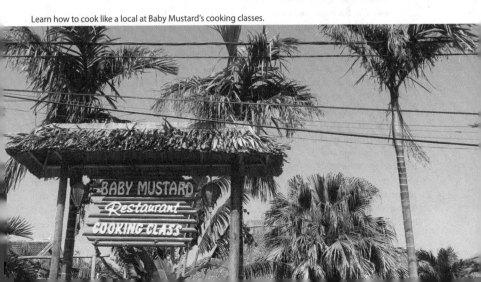

Local Cuisine: Hoi An

Hoi An is one place where you don't want to miss out on local cuisine. Boasting an array of dishes unique to the area, Hoi An's chefs take great pride in their creations.

- *banh vac* **(white rose):** Not unlike Chinese dim sum, these small, steamed shrimp dumplings are shaped like flowers, hence the name, and served with fish sauce.

- *banh xeo:* The town boasts its own version of these savory Vietnamese pancakes, which are smaller than their southern counterparts but just as tasty.

- *cao lau:* The most noteworthy of local meals, this is a meat and noodle dish sold on every street corner and in every restaurant in the old town and beyond. Topped with fresh greens, fried wontons, and as much—or as little—spice as you'd like, this particular meal is special because of its noodles, which are flat and much denser than average rice noodles, and can only be made with the water from Ba Le Well, the town's ancient Cham water source. While the uninitiated may not know the difference, Hoi An locals insist that they can tell the genuine article from its impostors.

- **fried wontons:** Borrowed from the Chinese, these fried wontons at first glance resemble tortillas, and are packed with pork, egg, or shrimp and topped with vegetables.

One of the old town's most popular restaurants, **Morning Glory** (106 Nguyen Thai Hoc, tel. 0235/391-1227, www.msvy-tastevietnam.com, 11am 10pm daily, VND55,000-250,000) is owned by the industrious Ms. Vy, also the mastermind behind Cargo Club and the large buffet-style Vy's Market Restaurant across the river. Its menu showcases a range of home-cooked Vietnamese meals, all of which are prepared in the open kitchen at the center of the restaurant. Diners watch as chefs put together dishes like grilled king prawns and an endless array of clay pot meats. Though portions run small, these delicious renditions of Vietnamese soul food keep customers coming back. The restaurant also runs **cooking classes** (VND705,000-990,000), which are taught by Ms. Vy, a third-generation chef. You'll now find a second Morning Glory location directly opposite the original to handle its growing clientele.

Housed in an enormous yellow building on the other side of the Thu Bon River, **Mango Mango** (45 Nguyen Phuc Chu, tel. 0235/391-1863, www.mangohoian.com, 9am-10pm daily, VND100,000-500,000) is a hub of activity in the evenings, when the town's night market gets under way next door and droves of diners fill up this mammoth riverfront spot. Beyond its swanky setting, Mango Mango sets itself apart through a creative menu featuring local ingredients with a contemporary twist, not to mention some delicious cocktails. Live music is often a part of Mango Mango's dining experience.

Street Food

There are few street stalls in the old town. But head a block or two outside the UNESCO zone and there are plenty of roadside eats along Phan Chau Trinh and beyond. Backpackers staying in the Ba Trieu area can take a stroll down Thai Phien to find cheap and tasty local fare.

For all the town's culinary specialties in one centrally located place, the food stalls within the **Hoi An Market** (Tran Phu and Nguyen Hue, sunrise-sunset, VND20,000-50,000) whip up a whole host of tasty local dishes, from *cao lau* (the local noodle specialty) and *mi quang* (rice noodle soup with shrimp and pork) to several other Vietnamese favorites. This is a good spot to survey all the options first. Check with your respective food vendor regarding the price beforehand, even if the amount appears to be posted, as these signs are sometimes ignored.

At the southern end of Tran Cao Van, **Madame Khanh the Banh Mi Queen** (115 Tran Cao Van, 7am-7pm daily, VND20,000) has been selling mouthwatering Vietnamese sandwiches for over 30 years. It's possible to pick and choose your ingredients, but Madame Khanh has her product down to an art, and tucking into a sandwich with all the fixings is your best bet. Prices run on the high side for a banh mi, but the resulting meal is worth every dong. Vegetarians should steer clear, as sandwiches feature several kinds of lunch meat. Be patient here; service can be slow.

With the colorful Ngu Bang Assembly Hall serving as a backdrop, Hoi An's best ★ *banh beo* (near Tran Phu and Hoang Van Thu, from 2pm daily, VND5,000; per piece) vendor sets up shop every afternoon just south of Tran Phu and slings hundreds of these heavenly steamed rice cakes in a miniature porcelain bowl, known as a *chen*, topped with a dollop of shrimp paste, some minced pork, and a few deep-fried *cao lau* noodles. Liberal amounts of fish sauce bring an added flavor. The low street-side seating is the perfect place to people-watch. For something truly unique, a "sweet" version of the rice cakes is available; it includes all the same savory toppings as the original and is only found in Hoi An. Look for the sign reading "Banh beo Ba Bay."

Not far from its namesake, **Ba Le Well** (45/51 Tran Hung Dao, tel. 0235/386-4443, 10am-10pm daily, VND120,000 pp) sits between the alley entrance off Phan Chau Trinh and Hoi An's famous water source. With conventional metal tables and plastic stools, this outdoor eatery offers a variety of local cuisine with a set menu of specialties that includes spring rolls, grilled pork, and *banh xeo* (savory Vietnamese pancakes), as well as fruit for dessert. Since it's designed with foreign visitors in mind, the restaurant does a nice job of covering all the bases and saves you the hassle of poring over a menu.

Cafés and Bakeries

Staffed by employees with hearing impairments, the **Reaching Out Tea House** (131 Tran Phu, tel. 0235/391-0168, 8:30am-9pm Mon.-Fri., 10am-8:30pm Sat.-Sun., VND45,000-120,000) is an extension of the nonprofit shop Reaching Out. Emphasizing local coffees and teas, the menu includes a variety of Fair Trade beverages (which can also

cao lau, a specialty noodle dish native to Họi An

be enjoyed in a sampler of three), small biscuits, and other goodies. Large wooden easy chairs and communal spaces make for a comfortable environment. Traditional tea sets and small bonsai trees are on display around the shop. Guests communicate with the staff by way of an order form, notepads, and small blocks with phrases like "water," "bill," and "thank you" printed on the front. With no music and no Wi-Fi, this shop is a charming and atmospheric spot.

Run by a coffee connoisseur, **Mia Coffee** (20 Phan Boi Chau, tel. 09/0555-2061, 6:30am-5pm daily, VND20,000-70,000) sits on a sunny corner at the eastern end of the old town. Small tables line the outer edge of the building, while a massive bean roaster keeps the interior smelling of coffee. The owner roasts and packages all his own beans, which are grown in the Central Highlands, and is an expert on caffeinated beverages. Swing by in the morning and you'll find plenty of early-risers getting their caffeine fix for the day.

International

One of Hoi An's best, the long-running ★ **Cargo Club** (107-109 Nguyen Thai Hoc, tel. 0235/391-0489, www.cargo-hoian.com, 9am-10:30pm daily, VND80,000-325,000) is a pretty colonial building with large shuttered windows and a cozy setup. Its exemplary baked goods run the gamut from croissants and crispy French breads to mouthwatering cakes. The dinner menu is noteworthy, featuring couscous, sesame crusted tuna, and lamb shank. With a mellow atmosphere and plenty of comfy chairs, Cargo is a prime spot for coffee or a full meal.

Halfway between Cua Dai Beach and the old town, the friendly and attentive staff at **Dingo Deli** (277 Cua Dai, tel. 012/0600-9300, www.dingodelihoian.com, 7:30am-9:30pm daily, VND75,000-200,000) dish out tasty Western food as well as imported groceries and sound travel advice. Outdoor patio seating and an air-conditioned indoor dining room are available. Burgers, pasta, sandwiches, and meat pies are on the menu, as are hearty Western breakfasts and regular daily specials.

Vegetarian

While meat-free restaurants are trickier to find, most of Hoi An's restaurants offer a vegetarian selection on the menu. **Dam Vegetarian**'s (alley between 69 and 71 Phan Chau Trinh, 7am-8pm daily, VND15,000-40,000) excellent rendition of the local noodle delicacy, *cao lau*, makes the small shop worth a visit. You'll find nothing special in terms of decor, but meals are tasty and affordable. Dam's massive metal street cart offers a nice selection of tofu and veggie dishes as well.

The meatless answer to Cafe 43 across the street, **Minh Hien** (50 Tran Cao Van, tel. 09/0566-7743, 9am-10pm daily, VND30,000-80,000) sticks strictly to tofu and veggies, offering the same laid-back outdoor seating and pleasant service surrounded by an impressive floor-to-ceiling collection of Vietnamese and Japanese comic books. Portions are on the small side, but at prices like these, you can order two mains apiece and still save money.

ACCOMMODATIONS

There are a few accommodations between the shops and restaurants of the old town, and droves of hotels north of the old town and along the road leading out to Cua Dai Beach. Budget options tend to be concentrated around Hai Ba Trung and Ba Trieu streets, along with a few dorm beds scattered across town. Standard budget amenities include hot water, air-conditioning, and Wi-Fi.

Most places in Hoi An are mid-range, with the majority of hotels charging upward of VND525,000. Depending on where you stay, this price can still represent great value, as the add-ons (hot water, air-conditioning, Wi-Fi, fridge, minibar, and coffeemaker) included in these accommodations are often much more than what you'd find in a VND210,000 hotel room.

Staying closer to the old town affords easy access to Hoi An's sights, restaurants, and ample shopping. As Hoi An's already astronomical tourism numbers soar, more than a few homestays have opened up. These are not authentic homestays, in which travelers shack up with a local family for the night, but more like a bed-and-breakfast. Many of these smaller family-owned places are excellent options and provide a more personal experience.

Old Town
VND1,050,000-2,100,000

Ha An Hotel (6-8 Phan Boi Chau, tel. 0235/386-3126, www.haanhotel.com, VND1,365,000-2,500,000, breakfast included) is a charming boutique hotel separated from the road by a lush courtyard garden. Rooms are bright white and well-appointed. The hotel's adjoining restaurant and café serves a range of Vietnamese and Western dishes throughout the day. Ha An operates its own tour outfit, which runs city tours and excursions beyond the old town, and also counts a swimming pool among its amenities.

Once the house of a Chinese merchant, the 200-year-old **Vinh Hung Heritage Hotel** (143 Tran Phu, tel. 0235/386-1621, www.vinhhunghotels.com.vn, VND1,785,000-2,270,000) oozes character from its sturdy columns and traditional carved wooden furniture. It's in the heart of the old town. Several high-profile guests have patronized the hotel, including foreign diplomats and actor Michael Caine. The six updated rooms include standard amenities as well as an in-room safe and a television. The suite rooms have a charming balcony overlooking the street. Breakfast is served at the Vinh Hung Restaurant next door.

OVER VND2,100,000

The rather grand **Hoi An Hotel** (10 Tran Hung Dao, tel. 0235/386-1445, www.hoianhotel.com.vn, VND2,650,000-10,500,000) is a beautiful, sprawling building with a lush interior garden and charming well-appointed rooms. A modern, sleek reception area gives way to the green courtyard and swimming pool. Guest rooms vary from comfortable

deluxe rooms to posh suites, all of which include basic amenities as well as tea- and coffee-making facilities and a minibar. Some rooms have a private balcony. A fitness center, spa, and tennis court are on-site.

North of Old Town
VND210,000-525,000

Hidden on the narrow part of Tran Cao Van, rooms at the **Hoa My II Hotel** (44 Tran Cao Van, tel. 09/0551-8569, www.hoamyhotel-hoian.com.vn, VND430,000-570,000) are average but clean and right for the price. Amenities include TV, Wi-Fi, air-conditioning, and hot water, as well as a hotel pool. The staff is pleasant, and this is one of the better value options. Rooms can get a little noisy in the mornings, and at night as Tran Cao Van sees a lot of action.

On a street packed with budget options, rooms at the **Hoa Binh Hotel** (107 Ba Trieu, tel. 0235/391-6838, www.hoabinhhotelhoian.com, VND115,000 dorm, VND363,000-410,000 d, breakfast included) are fitting for the price, providing clean beds and standard amenities like hot water, air-conditioning, Wi-Fi, TV, a fridge, and use of the downstairs pool. Plenty of backpackers turn up for the hotel's dorm beds, which come with personal lockers. A small travel outfit is on-site, and a café serves light meals throughout the day. This is a good spot for the budget crowd.

VND525,000-1,050,000

A mid-range option, **Vinh Hung Library Hotel** (96 Ba Trieu, tel. 0235/391-6277, www.vinhhunglibraryhotel.com, VND750,000-1,135,000, breakfast included) features a stylish interior and top-notch service. Even its smaller rooms, though windowless, feature a painted bamboo screen, a comfy bed, and the standard amenities, including use of the hotel pool. Deluxe and superior options are available.

Trim and tidy, **Thien Nga** (52 Ba Trieu, tel. 0235/391-6330, thienngahoianhotel@gmail.com, VND570,000-910,000, breakfast included) is a small mid-range spot offering both street- and garden-view rooms with hot water, air-conditioning, TV, a fridge, a safe, and Wi-Fi access. The rooms are pleasant, the location is nice, and the staff is friendly. The hotel also has a swimming pool.

VND1,050,000-2,100,000

Sporting a chic red-and-black interior, **Thien Thanh Hotel** (16 Ba Trieu, tel. 0235/391-6545, thienthanhhotel@dng.vnn.vn, VND1,250,000-1,475,000, breakfast included) comes in a step above the budget offerings on the block, providing more atmosphere as well as complimentary water and standard amenities. Decorative wall hangings made by Vietnam's highland minority people, pottery knickknacks collected from Thanh Ha village, and throw pillows and lampshades emblazoned with the Chinese symbol for happiness add to the hotel's charm. Several rooms feature balconies, and the garden patio has lovely views. Use of the outdoor pool is included in the rates.

Cua Dai Beach Road

Accommodations on the road to An Bang and Cua Dai Beaches run the gamut from budget to high-end, with several five-star resorts perched on the edge of the East Sea and a host of mid-range options in between. Some provide daily shuttles both into town and out to the beach. You can also hop on a bicycle and access either area in a matter of minutes.

UNDER VND210,000

One of Hoi An's backpacker hot spots, **Sunflower Hotel** (397 Cua Dai, tel. 0235/393-9838, www.sunflowerhotelhoian.com, VND150,000 dorm, VND390,000-525,000 d, breakfast included) sits a short way out of central Hoi An. Featuring clean, basic rooms with air-conditioning, Wi-Fi access, TV, and hot water, this spot is popular with the budget crowd, particularly its dorms, which offer lockers and en suite baths. Use of the swimming pool is included in the rates. Additional services such as laundry,

bicycle rentals, tours, and transportation can be arranged.

VND525,000-1,050,000

About 1.5 kilometers from the old town, **Hai Au Hotel** (576 Cua Dai, tel. 0235/391-4577, www.haiauhotels.com, VND630,000-882,000, breakfast included) is one of the most popular lodgings along the Cua Dai strip, in large part thanks to its excellent value for money and amiable staff. Rooms are clean, well-kept, and decorated in an eclectic array of colors and patterns. Both the swimming pool downstairs and the restaurant out front are open to guests, and amenities include hot water, air-conditioning, Wi-Fi, TV, a minibar, an in-room safe, and daily bottled water.

Just opposite the Hai Au, **Vaia Boutique Hotel** (489 Cua Dai, tel. 0235/391-6499, www.vaiahotel.com, VND795,000-1,250,000, breakfast included) is a trendy, sleek spot that offers well-appointed rooms with modern Asian elegance. Standard and deluxe options are available, with the former running on the small side, but the plush, sizeable beds make up for this. The usual amenities include air-conditioning, hot water, TV, a minibar, Wi-Fi, and an in-room safe. Bicycle use is included in the rates, and guests enjoy complimentary all-day coffee and tea as well as happy-hour cocktails.

VND1,050,000-2,100,000

The Earth Villa (380 Cua Dai, tel. 0235/392-6777, www.theearthvilla.com, VND680,000-1,180,000, breakfast included), a beautiful set of garden-facing buildings with cozy, well-appointed rooms, is 1.5 kilometers from Hoi An's old town and boasts a swimming pool and on-site restaurant. Rooms feature tea- and coffee-making facilities, TV, a fridge, Wi-Fi, hot water, and air-conditioning along with tasteful decor and a generous bath.

Bright, cozy, and well-appointed, rooms at the **Lotus Hotel** (330 Cua Dai, tel. 0235/392-3357, www.hoianlotushotel.com, VND1,552,000-2,700,000, breakfast included) are a reasonable size and are set in a traditional-style building that blends seamlessly into its surroundings. Each room comes with a balcony as well as hot water, air-conditioning, Wi-Fi, TV, a fridge, and tea- and coffee-making facilities. Breakfast is served downstairs, where you'll find pleasant views of the nearby fields. The hotel offers regular shuttles into town for guests and, slightly set back from the street, offers a quieter atmosphere than most.

OVER VND2,100,000

Billing itself as a "green retreat," secluded **Hoi An Chic** (Nguyen Trai, tel. 0235/392-6799, www.hoianchic.com, VND2,940,000-4,350,000) is 1.5 kilometers from the city center in a beautiful location amid verdant rice fields, making for a peaceful countryside experience. The simple sleek rooms are well-furnished with bright colors. Baths include both an indoor shower and outdoor stone bathtubs. A charming outdoor patio allows guests to enjoy the scenery. Breakfast is served in the breezy open-air restaurant, and guests can laze around the rooftop infinity pool. Free bicycle use and shuttles into the old town are available.

Vietnam's best seaside resort, ★ **Four Seasons Resort The Nam Hai** (Hamlet 1, Dien Duong Village, tel. 0235/394-0000, www. fourseasons.com/hoian, VND18,860,000-48,230,000, breakfast included) consistently rates among the top beach resorts in Southeast Asia. Sprawled across a manicured 35-hectare plot, the resort boasts 100 stunning villas that feature down duvets, plush sofas, private gardens, and outdoor rain showers. The smallest lodgings are 80 square meters. Guests have a choice of additional upgrades, such as a beachfront location or private pool. The Nam Hai features two restaurants, two bars, a spa, a fitness center, a private beach, a three-tiered infinity pool, and a kids' activity villa. Yoga, basketball, table tennis, and badminton are available to guests, as are regular shuttles to and from Hoi An.

INFORMATION AND SERVICES

Hoi An's official **tourist information center** (78 Le Loi, www.hoianancienttown. vn, 7:30am-9pm daily) doubles as a ticket vendor for the old-town sights. It doesn't offer much in the way of free information, and opening hours can be flexible. With so many independent operators in Hoi An and plenty of helpful hotel receptionists, you should be able to find solid travel advice by asking around.

You'll find a **Vietin Bank** (9 Le Loi, tel. 0235/221-2604, www.vietinbank.vn, 7:30am-11:30am and 1:30pm-5pm Mon.-Fri., 7am-11am Sat.), just north of the old town, that can assist with exchanges. ATMs are widely available on the streets lining the outskirts of the old town. Hoi An's central **post office** (6 Tran Hung Dao, tel. 0235/386-3333, www. hoianpost.com, 6:30am-8pm daily) handles all packages and post.

For minor bumps and bruises, the **Hoi An Hospital** (4 Tran Hung Dao, tel. 0235/391-4660) can fix you up, but anything major is best treated in Danang, about 30 minutes away.

GETTING THERE
Air

Visitors flying to Hoi An from Hanoi or HCMC will land at the **Danang International Airport** (DAD, www.danangairportonline.com), a 30-minute drive from town. Travelers should have no problem hailing a cab or *xe om* driver for the ride to town. Both cost around VND400,000.

Bus

Depending upon your point of departure, buses to Hoi An arrive at various points around the city. From Nha Trang, the ride costs VND499,000. From Hue to Hoi An is VND99,000-199,000, and from Danang, it's VND30,000.

While the town has its own long-distance bus station, local vehicles are aging, and you'll find more comfortable services through **Sinh**

Tourist (587 Hai Ba Trung, tel. 023/386-3948, www.thesinhtourist.vn, 6am-10pm daily), which offers routes throughout central Vietnam and beyond.

Local buses from Danang (30-50 minutes, VND30,000) drop riders off hourly at the public bus station (Le Hong Phong and Nguyen Tat Thanh, 5:30am-5:30pm daily).

Train

While Hoi An does not have a train station, more than a few travelers make the train trip up to Danang (from Hue, Hanoi, HCMC, or Nha Trang), then hop in a taxi or on the back of a *xe om* for the remainder of the journey, a 30-minute drive (VND400,000). Cabs and *xe om* drivers will be awaiting fares when the train arrives at the station. Be sure to confirm whether your taxi is operating on a flat rate or meter before hopping in.

GETTING AROUND

More than most Vietnamese destinations, Hoi An is a very walkable town. The old town, where the majority of travelers spend their time, can be covered on foot in an afternoon. There's really no need to bother with additional transportation, though renting a bicycle for the day and wheeling your way around is not a bad idea.

Taxi and *Xe Om*

You'll find *xe om* drivers camped out on street corners across town. During the daytime ban on motor vehicles in the old town area, you will have to walk a few blocks north to catch a motorbike ride. The same goes for taxis, but you'll find plenty of Mailinh (tel. 0235/392-9292) cabs hovering around the outskirts of the old town.

Bike

Bicycles, the preferred method of travel in this town, are readily available at most hotels and guesthouses, as well as through rental shops in the area. Rates usually start around VND30,000-40,000 per day and are a great way to wander around the old town and a little farther afield. For longer trips, you can find motorbike rentals around Hoi An, which run VND120,000-200,000 per day.

CHAM ISLAND

Boasting plenty of sunny, white-sand coast and a pagoda or two, Cham Island is often visited by snorkeling and scuba diving outfits, thanks to its attractive underwater landscapes. While these tours tend to be more expensive than the locally run sightseeing-and-snorkeling combos, you're better off paying the extra cash for the fancier excursion, as these usually offer more bang for your buck.

Tours are the most popular way to explore the islands. Most hotel travel outfits offer day trips to the island, but it's also possible to go on your own and spend the night on the island. Cham Island is a seasonal destination, with transportation to the island only really running March-September.

If you're pressed for time but determined to see the island, you can find ferry transportation at Cua Dai Harbor. Wooden boats depart around 8:30am and return from the island at approximately 11am. Passage on these vessels costs VND100,000-150,000 and can be hectic, so don't expect a comfortable ride.

Travelers with more time can look into island homestays, which are reasonably priced and help support the local community. Facilities are basic—a Western toilet, a cold shower, and a bed with mosquito net—and electricity can be touch-and-go. For those looking to escape the mainland hustle, accommodations on Cham Island are a worthy option. For more information on homestays, check out the website for Homestay Bai Huong (www.homestaybaihuong.com), which coordinates homestays (VND120,000 pp) with local island residents and travelers in addition to running a few tours of its own. These folks can also assist with transportation and other island recommendations. Bring enough cash for your trip, as there are no ATMs on Cham Island.

My Son Ruins

MY SON RUINS

Buried deep within the mountains west of Hoi An, the **My Son Ruins** (Duy Phu, Duy Xuyen, tel. 0235/373-1309, www.mysonsanctuary.com.vn, 6am-6pm daily, VND150,000) are a complex of Angkorian-age Hindu temples that have partially withstood the test of time, existing today as moss-covered, mystical stone structures. Before it was a tourist hot spot, a UNESCO site, or a thriving 18th-century port town, Hoi An belonged to the kings of Champa, a powerful matriarchal kingdom that worshipped several Hindu gods, most commonly Shiva, and began building temples in the My Son valley as early as the 4th century. Subsequent rulers added to the site's collection of religious structures, resulting in several eras of Cham architecture that make up the ruins.

By the time French explorers stumbled upon the temples in 1885, My Son was an overgrown, forgotten place. In the following decades, teams of French and Vietnamese architects studied and spruced up the site,

occasionally removing sculptures and other important pieces for posterity. Thirteen temple groups were discovered, with the original count numbering over 70 structures.

Scholars continued to study the area until World War II and the onset of the Franco-Vietnam War. As the country gained independence and Vietnam slid into another armed conflict, American bombs destroyed significant portions of the My Son complex, toppling a 28-meter tower, one of the site's most important structures. Thanks to the efforts of Polish architect Kazimierz Kwiatkowski (who was instrumental in helping Hoi An achieve its UNESCO status) and a Vietnamese colleague, Hoang Dao Kinh, My Son received a second facelift in the 1980s before gaining UNESCO recognition in 1999.

Today, visitors to the site often make the 40-kilometer journey by way of a day tour, many of which are offered at travel outfits in Hoi An. These trips vary in price, but all provide the added benefit of a local guide, as the site itself does not offer much in the way of historical information. For independent travelers, the road to My Son is fairly agreeable, and large, hard-to-miss signs direct you most of the way.

Once you arrive, you'll be required to purchase a ticket at the entry gate, where a pair of exhibition rooms display artifacts from the temples as well as a collection of historical images related to the temples' restoration. This is a must for independent travelers, as it helps you appreciate the history and architecture of the site. From here, drive another 1.5 kilometers up to the complex, where tour buses park and Cham cultural performances take place at 9:15am, 10:45am, 2pm, and 3:30pm daily.

A small footpath leads to the largest and most significant temple groups, B, C, and D, which are clustered together in a clearing. These structures date between the 7th and 13th centuries and feature some of the most intact temples at My Son. Two of the D temples now serve as miniature exhibits, showcasing well-preserved statues and other relics. These structures suffered under American ammunition: Look for a large, perfectly round bomb crater on one edge of the complex.

To the northeast, group A hails from the 9th century and used to house the complex's tallest temple, though you wouldn't know it from the modest structures in existence today. Farther on, group G bears the only written record of construction at My Son, its looping Sanskrit letters carved into a tablet to the left of the main temple. Groups E and F stand together at the edge of the grounds. Some of the oldest temples still in existence, these 8th-century structures bore the most damage from Vietnam's wars, with one or two now at risk of collapsing.

Most tours arrive at My Son around mid-morning. If you have your own set of wheels, it's best to visit before or after this time, as the crowds detract from My Son's appeal.

Extensive de-mining efforts have helped to remove most of the unexploded ordnance threat from the My Son area, but stick to the well-worn paths and Cham towers, as the lush rainforest around the site may still hold more than trees and temples.

The South-Central Coast

Highlights

★ **Po Nagar Towers:** These rust-hued Hindu temples date back as far as the 8th century and honor the ancient Cham goddess Po Nagar, Lady of the Kingdom (page 244).

★ **Nha Trang Beach:** These brilliant white shores and turquoise waters are the highlight of this sun-drenched southern hub (page 248).

★ **Nha Trang's Mud Baths and Hot Springs:** Get down and dirty in the thermal mud baths (page 252).

★ **Xuan Huong Lake:** The crown jewel of Dalat, this picturesque lake makes it into many photos of Vietnam's rustic highland resort town (page 270).

★ **Hang Nga Crazy House:** With its odd angles and warped facades, this building is a departure from architectural convention (page 271).

★ **Mui Ne's White Dunes:** This bizarre windswept landscape of sparkling white sands overlooks the ocean (page 288).

© AVALON TRAVEL

A vibrant, sun-soaked shoreline runs unbroken from the tumultuous cliffs of Quy Nhon down to Mui Ne's bizarre tropical sand dunes. The bulk of Vietnam's most-visited mainland beaches belong to this region.

Rounding out the belly of the *S*, this gently curving stretch of coast is a feast of greens and blues, with lush rainforest-green palms and azure waters, providing a picture-perfect backdrop for the region's sleepy fishing villages and bustling city thoroughfares. Whether you're an adventure junkie plying the surf of Mui Ne, a party animal living it up on the sands of Nha Trang, or just a traveler in search of some good old-fashioned rest and relaxation on the quieter shores of Phan Rang or Quy Nhon, there are plenty of places to lay your towel here.

Beyond the beach, the south-central coast boasts an equally colorful history as the former kingdom of Champa, an ancient Hindu civilization whose redbrick ruins still dot the shoreline today, and as a thriving part of the nation's fishing industry, awash with brightly hued wooden boats and kilometers of wispy white fishing net. Farther inland, 130 kilometers from shore, the highlands town of Dalat provides an excellent contrast to its coastal cousins, with the undulating mountains and dense forests inviting adventure travel.

The major stopover on the south-central coast is Nha Trang, the largest and flashiest of the region's cities, where sunny beach days give way to all-night parties. Some may venture away from the sand and on to Dalat, gateway to Vietnam's interior and home to mountainous adventure. Those seeking a more anonymous beach destination will be rewarded at Phan Rang or Quy Nhon, whose peaceful shores can be a much-needed escape from the buzz and chaos of Vietnam's larger cities without having to take a step off the beaten track.

HISTORY

For over 1,000 years, from the end of the 2nd century to the mid-1600s, Vietnam's south-central coast belonged to the powerful kingdom of Champa. Divided into four separate

---

Previous: Nha Trang Beach; Dalat's Valley of Love. **Above:** sand formations at Fairy Spring.

states, this matriarchal Hindu empire made its living off maritime trade, dealing in luxury goods like eaglewood and silk, in addition to constructing hundreds of soaring redbrick religious towers. The kingdom's original capital, situated just west of Hoi An, housed its major religious, political, and economic centers at the height of the Champa reign during the 9th century. This tenure was short-lived: the empire was often embroiled in military conflicts with the Khmer, their neighbors to the west, as well as the northern Dai Viet, ancestors of today's Vietnamese.

As outside forces began to overtake their land, the Cham were forced to flee south, their territory growing smaller and smaller until, in the 15th century, the Dai Viet dealt a fatal blow to the kingdom, destroying the Champa capital in what is now Binh Dinh province. Many escaped to Cambodia, scattering the Cham community across two countries, while the kingdom in Vietnam was reduced to a tiny portion of what is now Ninh Thuan and Binh Thuan provinces. As the Vietnamese and, later, the French took over, this once-great empire was reduced to a handful of often marginalized groups along the south-central coast and hidden away in the Mekong Delta.

Nowadays, the largely Vietnamese population makes its living offshore, with thousands of brightly colored wooden fishing boats plying the bountiful waters of the East Sea (as the Vietnamese refer to the South China Sea). Like the rest of the country, the south-central coast experienced hardships under French colonialism during the latter half of the 19th century and later fought the battles of the Franco-Vietnam and American Wars. While this region saw less violence than some others in the country, there are still places, particularly around Phan Thiet and Mui Ne, where land mines and other evidence of Vietnam's troubled past remain. Nonetheless, this coast continues to support a strong fishing industry in addition to a growing tourism industry and the country's best mainland fish sauce.

PLANNING YOUR TIME

Most travelers can hit all the highlights of this region in a little over a week, though you may need more time if you veer off the coast to Dalat. Spend 3-4 days in Nha Trang. If you crave beach time beyond that, spend 2-3 days in Quy Nhon or Phan Rang-Thap Cham. Mui Ne can be substituted as a quieter alternative to popular Nha Trang, as can the up-and-coming shores of Quy Nhon. Dalat is the polar opposite of the region's coast towns, and is worth a stay of 2-4 days. If you're planning to be here around the New Year during the Dalat Flower Festival (late Dec.-early Jan.), arrange accommodations in advance, as the city's hotels fill up quickly during this period.

This region spans a large swath of land, so travelers tend to town-hop. Nha Trang, the transportation hub of the region, is where you'll find vehicles heading toward Quy Nhon or Phan Rang-Thap Cham. Culture and history buffs will breeze through the area fairly quickly, making short stops in each destination to glimpse the pagodas and historical sites scattered along the shore, while beach-goers are sure to stick around longer, as this is Vietnam's prime mainland spot for sun and sand. Highway 1, the largest national road, is the major route for traveling between the region's cities.

While parts of this coast enjoy clear skies year-round thanks to a semi-arid climate, south-central Vietnam is at its best February-April, when the temperature has risen but the rain has yet to arrive. Sunshine prevails through the summer months until August, though the heat of late summer can get oppressive. Fall is rainy season, when winds pick up along the southern part of the coast and cooler weather settles in.

Quy Nhon

Quy Nhon is a pretty, peaceful town set amid the plunging seaside cliffs and soaring mountains of Binh Dinh province. Halfway between the hustle and bustle of Nha Trang and Vietnam's central cities, Hoi An, Danang, and Hue, this modest provincial capital has brilliant sun-kissed shores and plenty of genuine small-town charm, making it an inviting place to escape the madness of larger beach-front cities or break up the long journey down the coast. Quy Nhon's surroundings offer room for adventure in a less-trodden part of Vietnam, with the province's ever-present Cham towers dotting the nearby hills and vibrant green paddy fields spread out across the flatlands between.

Summer is a busy time, with affluent domestic tourists vacationing north of Nha Trang. Quy Nhon doesn't see much traffic the rest of the year, as temperatures drop and it rains November-February. Still, the town's quiet is sure to be short-lived. As mass tourism grows in Nha Trang, Quy Nhon has become a worthy spot for budget travelers seeking a quieter stretch of coast. Whether in town or slightly south of Quy Nhon along the shores of Bai Xep, local businesses are slightly more accommodating to foreign tourists these days, suggesting this sleepy seaside spot is an up-and-coming backpacker destination. Most travelers passing through Quy Nhon stick around for a few days at most before carrying on, as the main attraction is the beach.

SIGHTS

Beyond the beach, Quy Nhon does not offer much in the way of sights, though its nearby Cham towers make for an interesting and scenic adventure outside the city limits. Most travelers get around town just fine on foot.

Long Khanh Pagoda

Over 300 years old, **Long Khanh Pagoda** (141 Tran Cao Van, tel. 0256/374-9388, sunrise-sunset daily) is Quy Nhon's most famous Buddhist building and worth a look if you're wandering around town. Its entrance gate, just around the corner from the local football stadium, opens onto a soaring nine-tiered tower flanked by stone dragons and guarded by a statue of Quan Am. This building is the largest and newest on the premises, and has the least character. Inside the complex is a 17-meter blue-green Buddha standing at the center of the pagoda's bonsai garden. Caretakers and monks often hang out here during the day; you may have to ask one of them to let you into the often locked main hall, a squat

Quy Nhon

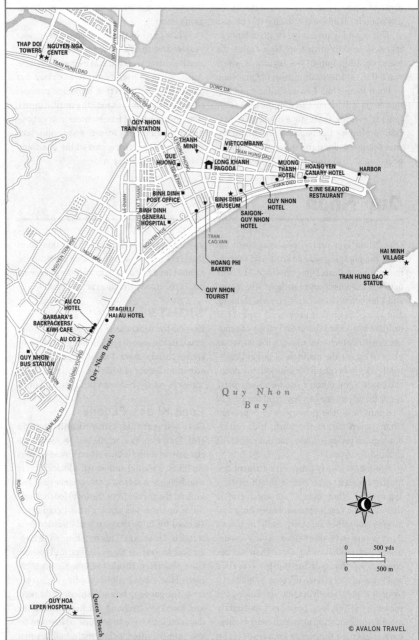

THAP DOI TOWERS

NGUYEN NGA CENTER

TRAN HUNG DAO

DONG DA

QUY NHON TRAIN STATION

THANH MINH

VIETCOMBANK

TRAN HUNG DAO

QUE HUONG

LONG KHANH PAGODA

MUONG THANH HOTEL

HOANG YEN CANARY HOTEL

HARBOR

BINH DINH POST OFFICE

BINH DINH MUSEUM

XUAN DIEU

C.INE SEAFOOD RESTAURANT

BINH DINH GENERAL HOSPITAL

SAIGON-QUY NHON HOTEL

QUY NHON HOTEL

TRAN CAO VAN

HOANG PHI BAKERY

HAI MINH VILLAGE

TRAN HUNG DAO STATUE

QUY NHON TOURIST

Quy Nhon Bay

AU CO HOTEL

SFAGULL/ HAI AU HOTEL

BARBARA'S BACKPACKERS/ KIWI CAFE

AU CO 2

Quy Nhon Beach

QUY NHON BUS STATION

0   500 yds

0   500 m

QUY HOA LEPER HOSPITAL

Queen's Beach

ROUTE 1D

NGUYEN HUE

LE DUAN

NGUYEN TAT THANH

NGO MAY

AN DUONG VUONG

HAI BA TRUNG

© AVALON TRAVEL

but beautiful bungalow with aging roof tiles. Inside, Long Khanh has two separate altars, each with a trio of statues lined up before a larger Buddha. The main hall is in reasonably good shape, considering its most recent construction was in the early 18th century. The caretakers are friendly and happy to give tours of the place.

Binh Dinh Museum

In a courtyard surrounded by cannons and old military vehicles, the oddly shaped **Binh Dinh Museum** (26 Nguyen Hue, tel. 0256/382-6997, 7am-11am and 2pm-5pm Mon.-Fri., VND5,000) houses the same exhibits you'd expect to find in a provincial museum, featuring sections on the history, industry, and people of the region, peppered with a few English signs to orient foreign visitors. Displays on the ethnic minorities of Binh Dinh and the Cham sculpture section at the back are particularly interesting, as is the revolutionary history exhibit on the right. The entire second level is reserved for photographs of Ho Chi Minh.

Thap Doi Towers

On a street corner heading northwest out of town, the **Thap Doi Towers** (Tran Hung Dao and Thap Doi, 6:30am-7pm daily, VND8,000) are a piece of 12th-century history surrounded by the present-day bustle of Quy Nhon. Sporting vegetation on the roof, the 18- and 20-meter towers have held up well over time, with the larger of the two still home to a massive stone linga-yoni (statue representing male and female energies).

So few Cham remain in the area that this site doesn't see many religious visitors. The local government has turned Thap Doi into a small park of sorts, with a handful of benches set up around the well-manicured lawn, and several tall willowy palm trees on the premises. While most other Cham towers along the Vietnamese coast are perched atop rocky hills or surrounded by arid landscapes, these two stand out against a vibrant green backdrop. Thap Doi's architecture is also

original, differing slightly from other Cham designs. Instead of the usual reliefs of Shiva that top many of these redbrick towers, Thap Doi's multitiered rooftop features the bird-like Garuda, a prominent creature in Hindu mythology.

Visitors are free to roam the park on their own. It doesn't take much time to explore the entire grounds. Across the street are a handful of cafés and street food stalls where you can stop for a quick coffee break or a snack.

Tran Hung Dao Statue

The mammoth **Tran Hung Dao statue** (Hai Minh village, sunrise-sunset daily), built in 1972, leans off the edge of Phuong Mai Peninsula facing the Quy Nhon shoreline and can only be accessed by boat. Tran Hung Dao, a 13th-century war hero and one of Vietnam's most famous military leaders, is credited with twice defeating the Mongol army led by Kublai Khan, first emperor of China's Yuan dynasty. Nowadays, the bright white letters emblazoned beneath his perch— "Statue of Tran Hung Dao"—are more visible from the beach than the statue itself, but a trip to this spot remains worthwhile.

To get to the statue, catch a boat at the **harbor** (Ham Tu) on the eastern edge of town. Some polite but stern haggling should bring the price down as low as VND30,000 one-way for an individual traveler. This is also a good time to arrange return transport, as boats to and from the village do not follow a regular schedule.

When you've made it safely across the sea, follow the shoreline to the right past Hai Minh's buildings to the rocky, forested edge of the peninsula. Hidden between the overgrown brambles and debris is a small, semi-paved path up toward the statue, which will be visible from the moment you land. Of course, the statue itself is worth a look, but the real showstopper here is the view of Quy Nhon from this vantage point, as you can see its coastline decorated with circular fishing boats and colorful wooden vessels. With more time, you can also wander the area to catch partial glimpses of the other side of Phuong Mai Peninsula as well as the nearby lighthouse.

Nguyen Nga Center

At first glance, the modest **Nguyen Nga Center** (884 Tran Hung Dao, tel. 09/1412-1168, www.nguyennga.org, 7am-10pm daily) appears to be nothing more than a souvenir shop: Its shelves are stocked with knickknacks and jewelry, handbags, artwork, and a few items of clothing. However the story behind this building and the people in it is an inspiring tale that makes the trip out here all the more worthwhile. Founded by the inimitable Ms. Nguyen Nga, this versatile facility functions as a training school and nonprofit organization for residents with physical disabilities across Binh Dinh province, teaching them a variety of skills, from sewing, tailoring, and music to English and computer classes. The center sells handicrafts and other products made by the students. Nguyen Nga also provides scholarships and employment opportunities to graduates, as well as offering microfinancing loans to locals with disabilities hoping to start their own business. Visitors, shoppers, and volunteers are always welcome to stop by for a chat with employees and residents.

fishing boats moored near Quy Nhon Beach

TOP EXPERIENCE

BEACHES

There are two main beach areas in Quy Nhon. Quy Nhon Beach is a very accessible main city beach yet manages to retain an air of quiet—except in the summer months when Vietnamese vacationers are on holiday. Even more peaceful are the secluded shores of Quy Hoa Beach, which lies just a few kilometers south of town between two mountains. Still farther south, you'll find a handful of resorts and guesthouses clustered around Bai Xep, a stretch of sand surrounded by friendly fishing communities that has become increasingly popular among the backpacker set. Travelers generally base themselves within walking distance of either Quy Nhon Beach or the shores of Bai Xep, though the drive between the two is only about 11 kilometers. Sand flies occasionally make an appearance here.

Quy Nhon Beach

Quy Nhon Beach (An Duong Vuong) is peaceful, accessible, and clean, making it a large part of the town's appeal. Stretching past the local university and alongside Children's Park, Quy Nhon's yellow sands remain uncluttered, affording easy public access to visitors and shores free from roving vendors or additional fees. On the northern end, fishing boats pull into the harbor, making this a less desirable place for swimming, but there are a few nice cafés and plenty of seafood restaurants nearby.

Around the middle of Xuan Dieu, heading toward An Duong Vuong, a set of volleyball nets and a lifeguard's tower hint at the action Quy Nhon sees during high season; there are some nice views here. The best place to lay out in the sun is past the large roundabout where Xuan Dieu ends and An Duong Vuong begins.

Fishing vessels are less common here, and this stretch of sand sees considerably less foot traffic during the day.

Quy Hoa Beach and Leper Hospital

Quy Hoa Beach, home to **Quy Hoa Leper Hospital** (south of Quy Nhon, tel. 0256/374-7999, www.quyhoandh.org.vn, 7:30am-11:30am and 1:30pm-5:30pm daily, VND7,000), is the last place in town you'd think to visit. The beach is a blustery, deserted shoreline where dramatic waves crash onto the white sand, and a few benches and other oddly shaped structures, including a guitar-shaped lookout, dot the coast.

Hidden between the mountains just off a coastal stretch of Highway 1, Quy Hoa began as a leper colony in 1929, with about 30 patients in the care of French Catholic priest Paul Maheure. Over the years, nuns were sent to help and additional buildings were constructed as the number of patients grew, housing a few famous Vietnamese figures with the disease, including poet Han Mac Tu. Nowadays, the center is a crucial part of local health care, serving the Central Highlands population, which often has little to no access to adequate health care.

Once you've paid the entrance fee, head left toward the beach and you'll pass the grave of Han Mac Tu. The celebrity park, a garden of statues near the water, is also decorated with busts of prominent doctors and scientists, both foreign and Vietnamese, who made notable contributions to leprosy research.

Quy Hoa is best reached by motorbike, whether on your own or with a hired *xe om,* as its narrow village roads tend to be too tight for larger vehicles. Follow An Duong Vuong south from Quy Nhon, bearing left up the hill when the road splits into several smaller lanes. A small pass brings you to the top of the mountain, where you'll keep an eye out for blue-and-white signs reading "Quy Hoa"; take another left down into the village and on to the hospital gates.

Bai Xep

If you're up for a day trip out of town, **Bai Xep** makes for a worthy jaunt south of the city. Surrounded by a sleepy fishing village, this peaceful stretch of coast has a growing number of tourists, mainly backpackers, and still retains much of its laid-back charm. Tucked in a small cove, Bai Xep's cool waters and relatively clean beach make for a great spot to spend an afternoon. You'll also find a handful of local eateries here, some more tourist-focused than others, as well as some notably friendly locals. Amenities like beach chairs are less prevalent here, but the unspoiled nature of Bai Xep's shores is part of its appeal. By taxi, the trip should take about 15 minutes from downtown Quy Nhon.

FOOD

Attached to Barbara's Backpackers, **Kiwi Cafe** (12 An Duong Vuong, tel. 0256/389-2921, 7am-9pm daily, VND40,000-150,000), serves both Western eats and tasty Vietnamese, as well as an ever-changing list of daily specials. While most backpacker-friendly places offer a selection of watered-down local dishes, meals at Kiwi Cafe have pizzazz, deviating from what you might expect in a delightfully appetizing way. Cheap beer and other cold beverages are also available, as is free travel information—ask about Barbara's Quy Nhon guide—and a book exchange.

A humble little spot, **Que Huong** (185 Le Hong Phong, tel. 0256/382-9395, 10am-8:30pm daily, VND50,000-170,000) is a good place to take a break from the coast's overabundance of seafood. This pleasant local eatery serves tasty chicken, beef, and pork dishes along with a few veggies and fish, offering plenty of selection at reasonable prices.

Dead-center on the main drag, **C.ine Seafood Restaurant** (94 Xuan Dieu, tel. 0256/651-2675, 10am-10pm daily, VND70,000-250,000) is one of several seafood eateries overlooking the beach and an obvious vendor of Heineken beer, as evidenced by the green-and-red advertisements plastered everywhere. Shrimp, squid, crab, fish, and hot pot dishes are listed on the menu, which comes in English as well as Vietnamese, though you'll likely have to point out your order for the staff, as few of the waiters speak English.

For vegetarians, the small, easy-to-miss **Thanh Minh** (151 Phan Boi Chau, tel. 0256/382-1719, 6am-8pm daily, VND15,000-50,000) is a narrow storefront complete with a street cart that serves tasty rice dishes with an array of sautéed vegetables and tofu. Thanh Minh makes a great spot for breakfast or lunch; arrive early, as food gets cold around 1:30pm-2pm.

A walk-up storefront not far from Le Hong Phong, **Hoang Phi Bakery** (74 Nguyen Hue, tel. 0256/381-2130, 8am-10pm daily, VND5,000-15,000) displays a lovely collection of Asian-style pastries and other sweet treats that work well as a snack or a compliment to your morning coffee.

ACCOMMODATIONS

Thanks to Quy Nhon's popularity among domestic tourists, hotels are readily available along the beachfront, which is likely where you'll want to stay during the summer months when the weather is best. A handful of good budget and mid-range options are found toward the center of town. Off-season travelers will find room rates heavily discounted.

Under VND210,000

Barbara's Backpackers (12 An Duong Vuong, tel. 0256/389-2921, VND115,000 dorm, VND230,000 d) offers bare-bones dorm beds at an unbeatable price. Mosquito nets and hot water are provided. No lockers are available, but valuables can be left at reception. A temperamental Wi-Fi connection exists in the open-air Kiwi Cafe out front, which serves Western and Vietnamese dishes and also boasts an up-to-date Quy Nhon city guide. Public access to the nice part of the beach is just across the road. English-speaking staff can help arrange guided tours, motorbike rentals, and bus and train tickets.

VND210,000-525,000

Opposite the four-star Seagull Hotel, **Au Co** (8 An Duong Vuong, tel. 0256/374-7699, VND340,000-680,000) is an oddly shaped corner building with generous rooms. Arched ceilings and stone columns add character to the place, not to mention its sturdy wooden beds. Large bay windows, hot water, air-conditioning, Wi-Fi, and TV are in each room, and most also have a balcony. You can also find a **second location** (24 An Duong Vuong) just a few steps down the road.

VND525,000-1,050,000

A pale-yellow art deco building overlooking the beach, the **Quy Nhon Hotel** (8 Nguyen Hue, tel. 0256/389-2401, www.quynhonhotel.com.vn, VND780,000-850,000) manages to provide a reasonable amount of ambience in its mid-range rooms. This government-run property offers several varieties of lodging, each featuring air-conditioning, Wi-Fi, hot water, and TV, not to mention complimentary breakfast in the hotel's restaurant. There is also a café on-site boasting wireless Internet. The staff can assist in travel arrangements and tours around Quy Nhon as well as the rest of the province.

Along with good value and location, the amiable folks at **Hoang Yen Canary Hotel** (13-17 Nguyen Hue, tel. 0256/389-1277, www.hoangyencanaryhotel.com.vn, VND600,000-800,000) make this a worthy mid-range spot, particularly on the upper floors where sea views are best. While the hotel is not splashy, each room is tidy and well-kept, featuring hot water and air-conditioning, Wi-Fi, TV, and complimentary breakfast. Many rooms come with a balcony, though these are cramped. This is also one of the few places where you'll find affordable front-facing sea views.

Complete with uniformed bellhops and a grand entrance hall, the regal **Muong Thanh Hotel** (2 Nguyen Hue, tel. 0256/389-2666, www.muongthanh.com, VND650,000-1,300,000) goes beyond the average mid-range hotel. Well-appointed modern rooms come with large flat-screen TVs, air-conditioning, hot water, and an in-room safe, as well as a view of the coast. Breakfast is included in the rates, as is use of the hotel swimming pool. You'll also find a whirlpool tub and tennis courts on the premises, making this the best-value hotel near the beach.

VND1,050,000-2,100,000

The **Saigon-Quy Nhon Hotel** (24 Nguyen Hue, tel. 0256/382-9922, www.saigonquynhonhotel.com.vn, VND1,800,000-4,200,000) is a stately place, if a little stuffy, and features a host of add-ons, from massage services to a swimming pool, travel assistance, a fitness center, and a restaurant. Rooms come with hot water, Wi-Fi, TV, air-conditioning, tea- and coffee-making facilities, and an in-room safe. A complimentary buffet breakfast is also provided downstairs. While the hotel lacks character, its level of service is a cut above. Like its other beachfront competition, sea views are equally stunning.

You'll find well-appointed rooms at the **Seagull Hotel** (Hai Au Hotel, 489 An Duong Vuong, tel. 0256/384-6377, www.seagullhotel.com.vn, VND1,400,000-2,600,000), just opposite Quy Nhon University and about as close to the ocean as you can get. Amenities include TV, air-conditioning, Wi-Fi, hot water, tea- and coffee-making facilities, a minibar, and complimentary breakfast. The balconies offer as good a sea view as any in town, and there are several restaurants on-site, not to mention a bar, a massage center, and a travel outfit. While the hotel itself isn't full of character, it is easily the best seaside option at this end of the beach.

Over VND2,100,000

Sixteen kilometers south of town, **AVANI Quy Nhon** (Bai Dai Beach, Ghenh Rang, tel. 0256/384-0132, www.avanihotels.com, VND2,310,000-3,650,000) features beachside lodgings along with a garden spa, an outdoor swimming pool, and a restaurant and bar. Combining Cham architecture and Vietnamese decor, accommodations are built into the hillside, with both deluxe room and junior suite options available. All spacious lodgings include TV, hot water, Wi-Fi, and air-conditioning as well as complimentary breakfast. A private beach bound by a pair of rocky escarpments is just steps away. The on-site spa also provides massage, facial, and body treatments.

INFORMATION AND SERVICES
Visitor Information

For a wealth of local information, **Barbara's** (12 An Duong Vuong, tel. 0256/389-2921, 7am-9pm daily) boasts its very own Quy Nhon guide for guests to peruse at their leisure. Recommendations cover restaurants, hotels, and sights, in addition to practical info regarding Internet access, banks, and postal services. This is a great spot for independent travelers seeking information on do-it-yourself trips in the city and around. You can also visit **Seagull Travel** (489 An Duong Vuong, tel. 0256/374-7747, 7am-11:30am and 1:30pm-5pm daily), attached to the Seagull Hotel, which hires out English guides (VND1,135,000 per day) and provides other travel- and transportation-related services. The folks at **Quy Nhon Tourist** (149A Nguyen Hue, tel. 0256/653-5959, www.quynhontourist.vn, 7:30am-11:30am and 1:30pm-5:30pm Mon.-Fri.) are also a helpful bunch, though you'll find English is limited here.

Banks

The **Vietcombank** (148 Le Loi, tel. 0256/382-1497, www.vietcombank.com.vn, 8am-11am and 1:30pm-4:30pm Mon.-Fri., 7am-11am Sat.), downtown, assists with currency exchange and has an ATM out front. There are plenty of ATMs situated near the university and outside of Seagull Hotel on the southern end of the beach.

Postal Services and Internet

The **Binh Dinh post office** (127 Hai Ba Trung, tel. 0256/382-1516, 7:30am-6:30pm Mon.-Sat., 8am-5pm Sun.) takes all mail and packages. For Internet access, head to one of the dozens of Internet shops in town.

Medical Services

The rundown **Binh Dinh General Hospital** (106 Nguyen Hue, tel. 0256/382-2184) is the closest you'll find to the beach, but facilities are dismal and English speakers will likely not be found here. If possible, head to Nha Trang or, better yet, Saigon.

GETTING THERE
Bus

Quy Nhon's **central bus station (Ben Xe Khach Quy Nhon)** (71 Tay Son, tel. 0256/374-6647, 6am-6pm daily) receives daily arrivals from as far as Saigon to the south and Danang to the north. The most comfortable option for the 14-hour trip from Saigon (3 times daily, VND250,000) is **Phuong Trang** (Quy Nhon bus station, tel. 0256/394-7947, www.futabus.vn), which has an office in the station. **Mailinh Express** (Quy Nhon bus station, tel. 0256/393-9393) also offers buses to and from Danang (6.5 hours, VND155,000).

Local minibuses serve the same routes, but they're often overcrowded, less comfortable, and less safe on the roads.

Train

Trains arrive daily at the **Dieu Tri station** (Nguyen Dinh Thu, tel. 0256/383-3255, 7am-5pm daily), 11 kilometers northwest of Quy Nhon, from northern destinations such as Danang (VND130,000-350,000) and Hanoi (VND525,000-1,100,000), as well as Nha Trang (VND90,000-260,000) and Saigon (VND205,000-720,000) to the south. From the train station, it costs VND150,000-200,000 for a taxi ride into town.

Though there is also a **Quy Nhon station** (Le Hong Phong, 7am-9pm daily), the city's downtown station only welcomes one arrival per day from Saigon. This train arrives at 8:45am and departs again for destinations south of Quy Nhon at 2:35pm.

Air

Though not many travelers opt to fly to Quy Nhon, it's possible to get here from Saigon, Nha Trang, Phu Quoc, Haiphong, and Hanoi. The **Phu Cat Airport (San Bay Phu Cat)** (UIH) is 32 kilometers north of downtown Quy Nhon and is served by Vietnam Airlines and budget carriers VietJet and Jetstar.

Taxis can transport you to and from town (VND250,000-350,000). It's also possible to hop on the **airport bus** (VND50,000), which runs regularly between Phu Cat Airport and 1 Nguyen Tat Thanh. The bus does not have a scheduled run time but rather operates whenever there is an incoming or outgoing flight. From the airport, it's easy enough to find the bus. However, if you choose this option when leaving Quy Nhon, make sure to arrive at 1 Nguyen Tat Thanh approximately 2-2.5 hours before your flight in order to catch the bus.

GETTING AROUND
Taxi and *Xe Om*

Xe om drivers camp out at intersections across town, particularly along Xuan Dieu. For taxis, you can call **Mailinh** (tel. 0256/379-7979) or simply flag one of their cabs down.

Bike and Motorbike

Barbara's (12 An Duong Vuong, tel. 0256/389-2921, 7am-9pm daily, VND150,000-200,000), at the top end of An Duong Vuong, has both motorbikes and bicycles available for rent. You can also ask your hotel or guesthouse, as they may have motorbikes or bicycles to rent out as well.

VICINITY OF QUY NHON

The undulating mountains and sun-bleached coastlines surrounding Quy Nhon are ripe with opportunities to get even more off the beaten path. Anyone with a motorbike can hop on the main road out of town and discover a slew of centuries-old Cham relics, as well as a few other less-frequented sights. Adventuresome travelers hanging around Quy Nhon for an extra day or two can hop on a bike and ramble across the Binh Dinh countryside.

Banh It Towers

The **Banh It Towers** (19 kilometers north of Quy Nhon on Highway 1, 7:30am-11:30am and 1:30pm-5:30pm daily, VND7,000), another relic of the Cham kingdom, are a 19-kilometer drive from town heading north. Overlooking lush rice fields and rolling mountains, these four hilltop structures date to the early 12th century. Despite its status as a well-preserved Cham structure, the place remains quiet, with only a few visitors passing through. The first tower is midway up a hill,

a small building dwarfed by the trio of structures above. The remaining towers each bear their own unique architectural traits. The tallest houses a large altar as well as a many-armed statue of Shiva. The repository boasts a boat-shaped roof, pointed at either end, and the smallest of the main structures, a short distance from the hilltop, resembles the gate tower down below.

If you aren't asked to pay at the main entrance, chances are you'll be approached by someone to collect the visitor's fee as you walk up the hill. Though the temple caretaker doesn't look very official, there is a sign listing the correct price out front.

Nha Trang

With sparkling blue waters and sun-bleached shores, frenetic traffic, and all-night parties, Nha Trang is one of mainland Vietnam's most popular beach destinations. Set amid a vibrant tropical landscape, this bustling metropolis plays the part of sunny seaside escape along the coast but maintains its local flavor farther inland, in the crowded markets and chaotic street stalls of the city.

Nha Trang's coastline is well equipped to entertain, with dozens of dive outfits, snorkeling excursions, and boat trips around the bay. A cluster of small islands near the southern edge of town host extensive marinelife, while Hon Tre Island, easily spotted from shore, boasts an island amusement park. On land, cultural attractions like the Po Nagar Towers, a prime example of ancient Cham architecture, and Long Son Pagoda, home to a 24-meter statue of the Buddha, do their part to occupy visitors, along with plenty of shopping, top-notch international cuisine, and a buzzing nightlife.

Nha Trang continues to expand beyond the borders of its small downtown backpacker district, sprouting new hotels and restaurants all along the coast. Over the past few years, the city has seen a shift in the makeup of its

foreign visitors, with more big tour groups rolling into town. Still, individual travelers hoping to catch some sun and party all night will appreciate the city's electric energy, which quickly seduces many into a few extra days on the beach. Those seeking a quiet seaside oasis should look elsewhere.

The best time to visit Nha Trang is March-September, as rain and wind take over the area October-January, making the waters rougher and the temperature a few degrees cooler. Whenever you go, three or four days in town is plenty of time to spend a day on the water, laze around on the beach, venture outside of town, and visit the local mud baths (a must-do in Nha Trang).

SIGHTS

Nha Trang's attractions stretch across the city and into the nearby countryside. Most sights within town are easily reached on foot, as is the main beach, while a handful of places north and south of downtown will likely require a taxi or *xe om*. The Po Nagar Towers to the north of town go well with a trip to the local hot springs or a visit to Bai Duong, while a southern jaunt to the Bao Dai Villas and the

Oceanography Museum can be paired with Vinpearl or, farther south, Bai Dai.

Downtown
LONG SON PAGODA

Backing onto nearby Trai Thuy Hill, **Long Son Pagoda** (20 23 Thang 10, tel. 0258/382-2558, sunrise-sunset daily) is home to a blindingly white 24-meter statue of the Buddha. Though it once stood at the top of the hill, the pagoda, originally built in 1886, was moved to safer ground after a storm in 1900 caused the building to collapse. The front entrance is adorned with interesting mosaics. Inside, the pagoda's muted tones give way to a riot of color, with bright religious flags and gilded woodwork lining the main hall. A lavish, many-armed Buddha sits at the front altar, backed by hundreds of tiny hands.

Ascend Trai Thuy Hill by walking past the right of the building up a set of stone steps. En route, you'll be greeted by a large reclining gray stone Buddha, just behind the main building, and the pagoda's bell, which weighs over 1,500 kilograms. For a small donation, visitors can sit inside the bell while a local monk performs a Buddhist chant.

At the top of the hill is another set of stairs, flanked by a pair of concrete dragons; the stairs bring you up to the largest statue. Towering above its surroundings, the pristine white Buddha sits on a lotus flower, eyes closed and smiling. Around its base are a series of reliefs commemorating the monks who protested Vietnam's southern government by lighting themselves on fire. Before the main incense urn at the very front of the statue is Thich Quang Duc, the first monk to self-immolate in 1963. You can also head around to the back of the giant hollow Buddha, where there is a small altar inside the statue's base.

NHA TRANG CATHEDRAL

The bell tower of the imposing **Nha Trang Cathedral (Nha Tho Nui)** (tel. 0258/382-3335, 8am-11:30am and 2pm-4pm Mon.-Sat.) soars 27 meters above the city, making this one of Nha Trang's more visible landmarks. The cathedral's gray faux-stone exterior, high arches, and ridged battlements give the appearance of a Gothic castle, along with the vibrant stained-glass reliefs occupying the front of the church.

The cathedral sits atop a hill, at the base of which is Ave Maria Square, a concrete clearing beside the city's six-way traffic circle. There, a sculpture of the Virgin Mary herself presides over a few palm trees and a

Buddha reclining on a hillside above Long Son Pagoda

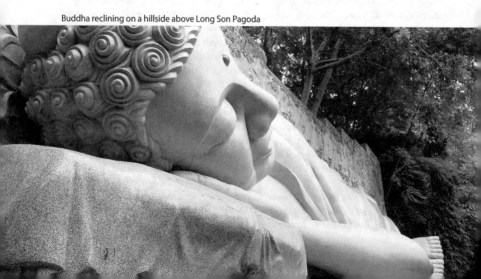

Vicinity of Nha Trang

DOC LET RESORT
WHITE SAND DOC LET RESORT

0   5 mi
0   5 km

Ba Ho Stream

MONKEY ISLAND FERRY

Monkey Island

SEE "DOWNTOWN NHA TRANG" MAP

PO NAGAR TOWERS

MUD BATH AND HOT SPRINGS
Bai Duong   HON CHONG

NHAT PHONG 3

SOUTHERN BUS STATION
NHA TRANG BEACH

LONG SON PAGODA
EVASON ANA MANDARA
VINPEARL LAND

SEE "SOUTHERN NHA TRANG" MAP
BAO DAI VILLAS
VINPEARL GOLF CLUB

Bach Dang Park

DIAMOND BAY GOLF
OCEANOGRAPHY MUSEUM

CAU DA HARBOR

ENTRANCE TO BAI DAI
THE SHACK

Bai Dai

CAM RANH AIRPORT

© AVALON TRAVEL

semicircle of park benches. Due to an uptick in large tourist groups, visitors are no longer permitted to venture upstairs to the cathedral except for mass (5am, 7am, 9:30am, 4:30pm, and 6:30pm Sun.), but visitors can take in the grand church and its surroundings from the courtyard below.

ALEXANDRE YERSIN MUSEUM

Tucked at the southern end of Nha Trang's Pasteur Institute, the **Alexandre Yersin Museum** (8-10 Tran Phu, tel. 0258/382-2406, www.pasteur-nhatrang.org.vn, 8am-11:30am and 2pm-4:30pm Mon.-Fri., VND20,000 adults, VND5,000 children) may not seem like much, but its exhibits manage to pack a great deal of information and scores of artifacts from the famed Swiss doctor's life into a few small rooms. Antique gadgets, from microscopes to old-school medical tools and test tubes from Yersin's study, are on display around the museum, as are dozens of letters, which he wrote to his mother and sister while living in Vietnam. Those keen on history and science will enjoy learning about one of the most influential Europeans of Vietnam's colonial era. All signage is in English, French, and Vietnamese.

LONG THANH GALLERY

A photographer since age 13, the man behind **Long Thanh Gallery** (126 Hoang Van Thu, tel. 0258/382-4875, www.longthanhart.com, 8am-5pm daily) began his career as an apprentice in his uncle's camera shop and has been snapping photos ever since. Using only analog machinery, Long Thanh's simple, evocative black-and-white portraits and countryside scenes have garnered him international acclaim as well as exhibits in Europe, the United States, and Australia. Long Thanh keeps to his gallery, down a quiet street north of the Nha Trang Cathedral, where the doors are open throughout the day, and visitors can drop in for a look at some of his best work. Long Thanh and his wife are usually around the shop, and the friendly pair is always up for a chat. Call ahead to arrange a private showing outside gallery hours.

North of Nha Trang
★ PO NAGAR TOWERS

About 1.5 kilometers north of town, the **Po Nagar Towers** (2 Thang 4, 6am-6pm daily, VND22,000) bear not one but two histories. Nha Trang may boast sleek modern buildings and swanky restaurants along its beachfront, but the intricate carvings and burnt red brick of the Po Nagar Towers hint at the region's ancient past. From the 8th to the 13th centuries, the Cham empire built these Hindu temples to honor Po Nagar, their most significant female deity. When the Vietnamese arrived in 1635, ending Cham authority, they adopted the towers and Po Nagar became Thien Y A Na, a young girl taken in by an elderly, childless couple who taught her people to farm rice. Perched upon a hill overlooking the Cai River, these towers continue to hold a special significance in Cham culture and are the site of an annual festival, which takes place from the 21st to 23rd of the third lunar month (late Apr.-mid-May) in honor of the namesake deity.

Inside the entrance gates are 22 columns (once 24). Here, amid a shadeless courtyard, the Cham would prepare offerings before hiking up the steep steps at the far end of the clearing. The tallest of the four sun-scorched towers is dedicated to Po Nagar and houses a black stone statue of the deity, which dates to AD 1050.

Beside the main tower, a slightly smaller structure belongs to Shiva (in the Cham version) or Thien Y A Na's husband (for the Vietnamese). Inside is the largest linga-yoni statue (symbols representing male and female energies) on-site.

The remaining two towers are more humble, each housing a smaller linga-yoni statue. The one beside the two large structures honors Skanda, first-born son of Shiva, as well as the adoptive parents of Thien Y A Na. Behind Po Nagar's main tower, the smallest structure is dedicated to Ganesh, second-born son of Shiva, and the children of Thien Y A Na, Princess Quy and Prince Tri. Look inside the exhibition room at the back, where replicas of the towers' statues are on display. Near the steps, Po Nagar also offers nice views of the Cai River.

Many tour groups and independent travelers pass through the towers. Respectful dress is a must inside the temples. Guests can use the gray robes located near the main

Po Nagar Towers

Downtown Nha Trang

tower, free of charge, if they are not dressed appropriately.

HON CHONG

Overlooking the sea, the rocky promontory of **Hon Chong** (Pham Van Dong, tel. 0258/628-9137, 6am-6pm daily, VND22,000) extends out from the southern end of Bai Duong Beach in a series of smooth stone formations. By the ticket booth, three traditional Vietnamese houses display local specialties and handicrafts, plus an array of musical instruments used by the region's ethnic minorities. Musical demonstrations occur when visitors arrive in large numbers.

Down a set of stairs, you'll clamber over a jumble of sandy rocks as you head toward the sea. Passing under the formation known as Heaven's Gate, in which a substantial rock hangs precariously between two larger stones, can be a nerve-racking experience. The formation has been this way for centuries without incident.

Towering above the rest, at the far end of the promontory, is Hon Chong, the stone after which the place is named. Legend has it that fairies used to bathe in the waters near Hon Chong. One day, while spying on these bathing beauties, a rather inebriated giant stumbled and nearly slipped off the rocks. The massive gouge in Hon Chong that resembles a handprint is where the giant caught himself and managed not to fall in. As you face the ocean, to your right is Hon Do, or Red Island, a small piece of land that houses a Buddhist pagoda, named for the color it turns at sunrise.

South of Nha Trang
OCEANOGRAPHY MUSEUM

The city's **Oceanography Museum (Bao Tang Hai Duong Hoc)** (1 Cau Da, tel. 0258/359-0036, www.vnio.org.vn, 6am-6pm daily, VND40,000) features several exhibits, some more interesting than others, covering the roughly 20,000 wildlife and plant specimens collected from Vietnamese waters by the research arm of the institute. A miniature aquarium is the highlight of the place, with large open pools home to dozens of saltwater creatures, including jet-black stingrays, massive sea turtles, a pair of seals, ropelike moray eels, colorful reef fish, and small sharks.

Farther on, a cavernous, tiled room catalogues the region's species with row upon row of creatures and plantlife. English signage is at most exhibits, though information can be sparse. You'll also find the 18-meter-long skeleton of a whale on display as well as the bones of the endemic dugong, a distant underwater relative to the elephant.

BAO DAI VILLAS

Visited for its breezy beach, seaside views, and history museums, the **Bao Dai Villas** (Cau Da, tel. 0258/359-0147, baodai@dng.vnn. vn, 8am-5pm daily, VND15,000) is a collection of five charming colonial buildings that once served as a vacation estate for Vietnam's last emperor, Bao Dai. Before they became home to royalty, these lemon-hued buildings briefly functioned as part of the Indochinese Institute of Oceanography. In 1926, the emperor was gifted two of the villas.

Nghinh Phong, one of the buildings, serves as a museum. It's perched on the edge of a seaside cliff amid ample greenery. While the exhibits within the villa are uninspired—no more than a few family photographs and a handful of the emperor's possessions—the history of Nghinh Phong's residents is rather interesting, and the panoramic views make the trip worthwhile, particularly for shutterbugs hoping to capture Nha Trang Bay and nearby Hon Tre Island from a different angle. The villa complex also houses two restaurants and the Queen's Beach, a small cove hidden from the wind where daytime visitors come to relax. The remaining four villas are currently rented out as hotel accommodations.

TOURS

With scores of local travel companies and plenty to do both in the water and on land, Nha Trang offers many day-long tours. The only way to access the nearby islands is via

Southern Nha Trang

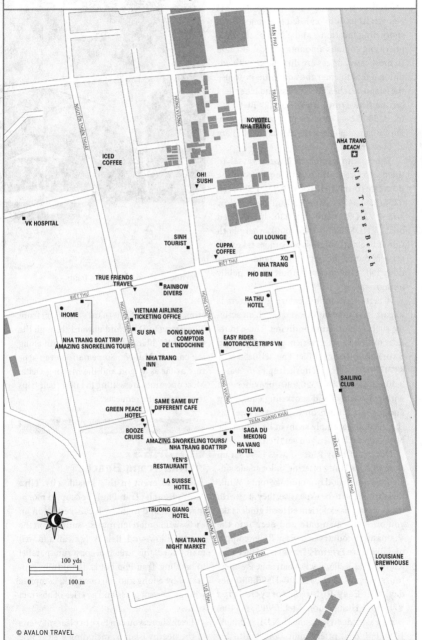

NHA TRANG BEACH ⊡

Nha Trang Beach

NOVOTEL NHA TRANG

ICED COFFEE

OH! SUSHI

VK HOSPITAL

SINH TOURIST

CUPPA COFFEE

QUI LOUNGE

XQ NHA TRANG

PHO BIEN

TRUE FRIENDS TRAVEL

RAINBOW DIVERS

HA THU HOTEL

IHOME

VIETNAM AIRLINES TICKETING OFFICE

SU SPA

NHA TRANG BOAT TRIP/ AMAZING SNORKELING TOUR

DONG DUONG COMPTOIR DE L'INDOCHINE

EASY RIDER MOTORCYCLE TRIPS VN

NHA TRANG INN

SAILING CLUB

SAME SAME BUT DIFFERENT CAFE

OLIVIA

GREEN PEACE HOTEL

BOOZE CRUISE

SAGA DU MEKONG

HA VANG HOTEL

AMAZING SNORKELING TOURS/ NHA TRANG BOAT TRIP

YEN'S RESTAURANT

LA SUISSE HOTEL

TRUONG GIANG HOTEL

NHA TRANG NIGHT MARKET

LOUISIANE BREWHOUSE

TRẦN PHÚ

TRẦN PHÚ

TRẦN PHÚ

HÙNG VƯƠNG

HÙNG VƯƠNG

HÙNG VƯƠNG

NGUYỄN THIỆN THUẬT

NGUYỄN THIỆN THUẬT

BIỆT THỰ

BIỆT THỰ

BIỆT THỰ

TRẦN QUANG KHẢI

TRẦN QUANG KHẢI

TUỆ TĨNH

TUỆ TĨNH

0   100 yds

0   100 m

© AVALON TRAVEL

boat tour. These generic trips receive mixed reviews, with most boat tours taking you around to a local fishing village, the Tri Nguyen Aquarium on Mieu Islet, one or two snorkeling locations, and a beach, all while providing copious amounts of local alcohol. In most cases, prices are dirt cheap, with additional fees to enter the aquarium or to use the island beaches. Red, white, and blue fliers for the **Nha Trang Boat Trip** (29 Biet Thu, tel. 0258/352-4471, www.nhatrangtour.com. vn, 8:30am-4:30pm daily, VND150,000) are all over town.

Those who prefer to have a vessel to themselves can hire private boats from the **Cau Da Tourist Harbor** (7 Tran Phu, tel. 0258/359-0479, 7am-5:30pm daily, slow boats VND300,000-800,000, high-speed boats VND800,000-1,400,000), where both slower boats and high-speed canoes take passengers out to the bay's four islands, essentially following the same route as the public tour groups.

A better option for seafaring travelers is to pair your time on the water with an activity, such as snorkeling or diving. These tours cater to all levels of experience. The **Amazing Snorkeling Tour** (29 Biet Thu, tel. 0258/352-4471, www.vietnamsnorkeling.com, 9am-3:30pm daily, VND350,000) provides you with reasonably good snorkeling equipment and a hearty lunch on the boat, as well as the freedom to simply swim or lie out on the boat's top deck when you get tired.

Dozens of Easy Rider outfits have set up shop in Nha Trang offering tailor-made single- and multiple-day motorbike tours. While these trips tend to be expensive, they are worth the price tag, as experienced local guides take you off the beaten path and deep into the Vietnamese countryside. Easy Rider companies like **True Friends Travel** (23C Biet Thu, tel. 09/0642-4266, www.nhatrangeasyrider-tours.com, VND1,370,000-1,590,000 per day) and **Easy Rider Motorcycle Trips VN** (7G/4 Hung Vuong, tel. 09/0538-4406, www.easyridertrips.com, VND1,360,000-1,700,000/day) offer single- and multi-day

palm trees and sun beds in Nha Trang

trips throughout Vietnam's interior, from Nha Trang to Dalat and onward through the Central Highlands to Hoi An or south along the coast to Mui Ne. Some outfits even venture as far as Saigon and the Mekong Delta. Most operators are willing to tailor their trips to your specific requests.

TOP EXPERIENCE

BEACHES
★ Nha Trang Beach

The main event in this seaside city, **Nha Trang Beach** (Tran Phu) is occupied morning, noon, and night by locals getting in an early swim or foreign tourists sunning on the coarse yellow sand. Relatively clean and well maintained, this stretch of coast runs parallel to bustling Tran Phu but is, thankfully, separated by a long and narrow park, complete with patches of grass and a series of abstract statues.

From shore, you can take in pleasant views of the nearby islands, including a clear line of sight toward the Hollywood-esque sign at Vinpearl Land, as well as the incredibly blue Nha Trang Bay. Beach chairs can be rented from independent vendors, or visit one of the many beachfront cafés and restaurants, where paying customers are given free use of the sun beds by the water. Traveling vendors—some friendly, some a little persistent—also make the rounds, offering food and drinks as well as souvenirs and other knickknacks. Keep an eye on your belongings, as theft on the beach is not unheard of.

Bach Dang Park

The sands of **Bach Dang Park** (Tran Phu near the Vinpearl ferry terminal) are a modest stretch of beach past the swanky Ana Mandara Resort. You'll find relative peace and quiet here compared to the crowded coastline farther north. While there isn't much in the way of services this far south, the park is only about two kilometers from the main part of Tran Phu, and the spot is pleasantly devoid of traveling vendors.

North of Nha Trang
BAI DUONG

On the other side of the small Hon Chong promontory, **Bai Duong** (Pham Van Dong) is barely a stone's throw from the downtown area but manages to avoid some of the chaos that characterizes the city's main beach. While many are happy to sit and sun amid the masses, those who prefer more peace and quiet but lack the time to make a trip out to Bai Dai will appreciate Bai Duong. The beach is still very much in the city, with a major thoroughfare zipping by at the back, but a low barrier and a few meters of sand put at least some distance between you and the traffic. Sun chairs are available for rent, and there are plenty of cafés and restaurants in the surrounding area. Unlike at the main beach, you'll have to get up from your seat in order to be served.

South of Nha Trang
BAI DAI

Half an hour south of Nha Trang, **Bai Dai** (Khu Du Lich Bai Dai) may not be quite as clean or as well-maintained as the city's main strip, but its wide empty beach and white-capped waters are ideal for novice surfers or those looking to spend an afternoon away from town. The shoreline is unpopulated, leaving travelers free to stretch out on their own.

At the top of the beach, stilted bamboo huts crouch together, slinging drinks, snacks, and seafood. **The Shack** (Bai Dai town, tel. 012/1666-3903, www.shackvietnam.com, 10am-7pm daily, VND40,000-200,000), a modest little hangout, hides inside the mix of makeshift eateries, offering Mexican food, surfing lessons, board rentals, and beach chairs.

Bai Dai lies roughly 21 kilometers from town, so it's worth at least a half-day trip. Taxis will be able to take you out for about VND250,000-300,000 one-way, but the drive can easily be done on your own via motorbike. Keep an eye out for the sign that reads "Khu Du Lich Bai Dai" as you pass Mia Resort, about 11 kilometers from the airport, where the road turns into a barren four-lane highway. Hang a left here and follow the dirt path in toward the beach.

ENTERTAINMENT AND EVENTS
Nightlife

Nightlife is a thriving part of Nha Trang's tourist neighborhood. While destinations like Phu Quoc or Mui Ne tend to draw a quieter crowd, visitors in this fast-paced seaside city are ready to party, and the foreign enclave carved out beside Nha Trang Beach does not disappoint. Packed into a few short city blocks you'll find thumping dance music and laid-back sports bars, classy cocktails, dirt-cheap street-side beer, and Nha Trang's version of the infamous "bucket," a mixed drink or three in a plastic jar. With so many places open late, travelers are free to stay out and party all night long, but it's important to stay safe.

BARS

While the name doesn't necessarily ooze class, **Booze Cruise** (110 Nguyen Thien Thuat, tel. 0258/352-1105, 7am-1am daily, VND15,000-150,000) is one of Nha Trang's finer casual hangouts, with friendly staff, a variety of sports channels, and a dance floor. Its spacious storefront and nearly all-afternoon happy hour convince most passing travelers to stop in at this blue-and-orange behemoth at least once for a cheap drink and some eats from the bar's Western menu.

Long after the sun sets, the breezy veranda at **Louisiane Brewhouse** (29 Tran Phu, tel. 0258/352-1948, www.louisianebrewhouse. com.vn, 7am-late, VND30,000-150,000) stays open late, offering drink specials and occasionally live music by the sea. While this place doesn't get as wild as the nearby Sailing Club, Louisiane offers a more relaxed atmosphere, perfect for a couple of end-of-day beers on the beach. Keep an eye out for drink deals and special events.

NIGHTCLUBS

The best party on the beach, **Sailing Club** (72-74 Tran Phu, tel. 0258/352-4628, www. sailingclubnhatrang.com, 7am-2am daily, VND60,000-200,000) turns the sands of Nha Trang into a loud and lively outdoor gathering every night, complete with DJs, cocktails, and plenty of room to dance. Drink prices are more expensive than most backpacker spots, and there is often a cover charge here, depending upon the event. Given the ambience and the beachfront location, the entry fee makes sense.

Boasting a swanky, palm-fringed outdoor patio as well as a chic indoor bar, **QUI Lounge** (62 Tran Phu, tel. 09/0696-1938, www.quilounge.com, 11:30am-1:30pm and 4pm-2am daily, VND90,000-500,000) is known for its handcrafted cocktails and top-shelf liquor selection. This upscale watering hole frequently plays host to DJs and other

performers, especially on weekends, and stays open into the wee hours.

Festivals and Events

Traditionally a Cham celebration, the annual **Thap Ba Festival** takes place from the 20th to the 23rd of the third lunar month, usually sometime in April. Over three days, hundreds of revelers visit the four Po Nagar towers just north of town, where a celebration is held in honor of the temple's namesake, Lady Po Nagar, a goddess credited with teaching the Cham people how to farm and earn a living. On the first day of the festival, a nearly 1,000-year-old statue located within the complex's main tower is undressed, bathed, and then dressed again in a new costume and crown for the coming year. Traditional dances and other cultural performances take place over the three days. On the final day, a more solemn worship rounds out the end of the celebration, as devotees from near and far pay their respects to the goddess and pray for protection and good fortune. The festival usually attracts a crowd of ethnic Cham as well as local Vietnamese residents, though anyone is welcome to stop by the Po Nagar Towers and observe the festivities.

SHOPPING

Most of the retail outfits in Nha Trang offer the same items you'll find in several other cities along the coast. Nha Trang is a popular spot for accessories made from ostrich and crocodile, such as purses, handbags, and belts. Those in search of beach essentials like sunscreen, swimwear, and other gear will find them scattered along Nguyen Thien Thuat and on Tran Phu near the Sailing Club. This main backpacker area around the beach features plenty of shopping for foreigners, from souvenirs and knickknacks to swimsuits and other essentials.

Markets

A sprawling, constant bustle of activity, the narrow streets surrounding **Dam Market** (Ben Cho, sunrise-sunset daily) are chock-full

Staying Safe After Dark

With dozens of tourists letting loose on the beaches, dance floors, and rooftops of Nha Trang, there are bound to be a few unsavory characters wandering the streets after dark. Pickpocketing, theft, and spiked drinks are common occurrences around Nha Trang's backpacker area and along the beachfront. When heading out for the night it's a wise idea to bring only the bare essentials and take care not to walk around alone.

One especially popular form of pickpocketing targets men. After a late night, guys leaving local bars will be approached by one or more friendly women, who proposition the victim before suddenly leaving. By the time the man realizes what's happened, the women are long gone with the full contents of his pockets. Xe om drivers, too, can pose a danger after dark. If you're planning to use local transportation to return to your hotel, it's best to use a taxi.

The most worrisome danger of Nha Trang's nightlife is drink-spiking. While the perpetrators tend to work independently, sometimes even local bartenders in a few of the city's less-reputable establishments get in on fixing a traveler's drink. More than a few backpackers have lost a night and woken up missing a phone or some cash. Avoid the area both in and around Why Not Bar after dark as acts of drink-spiking, theft, and violence are not uncommon here. While the Sailing Club is always a fun beachfront party, theft can occur on the sidewalks in front of this establishment. If you're heading home from here late at night, walk with a buddy or, better yet, grab a cab.

In the event that you feel you've been drugged, seek medical attention immediately. The **VK Hospital** (34/4 Nguyen Thien Thuat, tel. 0258/352-8866, www.vkhospital.com.vn), near the heart of the backpacker neighborhood, staffs English-speaking doctors and offers around-the-clock emergency services.

of produce and snack vendors, while the stalls within boast clothing, souvenirs, and more. If you wander long enough, you may even find one or two food stalls hidden within the maze of tented outdoor shops. Bargain for any purchases you make here.

Designed with tourists in mind, the local **night market** (alley 3 Tran Quang Khai, 5pm-10pm daily) gets going around sundown and hawks all manner of souvenirs, from clothing and jewelry to bags, notebooks, household items, and other knickknacks. Most of the goods on offer are standard Vietnam souvenirs, but the market atmosphere gives you the opportunity to bargain rather than shelling out what you might pay in a fixed-price shop.

Across the street from Tram Huong Tower along the city's main drag, the **Tran Phu Night Market** (Tran Phu beside Khanh Hoa Cultural Center, 5:30pm-11pm daily) runs throughout the evening and offers plenty of souvenirs, clothing, and even some dining options for hungry shoppers.

Gifts and Souvenirs

In case you missed the showrooms in Saigon and Dalat, the Nha Trang arm of the XQ empire, **XQ Nha Trang** (64 Tran Phu, tel. 0258/352-6579, www.xqvietnam.com, 8am-10pm daily), is hidden behind a series of snack stalls at the very top of Biet Thu and boasts a sizable collection of impressive hand-embroidered still lifes and portraits. A small souvenir shop on the far end of the complex also sells neat gifts, albeit expensive, with mugs, postcards, notebooks, and other items for sale. The hand embroidery, too, is available for purchase, but most images cost several hundred dollars.

A narrow storefront easily missed among the many small shops packed along Hung Vuong, **Dong Duong Comptoir de l'Indochine** (162 Hung Vuong, tel. 0258/352-3233, 10am-10pm daily) is unique in its range of carved stone jewelry boxes and other souvenirs, not to mention a host of propaganda posters and propaganda-style recreations of famous movie posters. Prices are reasonable, and the items inside offer something different than your standard Vietnam souvenirs.

SPORTS AND RECREATION

Nha Trang plays just as hard in the daylight as it does after dark. Scores of snorkeling and diving outfits catering to all levels of experience. Beyond the sea, a handful of onshore activities can keep you entertained, including a fast-growing massage and spa industry. A few other options include yoga sessions and cooking classes.

★ Mud Baths and Hot Springs

Nestled in the hills north of town, Nha Trang's spa-like hot springs and mud baths offer a unique way to spend an afternoon. Soak in private tubs of warm mud or hot mineral water before lounging around in the communal swimming pools. Spa and massage services can also be purchased. The experience is a relaxing escape from town and a must-do in Nha Trang.

There are two reputable hot springs in town. **Thap Ba** (15 Ngoc Son, tel. 0258/383-5335, www.tambunthapba.vn, 7am-7:30pm daily, VND200,000-700,000 pp) is the older and less expensive of the two, so it attracts a

higher percentage of Vietnamese holidaymakers and backpackers. If you don't mind spending the extra cash, the newer **i-Resort** (19 Xuan Ngoc, tel. 0258/383-8838, www.i-resort.vn, 8am-6pm daily, VND420,000-650,000 pp) has upscale facilities and better scenery as well as a few add-ons, including a restaurant and some nice private facilities. The best views are from the VIP rooms, which cost more. Fees vary depending on the package you choose. Each venue requires at least a few hours to go through the entire process. Both resorts are expansive, with a dozen or so baths built into the hillside overlooking Nha Trang. Since the mud baths are a big attraction, both resorts are always busy, but i-Resort gives more space and quiet to its customers.

Ask your hotel about transportation out to the hot springs, as many places offer a shuttle, or hop on the public bus. Each of the hot springs also offers its own electric car service, but these aren't really worth the cost; catch a taxi if you prefer to go on your own. Don't forget to bring your swimsuit.

Vinpearl Land Amusement Park

Plastered across the western side of Hon Tre Island are the bright-white blocky

freshwater pool at i-Resort

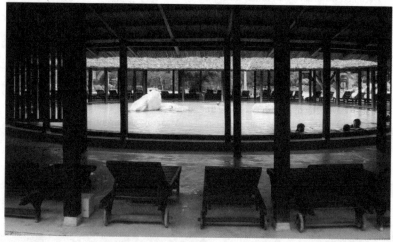

letters of **Vinpearl Land** (Hon Tre Island, tel. 0258/359-0611, www.vinpearlland.com, 8am-9pm daily, VND800,000 adults, VND700,000 children under 1.4 meters), Nha Trang's very own amusement park. Featuring an aquarium, several roller coasters, a water park, a beach, and arcade games, the island is a popular attraction for families with young kids as well as action-seekers. The island is reached by the world's longest sea-crossing cable car, which affords impressive views of the beach, the city, and the water. Tickets for the park cover both your cable car ride and access to Vinpearl's facilities. Most visitors make a day of the outing in order to get the most for their money.

Diving

Though it's not the most scenic underwater location in Vietnam, diving in Nha Trang is popular for its prices. Dozens of diving outfits are open in the backpacker area, providing travelers with everything from fun dives to PADI certification, but not all companies come with certified instructors or high-quality equipment. Both **Rainbow Divers** (19 Biet Thu, tel. 0258/352-4351, www.divevietnam. com, 6:30am-9:30pm daily) and **Sailing Club Divers** (72-74 Tran Phu, tel. 0258/352-2788, www.divenhatrang.com, 7:30am-8pm daily) are well-known and reliable outfits that offer a range of services to beginner and experienced divers.

Snorkeling

An all-day adventure with fun, sun, and plenty of underwater sights, the **Amazing Snorkeling Tour** (29 Biet Thu, tel. 0258/352-4471, www.vietnamsnorkeling.com, 9am-3:30pm daily, VND350,000) lives up to its name as one of the better budget tours available in town. Prices include a full day of snorkeling plus equipment, fruit, and a generous Vietnamese lunch on the boat. The tour guides are a cheerful and eclectic cast of characters with a sense of humor. The boat makes several stops near the local islands. Even if you're not a snorkeling enthusiast, this is a nice way to spend a day on a budget.

Surfing

While Nha Trang's main beach isn't ideal on account of its crowded waters, Bai Dai is a nice spot for novice surfers, as the waves are strong enough for newbies to practice without getting in over their heads. The surf is at its best November-March, after which the water starts to get too calm. In addition to food, Jet Ski rentals, bodyboards, and stand-up paddleboards, the folks at **The Shack** (Bai Dai town, tel. 012/1666-3903, www.shackvietnam.com, 10am-7pm daily, board rental VND200,000 per hour, surf lessons VND900,000 per hour) provide surf lessons and board rentals.

Golf

Nestled in the hills of Hon Tre Island, the **Vinpearl Golf Club** (Hon Tre Island, tel. 0258/359-0919, www.vinpearlgolf.com, 6am-6:30pm Tues.-Sun., VND1,900,000-2,460,000) is an 18-hole island course that looks out over Nha Trang Bay. Situated on the far side of Hon Tre, the course and its clubhouse offer impressive, uninhibited panoramas of the ocean as well as a moderately challenging course for beginners and experienced golfers. A driving range and pro shop are also here.

Taking advantage of the breathtaking coastline south of town, **Diamond Bay Golf** (Phuoc Ha Hamlet, Phuoc Dong Commune, tel. 0258/371-1722, www.diamondbaygolfvillas.com, 6am-7:30pm daily, VND2,100,000-2,800,000) is an 18-hole course surrounded by natural marshes and palm trees. The facility boasts a driving range, pro shop, restaurant, clubhouse, and villa accommodations.

Massages and Spas

New spas open up every day in the city, particularly around the backpacker area. Prices at even the most affordable spots are not as competitive as other coastal destinations in Vietnam. Tipping is expected at these facilities. The most professional businesses will either ask that the customer fill out a tip collection form, or won't ask at all. Either way, being solicited for tips without a form is not considered acceptable. If you find yourself being pestered for a gratuity after your trip to the spa, you have the right to politely decline.

A tall-and-narrow shop not far from Nha Trang Cathedral, **Sen Spa** (5 Ly Thanh Ton, tel. 0258/382-9899, www.senspanha-trang.com, 9am-8:30pm daily, VND150,000-700,000) offers reasonably priced massage and spa services with professional staff. Masks, facials, body scrubs, and massages are all on the spa menu, and the owners are an outgoing couple who do their best to ensure each customer's satisfaction. This is easily one of the best mid-range choices in town. Be sure to book ahead of time.

Su Spa (93AB Nguyen Thien Thuat, tel. 0258/352-3242, www.suspa.com.vn, 9am-11pm daily, spa treatments VND450,000-1,200,000) may charge Western prices, but this tranquil spa, in the middle of the back-packer district, does a good job of providing quality massages, manicures, and other spa treatments with a higher level of service.

FOOD

Thanks to the number of foreign tourists that visit Nha Trang, dining options around the backpacker area are varied in both price and cuisine. Those craving a taste of home can find steak, pasta, pizza, burgers, and burritos. Fresh fish, squid, and shrimp are popular and worthy choices. Nha Trang is also known for its *bun cha ca*, a rice noodle soup paired with pressed fish.

Prices in the backpacker area tend to be steep, with even a standard meal costing more than most other places in Vietnam. Street food is a good budget option. There are several rice stalls set up along Nguyen Thi Minh Khai. Ask the price first, or you may get overcharged.

Vietnamese

In a city with literally hundreds of shops specializing in *bun cha ca*, a tasty soup featuring rice noodles and pressed fish, ★ **Nguyen Loan** (123 Ngo Gia Tu, tel. 0258/351-5634, 5:30am-10:30pm daily, VND35,000) is a standout. Piping hot bowls of soup are

---

Edible Bird's Nests

Rare, fragile *yen sao* (edible bird's nests) are a hot item among Asian customers, as their consumption is said to have medicinal benefits. Made from the saliva of wild swiftlets, these nests can go for as much as US$2,000 per kilogram. They are difficult to come by, as the tiny creatures make their homes in hard-to-reach seaside caves along the south-central coast. They are sold in a few shops in Nha Trang and are usually dissolved into a soup before being eaten, although some keep the nest as a souvenir. The *yen sao* found in many local convenience stores is a bland, watered-down version. Shops that sell the actual nests will have signs emblazoned with *yen sao* out front.

---

accompanied by fresh greens, lime, and an array of sauces to compliment your personal taste, including the ultra-fishy, dark purple *mam tom* (fermented shrimp paste). The restaurant serves a few different styles of the dish, including one with thicker, rope-like *banh canh* noodles. It's best known for its *bun sua cha ca,* a variation which includes jellyfish.

A longstanding local haunt, **Pho 70** (112 Bach Dang, tel. 0258/351-2091, 6am-11:30am daily, VND30,000-45,000) has been turning out delicious bowls of Vietnam's favorite dish for over 50 years. The special beef pho is particularly tasty, and you'll find this modest spot filled with locals. Note, that you have to get up reasonably early to enjoy Pho 70, as the shop only operates during breakfast hours. If you turn up to late, never fear—there are plenty of other dining options along Bach Dang street.

Near Dam Market, **Nem Dang Van Quyen** (16A Lan Ong, tel. 0258/382-6737, www.nemdangvanquyen.com.vn, 8am-8:30pm daily, VND45,000-70,000) attracts foreigners and locals, thanks to its *nem nuong* (grilled pork sausage), which comes with a host of fixings for diners to create their own spring rolls. Fill your rice paper with greens, mango, cucumber, pickled carrots, and savory pork. A tasty special dipping sauce is a standard staple. They also have delicious noodle dishes, including *bun thit nuong* and *bun ca*, or rice noodles and fish.

You can smell the sumptuous barbecue at Lac Canh (44 Nguyen Binh Khiem, tel. 0258/382-1391, 9:30am-10pm daily, VND25,000-195,000) from a block away. This two-story open-front shop has been dishing out cheap, tasty Vietnamese meals since the 1960s, with a bustling atmosphere and bare-bones decor, not to mention one of the more affordable menus in town. Barbecue beef is the house specialty, but you'll find scores of other options here as well, including seafood, chicken, pork, and veggies.

On a street full of seafood restaurants, Nhat Phong 3 (63B Cu Lao Trung, tel. 0258/370-0233, 10am-10:30pm daily, VND50,000-300,000) is a popular local spot for grilled fish and other tasty Vietnamese dishes. Beside the ground floor dining area, waitstaff pluck your dinner from a series of large fish tanks; market prices are listed on a whiteboard above. The restaurant's specialty, grilled chicken with honey, is another excellent choice.

A charming yellow storefront down a quiet street, Yen's Restaurant (73/6 Tran Quang Khai, tel. 0258/652-1669, 10am-10:30pm daily, VND60,000-250,000) may run on the expensive side of local cuisine, but its tasty traditional dishes and pleasant ambience are worth a few extra dollars. The restaurant staff can offer recommendations.

Cafés and Bakeries

A super-skinny storefront wedged between a pair of high-rise hotels, Cuppa Coffee (4C Biet Thu, tel. 0258/352-4114, cuppavietnam@ yahoo.com, 7am-9pm daily, VND20,000-75,000) serves both European and Vietnamese coffee as well as tea, fruit smoothies, and a few desserts. A few stools line the narrow bar for customers, but most just grab and go.

One of the larger cafés in the backpacker area, Iced Coffee (49 Nguyen Thien Thuat, tel. 0258/246-0777, 6:30am-10:30pm daily, VND30,000-70,000) is a massive, air-conditioned building on Nguyen Thien Thuat with outgoing staff as well as European coffee, tea, smoothies, and Western food. It boasts a few locations around town, including another spot nearby at 146 Hung Vuong.

A delicious Asian-style bakery, Hoa Hung (39 Phan Boi Chau, tel. 0258/382-3141, 6am-10pm daily, VND8,000-30,000) stocks its

bun cha ca, a local specialty

shelves with eastern treats like sweet sticky rice cakes, mung bean pastries, and a wide variety of edibles featuring coconut, green tea, and other ingredients. Beware of the durian snacks; they're an acquired taste.

Brewpubs

Louisiane Brewhouse (29 Tran Phu, tel. 0258/352-1948, www.louisianebrewhouse. com.vn, 7am-late daily, VND80,000-310,000) makes its own beer from scratch, including a pilsner, a *witbier,* and a dark lager, as well as the odd seasonal brew. This classy beachside spot also serves top-notch seafood and Western cuisine, though at a price. Opt for sheltered seating on the veranda or camp out beneath the thatched umbrellas by the pool. This is a perfect spot for a splurge or a change from the usual Saigon Reds and 333s.

International

Same Same But Different (269 Nguyen Thien Thuat, tel. 0258/352-4079, ssbdcafe@ yahoo.com, 7:30am-10pm daily, VND50,000-150,000) is a classy establishment, sporting tablecloths and artistic photographs of countryside scenes on the walls, plus a nice mirrored bar at the back of the narrow restaurant. Prices are reasonable, and the menu boasts a decent selection of Vietnamese and Western food along with a few Thai dishes and a notably varied breakfast menu. Servers are particularly friendly and helpful, and a cooking class is offered.

Italian

The pizzas alone are reason enough to visit **Olivia** (14 Tran Quang Khai, tel. 0258/352-2752, 9am-11pm daily, VND75,000-300,000), a smart, affordable eatery not far from the beach. Dine inside, surrounded by simple but sophisticated exposed brick, or opt for covered outdoor seating with a genuine Italian café feel. The menu lists a variety of pastas and pizzas as well as gnocchi and other authentic European dishes.

Japanese

The narrow **Oh! Sushi** (17C Hung Vuong, tel. 0258/352-3139, 10am-11pm daily, VND50,000-400,000) bar boasts Japanese cuisine ranging from soba noodles and miso soup to sushi, hand rolls, and bento boxes for lunch. Indoors, a small bar lines the left side of the ground floor, from which diners have a perfect view of the restaurant's fresh ingredients. To the right, a few tables are huddled in the downstairs quarters, but you can also head up to the second floor for additional seating.

ACCOMMODATIONS

Most travelers prefer to camp out close to the beach for easy access. Whatever your price range, this city has the accommodations to match: in the low season, you'll find dorm beds for only a few dollars, while high-season prices at Nha Trang's luxury hotels will make a serious dent in your wallet.

Under VND210,000

The welcome greeting at ★ **Mojzo Dorm** (50 Nguyen Thi Minh Khai, tel. 0258/625-5568, www.mojzo-inn.com, VND160,000 dorm) is reason enough to shack up at this chic, well-appointed boutique hostel. From the moment you enter the building, Mojzo's staff remembers your name and treats you as part of the family. Modern six-bed dorms feature air-conditioning and hot water. There is unlimited free water and fruit in the cozy common area, where you can link up with fellow travelers or ask the staff for sound travel advice. Dorms include lockers and en suite baths with plenty of space for budget travelers. A notably tasty breakfast is served each morning, and Wi-Fi is available throughout the building.

The friendly folks at **iHome** (31/E2 Biet Thu, tel. 0258/352-1239, www.ihomen-hatrang.com, dorms VND115,000 dorm, VND460,000 double) run a top-notch hostel right in the heart of the backpacker neighborhood. Six-bed dorms feature en suite baths, lockers, and complimentary breakfast, while the hostel's common space is a great spot for meeting likeminded travelers. The front desk stays open 24 hours, and the friendly staff can help make recommendations on things to do, organize activities, and provide general information.

VND210,000-525,000

Tucked down an alley off the main road, **Truong Giang Hotel** (3/8 Tran Quang Khai, tel. 0258/352-2125, www.truonggianghotel. hostel.com, VND250,000-380,000) features basic, no-frills beds at excellent prices. Each modest room comes with air-conditioning, hot water, TV, a minibar, and Wi-Fi. You can also make use of the lockers downstairs to store your valuables. Guests have the option of accommodations with or without a window. Rooms on the higher floors are cheaper, as the hotel does not have an elevator.

Hidden behind Vietnam Xua restaurant in a quiet courtyard off the street, **Nha Trang Inn** (255 Nguyen Thien Thuat, tel. 0258/352-7527, tattravel_nt@yahoo.com.vn, VND300,000-350,000) is a bare-bones guesthouse, but its location is spot-on and Minh, the proprietor, is a welcoming guy. All accommodations come with air-conditioning, hot water, Wi-Fi, and TV, as well as a quieter atmosphere than most other places to stay on the block. With affordable prices and an excellent location, this is one of the better options on Nguyen Thien Thuat for budget backpackers.

Pho Bien (64/1 Tran Phu, tel. 0258/352-4858, www.phobienhotel.com.vn, VND450,000-700,000) stands out for a few reasons. From its unbeatable location directly opposite the beach to its clean rooms and exceptionally personable staff, this budget hotel does a great job of providing value as well as helpful travel advice. Rooms come with hot water, air-conditioning, Wi-Fi, a minibar, and TV.

In the same beach-side alley as Pho Bien, **Ha Thu Hotel** (64/2 Tran Phu, tel. 0258/352-2800, www.hathuhotel.com, VND300,000-500,000) is an equally worthy spot, with basic but adequate rooms with hot water, Wi-Fi, air-conditioning, and TV. Beds are a little hard, but balcony options are available overlooking the small alley out front, and many rooms have a sea view, though this is slightly obscured by the buildings across the street.

Rooms at the family-run **La Suisse Hotel** (34 Tran Quang Khai, tel. 0258/352-4353, www.lasuissehotel.com, VND435,000-630,000) may be a little aged but remain adequate and offer distance between your

Mojzo Dorm

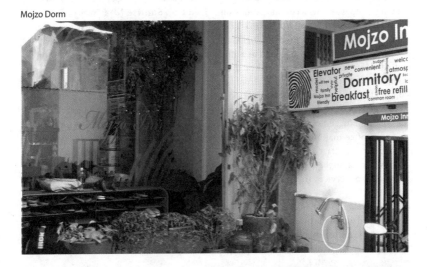

room and Tran Quang Khai's noisy main drag. In-room safes, minibars, air-conditioning, hot water, and TVs are standard amenities, and the hotel also includes breakfast in the rates as well as afternoon tea, coffee, and cake.

VND525,000-1,050,000

Though it's a little older than some of its competition, rooms at the **Ha Vang Golden Summer Hotel** (22-23 Tran Quang Khai, tel. 0258/352-6662, VND350,000-1,000,000, breakfast included) are clean, spacious, and well-kept with modern amenities, including hot water, TV, a minibar, and air-conditioning. The upper floors offer decent views of the ocean, though this is changing as more high-rise buildings go up in the area.

The staff and location make the **Green Peace Hotel** (102 Nguyen Thien Thuat, tel. 0258/352-2835, VND600,000-800,000, breakfast included) a worthy place to stay at the western end of Nguyen Thien Thuat, with hot water, air-conditioning, Wi-Fi, a fridge, and TV among the amenities in its well-appointed rooms. The standard room is cramped, so upgrade to a superior (VND100,000 extra). The nicest rooms also include a balcony.

VND1,050,000-2,100,000

Among the best-value accommodations on Tran Phu, the **Nha Trang Lodge** (42 Tran Phu, tel. 0258/352-1500, www.nhatranglodge. com, VND1,600,000-5,500,000) may be a little outdated, but its location can't be beat and, compared to the cost of other beachfront accommodations, rooms are a steal. All floors have superb views of the ocean, and you'll find air-conditioning, hot water, Wi-Fi, a minibar, tea- and coffee-making facilities, and TV in each room. Breakfast is included in the room rate, as is access to the hotel's pool. Additional travel and spa services are available.

Over VND2,100,000

Blessed with one of the nicest locations on the beach, the local **Novotel** (50 Tran Phu, tel. 0258/625-6900, www.novotel-nhatrang.com,

VND2,520,000-4,600,000) sits almost directly opposite Tram Huong Tower and affords top-notch views of the sea. Standard rooms include a small triangular balcony with partial views of the beach, while superiors boast some of the best panoramas in Nha Trang, with high windows and plenty of space, both indoors and out, from which to enjoy the scenery. All rooms feature sleek modern decor and come equipped with air-conditioning, Wi-Fi, hot water, a flat-screen TV, and a minibar. The hotel swimming pool, sauna, and fitness center are available to guests free of charge.

Surrounded by trendy cafés, ample beach views, and high-end shops, the **Sheraton Nha Trang** (26-28 Tran Phu, tel. 0258/388-0000, www.sheratonnhatrang.com, VND3,400,000-20,000,000) offers space and comfort along with a top-notch hotel staff. Its location farther down the coast means that beach-going travelers can enjoy a quieter stretch of sand. Amenities include air-conditioning, hot water, a flat-screen TV, minibar, coffee- and tea-making facilities, and an in-room safe. The hotel also boasts a fitness center, spa, several restaurants, and an incredible sixth-floor infinity pool with panoramic views of the bay and on-the-water lounge chairs.

A palatial building at the northern end of Tran Phu, **Sunrise Nha Trang** (12-14 Tran Phu, tel. 0258/382-0999, www.sunrisenhatrang.com.vn, VND3,390,000-8,700,000) pulls out all the stops in its decor, opting for lavish colonial grandeur and plush, well-appointed rooms. A beautiful circular swimming pool tops the roof of the ground floor, offering pleasant views of the bay. The hotel includes several restaurants, a spa, and a tour outfit. Sea views are available from every room, which include air-conditioning, Wi-Fi, hot water, a minibar, satellite TV, and an in-room safe.

Nha Trang's only seaside resort, **Evason Ana Mandara** (Tran Phu, tel. 0258/352-2222, www.sixsenses.com, VND6,050,000-16,615,000) is the pinnacle of luxury in this bustling beach town. Hidden from view, Ana

Mandara's 74 semidetached villas offer a beautiful, exclusive environment right in the middle of the city. Rooms feature clean, simple decor of earth tones and well-appointed furnishings. Both sea and garden views are available, as well as high-quality amenities and a host of additional services, from 24-hour in-room dining to the facilities at Ana Mandara's world-class spa.

INFORMATION AND SERVICES
Visitor Information

Free city maps and travel information are easy to come by in most hotels and tour agencies, though advice is usually influenced by whatever travel options that business offers. For slightly less biased news, check out local publications *Discover Nha Trang* (www.discovernhatrang.com) and *What's On Nha Trang* (www.whatsonnhatrang.net), a glossy magazine offering useful tips and recommendations about the city. You can usually find a stack of these at **Iced Coffee** (49 Nguyen Thien Thuat) alongside free city maps.

Banks

A **Techcombank** (Vincom Plaza, 44-46 Le Thanh Ton, tel. 0258/381-8177, www.techcombank.com.vn, 8am-11:30am and 1:30pm-5pm Mon.-Fri., 8am-11:30am Sat.) is in the Vincom Plaza near Nha Trang's backpacker neighborhood, complete with an ATM.

Postal Services and Internet

Nha Trang's central **post office** (2 Tran Phu, tel. 0258/382-1002, 7am-9pm daily) is located at the northern end of Tran Phu and provides postal services as well as Internet access.

Medical Services

The **VK Hospital** (34/4 Nguyen Thien Thuat, tel. 0258/352-8866, www.vkhospital.com.vn), located within the backpacker area, boasts English-speaking doctors and 24-hour emergency services.

GETTING THERE

Nha Trang can be accessed by regular buses, trains, and planes from all over the country. Budget airlines offer dirt-cheap flights from Saigon to Nha Trang. Cheap buses also make the trip from Ho Chi Minh City, while trains ply the route among Vietnam's coastal cities. Many bus and train services run at night, making an eight- or nine-hour journey feasible. There is a much greater distance between Nha Trang and its closest northern destinations, Hoi An and Hue, than between Nha Trang and Mui Ne, Dalat, or Saigon. If you're arriving from the north, a train or plane is recommended over a bus ride, which is less comfortable.

Air

Thirty-five kilometers south of Nha Trang, the **Cam Ranh Airport** (CXR, www.nhatrangairport.com) has daily flights from Saigon (1 hour) and Hanoi (2 hours) with Vietnam Airlines and budget carriers VietJet and Jetstar.

You can catch a taxi (VND350,000-400,000) into town or opt for the **airport shuttle bus** (tel. 0258/625-4455, 4:30am-7:55pm daily, VND50,000). If you take a taxi, clarify that the vehicle is metered or agree on a price before setting off. It's about 40 minutes into town from the airport.

For flight tickets in town, visit the **Vietnam Airlines ticketing office** (91 Nguyen Thien Thuat, tel. 0258/352-6768, www.vietnamairlines.com, 7:30am-11:30am and 1:30pm-4:30pm daily).

Bus

Sinh Tourist (90C Hung Vuong, tel. 0258/352-4329, www.thesinhtourist.vn, 6am-10pm daily) buses from Saigon (VND169,000), Mui Ne (VND99,000), Dalat (VND99,000), and Hoi An (VND249,000) arrive and depart at its office in downtown Nha Trang, in the heart of the backpacker area.

Phuong Trang (7 Hoang Hoa Tham, tel. 0258/381-2812, www.futabuslines.com.vn, 7am-10pm daily) buses from Saigon

(VND215,000) and Dalat (VND125,000) usually let off at the **southern bus station (Ben Xe Phia Nam)** (58 23 Thang 10, tel. 0258/382-0227, 4am-9pm daily).

For smaller destinations, such as Phan Rang or Quy Nhon, visit the Nha Trang bus station and hop on a local minibus. Be prepared to stand your ground on prices, as minibus drivers often overcharge foreign travelers. Ask your hotel's receptionist to call and inquire about the price ahead of time so that you arrive armed with the correct fare.

Train

The historical **Nha Trang train station (Ga Nha Trang)** (17 Thai Nguyen, tel. 0258/382-2113) has been around long enough to be considered a city relic. Daily trains run from Danang (10 hours, VND290,000-700,000), Hanoi (23 hours, VND600,000-1,360,000), and Saigon (8 hours, VND175,000-565,000).

GETTING AROUND

Taxi and *Xe Om*

You'll find plenty of *xe om* waiting for a fare on street corners in the backpacker area, while **Mailinh** (tel. 02583/838-3838) taxis are also widely available and easily flagged down in the street.

Bus

Nha Trang's public bus system is easily navigated and by far the cheapest transportation option. Look out for bright red and yellow buses, which ply six different routes around town, stopping near all of Nha Trang's major sights. Fares are posted on the side of the bus and run VND7,000-9,000, depending on your destination. Service usually stops around 7pm.

Nha Trang's largest and most central bus station is the **southern bus station (Ben Xe Phia Nam)** (58 23 Thang 10, tel. 0258/382-0227, 4am-9pm daily). This is also where long-distance local buses depart. Buses regularly travel Nguyen Thien Thuat and Tran Phu (the backpacker area), so it's unlikely a traveler will require a trip to the bus station in order to catch a local bus.

Bike and Motorbike

However you get around, check what options your hotel offers first, as rental companies typically want some sort of collateral, and hotels usually keep your passport anyway.

Motorbike and bicycle rentals are numerous in Nha Trang and are reasonably priced. Manual motorbikes start at around VND80,000 a day, while automatics may cost up to VND120,000. Most hotels offer **city bicycles** (around VND40,000-50,000), which are suitable for cycling around town.

TOP EXPERIENCE

DOC LET BEACH

Forty-eight kilometers north of Nha Trang, **Doc Let** is a spectacular expanse of white sand beach whose scenery and seclusion draw a growing number of day-trippers to its shores. Its pristine coastline and crystalline blue waters are bookended by fishing boats on one side and mountains on the other, and the wide beach affords plenty of room for visitors to spread out. Doc Let sees few visitors compared to the shores of Nha Trang; you won't find roving vendors or massive crowds.

The older **Doc Let Resort** (Ninh Hai Village, tel. 0258/384-9152, 7am-5pm daily, VND40,000) offers an array of services, all of which require an additional, often exorbitant, cost, from sun-bed and umbrella rentals to parasailing, Jet Skis, and kayaks. It's better to just bring your own towel, pay the fee for beach access, and spread out on the sand. You'll also find a restaurant on the premises, though it is only open intermittently, and a swimming pool (additional VND40,000) set back from the water.

Beside Doc Let Resort is its slightly more updated counterpart, **White Sand Doc Let Resort** (9 Dong Cat, Ninh Hai Village, tel. 0258/367-0670, www.whitesandresort.com.vn, 8am-5pm daily, VND40,000), a somewhat classier place to lounge around, though its services are equally overpriced. This resort also charges a fee for beach access.

The drive out to Doc Let is an experience

Ba Ho Waterfall

down the far side of the mountain, pooling into many small bodies of water. This has become an increasingly popular place to visit, as it offers travelers a pleasant, shaded hike and plenty of spots to stop and relax or go for a swim.

A rainforest trail (1.5 kilometers one-way) runs parallel to Ba Ho before dead-ending next to one of the stream's wider sections. From there, you can continue to the top of the waterfall by scrambling over the rocks that surround the water (though you'll need proper footwear). Along the path, several smaller dirt routes are carved into the underbrush, which allow you to stop and enjoy the scenery. A group of local women occasionally set up shop near the trail's end, selling barbecued chicken.

While Ba Ho's waters are most abundant during rainy season, the river still runs November-April, and it's possible to go for a swim. Independent travelers can hop on a motorbike and find the place themselves, or sign up with a tour group, such as **True Friends Travel** (23C Biet Thu, tel. 09/0642-4266, www.nhatrangeasyridertours.com), which includes a jaunt into the countryside as well as around Nha Trang proper. Rates start at US$40 per person for a group of two.

MONKEY ISLAND

Sometimes included in package tours to Doc Let and Ba Ho Waterfall, **Monkey Island (Dao Khi)** (tel. 0258/383-9067, www.longphutourist. com, 7:30am-5pm daily, VND150,000 adults, VND75,000 children), also known as Hon Lao, is a small islet off the coast north of Nha Trang where locals have trained a troupe of over 1,000 monkeys to perform circus acts for tourists. Most visitors find the place pretty depressing, as flagrant animal cruelty is not uncommon when the monkeys fail to successfully perform a trick, and the animals are so used to humans bringing food that they've become aggressive toward visitors, snatching items from tourists and, on occasion, scratching or biting. Safety standards in Vietnam are not the same as they might be at home, so visit the island at your own risk. Bear in mind that boats from the mainland to the islet stop at 3pm.

in itself, as the coastal road takes you past picturesque fishing villages and stunning rice paddies. A series of rocky seaside passes ascend the dramatic cliffs along the south-central coast before bringing you into the sleepy village of Ninh Hai, home to Doc Let Beach. For those comfortable on a motorbike, follow Tran Phu street north over the bridge and out of town, sticking to the coast until you reach the junction at Amiana World Resort, where you'll turn left and follow the markers for Ninh Hoa. A few billboards for White Sand Resort stand out among the other roadside advertising. Once you reach Ninh Hai village, a small concrete road takes you out to the beach.

BA HO WATERFALL

En route to Doc Let Beach, **Ba Ho Waterfall** (Khu Du Lich Suoi Ba Ho, 7am-5pm daily, VND50,000) punctuates the end of a dusty dirt track veering off the main highway south of Ninh Hoa. Flowing from the peak of Hon Son Mountain, Ba Ho ("Three Lakes") takes its name from the three segments of water that run

Phan Rang-Thap Cham

Hidden between Nha Trang's wild beach parties and the ever-multiplying resorts of Mui Ne, Phan Rang-Thap Cham is a winning mix of sunny, secluded shoreline and authentic local culture. Far less frequented than its neighbors to the north and south, this humble seaside town may not come with all the trappings of an international, tourist-friendly destination but it packs plenty of genuine Vietnamese food, history, and culture into its small city limits. In addition to the peaceful, palm-fringed beach, a handful of ancient rust-colored temples dot the nearby hillside, leftovers from the last Cham kingdom that fell to the Vietnamese empire in the late 1600s. Phan Rang's street-side cooks produce tasty and unique renditions of local fare. For travelers seeking a destination that ventures farther off the beaten path while still logging some quality beach time, look no farther than Phan Rang.

With rooms in Nha Trang and Mui Ne filling up fast and the hullabaloo, not to mention the prices, proving too much for some, Phan Rang's relative anonymity is poised to change: already, new hotels are beginning to appear just outside the town center near Ninh Chu Beach. For now, at least, this is a beautiful beach destination that is calm, quiet, and still easy on the wallet.

Thanks to its semi-arid climate, Phan Rang manages to remain fairly dry throughout the year, though it does heat up considerably in the summer months. Not much English is spoken; however, with a good sense of humor and patience, travelers should be just fine. The beach is the main attraction in this tiny town, so a few days here is sufficient.

SIGHTS

Phan Rang's handful of must-see monuments are located beyond the city center, with its nearest Cham towers sitting a few kilometers west of town. These sights are best accessed by motorbike, whether independently or on the back of a *xe om,* as some of the roads veering off the main highway very quickly turn into concrete pathways or dirt tracks. Taxis are also an option, though you may encounter more difficulty the farther you get from town. Quick jaunts back and forth to the beach are perfectly feasible in any vehicle.

There's not much in the way of landmarks, but Phan Rang is a likable little place, with plenty of charming old storefronts and angular Communist architecture. Near the central market, **Ong Pagoda** (beside Phan Rang Market, sunrise-sunset, days vary) is alive with color and boasts a beautifully detailed roof; though it is not always open, travelers can still appreciate the handiwork from outside. Farther down 16 Thang 4 street heading toward the beach, the sprawling parade ground at **16 Thang 4 Square** hints at the future of city planning in this small coastal town, with the massive **16 Thang 4 monument** and adjoining stone bleachers on one side and an eye-catching triangular building on the other, which now holds the **Ninh Thuan Museum** (16 Thang 4, tel. 0259/382-3695, 8am-11am and 1:30pm-5pm daily, free), showcasing the area's history, geography, and demographics. Back toward the city center, **16 Thang 4 Park** also makes for a nice spot to relax in town with its large fish pond and ample shade trees.

Po Klaung Garai

The most remarkable of the town's still-standing Cham towers, the 13th-century **Po Klaung Garai** (Bac Ai, 4.6 mi north of Phan Rang, tel. 0259/350-0971, 7am-5pm daily, VND15,000) sits northwest of the center and affords some nice views of the surrounding area. Perched atop Trau Hill, three imposing redbrick structures stand against the wind, with the smallest tower serving as an entrance gate onto the main sanctuary, a 20-meter-tall

Phan Rang-Thap Cham

temple honoring King Po Klaung Garai, former ruler of the Champa kingdom from 1151 to 1205. The doorway into Po Klaung Garai's shrine is guarded by a dancing Shiva and etched in the curling Sanskrit letters once used by the Cham. Through the narrow entryway you'll find a statue of the cow Nandin, a revered creature in Hinduism, facing the altar where the king's effigy lies. Painted onto the linga sculpture at the center of the temple is the human face of the king. During Kate, a celebration that gives thanks to the Hindu and Cham gods for bountiful harvests and prosperity, local Chams will "feed" the Nandin cow in order·to receive a successful harvest. Beside the entrance tower, Po Klaung Garai's third and final structure appears much the same as its contemporaries

but for a boat-shaped roof that peaks at either end. This is known as the fire tower, as it once held fires and prepared offerings for the main temple.

While Po Klaung Garai receives both devout followers and tourists, the temple's busiest time of year is during the Kate festival, when ethnic Cham come from near and far to give offerings and prayers to their former king. At the foot of the hill is a small exhibition room featuring photos of various Cham festivals and celebrations, as well as a small souvenir shop.

Ninh Chu Beach
Easily one of the south-central coast's best-kept secrets, **Ninh Chu Beach** (Yen Ninh) is likely to lose its anonymity in the future.

With five kilometers of secluded, pristine white sands and sparkling waters, the coast east of Phan Rang is blissfully devoid of roving vendors and mega-resorts, affording some stunning views of the curved shoreline and nearby mountains, along with the collection of fishing boats huddled at either end of the bay. Clean and undeveloped, there are several public access points available along the road parallel to Ninh Chu where travelers can simply walk onto the beach. A few resorts have also set up toward the north end of the beach with seaside restaurants, which are open to nonguests.

Po Ro Me

Removed from the city, the single tower at **Po Ro Me** (Ninh Phuoc, 20 kilometers from Phan Rang, sunrise-sunset daily) may not be as grand as Po Klaung Garai, its northern counterpart, but its location adds an air of mystery to the place. The journey to Po Ro Me takes travelers off the beaten path of Highway 1 and through a humble Cham village. At the foot of the hill, you can ascend the steep staircase along with the temple's caretaker, a friendly fellow who speaks some English, and, once you've reached the top, take in the panorama of paddy fields and small houses dotting the landscape. While the temple is usually locked, you can ask the caretaker to open it up for you. Once a wall of fluttering bats has cleared, you'll find two Nandin cows—one old and one new—sitting prostrate before a massive, six-armed statue of Champa's last king. In years past, additional statues were housed within the temple, but these have been lost to theft and the passing of time.

A trip to Po Ro Me requires the use of a motorbike or a *xe om* driver to bring you out to the towers. The journey itself can be a fun adventure. Bring a map, as things aren't always well marked and you're likely to get lost a few times before successfully reaching the temple. Keep an eye out for the blue sign on the left pointing you in the right direction.

Bau Truc Pottery Village

Several pottery shops are present in the dusty and otherwise unremarkable **Bau Truc Pottery Village (Lang Nghe Gom Bau Truc)**, where a small community of ethnic Cham make and sell their own pottery, formed by hand into all manner of creatures, pots, jars, jugs, ashtrays, and sculptures. These beautiful, authentic handicrafts are well made and dirt cheap compared to elsewhere. This is not a bad place to pull over en route to Po

A basket boat sits on shore at Ninh Chu Beach.

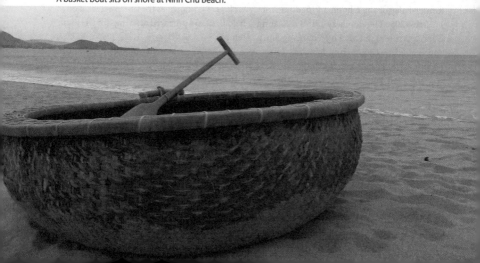

Local Cuisine: Phan Rang

While Phan Rang cuisine doesn't often make the list of Vietnam's most famous local cuisines, this sleepy town still has a variety of delicious specialties.

- *banh can:* The most popular of local dishes is this small savory cake made of grilled rice flour and egg. It's usually topped with pork, squid, or shrimp and served with fresh greens, and the mouthwatering, bite-size morsels can be consumed by the dozen. They're best enjoyed with *nuoc cham.*

- *banh xeo Phan Rang:* This local rendition of savory Vietnamese pancakes tweaks the national recipe to include seafood and is served with fresh greens and *nuoc cham.* You can easily find both of these dishes on the street, where women with scorching hot *banh can* pans (similar to muffin pans) churn out piles of the little snacks all day.

- *nuoc cham:* Local vendors in Phan Rang add peanuts into their *nuoc cham,* a lighter version of fish sauce used for dipping, making for a richer, more flavorful concoction.

Ninh Thuan province is also one of the only places in Vietnam to raise goats and sheep, both of which you'll occasionally find on local menus. These meats are often prepared in curries or hot pots. Thanks to its unusual climate, this area boasts garlic, grapes, and Vietnamese apples (a small green fruit with a miniature pit at the center), all of which you're sure to see for sale in the town market and along the roadside.

Ro Me, as it's only a few kilometers from the temple site.

FOOD

Phan Rang boasts several culinary specialties. Seafood is, of course, a local favorite in any beachfront town, but the cooks of Phan Rang have taken it upon themselves to incorporate these ingredients into traditional Vietnamese dishes like *banh xeo,* the local version of which is smaller—similar to the savory pancakes you'll find in the country's central region—and includes squid and shrimp, served with an appetizing peanut sauce. Another local specialty is *banh can,* small steamed rice-flour-and-egg cakes topped with meat, squid, or shrimp and again enjoyed with the same tasty sauce. For seaside eats, many of the resorts down the north end of Ninh Chu Beach have restaurants attached that welcome nonguests. Down the dirt road past Saigon-Ninh Chu Resort you'll also find a host of small seafood restaurants. In town, plenty of street food is available both around **Phan Rang Market** (Thong Nhat and Ngo Quyen, sunrise-sunset daily) and along Ngo Gia Tu south of 16 Thang 4.

The delectable *banh xeo Phan Rang* (Tran Quang Dieu opposite 16 Thang 4 Park, noon-late daily, VND30,000-50,000) can be found on the far side of the park at four or five small street stalls, where you'll get a glimpse of how *banh xeo* is made and what these scrumptious savory pancakes contain. Don't forget to throw in some fresh greens and make ample use of your dipping sauces.

A simple storefront, **Tri Tam** (Quan Tri Tam, 174 Thong Nhat, tel. 0259/382-0615, 10am-10pm daily, VND65,000-140,000) specializes in goat dishes, a local favorite. While you won't find an English menu, the Vietnamese version is posted on the wall and includes a tasty goat curry (*ca ri An Do*), goat hot pot (*lau de*), and grilled goat (*de nuong*). Each dish comes with either bread or rice.

A Phan Rang favorite, **Com Ga Khanh Ky** (61 Tran Quang Dieu, tel. 0259/383-8886, www.comgakhanhky.com.vn, 6am-8pm daily, VND25,000-60,000) is well known among locals for its chicken and rice. Several other items also feature on the menu, which one of the English-speaking staff will translate for you, but the restaurant's namesake dish is its best. Check out the precooked birds in the cart out front before you eat.

Sao Bien (end of 16 Thang 4, tel. 0259/389-1199, 9am-10pm daily, VND80,000-300,000) succeeds in both top-notch seafood dishes and a classy atmosphere. You'll find the catch of the day on display near the barbecue, an array that includes crab, squid, shrimp, and several kinds of fish. White wrought-iron furniture takes up the outdoor seating area. Inside, Sao Bien's well-lit dining room is grand as far as Phan Rang goes. English-speaking staff can assist you in making lunch or dinner choices. The large menu also includes a few meatless items.

While rooms at the Thong Nhat Hotel are nothing extraordinary, the **Thong Nhat Restaurant** (343 Thong Nhat, tel. 0259/382-7201, 6am-2pm daily, VND70,000-300,000) downstairs offers travelers a more conventional dining atmosphere, complete with tablecloths and a full place setting, a lengthy menu of Vietnamese dishes, and plenty of beverages. Seafood features heavily in the restaurant's offerings, but there are also chicken, beef, and a few tofu options available. The restaurant is primarily open for breakfast and lunch, but it is possible to order dinner with advance notice.

ACCOMMODATIONS

As a town still getting used to the notion of foreign tourism—and, indeed, still very much under construction for itself—Phan Rang boasts plenty of cheap and basic options, with fewer choices in the way of mid-range or high-end rooms, though the beachfront resorts along Ninh Chu try their best. The nicest digs are on the water, where several outfits, including the mammoth Saigon Tourist, have set up resorts catering largely to Russian tourists. Modest, family-run guesthouses and mini-hotels abound, leaving you with only location to worry about. To focus your trip on the Cham towers, opt for an in-town lodging for easier access to transportation; beachgoers should opt for lodgings closer to shore. With Ninh Chu Beach only a few kilometers from town, travelers should have no trouble gaining access to both the sea and the sights.

In Town
UNDER VND210,000

Newer than some of the other hotels on this road, **Dia Cau Xanh** (8 N3 16 Thang 4, tel. 0259/383-8939, VND150,000-250,000) is a particularly tidy place, with the standard hot water, air-conditioning, Wi-Fi, TV, and fridge amenities. The staff does not speak much English, but the hotel is fairly close to the beach and prices are reasonable.

VND210,000-525,000

Opposite the large Sao Bien restaurant, **Cong Luyn Hotel** (end of 16 Thang 4, tel. 0259/382-1111, VND300,000-450,000) is a reliable budget option. Rooms are cozy and well kept, with TV, a fridge, hot water, air-conditioning, and Wi-Fi. Its location also adds to Cong Luyn's appeal, as the hotel sits a short walk from the beach and from a handful of small local eateries around the corner on Yen Ninh.

On the Beach
VND210,000-525,000

For dirt-cheap but trim and tidy accommodations near the beach, **Huong Bien Hotel** (24 An Duong Vuong, tel. 0259/387-3044, VND340,000-455,000) offers rooms with decent beds and spotless baths, hot water, air-conditioning, TV, and Wi-Fi on the dirt road just past Saigon-Ninh Chu Resort. The cheerful receptionist speaks some English, and Huong Bien is just a short walk from both the beach and the cluster of seafood restaurants at the end of the road.

Right beside Huong Bien, **Dieu Hien Guesthouse** (26 An Duong Vuong, tel. 0259/387-3399, VND230,000) offers slightly less atmosphere but remains a clean and safe place to base yourself. Various configurations of hot water and cold water, air-conditioning, and fan rooms are available, as are second-floor rooms with small balconies.

VND1,050,000-2,100,000

With panoramic views of the ocean and the distant hills, **Saigon-Ninh Chu Resort** (Yen Ninh, tel. 0259/387-6001, www.

saigonninhchuhotel.com.vn, VND2,205,000-5,100,000) is nice but a little aged. The corridors could use new carpeting and the pool has seen better days. However, its spacious rooms offer great value and a decent level of service. Amenities include air-conditioning, Wi-Fi, hot water, TV, a minibar, and complimentary buffet breakfast. Add-ons range from a poolside bar to multiple restaurants, occasional beach barbecues, and one of the only tour outfits in town.

INFORMATION AND SERVICES

With a provincial tourism outfit nowhere to be found, the folks at Saigon-Ninh Chu Resort's **tourist information kiosk** are your next best option, offering free maps and useful information to guests as well as curious passersby. You can also consult the website for **Ninh Thuan Tourist** (www.ninhthuantourist.com) for more information on specific sights.

Phan Rang's main **Vietin Bank** (468 Thong Nhat, tel. 0259/382-1450, www.vietinbank.vn, 7am-11am and 1:30pm-4:30pm Mon.-Fri.) can assist with currency exchange and ATM services, while those closer to the beach can visit Saigon-Ninh Chu Resort (Yen Ninh, tel. 0259/387-6001, www.saigonninhchuhotel.com.vn), which has an official **Vietcombank** exchange counter in the lobby.

You'll find the city's **central post office** (217 Thong Nhat, tel. 0259/382-4430, 7am-7pm daily) able to assist with mail and packages.

The **Ninh Thuan General Hospital (Benh Vien Da Khoa Ninh Thuan)** (Nguyen Van Cu, tel. 0259/382-2660) can assist with minor medical emergencies, though don't expect to find English-speaking doctors here. More serious injuries and ailments should be referred to either Nha Trang or Saigon.

GETTING THERE
Bus

Buses from Saigon (VND125,000-170,000) and Nha Trang (VND60,000) arrive daily in Phan Rang at the **Ninh Thuan bus station** (3 kilometers from Phan Rang, Le Duan, tel. 0259/383-8043) on Highway 1. Reaching this seaside town can be tricky if you're coming from elsewhere.

The Ninh Thuan bus station is the only long-distance provider in the area. All its vehicles are aging minibuses. Buying your bus ticket from the station's official counter and looking for the fare posted on the side of your bus will ensure that you are not overcharged. Since few tourists visit this town independently, some fare collectors and touts will ask for more than the posted price. Remain polite but firm and insist on paying the standard fee; this usually settles the matter. Barring grossly oversize bags, there is no additional charge for luggage.

Train

Trains arrive at the **Thap Cham train station** (Minh Mang, tel. 0259/388-8084, 7:30am-11:30am and 1:30pm-5:30pm daily) from Saigon (6 hours, VND125,000-500,000) several times daily. You can also catch both north- and southbound trains along the coast from here. It is possible to purchase tickets at the station, about eight kilometers from downtown, or online at http://dsvn.vn.

GETTING AROUND
Taxi and *Xe Om*

You'll find some *xe om* drivers hanging around on the beach road, Yen Ninh, as well as along the main drag in town, 16 Thang 4. **Mailinh** (tel. 0259/389-8989) and **Phan Rang** (tel. 0259/362-6262) taxis also make the rounds.

Bike and Motorbike

Hiring a vehicle in Phan Rang can be difficult, as there are no official rental businesses. Ask your hotel for recommendations; they may even have a motorbike or bicycle lying around that they're willing to rent out. Check the quality of the bike and agree upon a daily rate before setting off.

Dalat

Far from the hot and humid beach towns of the south-central coast, Dalat is the gateway to Vietnam's interior, a wild and wonderful place brimming with lush mountains and cascading rivers, breathtaking panoramic landscapes, and a host of different cultures. The incredible scenery of Vietnam's mountainous region serves as a backdrop for rock climbing, canyoneering, mountain biking, trekking, and rafting. This is the home of Vietnam's original Easy Rider motorbike custom tours company.

As the most accessible town in the Central Highlands, Dalat is often the only place travelers stop in the area. For those who continue on to more remote towns, this is also a worthy spot to hire a guide or arrange tours deeper into the region, as you'll be hard-pressed to find English speakers or tourist services elsewhere in the Central Highlands. Three days is enough to take in the city's downtown sights and catch a glimpse of some of its nearby countryside attractions, but with outdoor excursions or other activities, you could spend up to a week here and still not explore everything. Easy Rider trips to Mui Ne and Nha Trang can take as little as two days, while adventures to Hoi An can run as long as a week or more.

While Dalat is never really cold by Western standards, its coolest months are in the winter, from November to January. The wetter season runs from April to November, but rain is much less intense here than in the low-lying areas of Vietnam. Even at its warmest, the town is still comfortable.

SIGHTS

For history and architecture enthusiasts, the downtown area has a handful of charming colonial houses, though these are beginning to disappear as modern buildings go up. Plenty of European-inspired facades populate the neighborhoods around the market, as does a miniature version of the Eiffel Tower, which serves as the city's radio transmitter.

Dalat has a more conspicuous Roman Catholic influence than most other Vietnamese cities. Several Gothic churches dot the nearby hillsides, including the downtown **Dalat Cathedral** (Nha Tho Con Ga, Tran Phu and Le Dai Hanh, Vietnamese mass 5:15am and 5:15pm Mon.-Fri., 5:15pm Sat., multiple masses 5:15am-6pm Sun.), the largest of the bunch. Also known as Chicken Church, so named for a miniature rooster atop its 47-meter bell tower, the cathedral can be seen throughout the city and stands as a solid example of most local churches, though it is rarely open outside mass. A handful of other Catholic structures farther afield provide more in history and design. The same goes for Buddhist pagodas, of which there are many. If you don't have time to leave the city limits, the **Linh Son Pagoda** (Nguyen Van Troi and Phan Dinh Phung, sunrise-sunset daily) is a fine example.

Plenty of day-trippers make the trek out to nearby Datanla Falls or up the low, sloping Lang Biang Mountain. More distant attractions are best approached with an experienced local guide to save the time and hassle of navigating the countryside.

Central Dalat

The downtown area is more accessible and fairly easy to get around, though some of the winding hillside streets can be disorienting.

Most pagodas, museums, and other sights within the city limits can be visited independently, but local operator **Dalat Tourist** (1 Le Dai Hanh, tel. 0263/382-2021, www.dalattourist.com.vn, 7:30am-11:30am and 1:30pm-6pm daily) offers basic day tours for those who prefer a guide.

Dalat

THIEN AN HOTEL

THÔNG THIEN HOC

LINH SON PAGODA

TRONG DONG

DOMAINE DE MARIE CONVENT

PHAT TIRE VENTURES

THI SÁCH

PHAM NGOC THACH

MY DREAM HOTEL

DREAMS 3

DREAMS 1

LAM DONG GENERAL HOSPITAL

FORTUNE DAI LOI

SEE "CENTRAL DALAT" MAP

PHAM NGOC THACH

TRUNG CANG/ SINH TOURIST

NEWLAND HOSTEL

V CAFE

PINK HOUSE HOTEL

HOTEL PHUONG THANH

HOÀNG DIEU

LONG HOA WINDMILLS CAFE

SACOMBANK

DALAT MARKET

L'ANG FARM

AU LAC VEGETARIAN

SCIMITAR EASY RIDER

AN CAFE

DALAT TOURIST

3 THANG 2

THANH THUY BLUE WATER

THÚ KHOA HUÂN

XUAN HUONG LAKE

Xuan Huong Lake

NGOC LAN HOTEL

DALAT CENTRAL POST OFFICE

SAIGON DALATHOTEL

3 THANG 2

TRAN QUOC TOAN

ANH SANG

Cam Ly Stream

HÀ HUY TAP

PHAM NGU LAO

DALAT PALACE HERITAGE HOTEL

CAFE DE LA POSTE

TRAN PHU

TRAN PHU

DALAT DU PARC

HANG NGA CRAZY HOUSE

DALAT CATHEDRAL

SAMMY HOTEL DALAT

0   200 yds
0   200 m

© AVALON TRAVEL

Central Dalat

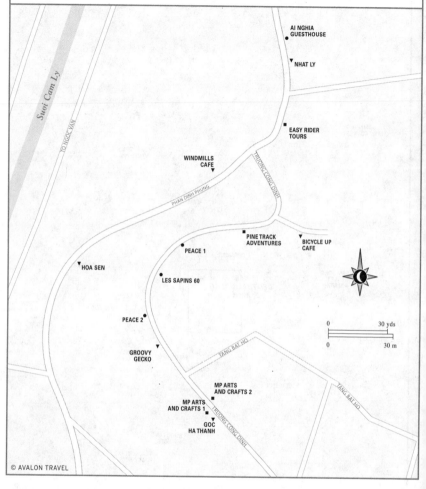

AI NGHIA
GUESTHOUSE

NHAT LY

EASY RIDER
TOURS

WINDMILLS
CAFE

PINE TRACK
ADVENTURES

BICYCLE UP
CAFE

PEACE 1

HOA SEN

LES SAPINS 60

PEACE 2

GROOVY
GECKO

MP ARTS
AND CRAFTS 2

MP ARTS
AND CRAFTS 1

GOC
HA THANH

Suoi Cam Ly

TO NGOC VAN

PHAN DINH PHUNG

TRUONG CONG DINH

TANG BAT HO

TANG BAT HO

TRUONG CONG DINH

0   30 yds

0   30 m

© AVALON TRAVEL

★ XUAN HUONG LAKE

The centerpiece of downtown Dalat, **Xuan Huong Lake** has inspired many a poet over the years. Once a modest stream winding through the valley, its calm blue waters exist as a vestige of French urban planning after the colonial powers decided to dam the stream in 1919 and create this 32-hectare lake. Draped in the greenery of Yersin Park and the Dalat Flower Garden, Xuan Huong features heavily in most photographs of the city and embodies the romantic air of this former colonial getaway. There's no doubt you'll catch a glimpse of Xuan Huong as you wander around town, as its size and proximity to Dalat Market make it hard to ignore. Many people are happy to go for a stroll around its five-kilometer perimeter, while others opt for renting bicycles to speed up their tour of the area. Others still prefer to sit at one of the local cafés on the water and simply take in the scenery.

DALAT FLOWER GARDEN

Covering 11 hectares near the northernmost point of Xuan Huong Lake, the **Dalat Flower Garden (Vuon Hoa Da Lat)** (3 Pham Ngu Lao, tel. 0263/382-1758, 7am-6pm daily, VND40,000) attracts hordes of domestic tourists year-round as well as a few curious foreigners and photography enthusiasts. Its sprawling grounds are exactly what you would expect: an array of vibrant blossoms tended by the park's army of gardeners. Each section boasts a combination of flowers from around the world as well as Dalat's trademark kitsch, namely horse-drawn carriages and pastel-drenched statues. To the back of the grounds you'll find a small pond, while up the stairs to the right the flower garden also has a sculpture section. Things really get busy around the end of December, when the Dalat Flower Festival brings thousands of visitors to the park for cultural performances.

★ HANG NGA CRAZY HOUSE

A weird, wonderful dreamscape of gnarled trees and spiderwebs, glittering mosaics, and eerie concrete animals, the **Hang Nga Crazy House** (3 Huynh Thuc Khang, tel. 0263/382-2070, www.crazyhouse.vn, 8:30am-7pm daily, VND50,000 adults, VND20,000 children) has become one of Dalat's—and, indeed, Vietnam's—most iconic buildings. Now over two decades in the making, its bizarre fusion of storybook influences, caricatured architecture, and riotous color have earned the Crazy House several mentions on lists of the world's most unusual structures. In 1990, construction began on the Crazy House, the brainchild of Russian-trained architect Dr. Dang Viet Nga. Its accomplished designer began dreaming up the warped walls and sharp angles of the building well beforehand: Inside the main entrance, you'll see the beautiful and intricate drawings that brought the Crazy House to life. Since its beginning, Nga's pet project has grown outward and upward, developing into a maze of shaded tunnels and narrow staircases that wind over and through its themed rooms, most of which are inspired by an odd array of creatures, including kangaroos, pheasants, bears, and termites.

Hidden in the depths of the main building, a contorted version of a traditional Vietnamese house, you'll also find a room devoted to Nga's parents: Her father, Truong Chinh, became the second president of Vietnam, succeeding the great Ho Chi Minh. Visitors are free to lose their way around the house, discovering its tiny niches and hollow,

Xuan Huong Lake

cave-like rooms. The shaded courtyard inside the gates gives off a wild overgrown feel that adds to the house's mystery and makes for a pleasant spot to take a break and admire the view.

EMPEROR BAO DAI'S SUMMER PALACE

Palace isn't necessarily a word you might associate with the blocky, art deco exterior of **Emperor Bao Dai's Summer Palace** (1 Trieu Viet Vuong, tel. 0263/383-1581, 7am-5pm daily, VND20,000), but nonetheless this solid concrete dwelling, completed in 1938, served as the summer home and, at one point, a permanent residence of Vietnam's last emperor. Combining the skills of a French and Vietnamese architectural duo, the 26 rooms of the palace are preserved to look much the same as they did in the 1940s, surrounded by large trees and ample topiary.

While the upholstery and bedroom furnishings are weathered, the photographs of the royal family lining the palace walls make it easy to imagine the emperor, his wife, Queen Nam Phuong, and their four children eating at the long dining room table or occupying the lavish sitting room. Several display cases on the ground floor hold antique dishware of the former royal family, as well as a few of the emperor's personal effects from his office.

The palace was originally used only in the summer months, when the emperor and his family stayed here to escape Saigon's brutal heat. From 1949 to 1954 it became Bao Dai's full-time residence while the queen took her children to France. Once the emperor had also been exiled to France, South Vietnam's second president, General Nguyen Van Thieu, briefly occupied the palace; his tenure, much like the South Vietnamese government, was short-lived.

DALAT RAILWAY STATION

Though it no longer connects to the rest of Vietnam's Reunification Line, the **Dalat Railway Station** (1 Quang Trung, tel. 0263/383-4409, 7am-6pm daily, VND5,000)

one of many staircases at Hang Nga Crazy House

remains open today, if only for curious tourists who stop to see the antique trains and throwback facades of this wide, low building. As more visitors have taken an interest in the train station, local tourism officials have invested in its upkeep, and vendors have opened souvenir shops and even a café in an old train car on the platform. The station does run one short section of the old rail line purely for travelers out to Trai Mat (multiple departures 6:55am-4:30pm daily, VND108,000-150,000 round-trip), not far from Linh Phuoc Pagoda. The journey takes about 20-30 minutes and requires a minimum of 25 passengers.

DU SINH CHURCH

Amid the incalculable number of Catholic churches scattered throughout Dalat, **Du Sinh Church** (12B Huyen Tran Cong Chua, grounds 7am-5pm daily) stands out for its distinctly Vietnamese architecture. Most churches you'll find in the city, and in much of Vietnam, mimic the grand cathedrals of France. But Du Sinh features a long, narrow building, not unlike the Cao Dai temples of the Mekong Delta, and intricate multihued rooftops that would not be out of place on a Buddhist pagoda.

The only French influence in the building is the statues, which depict a bright-white European Jesus sheltered by the ruddy tiles and ornate decoration of an Asian-style gazebo. Though the church itself is often closed, the grounds are usually open, and sometimes you'll find a parishioner who speaks some English. Du Sinh may not be the most awe-inspiring of churches in Dalat, but it's worth a look, if only to see Jesus Christ flanked by a pair of golden dragons atop the entrance gate.

DOMAINE DE MARIE CONVENT

The sloping grounds of the **Domaine de Marie Convent** (Ngo Quyen, near Pham Ngoc Thach, grounds 8am-11:30am and 2pm-5pm daily) would not be out of place in a small European village. This lofty stone-and-brick church boasts vaulted wooden ceilings and pretty pink-and-white living quarters for its residents, the local branch of the Daughters of Charity of Saint Vincent de Paul. Behind the church, a small garden courtyard is alive with colorful temperate flowers.

On one side of the square lies the grave of Suzanne Humbert, the wife of Jean Decoux, once governor of French Indochina. Humbert was a strong proponent of the church and one of its main benefactors; she died in a car accident en route from Saigon to Dalat in 1944. Upon her death, the sisters of Domaine de Marie constructed this grave. Today, around 40 nuns live and work at Domaine de Marie, providing outreach to women in the area as well as serving local blind and deaf people.

LAM DONG MUSEUM

En route to Linh Phuoc Pagoda, the extensive collection of artifacts at **Lam Dong Museum** (4 Hung Vuong, tel. 0263/381-2624, www.baotanglamdong.com.vn, 7:30am-4:30pm daily, VND15,000) covers the standard themes of a provincial museum, from geography and nature to current business production and local revolutionary history. Its most interesting displays are on Lam Dong's ethnic minorities, the Ma, the K'ho, and the Churu, who live in the highlands and practice traditional customs and ways of farming. English signage is present throughout the museum and is better than most. On the same grounds, you'll also find models of traditional Ma and K'ho houses, as well as a temple devoted to Nguyen Huu Hao, father of Queen Nam Phuong, Vietnam's last reigning queen.

ENTERTAINMENT AND EVENTS

Travelers who visit Dalat around the New Year may be able to catch the **Dalat Flower Festival** (late Dec.-early Jan.), a lively and colorful display of the region's best blossoms and a celebration of local culture. Held in the Dalat Flower Garden and around Hoa Binh Square, the four- or five-day festivities include cultural performances from Lam Dong province as well as other parts of the Central Highlands and focus on the traditions of local minorities as well as Vietnam's many heritage sites. In recent years, the festival has become an annual event, drawing thousands, and is now known nationwide. If you are here during this time, arrange your accommodations in advance, as the city's hotels can fill up quickly for festival weekend.

SHOPPING

Dalat has several local specialties. Beneath the shelter of Hoa Binh Square, the **Dalat Market** (end of Nguyen Thi Minh Khai, sunrise-sunset daily) displays an array of fresh fruits and vegetables piled high atop vendors' carts. Ply the ground floor to find bundles of fresh flowers and candied fruit, including berries, mangoes, bananas, and even kiwi. Head upstairs to explore stalls packed with scarves, shoes, and warm clothing. You'll also find a separate area for food vendors in this dizzying multi-level maze. Business starts in the early morning and carries through till evening, when a **night market** (5pm-10:30pm daily) takes over out front on Nguyen Thi Minh Khai.

Local minorities make a variety of authentic handicrafts, namely jewelry, bags, and clothing, which you'll find in shops around town. While many of these items can be purchased at the local market, prices are only cheaper if you bargain; if not, you may wind up paying far more than you would even at a souvenir shop. For those comfortable with haggling, head to Dalat's central trading center. If you prefer to deal in fixed prices, stick to the shops around the backpacker area.

MP Arts and Crafts (40D and 55 Truong Cong Dinh, tel. 0263/397-0240, mp.dalatshop@yahoo.com, 8am-10pm daily) offers a selection of souvenirs, handicrafts, clothing, maps, and a few other practicalities. The shop is roomy, covering several stories and has actually expanded across the street to cover both sides of Truong Cong Dinh.

For souvenirs from the hills of Dalat, **L'Ang Farm** (on the staircase beside Dalat Market, www.langfarmdalat.com, 7:30am-10pm daily) is a chain that has sprouted up all over town with high-quality packaged versions of the same local specialties you'll find in the market. In addition to dozens of teas and coffee, the shop also sells candied and dried fruits, local sweets, and jam, among other products. While you're sure to find the same products in the market at a cheaper price, for gifts L'Ang Farm's produce comes in sturdier, flashier packaging.

SPORTS AND RECREATION

Thanks to its hills, adventure sports are gaining ground in the Dalat area, as more travelers come to experience the untamed landscapes of Lam Dong province. The wilderness around the city provides ample opportunity for outdoorsy travelers to explore the countryside and try their hand at trekking, cycling, canyoneering, or white-water rafting. Most of these adventures—with the exception of trekking— require a guided tour, but even novices can join in the outdoor fun.

Adventure Tours

The folks at **Phat Tire Ventures** (109 Nguyen Van Troi, tel. 0263/382-9422, www.ptv-vietnam.com, 7:30am-8:30pm daily) specialize in mountain biking, white-water rafting, canyoneering, and trekking. Expertly trained guides run day trips to waterfalls and forests for the experienced and novices, as well as a handful of multi-day tours to destinations like Hoi An, Nha Trang, and Mui Ne. Customizable tours are also available. Phat Tire also has an office

Dalat Market is home to a host of fresh produce and candied fruits.

Easy Rider Tours

As Vietnam struggled to find its footing after the American War, a Dalat native named Mr. Toan was working as a porter and *xe om* driver at the local bus station. Once a student of theology, he was fluent in French and English. But behind the closed doors of postwar Vietnam there was little need for foreign languages. That is, until one day in the late 1980s when a pair of American tourists stepped off the bus in Dalat. The only English-speaker around, Toan struck up a conversation with the two. As more foreign visitors started coming to Dalat, Toan found his skill increasingly valuable. He began offering city tours to foreigners.

As tourism grew, Mr. Toan taught English to 15 other drivers, the original Easy Riders, a name they took at the suggestion of an American journalist. Drivers ventured beyond the city limits, bringing foreigners deep into the Central Highlands. By the time the Easy Riders received official recognition from local authorities as a legitimate enterprise, business was booming. These local guides and their heavy-duty motorbikes have become the face of homegrown tourism in the Central Highlands.

Nowadays, Mr. Toan has hung up his Easy Rider jacket, working instead as an English teacher in Dalat, but he remains a local celebrity. The original band of **Easy Riders** (70 Phan Dinh Phung, tel. 0263/382-9938, www.dalat-easyrider.com, 7am-8pm daily) operates out of a small shop on Phan Dinh Phung where it intersects with Truong Cong Dinh. Several members have gone off to start their own tour businesses and still more independent guides are present throughout Dalat.

For a single-day tour, most people do just fine finding a guide on the street or asking for a recommendation from their hotel. For longer trips, book ahead of time with a reputable company. The original team is a solid choice, as is **Scimitar Easy Rider Tours** (22/1 Hoang Dieu, tel. 09/0369-5165, www.easyrider-dalat.com, 7am-8pm daily), a 10-member group of local guides headed up by Mr. Hung, also known as Scimitar, one of the original crew. If you link up with an independent operator, your best bet is to take a day-long outing with the guide of your choice, then gauge whether to opt for a longer trip based on that experience.

Most tours leave from Dalat and venture into the less traveled areas between this Central Highlands town and destinations like Mui Ne, Nha Trang, Hoi An, and Buon Ma Thuot, the coffee capital of Vietnam. Fees usually run around VND570,000 for a single-day excursion, while longer trips hover between VND1,590,000 and VND1,820,000 per day. All rates cover entrance fees and accommodations, so travelers only pay for their food and drink on the trip.

in Hoi An and tours can be arranged through its website, where a regularly updated list of adventures is available.

One of the most established outfits in Dalat, **Groovy Gecko** (65 Truong Cong Dinh, tel. 0263/383-6521, www.groovygeckotours.net, 7:30am-8:30pm daily) offers a range of trekking, cycling, canyoneering, and rock-climbing tours around the Dalat area, varying from mild to adventuresome. Experienced local guides lead both single- and multiple-day trips covering Hoi An, Nha Trang, and Mui Ne as well as Dalat's nearby forests and waterfalls.

The easygoing Mr. Duan of **Viet Challenge** (64 Truong Cong Dinh, tel. 0263/354-6677, www.vietchallenge.com, 7am-9pm daily) is an expert in canyoneering and a nine-year veteran of the sport. Though it's one of the younger companies in town, his outdoor adventure outfit offers affordable day-long excursions (VND1,135,000) with experienced guides that combine hiking, rappelling, and canyoneering. All equipment is purchased from Europe or Singapore and meets appropriate safety standards. The company also offers mountain biking, trekking, and cycling trips, but canyoneering is by far the most popular.

Pine Track Adventures (72B Truong

Cong Dinh, tel. 0263/383-1916, www.pine-trackadventures.com, 8am-8:30pm daily) offers single- and multiple-day excursions around Dalat as well as cycling trips to Mui Ne, Nha Trang, and Hoi An. The company, which specializes in canyoneering, trekking, rafting, and cycling adventures, is staffed by highly qualified canyoneers with first-aid training. The emphasis is on fun, safe, physically challenging activities.

Trekking

With hundreds of trails crisscrossing the countryside around Dalat, trekking is a popular activity in the Central Highlands. Trips can last as long as a few days or as short as an afternoon, provided you go with a guide; there are also a handful of independent trekking options. Either way, these dirt paths bring travelers through the area's odd combination of temperate Asian rainforest and pine forest.

The trails leading up **Lang Biang Mountain** are a good place to start, with the steady, paved incline up to **Rada Point** as well as a notably more strenuous climb to the summit of Lang Biang. The woods around Truc Lam Pagoda and nearby Tuyen Lam Lake are another area for leisurely exploration, where visitors can stroll around the water's edge.

For more challenging treks, enlist the services of a guide. Adventure sports outfits like **Viet Challenge** (VND635,000-750,000), **Phat Tire Ventures** (VND930,000-2,065,000), and **Pine Track Adventures** (VND795,000-2,045,000) can be helpful in arranging single- and multiple-day guided treks.

Canyoneering

While tourists have long stood at the bases of Dalat's many waterfalls and snapped photos, more and more thrill-seekers are choosing instead to experience nature up close thanks to several canyoneering outfits in the area, which afford travelers the opportunity to rappel down the sheer cliffs hidden beneath these rushing waters. Most of the full-day excursions cater to first-time canyoneers, with a crash course in equipment and safety before descending on a few dry runs, literally, from practice slopes in the area. Most outfits will visit at least two waterfalls, almost always including a famous watery descent known as the Washing Machine, where rushing currents propel canyoneers down the final leg of a waterfall, spitting them out a few meters away.

Any reliable canyoneering company should

Rada Point, a popular trekking destination on Lang Biang Mountain be able to show you their equipment and give you a full rundown of the day's events, along with your guide's qualifications, beforehand. Dalat's two best-known canyoneering operators are **Groovy Gecko** (VND1,120,000-1,230,000) and **Phat Tire Ventures** (VND1,295,000-1,635,000). The newer **Viet Challenge** (VND1,135,000-1,705,000) also specializes in canyoneering. A typical canyoneering tour lasts 6-8 hours and includes all equipment, training, transportation, and lunch.

Cycling

Mountain biking trips depart daily from Dalat to dozens of trails throughout the countryside. Some of the more popular and challenging routes are located north of Dalat, including a 32-kilometer figure-eight loop that features rolling hills and top-notch scenery. The southern trails are more relaxed.

There are also downhill one- and two-day excursions toward either Nha Trang or Mui Ne. These trips include some time in a private van (you don't cycle the entire way); cruising down from the highlands on a mountain bike beats taking the bus. Most adventure sports outfits offer high-quality equipment and a range of excursions both easy and strenuous.

Having a guide for mountain biking excursions is important, since Dalat's surrounding forests are dense and it's important to have permission when passing through villages in the woods. Biking tours are provided by **Groovy Gecko** (VND630,000-945,000), **Pine Track Adventures** (VND770,000-1,700,000), and **Phat Tire Ventures** (VND885,000-1,295,000).

Golf

Located beside Xuan Huong Lake, the **Dalat Palace Golf Club** (Phu Dong Thien Vuong, tel. 0263/382-1201, www.dalatpalacegolf.com, 6am-4pm daily, VND1,400,000-1,500,000 for 9 holes, VND2,200,000-2,400,000 for 18 holes) has been a part of the local landscape since the 1930s. As early as 1923, plans for a golf course were factored into Dalat's construction, though no action was taken until Emperor Bao Dai returned from a trip to France, where he discovered the sport. The small six-hole course was used until 1945, when the emperor left for Hong Kong. Nine years later, its green was revived and expanded by a Hanoian doctor before shutting down again at the end of the American War.

When it was restored for a second time in the early 1990s, Dalat's golf course became an 18-hole playing field and now extends almost to the shores of Xuan Huong Lake. The clubhouse, a 1945 French colonial villa, is equipped with showers and locker rooms as well as a restaurant, bar, and pro shop. Golfers may book tee times either online or through the clubhouse. Course fees go up during weekends and holidays.

FOOD
Vietnamese

Goc Ha Thanh (53 Truong Cong Dinh, tel. 0263/355-3369, 11:30am-9pm daily, VND65,000-250,000) is a small eatery sandwiched between the many shops that run along Truong Cong Dinh. Specializing in Hanoian-style meals, the menu includes an array of Vietnamese options as well as a few tasty favorites, namely the *nem nuong* (grilled pork sausage), which is presented as a platter of do-it-yourself spring rolls. A handful of soups, sandwiches, and burgers also make their way onto the list, as do a few vegetarian plates. When in doubt, the friendly owners are happy to make recommendations.

For one of the best views in the city, grab a seat under the purple umbrellas at **Thanh Thuy Blue Water** (2 Nguyen Thai Hoc, tel. 0263/353-1668, 6:30am-11pm daily, VND65,000-400,000). With more quiet than some of the city cafés, Thanh Thuy is pricey by local standards but offers an endless variety of Vietnamese and Chinese cuisine as well as a prime spot on Xuan Huong Lake to observe downtown Dalat. The staff is especially cheerful. Both indoor and outdoor seating is available. This is also a nice spot for an evening drink, as it's right on the water but just far enough removed from the melee of the night market.

The quiet, cozy dining room at **Trong Dong** (220 Phan Dinh Phung, tel. 0263/382-1889, 11am-3pm and 5pm-9pm daily, VND50,000-100,000) combines a white-tablecloth setting with delicious renditions of standard Vietnamese fare. Vegetarian options are also available, as are local desserts and a range of meat, noodle, and rice dishes; the cheerful staff do their best to make you feel at home.

Thanks to its tasty local dishes, **Nhat Ly** (88 Phan Dinh Phung, tel. 0263/382-1651, 10am-9pm daily, VND60,000-350,000) sees regular foreign visitors as well as a few tour groups. Ranging from individual portions to family-style meals, this restaurant's fare tops many of the other eateries that cater to tourists. Try the particularly delicious *ca loc kho to* (braised fish in clay pot). Though the staff is not particularly warm, Nhat Ly's food makes up for it.

Just off Hoa Binh Square, **Long Hoa** (6 3 Thang 2, tel. 0263/382-2934, longhoarestaurant@yahoo.com.vn, 11:30am-2pm and 5pm-9pm daily, VND70,000-200,000) charms its guests with cozy ambience and delicious local meals. The tablecloths and framed menu posted out front help to give the place the feel of a European café. Both individual plates and family-style meals are served.

Street Food

You'll find ample street food within the **Dalat Market** (end of Nguyen Thi Minh Khai, sunrise-sunset daily). Take the stairs up to the second floor, where all manner of local fare is on offer. In the evenings, the night market also sees plenty of roadside vendors camp out along Nguyen Thi Minh Khai. Ask the price before dining, as these spots often charge higher prices for foreigners. Dozens of modest local eateries line Bui Thi Xuan, convenient for travelers based on the street, and Phan Dinh Phung, near the town's small backpacker area.

French

Set in the historical Triangle Building, an oddly shaped structure wedged between Tran Phu and Ho Tung Mau, **Cafe de la Poste** (12 Tran Phu, tel. 0263/382-5777, www.royaldl.com, 6am-9:30pm daily, VND80,000-600,000) has been a French bistro and an integral part of the famed Dalat Du Parc hotel since the 1950s. Bright-green walls lined with vintage French advertisements and high ceilings give the space a quaint feel. Dishes include a range of pizza, pasta, sandwiches, and salads, as well as main courses like steak, salmon, and pork tenderloin. European desserts also feature on the menu, as does an extensive wine list and several cocktails.

Cafés and Bakeries

As part of the nation's main coffee- and tea-growing region, you can't get more than a few steps in any direction without hitting a café. These places range from big to small, humble to extravagant. Scores of cafés along Le Dai Hanh and Nguyen Chi Thanh offer a higher vantage point from which to enjoy Xuan Huong Lake, while Phan Dinh Phung also boasts its fair share of small local hangouts.

A charming little spot hidden from street view, **Bicycle Up Cafe** (82 Truong Cong Dinh, tel. 0263/370-0177, 7am-10pm daily, VND12,000-55,000) is awash with old dog-eared books and antique typewriters, making it feel as if you've just walked into someone's study. Written in old storybooks, the café menu features your usual coffee and tea options, as well as fruit juices, shakes, and beer. Though seating is limited, this is a pleasant spot to grab coffee. Bicycle Up also offers a few light meals, but because of its busy decor, this place is better as a café rather than a restaurant.

Windmills Cafe (133 Phan Dinh Phung, tel. 0263/354-0808, 7am-10pm daily, VND25,000-70,000) is a popular and inviting little corner café decked out in white and green, serving a variety of coffee, tea, shakes, and sodas. Free Wi-Fi is available, and the staff is a particularly friendly bunch. If you're closer to the Dalat Market, there is also a second location (7 3 Thang 2, on the corner with Nam Ky Khoi Nghia), right by Hoa Binh Square.

Perched above a bustling road, **An Café** (63bis 3 Thang 2, tel. 09/7573-5521, www.an-cafe.vn, 7am-10pm daily, VND30,000-65,000) and its notably green surroundings make for a perfect place to get your morning caffeine fix or while away an afternoon. Grab a seat in the café's cozy interior or pull up a bench outside, where picnic-style tables shaded by trees overlook the city street below. In addition to coffee, you'll find an array of interesting teas, smoothies, and juices as well as light meals on the menu.

International

A popular tourist spot, **V Cafe** (17 Bui Thi Xuan, tel. 0263/352-0215, www.vcafedalatvietnam.com, 8am-10pm daily, VND55,000-200,000) serves soups, salads, pasta, pizza, some Latin food, and a selection of vegetarian dishes. Both indoor seating and an outdoor patio are available, and the restaurant offers breakfast until 11am. If you visit in the evenings, look for live music (from 7:30pm), which includes a range of acoustic, blues, folk, country, and rock-and-roll favorites.

The bright blue **Dalat Train Cafe** (Quang Trung, just past Dalat Railway Station, tel. 0263/381-6365, www.dalattrainvilla.com, 8am-9:30pm daily, VND89,000-275,000) is a charming, out-of-the-way diner in a restored 1910 French train car. Decked out in vintage railroad paraphernalia, this quaint little spot serves mostly Western fare, with salads, sandwiches, burgers, pizza, and a few fancier entrées. A host of wine options beyond the usual Vang Dalat are also available. If the train car is full, you can also grab a seat out front, where there is patio seating beneath the cover of a few large umbrellas.

Vegetarian

You'll find that most Western restaurants, as well as a few foreigner-friendly Vietnamese options, have a vegetarian section on their menu. If you prefer to go fully meat-free, the following eateries are great for local vegetarian food.

Au Lac Vegetarian (15 Phan Dinh Phung, tel. 0263/382-5054, 5am-9pm daily, VND20,000-50,000) serves noodles and steamed dumplings as well as an array of tofu, vegetable, and mock meat dishes out of its large open storefront on Phan Dinh Phung. The place may be bare-bones, but taste is the most important factor here.

A warehouse-like restaurant, **Hoa Sen** (62 Phan Dinh Phung, tel. 0263/356-7999, 8am-2pm and 4pm-9pm daily, VND10,000-45,000) is all-vegetarian, serving tofu as well as vegetables, noodles, soups, and rice. Meals are tasty and well-priced and there is ample space to stretch out. While the place usually closes for a few hours in the afternoon, on the 1st and 15th of the lunar month (religious days for Buddhists) you'll find Hoa Sen open all day.

ACCOMMODATIONS

There are a dizzying number of accommodations in and around downtown Dalat. Rooms run the gamut from budget beds to palatial luxury hotels. Base yourself within walking distance of Xuan Huong Lake, Dalat's focal point, as this will give you easy access to shops, restaurants, cafés, and the scenic downtown area. Most budget travelers prefer to stick around either the backpacker area near Truong Cong Dinh or slightly farther on Bui Thi Xuan. If you prefer more upscale accommodations, several of Dalat's high-end hotels lie farther afield, removed from the bustle of town. While peace and quiet are found in greater measures on the outskirts of Dalat, you will also likely require transportation to leave your hotel.

At 1,500 meters above sea level, Dalat is markedly cooler than most of the southern half of the country. Temperatures can actually become cold at night and, in dry season, stay chilly even during the day. For this reason, you'll find that some hotels do not include air-conditioning in their room amenities. In most cases, this should be just fine.

Under VND210,000

Rooms at the **Ai Nghia Guesthouse** (80 Phan Dinh Phung, tel. 0263/352-0529, VND200,000-250,000) are basic but clean and come with hot water, TV, and Wi-Fi. Noise levels can get bothersome for light sleepers, as this spot faces one of Dalat's busier streets. Larger, quieter rooms are toward the back.

VND210,000-525,000

A no-frills budget hotel, **Peace 2** (67 Truong Cong Dinh, tel. 0263/382-2787, peacedalat@gmail.com, VND230,000-275,000) supplies clean basic rooms to backpackers along with hot water, TV, and Wi-Fi. Decor is a little aged and the staff can be pushy at times, but the value of the place is what makes it popular. A small tour and motorbike rental outfit also operates downstairs. Avoid the hotel's sister outfit, Peace 1, farther down the road: Although its rooms are equally worthy, the nightclub next door blasts party music late into the night, keeping even the soundest of sleepers awake.

A little spartan but modern and tidy, the rooms at **Les Sapins 60** (60 Truong Cong Dinh, tel. 0263/383-0839, VND300,000-360,000) are well priced for what is offered. Equipped with comfy beds, hot water, TV, and Wi-Fi, this small budget spot on a bend of Truong Cong Dinh also runs a café and bar downstairs and can assist with travel inquiries. If you're lucky, you may land a room with a balcony, which looks out over the narrow street below.

With basic rooms featuring hot water, Wi-Fi, and TV, **My Dream Hotel** (213A Phan Dinh Phung, tel. 09/1856-4472, dorm VND80,000 dorm, VND252,000-294,000 d, breakfast included) manages a decent level of service and value. Opt for a smaller, quieter room at the back or a larger, brighter, front-facing bed with a small balcony. For solo travelers, the hotel also has dorms that feature an en suite bath and individual lockers.

The smartly decorated **Mint Homestay** (364 Phan Dinh Phung, tel. 09/3466-1066, VND350,000-400,000, breakfast included) may be about 1.5 kilometers from the city center, but its location next to the pretty hillside Ky Vien Pagoda. Bright, spacious rooms feature a personal safe, hot water, TV, a blow-dryer, a minibar, and Wi-Fi, and the cheerful owner can assist with travel inquiries.

The small but charming **Hotel Phuong Thanh** (4 Bui Thi Xuan, tel. 0263/383-6369, VND300,000-500,000) may not be as spacious as its competition, but rooms are clean, modern, and smartly decorated. Amenities include hot water, TV, and Wi-Fi. With Xuan Huong Lake only a few steps away, this mini-hotel's location is ideal for getting to the market area and around downtown without staying in the backpacker neighborhood. The staff is friendly and easygoing, though little English is spoken. Only double-bed rooms are available.

VND525,000-1,050,000

The **Pink House Hotel** (7 Hai Thuong, tel. 0263/381-5667, villapinkhouse@gmail.com, VND570,000-800,000) offers comfy rooms with balconies, TV, hot water, Wi-Fi, and an in-room fridge. Thanks to its location, a quieter atmosphere prevails, and the staff is happy to help with motorbike rentals and other travel services. The major draw is owner Rot's guests-only secret countryside tour. As the self-professed "only guy in town who speaks K'ho," a local minority language, Rot guides travelers through an authentic K'ho village. While the day-long trip costs extra, it's a must-do for guests.

Rooms at **Dreams 3** (140 Phan Dinh Phung, tel. 0263/383-3748, dreamshotel@gmail.com, VND680,000-800,000, breakfast included) feature plush beds and smart furnishings alongside the standard amenities. Massage services are available. For a cheaper option, **Dreams 1** (141 Phan Dinh Phung, VND460,000-680,000) is well furnished, if more basic. If you're staying in the latter, opt for a room on the upper floors, as street-level accommodations attract a lot of noise.

Perched on a bend in the road, **Fortune Dai Loi** (3A Bui Thi Xuan, tel. 0263/383-7333, www.dailoihotel.com, VND700,000-1,200,000, breakfast included) is another massive concrete building that looks slightly rundown on the outside but houses cozy, generous accommodations within. Rooms include plush beds, hot water, TV, and Wi-Fi. The decor is fairly elegant.

VND1,050,000-2,100,000

One of the largest accommodations in the city, **Saigon Dalat Hotel** (2 Hoang Van Thu, tel. 0263/355-6789, www.saigondalathotel.com, VND1,350,000-35,000,000) is at the corner of 3 Thang 2, about 1.5 kilometers from the market. Its stately, well-appointed rooms feature an in-room safe, tea- and coffee-making facilities, hot water, TV, Wi-Fi, a minibar, and fridge. Breakfast is served downstairs in the hotel restaurant, and guests can enjoy the heated pool on the ground floor as well as a fitness center. The hotel also runs a tour outfit in its grand reception hall.

Though the reception area at **Sammy Hotel Dalat** (1 Le Hong Phong, tel. 0263/354-5454, www.sammyhotel.vn, VND1,850,000-6,050,000, breakfast included) can feel cluttered upon arrival, the hotel's extravagant rooms have plenty of space, are furnished in upscale modern decor, and include TV, hot water, and a minibar. Rooms have Western-style bathtubs, and each room's wrought-iron balcony offers pleasant views of town. The downstairs restaurant also caters to nonguests.

Over VND2,100,000

Originally a cinema, the purple-clad **TTC Premium Ngoc Lan** (42 Nguyen Chi Thanh, tel. 0263/383-8838, www.ngoclan.ttchotels.com, VND2,200,000-3,800,000, breakfast included) is in an excellent location overlooking Xuan Huong Lake and boasts chic modern rooms with air-conditioning, hot water, Wi-Fi, an in-room safe, TV, and a minibar. The hotel also offers sauna and massage services, a tour desk, and a ground-floor restaurant, which often fills up for weddings and other functions.

Founded in 1932, the grandiose **Dalat Du Parc** (15 Tran Phu, tel. 0263/382-5777, www.dalathotelduparc.com, VND2,100,000-3,400,000, breakfast included) harks back to an earlier time. Its stunning French colonial exterior captures the original days of this former resort town. Inside, small touches like the still-functioning antique elevator in the lobby preserve the hotel's upscale ambience. Rooms feature beautiful wooden furnishings and lavish decor as well as a fan, hot water, TV, and Wi-Fi. If possible, opt for lodgings above the standard level, as these rooms are cramped, and pay a visit to the hotel's restaurant, Cafe de la Poste, across the street.

The **Dalat Palace Heritage Hotel** (2 Tran Phu, tel. 0263/382-5444, www.royaldl.com, VND4,000,000-8,600,000) has come through the nation's decades of war and civil unrest largely unscathed. Originally opened in 1922, this grand colonial hotel was once the largest building in Dalat. Today, rooms remain in much the same state as they were in the beginning, though with a few modern updates. Amenities such as hot water and Wi-Fi are provided, as well as TV, minibar, workspace, and tea- and coffee-making facilities. The hotel also runs an upscale restaurant, Le Rabelais.

INFORMATION AND SERVICES

Dalat Tourist (1 Nguyen Thi Minh Khai, tel. 0263/382-2520, www.dalattourist.com.vn, 8am-noon and 2pm-6pm daily), near the market, offers general travel advice in addition to a few package tours.

There are plenty of **ATMs** along Phan Boi Chau and around Hoa Binh Square near the central market. The local **Sacombank** (32 Khu Hoa Binh, tel. 0263/351-1082, www.sacombank.com.vn, 7:30am-11:30am and 1pm-5pm Mon.-Fri., 7:30am-11:30am Sat.) can also assist with currency exchange. The **Dalat central post office** (2 Le Dai Hanh, tel. 0263/353-2363, 7am-8:30pm Mon.-Sat., 7am-7:30pm Sun.) is able to handle Internet and postal needs.

Located near the city center, **Lam Dong General Hospital** (4 Pham Ngoc Thach, tel. 0263/382-1369, 7:15am-11:15am and 1:30pm-3:30pm daily) assists with minor injuries and illnesses.

GETTING THERE
Air

Though it is possible to fly into **Lien Khuong Airport** (DLI, Hwy. 20, Lien Nghia town, tel. 0263/384-3373), the largest in Lam Dong province, most travelers opt for the bus instead, as flight tickets are more expensive and, with the airport 29 kilometers south of Dalat, require an extra 30-minute drive to the city. Daily arrivals come from Saigon (45 minutes, VND300,000-650,000) and Hanoi (2 hours, VND1,055,000-2,225,000).

Arriving passengers can take the **shuttle bus** (tel. 09/1856-4686, 6am-6pm daily, VND40,000) or grab a taxi (VND250,000-300,000) into Dalat.

Bus

Buses from Can Tho, Hue, Nha Trang, Danang, and Saigon arrive at the **Phuong Trang bus station** (1 To Hien Thanh, tel. 0263/358-5858, www.futabuslines.com.vn, 24 hours daily), just under two kilometers south of the city center. The station is essentially run by Phuong Trang, but a few other local buses pull up here too. To get to Mui Ne, you'll have to visit **Sinh Tourist** (22 Bui Thi Xuan, tel. 0263/382-2663, www.thesinhtourist.vn, 7am-10pm daily) in the city center or ask your hotel for a booking.

GETTING AROUND

As usual, plenty of *xe om* and **Easy Rider** motorbike tours are about, many of them hoping to interest you in a tour around town or throughout the province. **Mailinh** (tel. 0263/383-8383) taxis are present throughout the city and surrounding areas.

Most hotels and guesthouses can help you to arrange **rental motorbikes.** Bicycles are also available, but, with all of Dalat's hills, a standard city bicycle is usually not a feasible option for getting around town. There are a few independent street-side outfits near Xuan Huong Lake that will hire out push bikes for the day, however the quality of these vehicles is often not worth the price, though the novelty of sharing a tandem bike with your travel buddy may trump bad brakes and rusty frames.

VICINITY OF DALAT
Datanla Falls

The rushing waters of **Datanla Falls** (Prenn Pass, Hwy. QL20, tel. 0263/221-2145, 7am-5pm daily, VND30,000 adults, VND15,000 children) draw foreign and domestic tourists. Follow the stone path that leads down to the base of the falls, where you'll find misty white waters and a handful of souvenir and drink vendors. Guests can also opt for a ride on the park's mini **roller coaster** (VND50,000), more like a two-person tram, or continue on to the **cable car** (VND40,000) that glides slowly above the water to a lower point on the river. Walkers will get as far as the park's third waterfall before they're forced to pay for the elevator down to another pathway below.

The first waterfall is easily the largest and most visually appealing, so there's not really much need to continue on to the few remaining falls. The farther you go, the more peace and quiet you'll find. Throughout the park, small cafés are situated around the various waterfalls, and the restaurant up top has affordable meals. There is also now a **ropes course** (7am-5pm, VND270,000 adults, VND150,000 children before 9am; VND250,000 adults, VND200,000 children after 9am) in the woods next to the falls featuring both high- and low-rope elements, if you're up for a bit of adventure. The six-kilometer trip out to Datanla Falls is easily covered by motorbike or taxi; it should cost around VND90,000-110,000 from downtown Dalat.

Truc Lam Pagoda and Cable Car

The understated **Truc Lam Pagoda (Truc**

Vicinity of Dalat

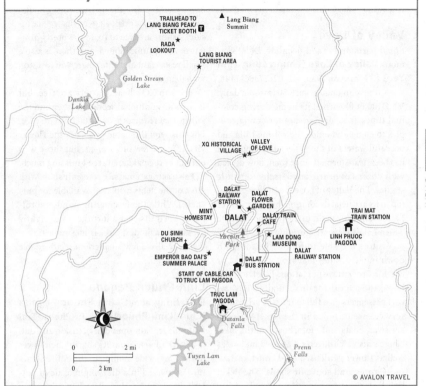

Lam Yen Tu) (7am-5pm daily) lacks the same vivid ornamentation that characterizes many older religious buildings. But its colorful array of flowers make the sprawling grounds something of a botanical garden set on the edge of Tuyen Lam Lake, a beautiful, secluded body of water that escapes much of the hustle and bustle surrounding its downtown counterpart.

Visitors to the pagoda can see its two main buildings, each featuring high ceilings, beautiful polished woodwork, and muted colors, before catching a glimpse of the pagoda living quarters, where over 100 monks reside. The most noteworthy part of a trip to Truc Lam is its natural surroundings, which include both bamboo groves and pine trees in the same short section of path. As the pagoda is often packed with people, a wander around the nearby area can be a pleasant way to escape the crowds and appreciate Truc Lam's surrounding nature. From the lake shore, it is also possible to hire a **boat** (Khu Du Lich Ho Tuyen Lam, 7:30am-4:30pm daily, VND300,000-500,000) around Tuyen Lam that travels a five-kilometer route out to a restaurant at the far end of the lake and back; the ticketing booth seems to spontaneously close at times, so be prepared to change your plans if the ticket vendor is out that day.

The most scenic way to get to Truc Lam is by **cable car** (Doi Ro Bin, tel. 0263/383-7938, 7:30am-11:30am and 1pm-5pm daily, VND80,000 round-trip adults, VND60,000 one-way adults, VND60,000 round-trip children, VND40,000 one-way children). Small, suspended pods travel a 1.5-kilometer route from Robin Hill to Truc Lam and back.

Valley of Love

Equal parts pretty and peculiar, Dalat's famous **Valley of Love (Thung Lung Tinh Yeu)** (7 Mai Anh Dao, tel. 0263/382-1448, www.tinhyeumongmo.vn, 8:30am-6pm daily, VND100,000) earned its name during colonial times as a popular spot for young couples to come and enjoy the rolling hills and peaceful waters of the valley. The landscape has been transformed since then, now dotted with dozens of hearts and kitschy romantic statues. The Valley of Love is a little over-the-top in its artificial decoration, but the views of Lang Biang Mountain in the distance and Da Thien Lake below are stunning nonetheless.

Visitors are able to follow the footpath down into the valley and around the lake or opt for other transportation. Electric cars, jeeps, and a tourist train (actually a bus) escort passengers on a full tour of the area; these services are included in the ticket price, as are swan boats and motorboats on the lake. There's also a children's play area on-site as well as flower gardens, a food court, restaurants, cafés, and souvenir shops. The ticket booth closes at 5pm, so give yourself plenty of time to explore.

XQ Historical Village

Just opposite the Valley of Love, **XQ historical village (Da Lat Su Quan)** (80 Mai Anh Dao, tel. 0263/355-2348, www.xqvietnam.com, 8am-5:30pm daily, free) celebrates traditional Vietnamese art and culture with a maze of exhibits featuring beautiful hand-embroidered pictures. These incredibly detailed, intricate images can take as long as several months to complete and, in some instances, require an entire team of women, who stitch each portrait by hand. Visitors are able to watch these craftswomen at work as they walk through XQ's many galleries, where portraits as large as a meter tall are on display. The village also showcases other aspects of Vietnamese art and culture, including the handicrafts of the region's ethnic minorities, jewelry, and traditional instruments. Though each room can be difficult to navigate once inside, visitors are free to roam the pretty miniature village uninhibited, and there is also a small restaurant and café where you can stop for a drink.

Trips to XQ's headquarters are free, but there is an additional section farther into the village that requires a VND100,000 entry fee. For this, you'll be able to access the flower village and a few other areas, but those who opt out of the paid area aren't missing much. XQ also acts as a massive souvenir shop, with most of the items displayed available for purchase. While the fascinating hand-embroidered portraits cost a fortune—and rightly so, as even a modest piece is no simple task—there are also a few smaller, more affordable items around.

Linh Phuoc Pagoda

Everything about **Linh Phuoc Pagoda (Chua Linh Phuoc)** (120 Tu Phuoc, Trai Mat village, 6am-6pm daily), inside and out, is a work of art. From its soaring bell tower to the long, wide main hall, the entire structure is covered in a dizzying mosaic of pottery shards and broken glass. Ten kilometers east of town, Linh Phuoc greets its visitors with a 36-meter tower, home to a massive bell weighing 8.5 tons. From the ground, ascend the narrow metal staircase up to the top, passing by different statues of the Buddha or Quan Am on each level. Above, you'll find pleasant views of the nearby valley as well as the pagoda's main hall, the front of which bears a large, ornate dragon. On the second floor of the tower, stacks of square papers sit beside the enormous bell: here, locals write out their prayers and paste them to the side of the chime for good luck.

Rounding out the other side of the square is the main hall. Flanked by row upon row of dragon-clad columns, the prayer area leads onto a large altar while, along the top section of the wall, scenes from the life of Buddha are

Linh Phuoc Pagoda

Lang Biang Mountain

In a region known for its natural beauty, the densely forested **Lang Biang Mountain** (13 kilometers north of Dalat, Khu Du Lich Lang Biang, tel. 0263/383-9088, www.dalattourist.com.vn, 6:30am-7pm daily, VND30,000 adults, VND15,000 children) is one of Dalat's most famous features. At 2,167 meters above sea level, Lang Biang can be seen clearly from higher vantage points in Dalat. Though there are several versions of how the mountain got its name, the most popular story goes that once, years ago, a boy called Lang and a girl named Biang were in love, but because they were each from different ethnic groups, their families forbade them to marry. The two pined for one another until death but were never able to get together. The mountain was named in their honor. Only later did the families of Lang and Biang understand their children's plight and changed their customs so that different ethnic groups could intermarry.

Lang Biang's two highest points offer striking panoramic views of Dalat and the dappled hills rolling off into the distance. Thanks to the local tourism board, the mountain's tourist area boasts several options for travelers, varying from easy to strenuous activity. Past the entrance gates and the group of horses grazing near Lang Biang's trademark sign, you can rent one of the park's **jeeps** (VND60,000 pp) for a relaxing visit. Drivers go up to the 2,064-meter **Rada Point,** which offers full views of a pastel-hued Dalat and the surrounding countryside and also has a restaurant.

If you're keen to get some exercise, follow the paved road on foot up to Rada. Though it's steep in some places, the wide, winding path makes it up to the lookout in about 1.5 kilometers. More enthusiastic hikers can veer off the main route and check in at the ticket booth for **Bidoup-Nui Ba National Park** (Da Nhim village, tel. 0263/374-7449, 7:30am-3:30pm daily), which manages the

rendered in vivid mosaic decoration. All of this makes for a stunning effect. Photography is forbidden inside the main hall.

Once you've seen the pagoda interior, head back outside to take in the entirety of Linh Phuoc's 49-meter dragon, which snakes along the right-hand side of the complex. Covered in roughly 50,000 shards of glass, the head of this massive creature watches over the square, while its three-dimensional body winds through the small area to the right of the pagoda. With more tourists coming to Dalat, this pagoda has now become a bona fide tourist attraction and draws its fair share of tour buses and curious travelers. Though the crowds can diminish its appeal, the sheer scale of the mosaic coverings is impressive. There is also ongoing construction here.

Though it's out of the way, Linh Phuoc can easily be reached from Dalat by motorbike or *xe om* and is often included on local tours. A tourist train also runs several times a day from the old Dalat train station to Trai Mat narrow rainforest-covered **Lang Biang Trail** (7:30am-3:30pm daily, VND40,000) up to the mountain's highest point. From there, the journey becomes more challenging, starting off with a modest incline at first before hurtling into the overgrown bush. Plenty of tree cover keeps the trail cool, which is needed given the rocky uphills and occasional felled tree you'll have to climb over. Throughout the path, signage is intermittent—sometimes nothing more than a red scrap of fabric tied around a branch—but the trail remains fairly visible even amid the thick foliage. As Lang Biang's grand finale, a steep wood-and-earth staircase brings you up the last section to the summit where, on a clear day, peak-baggers can see for kilometers, with beautiful views of Dalat as well as Rada Point down to your right.

For walkers, the journey from Lang Biang's main gate up to the summit is about a two-hour trip and can be completed solo. Hikers heading for the very top should bring proper shoes and plenty of water, as this is truly the wilderness and the trail can be rocky at times. Bug spray is useful, given that the shaded areas of the path can attract insects.

While the Lang Biang Trail is accessible year-round, travelers visiting during the rainy season may want to check with the guide at the ticket booth before committing to the peak, as this route can get slippery even in dry times. These same guides can also be hired for the trek (VND100,000-290,000, depending on the number of people): residents of Lat village, a minority town at the foot of the mountain, these men speak excellent English and are able to take travelers not only up to the Lang Biang summit but farther into Bidoup-Nui Ba National Park, as well as for a spin around their hometown, which is often visited by travelers en route to Lang Biang.

Waterfalls

The hills surrounding Dalat are awash with dozens of waterfalls, ranging from modest trickles to raging white-water descents. The most accessible and most visited of these is **Datanla Falls** (Prenn Pass, Hwy. QL20, tel. 0263/221-2145, 7am-5pm daily, VND30,000 adults, VND15,000 children), but visitors can also make the trip out to **Elephant Falls,** a natural spectacle 29 kilometers southwest of the city that pitches over the rocks in a half-moon shape, allowing you to walk behind the falls, though not without getting wet. Another 19 kilometers farther is **Pongour Falls** (VND10,000), the area's largest waterfall; it

a horse painted to look like a zebra at Lang Biang Mountain

is a hike to reach the place in a single day. Independent travelers can make the trip alone, although the road to these waterfalls has seen better days. Instead, many prefer to hop on an **Easy Rider day tour** (about VND570,000-800,000 full-day trip to Elephant Falls and Pongour Falls). **Groovy Gecko** (65 Truong Cong Dinh, tel. 0263/383-6521, www. groovygeckotours.net, 7:30am-8:30pm daily, VND675,000) also offers a day tour that brings travelers out to Elephant Falls in addition to exploring the nearby countryside.

Mui Ne

At the heart of Mui Ne's appeal is its natural beauty. Beyond sparkling turquoise waters and tranquil shores, the surrounding area boasts an unusual landscape, with shaggy palms and freshwater streams beside vast barren sand dunes. Tack on the Po Shanu Towers, a relic of the region's multicultural history and among the oldest Cham structures in Vietnam, plus a nearby provincial capital that produces some of the mainland's most prized fish sauce, and there's plenty to explore. As one of the windier coasts in the country, Mui Ne has become a major kitesurfing destination, and several kiting outfits also offer equipment for windsurfing or stand-up paddleboarding.

Once a sleepy, secluded beachfront, Mui Ne is now a well-trodden stop on the tourist trail and, in some ways, a smaller version of its northeastern neighbor, Nha Trang. Seaside resorts have materialized all along Nguyen Dinh Chieu, the 11-kilometer stretch of road parallel to the shore. This rapid development has its pros: a wider range of accommodations and dining options and a budding nightlife scene. The cons are that prices have soared, and overcharging is a particular problem.

On account of the area's strong winds and even stronger undertow, Mui Ne experiences a great deal of coastal erosion. Some seaside resorts, particularly those farther to the west, offer a genuine sand beach, while properties at the east end of Nguyen Dinh Chieu are fortified with concrete sea walls.

Dry season, November-April, is the best time to visit any of Vietnam's southern beaches, but Mui Ne experiences a conservative rainy season, with downpours occurring daily for only a few hours at a time. November-January, high season sees scores of Russian tourists, young families, backpackers, and couples, so book ahead and expect to pay slightly higher prices.

Travelers can catch some beach time en route to Saigon with a few days in Mui Ne. The area's few sights can be seen in a single day, leaving plenty of time for sunbathing.

ORIENTATION

Mui Ne is a small fishing town. All the attractions, hotels, and restaurants that bring travelers to Mui Ne are located on **Nguyen Dinh Chieu,** the coastal road in between Mui Ne and Phan Thiet. Once in Mui Ne, Nguyen Dinh Chieu becomes **Huynh Thuc Khang.**

SIGHTS

Most travelers come to Mui Ne for its beaches; the town doesn't offer many attractions. Most people base themselves on the coastal road that runs between Mui Ne and the larger town of Phan Thiet. Here you'll find plenty of shops and restaurants, all built within the last few years to cater to tourists. The closest sight is Fairy Spring, but for anything else you'll have to rent a motorbike or grab a taxi. It's a short drive out to the red sand dunes, with the larger and more impressive hills of the white dunes around 24 kilometers away. While some destinations in Vietnam require guided tours, Mui Ne is not one of them: you can easily see the main sights within a day and save the rest of your time for the beach.

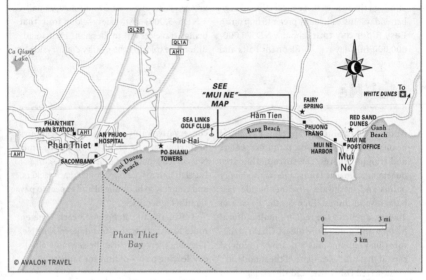

Mui Ne and Vicinity

Sand Dunes

RED DUNES

Ten kilometers from the beach, Mui Ne's **red dunes** (Provincial Rd. DT706B) are the most easily accessible of the area's sands, though not the most scenic. Spilling out onto the nearby highway, these gentle brick-red hills change with the wind, shape-shifting at the mercy of strong gusts. Some of the dunes' appeal has been lost in recent years, as a cluster of roadside drink shops have set up across the street and tend to be relentless in their sales pitch. The same goes for the droves of young kids trying to rent plastic sleds to tourists, which don't actually work on the sand. These dunes are a quick and easy stop for anyone exploring the area by motorbike.

★ WHITE DUNES

The **white dunes** (29 kilometers northeast of Mui Ne, 7am-5pm daily, VND15,000 adults, VND7,000 children) offer a more dramatic, windswept landscape than those closer to town. As you approach, you'll see these sun-bleached sands from afar, standing in stark contrast to the long and narrow turquoise lake at the edge of the dunes. A small footpath leads visitors into the hills, where you can trudge up the sands to catch a glimpse of the scenery. These dunes are also susceptible to regular changes from the breeze and, surrounded by redder sands and verdant shorelines, the barren hills become an interesting landscape.

Bring along a hat and sunscreen, as both the drive along the coast and the hills themselves offer no escape from the sun. This spot heats up as the day goes on, making the walk up to the dunes a little painful to do barefoot. Tucked between the lake and the dunes, a few small cafés sling coffee, beer, and other refreshments. It is also possible to rent ATVs (VND300,000-600,000 for 20 minutes) for a brief ramble across the dunes, though these are fairly expensive.

Visitors will have to pay a VND15,000 entry fee at the top of the path before entering, but this is subject to the time of day, as you may occasionally find the ticket booth empty and no one around to collect the entry fee. The dunes are easy to reach by motorbike;

Mui Ne

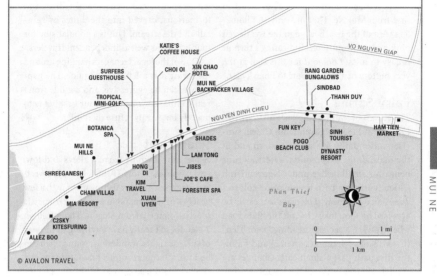

follow the road along the shoreline and turn left at the faded sign for Bau Trang.

Mui Ne Harbor

Passing through Mui Ne town en route to the white sand dunes, you'll come across **Mui Ne Harbor** (Huynh Thuc Khang), a pretty spot where hundreds of painted wooden fishing boats dock in the mellow waters of the bay. At the foot of the concrete steps leading down to the beach, groups of fishermen mend nets or hop in small, round boats, which are used to paddle out to the larger vessels. You can also occasionally catch fish drying in the sun along the sloped embankment that separates the street from the shore.

Po Shanu Towers

Built in the 9th century, the Hindu **Po Shanu Towers** (between Mui Ne and Phan Thiet, 6:30am-5:30pm daily, VND15,000) lean into Ba Nai Hill, a lookout five kilometers east of Phan Thiet. The three structures belong to the Cham, former rulers of Vietnam's south-central coast. From its first tower, perched on a hillside clearing, visitors can see directly across to the surrounding hills, where dozens of brightly hued headstones decorate the landscape. The 12-meter tower houses a modest altar along with a few other pieces. Continue the upward climb and you'll come to Po Shanu's soaring main structure, with a lavish altar bedecked with flowers, incense, and fruit, as well as massive stone linga-yoni statues. Next door, a squat tower complements the larger temple.

Ba Nai Hill's significance is not limited to these relics. Farther uphill, a large monument commemorates the 1947 Vietnamese victory over French forces, in which local soldiers disguised themselves in an ambush, killing or capturing 35 of their enemies as well as a cache of weapons. Continue to the top to this battle site and, on a clear day, some stunning views of the pastel-drenched Phan Thiet town, to your right beside the ocean. The dilapidated brick tower you'll find atop the hill is not a work of the Cham but a French duke by the name of de Montpensier who, in 1911, chose the site as his holiday home. For decades, locals referred to the lavish house as the Prince's Palace before French authorities set up a military outpost nearby in 1946, prompting the June 14 battle the following year.

The Po Shanu Towers aren't difficult to find from Mui Ne. They are only 10 kilometers west of the beach, though the weathered pink-and-red stone tablet indicating a turnoff is easy to miss. Look out for this sign at the very bottom of a hill en route to Phan Thiet.

Fairy Spring

The closest of Mui Ne's sights, **Fairy Spring** (**Suoi Tien**) (63A Nguyen Dinh Chieu, sunrise-sunset daily) sits at the eastern end of the main drag. This modest waterway runs beneath a small bridge under Nguyen Dinh Chieu, cutting a path beside some colorful dunes along the way. The place can easily be accessed on foot: take a left off the main road when you see a red sign reading "Suoi Tien" (the stream's Vietnamese name) and follow the dirt path past a small café. Chances are you'll find a jeep or two parked near the street, as small tour groups often make the rounds here. You can either enter the stream at the concrete steps immediately to your left or walk farther down to another point of entry. You'll need to take off your shoes in order to wade through the ankle-deep water. A 400-meter walk takes you out to the stream's deeper section, after which there's not much to see, but en route you'll catch desert-like landscapes of red, yellow, and white sand formations, carved into the dunes by rainfall and the stream. This is a popular stop for tour groups as well as independent travelers.

One of the local teenagers hanging around the spring may ask to be your guide. Their approach can be aggressive, and a guide won't really enhance your visit. Your best bet is to politely but firmly refuse their offer.

Phan Thiet

A pleasant town of narrow alleys and low, pastel houses, **Phan Thiet** is Mui Ne's western neighbor, a sleepy fishing town with a few beaches of its own, popular among domestic tourists, namely from Saigon. Though Phan Thiet doesn't really have anything in the way of specific sights, wandering around town can be a fun afternoon outing. En route to the city center, you'll pass a row of fish-sauce factories along Thu Khoa Huan street, where Phan Thiet's most famous product is made, bottled, and sold. Phan Thiet's resident city beach, **Doi Duong** is a breezy, tree-lined patch of sand far different from its bustling urban surroundings. This quiet spot is popular with young couples during the evening and has a

Mui Ne's white sand dunes

handful of cafés tucked at the western end of the beach. While it's not really the place for swimming, Doi Duong makes a worthy spot for a stroll or a peaceful afternoon drink.

BEACHES
Rang Beach
The one stretch of sand where most travelers spend their time is known as **Rang Beach.** This runs parallel to Mui Ne's main road and has mostly been gobbled up by seaside hotels and resorts, who stake their claim on the shoreline. A handful of bars and restaurants on the beachfront are open throughout the day, and it's perfectly acceptable to buy a drink and lounge around at one of these establishments for a few hours in order to take advantage of the ocean. Since Rang Beach, and, indeed, much of the Mui Ne coastline, suffers from an erosion problem, restaurants and accommodations farther east along the beach are less likely to have sand and more likely to have sun beds and umbrellas atop a concrete sea wall. Undercurrents are strong in Mui Ne, and waves can get big; exercise caution in the water.

Ganh Beach
On the other side of Mui Ne village is **Ganh Beach,** also known as Hon Rom. Much the same as its western counterpart, this coastal stretch is home to a handful of luxury accommodations but sees much less traffic than its neighbor and has not yet resorted to protective sea walls. You'll find a more traditional beach here, where a small point keeps the easternmost end of the coast from stronger winds and several restaurants cater to beachgoers. Beyond these, the place is quiet, with most visitors just driving up and laying down a towel. Ganh Beach also acts as the town's harbor for half the year, when boats from the more famous port on the other side of the village come to moor near this coast.

NIGHTLIFE
Though Mui Ne's nightlife isn't quite as lively as it used to be, the place still boasts a few spots for nighttime revelry. Most places close by midnight and the street quiets down considerably then. But night owls will find a handful of local watering holes that stay open until the last customer goes home.

In addition to some killer food, **Joe's Cafe** (86 Nguyen Dinh Chieu, tel. 0252/384-7177, www.joescafemuine.com, 7am-midnight daily, VND65,000-250,000) is a popular spot for a laid-back nightcap or happy-hour drink. With regular drink specials and live music on offer, guests can sit back and take in resident guitarists or play a game of billiards.

A psychedelic oceanfront hangout, **Pogo Beach Club** (138 Nguyen Dinh Chieu, tel. 09/0947-9346, 10am-late daily, VND20,000-200,000) is made up of a collection of lounge chairs and bean bags, wooden tables, cushions, and concrete benches. Putting together a fine burger and a handful of other meals during the day, the bar gets busy with young backpackers and kitesurfers around the time the sun goes down. Daily drink specials encourage guests to imbibe, and the resident DJs keep a steady stream of tunes coming.

After the sun sets, **Jibes** (90 Nguyen Dinh Chieu, tel. 0252/384-7405, www.jibesbeachclub.com, 7am-midnight daily, VND20,000-130,000) trades its sails and surfboards for beachside beer and happy-hour drinks. Tasty Western food (VND70,000-390,000) is also served, and the roadside storefront houses a host of windsurfing, sailing, kiting, and surfing gear, as well as the office of Jibes' rental and lesson outfit.

SHOPPING
In Mui Ne, authentic, locally made items center around three categories: seafood, fresh fruit, and textiles or pottery crafted by the local Cham minority. As a major *nuoc mam* (fish sauce) producer, Phan Thiet is a city known for its fish sauce, which is widely available both in town and along the Mui Ne strip. Dragon fruit is also a popular local

Fish Sauce

If you have even a single Vietnamese meal during your travels, there is no doubt that you'll encounter the country's most famous condiment: fish sauce. This is especially true in Phan Thiet, the fish sauce capital of the mainland, where the thick, reddish-orange sauce features heavily in most local fare.

Heading into town on the road from Mui Ne, you'll catch a whiff of the scores of fish sauce factories. Here, local manufacturers pack thousands of anchovies into massive wooden barrels, add salt, and allow the concoction to sit for at least a year. The liquid is then extracted from a tap at the base of the barrel, filtered, and bottled. Many shops both in Phan Thiet and along the Mui Ne strip sell local fish sauce, which tastes far better than it smells. Much like the island of Phu Quoc Phan Thiet's lower humidity and higher temperatures help to make its *nuoc mam* (fish sauce) some of the best in Vietnam.

specialty, and you'll no doubt see these cactus-like plants on your ride into or out of the area, as hundreds of orchards exist along the roadside. For Cham textiles or pottery, you can look into the souvenirs available on your visit to the Po Shanu Towers or keep an eye out when perusing the shops along the strip.

The majority of souvenirs are trucked in from Saigon, so the same gifts found in Ben Thanh Market or the Pham Ngu Lao area are on sale here at much higher prices. For standard souvenirs, you're better off waiting until you reach Saigon or Nha Trang. If you find something you like, don't be afraid to haggle. You can also find a few small independent shops that provide more unique items, though their price tags tend to be just as high, often without the bargaining option. For reading material, several of the small travel agencies on Nguyen Dinh Chieu double as used-book vendors.

SPORTS AND RECREATION

Going against Mui Ne's sleepy seaside reputation is its propensity for water sports. Considered Vietnam's kitesurfing capital, shorelines both east and west of the town are popular among both local and international kitesurfers, as well as other water sport enthusiasts. Boasting one of the windiest coasts in the country, this area makes an ideal spot for beginners and pros, with conditions changing throughout the day to suit every level of expertise. Other activities, from windsurfing to regular surfing and sailing, are also available, as are an odd assortment of non-beach-related activities.

Kitesurfing and Water Sports

Kitesurfers flock to this area in greater numbers each year. While Rang Beach remains the center of Mui Ne's kiting schools, more advanced riders are also able to get out beyond the crowded shores of the main beach to visit other areas. Thanks to a few helpful locals, the website **Kitesurfing Mui Ne** (www.kitesurf-ingmuine.com) keeps riders informed and updated on conditions, schools, and all the other ins and outs of the sport in Mui Ne.

Mui Ne's first and most established kite center, **C2Sky** (16 Nguyen Dinh Chieu, tel. 09/1665-5241, www.c2skykitecenter. com, 9am-5pm daily, equipment rental around VND1,815,000 per day, lessons VND2,270,000-13,620,000) has been here since the beginning, setting up shop on the windy shores of the south-central coast in 2006. Since then, the shop has hosted international kitesurfing events, turned several local riders into IKO-certified instructors, and taken scores of travelers out for a day on the waves. Instructors are experienced and welcome beginners and pros. High-quality equipment is provided. C2Sky's location can be a bit tricky to find from the road: Make sure you access the beach from Seahorse Resort and then turn right.

A chilled-out shop with excellent beachfront property, **Jibes** (90 Nguyen Dinh Chieu, tel. 0252/384-7405, www.jibesbeachclub.com, 7am-midnight daily) offers an array of water sport options, including windsurfing, sailing, and kiting lessons, as well as surfing and stand-up paddleboard rentals. Qualified instructors speak a host of languages and all equipment and safety precautions meet international standards. This is also a great spot to grab a quick bite or a drink after your day on the water, as Jibes boasts a friendly, easygoing vibe and also houses a restaurant and bar on the premises.

Golf

Nestled along the coast toward Phan Tiet, **Sea Links Golf Club** (Nguyen Thong, tel. 0252/374-1741, www.sealinkscity.com, tee times 5:30am-6:30pm daily, VND1,850,000-2,350,000) offers golfers a breezy seaside 18-hole course as well as a pro shop and driving range.

Hidden opposite the tail-end of Saigon-Mui Ne Resort, amateur golfers will appreciate **Tropical Mini-Golf** (97 Nguyen Dinh Chieu, tel. 0252/374-1184, www.minigolfmuine.com, 10am-11pm daily, VND100,000), an 18-hole concrete course fringed with greenery and complicated by an assortment of fake rocks. The place offers drink deals to golfers and has a restaurant and bar at the back of the property for afterward. Keep an eye out for the entrance, as it can be tricky to find from the street.

Massages and Spas

Hidden from view, **Botanica Spa** (85A Nguyen Dinh Chieu, tel. 09/4887-7203, noon-10pm daily, VND250,000-950,000) is a blissful open-air facility tucked behind the bustling restaurants and guesthouses of the main road. Set in a shaded garden and decked out in rattan and bamboo furniture, Botanica offers facials, massages, and hair and skin treatments at reasonable prices and with friendly staff.

The list of massages and spa treatments available at **Forester Beach Spa** (82 Nguyen Dinh Chieu, tel. 09/4995-2253, noon-10pm daily, VND250,000-1,270,000) may run a little on the expensive side, but this spot is definitely the best of the bunch along Nguyen Dinh Chieu. Overlooking the beach, Forester is a tranquil and professional environment complete with an array of body scrubs, full-body massages, and nail and hair treatments.

FOOD

Mui Ne's influx of foreign tourists have ushered in dozens of Western restaurants that offer dishes like pizza, pasta, and tacos in addition to Vietnamese fare. The local specialty is, of course, seafood, with a fresh catch every day and plenty of open-air joints near the water. You'll also find an array of international fare along the Nguyen Dinh Chieu strip.

Vietnamese

Beginning around the 15-kilometer mark, several open-air restaurants serve up delectable local **seafood barbecue** during the evening hours. These street food joints vary in cost and cleanliness, so browse before ordering. Some shops feature menus, which are helpful in factoring cost. Ask the price before ordering, as you don't want to wind up charged more than expected.

Though it's packed with backpackers on a budget, **Lam Tong** (92 Nguyen Dinh Chieu, tel. 0252/384-7598, 8am-10pm daily, VND20,000-100,000) manages to churn out tasty, authentic Vietnamese fare with the added benefit of being directly on the beach. In the middle of the Mui Ne strip, this restaurant has maintained both its prices and its basic beachside setup over the years, offering plenty of meat, seafood, and vegetarian options.

The cheerful crowd at **Choi Oi** (115 Nguyen Dinh Chieu, tel. 0252/374-1428, 8:30am-8pm daily, VND20,000-80,000) serves up simple but delicious Vietnamese fare, such as tofu in tomato sauce, chicken curry, spring rolls, and salads. Meals are a bit on the small side but the place is charming and the prices are right. Opt for a seat in the air-conditioning or on the comfy patio chairs out front.

Cafés and Bakeries

A trendy air-conditioned spot, **Katie's Coffee House** (115 Nguyen Dinh Chieu, 7:30am-10:30pm daily, VND30,000-120,000) serves well-made European-style coffee as well as a variety of teas. Food is available on the menu, but stick to drinks only. Wi-Fi is free, and unlike most places on the Nguyen Dinh Chieu strip, the indoor café offers a little more quiet.

Indian

The Mui Ne branch of a popular Indian chain, **Shree Ganesh** (57 Nguyen Dinh Chieu, tel. 0252/374-1330, www.ganesh.vn, 11:30am-10:30pm daily, VND75,000-300,000) prepares delicious renditions of Indian cuisine, ranging from vindaloos and curries to paneer, masala, and other tasty items. Look for the large white Ganesh statue up front to greet you as you enter the dining room.

International

A standout on the block, long-time resident **Joe's Cafe** (86 Nguyen Dinh Chieu, tel. 0252/384-7177, www.joescafemuine.com, 7am-midnight daily, VND65,000-250,000) provides a variety of seating options, from the shaded roadside patio to covered open-air seating near the bar with a line of sight toward the beach. A well-rounded menu lists Western favorites like pizza, burgers, and Mexican fare in addition to Thai and Vietnamese offerings. Though service can be sometimes attentive, sometimes not, the pizzas are some of the best in town and portions are generous.

Mediterranean

Though you could easily miss it, the miniature thatched-roof storefront of **Sindbad** (233 Nguyen Dinh Chieu, tel. 016/9991-5245,

11am-late daily, VND35,000-120,000), a humble eatery specializing in *doner* kebab (shawarma), has made waves on the strip with another dining option. Helmed by a cheerful, hard-working three-person team, the shop manages to turn out great kebabs as well as a few other Mediterranean dishes.

Quick Bites

A cheap but tasty roadside eatery not far from Surfer's Guesthouse, **King of Sandwich** (103B Nguyen Dinh Chieu, tel. 016/9785-8220, 8am-9pm daily, VND45,000-100,000) serves breakfasts, sandwiches, and other simple fare at reasonable prices. The staff is friendly, and delivery is available.

ACCOMMODATIONS

With hundreds of accommodations on the main strip, plenty of affordable options rub shoulders with higher-end boutique hotels and resorts. Upscale lodgings tend to be on the western end of the beach in the lower street numbers (usually under 100), while budget spots are spread throughout.

Hotels with even-numbered street addresses are located on the waterfront. If you stay on the other side of Nguyen Dinh Chieu, some odd-numbered hotels and guesthouses have pools, but will have to find a public access spot or beachside café in order to swim in the ocean. Due to erosion, some hotels may not have a sand beach on their property.

Under VND210,000

In the past few years, Mui Ne has become a bit more backpacker-friendly, with a handful of hostels popping up along the strip. One of the more social accommodations is **Mui Ne Backpacker Village** (137 Nguyen Dinh Chieu, tel. 0252/374-1047, www.muinebackpackervillage.com, VND45,000-140,000 dorm, VND340,0000-460,000 d). A range of 4- to 12-bed dorms are available as well as a handful of private rooms, all of which surround a swimming pool and sunbathing area. Dorms come with shared baths and lockers but no locks, though you can purchase one at reception. The front desk can help with on-ward travel and tour arrangements, and there is also a small café and bar in back.

Though **Xuan Uyen** (Nguyen Dinh Chieu, tel. 0252/387-4476, VND160,000-275,000) doesn't earn rave reviews for decor, its aged beachfront rooms remain clean and offer travelers the option of dirt-cheap, fan-only, cold-water rooms or fancier ones with hot water and air-conditioning. The location makes it worth mentioning, as this is one of the few budget ocean-side options. Guests will find a small restaurant attached to Xuan Uyen and some notably amiable owners.

While plenty of resorts have sprung up on the beach, **Mui Ne Hills** (69 Nguyen Dinh Chieu, tel. 0252/374-1707, www.muinehills. com) takes a different approach. Built into the surrounding hillside, these four friendly, modern budget accommodations are pleasantly removed from the buzz on the beach but with easy access to the Mui Ne strip. Shoestring travelers will appreciate **Mui Ne Hills Backpackers** (VND90,000-160,000 dorm, VND570,000 d), which features a generous swimming pool and communal activities like Ping-Pong and darts in addition to 4-, 8-, and 10-bed mixed dorms, or **Mui Ne Hills Budget** (VND90,000-140,000 dorm, VND500,000-570,000 d), which shares the same amenities. For a bit more privacy, try **Mui Ne Hills Villa** (VND795,000-1,025,000) or **Mui Ne Hills Bliss** (VND795,000-1,250,000), with slightly more plush accommodations as well as nice ocean views. Each room is decorated differently and features air-conditioning, hot water, Wi-Fi, TV, and a minibar. There is a blissful pool on the property as well.

VND210,000-525,000

Farther up the coast, **Thanh Duy Guesthouse** (243 Nguyen Dinh Chieu, tel. 0252/384-7077, thanhduy0602@gmail. com, VND230,000-275,000) is easily identified by its faded pink-and-purple sign out front. Featuring equally tacky bedspreads, the budget rooms are large and basic but clean, boasting generous street-facing windows on the upper floors and slightly smaller, quieter rooms downstairs. Hot water, Wi-Fi, air-conditioning, and TV are all standard with each room, and the guesthouse also has a travel agency out front and a restaurant next door.

The friendly folks at ★ **Hong Di** (70 Nguyen Dinh Chieu, tel. 0252/384-7014, hd-hongdi@yahoo.com, VND410,000-570,000) opened this no-frills guesthouse well before

Hong Di guesthouse

there were giant resorts and boutique hotels on the strip, and the place has remained a standout among budget accommodations. As one of the only affordable spots left on this side of the road, Hong Di offers basic but comfortable rooms with TV, Wi-Fi, hot water, and fan or air-conditioning. Those who opt for air-conditioning will also find a fridge in the room. The guesthouse also sells tours and rents vehicles.

VND525,000-1,050,000

Rooms at the **Surfers Guesthouse** (103B Nguyen Dinh Chieu, tel. 09/1805-7816, www.kitesurfing-vietnam.com, VND550,000) are basic, decked out in wooden furniture, and feature solar-powered hot water, a minibar, TV, and air-conditioning, tucked off the road just behind a trio of decent budget eateries, making its location equally worthy.

The charming **Rang Garden Bungalows** (233A Nguyen Dinh Chieu, tel. 0252/374-3638, www.rang-muine.com, VND630,000-950,000, breakfast included) is a collection of simple, spacious rooms equipped with TV, fridge, hot water, air-conditioning, an in-room safe, and Wi-Fi. The swimming pool sits in the middle of a peaceful courtyard. Out front is a restaurant as well as a souvenir shop stocked with unique silk creations. Rooms fill up fast, so book ahead. For a seaside view, you can also book a stay at **Rang Garden Beach Side** (128A Nguyen Dinh Chieu, tel. 0252/374-3787, www.rang-muine.com, VND1,200,000-1,725,000, breakfast included), directly on the waterfront.

One of Mui Ne's most popular mid-range accommodations, the fun and friendly **Xin Chao Hotel** (129 Nguyen Dinh Chieu, tel. 0252/374-3086, www.xinchaohotel.com, VND640,000-1,370,000) boasts smart, understated rooms with plush beds, hot water, TV, and air-conditioning. Both Wi-Fi and breakfast are included in the rates, and guests can use the courtyard pool at the center of the hotel. Xin Chao also manages **Indigo** (129 Nguyen Dinh Chieu, tel. 0252/374-3086, www.xinchaohotel.com, 7am-10pm

daily, VND50,000-160,000), a popular streetside restaurant at the front of the property that serves a decent mix of Vietnamese and Western dishes. Thanks to its great service, Xin Chao often finds itself with more customers than rooms; make sure you reserve your spot before heading to Mui Ne. Rates are also discounted heavily in the off-season; call or email ahead.

VND1,050,000-2,100,000

On the eastern end of the strip, **Dynasty Resort** (140A Nguyen Dinh Chieu, tel. 0252/384-7816, www.dynastyresorts.com, VND1,200,000-2,500,000, breakfast included) offers all the trimmings of a proper resort at prices that are slightly gentler on the wallet. Housed in a beautiful pale yellow building, rooms feature tasteful decor and high-quality amenities, including TV, air-conditioning, Wi-Fi, hot water, and charming balconies with beach-facing views. At the center of the resort is a spacious pool and bar overlooking the ocean.

The ultra-modern, teal-and-white **Shades** (98A Nguyen Dinh Chieu, tel. 0252/374-3235, www.shadesmuine.com, VND1,240,000-3,375,000) apartments are one of Mui Ne's trendier options, offering both short- and long-term rentals. Well-appointed accommodations range from standard doubles to fully equipped apartments with a kitchen, a lounge area, and a desk. All include Wi-Fi, air-conditioning, hot water, a minibar, and TV. Shades' higher-end lodgings offer a few more add-ons.

Over VND2,100,000

As soon as you enter **Allez Boo** (8 Nguyen Dinh Chieu, tel. 0252/374-3777, www.allez-booresort.com, VND1,800,000-9,785,000) on the western end of the Mui Ne strip, you'll be greeted by a beautiful high-ceilinged reception area, which opens onto the resort's stunning ocean-side pool. Owned by the same folks responsible for Saigon's Allez Boo restaurant and the infamous Go2 bar, this chic retreat is a classier establishment, boasting pristine rooms with a simple, sophisticated decor and high-quality amenities as well as complimentary breakfast. This full-service resort offers not only private pool and beach access but vehicle rentals, a spa, and a business center.

The idyllic **Mia Resort** (24 Nguyen Dinh Chieu, tel. 0252/384-7440, www.miamuine. com, VND3,600,000-11,000,000, breakfast included) is an oceanfront oasis among the many large resorts spread along Mui Ne's eastern end. With plush thatched-roof bungalows and generous beds, this seaside escape puts guests off the noise and chaos of the main road and closer to the nearby waves. Rooms are tastefully furnished and include both a fan and air-conditioning, TV, hot water, an in-room safe, tea- and coffee-making facilities, Wi-Fi, and a veranda.

A small but stunning boutique hotel, **Cham Villas** (32 Nguyen Dinh Chieu, tel. 0252/374-1234, www.chamvillas.com, VND3,950,000-5,205,000) doesn't appear to be much from the outside, but it affords guests ample privacy among lush palm trees and shaded walkways. Rooms are beautifully furnished and feature air-conditioning, TV, Wi-Fi, and hot water. A private pool and beach access are available. The staff can arrange tours, vehicle rentals, and other activities.

INFORMATION AND SERVICES
Visitor Information

For local sights, there are dozens of small outfits along Nguyen Dinh Chieu selling the same cookie-cutter tours, which include a visit to both sets of sand dunes, Fairy Spring, and the Po Shanu Towers. **Sinh Tourist** (144 Nguyen Dinh Chieu, tel. 0252/384-7542, www.thesinhtourist.vn, 7am-10pm daily) has free maps, though there is a better local map available at several businesses along the strip.

Banks

There is a **Vietcombank ATM** (beside Saigon-Mui Ne Resort, 24 hours daily) and several other ATMs, including a pair beside

Tien Dat Resort, along the strip. For additional services, visit the **Sacombank** (364 Tran Hung Dao, tel. 0252/383-2424, www.sacombank.com.vn, 7:30am-11:30am and 1pm-5pm Mon.-Fri., 7:30am-11:30am Sat.) in town. To avoid this trip, change currency before you arrive. U.S. dollars are often accepted by local hotels and restaurants along this strip, but be wary of the exchange rate.

Postal Services and Internet

You'll find the nearest **post office** (2 Ho Xuan Huong, tel. 0252/384-8101, 7am-11:30am and 1:30pm-5pm daily) in Mui Ne just east of the main beach.

Medical Services

For ailments, visit **An Phuoc Hospital** (235 Tran Phu, Phan Thiet, tel. 0252/338-1056, www.anphuochospital.com) in Phan Thiet, or, better yet, head to Saigon.

GETTING THERE
Bus

From Saigon, both **Sinh Tourist** (144 Nguyen Dinh Chieu, tel. 0252/384-7542, www.thesinhtourist.vn, 7am-10pm daily) and **Phuong Trang** (20 Huynh Thuc Khang, tel. 0252/374-3113, www.futabuslines.com.vn, 6am-10pm daily, VND130,000) run daily buses to Mui Ne, which arrive at their respective offices along the main strip, Nguyen Dinh Chieu (which turns into Huynh Thuc Khang in Mui Ne town). The trip takes 4-6 hours, depending on traffic. Sinh Tourist can also arrange buses to Mui Ne from Dalat (VND99,000) and Nha Trang (VND119,000).

Train

A morning train leaves from Saigon (4 hours, VND150,000-180,000) at 6:40am featuring soft-seat, air-conditioned cars and arrives at the **Phan Thiet station** (1 Le Duan, Phan Thiet, tel. 0252/363-6115, 7am-8pm daily). From there, it's another 16 kilometers to Mui Ne by taxi (VND285,000).

GETTING AROUND
Taxi and *Xe Om*

You'll find most *xe om* hanging around the front of larger resorts down the western end of Nguyen Dinh Chieu. They usually begin the bargaining high, so be prepared to haggle. **Mailinh** (tel. 0252/389-8989) taxis regularly ply Nguyen Dinh Chieu and have a habit of honking at any foreigner they see, which, in Mui Ne, is pretty much everyone.

Bike and Motorbike

Hiring a bicycle or motorbike to get around Mui Ne and the surrounding area is not a bad idea, particularly if you're heading out to the sand dunes or Po Shanu Towers. Most hotels and guesthouses will happily rent out bicycles at reasonable rates. Don't bother with the makeshift motorbike setups outside some of the larger resorts, as they start their asking prices as high as VND250,000. You should never need to pay more than VND150,000 for a motorbike rental, regardless of whether the vehicle is semi- or fully automatic. **Kim Travel** (72 Nguyen Dinh Chieu, tel. 0252/655-2179, 9am-9pm daily) is a reliable provider, where you can arrange both short- and long-term rentals.

Despite the strip's easygoing vibe, this is a notably dangerous stretch of road on which two-wheeled vehicles and enormous transport trucks roar past each other at breakneck speeds. More than a few traffic fatalities have occurred here, and following the death of a Russian tourist in 2013, local authorities are cracking down heavily on Mui Ne's traffic safety in general and foreign drivers in particular. The same road rules apply here as in the rest of Vietnam and are more often enforced. All drivers and passengers must wear helmets by law, observe the speed limit, and stick to no more than one passenger on the back of a bike.

Since Mui Ne's main strip is slightly removed from the nearest town, the area's only proper gas station lies at the far end of Nguyen Dinh Chieu heading toward Phan Thiet. Instead of driving out to this spot, many local shops will sell fuel from old-school gas pumps on the roadside. These independent shops tend to be more convenient but also more expensive.

Ho Chi Minh City

Look for ★ to find recommended
sights, activities, dining, and lodging.

Highlights

★ **Reunification Palace:** This opulent palace was once home to the presidents of the short-lived Republic of Vietnam (page 305).

★ **Ben Thanh Market:** Frenetic and fast-paced, the city's iconic market hosts dozens of multilingual vendors and thousands of stalls packed to the ceiling with everything you could imagine (page 308).

★ **War Remnants Museum:** Thoughtful and at times harrowing, Saigon's best museum provides insight into life during and after the American War (page 313).

★ **Thien Hau Pagoda:** A centuries-old Chinese pagoda in the heart of bustling District 5 was built by Chinese refugees in thanks to the goddess of the sea after their treacherous emigration (page 316).

★ **Ho Chi Minh City's Nightlife:** The party starts in Saigon when the sun goes down (page 319).

★ **Ho Chi Minh City's Street Food:** The best of Vietnamese cuisine finds its way to the dented metal carts and bamboo poles of Saigon's street vendors (pages 337 and 339).

Ho Chi Minh City (HCMC)—still known to locals as Saigon—packs all of southern Vietnam's best food, art, culture, and diversity into the jumbled houses and narrow alleyways of the country's most ambitious metropolis.

Shackled by heavy-handed governmental policies after the Vietnam War, HCMC hit the ground running in the mid-1980s, as the nation's *doi moi* economic reforms flung open the door to international business and trade. A decade of pent-up energy was unleashed, sending the city on a frantic, determined mission to become Vietnam's cosmopolitan leader.

Settled on the sticky, humid, pancake-flat marshland just east of the Mekong Delta, the city began only a few centuries ago but has exploded in population over the past two decades. Even today, immigrants travel from near and far, hoping to make a home and a living amid the bustle of Vietnam's largest city. National government statistics put the urban population at around 8.3 million residents and counting, but this number hardly seems enough when you sit bumper-to-bumper in midday traffic or squeeze onto a tiny patch of sidewalk for a nighttime *ca phe bet*

(street-side coffee). City statistics put the actual population as high as 13 million people. Whatever the number, HCMC shows no signs of stopping. Already, outlying districts are swallowing up nearby towns like Di An and Bien Hoa, and the population of the greater metropolitan area is expected to grow in the coming years.

HISTORY

The outlines of modern-day Saigon began to take shape in 1674, as communities settled along the Ben Nghe River. To the east, Vietnamese farmers raised buffalo in what is now District 1, while a large, business-minded community of Chinese refugees, who had fled the persecution of the Ming dynasty, appeared in present-day District 5. Over the next 200 years, these two settlements grew closer to one another, forming the boundaries of Vietnam's largest metropolis.

After the French arrived in 1859, the city

Previous: fishing boats docked in Vung Tau; HCMC's Central Post Office. **Above:** *banh khot,* a Vung Tau specialty.

Ho Chi Minh City

TAN SON NHAT INTERNATIONAL AIRPORT

DHL

UPS

PHU NHUAN

VAN THANH POOL

BINH THANH

TAN BINH

SEE "DISTRICT 1" MAP

SEE "DISTRICT 3" MAP

HO CHI MINH CITY'S STREET FOOD

HO CHI MINH CITY'S NIGHTLIFE

GIAC LAM PAGODA

FITO MUSEUM

DISTRICT 3

WAR REMNANTS MUSEUM

DISTRICT 1

DAM SEN WATER PARK

DISTRICT 10

REUNIFICATION PALACE

BEN THANH MARKET

DISTRICT 2

Saigon River

DISTRICT 11

QUAN THIEN THIEN

CA RI MUSA

MINH HUONG PAGODA

AN DONG MARKET

TIEM CHAY TUONG VIEN

THIEN HAU PAGODA

BINH TAY MARKET

CHO LON MOSQUE

DISTRICT 5

DISTRICT 4

Te Canal

DISTRICT 8

Bang Canal

CHAOZHOU ASSEMBLY HALL/ NGHIA AN HOI QUAN PAGODA

FV HOSPITAL

underwent major changes. Few were quick to welcome the French to Vietnam, but colonialism provided Saigon with several important and lasting things. At the center of town, the French erected churches, theaters, government buildings, and a post office, many of which remain in use today. To the west, much of the Chinese neighborhood was left as a separate entity, and so its residents carried on living as they had prior to colonization.

While Saigon's Chinese residents were able to live undisturbed, the Vietnamese resented European authority. Tensions rose steadily between foreign and local residents. By the

1940s, a healthy opposition force had grown. Their efforts briefly stalled during World War II, when Japanese forces wrested power from the French for a short time in 1944.

When the French finally left in 1954, South Vietnam set up its own government, with Saigon as the capital. Aided by the United States, the Republic of South Vietnam began in the spirit of democracy but quickly grew unpopular thanks to the policies of its leader, Ngo Dinh Diem. Once again, dissent turned the city into a staging ground for protests and other acts of political opposition. Rallies were held, Buddhist monks self-immolated in protest, and, across the city, plots to overthrow the government were plentiful. Finally, in 1963, Diem and his brother, Ngo Dinh Nhu, met their end after hiding out in a church in District 5, and the country quickly rolled into armed conflict.

For the better part of the American War, Saigon remained safe, and foreign journalists flocked to the city to cover the conflict, making the city something of an international hub. That is, until Communist forces crashed through the Independence Palace gates on April 30, 1975, officially ending the war. From then on, the southern hub became Ho Chi Minh City in honor of the man who crusaded for Vietnam's independence.

Closed to the world and still reeling from decades of battle—against the French, Americans, Cambodians, and Chinese—Vietnam began to rebuild. Economic reforms in the mid-1980s allowed HCMC to begin realizing its full potential, with brightly colored billboards and trendy foreign shops opening across town. By the 1990s, an ever-growing number of foreign tourists began to visit HCMC, and since then the city has taken off.

PLANNING YOUR TIME

Though the jumble of traffic and mismatched buildings can seem infinite, the city's downtown area is small. Most of the major sights and activities can be covered in 4-5 days, as attractions tend to be concentrated around Districts 1 and 5.

Do your sightseeing in the morning to avoid the heat, especially if you're visiting pagodas and other non-air-conditioned places. Afternoons are great for activities, eating, and taking in the buzz of the city. Though businesses stay open at lunchtime, many Vietnamese siesta around noon, particularly those working at museums and government-run buildings, so avoid these places at midday. Once the sun goes down, street vendors set up along sidewalks, restaurants open, and tiny roadside stalls sling beer and *do nhau* (drinking food). The heat also lets up, making the evening a perfect time to wander through a night market, grab a bite, or delve into the city's nightlife.

You should have no trouble finding English speakers downtown in HCMC, though you may occasionally have to rely on the pick-and-point method. When heading out for the day, grab a business card from your hotel or jot down the address of wherever you're headed: While most taxi and *xe om* (motorbike taxi) drivers know the city's major landmarks, it pays to have the address and district on hand for lesser-known locations.

The biggest holiday of the year is Tet (Lunar New Year, late Jan.-mid-Feb.), a day when everyone in Vietnam returns to their hometown to celebrate. During this time, HCMC is virtually a ghost town. Most streets are empty and businesses deserted. Many services are not available or if they are prices go up considerably to compensate.

Set aside a day or two to escape the downtown area and pay a visit to the Cu Chi Tunnels and Tay Ninh's mammoth Cao Dai temple.

If you have an extra few days, you might consider hopping the border into Cambodia to visit Angkor Wat and its surrounding temples; the gateway town of Siem Reap is just a quick flight from HCMC.

ORIENTATION

Ho Chi Minh City is divided into 19 districts and five communes. The majority of visitors only make it to a few of the more centrally located neighborhoods.

District 1

At the heart of the city is District 1 (considered the city's downtown), perched on the banks of the Saigon River, where the best shopping, nightlife, hotels, restaurants, and trendy cafés can be found. **Ben Thanh Market,** one of HCMC's most famous landmarks, and **Pham Ngu Lao street** (the **backpacker district,** where most travelers stay) are located in the southwestern part of this district. Several of the city's other famous sights, such as the **Reunification Palace** and

District 1

HOÀNG SA

CỤC GẠCH QUÁN

CRAIG THOMAS GALLERY

ĐINH TIÊN HOÀNG

ĐIỆN BIÊN PHỦ

TRƯỜNG SA

Thi Nghe Canal

TRẦN QUANG KHẢI

JADE EMPEROR PAGODA

NGUYỄN THỊ MINH KHAI

LUNCH LADY

TAN DINH MARKET

BANH XEO 46A

HAI BÀ TRƯNG

Le Van Tam Park

QUAN MIEN CUA 94 CU

GALERIE QUYNH

LAU NAM CHAY N NHIEN

NGUYỄN VĂN THỦ

KOTO

SAIGON ZOO AND BOTANICAL GARDEN

NAM KỲ KHỞI NGHĨA

PHẠM NGỌC THẠCH

TOKYO DELI

ĐINH TIÊN HOÀNG

HISTORY MUSEUM

HUNG KINGS TEMPLE

NGUYỄN BỈNH KHIÊM

VÕ THỊ SÁU

HO CHI MINH CITY'S STREET FOOD

MẠC ĐĨNH CHI

HO CHI MINH CITY'S NIGHTLIFE

SAIGON SQUARE 3

DISTRICT 3

Turtle Lake

PASTEUR

US CONSULATE

LÊ QUÝ ĐÔN

LÊ DUẨN

DISTRICT 1

LUSH

PIZZA 4PS

SEE "OPERA HOUSE AREA" MAP

LÊ QUÝ ĐÔN

FAMILY MEDICAL PRACTICE

WAR REMNANTS MUSEUM

VŨ XUÂN

ĐIỆN BIÊN PHỦ

TRƯƠNG ĐỊNH

TRẦN QUỐC THẢO

COLUMBIA ASIA INTERNATIONAL CLINIC

NOTRE DAME CATHEDRAL

CENTRAL POST OFFICE

LÊ THÁNH TÔN

NGÔ THỜI NHIỆM

NGUYỄN ĐÌNH CHIỂU

30-4 Park

HAI BÀ TRƯNG

REUNIFICATION PALACE

AU PARC/ PROPAGANDA

CÁCH MẠNG THÁNG TÁM

GOLDEN DRAGON WATER PUPPET THEATER

Tao Dan Park

NGON RESTAURANT

LÝ TỰ TRỌNG

VÕ VĂN TẦN

SEE "BEN THANH MARKET AREA" MAP

NGUYỄN DU

NAM KỲ KHỞI NGHĨA

PASTEUR

NGUYỄN THƯỢNG HIỀN

CINNAMON HOTEL SAIGON

BEN THANH MARKET

NGUYỄN HUỆ

TÔN ĐỨC THẮNG

TOWNHOUSE 50

ONO SAIGON HOTEL

BÙI THỊ XUÂN

ZEN PLAZA

CALMETTE

HÀM NGHI

NGUYỄN THỊ MINH KHAI

SNUFFBOX

THỦ THIÊM TUNNEL

CÔNG QUỲNH

SEE "PHAM NGU LAO STREET" MAP

23-9 Park

PHẠM NGŨ LÃO

BÙI VIỆN

NGUYỄN THÁI HỌC

KÝ CON

PHÓ ĐỨC CHÍNH

ROGUE SAIGON

DAN SINH MARKET

BẾN VÂN ĐỒN

NGUYỄN TẤT THÀNH

NGUYỄN CƯ TRINH

YELLOW HOUSE HOTEL SAIGON

CÔ BẮC

0   500 yds

AVA SAIGON 2

CÔ GIANG

0   500 m

NGUYỄN TRÃI

CAT MOC SPA

HOÀNG DIỆU

© AVALON TRAVEL

Notre Dame Cathedral, are slightly farther north. The Opera House is a destination for high-end shopping and numerous nightlife spots. Also within District 1 is Nguyen Hue street, a large open pedestrian-only square featuring high-end shops, cafés, snack vendors, and street performers.

The northern part of the district has a quieter web of streets packed with plenty of mouthwatering Vietnamese cuisine and a handful of sights, including the Jade Emperor Pagoda.

District 3

Also in the middle of the action, District 3, to the northwest of District 1, is quieter. District 3 contains the War Remnants Museum, Vinh Nghiem Pagoda, Turtle Lake, and the historic Xa Loi Pagoda. (Some of these sights are on District 3's border with District 1.) This area is home to excellent restaurants at more affordable prices than its downtown counterpart.

Cho Lon

The city's famous Chinatown, also known as Cho Lon, is a haze of noise, light, and traffic. Here you'll find the vast majority of HCMC's vibrant Chinese-Vietnamese community, along with scores of pagodas, temples, and assembly halls. Cho Lon literally means "big market," named after the enormous Binh Tay Market. This neighborhood lies across Districts 5 and 6. This area became a safe haven in the 16th and 17th centuries for Chinese refugees fleeing the persecution of the Ming dynasty and, later, the Tay Son rebellion.

Sights

Ho Chi Minh City has seen a lot in its short history. Its sights are a testament to its diverse and intricate past. The streets are brimming with churches, temples, markets, museums, and everything from French-inspired halls to Chinese-style pagodas, offering proof of its many cultural intersections.

HCMC is not the place for grand photo ops or immense, awe-inspiring structures. Though there are some stunning sights within the city limits, it is the stories of these places and the ways in which they continue to function today that make them worth appreciating. Hop on a motorbike and jet out to Cho Lon, the city's Chinatown and one of the most hectic districts. Write a friend—or yourself—a postcard in the Central Post Office, a lasting relic of an earlier time, or grab a coffee outside the striking Notre Dame Cathedral and see how people live in the country's biggest metropolis.

REUNIFICATION PALACE AREA
★ Reunification Palace

The Reunification Palace (135 Nam Ky Khoi Nghia, D1, tel. 028/3822-3652, www.dinhdoclap.gov.vn, 7:30am-11am and 1pm-4pm daily, VND40,000) is a colossal white building that punctuates the end of Le Duan Boulevard. Set on 12 hectares of shaded, well-manicured lawns, the palace once served as the seat of government for both the French colonial regime and the short-lived Republic of Vietnam. Its interior remains almost exactly as it was 43 years ago, from the pale pink rotary phones in the situation room to the art deco ambience of the upper floors.

Named Norodom Palace in 1868, it was an official dwelling until World War II, when Emperor Bao Dai, Vietnam's last king, abdicated. Once the war ended, the French reclaimed the palace until 1954, when power was officially transferred to politician Ngo Dinh Diem, who became South Vietnam's first president the following year. Diem

Three Days in Ho Chi Minh City

As one of Vietnam's younger cities, Ho Chi Minh City has infectious energy. When experienced like a local, this massive, fast-paced behemoth is a wonderful place. Plan for three action-packed days around town, whizzing past the city's sights and enjoying the sounds, smells, and vibrancy of life in Vietnam's largest metropolis.

DAY 1

Start your adventure at the **Reunification Palace** with a free guided tour. When you've finished, stroll through **30-4 Park,** stopping for a *ca phe bet* (sidewalk coffee) if you need a caffeine fix, or popping into one of the upscale air-conditioned cafés nearby. The opposite end of the park opens onto **Notre Dame Cathedral** and the **Central Post Office.** From here, walk up toward **Turtle Lake** for lunch. There are plenty of options overlooking the roundabout and on the side streets surrounding 30-4 Park. You can also head west to **...hum** before spending the afternoon at the **War Remnants Museum.**

Head back toward the backpacker district as the day winds down, passing through **Tao Dan Park** en route. Stop by **Chill Skybar** or **OMG** for cocktails and bird's-eye views of the city, or simply rest up before heading off for dinner. District 1's Tan Dinh neighborhood is a good choice. For street food, **Banh Xeo 46A** offers a great introduction into local cuisine, while **Cuc Gach Quan** adds an upscale environment to its delicious Vietnamese menu. Not far from this area, seafood lovers will also appreciate **Quan Mien Cua 94 Cu.**

After dinner, return to the backpacker neighborhood for cheap bottles of beer sold on the street, a laid-back drink at **The View,** or craft beer at **East West** or **Rogue Saigon,** a short walk from the Pham Ngu Lao area.

DAY 2

Jet out to **Cho Lon** first thing in the morning to explore Chinatown's enormous wholesale market. You can grab breakfast from one of the many market vendors before hitching a *xe om* ride over to **Thien Hau Pagoda,** stopping in at the nearby **Chaozhou Congregation**

---

renamed it the Independence Palace and installed his family in the house, which included a rooftop dance floor, several sitting rooms, dining areas, offices, a kitchen, and a series of underground bunkers. Following an assassination attempt in 1962, Diem commissioned Vietnamese architect Ngo Viet Thu to build a new structure in its place. This served as the headquarters of the South Vietnamese government until Communist forces crashed through the palace gates on April 30, 1975, officially putting an end to the American War.

Enter the palace to the left of the main gates and head toward the left side of the building, where free guided tours are offered regularly 7:45am-11am and 1:15pm-4pm daily. Signage is virtually nonexistent, so it's a good idea to take the tour. It takes about an hour to see the palace's four floors as well as its eerie

bomb-shelter basement. There is also an educational video offered at the end of the tour, but you can skip it. The palace gardens make for a pleasant stroll back to the entrance. To the right of the building are two tanks parked at the edge of the lawn. These vehicles were among the group that broke through the palace gates in 1975.

Notre Dame Cathedral

Set amid the bustle of downtown is the imposing figure of **Notre Dame Cathedral** (1 Cong Xa Paris, D1, tel. 028/3822-0477, 8am-11am and 3pm-4pm daily). Completed in 1880, this iconic Roman Catholic church is known for its soaring Gothic arches. Every item that went into Notre Dame's construction was imported from France. The famous redbrick exterior is a product of Marseille.

Hall and **Cho Lon Mosque** while you're there. When you've had your fill of District 5, head back downtown to bustling **Ben Thanh Market** for shopping and lunch. Wander down **Le Loi** street, passing by the city's charming colonial **Hotel de Ville** building and the **Opera House** as you reach a more upscale part of town.

Enjoy a sunset drink from the rooftop of **Broma** or grab a cocktail at the swanky **Racha Room.** Dinner in this neighborhood is an international affair, with **Ciao Bella, The Refinery,** and **Pizza 4Ps** within walking distance, as well as a few local eateries, such as **Bo Tung Xeo** and **Temple Club.**

For a night on the town, **Layla,** a classy cocktail lounge, is nearby, as is **Phatty's,** an expat sports bar, and the dance floor of **Apocalypse Now.** The city's best live music venues are **Yoko** and **Acoustic Bar.**

DAY 3

Spend your last day in the city with a local. Art enthusiasts can sign up for **Sophie's Art Tour** to learn more about Vietnam's history through the eyes of its artists. Foodies will appreciate **Back of the Bike Tours,** which go around town, savoring all the best local fare. If you prefer an activity, you can spend the morning honing your culinary skills with a **cooking class** or treat yourself at one of the city's **spas.**

When you're ready for lunch, pay a visit to the famous **Lunch Lady** for one of her tasty soups before walking to the **Jade Emperor Pagoda** nearby. From here, spend the rest of the afternoon unwinding at a café or wandering around the city.

Notre Dame Cathedral

The pair of 58-meter bell towers were added in 1895 and still house functioning but rarely used bells.

In front of the church is the **Our Lady of Peace statue,** completed in 1959 by an Italian sculptor and shipped from Rome. This is the second sculpture to stand in its place. The first was a statue of the Bishop Pigneau de Behaine, who helped Emperor Gia Long rise to power. The bishop's statue was removed in the 1940s. The red marble base on which Our Lady of Peace stands is a leftover from this original work.

Our Lady of Peace is one of Saigon's biggest celebrities. Early in the morning, you can see local Catholics before the statue, hands folded in prayer. By the afternoon, she is the subject of countless tourist photos.

Notre Dame is most impressive when viewed from outside. Inside, a set of arched door frames give way to high ceilings crisscrossed with a wooden detail. Visitors are forbidden beyond the back area of the church, but it is still possible to see a few stained glass panels as well as a figure of Jesus above the altar. The alcoves on either side of the entrance house statues of the Virgin Mary and Saint Anthony. Around each statue, stone tiles express reverence in French, English, and Vietnamese. To see the building in its entirety, attend the English version of Sunday mass at 9:30am, during which time you can gain full access to the main hall.

Central Post Office

On the eastern side of the Cong Xa Paris square is another vestige of French colonialism, the **Central Post Office** (2 Cong

Xa Paris, D1, tel. 028/3822-1677, www.hcm-post.vn, 7am-7pm Mon.-Fri., 7am-6pm Sat., 8am-6pm Sun.). More reminiscent of a train station, this large building was designed by Gustave Eiffel. The massive clock and grand entrance are a favorite photo op among tourists. High yellow-and-green arches line either side of the vast hall. The two maps near the main entrance depict the Vietnam of an earlier time. No matter where you stand, you're sure to catch a glimpse of modern Vietnam's founding father, Ho Chi Minh, affectionately known as Uncle Ho, who watches over the building from a portrait mounted on the back wall.

The Central Post Office functions as the city's main postal hub. A number of other services are also available here, including international phone calls, which can be made from a tiny antique wooden phone booth. There are also postcards for purchase and a set of writing desks farther back if you want to send your postcard on the spot. You might also catch Duong Van Ngo, Saigon's last professional letter writer, hard at work. A post office employee since 1946, Ngo is fluent in English, French, and Vietnamese and specializes in both translating and writing letters.

OPERA HOUSE AREA

A block away from bustling Nguyen Hue, dapper security guards and lavish store displays signal a more upscale part of town.

Opera House

At the end of Le Loi Street, Saigon's **Opera House** (7 Cong Truong Lam Son, D1, tel. 028/3823-7419, www.hbso.org.vn), also known as the Municipal Theater, is a well-preserved historical gem and one of the city's oldest supporters of the arts. When the opera house opened in 1900, it became Saigon's premier center for the arts, hosting scores of ballets and musical acts, as well as other performances.

Following the end of the French colonial government, the building was transformed from a cultural center into the Lower Assembly of the Republic of Vietnam as part of the south's new administration. It remained a government office until the end of the war in 1975.

After reunification, the Opera House was restored to its original function as a performance space. Renovations later brought back its former architectural glory as well, and today it continues to hold cultural events, showcasing both domestic and international performers. Except for performances, the Opera House is closed to the public. Its exterior is the most impressive aspect, with a wide set of front steps and a massive arched facade.

Hotel de Ville

Positioned at the end of Nguyen Hue's long, open pedestrian street is the **Hotel de Ville** (86 Le Thanh Ton, D1), a stunning colonial building from the turn of the 20th century. Set amid the old-world grandeur of the nearby buildings, the Hotel de Ville remains a piece of colonial Indochina in the modern age. The Vietnamese flag flies high above the French-made building. Now the home of the local People's Committee and the center of city government, the building is not open to the public.

BEN THANH MARKET AREA
★ Ben Thanh Market

Easily the most recognizable structure in Saigon, **Ben Thanh Market** (Le Loi and Tran Hung Dao, D1, tel. 028/3829-9274, 6am-6pm daily) is the original commercial heart of the city and a prime spot for souvenir shopping, with over 3,000 small businesses and an army of multilingual vendors. Using the city's waterways to transport goods, Ben Thanh became the Vietnamese answer to Chinatown's Binh Tay Market, with each attracting traders from their local communities and neighboring states. When the French arrived and began to incorporate their architecture into Saigon's landscape, the market was formalized as a large, thatched-roof building near the river. Ben Thanh's present-day site is at

Opera House Area

INTERCONTINENTAL SAIGON

QUI LOUNGE

Children's Hospital No 2

THAI VAN LUNG

HEM 158

NGUYEN DU

BO TUNG XEO

L'USINE LE THANH TON

HEM 3A

LY TU TRONG

LE THANH TON

HAI BA TRUNG

THE REFINERY

SAIGON COOKING CLASS

VINCOM CENTER B

CAO BA QUAT

NGUYEN SIEU

THI SACH

Cong Vien Chi Lang

SAIGON TOURIST LE THANH TON

APOCALYPSE NOW

...HUM LOUNGE

HOTEL DE VILLE

OPERA HOUSE

CARAVELLE SAIGON

DONG DU

CIAO BELLA

Vuon Hoa Tuong Dai Bac Ho

LE LOI

DONG KHOI

RACHA ROOM

THE REX HOTEL/ THE REX HOTEL ROOFTOP BAR

LE LOI

L'USINE

LAYLA

MAC THI BUOI

PHAN VAN DAT

PASTEUR STREET BREWING COMPANY

NGUYEN THIEP

SAIGON RIVER BOUTIQUE HOTEL

PHAM MINH TAILOR

SAX N ART

HEM CM

LE LOI

SAIGON TOURIST

TAN HOANG LONG

HO HUAN NGHIEP

TON DUC THANG

AUTHENTIQUE INTERIORS

LAC THAI

LE LOI BOULEVARD

PASTEUR

NGUYEN HUE

NGO DUC KE

SRI THENDAYUTTAPHANI HINDU TEMPLE

Pho di bo Nguyen Hue

NGUYEN HUE

SAIGON CENTER

PHATTY'S

TON THAT THIEP

NAM KY KHOI NGHIA

SAIGON KITSCH

TEMPLE CLUB

HO TUNG MAU

BROMA

HOTEL MAJESTIC

TON DUC THANG

HUYNH THUC KHANG

TON THAT DAM

NHAN SUSHI

NGO DUC KE

BACH DANG TOURIST WHARF

0   100 yds

0   100 m

Cao Thang Technical College

★ SAIGON SKYDECK, EON 51

HAI TRIEU

© AVALON TRAVEL

Ben Thanh Market Area

© AVALON TRAVEL

the north edge of Quach Thi Trang round-about. The building was completed in 1914 and dubbed the "New Ben Thanh Market."

Since its inception, Ben Thanh has been a major commercial hub and the site of many historical events. During the tumultuous 1950s and 1960s, several significant protests occurred outside its massive gates. The most notable of these occurred on August 25, 1963, when thousands of students and Buddhist monks gathered at the roundabout in front of the market to protest American forces and the presidency of Ngo Dinh Diem. As the protest

grew in size and strength, shots were fired to subdue the crowd and one young protester, 15-year-old student Quach Thi Trang, was killed. Since then, the traffic circle has been referred to as Quach Thi Trang traffic circle.

Vendors begin setting up as early as 4am each day. The outer shops open their doors first, followed by the market's main gates. Once the day market has closed its doors to the public, an equally popular night market sets up shop around the building on Phan Chu Trinh and Phan Boi Chau streets from 6pm until about midnight daily.

Mariamman Hindu Temple

The **Mariamman Hindu Temple** (45 Truong Dinh, D1, 7am-7pm daily), northwest of Ben Thanh Market, comes as a surprise with its colorful towers rising high out of the downtown traffic. The largest of three Hindu temples in the city, this shrine is dedicated to Mariamman, the fickle south Indian goddess of rain and disease.

This temple was built in the late 19th century by Tamil immigrants and is today visited by the small remaining Hindu community and many local Vietnamese. Mariamman is housed inside a large central sanctuary and flanked by her two guardians: Maduraiveeran on the left and Pechiamman on the right. A walk around the back of these shrines reveals a series of brightly hued statues carved into the far wall.

Beside the entrance is a lion statue, which was once used for Hindu processions around the city. An impressive and beautifully decorated *rajagopuram* (tower) stands nearly 12 meters high, the tallest Hindu structure in Saigon, and features images of the temple's guardian as well as other Hindu deities.

Dress modestly when visiting and remove your shoes on the raised platform. Silence is observed indoors, and it is forbidden to enter the gated area surrounding the central sanctuary.

NGUYEN HUE STREET

Saigon Skydeck

Saigon Skydeck (2 Hai Trieu, D1, tel. 028/3915-6156, www.bitexcofinancialtower. com, 9:30am-9:30pm daily, VND200,000), 49 stories above the city, is the official viewing platform of the lotus-shaped Bitexco Financial Tower. Standing at 260 meters, this is the tallest building on the city skyline, with 68 floors, a shopping mall, several restaurants, and a helipad topped with a Vietnamese flag so large that it is visible from the street below.

The Bitexco opened its doors for the first time in 2010. A year later came the inauguration of the Skydeck, providing a unique opportunity to see the city from above. Since most of Saigon's buildings are low-lying structures, finding a bird's-eye view like this is no easy feat. On the 360-degree viewing deck, a series of displays help to orient visitors, offering snippets of historical information about the landscape and the buildings below. You can catch a close-up look at the city's more famous sights through the binoculars situated around the platform.

If you're looking for nice views and some peace and quiet, head a few floors up to **Eon 51** (tel. 028/6291-8751, www.eon51.com, 10:30am-late daily, VND140,000-500,000), which spans the 50th to 52nd floors and includes a bar, café, and restaurant. Prices are higher than other bars, but instead of shelling out cash to stand on the 49th floor, you get the added benefit of a seat and a drink slightly higher up. Hours of operation vary depending upon the venue. The café is open longest, from 10:30am, while the restaurant has more limited lunch and dinner hours; check the website.

Sri Thendayuttaphani Hindu Temple

The **Sri Thendayuttaphani Hindu Temple** (66 Ton That Thiep, D1, 6am-7pm daily) is an interesting fusion of Hindu and Buddhist traditions. Built over 100 years ago, this structure is the work of a once-thriving south Indian community. In its heyday, the temple was regularly used, and Hindu processions took place in the streets of Saigon. After 1975, racial and religious persecution escalated, and many south Indians fled the country.

The Sri Thendayuttaphani Temple is for worship of both Hindu and Buddhist deities. In the main sanctuary, a statue of Thendayuttaphani, also known as Lord Muruga, sits at the center of the temple. Images of Hindu deities line the surrounding walls alongside famous Indian faces. Most notable is the photograph featuring former Indian Prime Minister Jawaharlal Nehru in a meeting with Ho Chi Minh. A statue of Quan Am, a popular Buddhist bodhisattva, sits on the right side of the courtyard. Hidden at the back of the temple is a statue of the Buddha.

Wear appropriate clothing and, when stepping onto the raised platform, remove your shoes. Before you leave, take the narrow staircase on the right up to the roof, where a single blue-and-white incense pot sits before the temple's colorful tower, covered with depictions of Hindu gods and goddesses.

NORTHERN DISTRICT 1
Saigon Zoo and Botanical Garden

Rounding out the eastern end of Le Duan Boulevard is the **Saigon Zoo and Botanical Garden** (2B Nguyen Binh Khiem, D1, tel. 028/3829-1425, www.saigonzoo.net, 7am-6:30pm daily, VND50,000), one of the oldest zoos in the world. Part menagerie, part beautiful park, and part children's carnival, this is a nice place to trade the urban chaos for a rare glimpse of nature in the bustling city. Once one of Saigon's nicest features, the zoo was first developed in 1864. Louis Adolph Germain, a military veterinarian with the French Expedition Army, was tasked with developing the 12 hectare park's roads, animal cages, and nurseries.

The zoo section of the park has not retained its former glory. While the various plants, trees, and flowers packed onto the grounds provide a gorgeous backdrop for an afternoon stroll, the zoo would likely not be considered humane by Western standards due to small and crowded enclosures. Anyone sensitive to animal rights should avoid this part of the park.

Instead, stick to the shaded walkways and stone benches of the botanical garden or the butterfly garden, an enclosure often brimming with dozens of the brightly colored creatures. If you prefer a quiet stroll around the gardens, it's best to go during the week.

HISTORY MUSEUM

Within the gates of the Saigon Zoo and Botanical Garden, the city's **History Museum** (2 Nguyen Binh Khiem, D1, tel.

028/3829-8146, www.baotanglichsuvn.com, 8am-11:30am and 1:30pm-5pm daily, VND30,000) has seen several iterations, from ancient Asian art museum to the country's national museum. It's been the History Museum since 1979. The beautiful grounds surrounding the building add to its already-stunning colonial architecture, which bears the telltale yellow paint and sloping roof of many early-20th-century structures in the city.

The museum's exhibits are divided into two parts: Vietnam's cultural history, from 5,000 years ago until the mid-20th century; and the ancient art of some of Vietnam's southern minorities, including the Champa and the Oc Eo. Though many of the more modern exhibits feature beautiful, functional pieces—lacquer trays, ceramic vases, ivory trinkets—there is little signage or additional information. The most educational exhibits are the Champa and Oc Eo sections, in which a few simple placards guide you through the Hindu and Buddhist influences that helped create these works of art.

There are no photographs allowed without a photo ticket (VND40,000), though most visitors won't feel the need.

Directly across from the museum is the **Hung Kings Temple,** which is guarded by a famous Ho Chi Minh quotation carved onto a large stone slab: "The Hung Kings built this country; we must uphold it." This building once served as a memorial honoring the Vietnamese soldiers who died during World War I. After 1954, locals began coming here to worship the historic Hung Kings. The temple is an impressive structure, particularly inside, where its walls and ceiling are full of ornate red-and-gold carvings. Taking photos is allowed within the temple, but ask permission first.

Jade Emperor Pagoda

Just off busy Dien Bien Phu street sits the **Jade Emperor Pagoda (Chua Phuoc Hai)** (73 Mai Thi Luu, D1, 7am-6pm daily), one of Saigon's more prominent places of worship. Cantonese immigrants completed the building in the late 19th and early 20th centuries, though it was never meant to be a pagoda. Phuoc Hai originally belonged to followers of Minh Su, one of the five syncretic religions brought to Vietnam by the Chinese, and was only later handed over to the Buddhist Association to ensure its preservation.

Inside, massive wooden warriors loom just beyond the main doorway, guarding the entrance to the pagoda. Locals usually pay respects to these imposing figures before heading into the main hall, where the King of Heaven and his court sit, waiting to decide who is admitted into paradise. On the left side of the hall, a series of wood carvings depict the 10 levels of hell in gruesome detail.

Turn right out of this room, follow the signs reading "Dien Quan Am," and take the wooden staircase up to where the goddess of fertility resides. Less fearsome than her counterparts downstairs, she is often visited by pregnant women and those hoping to conceive. A small balcony at the top of the staircase offers up-close views of the pagoda's elaborate roof.

Outside the narrow corridor beside the main hall is a small pond brimming with turtles of varying size; this is why the pagoda is also called the Tortoise Pagoda. Out front, vendors sell fish and baby turtles, which can be released into their respective ponds. With Phuoc Hai's already-overcrowded waters, it's better to leave these creatures where they are.

DISTRICT 3
Turtle Lake

Turtle Lake (Cong Truong Quoc Te, D3, 24 hours daily), an enormous circle surrounded by several cafés, used to be known as Soldier's Park, where bronze statues honored the fallen French soldiers of World War I. Not long before his assassination in 1963, then-president Ngo Dinh Diem did away with the French park, and his successor, General Nguyen Van Thieu, used the land to erect the monument you see today: a large, somewhat murky pond sitting beneath a series of concrete walkways and a statue of a towering lotus, the national flower of Vietnam. The park originally included a statue of a turtle, but it was destroyed shortly after Saigon fell in 1975. The statue was never replaced, but the name stuck.

During the day, vendors gather around the park, selling snacks and refreshments to office workers and students. The higher floors of the surrounding cafés make a good spot to take a break and people-watch over a *ca phe sua da* (Vietnamese iced coffee with milk). This is a good stop en route to the War Remnants Museum and the rest of District 3's sights.

★ War Remnants Museum

The **War Remnants Museum** (28 Vo Van Tan, D3, tel. 028/3930-6664, www. baotangchungtichchientranh.vn, 7:30am-6pm daily, VND40,000), located behind the Reunification Palace, is one of the city's most-visited sights. This museum serves as an important reminder of Vietnam's recent past and a conflict that many locals remember firsthand.

During the years between the end of the American War and the country's normalization of relations with the United States in 1995, this building housed the Museum of Chinese and American War Crimes. Though the name has changed, the sentiment remains largely the same: Each floor of the building touches upon a different topic, from the global community's fierce opposition toward U.S. involvement in Vietnam to the atrocities committed by American soldiers against Vietnamese civilians. Though several of these exhibits are laden with propaganda, they paint an accurate picture of the struggles that many Vietnamese endured during the war and continue to face today.

Outside the main building, military vehicles line the border of the property, including a helicopter and different types of tanks, all of which were used during the conflict. There is also a smaller exhibit dedicated to tiger cages, the brutal form of punishment once used at the infamous Con Dao and Phu Quoc prisons, where thousands of Vietnamese were tortured and often died at the hands of their captors.

District 3

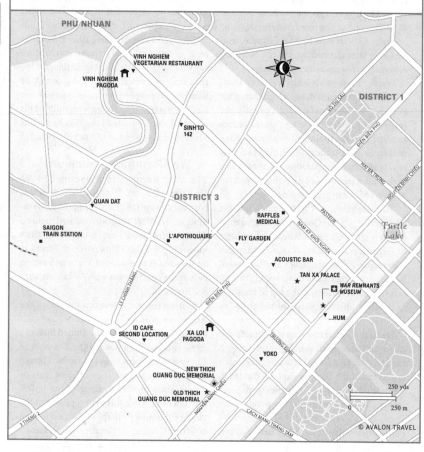

While this is a valuable and eye-opening experience for locals and foreigners, it is not an easy place to visit. Families with children may want to steer clear, as some of the exhibits are graphic.

Tan Xa Palace

The oldest private residence in the city is **Tan Xa Palace** (180 Nguyen Dinh Chieu, D3, 8am-5pm daily), a small, one-room building hidden in the shadow of the lavish Archbishop's residence. Now a chapel, this modest structure is credited to the man who would later become Emperor Gia Long. Before

ascending the throne, Nguyen Phuc Anh arranged its construction in 1790 as a thank-you gift to then-Bishop Pigneau de Behaine for his help in reclaiming the Nguyen dynasty's power after the Tay Son rebellion. The place later became a home for missionaries and bishops before being converted into a chapel.

It is possible to see the palace up close, but you can also get a good feel for it from the street, where you can look through the fence to see the decaying wood of the structure. To get on the property, check with the security guard at the side gate, located on Tran Quoc Thao street, before entering. The chapel itself is no longer in use and no one is permitted inside, but the neighboring buildings are functioning offices for the local Catholic church.

Vinh Nghiem Pagoda

Before you can even see the building, the 40-meter seven-tiered tower of **Vinh Nghiem Pagoda** (339 Nam Ky Khoi Nghia, D3, tel. 028/3896-6798, www.vinhnghiemvn.com, 6:30am-11:30am and 1pm-6pm daily) alerts you to the largest Buddhist structure in Saigon. Built in 1971, this fairly modern complex comprises not only a pagoda but also a library and classrooms for Buddhist study. Three staircases lead up to the main hall, an open space that becomes jam-packed during holidays and special occasions. Inside, the front half of the pagoda is used for Buddhist ceremonies and worship, with religious paintings and other artwork lining the walls. A walk around the main altar reveals hundreds of tiles, kept behind glass at the back, that commemorate the dead.

Outside, the corners of the pagoda's impressive roof curl skyward in the northern style, and its stark, gray tower rises high above the surrounding structures. Though it is not possible to enter the tower itself, visitors can look out over bustling Nam Ky Khoi Nghia street from the balcony and admire the maze of Buddhist flags zigzagging across the complex.

Xa Loi Pagoda

Xa Loi Pagoda (89B Ba Huyen Thanh Quan, D3, tel. 028/3930-0114, www.chuaxaloi.vn, 7am-11am and 2pm-5pm daily) has seen a lot in its short history. Originally built to house sacred relics of the Shakyamuni Buddha, this pagoda is known as a major center of Buddhist study. Today the sacred relics can be seen in a red compartment above the enormous Buddha residing in the main hall.

Xa Loi is also known for its outspoken opposition to the government of South Vietnam in the early 1960s. Most notably, on the morning of June 11, 1963, the Venerable Thich Quang Duc, a senior monk at Xa Loi, sat in the middle of a busy downtown intersection and, surrounded by supporters, lit himself on fire in response to President Ngo Dinh Diem's religious persecution. He was the first of several monks who undertook this act of protest against Diem's government.

Today, Xa Loi is a quiet place, equipped with a library and study center. Two massive staircases curve up to the main hall of the pagoda, an airy room that houses one large

War Remnants Museum

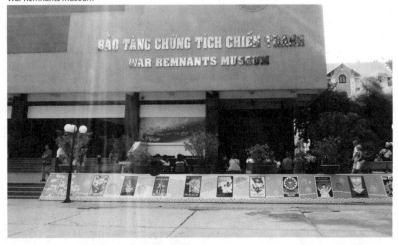

floor-to-ceiling Buddha as well as several smaller statues. Both outside and in, Buddhist flags sway in the breeze, and a smaller statue honors Quan Am, the most well-known female bodhisattva in Mahayana Buddhism. A short walk down the road leads to the **Thich Quang Duc Memorial** (Cach Mang Thang Tam and Nguyen Dinh Chieu, D3), honoring the fallen monk.

CHO LON

If you think District 1 is busy, meet its noisy neighbor to the west. The farther you travel along the Saigon River, the faster the motorbikes begin to move, speeding down wide and hectic Vo Van Kiet street. Buses blare their siren-like horns into the fray, followed by cars, transport trucks, and the occasional motorized tractor, chugging along with its cargo.

Binh Tay Market

One look at the massive entrance of **Binh Tay Market** (57A Thap Muoi, D6, tel. 028/3857-1512, 6am-7pm daily) is all it takes to understand how the trading center got its name. Still known by locals as Cho Lon—"big market" in Vietnamese—this mammoth building was constructed in the late 1800s. Cho Lon drew traders and businessmen from across the city as well as from neighboring countries, such as Cambodia, Malaysia, and India. Cho Lon fast grew into the wholesale market of the south. After the original location grew too large, the new Cho Lon was constructed, using a combination of Chinese-style architecture and French building techniques. A small bust of Quach Dam, the market's founder, stands in the center of the market.

Binh Tay is a major commercial center in the city, housing over 2,300 separate stalls and serving not only the large Chinese-Vietnamese community nearby—roughly a quarter of the vendors within the market are ethnic Chinese—but also the rest of the city. The bustle inside the market embodies much of the pace at which this part of Saigon moves, buzzing with activity from morning until night. At the time of writing, Binh Tay

is closed for renovations and its stalls have shifted to a series of temporary structures; it's unclear how long these upgrades will take, but the makeshift version of the market isn't quite as impressive, so ask around about its status before you visit.

★ Thien Hau Pagoda

The teetering, haphazard, multistory houses of Chinatown mix with the shops and offices of a modern city. But stuck firmly in a bygone era is **Thien Hau Pagoda** (710 Nguyen Trai, D5, 6am-5:30pm daily, free), a beautiful building constructed in 1760. Southern Chinese refugees arrived in southern Vietnam and began to settle around the Cho Lon area, then known as Tai Ngon. The Chinese expressed their thanks to Thien Hau, goddess of the sea, by crafting the ornate wood carvings and terra-cotta scenes depicted around this pagoda. This single-story structure shows its age gracefully in the worn exterior and intricate designs on the roof.

Before you step inside you'll be accosted by a wave of incense, which burns ceaselessly from the massive pots indoors, not to mention a collection of incense coils that hang from the ceiling. Flanking the walls on either side of the pagoda are stone engravings that list the building's benefactors over the years. The final third of the main hall is easily the most impressive. Vivid red and gold adorns the building's columns, while up above countless incense coils twist and flutter in the breeze. Dozens of locals and foreigners pay their respects with incense sticks, candles, and other offerings, which are available for purchase. A statue of Thien Hau sits at the back, ornate and heavily decorated. The pagoda is one of the more unique buildings in Saigon. Despite the click of cameras and the curious tourists, locals are friendly and seemingly unaffected by the many foreign visitors.

Chaozhou Congregation Hall

A short walk down the road from Thien Hau Pagoda is the newer and bigger **Chaozhou Congregation Hall (Nghia An Hoi Quan)**

(678 Nguyen Trai, D5, 6am-6pm daily), obscured by a high stone wall. Honoring the great Chinese general Quan Cong, this structure is the work of the local Chaozhou Chinese Congregation. The gilded woodwork of the exterior forms a splash of color that runs along the thick cylindrical beams of the building and up to the detailing on the roof.

Inside, a statue of a red-faced Quan Cong sits, beard in hand, at the center of the pagoda, with his horse tucked on the left of the entrance. Farther into the pagoda, bright neon hues contrast against a pair of stone walls. Remove your shoes as you step onto the raised platform at the back, where a larger statue of the general sits, flanked by towers of golden figurines and other ornamentation. Look up: Much of this building's stunning decor and architecture is tucked inside the rafters of the high-ceilinged structure.

Cho Lon Mosque

A marked contrast from the colorful ornamentation of nearby pagodas, the pastel blue **Cho Lon Mosque** (641 Nguyen Trai, D5, 4:30am-6:30pm daily) is easy to miss amid the hectic market outside its front door. This no-frills building became a house of worship for Tamil immigrants in 1935. After 1975, much of the Tamil community left Vietnam. Today, the mosque serves mostly Malaysian and Indonesian Muslims living in the city, though there are also a few Vietnamese believers. To the left of the entrance is an ablutions pool, where the religious wash before praying, and opposite the entrance of the mosque is a Halal restaurant serving mostly Malaysian dishes.

Minh Huong Pagoda

Near the corner of Thuan Kieu street just a block north of the string of pagodas lining Nguyen Trai is the **Minh Huong Pagoda** (184 Hong Bang, D5, 6am-5pm daily, free), also known as the Phuoc An Assembly Hall. Originally completed in the late 19th century by immigrants from the Guangdong, Fujian, and Zhejiang provinces of China, this vibrant building once stood beside the Cho Lon

Railway Station. In the small courtyard out front, statues of the Buddha and Quan Am, a popular Buddhist bodhisattva, flank the main entrance. The pagoda's front door features a beautiful, iridescent red lacquer, but its most unique element is the collection of mosaic incense pots throughout the pagoda. Carefully tiled with colorful patterned pieces of broken china, these massive standing pots catch your eye amid a main hall full of vivid embellishment. At the back of the hall, famous Chinese general Quan Cong sits in the middle, accompanied by Ong Bon, a Fujianese god, on the left and the Ngu Hanh goddesses of the five elements on the right. Above the red, yellow, and green decor, enormous incense coils burn slowly, taking as long as a full month to burn down.

Fito Museum of Traditional Medicine

Slightly off the beaten path, the **Fito Museum of Traditional Medicine** (41 Hoang Du Khuong, D10, tel. 028/3864-2430, www.fitomuseum.com.vn, 8:30am-5pm daily, VND120,000) is an unusual and worthy attraction that is slowly gaining popularity among tourists. It's owned and operated by the Fito Pharmaceutical Company, which produces and sells traditional Vietnamese remedies. The energetic museum staff are eager to educate visitors on the nation's long history of traditional medicine. Designed to reflect Vietnamese architecture in various parts of the country, from the northern structures of Hanoi down to Mekong Delta-style houses, the museum is filled with dozens of artifacts dating as far back as thousands of years. Free guided tours cover the origins of Vietnamese medicine, the many plant and animal ingredients involved in traditional remedies, and the practices of traditional Vietnamese pharmacists. The tour ends downstairs with a cup of tea and a chance to peruse the museum's small shop of traditional medicine, including teas and oils.

Though it's never busy, the museum sees a steady stream of visitors; there is almost always someone available to lead a tour. Informational pamphlets are available at the front desk for guests who arrive after a tour has begun. Photos are also allowed here and even encouraged on the third floor, where visitors can try on traditional Vietnamese garb and snap a picture with the museum's collection of grinding apparatuses, once used by pharmacists.

If there's time, swing by Hai Thuong Lan Ong street near Binh Tay Market, better known as the traditional medicine street, where dozens of traditional pharmacists sell their remedies.

GIAC LAM PAGODA

About six kilometers outside of downtown, **Giac Lam Pagoda** (565 Lac Long Quan, D Tan Binh, 6am-noon and 2pm-8pm daily, free) is the city's oldest pagoda. A large, open complex made up of several buildings, the grounds of Giac Lam boast over 100 statues of the Buddha as well as a staggering collection of shrines honoring the relatives of local residents.

In the seven-tiered tower just inside the gates, each floor houses a different statue of the Buddha or a popular bodhisattva. This is one of the only Buddhist towers in the city that you can ascend. Though the very top is off-limits to visitors, a narrow balcony on each floor offers a nice view of the surrounding area.

Beyond the tower is a small garden decorated with dozens of miniature idols as well as a large statue of Quan Am, one of Buddhism's most famous bodhisattva. A second set of gates leads into the main building, where dozens more Buddhas are on display, as well as headstones and nameplates with ages and birth dates scrawled across lacquer plaques and stone carvings.

The largest statue of all, a towering white Buddha, sits cross-legged to the right of the main walkway. Another small garden precedes the main pagoda, while the far end of the complex is home to a series of ornate tombs belonging to the pagoda's founders.

TOURS

There are scores of travel agencies in the city that offer half- and full-day tours. Larger companies like **Sinh Tourist** (246-248 De Tham, D1, tel. 028/3838-9593, www.thesinhtourist.vn, 6:30am-10:30pm daily) and **TNK Travel** (220 De Tham, D1, tel. 028/3920-4766, www.tnktravelvietnam.com, 6:30am-10pm daily) provide inexpensive, cookie-cutter tours to most of the city's major sights (VND150,000-500,000). Though by far the most inexpensive option, these tour buses often shepherd groups of 20-30 people around town. Being on such a large tour diminishes the experience, as it can be difficult to hear the tour guide or get much of the benefit that paying for a tour is meant to provide.

Motorbike Tours

Hands down, the ultimate way to experience the city is as most locals do—on a motorbike. **XO Tours** (tel. 09/3308-3727, www.xotours.vn, 9am-10pm daily, VND1,100,000-1,700,000) does just that, ferrying visitors around town on the back of a scooter. In addition to visiting the city's major sights, XO provides tours tailored to food, nightlife, and shopping, all with experienced, traditionally clad local guides who double as motorbike drivers. The same goes for **Vietnam Vespa Adventures** (169A De Tham, D1, tel. 012/2299-3585, www.vietnamvespaadventures.com, 7am-2am daily, VND1,700,000-2,180,000), which runs food and nightlife city tours as well as one-day trips to the Mekong Delta.

Foodies should book a trip with **Back of the Bike Tours** (tel. 09/3504-6910, www.backofthebiketours.com, 9am-10pm daily, VND960,000-3,000,000), the brainchild of husband-and-wife team Chad and Thuy Kubanoff, a pair with a serious passion for the city and its delectable street food. Tours leave from District 1 and take guests outside of Saigon's central area to dine in some of the less-visited neighborhoods, offering a more unique, authentic take on Vietnam's southern hub.

Cultural Tours

For a unique perspective on Vietnamese history and art, sign up for **Sophie's Art Tour** (tel. 09/3375-2402, www.sophiesarttour.com, 9am-1pm Mon.-Sat., VND1,500,000). A long-time Saigon resident and the former curator of local Galerie Quynh, Sophie Hughes spent over a year researching and compiling this living project, which tells the tumultuous history of 20th-century Vietnam through its greatest artists. Divided into four chapters, the tour whisks visitors to a series of private galleries as well as the Fine Arts Museum, focusing on different aspects of local history before and after colonialism and the American War. Sophie's interactive approach and continuing research keep the story fresh, adding new anecdotes and information all the time and encouraging visitors to get involved. The tour leaves from a small café in District 3 and its fee includes transportation as well as admission to museums, cold drinks, and, of course, the expertise of a local resident.

Entertainment and Events

★ NIGHTLIFE

As the sun sets over Saigon, street barbecues and curbside watering holes pop up all over town, serving a variety of *do nhau* (drinking food) and slinging bottles of Saigon Red and Tiger beer.

Though there are hundreds of bars across town, the best of the city's nightlife is in District 1. For backpacker bars and nonstop activity, head to Bui Vien, where there is always a party. Drinks are dirt-cheap and most places have nightly specials. More spacious and slightly more expensive environments can be found down the narrow streets surrounding Nguyen Hue and the Opera House, where laid-back lounge options abound, not to mention larger expat bars and a handful of trendy nightclubs. Saigon is big on rooftop venues, which are a nice place to take in the city at night, removed from the bustle down below.

Petty theft is common at night. When heading out on the town, take only the essentials, travel in groups, and opt for taxis over motorbikes where possible. There have been instances in which passengers have been accosted on a *xe om* and robbed, sometimes by a thief in cahoots with the motorbike driver. Though it's just as likely you won't have trouble in the evening, it's best to keep your wits about you and an eye on your belongings at all times.

Bars

OPERA HOUSE AREA

Up a flight of stairs, the chic **Layla** (2nd floor, 63 Dong Du, tel. 028/3827-2279, 4pm-1am Mon.-Thurs., 4pm-2am Fri.-Sat., 1pm-1am Sun., VND60,000-390,000) is often crowded with hip young Saigon socialites catching up over cocktails. Spread across several rooms, with both indoor and outdoor seating, it's known for handcrafted beverages and friendly service. Layla also has a pool table.

NGUYEN HUE STREET

On the corner of Ngo Duc Ke and Nguyen Hue, **Broma** (41 Nguyen Hue, D1, tel. 09/0144-1955, 5pm-2am daily, VND80,000-200,000) has made a name for itself among the younger Vietnamese and expat crowds, mostly for its laid-back rooftop seating. Take the narrow staircase up to the roof and you'll find a small-but-steady flow of people enjoying the cozy open-air terrace, which is decked out in tea lights and greenery. The bar is usually open late; closing time depends on the number of customers, so don't be surprised if you arrive in the wee hours to find that they've already closed for the evening.

Saigon's original craft brewery, **Pasteur**

Street Brewing Company (144 Pasteur, D1, tel. 028/3823-9562, www.pasteurstreet.com, 11am-11pm daily, VND70,000-200,000) combines American-style brewing techniques with Vietnamese ingredients to create some of the city's tastiest and most innovative beer. Whether it's the signature jasmine IPA, featuring dried jasmine flower, or more adventurous seasonal refreshments like the jackfruit wheat ale or a surprisingly pleasant durian beer, Pasteur Street always has an array of brews on tap, and its cozy second-floor bar makes for a nice spot to enjoy a drink, as does the new taproom across the alley.

For more of a sports-bar atmosphere, **Phatty's** (46-48 Ton That Thiep, D1, tel. 028/3821-0796, 8am-midnight daily, VND40,000-320,000) is a popular expat haunt just off Nguyen Hue. Serving beer, cocktails, and hearty pub food, the bar keeps a schedule of major sporting events, which it plays on the multiple televisions around the bar, and exudes a bit more class than its Pham Ngu Lao counterparts.

On a rooftop overlooking the downtown area, **Rogue Saigon** (13 Pasteur, 2nd fl., D1, tel. 09/0236-5780, www.saigonoutcast.com, 4pm-midnight Sun.-Thurs., 4pm-2am Fri.-Sat., VND40,000-150,000) is a modest downtown watering hole that serves several of Saigon's ever-growing array of craft beer. The spot is bare-bones, but there's a nice little balcony overlooking the street as well as outdoor seating upstairs. Rogue's owners keep things interesting with regular DJs and the occasional live music night.

BEN THANH MARKET AREA

Starting around late afternoon, dozens of plastic stools begin to appear on Bui Vien. This is a good place to start, as beer is inexpensive and the setup makes it easy to meet other travelers. As the evening goes on, the crowd of backpackers creeps out onto the street, making it hard to tell that this real estate actually belongs to several different businesses. Each small shop slings a variety of cheap local beer. To get an idea of the chaotic ambience and shoulder-to-shoulder seating, head to **Bia Sai Gon** (73 Bui Vien, D1, 5pm-1am daily, VND12,000-50,000) for an ice-cold brew and a street-side view of the action.

Craft beer enthusiasts will appreciate **East West** (181-185 Ly Tu Trong, D1, tel. 09/1306-0728, www.eastwestbrewing.vn, 11am-midnight Sun.-Wed., 11am-1am Thurs.-Sat., VND90,000-200,000), a local brewery offering its own line of beverages. The atmosphere may be more refined than its street-side counterparts, but East West's staff is friendly and laid-back, and the beer is worth a visit.

Just off Bui Vien near the looming neon sign of Crazy Buffalo, **Thi Bar** (224 De Tham, D1, tel. 028/2210-2929, 5pm-12:30am Sun.-Thurs., 5pm-2am Fri.-Sat., VND60,000-180,000) has the best of both worlds, with a lively bar area downstairs and relaxed comfortable seating up top. The house band starts to play around 10pm nightly, turning the narrow area around the bar into a dance floor and sending the noise level through the roof.

For a rooftop view without the sky-high prices, Duc Vuong Hotel's **The View** (Duc Vuong Hotel, 195 Bui Vien, D1, tel. 028/3920-6992, www.ducvuonghotel.com, 10am-1am daily, VND30,000-180,000) offers cheap beer and cocktails to the budget traveler set. Its heavily decorated rooftop area, which overlooks the backpacker neighborhood, is a pleasant escape from the bustle at street level, and the friendly atmosphere makes this an easy place to make friends.

While it's not quite as high up as other rooftop watering holes, **OMG** (15-19 Nguyen An Ninh, D1, tel. 09/3720-0222, 5pm-1am daily, VND80,000-250,000) has an incredible view of both Ben Thanh Market and Quach Thi Trang roundabout. Located on the top floor of Tan Hai Long Hotel, the bar offers both indoor and outdoor seating, but no matter where you sit you'll be able to take in the view, thanks to the floor-to-ceiling glass windows facing the traffic circle.

Twenty-six stories above the city, **Chill Skybar** (76A Le Lai, AB Tower, 26th and 27th Fl., D1, tel. 028/7300-4554, www.chillsaigon.

com, 5:30pm-2am Sun.-Thurs., 5:30pm-4am Fri.-Sat., VND150,000-400,000) is worth a visit for its view. Drink prices are steep, but the outdoor bar boasts a 180-degree panorama of the downtown area, impressive at night. To save a little cash, visit 5:30pm-8pm, when happy-hour specials make cocktail prices reasonable. Be aware that the bar enforces a strict dress code, which Chill describes as "smart casual": no flip-flops, shorts, athletic clothing, or men in sleeveless tank tops. There is an indoor lounge and restaurant area if you prefer to admire the view from inside, though these are equally overpriced. For a quieter but equally upscale atmosphere, grab a drink just downstairs at **Sorae** (24th Fl., AB Tower, 76A Le Lai, D1, tel. 028/3827-2372, www.soraesushi.com, 11:30am-2pm and 5:30pm-1am daily).

Lounges
OPERA HOUSE AREA

A short jaunt away from Nguyen Hue's walking street, **Racha Room** (12-14 Mac Thi Buoi, D1, tel. 09/0879-1412, http://theracharoom. com, 11:30am-midnight Mon.-Fri., 4pm-midnight Sat.-Sun., VND80,000-300,000) is the perfect place for a happy-hour refreshment. Its exposed brick interior, dim lighting, and dark red upholstery add a bit of class, as do its array of expertly crafted signature cocktails. While the upscale vibe attracts a sophisticated clientele, the place lacks pretense, making this an excellent spot to while away an evening. You're best to visit during happy hour (5pm-8pm Mon.-Sat.), when cocktails are half-price.

NGUYEN HUE STREET

Hidden in an old French colonial apartment building, **Snuffbox** (14 Ton That Dam, D1, tel. 09/4170-1888, 6pm-3am daily, VND80,000-250,000) is Saigon's only speakeasy. The door to the laid-back lounge is unassuming, but indoors the venue gives off a vintage vibe that feels straight out of the Roaring '20s, complete with art deco accents and plush furniture. At the bar you'll find beer, wine, and hand-crafted cocktails, while the seating arrangement allows for large gatherings downstairs and more intimate conversations in the tiny upstairs loft.

Nightclubs
OPERA HOUSE AREA

Thumping music and spacious dance floors have turned **Apocalypse Now** (2B Thi Sach, D1, tel. 028/3825-6124, www.apocalypsesaigon.com, 7pm-4am daily, VND80,000-200,000) into a local institution. The self-proclaimed "first nightclub in Saigon" is slightly removed from Pham Ngu Lao, but is still frequented by the backpacker set, blasting bass-filled hits well into the night. Its smaller outdoor area makes for a good spot to relax, but most of the action happens indoors, where several rooms play different genres of music.

A massive compound on the corner of Dinh Tien Hoang, **Lush** (2 Ly Tu Trong, D1, tel. 09/4876-7676, 8:30pm-4am Tues.-Sun., VND90,000-250,000) is one of the city's best-known clubs due to its "ladies' nights" (9pm-midnight Tues.), during which time women drink for free. When it gets busy around 10:30pm, it brings together a handful of tourists with expats and locals. The DJ sets up just beyond the large circular bar at the center of the room. There are quieter areas to sit at the back of the club and just beside the main entrance. Ladies' night is a fun, cheap night on the town, but it's not worth visiting on other days, as it gets less crowded and drinks are overpriced. The dress code requires semiformal attire.

If you're up for a night on the town, **Qui Lounge** (22 Le Thanh Ton, D1, tel. 028/3828-8828, www.quilounge.com, 11am-2:30pm and 5:30pm-2am Mon.-Fri., 5:30pm-2am Sat.-Sun., VND130,000-400,000) gets busy on weekends, when the city's social butterflies come out to drink and dance. The layout of the place makes busting a move a little tricky—in Vietnam, clubgoers often prefer lounging to dancing—but the DJ spins plenty of danceable tunes until late. Drinks are expensive, as in most local clubs, and a more formal dress code is enforced.

Live Music

One of Saigon's pioneer music venues, **Yoko** (22A Nguyen Thi Dieu, D3, tel. 028/3933-0577, 8am-midnight daily, VND80,000-180,000) was once an intimate one-room venue packed with couches and a precarious wooden balcony. Nowadays, the venue boasts a bigger stage and more comfortable seating, not to mention both original local acts and the odd international performer. The atmosphere is very laid-back and the venue remains cozy enough that you can enjoy the show no matter where you sit. Talented musicians appear nightly from 9pm, performing rock-infused covers of old and new hits as well as original music.

Easily the only venue of its kind in the city, **Sax N Art Jazz Club** (28 Le Loi, D1, tel. 028/3822-8472, 6pm-midnight daily, VND100,000) is the pet project of master saxophonist Tran Manh Tuan, one of Vietnam's renowned jazz musicians. With eight solo albums to his credit, Tuan operates and often performs at the club. The long, narrow building makes for a great performance space, and a rotating group of Vietnamese and foreign musicians joins the mix. Live music begins at 9pm, at which time a cover charge is enforced.

A popular, if a little cramped, live music venue is **Acoustic Bar** (6E1 Ngo Thoi Nhiem, D3, tel. 012/7677-7773, 7pm-midnight daily, VND70,000-150,000), set at the back of an alley packed with cafés and karaoke lounges. While Acoustic often features sugary pop-fueled performances. The bar feels intimate, with a lively audience lined up shoulder-to-shoulder in front of the stage. Live music starts at 8pm daily, and you'll catch a crowd of young Vietnamese hanging out here.

THE ARTS

A burgeoning community of painters, film-makers, visual artists, and enthusiastic supporters of the arts call Saigon home. While more traditional performances and cultural showcases have long been a mainstay at the Opera House, smaller venues like cafés and independent galleries also exhibit artwork and hold regular film nights as well as artist workshops. Keep an eye out for these smaller events through the calendar on **Saigoneer** (www.saigoneer.com). Several regularly scheduled film screenings like **Future Shorts** (www.futureshorts.com), a quarterly international short film festival, also take place.

Performing Arts

Most of the city's English-language theatrical performances take place at the historic **Opera House** (7 Cong Truong Lam Son, D1, tel. 028/3823-7419, www.hbso.org.vn). A regularly changing schedule of shows passes through the theater, from plays, ballets, and circus acts to cultural shows and musical performances. Box office hours vary with the show; book your tickets through the opera house or through **Saigon Tourist** (45 Le Thanh Ton, D1, tel. 028/3827-9279, www.saigon-tourist.com, 8am-7pm daily).

The labor of a group of talented Vietnamese-European musicians and circus performers, **AO Show** (tel. 012/4518-1188, www.luneproduction.com, box office 9:30am-6pm daily, VND630,000-1,470,000) is Vietnam's answer to Cirque du Soleil. Inspired by the rapidly changing pace of Vietnam, from the quiet laid-back life of the countryside to the mayhem of its cities, this hour-long show, performed at the Opera House, has received rave reviews from local media and visiting travelers for the acrobatics and agility of its performers, as well as the cultural element it brings to a circus-based show. AO Show takes place in the evenings several times a week. When the main show is traveling, a trio of similar shows—Lang Toi, The Mist, and Teh Dar—each created by the production company behind AO, also play at the city's opera house.

A long-standing northern tradition, the colorful wooden puppets of *roi nuoc* (Vietnamese water puppet theater) have been around since the 11th century. This unique form is one of the more popular cultural performances in town. The **Golden Dragon Water Puppet Theater** (55B Nguyen Thi

Minh Khai, D1, tel. 028/3930-2196, box office 8:30am-11:30am and 1:30pm-7:30pm daily, VND200,000), located within the grounds of the Labor Cultural House, holds performances at 5pm and 6:30pm daily. Musicians play traditional Vietnamese instruments such as the *dan nhi,* a two-stringed violin, and lend their voices to a lively cast of characters, who splash around in the miniature pool that serves as a stage. Hidden behind a bamboo screen are the show's masterful puppeteers. The show runs 50 minutes, and each scene is accompanied by music and vocals. Though the performance is entirely in Vietnamese, no translation is required. Reserve your ticket at least one day in advance, as seats fill up quickly. Request a seat behind the front row if you prefer to stay dry during the performance—the puppets can get rowdy. Call the theater's hotline or visit their box office in order to get the best price.

Galleries and Museums

The **Fine Arts Museum** (97A Pho Duc Chinh, D1, tel. 028/3829-4441, 9am-5pm Tues.-Sun., VND30,000) is housed in the former residence of a wealthy Chinese family. This three-story colonial-style building dates to 1929 and was the first building in the city to feature an elevator, on display on the ground floor. Since its opening in 1992, the museum has housed permanent exhibits in the main house as well as a rotating collection of special exhibits, which are on display in a smaller building nearby. The exhibits are organized chronologically, beginning with ancient Champa and Oc Eo sculpture from the 7th to 17th centuries and continuing through modern-day Vietnamese art. There is also a display of what's called "combat art." During the American War, artists followed rebel forces to the front lines and drew the people and battles before them. These works are displayed in the second-floor corridors. Allot a few hours here, as the collection is deceptively large. There are information desks located at the front of the main building.

For a constantly changing lineup of both local and international artists, **Galerie Quynh** (118 Nguyen Van Thu, D1, tel. 028/3822-7218, www.galeriequynh.com, 10am-7pm Tues.-Sat.) regularly curates new exhibits from around the world. The joint effort of Vietnamese-American art critic Quynh Pham and Englishman Robert Cianchi, Galerie Quynh has been working to promote contemporary art in Vietnam and the larger region since 2000, when it first came on the scene as an online entity showcasing the talents of local artists. The gallery boasts a modern space that is at the forefront of contemporary art in southern Vietnam.

A major player in the local art scene is the **Craig Thomas Gallery** (27I Tran Nhat Duat, D1, tel. 09/0388-8431, www.cthomasgallery.com, 11am-6pm Mon.-Sat., noon-5pm Sun.), tucked at the back of a wide alley in northern District 1 not far from Tan Dinh Market. Inside the gallery gates, golden bicycles scale the front wall of the building, up and over its awning. Indoors, two high-ceilinged rooms showcase the work of talented contemporary Vietnamese artists. Gallery founder Craig Thomas has been an active member of the Vietnamese art scene since 2002, mentoring young Saigon artists working in all mediums, and fostering the nascent artistic community of southern Vietnam. The gallery regularly changes its exhibits and is willing to open for private showings (call to arrange).

FESTIVALS AND EVENTS

Roughly a month after the Western world ushers in a new year, the entire nation of Vietnam takes a long holiday in honor of Tet, the Lunar New Year. During this time, Saigon is an empty city, deserted by many of its year-round residents who return home to enjoy the holiday with their extended families. Despite the mass exodus, HCMC still holds a well-known annual **Flower Street Festival** (Jan.-Feb.), at which time the length of Nguyen Hue Boulevard is shut down in order to accommodate an impressive floral display, usually featuring the Vietnamese zodiac animal of that year. Gardeners will twist and shape these colorful plants into a dragon, a cat, or a slithering snake. The flower festival is the one thing that draws people out of their homes at Tet to admire the vivid decorations along Nguyen Hue.

Though the **Mid-Autumn Festival** (mid-late Sept.) is a holiday celebrated throughout the country, Saigon's festivities are particularly lively. Beginning about a month before the holiday, the tiny street of Luong Nhu Hoc in District 5 becomes a *pho long den* (lantern village). Vendors sell colorful paper lanterns and decorations in honor of the coming day of festivity. Go in the evening, after sunset, to get the full effect of the lanterns. The closer the holiday is, the more likely it is to be packed with people.

Shopping

From droves of street peddlers on Pham Ngu Lao to the high-end boutiques and colossal shopping centers of District 1, Saigon is the commercial heart of Vietnam. The city's shopping obsession runs deep, extending out into the frenzied markets of Chinatown and down narrow streets that specialize in everything from guitar-making to used bicycles to high-quality fabrics. Designer clothes line Nguyen Hue and Dong Khoi streets. Closer to the backpacker area, shopping hubs like Ben Thanh Market and Saigon Square are packed with inexpensive souvenirs and colorful clothing. Bargaining is a common practice, giving you the opportunity to hone your haggling skills while picking up a new wardrobe.

MARKETS

Market culture is alive and well in Saigon. It is in the mayhem of these open-air buildings that many locals do their shopping. Vendors sit outside their stalls and call to passing shoppers, advertising T-shirts and fabric, souvenirs, shoes, and every food under the sun.

Ben Thanh Market

A Saigon institution, **Ben Thanh Market** (Le Loi and Tran Hung Dao, D1, tel. 028/3829-9274, 6am-6pm daily) is a symbol of the city. The current market, built in 1914, houses every item imaginable, from souvenirs and clothing to accessories, electronics, packaged food, and foreign items that can't be found elsewhere in the city. Squeeze your way through the aisles of fabric stalls or peruse the coffee selection along the main corridors. The majority of the market's outer shops, which line the perimeter of the building, try to maintain a fixed-price policy. Still, you do have some room to bargain, particularly if you are buying multiple items at a time. Inside, vendors beckon from all sides. The food area is concentrated close to the middle, and there are a handful of luggage and backpack shops on the very exterior of the building near the northern entrance.

At 6pm, Ben Thanh closes its doors, but a busy outdoor **night market** begins, going until about midnight. The night market is considerably smaller, though it does have a good number of outdoor dining options and some shopping.

Located near the northern entrance to Ben Thanh Market, **Dung Tailor** (221 Le Thanh Ton, D1, tel. 028/3829-6778, dung-tailor@hcm.vnn.vn, 8am-7:30pm daily) designs suits, button-up shirts, and other dress clothes specifically for men. The shop is clean and comfortable with a range of ready-made items to choose from as well as plenty of fabric options. Prices are expensive, with a men's button-up shirt going for about VND600,000, but the quality of the work is undeniable and it's worth the investment.

Even with its close proximity to Ben Thanh, it would be easy to miss **The House of Saigon** (258 Le Thanh Ton, D1, tel.

028/3520-8178, www.thehouseofsaigon.com, 8:30am-9pm daily), as it's not directly surrounding the market. The housewares, jewelry, clothing, and knick-knacks sold here make it worth a visit. Though prices are steeper than in the market, items are of high quality and beautifully made, from wicker-and-porcelain serving dishes to buffalo horn chopsticks. The shop also features clothing and souvenirs.

Binh Tay Market

The large and imposing **Binh Tay Market** (57A Thap Muoi, D6, tel. 028/3857-1512, 6am-7pm daily) boasts an ornate Chinese-style roof visible from kilometers away. This is the heart of Cho Lon, home to Saigon's large ethnic Chinese population. The mammoth market houses dry goods, clothing, fabrics, food, cosmetics, and household items. It's more of a local market than the foreign-influenced Ben Thanh. Inside is a small courtyard devoted to Quach Dam, a wealthy Chinese immigrant and the benefactor of modern-day Binh Tay. Beyond and around that, the market is a flurry of activity that features Chinese products as well as local offerings. Binh Tay closes in the evening but the area remains busy well into the night. For practical items or specific Vietnamese goods, Binh Tay is a better place to go than Ben Thanh, as its prices are often cheaper. At the time of writing, Binh Tay is undergoing renovations and is closed. It's unclear how long these upgrades will take. Ask around about the market's status before you make the trek.

Tan Dinh Market

Considerably smaller than other downtown markets, **Tan Dinh Market** (Hai Ba Trung and Nguyen Huu Cau, D1, tel. 028/3829-9280, 6am-6pm daily) houses the usual smorgasbord of household goods, clothes, and food items but is best known for the fabric vendors in the market and across the street on Hai Ba Trung and Nguyen Huu Cau. Stalls are packed to the ceiling with silk, cotton, and other materials, from plain colors to intricate, sequined patterns. Around the market's exterior along Hai Ba Trung, fruit vendors set up a nice display to attract passing customers.

An Dong Market

If you're on the lookout for wooden or lacquer handicrafts, visit **An Dong Market** (34-36 An Duong Vuong, D5, 6am-6pm daily). This ancient building doesn't see nearly as much traffic as An Dong Plaza, its newer, fancier

a vegetable vendor's produce on display in downtown Saigon

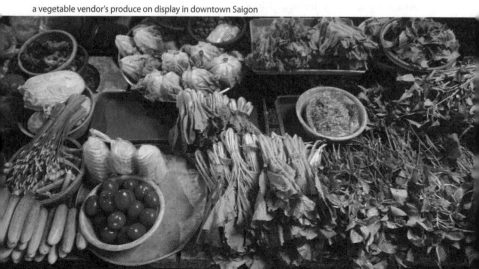

What a Bargain!

Bargaining in Ho Chi Minh City's markets is almost always acceptable. In bigger, more central markets, prices are higher and room for negotiation is greater. In Ben Thanh Market, for instance, you may be able to drive the price down as much as 40-50 percent. Vendors in these heavily touristed areas tend to sell the same products, which gives you more bargaining power. If you attempt to haggle with a local vendor and are unsuccessful, you can move next door and find the same things on offer.

Many travelers find their first trip to the local market overwhelming. Stalls are small and cluttered, cramming innumerable items into one space, and, particularly in tourist areas, vendors can be pushy. Remain patient and only bargain seriously for something you really want. The most important thing to remember when bargaining is that as long as both you and the vendor are pleased with the transaction, then the price is acceptable. You may pay slightly more than a local might, but there's a good chance it's still cheaper than what you would pay at home.

counterpart down the block, but it boasts a wider selection of statues, dishes, and other handicraft items. The first floor of the market is mostly food stalls; upstairs is an array of fabric, shoes, purses, clothing, and handicrafts. This is a quieter, more relaxed bargaining environment than Ben Thanh Market, and vendors tend to be friendlier.

Dan Sinh Market

Dan Sinh Market (104 Yersin, D1, tel. 028/3825-1130, 6am-6pm daily), sometimes known as Yersin Market, sells an eclectic combination of construction materials and war memorabilia. Tucked in the heart of this dank makeshift building are a plethora of stalls carrying army gear and personal effects of soldiers from both sides of the American War. In addition to combat helmets, compasses, bullets, canteens, and all manner of camouflage, you'll find rusted antique lighters and cameras as well as piles of photographs once carried by Vietnamese soldiers. The market offers authentic antiques as well as cheaper reproductions of most items.

SHOPPING DISTRICTS
Nguyen Hue and Le Loi Streets

On the eastern side of Ben Thanh Market is **Le Loi,** a street devoted almost exclusively to shopping and geared toward the tourist crowd.

Many of the same souvenirs sold inside Ben Thanh are featured here, but alongside more expensive local shops as well as international brands. Intermixed with these smaller boutiques are one or two shopping malls, including the flashy **Saigon Center** (65 Le Loi, D1, tel. 028/3829-4888, www.saigoncentre.com.vn, 9:30am-9:30pm Mon.-Thurs., 9:30am-10:30pm Fri.-Sun.), a seven-level shopping complex adjoining the Japanese department store Takashimaya. Farther down the street, take a right onto Nguyen Hue and you'll find more retail shops squeezed in among the nicer hotels and Western restaurants.

For cheap local fashions, visit the gargantuan **Saigon Square** (77-89 Nam Ky Khoi Nghia, D1, 9am-9pm daily), a cross between a local market and a Western-style shopping mall. Here you'll find boatloads of inexpensive souvenirs, bags, coffee, clothes, and various electronic odds and ends. Haggling is acceptable and, though the place is usually a madhouse, it is slightly more organized than nearby Ben Thanh Market. There is also a second location, known as **Saigon Square 3** (179-183 Hai Ba Trung, D1, 9am-9pm daily), which is equally hectic.

The folks at **Saigon Kitsch** (43 Ton That Thiep, D1, tel. 028/3821-8019, saigonkitsch@gmail.com, 8am-9pm daily) take old propaganda images and spruce up T-shirts, notebooks, drinking glasses, magnets, and other odds and ends, including propaganda-style renditions of famous movie posters.

Pham Minh Tailor (132 Pasteur, D1, tel. 09/0378-2220, phamminhtailor@yahoo.com. vn, 8am-7:30pm daily) is a reputable tailor for men and women. This store boasts fabrics from all over the world, including Vietnam, India, Italy, and China. The experienced seamstresses can complete a job on a tight deadline, though it's important to be clear about your travel plans from the beginning in order to ensure your order is completed on time. You may be able to pay a visit to Ben Thanh Market with the tailor to choose your fabric.

Mekong Quilts (68 Le Loi, tel. 028/2210-3110, www.mekong-creations.org, 9am-7pm daily) carries plush, colorful quilts as well as bamboo and papier-mâché products, handmade by women in southern Vietnam and Cambodia. This nonprofit enterprise employs over 300 people. Designs come from the women themselves as well as professional designers, and 50 cents of each dollar spent at the shop goes directly back to the villages, providing each employee with a sustainable income.

Pham Ngu Lao Street

Also known as the backpacker area, **Pham Ngu Lao** is home to a wide variety of reasonably priced souvenir and clothing shops, as well as street vendors carrying everything from knock-off Ray-Bans to photocopied books, fans, and other goods. This neighborhood provides the same products as Ben Thanh Market with a slightly lower degree of chaos and fewer bargaining opportunities.

Nearly every shop in this neighborhood has a section devoted to travel necessities like outlet adapters, headphones, backpacks, sleeping bags, and camera gear. It's also a good spot for buying bootleg DVDs and boxed sets, as well as English-language books. Shops are open from early morning to late at night. If you see a price tag on an item, it is not up for negotiation. If the product does not have a listed price, there is a chance you can bargain.

The **Ginkgo Concept Store** (254 De Tham, D1, tel. 028/3838-6161, www.ginkgovietnam.com, 8am-10pm daily) sells well-made, locally produced souvenirs like buffalo horn jewelry and lacquer dishware, in addition to its signature T-shirt line. The company is a fair-trade enterprise, so the higher prices for T-shirts go to providing workers with a sustainable living. There is a second location (54-56 Bui Vien, D1, tel. 028/3837-3077, www.ginkgo-vietnam.com, 8am-10pm

street vendors

Pham Ngu Lao Street

daily) in the Pham Ngu Lao area as well as a larger location on Le Loi (92-96 Le Loi, D1, tel. 028/3823-4099, www.ginkgo-vietnam.com, 8:30am-10pm daily).

On Bui Vien is a massive sign advertising "Old Propaganda Posters." This is the **Hanoi Gallery** (79 Bui Vien, D1, 9am-8pm daily), where high-quality reproductions of Communist propaganda are sold at bargain prices. Prices aren't listed on the items, so it's possible to bargain, especially if you purchase more than one. Take a peek upstairs, where there are more prints available for sale. Beware of "original" posters: There are

very few remaining originals left in Vietnam. Chances are it's just a good reproduction for several times the normal cost.

Dong Khoi Street

Beginning at Notre Dame Cathedral and running south toward the Saigon River, **Dong Khoi** and the maze of narrow streets that surround it are full of interesting and unique local handicrafts, antiques, and artwork, and a handful of local designers specializing in silk and other fine fabrics.

A prominent part of the city's current skyline, the **Vincom Center B** (72 Le Thanh

Ton, tel. 028/3936-9999, www.vincom.com.vn, 9:30am-10pm daily) houses several notable Western brands like Zara, Marks & Spencer, and Yves Rocher as well as homegrown retailers. Though you wouldn't guess it from the outside, Vincom's shopping facilities are surprisingly large, with several underground floors that offer shopping, a food court, and a supermarket.

Crisp white walls, exposed lightbulbs, and an industrial decor make **L'Usine** (151/1 Dong Khoi, D1, tel. 028/6674-3565, www.lusinespace.com, 7:30am-10:30pm daily) the city's center of cool. This café-restaurant-boutique sells a variety of men's and women's clothing as well as Lomography cameras, shoes, and jewelry. Housed in a French colonial building, L'Usine pulls its look into the 21st century with an eclectic clothing selection, drawing upon contemporary designers from Vietnam, Europe, and beyond. Prices are quite high for Vietnam, but the shop also stocks a unique range of products. L'Usine also has a second location (70 Le Loi, D1, tel. 028/3521-0702, 7:30am-10:30pm daily) closer to Ben Thanh Market as well as an outlet (19 Le Thanh Ton, D1, tel. 028/3822-7138, 7:30am-10:30pm daily) near the city's Japanese neighborhood.

Nga Art & Craft (91 Le Thanh Ton, D1, tel. 028/3823-8356, www.huongngafinearts.vn, 8am-9pm daily) provides home furnishings in unique designs and colors, adding contemporary flair to the age-old lacquer-ware tradition. After harvesting, pieces undergo a lengthy lacquering process—even something as small as a tray requires at least 75 days to create. The resulting products are unique and durable. Larger items like dressers and coffee tables can be purchased and shipped, but there are plenty of smaller creations like dishes, paintings, and frames.

For beautifully made ceramics, **Authentique Interiors** (71/1 Mac Thi Buoi, D1, tel. 028/3823-8811, www.authentique-home.com, 9am-9pm daily) produces and sells plates, bowls, and teapots, from simple monochromatic sets to intricately patterned pieces. Downstairs is kitchenware, including utensils, while upstairs holds a small selection of bedding and table runners. Items are affordable and high in quality. The shop also has a second location (113 Le Thanh Ton, D1, tel. 028/3822-8052, 9am-9pm daily).

Nguyen Trai Street

From morning to night you'll see the flashing lights of **Nguyen Trai** advertising brand-name clothes as well as knock-off handbags and other bargain items. Companies like The Gap, Banana Republic, and Nike have factories in Vietnam, so there are lots of discounted clothes here that are either the real deal or a good imitation of it. Brand names from other Asian countries also make an appearance on this stretch, particularly closer to the backpacker area. In addition to air-conditioned stores and shopping malls, vendors set up along the sidewalk, hawking helmets, shoes, purses, and other goods. This is a decidedly more local shopping area, with lower prices but also Vietnamese-only sizes; if you're taller than the average local, you might need to stick to the tourist trail.

Roughly a block away from the massive roundabout that houses Vietnam's original Starbucks location, **Zen Plaza** (54-56 Nguyen Trai, D1, tel. 028/3925-0339, www.zenplaza.com.vn, 9:30am-10pm daily) is an eclectic combination of Asian brands packed into a tall narrow building. With loads of women's and men's clothing, some from major brands like Nike and others from small designer labels, this shopping mall is compact, unique, and close to Pham Ngu Lao and the shopping street of Nguyen Trai, making it worth a quick visit.

Hai Ba Trung Street

Busy **Hai Ba Trung** offers a more local collection of shops. Here, you'll find a large selection of fabrics in and around Tan Dinh Market, whose southern side faces a row of tailors capable of stitching together anything from men's suits and women's dresses to *ao dai* (the traditional garment of Vietnam). This area is particularly well known for its fabrics, but there are also shops dedicated to skin care and ready-made clothes. Farther down the road, **Saigon Square 3** (179-183 Hai Ba Trung, D1, 9am-9pm daily) is bustling day and night with local shoppers.

Sports and Recreation

Though it's not an especially sporty place and the great outdoors are rare, Saigon maintains its fair share of parks, swimming pools, and day spas, all of which offer a great way to unwind and experience local culture.

PARKS

Saigon's parks are oases amid a chaotic urban landscape. It's worth paying a visit to these well-manicured green spaces in the morning, when locals flock to the park for their daily exercise. Men stretch and practice tai chi while groups of women gather around a massive speaker on wheels, bouncing to the beat of techno music during their daily aerobics class. Still more groups hone other skills, from martial arts to ballroom dancing, or play a rousing game of badminton.

Tao Dan Park

One of the larger parks in District 1, **Tao Dan Park** (Truong Dinh and Nguyen Thi Minh Khai, D1), is bisected by the fast-paced traffic of Truong Dinh. The park stays busy from dawn to dusk, but the early hours are particularly hectic, with locals tracing the paths that loop around the park. On the western side, foliage helps to shelter the grounds from traffic.

Manicured topiaries line the walkway up to the Hung Kings Temple at the center of the grounds. Flanked by two dragons sculpted out of the greenery, this temple is an homage to the first kings of Vietnam, who ruled during the Hong Bang dynasty (2879-258 BC). The temple is small but popular. Visitors come to burn incense or offer fruit.

Tao Dan Park

To the east, the sidewalk winds through a series of angular stone statues. It's a quiet, pleasant change from the mayhem of traffic that buzzes outside its grounds.

23-9 Park

Sandwiched between Pham Ngu Lao and Ben Thanh Market, **23-9 Park** (Pham Ngu Lao and Nguyen Thi Nghia, D1), also known as Lover's Park, holds regular events, from food festivals and cultural performances to dance recitals and concerts. While locals sometimes use it for their morning exercise routines, this park sees the most activity at night, when young Vietnamese gather here. The long, narrow grounds are sometimes occupied by local students hoping to practice their English with a foreigner; you are sure to attract at least one conversation partner if you decide to sit beside the lotus pond. Just beside the park is **Sense Market** (23-9 Park, tel. 028/3836-4057, ext. 100, 10am-10:30pm daily), an underground food court and shopping complex.

Le Van Tam Park

Farther north and east in District 1 is **Le Van Tam Park** (Hai Ba Trung and Dien Bien Phu, D1), one of the nicer fresh-air spots downtown. Le Van Tam maintains beautiful well-kept grounds that can be a peaceful escape from the din of the surrounding streets. A long flowered walkway leads to the park's main gathering area, at the center of which stands a large Communist-era statue. At the back of the park are a handful of coffee stalls and a playground. At time of writing, half the park was cordoned off for metro construction, which is expected to take several years.

This park is named after national hero Le Van Tam, who, as a teenager, dressed in gasoline-soaked garments and lit himself on fire before running into a gasoline depot owned by the French, destroying the structure in protest of colonial rule. It has since been revealed that the story was propaganda invented to boost public support of the anticolonial revolutionary cause.

30-4 Park

Bordered on one side by the sweeping grounds of the Reunification Palace and on the other side by the imposing structure of Notre Dame Cathedral, **30-4 Park** (Nam Ky Khoi Nghia and Le Duan, D1) is a lush, green area zigzagged with walkways and park benches where young people gather to enjoy a *ca phe bet* (sidewalk coffee) or mid-afternoon snack in the shade.

AMUSEMENT PARKS

To cool off and get away from the noise and chaos of city traffic, pay a visit to **Dam Sen Water Park** (3 Hoa Binh, D11, tel. 028/3858-8418, www.damsenwaterpark.com.vn, 8am-6pm Sat.-Thurs., 9am-6pm Fri., VND160,000). The huge venue, located northwest of the city center, boasts a well-manicured wooded area as well as a water park, where local and foreign visitors flock on hot days to enjoy the slides, rides, and cool water of the wave pool. All rides are supervised by park staff, and changing rooms are available. The cost of entry goes down after 4pm (VND140,000), though it's better to make an afternoon of the trip, as Dam Sen is far from downtown. There is also an on-site restaurant.

SWIMMING

The pool at **Van Thanh Tourist Area** (48/10 Dien Bien Phu, D Binh Thanh, tel. 028/3512-3026, 6am-8pm daily, VND70,000-80,000 adults, VND40,000-50,000 children) is the perfect way to escape the city without actually having to leave the city. Hidden down an alley off Dien Bien Phu street in Binh Thanh District, Van Thanh is a pleasant surprise, with lush green lawns and tree-lined walkways that create the illusion that you've left Saigon behind. The pool is clean and big, with a separate, smaller swimming pool for young children, and there are plenty of lounge chairs nearby. Van Thanh has a restaurant and several activities for young kids. The place gets crowded on weekends and holidays.

MASSAGES AND SPAS

Massages are all the rage in Saigon, with dozens of spas located in the District 1 area alone, ranging in price from dirt-cheap to exorbitant. Many hotels and guesthouses also offer spa services, but these are often overpriced and, in truth, you're usually better off visiting a spa on your own. While tipping is not common in restaurants or cafés, it is expected that you offer a 15-20 percent tip to a masseuse or masseur. In some places, masseuses will have a tip form for you to fill out, noting the amount you are giving. While this can be uncomfortable for some—having to write down your tip amount and give it to the masseuse before you pay—it is the norm in many places here.

Less expensive without sacrificing quality, **Hoang Thy Spa** (35 Do Quang Dau, D1, tel. 028/3836-4404, 8am-9pm daily, VND50,000-300,000) is a great spot for a massage or manicure. The facility itself is pretty bare-bones, but the staff are incredibly friendly and the spa's services, from hair and nails to massages, waxing, foot care, masks, and facials, are inexpensive. A manicure or pedicure will set you back around VND50,000, while body massages cost VND120,000-300,000.

If you don't mind venturing a few more blocks outside the backpacker area, **Cabana Health Spa** (36-38 Nguyen Cu Trinh, D1, tel. 028/2220-2132, www.cabana.vn, 9:30am-10:30pm daily, VND50,000-860,000), formerly known as Ngoc Anh Spa, has a range of affordable massage services beginning at VND200,000, tips excluded. This massive building has separate floors for men and women, as well as a sauna and steam room, and the masseuses are well trained and speak some English.

The mid-range **Cat Moc Spa** (61-63 Tran Dinh Xu, D1, tel. 028/6295-8926, www.catmocspa.com, 9am-10pm daily, VND120,000-840,000) is an excellent value. The modest storefront belies the spa's impeccable service. Guests are greeted with a glass of iced tea in the cozy seating area before choosing from massages, body scrubs, facials, hair care, and waxing. The friendly and experienced staff speak English. Afterward, you'll be offered a glass of chanh muoi (lemon juice and salt), a refreshing local treat. Spa packages (VND548,000-1,628,000) are available for those looking to make a day of it.

The cheerful, purple-clad staff at **L'Apothiquaire** (64A Truong Dinh, D3, tel. 028/3932-5181, www.lapothiquaire.com, 9am-9pm daily, VND320,000-1,200,000) carry their own line of skin care products, as well as offering massages, wraps, facials, manicures, pedicures, and waxing services. Packages can be purchased to combine several services for a full day at the spa. Walk-ins are welcome, but book ahead in order to receive the best service possible.

COOKING CLASSES

There are a handful of excellent culinary courses offered in Saigon. Class prices are higher here than other places, so you may be better off waiting, particularly if you are also traveling to central coast cities like Hue and Hoi An.

The most well-known culinary course is **Saigon Cooking Class** (74/7 Hai Ba Trung, D1, tel. 028/3825-8485, www.saigoncookingclass.com, 8am-5pm Tues.-Sun., VND870,000-990,000 adults, VND550,000-616,000 under age 12), which operates out of Hoa Tuc, an upscale Vietnamese restaurant. The three-hour hands-on course teaches students how to prepare a three-course Vietnamese meal, with the dishes changing daily. An English-speaking Vietnamese chef gives instruction. For an extra fee, you can accompany the chef to the market, where he shows students how to select and purchase the necessary ingredients. Classes are capped at 12 people, and children age seven and up are welcome.

For a slightly more affordable option, the **Cyclo Resto Cooking Class** (6/28 Cach Mang Thang 8, D1, tel. 028/6680-4235, www.cycloresto.com.vn, 11am-10pm daily, VND900,000) combines a market visit and cooking class with sightseeing. Ride to the local market in a cyclo, taking in the city as you go, before exploring the stalls of fresh produce and meat. A taxi ferries you back to the cooking center, where you'll learn several dishes from a professional and knowledge-able English-speaking staff. Cyclo Resto has smaller class sizes and more one-on-one interaction.

Food

Saigon is obsessed with food. Everywhere you turn, people are crouched over bowls of noodle soup or picking at fruit and *banh trang tron* (a salad-like mix of rice paper, dried meat, green mango, and seasonings eaten from a plastic bag with chopsticks) in the park. Women hustle across intersections, bamboo poles bouncing beside them, as they carry mobile kitchens from one location to the next; empty stretches of sidewalk become a maze of tiny tables at lunchtime.

While the southern city doesn't have many specialties to call its own, HCMC has man-aged to appropriate the best of Vietnam and the world so that you can find just about any-thing to please your palate. Dine in the quiet garden courtyard of an upscale eatery or share tables with a stranger amid the chaotic buzz of a street food stall—wherever you are, there's a solid chance you'll find yourself going back for seconds.

REUNIFICATION PALACE AREA
Vietnamese

Ngon Restaurant (160 Pasteur, D1, tel. 028/3827-7131, 7:30am-10:30pm daily, VND40,000-200,000) is a tourist favorite and the perfect spot for a crash course on local food, offering every meal under the sun at reasonable prices. This large, colonial-style building boasts spacious seating and gives the restaurant a marketplace feel, with cooks set up along the outer edges of its open-air court-yard so that guests can peruse their options before ordering.

a local sidewalk café

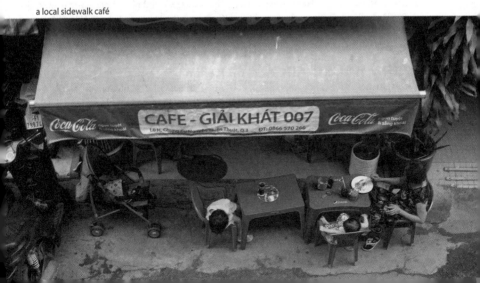

Saigon's Best Meals

- **Pizza 4Ps:** Boasting the city's best pies and a trendy setting, Pizza 4Ps combines fresh ingredients—including homemade artisanal cheeses from its farm in Dalat—to create a menu of both traditional and innovative Neapolitan-style pizzas.

- **Quan Mien Cua 94 Cu:** Amid the bustle of District 1, this long-standing eatery focuses on one main ingredient: soft-shell crab. Whether accompanied by a mountain of glass noodles or steamed in a savory tamarind sauce, this makes for a hearty meal.

- **Street food:** For a primer on the city's roadside dining, check out the famed **Lunch Lady**, who serves up a different Vietnamese noodle soup for lunch every day; swing by **Banh Xeo 46A** for a helping of southern-style *banh xeo*, savory Vietnamese pancakes featuring shrimp, pork, and bean sprouts; or head to Chinatown's **Quan Thien Thien** for the *mi sui cao*, dumplings with egg noodle soup.

Mediterranean

Exactly as the name suggests, **Au Parc** (23 Han Thuyen, D1, tel. 028/3829-2772, www.auparcsaigon.com, 7:30am-11pm daily, VND115,000-295,000) boasts a beautiful location overlooking 30-4 Park. This chic café serves up Mediterranean dishes like hummus, baba ganoush, and shish kebabs. This is also a great place to enjoy a morning coffee or tuck in to either of the Turkish or New York brunches, which are served every weekend. For more local fare, you can also pop in next door at Au Parc's sister restaurant, **Propaganda** (21 Han Thuyen, D1, tel. 028/3822-9048, 7:30am-10:30pm daily, VND50,000-175,000), for fresh spring rolls and modern Vietnamese cuisine.

OPERA HOUSE AREA
Vietnamese

Guests become chefs at **Bo Tung Xeo** (31 Ly Tu Trong, D1, tel. 028/3825-1330, 10am-10pm daily, VND120,000-430,000), a spacious open-air spot, with an extensive menu of do-it-yourself barbecue dishes. Sturdy clay pot fires are brought to your table, along with a grill and a plate of raw meat. Barbecue your own meat as you like it and choose the accompanying side dishes. Stick to tried-and-true beef, fish, and chicken or try crocodile, ostrich, deer tendon, or goat breast. Meals are reasonably priced and the waiters keep a steady flow of Saigon Red coming.

French

Formerly the Saigon Opium Manufacture, **The Refinery** (74 Hai Ba Trung, D1, tel. 028/3823-0509, www.therefinerysaigon.com, 11am-late daily, VND130,000-420,000) has come a long way from its past involvement in the drug trade. The restaurant offers French cuisine and is outfitted in the style of a Parisian bistro. Meals are top-notch, featuring barbecued swordfish, steak frites, gourmet cheeseburgers, and homemade pasta dishes. Come for the weekend brunch (11am-4pm Sat.-Sun.), when a complimentary chocolate fountain occupies the front dining room.

Italian

An affordable white-tablecloth affair, the atmosphere at **Ciao Bella** (11 Dong Du, D1, tel. 028/3822-3329, www.ciaobellavietnam.com, 10am-11pm daily, VND125,000-575,000) is cozy and communal. With New York-style Italian dishes and an intimate dining space, this restaurant prides itself on its diverse menu and constantly changing list of specials, featuring old favorites such as spaghetti al pomodoro and chicken parmesan as well as more unique dishes. Entrées are generous, and servers are attentive. A nice wine selection is also on offer.

Pizza

With hip European decor and an excellent handle on Italian food, ★ **Pizza 4Ps** (8/15 Le Thanh Ton, D1, tel. 028/3622-0500, www. pizza4ps.com, 10am-11pm daily, VND90,000-420,000) is, surprisingly, a Japanese creation. Only when you flip past the margherita and quattro formaggi to toppings like calamari seaweed and salmon miso cream do the restaurant's roots become apparent. Meals at 4Ps are more expensive than other local Italian places, but the extra cost is worth it. Book a table before you go, as this is one of the only places in town that requires a reservation. You can also grab a pie at the **Ben Thanh location** (8 Thu Khoa Huan, D1, tel. 028/3622-0500, 10am-2am Mon.-Sat., 10am-11pm Sun., VND90,000-420,000).

NGUYEN HUE STREET
Vietnamese

The narrow corridor leading up to the **Temple Club** (29-31 Ton That Thiep, D1, tel. 028/3829-9244, www.templeclub.com.vn, noon-midnight daily, VND140,000-285,000) is a step back in time. Lined with white elephant statues and Chinese wood carvings, the red-tiled entryway leads to an opulent dining room, where dark wooden furniture and deep red curtains create an old-world feel. The menu features expertly prepared Vietnamese, Chinese, Khmer, and French cuisine. Though prices are slightly higher than other local restaurants, the upscale atmosphere and food are worth it. Book a table before going, as dinnertime can be very busy.

Japanese

Expensive, but worth every penny, **Nhan Sushi** (62 Ngo Duc Ke, D1, tel. 028/3915-2280, nhansushibito@gmail.com, 11am-2pm and 5pm-11pm Mon.-Fri., 10am-2:30pm and 5pm-11:30pm Sat.-Sun., VND75,000-350,000) is a tiny restaurant opposite the Bitexco Tower. Its menu features an impressive list of authentic Japanese fare, including a handful of excellent lunch sets. Reservations are a good idea

in the evenings, as the place fills up once the work day ends.

Thai

Squeezed down a narrow alley off Mac Thi Buoi, **Lac Thai** (71/2-71/3 Mac Thi Buoi, D1, tel. 028/3823-7506, www.lacthairestaurant.com, 10am-2pm and 5pm-10pm daily, VND130,000-280,000) offers some of the most authentic Thai food in the city. From noodles and tom yum soup to Thai curries, the menu runs from conventional to unexpected, and the intimate dining area is decked out in plush sofas and low tables. Both upstairs and downstairs seating are available. Its hidden location gives the place a serene, laid-back vibe.

BEN THANH MARKET AREA
French

Just behind Ben Thanh Market is the French-owned and operated **Une Journee A Paris** (234 Le Thanh Ton, D1, tel. 028/3827-7723, www.une-journee-a-paris.com, 7am-7pm Mon.-Sat., 7am-2:30pm Sun., VND80,000-200,000), a Parisian-style bakery and sandwich shop decked out in pink and purple. Its glass display case features *pain au chocolat* and croissants as well as cakes, all of which are made fresh. Sandwiches are served on European-style baguettes.

Cafés and Bakeries

Calm, cool, and centrally located, **ID Cafe** (34D Thu Khoa Huan, D1, tel. 028/3822-2910, www.idcafe.net, 7am-11:30pm daily, VND35,000-150,000) is a trendy café not far from Ben Thanh Market that is popular among locals and foreigners. Customers gather around its solid wood tables for coffee, smoothies, and decent Vietnamese food. Vintage records decorate the walls and mood music plays in the background, adding to the laid-back vibe. There is also a larger **second location** (61B Tu Xuong, D3, tel. 028/3932-0021, 7am-11:30pm daily) in District 3.

It only takes two words to convince most people to pay a visit to **Maison Marou**

Street Food in Saigon

No trip to Saigon is complete without experiencing its street food. From morning to night, locals crowd around plastic tables and miniature stools on every sidewalk in town. Some of the best food in the city comes from a cart. A visit to these mobile businesses brings you the best of Hue, Nha Trang, Can Tho, or Hanoi, all with a southern twist. People from all walks of life flock to these makeshift eateries for a quick banh mi or a bowl of pho.

There are several good streets where the food masters congregate. **Huynh Man Dat** in District 5, not far from Nguyen Trai, does a fair turn in Chinese-style street food, while **Nguyen Thuong Hien** in District 3, north of Nguyen Thi Minh Khai, is a popular street for delicious rice and noodle dishes. The stalls of District 1's **Co Giang,** south of Pham Ngu Lao Street, are also packed with local favorites that are both delicious and easy on the wallet.

Eating street food can be safer than dining in a local restaurant. Because the kitchen is visible and the meal you're about to enjoy is already on display, you can tell whether or not the cart in question is clean, safe, and worth a visit. Street food is best consumed hot; things like soups are a solid choice because the broth is cooking constantly, but anything being prepared on the spot rather than sitting out in metal trays is likely a safer choice. Also, there's safety in numbers: Any street food venue that's packed with diners is usually a good choice. In some cases, you can also hang around for a moment near the street cart and just observe how the vendor handles the food (for instance, using plastic gloves or tongs rather than bare hands). Rice stalls usually receive most of their business around lunch time, so even though their prepared food is sitting out, it's generally fine around midday hours (11am-1pm) but probably worth skipping in the mid- to late afternoon.

(167-169 Calmette, D1, tel. 028/7300-5010, www.maisonmarou.com, 8am-10pm daily, VND70,000-200,000): fresh chocolate. Founded by two French transplants, Marou's single-origin chocolate bars have become famous in the country and abroad, springboarding Vietnam's cacao industry onto the global stage. Not far from the Fine Arts Museum and Ben Thanh Market, the gourmet café stocks all of Marou's signature single-origin products and a few flavored bars, as well as has a patisserie full of decadent chocolate desserts and other creations.

PHAM NGU LAO STREET
Indian

The masterful chefs at **Baba's Kitchen** (164 Bui Vien, D1, tel. 028/3838-6661, www.babaskitchen.in, 11am-10:30pm daily, VND60,000-160,000) supply Saigon with cheap, authentic Indian food smack-dab in the heart of the backpacker district. The menu lists standard Indian fare, including masalas, curries, dals, and vindaloos, and everything is made in-house, including the paneer. Though there are a couple of more upscale Indian ventures in town, this is the best.

Vegetarian

The An Lac Pagoda, located in Pham Ngu Lao, has drawn a handful of vegetarian restaurants into the area, including **Ngoc Tho** (175/9 Pham Ngu Lao, D1, tel. 028/3836-0162, 8am-11pm daily, VND30,000-300,000). This no-frills eatery churns out delicious meat-free Vietnamese food, and has recently expanded its menu to include Western dishes and some carnivorous fare.

Western

A narrow, barely there shop on the far side of Pham Ngu Lao, the **Hungry Pig** (144 Cong Quynh, D1, tel. 028/3836-4533, 7am-9pm daily, VND70,000-150,000) shows great potential with its varied lineup of bacon sandwiches. Beyond the fat pink pig emblazoned across the shop's awning, a large menu on the back wall lists sandwich combinations as well as a build-your-own menu with different types of bacon, cheese, veggies, and sauces. Solid iron-and-wood picnic-style furniture takes up most of the space indoors and out. The walls feature antique black-and-white portraits of—you guessed it—pigs.

NORTHERN DISTRICT 1
Vietnamese
★ **Quan Mien Cua 94 Cu** (84 Dinh Tien Hoang, D1, tel. 028/3910-1062, 10am-10pm daily, VND80,000-500,000) is a well-known local spot that specializes in soft-shell crab. A row of live crabs sits outside the storefront, waiting to be turned into soup or spring rolls, fried or steamed. The *mien xao cua* (crab with glass noodles) and tamarind soft-shell crab are particularly noteworthy. Note a few impostors are located nearby; Quan Mien Cua 94 Cu is the shop just before the corner, not directly on it.

Cuc Gach Quan (9-10 Dang Tat, D1, tel. 028/3848-0144, www.cucgachquan.com.vn, 9am-11:30pm daily, VND80,000-220,000) is a return to the basics. Inspired by his grandmother's street food stall, owner and architect Tran Binh transformed this French colonial house into an intimate restaurant serving traditional countryside fare. Each meal is arranged on antique earthenware dishes, and chopsticks are kept in recycled milk tins. The menu may overwhelm, but knowledgeable servers will recommend dishes like pork stewed in a clay pot, morning glory sautéed in garlic, or homemade fried tofu with chili and lemongrass. Binh's pledge to "eat green, live healthy," means that ingredients are all natural, down to the drinking straws, which are hollow vegetables. All meals are served family-style.

★ Street Food
Ever since Anthony Bourdain visited HCMC in 2009, Nguyen Thi Thanh, better known as ★ **The Lunch Lady** (23 Hoang Sa, D1, from 11am daily, VND40,000-50,000), has become a local celebrity. Her cart, at the edge of a clearing not far from the Saigon Zoo, serves up a different soup every day, from spicy *bun bo Hue* (soup with beef and rice noodles) to pho or Cambodian-style *hu tieu* (rice noodle soup). Around noon the sidewalk becomes a mess of diners hoping to get a bowl. The Lunch Lady has no set closing time and sells her soup until it's sold out: Arrive no later than mid-afternoon.

Just north of the massive Tan Dinh Church is **Tan Dinh Market** (Hai Ba Trung and Nguyen Huu Cau, D1, 6am-6pm daily, VND20,000-75,000), which houses several food stalls along Nguyen Huu Cau. A variety of local dishes are available, including vegetarian fare, as well as juices and smoothies. One of its best offerings is *banh canh cua* (crab soup with thick, rope-like rice noodles).

The namesake specialty at ★ **Banh Xeo 46A** (46A Dinh Cong Trang, D1, tel. 028/3824-1110, 10am-2pm and 4pm-9pm daily, VND60,000-180,000) is the star here. Cooks crouch over piping hot pans, dishing up large *banh xeo* (southern-style Vietnamese pancakes). A deft waiter will rush over with a pile of fresh greens, fish sauce, and pickled vegetables, and from there it's up to you. Roll your pancakes up in the accompanying lettuce leaves, throw in a few herbs for flavor, dip in fish sauce, and enjoy. The pancakes come in regular and large sizes and can easily be split between two people. A handful of other items, like fresh and fried spring rolls and barbecued meat, are also available.

Vegetarian
With an emphasis on Buddhist tenets and healthy living, the folks at **Lau Nam Chay An Nhien** (94 Nguyen Van Thu, D1, tel. 028/3910-1129, www.launamchayannhien. com, 9:30am-9:30pm daily, VND30,000-250,000) create delicious vegetarian dishes without mock meat or any artificial products, instead using mushrooms and other all-natural ingredients. The menu runs the gamut from spring rolls and southern specialties like *hu tieu My Tho* (rice noodle soup) to a

meatless hot pot and an excellent, aromatic rendition of pho. The dining area is clean, spacious, quiet, and comfortable. Best of all, prices are affordable, with most one-person dishes no more than VND50,000.

DISTRICT 3
Vietnamese

Slightly removed from downtown, **Quan Dat** (16 Truong Dinh, D3, tel. 028/3843-7390, 10am-10pm daily, VND70,000-200,000) serves incredible, affordable meals to a local crowd. Mastering the art of Phan Rang cuisine, seafood-infused southern food featuring a savory peanut sauce, Quan Dat's most popular dishes are *banh can* (small egg-and-rice-flour cakes topped with meat or seafood) and a smaller seafood version of *banh xeo* (savory Vietnamese pancakes). Sit downstairs near the window overlooking the street or in the spacious second-floor dining area, where wooden tables and chairs line the room.

Cafés and Bakeries

An extension of the Fly Cupcakes chain, **Fly Garden** (25A Tu Xuong, D3, tel. 028/3932-2299, 7am-11pm daily, VND40,000-130,000) is a cross between a Western coffee shop and a Vietnamese *san vuon* (garden) café. The

bakery, lined with stringed lights in cupcake wrappers, offers sweets like cream puffs, tarts, and cupcakes. The wall of vines outside brings a hint of green to the city, while inside the whimsical decor and mellow music make this a pleasant place to unwind. There is an eclectic food menu featuring Vietnamese, Western, and Japanese items.

A local institution, the perpetually busy **Sinh To 142** (142 Ly Chinh Thang, D3, tel. 028/3848-3574, www.sinhto142.vn, 8am-11pm daily, VND20,000-50,000) is exactly like a local café but without the coffee. From sunup to sundown, this open-front shop slings an assortment of fresh smoothies and juices, ranging from conventional single-fruit drinks to more unusual combinations, like avocado-mung bean, tomato-mango, or the deceptively delicious carrot-coconut.

Japanese

For cheap Japanese cuisine, visit **Tokyo Deli** (187 Dien Bien Phu, D1, tel. 028/3827-7755, www.tokyodeli.com.vn, 11am-10pm daily, VND40,000-180,000), a popular sushi chain with multiple locations around Districts 1 and 3. These large restaurants have prix-fixe lunches (about VND100,000) and also offer an à la carte menu throughout the day. The

Quan Dat restaurant

service isn't stellar, but the space is nice and the prices worthwhile.

Vegetarian

Located inside the grounds of the Vinh Nghiem temple, **Vinh Nghiem Vegetarian Restaurant** (339 Nam Ky Khoi Nghia, D3, tel. 028/3848-1829, www.vinhnghiemchay. vn, 7am-8pm daily, VND40,000-120,000) is one of the city's best-known vegetarian restaurants and, due to its location, also one of the more peaceful places to sit and have a quiet meal. The restaurant serves up a range of Vietnamese dishes without the meat, including soups, tofu, and fried rice options.

With its placid courtyard and back-to-basics philosophy, **...hum** (32 Vo Van Tan, D3, tel. 028/3930-3819, www.humvietnam. vn, 10am-10pm daily, VND65,000-180,000) is a pleasant escape from the roar of the city. Concealed by a high wall, a floating walkway leads over a mossy pond and into the courtyard. The decor is simple, with wooden furniture and chopsticks wrapped in pandan leaves. The menu lists tofu and vegetable dishes, and explains the specific health benefits of each meal. The spring rolls and spicy tofu are especially good. In addition to the flagship location, a slightly trendier lounge downtown (2 Thi Sach, D1, tel. 028/3823-8920, 10am-10pm daily, VND65,000-180,000) also serves the same delicious dishes in a hip setting.

CHO LON
★ Street Food

Well off the beaten path and a challenge to find, **Ca Ri De Musa** (001 Bldg. B, Su Van Hanh Apts., D5, tel. 028/3833-9167, 10am-11pm daily, VND50,000-150,000) is a small bustling eatery that does an excellent rendition of *ca ri de* (goat curry). Take a seat at one of the many metal tables indoors or out and tuck into a hearty helping of the dish, accompanied by a baguette. Foreigners are few here, so you might draw attention during your visit. To find the restaurant, look for the flashing red-and-blue sign reading "Ca Ri An Do" beside 202A Su Van Hanh.

On a street packed with dumpling shops and touts waving at passersby, the ★ **Chinese noodles** (193 Ha Ton Quyen, D11, 11am-midnight daily, VND15,000-50,000) at **Quan Thien Thien** are the best of the best. Order a piping hot bowl of *mi sui cao* (dumplings with egg noodle soup) with Chinese-style dumplings and take in the bustling chaos of this eating street. The shop—which has tables on both sides of the street due to the high volume of customers—is out of the way, but the reward is an authentic mouthwatering bowl of noodles. Make sure to grab a *tra hong* (sweet tea) to go with your meal.

Vegetarian

Off the beaten path, **Tiem Chay Tuong Vien** (58-62 Huynh Man Dat, D5, tel. 028/6275-8938, 6am-9pm daily, VND25,000-50,000) is like any local restaurant but for its lack of pork, beef, or chicken. This humble shop serves everything from mock-meat barbecue to vegetarian pho and Chinese-style stir-fried noodles. Prices are easy on the wallet, and at lunchtime you'll find impressive mock-meat renditions of many Vietnamese dishes, including vegetarian clay-pot catfish and barbecued pork. Their menu does not have an English version; just point at what you want to order.

Accommodations

From the bare-bones hostels hidden down the alleys off Pham Ngu Lao to the high-end hotels overlooking the Saigon River, accommodations in HCMC run the spectrum. Dorm beds cost as little as VND100,000, while the peak of luxury will set you back several hundred dollars.

Base yourself in District 1, where the majority of the city's sights, shopping, restaurants, and English-speaking services are located. Due to the many hotels in this area, making a reservation is usually unnecessary, though you may want to check availability ahead of time if you're in town during a holiday.

Most budget travelers base themselves in Pham Ngu Lao, the backpacker neighborhood. Just outside of the backpacker area, Nguyen Trai is an excellent choice if you're looking to get away from the nonstop noise of Pham Ngu Lao but still remain close to the heart of downtown. Mid-range accommodations are packed onto the streets around Ben Thanh Market. Several historic five-star hotels are close to the Opera House.

Light sleepers should be extra selective, as Saigon's noise pollution is second to none. Hotels located in alleys tend to be quieter than those on the street. Conversely, hotels on busy streets are safer at night, where front doors are more visible and well lit.

If rates are listed higher than VND500,000, check if the hotel gives a discount for booking ahead of time. Budget accommodations often discount their rates for someone walking in off the street in order to fill rooms.

OPERA HOUSE AREA
VND525,000-1,050,000

Clean and spacious, rooms at the **Tan Hoang Long Hotel** (84 Mac Thi Buoi, D1, tel. 028/3827-0006, www.tanhoanglong-hotel.com, VND980,000-1,590,000, breakfast included) are a good value, with plenty of natural light and a private working desk as well as daily coffee, tea, and bottled water. In some of the larger rooms, sofas and street views are available. The staff is courteous and the hotel's location is close to the downtown shopping area, Dong Khoi, and the market.

VND1,050,000-2,100,000

Boasting colorful decor and large rooms, the ★ **Saigon River Boutique Hotel** (58 Mac Thi Buoi, D1, tel. 028/3822-8558, www.saigon-riverhotel.com, VND885,000-1,890,000) provides more upscale lodgings with an exceptional level of service and cleanliness, with modern facilities and amiable staff. Each room includes a safe, cable TV, free Wi-Fi, toiletries, and air-conditioning. For a bit more, you can get a room with a balcony at the front of the hotel, where there are nice views of the street below. The hotel has a restaurant serving Asian and Western dishes as well as a rooftop bar and café.

Over VND2,100,000

The five-star **Hotel Majestic** (1 Dong Khoi, D1, tel. 028/3829-5517, www.majesticsaigon.com, VND3,970,000-17,000,000) has been in business since 1925, located at the intersection of Ton Duc Thang and Dong Khoi, formerly the famous Rue Catinat. The stunning arches and ornate detail of the building's exterior are a fitting welcome. The interior boasts equally impressive decor, with rich wooden surfaces and opulent antique furniture. Riverview rooms include a balcony, and each room comes equipped with a safe and spacious marble baths. The hotel has fitness facilities, a serene outdoor swimming pool, and the grandiose Catinat Lounge.

The Rex Hotel (141 Nguyen Hue, D1, tel. 028/3829-2185, www.rexhotelvietnam.com, VND2,860,000-20,450,000, breakfast included) is a Saigon institution. Topped with its iconic crown and featuring high-end

Saigon's Best Hotels

- **Saigon River Boutique Hotel:** The staff at this charming abode goes above and beyond to make guests feel welcome.

- **Hong Han Hotel:** An oasis of relative calm amid the chaos of the city's backpacker district, this budget option is a find with its central location, comfortable beds, charming communal balcony, and friendly staff.

- **NN99 Hotel:** In a prime location not far from Pham Ngu Lao's best nightlife, NN99 offers proximity to all the action as well as cozy, affordable rooms and an easygoing staff eager to help.

- **Town House 50:** Accommodations here manage to be both cost-effective and stylish, with well-appointed dorm rooms and bright, colorful design.

- **Cinnamon Hotel Saigon:** From its elegant and inviting reception area to the beautiful, spacious, cinnamon-scented rooms, this swanky red-and-black hotel stands apart in many ways.

designer shops on the ground floor, the Rex is best known as the site of daily press briefings from the American Information Service during the Vietnam War. The deluxe hotel boasts 286 rooms as well as a top-notch spa and fitness center, a rooftop pool and bar, and several restaurants. Each room comes with plush queen or king beds, shower and bathtub, and daily newspaper service.

On the far side of the Central Post Office, the beautifully furnished **InterContinental Saigon** (Corner Hai Ba Trung and Le Duan, tel. 028/3520-9999, www.intercontinental.com/saigon, VND3,700,000-44,600,000) features modern facilities with an Asian-inspired decor. Its sleek guest rooms boast plush beds and spacious baths. The hotel features on-site fitness facilities, a concierge, room service, and a rooftop swimming pool. Next door, the Kumho Asiana Plaza offers a variety of restaurants and high-end shopping.

Beside the Opera House, the **Caravelle Saigon** (19-23 Lam Son Square, D1, tel. 028/3823-4999, www.caravellehotel.com, VND4,065,000-10,700,000) is one of the city's largest and best-known five-star hotels. In the heart of downtown, this enormous building served as a meeting place for foreign journalists during the war. The original 10-story structure has been joined with a larger 24-floor tower. The well-known Saigon Saigon Bar is found on the roof of the smaller building. The Caravelle boasts 335 guest rooms, as well as six different eating and drinking venues, a spa, pool, and fitness center. Deluxe rooms are plush and comfortable and include standard amenities. Higher-end rooms on the Signature Floor include breakfast and evening cocktails, and spacious suites have sweeping views of the city and a comfortable living room.

BEN THANH MARKET AREA
VND525,000-1,050,000

Down a side street is **Vuong Tai Hotel** (20 Luu Van Lang, D1, tel. 028/3521-8597, vuongtaihotel@gmail.com, VND905,000-1,125,000, breakfast included), which offers service well above its two-star label. Rooms range from deluxe to VIP and include complimentary bottled water, cable TV, and a safe. Higher-end rooms feature bathtubs and a desk. All guest rooms have windows.

VND1,050,000-2,100,000

A high-quality three-star facility, the **Alagon Western** (28-30 Nguyen An Ninh, D1, tel.

028/3823-2999, www.alagonhotels.com, VND1,130,000-2,485,000, breakfast included) boasts well-appointed rooms with contemporary decor and modern facilities. Larger rooms include a small sitting area as well as city views and standard amenities like air-conditioning and toiletries.

The bright and spacious **Sanouva Hotel** (177 Ly Tu Trong, D1, tel. 028/3827-5275, www.sanouvahotel.com, VND1,310,000-2,500,000, breakfast included) is close enough to Ben Thanh to be convenient without the added noise that comes with staying directly beside the market. Each room has natural light, as well as chic contemporary decor, large baths, and the usual amenities, including toiletries and cable TV. Larger rooms feature a small sitting area. The staff is exceptionally helpful.

Rooms at the **Blue Diamond Hotel** (48-50 Thu Khoa Huan, D1, tel. 028/3823-6167, www.bluediamondhotel.com.vn, VND1,150,000-3,220,000, breakfast included), just north of the market, are spacious with plush, cozy beds and plenty of natural light. All rooms include a large bath with a bathtub, a daily newspaper, free Wi-Fi, air-conditioning, and complimentary bottled water, tea, and coffee. A small fitness center is available, as are professional foot massages. The on-site restaurant serves Vietnamese and Western cuisine.

The **Lan Lan 2 Hotel** (46-46bis Thu Khoa Huan, D1, tel. 028/3822-7926, www.lanlanhotel.com.vn, VND960,000-2,380,000, breakfast included) boasts five different types of rooms, from small but adequate standard rooms to large suites. The hotel is decorated in dark wood and rich colors. Each of its 100-plus rooms includes cable TV and air-conditioning. The hotel also has a small fitness center, a restaurant, room service, and laundry.

PHAM NGU LAO STREET

Pham Ngu Lao is the most inexpensive area to stay, although it is also party central. The main streets in the backpacker area—De Tham, Bui Vien, and Pham Ngu Lao, along with their respective alleys—are brimming with budget hotels that do most of their business in walk-in customers.

Pham Ngu Lao is a loud and happening place morning, noon, and night. Don't shell out more than VND1,000,000 per night for hotels in this area. For more upscale rooms, head to the Ben Thanh Market area or downtown, where there is a little more flash and a little less debauchery.

The Rex Hotel

Hong Han Hotel

Under VND210,000

Hidden in one of Pham Ngu Lao's alleys, the **Saigon Youth Hostel** (241/32 Pham Ngu Lao, D1, tel. 028/3920-3665, www. saigonyouthhostel.com, VND140,000 dorm, VND340,000-455,000 d, breakfast included) has mixed and all-female dorms, as well as private single and double rooms. Clean and comfy beds are available, and the hostel provides lockers for dorm guests and each private room features an en suite bath with hot water. Two computers are available for guest use, and the common room is well stocked with DVDs, reading material, and a foosball table.

The entrance to alley 373 of Pham Ngu Lao is down the road from the heart of the backpacker area. The beds and staff at **Phan Anh Hostel** (373/6 Pham Ngu Lao, D1, tel. 028/3920-9235, www.phananhback-packershostel.com, VND185,000 dorm, VND545,000-680,000 d, breakfast included) make it worth the walk. Clean, comfortable, and reasonably priced, each room features basic amenities, including air-conditioning

and free Wi-Fi. The eight-bed dormitories have en suite baths and lockers, and there is a common room with a flat-screen TV. Unlike other hostels, Phan Anh has an elevator.

VND210,000-525,000

★ **Hong Han Hotel** (238 Bui Vien, D1, tel. 028/3836-1927, www.hochiminhguesthouse. com, VND500,000-710,000, breakfast included) offers clean and spacious rooms as well as a nice communal balcony. The guesthouse has a variety of room options, from double and twin beds to triple rooms, all of which have air-conditioning, hot water, cable TV, and free Wi-Fi. The staff goes out of their way to be hospitable and are happy to offer advice and local recommendations.

Though the rooms are not as modern or well-appointed as others in town, the staff and value at **Ava Saigon 2** (126 De Tham, D1, tel. 028/3920-8647, www.avasaigon.com, VND390,000-860,000, breakfast included) make it a nice place. The hotel offers complimentary laundry services, international phone calls, and Wi-Fi. Ava 2 is located just across Tran Hung Dao, close to the backpacker area without being directly at the center of the noise. Though there are cheaper standard rooms available, spring for a room with a window, as it's a better deal.

VND525,000-1,050,000

Away from the heart of the backpacker area, the **Yellow House Saigon Hotel** (114/32 De Tham, D1, tel. 028/3920-6503, yellowhouse-hotel@gmail.com, VND725,000-945,000) boasts a plethora of options, from standard rooms (with or without a window) to spacious superior and deluxe offerings. Standard rooms are smaller than average, but the baths are larger. Upgrade to a superior for more space and light.

Rooms at the ★ **NN99 Hotel** (99 Bui Vien, D1, tel. 028/3836-9723, www.nn99ho-tel.com, VND550,000-750,000) are a steal. Though small, NN99 features large beds, cable TV, air-conditioning, and modern decor. The staff is helpful and attentive. In addition to free Wi-Fi throughout the building, there is a computer in the lobby for guest use. Don't bother spending the extra money for a room with a balcony, as it's small.

The **Beautiful Saigon Hotel** (62 Bui Vien, D1, tel. 028/3836-4852, www.beautiful-saigonhotel.com, VND680,000-1,600,000) is a good value with modern, if small, rooms. Each room comes equipped with cable TV and air-conditioning, and has a window. The hotel is on the main drag, so opt for a higher floor for quiet. The superior and deluxe rooms have in-room computers, bathtubs, and complimentary fruit baskets. As part of a larger hotel chain, guests also have access to a swimming pool down the road at Beautiful Saigon Boutique Hotel.

Though there are clean, comfortable rooms and a nice reception area, it is the staff that makes the experience at **Nguyen Khang Hotel** (283/25 Pham Ngu Lao, D1, tel. 028/3837-3566, nguyenkhanghotel283@gmail.com, VND410,000-795,000). Down an alley, removed from the city noise, Nguyen Khang has rooms with and without windows as well as free Wi-Fi, cable TV, and air-conditioning. The friendly receptionists can recommend restaurants and activities. Book in advance, as the hotel's 15 rooms fill up quickly.

With the assurance that it's "not an ordinary one-star hotel," the **Cat Huy Hotel** (353/28 Pham Ngu Lao, D1, tel. 028/3920-8716, www.cathuyhotel.com, VND685,000-820,000, breakfast included) does not disappoint. Featuring large, well-decorated rooms and impeccable service, this family-owned mini-hotel is an excellent spot, near enough to the backpacker area but tucked down an alley. All rooms have air-conditioning, free Wi-Fi, and cable TV. The hotel also offers services such as laundry and travel arrangements.

While rooms at the **Saigon-Europe** (207 De Tham, D1, tel. 028/3837-3879, www.beautifulsaigonhotel.com, VND700,000-1,500,000, breakfast included) are on the small side, modern decor and impeccable cleanliness more than compensate, not to mention the flat-screen TVs and computers in each room. Rooms (with or without windows) come with in-room safes, toiletries, a minibar, and a complimentary fruit basket. The friendly staff assist with additional services such as laundry and motorbike rentals. As part of a larger hotel chain, guests are also free to use the swimming pool at Beautiful Saigon Boutique Hotel around the corner.

Over VND2,100,000

On the edge of one of Saigon's busiest traffic circles, the **New World Hotel** (76 Le Lai, D1, tel. 028/3822-8888, www.saigon.new-worldhotels.com, VND3,880,000-7,000,000) boasts over 500 of the nicest rooms in town. Its tower offers sweeping views of the city from the perfect vantage point, not far from Ben Thanh Market. Each plush guestroom features a marble bath, a large bed, and satellite TV. The hotel has two restaurants serving Western and Asian cuisine, as well as a spa, an outdoor swimming pool, a fitness center, and tennis courts.

NGUYEN TRAI STREET
VND525,000-1,050,000

Down an alley, **Ono Saigon Hotel** (7/8 Nguyen Trai, D1, tel. 028/3925-2345, onosaigon@gmail.com, VND500,000-700,000) is spare in its decor but clean, comfy, and spacious. Basic amenities such as air-conditioning and television are available, as well as hot showers and free Wi-Fi. Ms. Rose, the general manager, is always willing to recommend restaurants and other activities.

Bright and cheery ★ **Town House 50** (50E Bui Thi Xuan, D1, tel. 028/3925-0210, www.townhousesaigon.com, VND250,000 dorm, VND795,000-885,000 d, breakfast included) is a pleasant surprise. Set back from the street, this beautiful mini-hotel is decorated in vibrant colors. Though dorm lodging is more expensive than in Pham Ngu Lao, beds are comfy and spotless. This is one of only a few places to offer all-female dorms. The massive common area has a homey feel.

Staff is knowledgeable and can offer recommendations on eating, sightseeing, and other activities. Private rooms are more expensive but equally clean and spacious, with large en suite baths, air-conditioning, hot showers, cable TV, and free Wi-Fi. You can also find **Town House 23** (23 Dang Thi Nhu, D1, tel. 028/3915-1491, www.townhousesaigon.com, VND250,000 dorm, VND730,000-840,000 d) a bit closer to Ben Thanh Market and **Town House 373** (373/45 Pham Ngu Lao, tel. 028/3838-6020, www.townhousesaigon.com, VND195,000 dorm, VND615,000-685,000 d), which provides both private rooms and all-female dorms in the backpacker area.

VND1,050,000-2,100,000

Despite its modest sign and inconspicuous location, ★ **Cinnamon Hotel Saigon** (74 Le Thi Rieng, D1, tel. 028/3926-0130, www.cinnamonhotel.net, VND1,815,000-2,090,000) exceeds expectations. Dressed in red-and-black *ao dai* (traditional Vietnamese garments), employees are outgoing and personable. Each of the hotel's beautifully furnished, cinnamon-scented rooms feature large beds and great attention to detail, with even the air-conditioning units masked by crafty embellishments. From the sumptuous breakfast to the occasional complimentary foot massage and the service-minded staff, this spot is worth the extra cash. Service charges and tax are not included in the rates, and note that the hotel does not have an elevator.

Information and Services

VISITOR INFORMATION

Saigon Tourist (23 Le Loi, D1, tel. 028/3829-2291, www.saigon-tourist.com, 8am-7pm daily) is able to provide helpful information, as well as free city maps. It is a for-profit entity, so your questions may be answered with a pamphlet or a travel brochure. There is also a second office near the corner of Dong Khoi (45 Le Thanh Ton, tel. 028/3827-9279, 8am-7pm daily).

Most hotels in the backpacker area have travel agencies attached to them, and even if you don't purchase a trip through their business, chances are the receptionist can give you practical information.

If you're looking for information about transportation or day trips outside the city, a better spot to visit is **Sinh Tourist** (246-248 De Tham, D1, tel. 028/3838-9593, www.thesinhtourist.vn, 6:30am-10:30pm daily) near Pham Ngu Lao. This massive company provides travel services within Saigon, throughout the country, and into Cambodia. Employees speak English well and are helpful in presenting options, though this is a for-profit company so you will likely be encouraged to book a tour. **Vinaday goREISE** (228 De Tham, D1, tel. 028/3838-8382, www.goreise.com, 7am-10pm Mon.-Sat., 7am-9pm Sun.) is another reliable and friendly source in the backpacker area that provides helpful information to travelers, even if you forgo their tours and venture out on your own. The company also handles hotel reservations and other logistical services.

BANKS AND CURRENCY EXCHANGE

ATMs are plentiful in the city. Drawing money directly from your account is often a better deal and less hassle than trying to exchange dollars or traveler's checks at a local bank.

There are countless currency exchange kiosks advertised around District 1, particularly in the Pham Ngu Lao area and around Nguyen Hue. You can also visit one of the gold shops near Ben Thanh Market to exchange currency. **Ha Tam Jewelers** (2 Nguyen An Ninh, D1, tel. 028/3823-7243, 8am-8:30pm daily) is a reliable place to buy and sell foreign bills.

International banks like **ANZ, HSBC,** and **Citibank** follow the typical business day, opening 8am-5pm Monday-Friday; the majority of local banks in Saigon keep odd hours, breaking for lunch in the middle of the day and opening again for only a few hours in the afternoon. A trip to a local bank can often be a tedious affair. But, if you need a local bank, visit **Vietcombank** or **Techcombank.** Several of these institutions provide Western Union wire services. For the most part, you're better off visiting an institution with some foreign affiliation.

While a growing number of high-end boutiques, restaurants, and hotels in Saigon have begun to accept credit cards, Vietnam remains, for the most part, a cash-only country, so check before trying to use your card.

POSTAL SERVICES AND INTERNET

A handful of shops in District 1 sell postage stamps, but there are no mailboxes in Vietnam. To send mail, you'll need to go to a post office. Pay a visit to the **Central Post Office** (2 Cong Xa Paris, D1, tel. 028/3924-7247, 7am-7pm Mon.-Fri., 7am-6pm Sat., 8am-6pm Sun.) near Notre Dame Cathedral. In addition to being a worthy sightseeing spot, it is the city's main post office.

There is a **DHL** (6 Thang Long, Tan Binh, tel. 1/800-1530, www.dhl.com.vn, 8:30am-6:30pm Mon.-Tues. and Fri., 8am-6pm Wed.-Thurs. and Sat.) drop-off point in downtown Saigon as well as a **UPS** (18 Cong Hoa, Tan Binh, tel. 028/3811-2888, www.ups.com, 7:30am-6pm Mon.-Sat.) farther from the city center. Sending large or expensive items from Vietnam is not advised. Even reputable international companies have been known to tack on additional fees, and prices change inexplicably.

Wireless Internet is available throughout the city at most hotels, cafés, and restaurants; all you need to do is ask for the password.

Many hotels keep a desktop computer in their lobby for guests to use.

PHONE SERVICE

For anyone planning to stay in Vietnam beyond a couple weeks, a mobile phone is a good idea. Cheap but reliable Nokia phones can be purchased new or secondhand at **The Gioi Di Dong** (136 Nguyen Thai Hoc, D1, tel. 1/800-1060, www.thegioididong.com, 8am-10pm daily) starting from VND350,000. Tourist SIM cards are available in the Pham Ngu Lao area and at the post office for around VND90,000. These are less expensive than a regular SIM, but only make domestic calls. Vietnamese mobile service runs on a pay-as-you-go basis, and phone credit is sold throughout the city. There are several carriers, most notably Viettel, Vinaphone, and Mobifone; look for these names posted outside *tap hoa* (convenience stores). Credit can be purchased in VND20,000, VND50,000, VND100,000, and VND200,000 increments.

EMERGENCY AND MEDICAL SERVICES

Vietnam has no single phone number for general emergency services. Dial 113 for the police, 114 for the fire department, and 115 for a local ambulance. Don't expect any of these operators to speak English or for help to come quickly. Emergency services in Vietnam are not often helpful and can be more hassle than they're worth.

In the event of a medical emergency, go directly to a foreign medical center. Local hospitals have aging and overcrowded facilities, and it is doubtful that you'll find an English-speaking doctor. All of the best-equipped facilities in town have 24-hour emergency services. **Family Medical Practice** (Diamond Plaza, 34 Le Duan, D1, tel. 028/3822-7848, www.vietnammedicalpractice.com, 24 hours daily) operates a 24-7 emergency hotline (tel. *9999) and medical staff are always on standby. Family Medical is also the only facility in town equipped with proper ambulances. **Raffles Medical Clinic** (167A Nam

Ky Khoi Nghia, D3, tel. 028/3824-0777, www. rafflesmedicalgroup.com, 24 hours daily) also provides routine check-ups as well as emergency services. Both of these clinics are reputable and staffed by well-qualified doctors. The largest and most sophisticated facilities are located at **FV Hospital** (6 Nguyen Luong Bang, D7, tel. 028/5411-3333, www.fvhospital. com, 24 hours daily), which is reminiscent of a standard Western hospital. Due to its size, the facility is located farther from the city center, in District 7. The hospital operates a **24-hour emergency hotline** (tel. 028/5411-3500).

For nonemergencies, **Columbia Asia International Clinic** (8 Alexandre de Rhodes, D1, tel. 028/3823-8888, www.columbiaasia.com/saigon, emergency room 7:30am-9pm Mon.-Fri., 8am-5pm Sat.-Sun.) is located downtown between Notre Dame Cathedral and the Reunification Palace. The clinic also offers emergency services, though it closes at night.

Pharmacies (*nha thuoc tay*) are common throughout the city and carry all manner of prescription and over-the-counter drugs. Most pharmacies within District 1 have at least one English-speaking staff member. **Pharmacy 22** (214 De Tham, D1, tel. 012/8472-3669, 7am-9:30pm daily) on the corner of De Tham and Bui Vien is reliable and sells hard-to-find products like contact solution and tampons. You can also look out for **Pharmacity** (173 Pham Ngu Lao, tel. 1/800-6821, www.pharmacity.vn, 6am-midnight daily) locations throughout Saigon.

DIPLOMATIC SERVICES

The massive, heavily guarded **U. S. Consulate** (4 Le Duan, D1, tel. 028/3520-4200, www.vn.usembassy.gov) provides assistance in emergency situations such as arrest, destitution, or serious illness in addition to dealing with passport-related issues. Appointments are required, and the consulate keeps separate hours for specific nonemergency services, so check online for hours. The consulate is closed on both Vietnamese and American holidays. In the event of an emergency, consulate officers will assist U.S. citizens 8am-5pm Monday-Friday using the phone number above. After 5pm, you should phone the embassy's **emergency hotline** (tel. 024/3850-5000).

Getting There

AIR

Ho Chi Minh City is connected to the rest of the world via **Tan Son Nhat International Airport** (SGN, tel. 028/3848-5383), located just six kilometers north of the city center. This is the country's largest airport, with over 30 million passengers per year. Local carriers Vietnam Airlines, Vietjet, and Jetstar offer multiple daily flights between Saigon and Hanoi, with fares usually hovering around VND1,120,000-2,000,000. The trip takes just over two hours and is the fastest, most convenient way to travel between the two cities.

In recent years, overcrowding has become a problem at Tan Son Nhat. While immigration and processing lines move at a steady pace, be prepared to wait if you are receiving your visa stamp at the airport. Traffic around the airport has also become increasingly congested, so it's important to budget enough time to get to Tan Son Nhat when you have a flight to catch. The evening rush hour is particularly busy, so you'll want to tack on an extra 30 minutes or so if you're leaving around this time.

Taxi from the Airport

This is the easiest way to get downtown. Outside the arrivals area are dozens of taxis waiting to ferry passengers into the city. Cab drivers can be persistent, so turn left down to the end of the sidewalk and find a dispatcher from either Mailinh or Vinasun companies. (There are occasional reports of tourists being overcharged or meters running faster than they should when using lesser-known companies.) Forming lines is an oft-ignored concept in Vietnam, so be proactive and let the dispatcher know where you're going. Getting to downtown District 1 takes about 30-40 minutes, depending on traffic, and costs VND150,000-180,000. Rides from the airport are metered, not flat rate.

Xe Om from the Airport

Though it requires a bit of a walk, you can take a *xe om* (motorbike taxi) directly from the airport. If you're a lone traveler, it's cheaper than grabbing a cab. Exiting the arrivals area, look for an overpass. (From the international terminal, it's ahead and to the right; for domestic arrivals, it is ahead and to the left.) Follow the other people walking past this structure toward the road. There is a parking garage on the right and, beyond it, bustling Saigon traffic. *Xe om* drivers will start to approach at this point. Agree on the fare before you set off. A typical ride to the Pham Ngu Lao area should take about 25 minutes and cost no more than VND80,000. If you'd rather not haggle, you can also hail a **GrabBike** (VND30,000-50,000) via smartphone, but you must leave the airport terminal first and head toward the road, as two-wheeled vehicles are not allowed at Tan Son Nhat.

Public Bus from the Airport

If you're up for traveling like a local, you can take the bright yellow **public bus 109** (5:30am-1:30am daily, VND20,000) from the airport directly to Ben Thanh Market, a stone's throw from the backpacker area. This is the cheapest transportation option and takes about 45 minutes to reach the market. Don't expect anyone on the bus to speak English.

TRAIN

The **Saigon Train Station (Ga Saigon)** (1 Nguyen Thong, D3, tel. 028/3843-6524, www.dsvn.vn) sits just south of the Nhieu Loc Canal in District 3 and is the final destination for all domestic trains. The country's north-south Reunification Line runs along the coast from Hanoi with major stations in Hue, Danang, and Nha Trang before reaching HCMC. Trains from Hanoi to Ho Chi Minh City depart several times a day, primarily in the morning and evening, and takes a staggering 32 hours. Tickets cost VND885,000-1,450,000, but you'll want to spring for a sleeper car on this ride, given the length of the trip. Trains arrive from Nha Trang in the early morning or Phan Thiet in the evening. There are always taxi drivers and *xe om* drivers waiting outside the station's main entrance; it's about 15 minutes via taxi or *xe om* to downtown. Public buses 65 and 149 can also take you to the bus station at 23-9 Park (30 minutes, 4:30am-8pm daily, VND5,000).

BUS

The majority of tourist buses coming from Can Tho, Nha Trang, Dalat, and Mui Ne drop off passengers in the Pham Ngu Lao area of District 1. Tour operators usually park their vehicles around 23-9 Park or on De Tham, right in the heart of Pham Ngu Lao. **Phuong Trang** (272 De Tham, D1, tel. 028/3838-6852, www.futabuslines.com.vn, 5am-1am daily) is a major bus provider, as is **Sinh Tourist** (246-248 De Tham, D1, tel. 028/3838-9593, www.thesinhtourist.vn, 6:30am-10:30pm daily). While bus travel is a convenient and affordable mode of transportation for nearby destinations such as Dalat, Mui Ne, Nha Trang, and the Mekong Delta region, long-distance bus rides are not recommended in Vietnam. A trip from Hanoi to Saigon, for instance, would require multiple bus tickets and take about 32 hours nonstop. During long-haul trips, many companies attempt to cover as much ground as possible in a short amount of time, and passenger safety can be compromised by sleep-deprived or distracted drivers. If you're heading to Saigon from anywhere farther than Nha Trang, a train or plane is recommended.

There are three main stations used by local buses. To the northwest is **An Suong bus station (Ben Xe An Suong)** (Quoc Lo 22, D Hoc Mon, tel. 09/8557-3573), 14.5 kilometers from the city center, just beyond the airport where Truong Chinh street turns into Highway 22. Also 14.5 kilometers from the city center is the **Western bus station (Ben Xe Mien Tay)** (Kinh Duong Vuong, D Binh Tan, tel. 028/3877-6594), which sits farther south and serves the Mekong Delta. For all other destinations, Saigon's **Eastern bus station (Ben Xe Mien Dong)** (292 Dinh Bo Linh, D Binh Thanh, tel. 028/3899-1607) is a mere 6 kilometers from town. It is unlikely that you will need to visit any of these places, but if your bus drops you at one of these stations, the usual modes of transportation—taxis, *xe om*, ride-hailing apps, and the public bus—are all good ways to get downtown.

MOTORBIKE

The most direct—and congested—route into the city is National Highway 1, a gritty, chaotic road that runs into town from the Mekong Delta on the western side and Phan Thiet on the eastern end. Highway traffic is usually a mess, full of massive trucks, buses, cars, and motorbikes, and the flow of vehicles becomes more backed up as you approach the city, particularly during the evening rush hour.

Coming from the east, things start to get better once you reach the Saigon Bridge, which takes you out of District 2 and, from there, into the city center. If you're approaching from the Mekong Delta, Highway 1 curves north to avoid Saigon. Make a right onto Vo Van Kiet (look for signs), and follow the road straight into town, getting off at the Ben Thanh Market exit. If you go too far, you'll know it—the Thu Thiem tunnel leads right back out of town and into District 2.

Getting Around

When driving around town, there are essentially no rules. People drive while texting, neglect to use the correct turn signals (if they use them at all), routinely speed in the opposite direction down a one-way street, and generally disregard lane markings. Exercise caution on the road and obey stoplights and traffic laws as you would at home, even if others don't.

TAXI

When traveling in the city, it's best to hail a green-and-white **Mailinh** (tel. 028/3838-3838) or green, white, and red **Vinasun** (tel. 028/3827-2727) cab, particularly at night. These vehicles are clean and well kept, the drivers are knowledgeable, and the meters correct. Other cab companies are okay to use during the day.

Cab drivers occasionally try to beat the system by taking a longer route than necessary. The most trusted cab companies in Saigon are Vinasun and Mailinh, so it's a safe bet to stick with them. Never bargain for a cab ride in Vietnam. All taxis are metered and it is always to your benefit to use the meter.

It's easier to hail a cab from the street rather than calling for one, but if it's late at night or no taxis are around, then ask a Vietnamese speaker to call for a Mailinh or Vinasun taxi. Vinasun also has its own ride-hailing app, a helpful service for non-Vietnamese speakers.

RIDE-HAILING APPS

Regional ride-hailing app **Grab** (www.grab.com) has made its mark on Saigon traffic, much to the ire of both traditional *xe om* drivers and cabbies alike. It offers riders dirt-cheap rates in both two- and four-wheeled vehicles. While Grab drivers can be a mixed bag—your driver might be a knowledgeable local, a whiz with the GPS, or someone who just moved to the city yesterday—the service is generally safe and prices are unbeatable. You can also opt to pay by credit card or in cash in Saigon.

XE OM

As you wander around the city, you will hear cries of "You! Motorbi-i-ike!" These are Saigon's *xe om* drivers, an impressive and eclectic fleet of motorbike drivers that ferry people from place to place. This is the most efficient way to get around town, though it is not for the faint of heart. *Xe om* drivers drive fast and are just as likely as the rest of the population to break traffic laws. Always agree on a price before embarking and stand firm on that agreement, as drivers sometimes attempt to glean extra cash from you later on.

The going rate for a *xe om* fluctuates depending on where you're headed, so ask a local what they might pay to get an idea of a fair price. At night, stick to taxis.

CYCLO

Hopping on a cyclo can be a nice way to see the city. Muscular cyclo drivers will pedal you around the downtown area and past some of the city's most popular sights. Many drivers speak English well, as these pedal-powered vehicles are more likely to be used by visitors for tours of District 1 than by the local population, who prefer to get around on a motorbike. Prices are negotiable, though you should be prepared to pay more than you would for a *xe om,* as your driver will also be your guide around town and he is doing a lot more legwork than someone on a motorbike. The experience is fun and something that many visitors to HCMC enjoy, but this is not a method of transportation for someone in a hurry.

BUS

An efficient army of city buses roams Saigon's streets. Buses generally run 5am-7:30pm, but some may go as late as 9pm. It can be difficult to navigate the dizzying maze of bus routes that crisscross the city, though there is a handy interactive bus map online (www. buyttphcm.com.vn) that helps. If all else fails, ask a Vietnamese speaker to help out.

Buses vary in size from minibuses to large air-conditioned vehicles. Bus stops are either a small, navy blue sign listing that stop's buses, or full covered stops with a bench and route map.

A trip within the city limits will usually set you back about VND5,000. If you're heading farther afield, prices go up according to your destination.

MOTORBIKE

Motorbikes are available for hire (VND100,000-120,000 per day) throughout the Pham Ngu Lao area. Before heading out, give the bike a short test-drive and check that you have the vehicle's registration card. **Chi's Cafe** (40/31 Bui Vien, D1, tel. 09/0364-3446, www.chiscafe.com, 9am-10pm daily, VND100,000-120,000) has good, reliable vehicles, both automatic and semi-automatic, and offers daylong and long-term rentals (only for visitors staying in the city). **Trung's Motorbikes** (185 Pham Ngu Lao, D1, tel. 09/0330-8466, trung_motorbike@yahoo.com, 7am-9pm daily, VND100,000-130,000), a tiny green shop on the corner of a small alley, also has rentals available.

If you're looking to buy a bike for a longer trip around the country, signs advertising heavy-duty vehicles for sale can be found in the backpacker area. Make sure to have the bike checked by a mechanic before finalizing the purchase.

Vicinity of Ho Chi Minh City

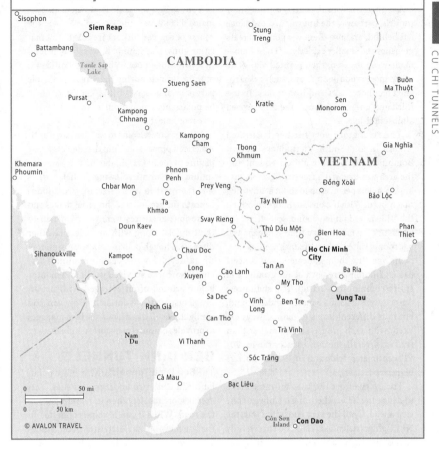

© AVALON TRAVEL

Cu Chi Tunnels

Considered one of the greatest tactical achievements of the southern insurgency during the American War, the **Cu Chi Tunnels** (Ben Dinh, Nhan Duc Commune, Cu Chi, tel. 028/3794-8830, www.diadaocuchi.com.vn, 7am-5pm daily, VND110,000) spiderweb beneath kilometers of paddy fields and fertile farmland all the way from Ho Chi Minh City to the Cambodian border. As early as the 1940s, members of the Viet Minh resistance army (later the National Liberation Front, or NLF) began digging out these cramped crawl spaces by hand. With technology and firepower far inferior to their French enemies, the tunnels allowed Ho Chi Minh's rebel forces to communicate with nearby villages and bases undetected. By the time the American War arrived in the 1960s, a 250-kilometer underground network existed.

Initially, the tunnels were meant to provide

escape routes and shelter during American bombing raids. As soon as the skies were clear, guerrillas would emerge from their tunnels, cart away the unexploded ordnance left behind, and use these weapons to create grenades and smaller explosives. These home-made weapons were then planted alongside other, more crude booby traps, such as sharp-ened bamboo sticks and iron spikes. In the thick and unfamiliar forest, the NLF proved almost invisible.

The retaliatory acts further frustrated American and South Vietnamese troops. Bombing raids became more frequent and the area was deemed a free-strike zone, giv-ing U.S. pilots permission to shoot at anything that moved. With the onslaught of explosives, the NLF moved underground, sometimes for weeks or even months at a time. Kitchens and bedrooms were constructed, as well as hos-pitals, meeting rooms, theaters, and concert halls. Children were born below ground and entire communities set up. The shallowest tunnels were at least 1.5 meters underground, but four different levels of passageways ex-isted, with each progressively smaller than the last. Overall, the crawl spaces ranged 70-120 centimeters wide and 70-180 centimeters high.

For every effort the U.S. military made to defeat the NLF, rebels in Cu Chi were one step ahead. Until the very end of the war, the NLF fighters defended their land successfully against the Americans and South Vietnamese.

Today, the government-run tourist area encompassing the Cu Chi tunnels features exhibits, guided tours, and a variety of other attractions. Weapons displays illustrate the gruesome methods of the NLF and hint at the hardships of those who lived underground.

Park guides escort you through the tun-nels, telling of the history and people of Cu Chi. At each of the two tunnel sites, Ben Dinh and Ben Duoc, the narrow passageways have been lit and widened to accommodate visitors. Larger subterranean rooms are occasionally furnished with mannequins and other items.

The history of the Cu Chi tunnels is more interesting than a visit to the tunnels them-selves. The present-day memorial site is a bit of a circus. On the same land where an esti-mated 45,000 men and women died over the course of the war, visitors are able to fire ma-chine guns, play paintball, or splash around in a swimming pool. While the significance of these tunnels during the war is a valuable part of local history, visiting Cu Chi tends to be polarizing among tourists: people either love it or hate it.

Visitors are welcome to watch a harsh anti-American propaganda film that depicts a rosy picture of life in Cu Chi during the war, with smiling NLF women plowing the fields, rifles slung across their backs. In reality, conditions beneath the ground were horrific: snakes and poisonous creatures were rampant within the tunnels, along with malaria and other diseases. Though collapses were uncommon, when they did occur, death was almost cer-tain. Those who survived weeks and months below ground often emerged with health problems, largely from lack of oxygen and sunlight. For all these flaws, the film manages to provide some useful historical information.

BEN DINH TUNNELS

The **Ben Dinh Tunnels** are the more popu-lar of Cu Chi's two underground sites. This area is more touristy than its counterpart up the road. While it can become congested in the late morning and early afternoon, guides and other park staff at Ben Dinh speak more English than those at Ben Duoc. The web of tunnels and exhibits at Ben Dinh is more com-pact, allowing for visitors to get around more easily.

A souvenir shop hawks mass-produced tchotchkes, and a handful of restaurants sit across the road from the Ben Dinh entrance. There are also vendors within the grounds selling snacks and light meals at slightly in-flated prices.

BEN DUOC TUNNELS

Farther down the road, the older **Ben Duoc** site is less frequented than Ben Dinh. It contains near-identical tunnels and weapons displays but is significantly more spread out than Ben Dinh. If you wish to visit other parts of the Cu Chi tourist area—such as the AK-47 shooting range—you will be required to take an electric car, which is available for hire near the park entrance. There are a handful of on-site restaurants serving light meals (VND20,000-100,000) as well as a few souvenir vendors just beyond the entrance.

TAY NINH HOLY SEE

A colorful, sprawling complex in an otherwise sleepy town, the **Tay Ninh Holy See** (Ly Thuong Kiet, Hoa Thanh Town, tel. 0276/384-1193, www.caodai.com.vn, 6am-6pm daily) is the epicenter of Caodaism. Built in 1933 by a devout group of followers, the holy city's main temple stands at the end of a long, narrow parade ground, flanked on either side by banks of stadium-style seating. This is the most ornamental and visually interesting piece of architecture within the Cao Dai complex.

Leave your shoes at the edge of the raised sidewalk surrounding the building. The temple's exterior has an ornately decorated entrance and a long three-tiered roof. Inside, the building is divided into three separate areas that pay tribute to the three main branches of Caodaism: the legislative branch, the administrative branch, and the spiritual branch. The small area at the front belongs to the three protectors and upholders of Caodaist law: Ho Phap at the center, and his right- and left-hand men, Thuong Sanh and Thuong Pham. The three are represented by a set of colorful statues inside the main hall. On the opposite wall, facing the temple's main entrance, a painting depicting three of Caodaism's most famous saints: poet Nguyen Binh Khiem, Sun Yat-Sen, and Victor Hugo, shows the trio writing the phrases "God and humanity" and "Love and justice" in French and Chinese.

The administrative branch of Caodaism is represented in the long airy main hall where Caodaist followers, known as adepts, participate in religious proceedings. This is the most colorful and decorative section of the temple.

Wide-eyed, multihued dragons snake down the endless rows of pillars, while the ceiling is painted to reflect a bright blue sky with silver stars. The all-seeing eye, the central symbol of Caodaism, is featured heavily upon the walls, surrounded by lotus flowers and repeating up all nine of the main hall's steps to the altar. Here, a large blue orb adorned with stars and a single image of the all-seeing eye sits at the center of a large table, upon which offerings of fruit, tea, alcohol, and other items are presented.

Religious ceremonies take place at 6am, noon, 6pm, and midnight daily. Most guided tours arrive at the temple in time for the midday procession, in which men and women file into the temple from separate sides and take their place within the main hall. The entire length of the building is divided into nine steps, each of which represents part of the hierarchy within Caodaism. Only about six steps are used, while the rest remain empty, including a series of red-and-gold lacquer chairs at the very front, which are reserved for the pope and other high-ranking members of the religion. During prayer, men take the right side of the temple and women the left. The adepts complete a series of prostrations before the altar as well as several religious chants, usually accompanied by a band of traditional Vietnamese musicians, who sit on the balcony.

Due to the large volume of visitors at the temple, adepts usher you along after some time to allow for other visitors to watch the ceremony from above. You'll also be able to wander around the main entrance of the temple. If you stick around long enough, the adepts file out after prayer and a smaller group returns with another altar, this time filled with incense, fruit, and other offerings, which is blessed on each step up to the altar before being placed in front of the all-seeing eye.

On your way out of the building, take a look across the parade grounds into the distance to find another cluster of sparkling, intricate towers devoted to the trio of protectors who guard the laws of Caodaism. If you've got time and want to ask questions, local adepts are friendly and willing to chat, though few of them speak English.

There have been some reports of shoe theft outside the temple, so you can remove your shoes and carry them inside, though it's better to stick them in your bag and out of sight, or you may be told to leave them.

TOURS

For dirt-cheap mass tours, **Sinh Tourist** (246-248 De Tham, D1, tel. 028/3838-9593, www.thesinhtourist.vn, 6:30am-10:30pm daily, VND129,000-499,000) offers half-day trips to the tunnels or full-day tours combining Cu Chi with a visit to the Cao Dai temple at Tay Ninh or a trip to the Mekong Delta. Admission to the tunnels is not included in the price, but you are spared the hassle of navigating the public bus system and a tour guide is provided. Groups tend to be 30-40 people; get a spot at the front if you want to hear what your guide has to say.

Ho Chi Minh City Urban Adventures (tel. 09/0990-4100, www.hochiminhcityurbanadventures.com, VND885,000) runs a tour from the city to Cu Chi for a maximum of 16 people, allowing for additional one-on-one time with the guide and more than the cookie-cutter speeches provided by the guides at the park. HCMC Urban Adventures prides itself on creating tourism that benefits the local community, and so its tours often include extra off-the-beaten-track stops, which allow travelers to see how the local population lives. The company books its tours via the website or phone reservations; travelers can call at any time to book a tour.

More expensive but also more relaxing is a tour with **Les Rives** (Me Linh Point Tower, Ste. 2105, 2 Ngo Duc Ke, D1, tel. 012/8592-0018, www.lesrivesexperience.com, 10am-10pm daily, VND1,899,000-3,599,000), a company that provides on-the-water excursions to a handful of nearby sights, including the tunnels. The company offers half-day

tours to Cu Chi in both the morning and afternoon with an array of extra features, from an additional bicycle trip to a "hidden HCMC" tour that includes a trip to the tunnels. Meals are served, along with unlimited fruit and refreshments, and the hour-long boat ride to the tunnels eliminates the stress of inching through the bumper-to-bumper traffic that often crowds the outskirts of the city. Hotel pickup and all park entrance fees are included in the tour price.

TRANSPORTATION
Bus

Public buses run regularly to Cu Chi District from downtown Saigon's 23-9 Park bus station. Take the number 13 bus to Cu Chi bus station (1.5 hours, VND7,000). From there, bus 79 will bring you to the Ben Duoc bus station (45 minutes, VND8,000) directly in front of the tunnels. The last bus from Ben Duoc leaves at 5:30pm.

Motorbike

The Cu Chi tunnels are located along Provincial Road 15. From Saigon, take Truong Chinh street in Tan Binh District out past An Suong bus station on Highway 1, labeled QL22 on the kilometer stones. Roughly five kilometers past the bus station, make a right onto Ba Trieu street. Once you reach the Hoc Mon Market, this road changes names a few times, from Trung Nu Vuong to Do Van Day, but will eventually turn into Provincial Road 15. Stay on this route for another 32 kilometers and you'll find yourself at the tunnels. The drive takes 1.5-2 hours.

While it is possible to reach the tunnels on your own, this trip is not recommended for novice drivers, as it involves a stretch along Highway 1, the nation's busiest and most dangerous road. Unless you have a hired driver at your disposal, save yourself the hazard and the headache and hop on a tour or a public bus instead.

Vung Tau

Stretching out into the ocean, Vung Tau was not always the buzzing tourist town it has become. Well before droves of domestic visitors began to flock here for weekend getaways and summer vacations, Vung Tau played a significant role in the military history of most powers to occupy Vietnam. For centuries, its view of Can Gio, the entryway into the Saigon River, made it a valuable strategic outpost for several different armies, from the Vietnamese battling against colonial invasion in 1859 to the French army, a brief occupation by the Japanese during World War II, and the extended presence of the Australian military throughout the American War.

In the 19th and 20th centuries, French colonists identified this sleepy beach town as the ideal spot from which to keep an eye on Saigon. It was armed with artillery cannons and military forts, hidden deep in the thick tangle of rainforest, which still obscures many of its mountainsides today. Later, when the NLF and Communist forces were battling against Western troops, the Australian military, who had come to assist their American allies, set up a logistics base in the area, stationing its soldiers all over Ba Ria-Vung Tau province. Throughout the region, tunnels were dug, forts built, and several significant battles played out within the mountains.

Years of missionary proselytizing created a strong Roman Catholic following alongside Buddhist traditions. Every other building is an eye-popping, brightly decorated pagoda or a towering stark-white statue of Jesus or the Virgin Mary. One of Vung Tau's most famous attractions is the gigantic Christ of Vung Tau, believed to be among the largest statues of Jesus in the world.

Vung Tau is regarded as a weekend tourist hot spot, packed with domestic visitors and overpriced goods. Avoid Vung Tau on Saturday, Sunday, and public holidays. Its beaches have a reputation for being on the seedy side, due to some harassment of women in revealing swimsuits. Focus on the town's sights and you'll be fine.

Christ of Vung Tau

Vung Tau

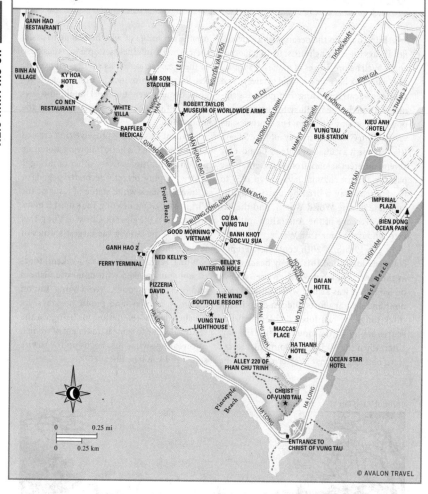

GANH HAO RESTAURANT

BINH AN VILLAGE

KY HOA HOTEL

CO NEN RESTAURANT

WHITE VILLA

RAFFLES MEDICAL

LAM SON STADIUM

ROBERT TAYLOR MUSEUM OF WORLDWIDE ARMS

VUNG TAU BUS STATION

KIEU ANH HOTEL

IMPERIAL PLAZA

BIEN DONG OCEAN PARK

CO BA VUNG TAU

GOOD MORNING VIETNAM

BANH KHOT GOC VU SUA

GANH HAO 2

FERRY TERMINAL

NED KELLY'S

BELLY'S WATERING HOLE

DAI AN HOTEL

PIZZERIA DAVID

THE WIND BOUTIQUE RESORT

VUNG TAU LIGHTHOUSE

MACCAS PLACE

HA THANH HOTEL

OCEAN STAR HOTEL

ALLEY 220 OF PHAN CHU TRINH

CHRIST OF VUNG TAU

Pineapple Beach

Back Beach

Front Beach

ENTRANCE TO CHRIST OF VUNG TAU

0   0.25 mi

0   0.25 km

© AVALON TRAVEL

CHRIST OF VUNG TAU

Vung Tau's most famous monument, the enormous **Christ of Vung Tau** (2 Ha Long; main gates 6:30am-5pm daily; statue 7:30am-11:30am and 1:30pm-4:30pm Sat.-Thurs., 7:30am-11:30am and 1:30pm-4pm Fri.) is among the largest statues of Christ in the world. Nestled partway up Small Mountain, this sculpture is 32 meters tall, with an 18-meter wingspan. Vung Tau's statue is taller than the Christ the Redeemer statue in Rio de Janeiro. Visitors can ascend the narrow interior, going 133 steps up for a stunning 360-degree view of Vung Tau and the ocean.

Construction began in 1974, before the end of the American War. A year later the statue was complete, but the 800-odd steps from the base of Tao Phung to the base of the statue had yet to be finished. Construction was suspended over the next decade, and the statue sat partially hidden in the thick brush of the mountain. When it was discovered that the statue's lightning rod system—the metal points of the halo—had been stolen, the Catholic church was allowed to complete the project. In 1994 the statue and walkway were opened to the public.

Make the long hike to the statue in the early morning or late afternoon, as the sun can be brutal. There is also a back passage up to the statue. It begins from alley 220 of Phan Chu Trinh and ends at the last 200 steps up to the statue. This is no less challenging for hikers, but a skilled motorbike driver could take the narrow path up here.

Before entering the statue, take your shoes off and leave all bags at the door. On either side of the main monument are two massive French artillery cannons. Beyond the statue, small bridges arch over a waterless canal: This is where the French transported ammunition to the cannons, loading the magazines from below.

Anyone wearing short shorts or a tank top will be turned away from the statue; shoulders and knees must be covered. Note that even though the main gates stay open until 5pm, the parking lot closes at 4pm—so if you've got your own set of wheels, make sure you visit earlier in the day.

FRENCH FORT RUINS

A lesser-known but equally fascinating relic of Vung Tau's history are the French Fort Ruins scattered across Big and Small Mountains. From as early as the late 19th century, the French colonial government recognized Vung Tau as a valuable military outpost, affording them a clear view toward the mouth of the Saigon River. Several separate forts were built, each extensively armed. Soldiers kept watch from their on-site living quarters, and underground rooms were built to accommodate ammunition stores. During World War II, the Japanese also made use of these posts. Following the end of French colonial rule, many of the military forts were abandoned. Several of these hidden forts remain forgotten, covered in plant life and crumbling on the

mountainsides of Vung Tau. The local authorities have done little to maintain these sites, giving the old forts an eerie feel.

One of these military forts exists on the back passage from Christ of Vung Tau, which begins on alley 222 of Phan Chu Trinh street. At the entry to the ruins is a battery of artillery guns as well as the remains of a well and some living quarters. Below, the dark, cave-like opening leads beneath the guns. If you've got a flashlight handy, you can venture inside (though it's more than a bit spooky) and see where and how the guns were loaded, feeding ammo up through a metal chamber at the center of the back room. If you visit the statue of Christ of Vung Tau on foot, it is also possible to hike down to these ruins, as they're not too far from the stone steps. From the statue, drive across the stone path and down to the left. The ruins will be on your left but are barely visible from the path, appearing as only a bit of stone wall and a hollow doorway. Park your bike and walk up the steps beside the darkened entryway.

The other, more easily accessible fort ruins exist off alley 444 of Tran Phu street. The trip up the mountain is pleasant, passing by brightly hued houses and locals raking out their catch of shrimp to dry in the sun. Scenic views abound. There is a plaque providing some general information about the fort, and then two batteries of weapons, one with six artillery guns, the other with three. The road up to these ruins is paved the entire way, making the trip a much easier feat, whether on foot, on a motorbike, or via a hired xe om driver.

These historical sites are free to visit and open to the public. Note that on weekends you'll find a healthy crowd of picnic-goers at the fort off Tran Phu street, making for a slightly less peaceful visit.

ROBERT TAYLOR MUSEUM OF WORLDWIDE ARMS

Housed within a grand colonial-style villa, the extensive collection at the Robert Taylor Museum of Worldwide Arms (98

Tran Hung Dao, tel. 0254/381-8369, www. baotangroberttaylor.com, 8am-5pm daily, VND100,000) comes as something of a surprise. Featuring weapons and military uniforms from across the globe, the museum's mannequins don the colors of China, Japan, Mongolia, England, Scotland, and France, while every wall of the space is covered in intricately detailed weapons dating back centuries. Englishman Robert Taylor has spent years cultivating his collection of military memorabilia.

VUNG TAU LIGHTHOUSE

Though the **Vung Tau Lighthouse** (end of Hai Dang on Small Mountain, 7am-11am and 2pm-6pm daily) is rather unimpressive on its own, its views of the town and the beach, as well as of the Christ of Vung Tau statue, make this a nice spot to visit. Perched 170 meters above sea level atop the summit of Small Mountain, this modest white tower was built in 1910 in order to guide ships leaving and entering the Saigon River. Visitors are not allowed inside, but the views from the ground are pleasant and the breeze is refreshing.

WHITE VILLA

Perched atop a small hill between Front Beach and Big Mountain, **White Villa (Bach Dinh)** (4 Tran Phu, tel. 0254/351-1608, 7am-5pm daily, VND15,000) was built as a holiday residence for the Governor General of Cochinchina, Paul Doumer, in 1898. The six-hectare plot of land originally housed Phuoc Thang Fort, a military base. After colonization, Phuoc Thang was destroyed to make way for the two-story structure that exists today. During its heyday, Bach Dinh served as the living quarters of not only Governor General Doumer but also Emperors Thanh Thai and Bao Dai, Vietnam's final king. With its intricate mosaics and detailed ceramic accents, the grounds surrounding Bach Dinh are surprisingly lush for being so close to the center of town.

A lasting relic of Vietnam's colonial history, the house is most impressive from outside.

Inside, the ground floor exhibit is filled with late 17th- and early 18th-century Chinese ceramics and porcelain discovered from a shipwreck bound for Europe that sank just off the Con Dao Islands. Upstairs is a preserved version of the house's former glory, though the solid wooden furniture and moldy drapes are worse for wear. There is also a nice spot to take in a sea view from above.

A long, well-covered path runs out to a headstone honoring Emperor Thanh Thai, who became emperor at the age of 10. In his later years he grew unpopular with the French due to his resistance to colonial power. In 1907 he was placed under house arrest here at Bach Dinh, living under the watchful eye of the French government until 1916, when he was sent to Reunion, another French colony off the eastern coast of Madagascar. The stele, emblazoned with a dragon at the top, bears one of the emperor's poems, written in Vung Tau.

BEACHES
Front Beach

Between the ferry port and Big Mountain, **Front Beach** (Quang Trung and Ha Long streets) is directly at the center of the action. Front Beach Park acts as a buffer between the main road and the water, which comes all the way up to the sea wall. The park is a nice place to stop and relax in the shade with swaying palm trees blocking out the midday sun. While Front Beach is fine for swimming and markedly less crowded than Back Beach on the weekends, its flaw is its lack of sand. In the early morning and late afternoon, when the sun is less fierce, this is a lively spot full of local vendors.

Back Beach

For sunbathing and as much R&R as can be gleaned from the well-touristed shores of Vung Tau, **Back Beach** (Thuy Van between Phan Chu Trinh and Nguyen An Ninh) is the place to go. Spanning three kilometers—longer than Vung Tau's other main beaches—and boasting plenty of room to lay down a towel, this is a quieter spot during the weekdays and sees more of the foreign tourist crowd, though you are still likely to get a few stares. The beach itself is nothing stunning, but its close proximity to the rest of town make it a nice escape. There are several tourist areas based on the beach, including **Bien Dong Ocean Park** (8 Thuy Van, tel. 0254/381-6318, www.khudulichbiendong.com, 6am-10pm daily), which features a restaurant, a swimming pool, and beach chairs, and is free to enter.

SHOPPING

If you're in need of good beach clothing or a bathing suit, the ultra-modern **Imperial Plaza** (159-163 Thuy Van, tel. 0254/352-6688, www.imperialplaza.vn, 9am-9:30pm Mon.-Fri., 9am-10pm Sat.-Sun.) is the place to go. The shopping center has several floors of well-priced local and foreign brand-name clothing, swimsuits, and souvenirs, as well as a small food court on the top floor with mainly Vietnamese food and a café out front. Only Vietnamese sizes are offered here.

SPORTS AND RECREATION
Golf

Part of a larger resort complex, **Paradise Golf Vung Tau** (1 Thuy Van, tel. 0254/385-3428, www.golfparadise.com.vn, 5:30am-4:30pm daily, VND1,400,000-2,100,000 for 18 holes) is the town's only golf course. Located about three kilometers from the town center, the seaside course features three separate areas with a total of 27 holes and offers caddies, golf carts, and rental equipment. Guests can call to book a tee time for 18 holes; fees are higher on weekends.

Dog Racing

A lesser-known attraction in Vung Tau takes place every weekend at **Lam Son Stadium** (15 Le Loi, tel. 0254/380-7309, 7:15pm-10pm Sat., VND60,000-120,000), the city's only venue for greyhound racing and one of the few places where gambling is legal for Vietnamese. Every Saturday, a healthy crowd of spectators flocks to the stadium to watch the races and wager. Purchase a cheap ticket and hang out with the masses, or spring for a VIP air-conditioned balcony view. Drinks and snacks are available inside.

FOOD

Being a beach town, Vung Tau is known for its seafood. However, the main culinary specialty is a dish called *banh khot,* which is something like a miniature version of the

Vung Tau's Back Beach

large, hang-over-the-plate southern-style Vietnamese pancakes you might find in Saigon, or their smaller cousins up in the central region. Bite-size and accompanied by all the same fixings, these fried morsels of rice flour are often topped with shrimp but can also be served with meat or other seafood, usually squid. A healthy serving of fresh greens, pickled veggies, and fish sauce are added to the mix, making for a delectable, authentic Vung Tau meal.

Famed throughout Vung Tau and beyond, the *banh khot* at ★ **Banh Khot Goc Vu Sua** (14 Nguyen Truong To, 7am-2pm Mon.-Fri., 7am-8pm Sat.-Sun., VND50,000) is considered the best in town. Packed at all hours, this restaurant is just a few metal tables and plastic stools tucked into an outdoor space with pale-blue chain-link "walls." Fresh greens and veggies come standard with every order, as does fish sauce and as much crushed chili pepper as you can stomach. Grab a lettuce leaf; toss in your *banh khot*; add some pickled carrots and daikon, mint leaves, and other herbs; wrap; dip; and enjoy. Order a refreshing *nuoc mia* (sugarcane juice) to go with your meal and bring your patience, as service can take a little while given the customer volume.

For more variety, **Co Ba Vung Tau** (1 Hoang Hoa Tham, tel. 0254/352-6165, www. cobavungtau.com, 6:30am-10pm daily, VND45,000-180,000) serves equally delicious *banh xeo* (Vietnamese pancakes) as well as *banh khot,* the Vung Tau specialty, and *banh beo,* a steamed rice-flour cake similar to its fried counterpart, all in an open-air setting. All meals are reasonably priced, and the open kitchen allows diners to watch the food being prepared.

Right in the thick of the cafés and restaurants that surround the cable car to Big Mountain, **Co Nen** (20 Tran Phu, tel. 09/0709-0606, www.quannuongconen.com, 4pm-11pm Mon.-Fri., 10am-11pm Sat.-Sun., VND60,000-280,000) is a right-on barbecue joint serving a variety of seafood and meat as well as hot-pot dishes. Its decor is limited to the bare essentials, with metal tables and creaky chairs, but

banh khot

the grilled octopus here is incredible and well worth enduring the loud music blaring from the café nearby and the flashing lights of the smoothie and snack stands across the way.

Excellent seafood and views of the water can be found at **Ganh Hao** (3 Tran Phu, tel. 0254/355-0909, www.ganhhao.com.vn, 9am-10pm daily, VND95,000-900,000), located past the cable car to Big Mountain. The restaurant's huge menu includes everything from squid, fish, shrimp, snails, and several types of crab to Vietnamese meat and vegetable dishes. The restaurant's outdoor dining area is perched right at the edge of the sea. Dishes at Ganh Hao are affordable, with a few higher-cost items available. There is also a **second location** (9 Ha Long, tel. 0254/357-7777, www.ganhhao.com.vn, 9am-10pm daily, VND95,000-900,000) closer to town.

★ **Pizzeria David** (92 Ha Long, tel. 0254/352-1012, 9am-10:30pm daily, VND145,000-235,000) turns out top-notch classic pies, including a delicious *quattro formaggi* as well as prosciutto and mushroom.

Two floors of open-air indoor and outdoor seating are available, with cozy low tables and patio furniture reminiscent of a European café. Add to this the exposed brick exterior and you might forget you're on the other side of the world. David's also boasts an impressive wine list as well as pasta dishes, ice cream, and Italian desserts.

A cozy little spot near Tran Hung Dao Park, **Good Morning Vietnam** (6 Hoang Hoa Tham, tel. 0254/385-6959, 8am-10pm daily, VND50,000-270,000) is another anomaly among Vung Tau cuisine, serving unexpectedly delightful Italian food at affordable prices. Its menu runs the spectrum from standard pastas and pizzas to dishes like gnocchi, risotto, and authentic fish and poultry fare, all accompanied by a healthy wine list. Add to that linen tablecloths and its breezy corner real estate and this tiny Italian eatery is worth a visit.

Overlooking the sea, **Ned Kelly's** (128 Ha Long, tel. 0254/351-0173, 7:30am-midnight daily, VND35,000-300,000) is a ramshackle little Aussie expat bar with cold beer and an assortment of Western dishes. The open-air watering hole serves breakfast, lunch, and dinner as well as a variety of drinks and is open later than most bars in town.

ACCOMMODATIONS

Vung Tau is a small town. Most accommodations are within 5 or 10 minutes' drive of its major sights and beaches. The majority of budget accommodations are located on or around Back Beach, while you'll find fancier, more expensive digs near the Front Beach area. Visiting Vung Tau on the weekend is not a great idea, as the city is flooded with local tourists; book your hotel in advance if you do so, as rooms fill up quickly. Many hotels increase their room rates on the weekends (Sat.-Sun. nights, sometimes Fri. nights).

VND210,000-525,000

No-frills but clean and adequately appointed, the **Dai An Hotel** (151A Hoang Hoa Tham, tel. 0254/625-3299, weekdays VND350,000-650,000, weekends VND600,000-1,100,000) is minutes from Back Beach and a decent value for the money. Each room includes a fan, air-conditioning, hot water, and TV. Baths are spacious, and the hotel staff are kind and easygoing.

Slightly removed from the beachfront tourist zone, ★ **Maccas Place** (31 Lac Long Quan, tel. 0254/352-7042, www.maccashotel.com, VND300,000-400,000) more than makes up for its lack of oceanfront property by providing comfortable, tidy rooms with high ceilings and plenty of light. The staff at this family-owned guesthouse is especially friendly and gives the place a homey feel. Each room has a fan, air-conditioning, TV, hot water, and a minibar; larger rooms have a balcony. A small café downstairs serves light meals and drinks. Maccas Place rents out motorbikes and is willing to help with travel arrangements for sightseeing around Ba Ria-Vung Tau province.

VND525,000-1,050,000

Overlooking the enormous Martyrs' Memorial roundabout, the decor of the **Kieu Anh Hotel** (257 Le Hong Phong, tel. 0254/356-3333, www.kieuanhhotel.vn, VND350,000-1,600,000) is nothing special, but its large rooms offer a beautiful view of the monument at the center of the roundabout as well as the manicured grounds. Beds are large and rooms are clean and quiet. Though the hotel seems isolated, the beach is just a short walk down Le Hong Phong street on the other side of the roundabout. Prices top out at VND950,000 during the week and go up on the weekends.

A beautiful building with well-appointed rooms, the **Ocean Star Hotel** (43A Thuy Van, tel. 0254/358-9589, www.oceanstarhotel.vn, weekdays VND670,000-1,050,000, VND1,000,000-1,450,000) is located right in the heart of Back Beach and offers pleasant views of the ocean. The hotel offers great value for money, as its staff are particularly friendly, and each room comes equipped with modern facilities such as a minibar, hot water, air-conditioning, and a large bath.

VND1,050,000-2,100,000

For a step above average, the **Ky Hoa Hotel** (30-32 Tran Phu, tel. 0254/385-2579, www.kyhoahotel.com.vn, VND1,160,000-2,760,000), just beyond the cable car to Big Mountain, boasts large, modern rooms and excellent views of the sea. All rooms feature air-conditioning, hot water, a TV, and large beds, and the hotel has an on-site restaurant and a pool where guests can soak up the sun just opposite the sea. Built into the mountainside, Ky Hoa has plenty of rooms with a view. Superior-level and higher rooms have better views and include a small balcony.

Over VND2,100,000

With peaceful, shaded grounds, stunning rooms, and a stellar view of the sea, it's hard to believe that a resort like **Binh An Village** (1 Tran Phu, tel. 0254/351-0732, www.binhanvillagevungtau.com, VND1,135,000-3,750,000) exists so close to town. Each spacious room features opulent traditional Vietnamese decor and plush beds along with a sitting area and a large bath. While the smaller rooms are spacious well beyond average, Binh An's larger guest suites include a private garden as well as a separate bathtub and shower. The resort boasts both freshwater and saltwater swimming pools, with the latter built into the ocean and naturally maintained by the ebb and flow of the sea.

INFORMATION AND SERVICES

For medical emergencies, the **Raffles Medical Clinic** (1 Le Ngoc Han, tel. 0254/385-8776, www.rafflesmedicalgroup.com, 8am-5pm Mon.-Fri., 8am-noon Sat.) keeps physicians on-site 24 hours daily. The clinic has regular hours for nonemergency medical consultations.

GETTING THERE
Boat

A handful of high-speed boat companies in HCMC offer departures from **Nha Rong Wharf** (5 Nguyen Tat Thanh, D4) just over the bridge from District 1, with boats leaving roughly every two hours 8:30am-3:30pm daily. **Greenlines DP** (tel. 09/8690-8907, www.greenlines-dp.com, 8am-4pm daily, VND250,000 adults, VND120,000 ages 6-11) makes the trip from Saigon to Vung Tau at 8am, 10am, noon, and 2pm daily, with additional trips at 9am and 4pm on Saturday-Sunday. Vessels depart for the return trip from Vung Tau at 10am, noon, 2pm, and 4pm daily, with extra trips at 1pm and 3pm Saturday-Sunday. The trip takes about an hour and 20 minutes and drops you at the centrally located **Ferry Terminal** (Tran Phu) in Vung Tau, just a stone's throw from Front Beach.

In most cases, it is possible to show up at the wharf a half-hour or so beforehand and purchase the ticket then, but if you're visiting Vung Tau on a holiday or weekend, it's best to reserve your seat ahead of time, as this is a popular destination for city folks taking a long weekend. Fares sometimes go up on weekends and holidays. If you plan to buy a ticket on the day of departure, check the website to confirm that the time you want is still available.

Bus

From HCMC, tourist buses heading to Vung Tau depart regularly from the Pham Ngu Lao area and the **Eastern bus station (Ben Xe Mien Dong)** (292 Dinh Bo Linh, HCMC, tel. 028/3899-1607). Several reputable companies make the trip, including **Phuong Trang** (272 De Tham, HCMC, tel. 028/3838-6852, www.futabuslines.com.vn, 5am-1am daily, VND95,000) and **Kumho Samco** (239 Pham Ngu Lao, HCMC, tel. 028/3511-2112, www.kumhosamco.com.vn, 4:30am-7pm daily, VND95,000). The trip takes 2.5-3 hours, and buses arrive at the **Vung Tau bus station** (192 Nam Ky Khoi Nghia, HCMC, tel. 0254/385-9727), about 1.5 kilometers from both Front and Back Beaches. Equally reliable is **Hoa Mai** (44 Nguyen Thai Binh, HCMC, tel. 0254/351-5200, 4am-7pm daily, VND90,000), which runs minibus shuttles to Vung Tau 4am-7pm daily and has an office in downtown Saigon.

GETTING AROUND

Because of all the tourists, taking a cab in Vung Tau is notably more expensive than in HCMC. If you're in a larger group it may still be cost-effective to hop in a **Mailinh** (tel. 0254/356-5656) or **Vinasun** (tel. 025/3727-2727) taxi when getting around town; opt for a *xe om* if you're traveling solo or in smaller numbers.

It's necessary to bargain for *xe om* rides in Vung Tau. The town is small, so a ride around town should cost VND30,000-40,000, though be prepared to pay more if you go farther out of the town center. Most hotels in town can arrange a **motorbike** for hire. Prices should range VND100,000-175,000 per day.

Con Dao Islands

Arriving in Con Dao is a surreal experience. After the claustrophobic cities of Vietnam's southern coast, the sight of lush, wild green hills and rocky precipices is like a postcard. Made up of 16 individual islands, Con Dao is one of the best-kept secrets in Vietnam: a spectacular combination of white sand beaches, thick forests, and sharp sun-bleached cliffs plunging into the turquoise sea. With 80 percent of Con Son, the main island, a protected national park, there are dozens of opportunities for the adventurous traveler, including hiking, diving, and snorkeling. Endemic species such as the giant black squirrel and bow-fingered gecko can be found along national park trails with monkeys and several species of birds.

Con Dao was once the site of several of the nation's most brutal prisons, built by the French during the colonial era and used through the American War to house political prisoners. These horrific places claimed the lives of 20,000 Vietnamese from 1862 until the late 1970s. A look at the surviving prisoners is a who's who of the Communist party. Only a handful of the country's prime ministers since reunification did not see the inside of a Con Dao prison. Though locals also venture here for the stunning natural scenery, a visit to the prison cemetery and the shrine of Vo Thi Sau, the first Vietnamese woman to be executed by the French, is all but required for Vietnamese.

Con Dao's relative isolation from the tourist crowds of the mainland means some initiative is required to make your own fun. English speakers on Con Son are few. Locals are friendly, and good humor and a few charades go a long way in communication. As a result of its remoteness, certain costs differ from the mainland. Accommodations tend to be cheaper—though more limited—than you might find elsewhere, but food is usually more expensive. Unless you're willing to spend big at Six Senses, the island's sole five-star resort, restaurants serve only Vietnamese cuisine. The main town on Con Son is very small. It makes little difference where you stay, and most resorts are located on the coastal road; budget options are set farther back into town.

SIGHTS

With the exception of the prison complex, most of the sights around Con Dao are located within the national park.

Museums

Set amid a large clearing just north of Vo Thi Sau Park, the **Con Dao Museum** (10 Nguyen Hue, tel. 0254/383-0517, 7:30am-11:30am and 1:30pm-4:30pm Mon.-Sat., free) is a modern take on the islands' older Revolutionary Museum. This museum possesses decent English signage and takes visitors through the history of the islands, from its first European

Con Son Island

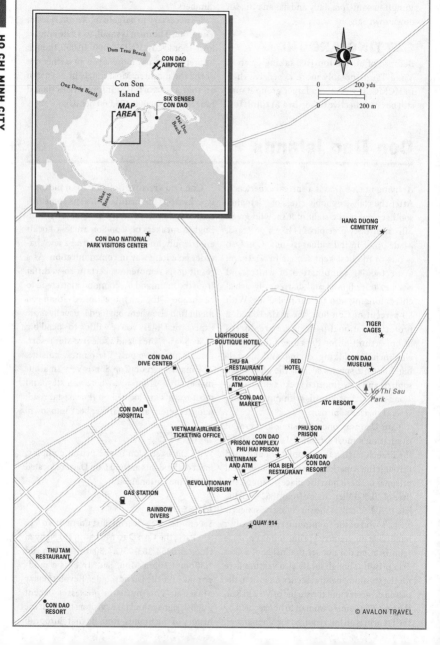

Dam Trau Beach

CON DAO AIRPORT

Con Son Island

Ong Dung Beach

MAP AREA

SIX SENSES CON DAO

Dat Doc Beach

Nhat Beach

0   200 yds
0   200 m

HANG DUONG CEMETERY

CON DAO NATIONAL PARK VISITORS CENTER

TIGER CAGES

LIGHTHOUSE BOUTIQUE HOTEL

CON DAO DIVE CENTER

THU BA RESTAURANT

RED HOTEL

CON DAO MUSEUM

TECHCOMBANK ATM

CON DAO MARKET

Vo Thi Sau Park

CON DAO HOSPITAL

ATC RESORT

VIETNAM AIRLINES TICKETING OFFICE

PHU SON PRISON

CON DAO PRISON COMPLEX/ PHU HAI PRISON

VIETINBANK AND ATM

HOA BIEN RESTAURANT

SAIGON CON DAO RESORT

REVOLUTIONARY MUSEUM

GAS STATION

RAINBOW DIVERS

QUAY 914

THU TAM RESTAURANT

CON DAO RESORT

© AVALON TRAVEL

settlers in the early 1500s through the brutal Con Dao prison system and into the present day. While these exhibits encompass all of Con Dao's past, it is the island's penal history that features most heavily in the museum. In-depth displays cover everything from the daily lives of inmates to the facility's development as a revolutionary school and the harsh mistreatment suffered at the hands of Con Dao's prison guards. If you have the time and interest, this location does an admirable job of providing visitors with detailed information on one of the darkest eras in modern Vietnamese history.

The older, more abridged version of Con Dao's prison history is at the **Revolutionary Museum** (Ton Duc Thang opposite Quay 914, tel. 0254/383-0517, 7:30am-11am and 2pm-4:30pm Mon.-Sat., VND40,000), where exhibits feature more photos and historical write-ups than actual artifacts. The majority of these images appear at the newer Con Dao Museum as well, so a visit to both venues is unnecessary. If you're looking for a more condensed version of the island's history, this is the place. Entry tickets for this museum are also valid for the prison complex, so hang onto your receipt to show the guides at each respective location.

Con Dao Prison Complex

Perched on the northeastern edge of town, the mossy crumbling stone exterior of the **Con Dao Prison Complex** (Le Van Viet, tel. 0254/383-0517, 7:30am-11am and 2pm-4:30pm Mon.-Sat., VND40,000) serves as a reminder of the island's grim history. From as early as 1862, the cells within these high-walled structures housed Vietnamese political prisoners banished to the island for acting out against the French colonial government. Kilometers away from the mainland and public view, guards quickly became known for their harsh treatment and torture of prisoners, which included forced labor, beatings, and starvation. The conditions of the prison's dank cells were equally miserable, with dozens of inmates crammed into dimly lit rooms and often shackled at the ankles, unable to move. As the number of political dissidents grew, so did the facilities on Con Dao. At its height, the island contained eight separate facilities, each as cruel and unforgiving as the next.

While it is still possible to visit most of the prisons on the island, the main facilities are Phu Hai and Phu Son, located beside one another on Le Van Viet street, as well as the infamously brutal tiger cages a little farther out of

fishing boats off Con Dao

The Island Prison of Con Dao

Vietnam is eager to cast off the darker days of the 20th century, opting instead to look toward the future. Many of its wartime sites have been transformed into tourist attractions. While there are plenty of past hardships that the nation seems ready to shrug off, Con Dao still weighs heavily upon Vietnam's collective psyche.

In 1862, a few years after the French wrested control from Vietnam's emperors, the colonial government went to great pains to suppress political dissent. Outspoken locals were imprisoned on the small island of Con Son, 179 kilometers from mainland Vietnam. Until the end of the American War, inmates were mercilessly beaten, tortured, starved, and worked to death. The French guards were ruthless, enacting cruel and severe punishments. Forced labor built many of the island's roads and structures, including Quay 914, whose name comes from the 914 prisoners who died over the course of its construction. The miserable living conditions and meager rations were so bad that diseases like leprosy spread rapidly, killing some and leaving others permanently disfigured. The Con Dao prisons claimed 20,000 Vietnamese lives.

Though widely regarded as the most terrible of the prison facilities, the island's infamous tiger cages were but one of a wider array of punishments, along with solitary confinement units, in which prisoners were forced to exist in ghastly and unsanitary conditions. Built in 1907 to accommodate the offenders of a student uprising, the tiger cages allowed guards to survey their prisoners from above and permitted inmates very little light or space to move. Those who managed to survive these dank cells often left with debilitating physical injuries, their muscles atrophied from being shackled in the same place for weeks or months at a time.

After the French left, the American-backed South Vietnamese government took over the prison, maintaining the policies of torture and abuse. American officials swore throughout the 1960s and 1970s that Con Dao's tiger cages were no longer in use—until 1970, when photographer Tom Harkin and two American congressmen, Representatives Augustus Hawkins and William

town on Nguyen Van Cu. Phu Hai, Con Dao's original prison, is the largest of these buildings and depicts the harsh living conditions of its former inmates with the help of mannequins, which are shackled in the same place where many prisoners once sat. Next door, Phu Son is similar but holds added notoriety as one of the main centers of Communist training within the prison system. Farther afield, the tiger cages sit eerily empty; guests are free to wander around on their own, treading the catwalk above these dark, isolated cells, just as the prison guards would have.

Entrance tickets can be purchased at any of the prisons or at the **Revolutionary Museum** (Ton Duc Thang opposite Quay 914, tel. 0254/383-0517, 7:30am-11am and 2pm-4:30pm Mon.-Sat., VND40,000) and are valid for all locations as long as you keep the ticket handy to show the gatekeepers. There is little to no signage in most of these places, which

is why a visit to either the Revolutionary Museum or the Con Dao Museum is recommended in order to have a better understanding of the history associated with these aging buildings.

Vo Thi Sau Park

The island's most famous in a long list of revolutionaries, Vo Thi Sau was just 14 years old when she joined a Communist volunteer police outfit. Despite her youth, she became involved in plots to attack and kill French officials, some of which succeeded. In 1950, at 17, Vo Thi Sau was arrested by the French. Due to her age and the harsh public reaction an immediate execution was sure to produce, officials waited until she was 19 before carrying out the young woman's death penalty in 1952. This made Vo Thi Sau the first Vietnamese woman to be executed by the French. Today, she is deeply revered by locals and nearly

Anderson, visited the prison on a government-led tour. Armed with a map drawn by a student who had just been released from the tiger cages, the men discovered the prison's entrance, masked by a vegetable garden. Harkin's photos were published in *LIFE* magazine in July 1970 and served as another blow against American involvement in Vietnam.

Con Dao's overcrowded facilities fast became a de facto training school for the opposition. Shackled side-by-side for hours at a time, the prisoners studied Communist theory and, during the American reign, even published several news magazines, with the written materials smuggled out of the prisons, printed, and then returned to the grounds, where they were disseminated among the inmates. Many of the Communist party's most famous players did time at Con Dao. In a country where most streets and public spaces are named after national heroes, nearly all of the island's roadways bear the name of a former prisoner who went on to greatness.

the Con Dao Prison Complex

When the American War ended in 1975, word traveled quickly to Con Dao, where frightened prison guards fled at the news, leaving the island to the Communist captives. On May 4, 1975, nearly 7,500 prisoners walked out of their cells, free at last, to greet the arrival of the Vietnamese navy. Today, visiting the prisons is a rite of passage among locals, who come to pay their respects to the collective ancestors who struggled for national independence.

every Vietnamese visitor to the island pays their respects at her grave. Though the **Vo Thi Sau Park** (in front of Con Dao Museum, Ton Duc Thang and Nguyen Hue) is small and far less ornamental, there is a small building on the grounds dedicated to offerings for the young revolutionary.

Quay 914

At the center of town, a long sandy walkway protrudes out into the harbor just beyond Saigon Con Dao Resort. This is **Quay 914** (intersection of Ton Duc Thang and Le Duan), not an impressive sight but a historical one. During the brutal years of French rule, prisoners were forced to construct this pier, beginning in 1873 and carrying on for decades. When prisoners faltered or refused to continue work they were beaten severely, causing 914 deaths during the pier's construction. Today, the quay still functions as an integral

part of the harbor. A small plaque honoring the fallen prisoners stands at the entrance.

Hang Duong Cemetery

Though it wasn't constructed until after reunification, the **Hang Duong Cemetery** (Nguyen An Ninh, tel. 0254/383-0517), just outside of town, serves as a final resting place for many of Con Dao's deceased prisoners. In the same spot where, years before, French and American guards had carelessly disposed of Vietnamese bodies, the manicured grounds of Hang Duong are now a peaceful green space with winding pathways.

A walk up the main road brings you to the cemetery's large martyr's monument, a towering stone structure. Hang Duong's most famous resident resides to the left of the main path. Amid a sea of modest red-and-yellow headstones, the large black tomb of Vo Thi Sau, the first Vietnamese woman to be executed by the French, lies in sharp contrast to the other graves in the area. Its sleek exterior is laden with offerings, from fruit and drinks to flowers, incense, and prayers. Beyond the young revolutionary's resting place, the sight of so many headstones in one area helps to illustrate just how many prisoners succumbed to the harsh conditions on Con Dao.

Con Dao National Park

The largest attraction on Con Son, **Con Dao National Park** (visitors center 29 Vo Thi Sau, tel. 0254/383-0669, www.condaopark. com.vn, 7am-11:30am and 1:30pm-5pm daily, VND60,000 adults, VND20,000 children) is home to approximately 160 species of animals, including three found only on the islands, as well as over a 1,000 marine species. The park boasts hiking trails, snorkeling beaches, camping, and bird-watching excursions. Stop by the visitors center to arrange guides, hire boats, or book tours to the different areas of the park. Make your booking at least a day in advance. Given the temperamental weather of the island and the limited organization of the park offices, guides and tours are subject to sudden changes or cancellations; head to the national park office as soon as you arrive in order to allow enough time for any scheduling hiccups that may occur. At the time of writing, there was no entry fee to the park for hikers; this is expected to change in the near future.

TOP EXPERIENCE

BEACHES

While there are a handful of sandy stretches along the main drag that are largely used for fishing, the best of the island's beaches lie farther afield. Wherever you lay out your towel and catch sun, there is little chance you'll be disappointed, with far fewer people and far less pollution than on the mainland. Locations range from easily accessible to a few hours' trek. Always bring insect repellent, as the sand flies can be a major issue.

Dat Doc Beach

Stretching along the southern coast just before you enter town is **Dat Doc Beach,** a beautiful patch of white sand framed by dramatic cliffs and rocky precipices. Hidden from view by a wall of shaggy trees and underbrush, this quiet beach comes in just close enough to make it easily accessible from town but remains far enough away that the harbor is invisible from here, and so you are left with the company of blue skies, turquoise seas, and a glimpse of the ultra-swanky interior of Six Senses, the island's only five-star resort.

Nhat Beach

Rounding out the other end of town, **Nhat Beach** sits just beside Con Son's ferry docks, slightly rocky and more visible from the road but still gifted with the same awe-inspiring views of the sea and the sharp rise and fall of the island's cliffs. This is a beautiful place from which to take in a good island vista, but not the best for swimming on account of its terrain.

Ong Dung Beach

The most easily accessible beach on the northern shore, **Ong Dung Beach** is a 20- to 30-minute hike from the end of Vo Thi Sau street, just past the national park office, and is a popular spot among visitors. Follow the path down to the water to swim, snorkel, and enjoy the beach. This particular stretch is not ideal for sunbathing, as the sandy area is small. It does make for great snorkeling farther out, with an array of colorful sea creatures on the reef. Snorkeling gear can be rented from the national park outpost here; the more adventurous can make a full loop from the thick rainforest of So Ray down to the beach and then back around into town on Vo Thi Sau street.

Dam Trau Beach

Popularly known as Airport Beach, **Dam Trau** is the pristine white-sand ribbon you see stretched across the north shore when approaching Con Dao from the sky.

Picture-perfect and surrounded by emerald green palm trees, this beach is the ideal oasis for travelers hoping to lay out a towel and catch some rays. Stunning and secluded, Dam Trau is a more peaceful option than Ong Dung—with the exception of a small number of daily plane departures. It has a beautiful area for swimming, though don't bother snorkeling here, as you'll find the fish are few and far between.

SPORTS AND RECREATION
Diving

Though the islands themselves are quiet, Con Dao is known as the best diving spot in Vietnam. Even so, the slow-but-steady trickle of visitors has only managed to keep a couple diving outfits in business, and with a recent dip in tourists to the island, even those are struggling. All of Con Dao's diving outfits require you to have comprehensive dive insurance before going out, as the islands are remote and any serious medical treatment means an airlift to Saigon. If you don't purchase insurance beforehand, it's possible to buy coverage on-site. Given the temperamental weather of the islands, if you plan to dive, contact a Con Dao dive outfit ahead of time to make sure that you will be able to dive during your stay on the island.

Rainbow Divers Con Dao (40 Ton Duc Thang, tel. 09/0557-7671, www.divevietnam.com, 9am-9pm daily, VND1,100,000-12,520,000) sets up shop on the island every year March-September and staffs qualified dive instructors and guides. In addition to recreational dives and snorkeling trips, the shop also runs PADI certification and advanced courses for more experienced divers.

For year-round diving, the **Con Dao Dive Center** (Bar200, Nguyen Van Linh, tel. 09/3700-8483, www.divecondao.com, 10am-2pm and 5pm-10pm daily, VND1,000,000-11,550,000) is the only other option on the island. Certified instructors and guides lead everything from try dives and snorkeling excursions to longer scuba trips and PADI courses.

Hiking

From the center of town there are several hiking trails that you can take through the national park area that allow for wildlife-spotting and beach time. Most treks can be done without hiring a guide. Wear decent shoes and stick to the trails. Hikes to So Ray, where monkeys, birds, and the endemic black squirrel can be seen, take about 45 minutes and require a moderate level of fitness, while the trek to Ong Dung Beach is an easy 30-minute walk. Farther afield near the airport, a two-hour hike to Dam Tre Bay is possible, though it is required that you hire a guide for this journey, as changing tides and weather conditions make it necessary to have a local on hand. Guides can be hired at the **national park office** (visitors center 29 Vo Thi Sau, tel. 0254/383-0669, www.condaopark.com.vn, 7am-11:30am and 1:30pm-5pm daily) for VND300,000-500,000. Most don't speak English but are knowledgeable about the terrain and conditions along these routes.

Wildlife-Watching

Turtle- and bird-watching trips can be booked through the national park office. The best time for bird-watching is in the summer months. It is recommended that you steer clear of Con Dao's turtle-watching excursions, as there have been reports of animal abuses within the park.

FOOD

Con Dao has little in the way of proper eateries, and the only cuisine served is Vietnamese. There are a cluster of **street food vendors** selling broken rice, pho, banh mi sandwiches, rice porridge, and other cheap local meals around the intersection of **Ton Duc Thang and Nguyen Hue** streets as well as near the market. Many of the nicer hotels, including Saigon Con Dao, have restaurants attached, which you can patronize even if you're not a guest, and the **local market** (corner of Vo Thi

Sau and Tran Phu) sells fruit and snacks from the wee hours of the morning, though there is a noontime siesta.

With very few restaurants in town and even fewer that offer a decent selection, **Thu Ba Restaurant** (Vo Thi Sau, tel. 0254/383-0255, 10am-10pm daily, VND70,000-350,000) stands out as a more diverse eatery than most. Its menu goes beyond the standard seafood options that occupy most menus on the island to include pork, beef, chicken, and vegetarian dishes. Servers speak some English and are friendly and easygoing.

At the far end of the Saigon Tourist line of properties, **Hoa Bien Restaurant** (Ton Duc Thang, tel. 0254/383-0336, 6am-10pm daily, VND80,000-400,000) has a nice view of the ocean and decent Vietnamese fare. Seafood features heavily on the menu, but other options are also available. Open-air dining looks out onto the picturesque Con Dao harbor, and portions on the family-style menu are generous.

A more diversified option, **Thu Tam** (Nguyen Duc Thuan, tel. 0254/360-8040, nhahangthutam@yahoo.com.vn, 8:30am-10pm daily, VND50,000-300,000), located directly opposite of Con Dao Seatravel Resort, features a plethora of breakfast, lunch, and dinner items with friendly service. The dining room is a large, open-air area where those who opt for seafood dishes are able to choose their meal from a series of small fish tanks lining the far wall. Prices are reasonable and the restaurant is open late.

ACCOMMODATIONS

There is a large divide between high-end resorts and dirt-cheap budget hotels. Some accommodations have less-than-stellar business practices and, with so few options available, it's easy to wind up with a bad apple. Larger hotels have information listed online and arrange airport pickup for guests. Smaller, more inexpensive guesthouses tend to have fewer reviews and recommendations, though there are a handful of reliable places in town.

VND525,000-1,050,000

Farther from the beach and closer to the national park office, **Lighthouse Boutique Hotel** (10 Ho Thanh Tong, tel. 0254/350-8077, VND500,000-800,000) is clean, quiet, and affordable. Rooms are basic, featuring Wi-Fi, TV, air-conditioning, and a fan; the beds are large. The hotel assists with additional travel arrangements, such as tour bookings and ferry tickets.

Clean, if a bit cramped, rooms at the **Red Hotel** (17B Nguyen An Ninh, tel. 0254/363-0079, VND570,000-800,000) feature two twin beds apiece, decent baths, Wi-Fi, cable TV, and plenty of light. Rates vary with the number of people. The hotel staff assist guests with tour arrangements and motorbike rentals.

VND1,050,000-2,100,000

Housed in a beautiful, expansive set of colonial-style villas, **Saigon Con Dao** (18-24 Ton Duc Thang, tel. 0254/383-0336, www.saigon-condao.com, VND1,590,000-3,390,000) resort is a property of the mammoth Saigon Tourist company. Featuring a large swimming pool, two restaurants, and a tropical garden, the hotel has rooms that are a little dated but nice and spacious with large baths and, in some cases, a sitting room. Breakfast is included in the rates, as is airport pickup and drop-off. The hotel offers motorbike rentals, tour information, and flight ticket services.

Beyond the shore-hugging street of Ton Duc Thang, **Con Dao Resort** (8 Nguyen Duc Thuan, tel. 0254/383-0979, www.condaoresort.vn, VND1,900,000-4,200,000) features tasteful rooms with enclosed showers and private balconies as well as a pool, tennis courts, and a pristine private beach that runs along the far edge of the harbor. Breakfast and airport pickup are included in the rates, and the staff speak decent English.

ATC Resort (8 Ton Duc Thang, tel. 0254/383-0456, www.atcresort.com, VND730,000-5,515,000) boasts a friendly and conscientious staff on top of its spacious well-appointed rooms, which include air-conditioning, cable TV, Wi-Fi, breakfast, and airport pickup. ATC is located across the street from the harbor beach. There is a private outdoor pool hidden by the surrounding buildings for guests to use. Each room comes with a private balcony with a view of the pool, garden, or sea.

Over VND2,100,000

The island's sole luxury lodging, **Six Senses Con Dao** (Dat Doc, tel. 0254/383-1222, www.sixsenses.com, VND17,300,000-70,000,000) is a secluded beachfront property whose lavish rooms and exclusivity are second to none. Each split-level villa comes with a private infinity pool and panoramic ocean views as well as high-end amenities, including satellite TV, a BOSE sound system, and butler service. Six Senses also counts a spa, several restaurants, and activity services in its offerings.

INFORMATION AND SERVICES

The **Vietnam Airlines ticketing office** (44A Nguyen Hue, tel. 0254/383-1831, condaobranch@vasco.com.vn, 7:30am-11:30am and 1:30pm-5pm Mon.-Fri.) can help arrange and confirm flight reservations.

There are two ATMs on the island, a **Techcombank ATM** (corner of Vo Thi Sau and Tran Phu, opposite the market) and one beside **Vietin Bank** (2 Le Duan, tel. 0254/383-0162, www.vietinbank.vn, 7:30am-11:30am and 1:30pm-4:30pm Mon.-Fri., 8am-11am Sat.). These ATMs are prone to malfunction, so bring enough cash for your entire stay. Foreign currencies cannot be exchanged on the island.

Con Dao's only **hospital** (corner of Le Hong Phong and Pham Van Dong, tel. 0254/383-0128, 7am-11:30am and 1:30pm-5pm daily) is located just north of the town's only roundabout, and facilities are about as rudimentary as they come. The staff do not speak English. While minor injuries and illnesses may be treatable here, anything beyond that will require a trip to the mainland.

GETTING THERE
Air

Despite its growing popularity, Con Dao is still a very difficult place to reach. **Vietnam Airlines** (ticketing office 44A Nguyen Hue, tel. 0254/383-1831, condaobranch@vasco.com.vn, 7:30am-11:30am and 1:30pm-5pm Mon.-Fri.) is the only carrier to serve the small **Con Son Airport** (VCS, Khu Dan Cu 1, Con Dao). Flights run several times a week, with fewer options than you might have for other destinations. Tickets cost VND1,000,000-2,000,000 each way. The flight is 45 minutes and arrives at Con Dao airport, 14.5 kilometers from town. Most hotels on the island offer airport pickup if you book in advance. You can also jump on several of the hotel minibuses for VND50,000 and they will take you where you want to go. Don't bother with hailing a taxi—a fare from the airport into the center of town runs about VND300,000.

Boat

In 2017, local speedboat operator **Superdong** (Le Duan, tel. 0254/363-0138, www.superdong.com.vn, 7am-5pm daily, VND310,000) opened a route between downtown Con Dao and the Mekong Delta province of Soc Trang. While the mainland drop-off point is not in an especially convenient location, speedboat tickets cut the cost of a trip to Con Dao significantly. Vessels depart from Soc Trang at 8am and 1:15pm daily and reach the shores of Con Son in 2.5 hours.

GETTING AROUND

Since the island is so small, the best way to explore is on two wheels. Hiring a bicycle or motorbike gives you the freedom to head out on your own and appreciate the island scenery. Due to the island's size, most roads are easy to navigate both in and out of the main town. Due to its location, weather on Con Son is very temperamental and strong gusts can be dangerous when driving. Especially during the last few months of the year, when Con Dao is at its windiest, pay special attention to the roads, as accidents do happen.

Taxi

There are a handful of **taxis** (tel. 09/1807-6345) that make their rounds on the island at a much higher cost than the ones you'd find on the mainland. Base rates are roughly double what you'd pay elsewhere in Vietnam, starting at VND25,000 just to enter the taxi.

Bike and Motorbike

Once on the island, the easiest and most cost-effective way to get around is by renting a motorbike or bicycle. Most guesthouses rent out either vehicle for a daily fee; check the quality of your bike before setting out on a long trip.

Con Son has only one **gas station** (corner of Nguyen Hue and Ngo Gia Tu, 6am-11:30am and 1:30pm-8pm daily). Also beware that driving on the coastal roads can be a challenge in strong winds, especially if you're traveling by pedal power. Proceed with caution and always take it easy on the turns.

Excursion to Angkor Wat

TOP EXPERIENCE

From Vietnam, travel to Cambodia, and specifically to Siem Reap, the gateway to Angkor Wat, has become notably more affordable and accessible in recent years, as budget airlines open routes to the area and with regular flights from Ho Chi Minh City and Hanoi. Overland travel is also possible, though the ride from Saigon to Siem Reap is a long and arduous journey.

As the largest religious site in the world and one of the most famous monuments in Southeast Asia, the sprawling network of temples at Angkor is a cherished symbol of the Khmer people. Spread over 400 square kilometers, this ancient city once served as the center of the Khmer empire, a powerful kingdom whose scope expanded beyond Cambodia's present-day borders into neighboring Thailand, Laos, and Vietnam.

Home to a complex system of temples, roads, and hydraulic structures, the Angkorian period began in the early 800s AD and lasted until the middle of the 15th century. During this time, Khmer kings created a city to rival the size of Cambodia's present-day capital, Phnom Penh, making Angkor the largest empire on earth in the 12th century. Some of the area's most famous temples, including Angkor Wat, Bayon, and Ta Prohm, were built in the 12th century.

Though Khmers have always revered the complex and its temples as a national symbol—Angkor Wat features prominently on the Cambodian flag—outsiders knew little of the city during its heyday. In fact, only a handful of foreign accounts exist from the height of the empire, namely the 13th-century report of Chinese trader Zhou Daguan, who visited Angkor in 1296 to find a thriving prosperous city. Europeans did not know of the empire until the 1800s, when France colonized Cambodia and took an intense interest in the area's then-overgrown temples, specifically Angkor Wat. Throughout the early 20th century, a group of archaeologists and philologists known as the Ecole Francaise d'Extreme Orient conducted research on the temples and their surrounding structures.

Toward the end of the 20th-century, as the Khmer Rouge came to power and war broke out in Cambodia, Angkorian temples suffered theft and destruction, but research resumed in the 1990s and archaeologists continue to uncover new information about the complex to this day.

Though researchers have several theories on the matter, the fall of the Khmer empire remains a mystery. Some believe the neighboring Ayutthaya, or Thai, empire sacked the city and drove its inhabitants out, putting an end to Khmer rule. Others think climate change was Angkor's downfall, arguing that a long drought followed by heavy monsoon rains

Siem Reap and Angkor

ANGKOR

- PREAH KHAN ★
- NEAK PEAN ★
- BANTEAY SREI ★
- TERRACE OF THE LEPER KING ★
- PHIMEANAKAS ★
- TERRACE OF THE ELEPHANTS ★
- BAPHUON ★
- BAYON ★
- TA PROHM ★
- SRAH SRANG ★
- ANGKOR THOM SOUTH GATE ★
- BANTEAY KDEI ★
- PHNOM BAKHENG ★
- BLUE PUMPKIN ANGKOR CAFÉ ▼
- ANGKOR WAT ★
- GRAND CIRCUIT/PETIT CIRCUIT

0   600 yds
0   600 m

SEE "ANGKOR" DETAIL

- PREAH KHAN ★
- BAYON ★
- PRE RUP ★
- ANGKOR WAT ★
- GRAND CIRCUIT
- PETIT CIRCUIT

SIEM REAP INTERNATIONAL AIRPORT ✈

SEE "SIEM REAP" DETAIL

APSARA AUTHORITY TICKETING OFFICE

STREET 52

KROVAT KRONG

0   2 mi
0   2 km

NATIONAL ROAD 63

TONLE SAP BOATING DOCKS

SIEM REAP

- ANGKOR NATIONAL MUSEUM
- 6
- PARKLANE HOTEL
- RAFFLES GRAND HOTEL D'ANGKOR
- CHARLES DE GAULLE
- KOMAY RD
- TEP VONG ST
- OUM KHUN ST
- TAPHUL ST
- SIVATHA BLVD
- POKAMBOR ST
- WAT BO RD
- 0   250 yds
- 0   250 m
- GREEN E-BIKES
- ACHAMEAN ST
- SISTER SREY CAFÉ
- THE WHITE BICYCLES/ SORIA MORIA BOUTIQUE HOTEL
- GIANT IBIS SIEM REAP
- HOSPITAL ST
- KONH SEN ST
- GRASSHOPPER ADVENTURES
- DIAMOND D'ANGKOR
- SOK SAN RD
- ROHATT CAFÉ
- 72
- BOUTIQUE DORMITORY KOCHI-KE
- KING'S ROAD ANGKOR
- 7 MAKARA
- NIGHT MARKET
- STREET 52
- CUISINE WAT DAMNAK ▼
- APSARA CENTREPOLE
- 63
- OLD MARKET
- CHAMKAR HOUSE
- AMOK

© AVALON TRAVEL

Tourist Visas

All visitors to Cambodia are required to purchase a visa, which can be done on arrival at a border gate, at the airport in Siem Reap, or online (www.evisa.gov.kh). One-month single-entry tourist visas cost US$30 and require you to fill out paperwork and have your fingerprints scanned. Do not confuse these with the US$35 "ordinary visa," which is unnecessary unless you plan on staying in Cambodia for an extended period of time; it also allows for a one-month stay, but can be extended indefinitely as it's intended for those planning to work, study, or settle in the country. All visas to Cambodia must be paid for in American currency, so have U.S. dollars and at least one passport photo on hand when you arrive. If you show up without a passport photo, you may be asked to pay an additional US$2 fee.

Online applicants should bear in mind that e-visa pickup is only available at certain border crossings. Both Siem Reap and Phnom Penh international airports support the e-visa system, as does Vietnam's Moc Bai-Bavet border crossing, the typical route for travelers entering Cambodia from HCMC. If you enter Cambodia through most other border gates, however, you will not be able to claim your e-visa on arrival. For an updated list of border crossings that support the e-visa system, check the Cambodian government's e-visa website. E-visa applications typically take three business days to process, and travelers are required to pay a US$6 fee for the online application.

Should you choose to apply for a visa on-arrival, the process is relatively quick and easy. This option is available at all airports and border crossings into Cambodia. For overland travelers coming from Vietnam, note that most cross-border bus services charge an additional US$5 for the convenience of arranging your visa.

rendered much of the area's hydraulic system unusable, forcing inhabitants to leave. Still others believe factors like the mass conversion of Angkorians to Theravada Buddhism, the rise of maritime trade, and the city's growing population all contributed to its demise.

Whatever the reason, Angkor remains a deeply significant part of Khmer history and culture. For Cambodians, the temples are a symbol of national identity. For outsiders, the sophisticated architecture, lasting construction, and incredible scale of the temples at Angkor make it a sight unlike any other.

Today, the area is relatively well preserved, with international funding allotted to numerous preservation projects throughout the park, but the Angkor complex continues to struggle with high visitor numbers as more travelers come to experience the wonder of the temples—a whopping 2.5 million visitors came in 2017. During sunrise and sunset hours, park officials have begun to regulate the number of tourists atop certain temples

in an effort to minimize their impact on the structures.

For more detailed information on Angkor Wat, see *Moon Angkor Wat* by Tom Vater.

SIEM REAP

When it comes to sights, nothing in Siem Reap quite compares to the Angkorian temples just north of town, but if you're looking to while away a few hours, this sleepy little town has a handful of attractions to keep you occupied. Situated on the western side of a river, the town center is packed with bars—Pub Street has a reputation as a party street, and its bars are particularly lively—restaurants, and souvenir shops, as well as the Old Market located directly on the riverfront. Move a little further north and you'll come across the Angkor National Museum and a collection of grander accommodations lining the route into Angkor Archaeological Park. A quick jaunt across the river to the east provides a slightly mellower version of Siem Reap, with local eats and quieter streets.

Angkor National Museum

The regal **Angkor National Museum** (968 Vithei Charles de Gaulle, tel. 06/396-6601, www.angkornationalmuseum.com, 8:30am-6pm daily Apr.-Sept. and 8:30am-6:30pm Oct.-Mar., US$12 adults, US$6 children 6-11) provides ample explanation of the religious, cultural, and historical complexities of the kingdom's most famous sights in its seven well-organized exhibition halls. Audio guides are available for US$5 to provide further background. If you're not a major history buff, this museum isn't a must-see—the temples themselves are far more impressive—but for those who plan to visit the Angkor park without a guide, this is worth a visit ahead of your temple-touring.

Markets

Around 5pm, the streets of downtown Siem Reap come alive for the **Angkor Night Market** (5pm-10:30pm daily), a bustling tourist attraction that covers several sidewalks with snack stalls, mobile drinking venues, and souvenir hawkers. Just west of Pub Street, the night market has a lively atmosphere and makes for a nice evening stroll, offering both shopping and entertainment. Many vendors begin to pack up around 10:30pm, though some stick around until 11pm. Nearby, the riverfront **Old Market** (10am-8pm daily) also sells souvenirs and is open throughout the day. More souvenirs, accessories, clothing, and other knickknacks are also available directly across the river at **King's Road Angkor** (corner of 7-Makara and Achar Sva, tel. 01/034-5643, http://kingsroadangkor. com, noon-10pm daily), with goods made in Cambodia. Starting around midday, it offers a high-quality showcase of local designers' products in addition to housing a handful of upscale restaurants.

Food

Siem Reap's eats run the gamut from cheap local roadside fare to high-end reservation-only fine dining. Plenty of local restaurants along Sok San Street have the most affordable meals. In the evenings, the area around Pub Street is full of snack carts and inexpensive barbecue joints, as is the sidewalk along the river. Whatever you do, make sure to try *phnom pleung*, the mouth-watering Cambodian version of do-it-yourself barbecue.

Cheerful **Sister Srey Café** (200 Pokambor, tel. 09/7723-8001, www.sistersreycafe.com, 7am-6pm Tues.-Sun., US$1-6) serves an array of healthy breakfast and lunch options as well as beverages from a charming open-air storefront along the river. Prices are reasonable, and the laid-back atmosphere makes this a good spot to start your day.

Boasting a leafy green terrace and quiet indoor seating in the King's Road market, **Rohatt Café** (Vithei Acha Svar, tel. 09/388-8500, 7am-11pm daily, US$4-13) serves an impressive variety of Khmer dishes as well as a few Western options. Prices are more reasonable than the tourist restaurants across the river, and the staff is friendly and attentive.

Though it's definitely geared toward tourists, the brightly-colored **Amok** (Street 9, tel. 08/550-6396, www.amokrestaurant.com, 8am-11pm daily, US$4-15), named after Cambodia's most famous dish, is a solid option for those hoping to get acquainted with Khmer cuisine. The menu features exclusively Khmer dishes, including a discovery menu that includes a starter, main, and dessert. À la carte options include an array of skewers, curry, and other delights. Both sides of the restaurant's dining area are decked out in vibrant patterns, but those seeking peace and quiet will appreciate the alley-side dining room, which is a bit quieter than the bustling roadside area out front.

Vegetarian diners can experience Khmer cuisine at **Chamkar House** (Khum Svay Dangkum, tel. 09/273-3150, chamkarangkor@gmail.com, 11:20am-10:30pm Mon.-Sat., 4:30pm-10:30pm Sun., last order 10pm, US$3-6). Its menu features a range of fresh, healthy Khmer dishes minus the meat, and the restaurant prides itself on using high-quality local produce. Sit downstairs in the cozy ground-floor dining room and people-watch, or head up top for a quieter setting.

For a fine dining experience, **Cuisine Wat Damnak** (between Psa Dey Hoy market and Angkor High School, tel. 07/734-7762, www.cuisinewatdamnak.com, 6:30pm-9:30pm Tues.-Sun., US$27-31) hits the mark with a combination of impeccable service and contemporary Khmer cuisine. Five- and six-course dinner menus are offered, changing every few weeks to keep abreast of what's available in the local markets. Reservations are strongly advised.

Accommodations

Accommodations in Siem Reap reflect the universal appeal of the Angkor temples with a range of hotels, guesthouses, resorts, and hostels that will please everyone from backpackers on a shoestring to luxury travelers. You'll find accommodations throughout the downtown area and beyond, but it's best to base yourself either in Siem Reap or somewhere north of town en route to Angkor Archaeological Park.

UNDER US$25

Beds at **Boutique Dormitory Kochi-Ke** (Angkor Night Market St., tel. 09/060-9060, www.kochi-ke.asia, US$4-5 dorm, US$10-12 private room) are a bargain for the backpacker crowd. Choose between fan or air-conditioned dorms, complete with lockers and shared baths, or splurge for a private bed with an en suite bath. A few inviting common areas also give travelers a place to connect, and staff are able to provide sound travel advice.

The no-frills **Parklane Hotel** (Street Taphul, tel. 06/396-7676, www.parklanehotel.asia, US$19-25) sports an array of patterned wallpapers in its lobby and sparse, spacious rooms upstairs, but its large beds are comfy, and the staff is willing to assist with travel and tour information. Breakfast is available but not included in every booking, so be sure to clarify this beforehand.

US$25-50

The swish, modern **Apsara Centrepole** (522 Svay Dangkum, tel. 06/396-8096, www.apsaracentrepole.com, US$35-80) combines chic contemporary design with Khmer flourishes. Each double comes with a small terrace or balcony as well as generous beds. A trendy terrace café serves food and drinks, while the lush green pool area includes sun beds and umbrellas.

US$50-100

The charming **Diamond d'Angkor** (50 Sok San, tel. 01/637-0777, www.diamondangkor.com, US$50-105) boasts large beds, beautiful Khmer accents, and natural design elements in each spacious room. A cozy swimming pool area hugs one side of the building, while breakfast is served in the open-air dining room and front hall. The hotel staff is professional, attentive, and on hand to assist with tour bookings and travel advice.

OVER US$100

The historic **Raffles Grand Hotel d'Angkor** (1 Vithei Charles de Gaulle, tel. 06/396-3888, www.raffles.com/siem-reap, US$280-910) first opened its doors in 1932 and is considered one of Cambodia's finest accommodations. Situated in the posh neighborhood near Siem Reap's Royal Palace, the Grand Hotel d'Angkor spans six hectares and includes a lush tropical garden as well as the country's largest swimming pool. Accommodations range from plush standard rooms to romantic cabana suites, which include direct pool and garden access, and generous two-bedroom villas, complete with personal butler service. The hotel also holds afternoon tea as well as dinner and entertainment at its Apsara Terrace restaurant.

Information and Services

Tourist SIM cards are available at dirt-cheap prices. **Metfone,** located at the Siem Reap airport, offers 7- to 30-day plans with unlimited Internet and some calling for US$4-16, depending on the duration. A handful of other mobile providers also have kiosks outside the airport.

Getting There
AIR

The fastest, easiest way to reach Siem Reap from Vietnam is by air. Flights take about 1 hour from HCMC and 1.75 hours from Hanoi. And with a handful of budget carriers expanding regional coverage, the flight to **Siem Reap International Airport** (REP, National Hwy. 6, http://corp.cambodia-airports.aero) is now more affordable. From Hanoi, **VietJet Air** (www.vietjetair.com) offers direct once-daily flights for as low as US$50 one-way, while **Cambodia Angkor Air** (www.cambodiaangkorair.com) serves travelers in Ho Chi Minh City with direct trips 4-5 times daily for around US$80 one-way. Vietnam's national carrier, **Vietnam Airlines** (www.vietnamairlines.com), also provides direct flights from both Hanoi (18-plus flights daily) and HCMC (2-8 flights daily) for around US$150 one-way.

On arrival in Siem Reap, you'll find a handy transportation kiosk directly outside the airport, where you can purchase transportation tickets for your choice of motorbike, tuk-tuk, car, or van. Between 6:30am and 11pm, flat rates to the downtown area run US$9-15, depending on your chosen mode of transportation. Those rates climb to US$14-20 later, 11pm-6:30am. All drivers are certified through the service. Be sure to have the name and contact information of your hotel on hand in case directions are required.

BUS

From Ho Chi Minh City, travelers can reach Siem Reap overland via Phnom Penh. **Giant Ibis** (237 Pham Ngu Lao, HCMC, tel. 012/0890-2333, www.giantibis.com, 7am-8:30pm daily) runs safe, reliable shuttles (US$15-18 one-way) between Ho Chi Minh City and Phnom Penh as well as from Phnom Penh to Siem Reap (Sivatha Blvd, Siem Reap, tel. 09/6999-3333, www.giantibis.com, 7am-10pm daily). Buses to Siem Reap leave in the morning as well as late at night. Bear in mind that if you plan to make the entire trip by bus, it's not a bad idea to spend at least a night in Phnom Penh. Each leg of the journey is about six hours, and by the time you make it past the border and into Cambodia's capital city, you will likely be ready for a break.

aerial view of Angkor Wat temple complex

ANGKOR ARCHAEOLOGICAL PARK

Sprawling Angkor Archaeological Park is awash in both ancient temples and lush greenery. Visiting hours begin at 5am daily, when early risers can head to one of the designated sunrise-viewing areas, and end at 7pm daily. Note that although these are the park's general opening hours, temple opening hours are different. Only Angkor Wat, Phnom Bakheng, Srah Srang, and Pre Rup are open from 5am for sunrise, while Phnom Bakheng and Pre Rup remain open until 7pm for sunset. Banteay Srei is open 7:30am-5pm, and Kbal Spean from 7:30am-3pm daily. Otherwise, all temples are open 7:30am-5:30pm daily.

All tickets must be purchased through the Angkor ticketing office (corner of Apsara Rd. and Street 60, tel. 01/260-6852, www.angkorenterprise.gov.kh, 5am-5:30pm daily) southeast of the park. Legitimate passes are only available through this office; passes bought from a third-party vendor will not be recognized by ticket control. One-, three-, and seven-day passes are available for US$37, US$62, and US$72, respectively. Children under 12 are not required to purchase an individual ticket, though you will be asked to show the child's passport. Apsara Authority ticket counters will accept cash as well as Visa, Mastercard, UnionPay, and Discover cards. Once you've secured your ticket, three-day passes can be used on any 3 days within a 7-day period, while 7-day passes can be used on any 7 days within a 30-day period.

When you purchase your Angkor ticket, your photograph will be printed on the pass to ensure visitors don't swap or share passes. Be sure to keep your pass in a safe, dry place while moving around the park: Ticket control is quite strict, and employees are present outside most temples, even smaller ones. Any tickets that are torn or severely damaged may not be accepted, and if you lose your pass you will be required to purchase a new one. Visitors found in the park without a valid pass can be fined US$100-300.

Given that the ticketing office is a bit out of the way, your best bet is to turn up at 5pm the day before you wish to visit the park. All tickets purchased after 5pm are valid for the following day, and ticket buyers are then free to enter the park after 5pm for sunset on that same day.

While there are too many Angkorian temples to see in one day, many visitors opt for one of two routes to make the most of their visit: the Small Circuit, an 18-kilometer loop which includes Angkor Wat, Angkor Thom, and Ta Prohm, or the Grand Circuit, a slightly larger 27-kilometer loop that encompasses those same temples along with several others, such as Phnom Bakheng.

During your visit, you'll want to bring along sunscreen as well as a hat or some other form of sun protection. Drinking water is available throughout the park. Public restrooms are available in the park, though they can be tricky to find; look for the blue-and-white signs. The clutch of restaurants opposite Angkor Wat also has restrooms. One of the purple-clad ticket-control officers should be able to point you in the right direction.

You'll notice the many vendors outside Angkor's temples. Should you find yourself the center of unwanted attention, be polite but firm and move along; promising to return or buy something later will only delay this pressure to purchase. It is also advisable not to buy snacks or souvenirs from children, as this encourages the practice of employing young kids.

Respectful dress is a must. Cover your shoulders and knees. Slip-on shoes are not necessary but still a good idea, as you will often be required to remove your shoes when entering certain religious buildings. While enforcement of the dress code isn't necessarily consistent in Angkor Archaeological Park, there are certain sights—Angkor Wat itself, for instance—where it's strictly observed, and you may be denied access if you're dressed inappropriately.

Angkor Wat

Though scholars and historians are unsure of the temple's actual name, **Angkor Wat**—literally "City Temple"—earns its reputation as one of the most famous religious monuments in the world. The sprawling complex is remarkably well preserved compared to the area's other structures and sees scores of tourists venturing across its moat and into the temple every day. Yet, for all that is known about Angkor Wat, much of its story remains a mystery. While many believe the structure is a temple dedicated to Vishnu, protector of the universe, some historians believe Angkor Wat is, in fact, a mausoleum for King Suryavarman II. Either way, the structure was originally built as a Hindu monument and later transitioned into a Buddhist site around the 15th or 16th century.

Angkor Wat covers an area of 500 acres, including the temple itself plus its causeway, main entrance, and library structures. The main building consists of three levels. Once you've passed over the moat leading to Angkor Wat's front entrance, you'll be greeted by the complex's five iconic towers, meant to represent Mount Meru, mythical home of the Hindu gods. Surrounding the building's exterior are several bas-reliefs relaying several epic stories from Hindu mythology, while the **Thousand Buddha Gallery** inside holds fewer statues of its namesake today but manages to remain captivating for its symmetrical architecture and the intricate patterns carved onto its surfaces. Continue your walk to the next level, which holds a gallery filled with *apsaras*, or Hindu nymphs. On the next level is a gallery and a very steep set of steps to **Bakan**, Angkor Wat's central sanctuary and tower, 213 meters tall, once reserved solely for kings and high priests. Due to its small area, park employees restrict the number of visitors to the Bakan, so expect a brief wait in line, and be sure to cover up; there is a dress code loosely in effect throughout the park but in the Bakan, the most sacred part of the park's most famous temple, covered shoulders and knees are a must.

If you've chosen to visit the park on your own, an **audio guide** (tel. 01/077-7767, www. angkoraudio.com, 8:30am-5pm daily, US$7) specifically for Angkor Wat is available across the road near the southwest corner of the main entrance. You will be required to leave either your passport or a US$50 deposit in order to take the audio guide, which provides comprehensive information on all areas of the Angkor Wat complex.

In order to get the full experience, from its main entrance through the temple and up to the very top of Bakan, budget 2.5-3 hours at Angkor Wat.

Angkor Thom

The enormous **Angkor Thom** is a walled complex encompassing several temples and other sights. Built around 1200 by King Jayavarman VII, the "Great City," as its name translates, is a 145-hectare square bordered on each side by laterite walls. There are five gates into the complex—one on each side plus an extra gate on the eastern wall that leads onto the Terrace of Elephants. The most famous of these is the **South Gate,** whose causeway has been restored to its original glory through a combination of preservation and reconstructed sculptures. This narrow stone path is lined on either side with statues of gods and demons locked in a tug-of-war; they hold on to a *naga*, or mythical serpent, referencing the tale of the Churning of the Sea of Milk, an important story in Hindu mythology.

While Angkor Thom houses many temples, its most famous structure, **Bayon,** is often remembered for its many-faced towers. Built sometime in the 12th or 13th century by King Jayavarman VII, Bayon rises from the center of Angkor Thom. This three-tiered temple consists of two levels of bas-relief galleries as well as a central sanctuary. The top floor is a maze of 54 stone towers, each featuring the same smiling face on all four sides. This is believed to be the face of Avalokitesvara, a prominent Buddhist bodhisattva.

Farther north in Angkor Thom lies the long walkway to **Baphuon,** a generous

11th-century structure whose upper floors make for a nice view of the complex. Farther along, the **Terrace of the Elephants** overlooks Angkor Thom's Royal Square, once serving as a viewing platform from which royals could observe any passing festivities. Next door, the **Terrace of the Leper King** is so named for the large, discolored statue that once occupied the platform and was thought to be a legendary leper king. Today, researchers believe the figure represents Yama, god of the underworld. **Phimeanakas,** or the Celestial Palace, sits behind the Terrace of the Elephants and affords some top-notch views of Bayon from afar.

Beyond these structures—for which you should budget about 3-3.5 hours—you could easily while away a few more hours in Angkor Thom's remaining temples. While the complex draws a considerable number of visitors, Bayon is really the only temple that becomes completely overrun with tourists (come in the late afternoon for fewer crowds); if you prefer more peace and quiet, find your way to some of Angkor Thom's smaller temples and you'll be just fine. **Tep Pranam** and **Preah Palilay,** just north of the Terrace of the Elephants, as well as **Prasat Suor Prat,** opposite the Terrace of the Elephants are recommended.

Ta Prohm

While some Angkorian temples remain remarkably intact, nature's influence on **Ta Prohm** is part of its appeal. Tree roots have wound around, under, and through the incredible 12th-century stone temple, damaging Ta Prohm in some places and propping it up in others. King Jayavarman VII built the structure in 1186 in dedication to his mother, and at its height, the maintenance of Ta Prohm required nearly 80,000 Buddhist devotees.

The temple's fusion of nature and history makes for excellent photographs, particularly if you arrive early in the morning or later in the afternoon when the crowds are smaller. Be mindful of the wooden platforms and barriers erected to preserve the temple as a result of Ta Prohm's trees. You'll also want to keep your eyes peeled for the chest echo tower, a tall, narrow, unmarked structure that looks unassuming from the outside. Step inside, lean your back against the wall, and hit your chest three times for luck: The tower acts as an echo chamber, generating a low hum around you as you hit your chest.

Allot around 45 minutes to an hour for your visit, as it takes some time to wander

Ta Prohm temple

through the entirety of the temple, and Ta Prohm is especially photogenic.

Srah Srang

Srah Srang is one of the only areas in the park open for sunrise and an excellent spot to do so at Angkor without the crowds. Surrounded by sugar palms and lush greenery, this large reservoir is especially peaceful in the mornings before tour groups begin to arrive. Take in views from its cross-shaped stone platform overlooking the water.

Neak Pean

Neak Pean sits amid the massive Jayatataka Reservoir. Walk down the temple's narrow causeway across the reservoir and you'll find a modest sanctuary at the center of an artificial pond. Though it doesn't take long to visit, the view from the causeway is particularly stunning.

Preah Khan

North of Angkor Thom, Preah Khan is another well-preserved example of Angkorian architecture built by King Jayavarman VII and dedicated in 1191. Also known as the "Sacred Sword," one of this temple's most impressive features is its Hall of Dancers, home to countless carvings of *apsaras*, Hindu nymphs.

Phnom Bakheng

A standout along the Grand Circuit is Phnom Bakheng, a towering structure between Angkor Wat and Angkor Thom and one of the first temples built in the Angkor area. Sitting atop a hill of the same name, Phnom Bakheng's top level is now a popular spot to watch sunset over Angkor Wat, but tourist numbers at the temple are restricted to no more than 300, so you'll want to arrive by 4pm in order to get a spot.

Pre Rup

Many visitors choose to finish off their day at Pre Rup, a popular sunset viewing spot. Completed in 961, this pyramidal temple-mountain features five towers that rise above its base. Its name translates to "turn the body," and the structure is believed to have once served as a crematorium. Again, note that this temple becomes quite busy around the sunset hour, so you'll want to arrive by 4pm to stake out a spot.

Banteay Srei

Known as the Citadel of the Women, the stunning pink sandstone carvings of Banteay Srei lie 40 kilometers north of Siem Reap. Constructed in the 10th century, the modest temple is remarkably well preserved and covered with the graceful figures of *apsaras*. Its intricate carvings and intense detail help Banteay Srei stand out from its Angkorian contemporaries. Though the temple is farther afield, many travelers find a journey here worth the effort. Entry to Banteay Srei is included in your Apsara Authority ticket, but you'll need to enlist the services of a driver to get here. Tuk-tuks make the journey for around US$25 from Siem Reap, while the cost of a car runs closer to US$40.

Food

You'll find refreshment stalls outside nearly every temple in the main area of the park, as well as a handful of snack vendors. For proper meals, there are several restaurants opposite the entrance to Angkor Wat as well as a few along the route between Ta Prohm and Angkor Wat. Be sure to drink plenty of water, as the complex is hot and shadeless year-round, and you'll have ample opportunity to buy beverages from the eager vendors in the park.

For air-conditioning and a combination of Khmer and Western meals, try the Blue Pumpkin Angkor Café (tel. 01/769-2370, www.bluepumpkin.asia, 6am-6pm daily, US$3-12). Just opposite the entrance to Angkor Wat, this place sees plenty of traffic throughout the day, and its prices are a higher than other nearby venues, but the meals are decent and comfortable seating and cooler indoor temperatures make for a nice break from the heat and action outside.

Getting There

Angkor Archaeological Park lies about seven kilometers north of Siem Reap and is easily accessible by bicycle, motorbike, tuk-tuk, or car. For those who hire a vehicle to explore the park, drivers sometimes double as guides. It takes about 20 minutes to reach the park by motorized transport.

VEHICLES FOR HIRE

When traveling around the Angkor park, your best option is to hire a set of wheels. While open-air vehicles are recommended to get the full experience, those who prefer riding in air-conditioning can hire a car or van. This is an especially good option if you plan to visit some of the temples farther afield, such as Banteay Srei. You can hire a car and driver through the **Tourist Transport Association** (tel. 06/396-3572, www.siemreap-airport-taxi.com), which has a 24-hour kiosk at the Siem Reap airport. It provides transport to and from the airport. The company has set rates (US$40/day for cars) as well as English-speaking drivers, and you can inquire about bookings online through its website.

TUK-TUK

If you're planning to hire a motorized vehicle for your Angkor excursion, the most affordable option is a tuk-tuk. These three-wheeled vehicles can usually seat up to four travelers, and their open sides and covered roofs provide ventilation and coverage from the sun. Tuk-tuk hires are easily arranged through most hotels, but you'll no doubt find a few free-lancers on your own while wandering about town. Day rates usually run US$20-25. Agree on an itinerary before setting off. Or you could also book through **Tourist Transport Association** (tel. 06/396-3572, www.siem-reap-airporttaxi.com), which has set rates (US$20/day for tuk-tuks) as well as English-speaking drivers, and you can inquire about bookings online.

BIKE

When it comes to pedal-powered transportation, travelers in Siem Reap are spoiled for choice. Cyclists on a budget can find basic push bikes at most hotels and guesthouses, and rentals typically go for US$1-2 per day.

On the off-chance you can't secure a bike through your hotel, **The White Bicycles** (www.thewhitebicycles.org, US$2 per day) is a nonprofit organization that rents bicycles to tourists, using the proceeds to fund clean water projects and scholarships for local students. Its bicycles can be found at a number of hotels around town, including the **Soria Moria Boutique Hotel** (Wat Bo, tel. 06/396-4768, www.thesoriamoria.com). A US$20 deposit is required, and overnight rentals are not permitted. For a more serious set of wheels, **Grasshopper Adventures** (Street 26, tel. 01/246-2165, www.grasshopperadventures. com, 7am-8pm daily) offers high-quality mountain bikes for hire. Guests can rent a bike for six hours (US$8), a full day (US$12), or overnight (US$18). All rentals include a bicycle lock and helmet as well as bottled water. A passport is required as collateral.

For a less labor-intensive mode of two-wheeled transportation, Siem Reap's **Green E-Bikes** (Central Market, C11, tel. 09/570-0130, www.greene-bike.com, 7:30am-7pm daily, US$10 per day) are a clean, convenient way to get around town and out to the main Angkor temples. Rentals last 24 hours and include a bike lock, a helmet, and a battery charger. Electric bicycles can travel up to 40 kilometers on a single charge, and there are 12 free charging points available throughout Siem Reap, as well as 4 charging points located within the Angkor Archaeological Park. Note that a passport is required for e-bike rental, and users must be age 16.

MOTORBIKE

You can rent a motorbike through **Tourist Transport Association** (tel. 06/396-3572, www.siemreap-airporttaxi.com), which has set rates (US$20/day for motorbikes). Inquire about bookings online.

The Mekong Delta

Can Tho 388
Mekong River Islands 397
Vinh Long 408
Tra Vinh 414
Tram Chim National Park
  and Vicinity 421
Sa Dec....................... 426
Chau Doc..................... 430
Rach Gia and Ha Tien 439
Phu Quoc Island 451

Look for ★ to find recommended
sights, activities, dining, and lodging.

Highlights

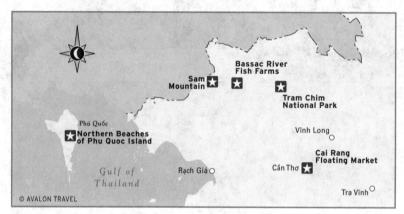

★ **Cai Rang Floating Market:** Experience the melee of rice barges and fishing boats trading in fresh fruits and vegetables along the Can Tho River (page 390).

★ **Tram Chim National Park:** In this stunning landscape of flooded plains and wiry cajuput trees is a quarter of all bird species in Vietnam, including the redheaded sarus crane, the world's tallest flying bird (page 421).

★ **Bassac River Fish Farms:** Entire communities of colorful floating fish farms provide

both shelter and a living for many residents of the Delta (page 432).

★ **Sam Mountain:** Follow a dizzying maze of temples, pagodas, and shrines up to the summit for incredible views of Chau Doc and its surrounding rice fields (page 434).

★ **Northern Beaches of Phu Quoc Island:** Secluded beaches like the stunning Ganh Dau Beach offer an unparalleled piece of paradise (page 458).

At first glance, the geography of the Mekong Delta is almost incomprehensible. Awash with emerald rice paddies, serpentine rivers, lush palms, and creaky cajuput trees, the entire region is as much water as it is earth.

Its fertile farmland, which stretches south and west from Ho Chi Minh City all the way to the Cambodian border, rises tentatively from a maze of tributaries known in Vietnamese as the River of Nine Dragons. Amid flooded plains and shape-shifting islands, the mighty Mekong flows to the sea, providing one of the country's most heavily populated areas with its defining geographic feature and an altogether different way of life.

On land, the region's unparalleled annual rice harvest has earned it an affectionate nickname as Vietnam's "rice bowl," a major player in the third-largest rice-exporting nation in the world. But more than its farming exploits, life in the Mekong Delta revolves largely around water. At the mouth of one of Asia's longest rivers—which winds from the Tibetan Plateau through China, Myanmar, Laos, Thailand, and Cambodia before arriving in southwestern Vietnam—local residents travel just as often by water as by land, navigating narrow palm-fringed canals on wooden sampans or jetting to another part of the coast via speedboat. The Delta's low-lying terrain and a complex web of estuaries mean that it's not uncommon for local families to anchor their house within the river or earn a living in one of the region's famed floating markets. For many travelers, the Mekong's main appeal lies here, in its verdant landscapes and unassuming pace. Beyond scenery, a diverse population only adds to the many intricacies of the Delta, as Vietnamese residents live alongside ethnic Chinese, Khmer, and Cham communities, each of which brings its own distinct culture and traditions to the area.

Tourism in the Mekong Delta is fairly spread out, with travelers venturing as near as the river islands between My Tho and Ben Tre or as far as the westernmost reaches of Ha Tien and Chau Doc. Those with an interest in local culture and a sense of adventure will appreciate the freedom of the Delta, where

The Mekong Delta

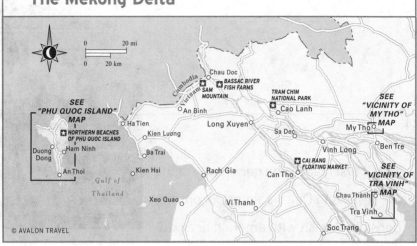

© AVALON TRAVEL

travelers can blaze their own trails without the confines that come with large foreign crowds. Exploring western Vietnam allows for more interaction with locals and a more authentic glimpse of daily life than many other destinations along the coast, though a good deal more patience is required in a region where tourism is less developed and English speakers are few.

HISTORY

With its modern history dating from the late 1600s, the Mekong Delta is Vietnam's youngest region. For centuries, while rulers in Hanoi and Hue vied for supremacy and the Nguyen Lords pushed south toward Saigon, these low-lying wetlands sat uninhabited, thick with rainforest and wild animals. Though several ancient kingdoms once laid claim to the area, the Khmer were last in control before the Vietnamese slowly moved westward from Saigon, edging their neighbors out of the region and establishing independent towns and communities. As early as the late 17th century, the land then known as Kampuchea Krom, or Lower Cambodia, began to fall into Vietnamese hands, with key players like Nguyen Huu Canh, a nobleman who helped

bring order to the Delta's then-remote communities, and Mac Cuu, the Chinese merchant, explorer, and founder of Ha Tien town, proving instrumental in the development of the area.

Despite this progress on the part of the Vietnamese, life in the Mekong Delta was not without its challenges, as harsh conditions and tentative relationships with the neighbors prevailed, particularly around the border. Thai pirates routinely crossed the frontier to loot and pillage the country's western settlements, and the Khmer Krom, still smarting from the loss of their land, did not take kindly to an increased Vietnamese presence. By the time Mac Cuu sought protection from the Nguyen Lords in 1708, hoping to save Vietnam's western border from capture or destruction, the nation's boundaries had been set, and armed defense supplied by the Nguyens only solidified the status of the country's youngest settlements as an official part of Vietnam.

After France launched its takeover in the middle of the 19th century, residents of the Delta were particularly outspoken in their disapproval, acting as an important center of opposition against colonial powers in Saigon. Southern members of the Viet Minh, Ho Chi

Minh's Communist resistance army, took refuge in limestone caves and cajuput forests across the region, constructing military bases and training schools that were all but undetectable to their enemies.

Amid the Delta's lush rainforest and tropical humidity, the Viet Minh's crude weapons and guerrilla tactics turned them into a formidable power. After independence was won, it took only a few short years before Ngo Dinh Diem and the South Vietnamese government stirred southern revolutionaries to action again, reforming as the National Liberation Front (NLF). Well-hidden within the Delta landscapes and skilled at repurposing American weapons against the enemy, southern guerrillas fast earned a reputation as one of the United States' strongest adversaries. This distinction came at a price: some of the most intense fighting to take place in southern Vietnam played out in paddy fields and hamlets across the Mekong Delta.

Following the end of the American War, Vietnam's southwestern frontier remained a battleground, as a border conflict with Cambodia in the late 1970s escalated into two years of full-blown war against Pol Pot's brutal Khmer Rouge regime. Once the violence dissipated and the country began to focus on rebuilding from within, local residents gave up their guns to return to the land, working the Delta's rivers and rice fields. Today, the region is responsible for the vast majority of Vietnam's rice exports, which are among the highest in the world, as well as thriving fishing and fruit industries.

PLANNING YOUR TIME

The region's major attractions can be packed into a few days. Travelers in the Delta are free to pick and choose their destinations, as tourism here is not about specific sights or attractions so much as it is about experiencing the local way of life.

Those planning to spend more than a day in the Delta begin their journey in tourist-friendly Can Tho, using this hub to arrange bus transport to more remote destinations. Stay overnight here to experience the city's first-rate floating market.

The more popular tourist hubs are Chau Doc, Phu Quoc, and (to a lesser extent) Vinh Long. Allot 1-2 days each to visit Chau Doc and Vinh Long. Budget at least 3-4 days to visit Phu Quoc because it requires either more money (for the plane ticket) or more time to get there (by way of a speedboat).

Beyond the primary destinations, travelers can spend as little as a single day in the area or as long as a few weeks. Add an extra day each to explore the Khmer pagodas of Tra Vinh, bird-watch at Tram Chim National Park, and sightsee in Sa Dec, or tack on an extra day or two in towns like Rach Gia and Ha Tien to explore the surrounding area. If you're pressed for time, it's also possible to take day trips from Saigon to towns like My Tho, Ben Tre, or Vinh Long.

While the Mekong Delta is a popular destination as a whole, tourism here is spread out. Major destinations like Can Tho and Phu Quoc work well as tourist hubs, but most places west of Saigon have little tourism infrastructure. This means that English speakers and Western services are at a minimum, and you'll need extra time and patience. Expect to have a few communication hiccups and to spend time on less-than-comfortable buses when traveling between many of the region's cities.

The best time to visit is outside the rainy season, as steady downpours bury much of the landscape April-October and flooding can be extreme.

Can Tho

The economic, political, and cultural heart of the Mekong Delta, Can Tho is a large city that feels like a small town. Along Ninh Kieu Park, its main riverside promenade, you'll find the pace of this southwestern nerve center low-key and pleasantly unhurried, particularly when coming from Saigon. For most travelers, Can Tho is an important stop for a few reasons: as the area's largest and most developed city, it is here that you'll find the majority of useful travel information, English speakers, and Western amenities. This sun-drenched town boasts its own share of cultural attractions, showing the region's intricate demography in the beautiful Chinese assembly hall nestled between hotels and restaurants along Hai Ba Trung, as well as a pair of gilded Theravada Buddhist pagodas that would not be out of place on the other side of the Cambodian border. Like any town in the Mekong Delta, a snaking web of rivers and canals burrows deep into the surrounding countryside, shaded by drooping palm fronds and plentiful fruit trees, and every morning as the sun comes up boats depart from the local tourist pier for Cai Rang, the largest and most active of the Delta's famed floating markets, as well as its smaller counterpart, Phong Dien.

Visiting Can Tho, if only for a day or two, is worth it for the city's on-the-water attractions and for some R&R before setting off deeper into the Delta. For its part, some of the city's more enterprising young locals have also taken it upon themselves to provide more unique and authentic opportunities for foreign visitors to experience life in the Delta, with a handful of small independent tour outfits beginning to crop up around town that take travelers farther off the beaten track. Regardless of how long you stay in the city, at least one overnight is necessary in order to rise early enough for the floating market. There are several other sights on land, though even street vendors and boat pilots call off the chase at midday to escape the city's sweltering, shadeless avenues.

Temperatures reach their peak around late April or May, as the dry weather gives way to daily rains. From mid-November to early April the city is slightly cooler. But, coming from abroad, you'll likely still find it hot.

SIGHTS

From the waterfront, all of Can Tho's on-land sights are easily accessible and can be reached on foot or, if you prefer, by bicycle. Dress appropriately when visiting pagodas. For water sights, boats are available for hire from hotels and travel agencies as well as through independent drivers at Ninh Kieu Pier.

Ong Pagoda

You could spend an afternoon studying the dizzyingly intricate exterior of **Ong Pagoda** (32 Hai Ba Trung beside Mekong Restaurant, 6am-6pm daily, free), a riverfront property built in 1896 by the city's then-sizable Chinese population. Honoring the red-faced beard-twirling Chinese general Quan Cong, a figure who represents loyalty, cleverness, virtue, and courage, among other things, the pagoda's layout is inspired by the stiff lines and angles of the Chinese character for "nation." As soon as you pass through the main doors, you'll be greeted by two figures: the Goddess of Fortune on the right and the wide-eyed General Ma Tien and his horse on the left. Beyond the entrance hall, incense burns in a small clearing at the center of the pagoda, also known as the celestial well, above which dozens of large, smoldering incense coils sway in the breeze. The main altar at the back is where Quan Cong himself resides, flanked by the God of Earth and the God of Finance. Nowadays, this pagoda still functions as the Guangzhou Assembly Hall, bringing together the community that created it, despite the fact

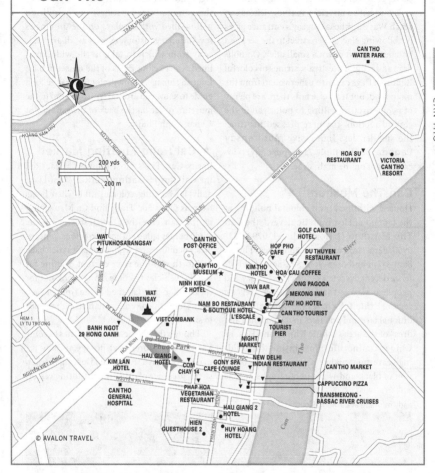

Can Tho

that Can Tho's Chinese population has declined considerably in recent decades.

Wat Pitukhosarangsay

Squeezed down a narrow lane near Xang Thoi Lake, **Wat Pitukhosarangsay** (17/28 Mac Dinh Chi, 7am-7pm daily, free) is tangible proof of the Mekong Delta's Khmer connection. Complete with all the gold-edged trimmings of a typical Theravada Buddhist pagoda (the sort you might find in Thailand or Cambodia) this *wat* is packed to the rafters

with sparkling statues of the Buddha, most of which were brought across the border from neighboring countries. Its three stories of intricate neon-hued murals and overflowing altars make this one of the taller buildings in the neighborhood, and a climb up to the top floor is rewarded with nice views of residential Can Tho and the nearby lake, as well a close-up of the pagoda's ornately detailed roof. There are also a handful of outgoing monks who can give you a short tour of each floor before bringing you up to the attic library, where dozens of religious texts are stored, each penned in the Khmer or Thai script.

Though it's a bit tricky to find, visitors can reach Wat Pitukhosarangsay's entrance gates by following Ngo Quyen street to the very end and bearing left down a small alley. On holidays and religious festivals, strings of colorful Buddhist flags can also usher you in from the main road, but if all else fails there are plenty of people around willing to point you in the right direction. If you're pressed for time, the smaller, less-impressive **Munirensay Pagoda** (36 Hoa Binh, 7am-7pm daily) is located right on the main drag.

Can Tho Museum

Housed within a grand colonial building at the far end of Hoa Binh Boulevard, the **Can Tho Museum** (1 Hoa Binh, tel. 0292/382-0955, 8am-11am and 2pm-5pm Tues.-Thurs., 8am-11am and 6pm-9pm Sat.-Sun., free) offers a decent overview of the city's history and people as well as that of the larger Mekong region. Exhibits include everything from traditional farming practices to the customs and dress of the area's ethnic Khmer and Hoa, or Chinese, minorities. Just inside the building's cavernous main entrance, a faded collection of black-and-white photographs depicts turn-of-the-century Can Tho, providing insight into just how much has changed since the colonial era. Upstairs, the exhibition hall is filled with displays on the province's revolutionary history, as well as an airy balcony from which to take in the wide, tree-lined street below. Parts of the museum have English signage. If you prefer to arrange for a guide to show you around, you can head to the museum office on the back of the grounds at 6 Phan Dinh Phung.

★ Cai Rang Floating Market

Easily Can Tho's most popular attraction, the **Cai Rang Floating Market** (5am-11am daily) is a bustling, colorful affair where boats from as far as Soc Trang and Ca Mau gather on the Can Tho River to sell fresh produce. Wide barges laden with watermelons, pineapples, coconuts, and fresh vegetables rock back and forth with the river current, waiting for smaller vehicles to come along. Look out for the bamboo pole fastened to the front of each boat, from which vendors hang their produce to show what's available.

Though this particular market has become a hot spot for foreign visitors, Cai Rang remains every bit a traditional floating market, so the presence of other tourist-toting vessels

early morning at Cai Rang Floating Market

Floating Markets

Each morning, as the sun rises over southwestern Vietnam's maze of waterways, dozens of wooden boats congregate along the river to take part in one of the Mekong Delta's many famed floating markets. Wide barges and hollow-hulled boats laden with fresh produce and hundreds of river fish travel from near and far to reach these on-the-water trading posts. River vendors typically sell bulk amounts of one or two items, which they advertise to other shoppers by hanging a sample of the available goods atop a bamboo pole that sits at the front of the boat. Even smaller, motorized canoes join in on the action, zipping around the larger barges with coffee, tea, and snacks for sale.

The most famous of the Delta's markets exist in and around Can Tho: **Cai Rang Floating Market,** easily the most popular of the bunch, and **Phong Dien market,** another large floating business center. Farther north, **Cai Be floating market** is a smaller version. Set just before the charming spire of the town cathedral, this market makes for a nice photo-op. **Chau Doc floating market** still has a ways to go, with only a few boats turning up in the morning, more for show than anything else.

doesn't much detract from the atmosphere. Get in on the action by grabbing a coffee on the water or haggling for fresh fruit from one of the smaller vessels. Half the fun of visiting the market is the ride out to Cai Rang, as this allows you to travel along the banks of the Can Tho River, passing by throngs of local houseboats and floating gas stations, fishing vessels, and shops with waterside service.

Visitors can arrange to depart from Ninh Kieu Pier at any time, though it's best to go in the early morning, as Cai Rang's vendors disappear as the day wears on. Boats leave for the market as early as 5am and can be hired either through local hotels and travel agencies or with any of the freelance drivers around Ninh Kieu Park. It's best to leave from Ninh Kieu at 5am-5:30am, as this allows you to beat the tourist rush but also have enough sunlight to snap decent photographs. Freelancers are usually more affordable and their smaller boats allow you to get closer to the action than some of the larger tourist vessels. If you go this route, agree upon an itinerary and a price before setting off. Freelance boat trips can run as cheap as VND200,000-250,000 for a straight out-and-back ride to the floating market, while longer journeys into the surrounding countryside and along Can Tho's many narrow canals

come at a higher price. Larger, organized boats begin at VND360,000 for a standard floating market trip.

Many travelers combine a trip to Cai Rang with a wander down the area's narrow canals, populated with lush greenery and plentiful fruit orchards. This can be arranged either through a guided tour or with a freelance driver. Some even tack on the longer journey out to **Phong Dien market,** a smaller floating market that lies farther down the river, about 19 kilometers from town, which sees fewer visitors than Cai Rang.

Sightseeing Tours

With so many travelers drawn to Can Tho for its waterways, guided boat tours to the nearby floating markets and the surrounding area are a popular activity. **Can Tho Tourist** (50 Hai Ba Trung, tel. 0292/382-1854, www. canthotourist.vn, 7am-6pm daily), the city's government-run travel outfit, supplies a standard trip out to Cai Rang market and back (VND740,000 per boat for 2 people) combined with a visit to a local rice noodle factory and jaunt down some of the area's smaller canals. There are also several longer tours that tack on a handful of additional sights, such as Phong Dien floating market. Cost depends upon the number of people on board; this is not the best option for solo travelers, as prices begin at VND670,000.

For a closer look at local culture and the Delta countryside, the friendly folks at **Open Tour CT** (tel. 09/6262-1119, www.opentourct.com, VND730,000-865,000) do not disappoint. This promising young tour outfit pairs travelers with local guides both on land and on the water, taking you for a ride around the city or farther afield for an authentic look at Delta life. In addition to its own tour itineraries, the most popular of which is a half-day adventure into the countryside. Open Tour CT provides private guides, giving you all the tools to create your own travel plans. The company also runs affordable floating market trips out to Cai Rang and Phong Dien, with both private and group tours; opt for the private boat if possible, as this allows you to set your own schedule.

NIGHTLIFE

As a whole, the Mekong Delta is a region of early risers. Nighttime in Can Tho still draws a fair number of locals to Ninh Kieu Park, where couples sit on park benches and groups of friends peruse the nearby **night market** (Nguyen Thai Hoc and Vo Van Tan streets, 5pm-11:30pm daily). The street lining the river gets busy around 6pm and stays that way until later in the evening, quieting down around 10pm-11pm. Many people meander the maze of **snack carts** (Phan Boi Chau and Phan Chu Trinh streets, 5pm-late daily) near Can Tho Market, where quick bites like sticky rice, grilled meats, and local desserts are on offer, before heading to the waterfront.

For anything more than a park bench, options are pretty slim along the river: **Mekong Restaurant** (38 Hai Ba Trung, tel. 0292/382-1646, 3pm-10pm daily, VND16,000-150,000) slings local beer and a bit of hard liquor in a casual atmosphere. For a fancier crowd, **Hoa Cau Coffee** (4 Hai Ba Trung, tel. 0292/365-6999, 6am-11pm daily, VND20,000-80,000) has a list of beer and cocktails in addition to its standard coffees and teas. There are a few local *bia hoi* (Vietnamese beer) vendors stuffed in between the dozens of local restaurants along De Tham street as well as around Xang Thoi Lake.

SHOPPING
Can Tho Market

Packed with local handicrafts and clothing, the waterfront **Can Tho Market** (Hai Ba Trung, 7am-10pm daily) is your go-to spot for knickknacks and backpacker gear. Plenty of T-shirts, knapsacks, and loose clothing are available, as well as locally made hand fans, scarves, and other souvenirs. Though it now functions as a tourist market, this once was the main trade center of the city and saw hordes of shoppers, both by land and by river.

Night Market

After sunset, the fun continues at Can Tho's **night market** (Nguyen Thai Hoc and Vo Van Tan streets, 5pm-11:30pm daily), where vendors hawk mostly clothing, sunglasses, and jewelry. Don't forget that you can haggle for your purchases here, though most vendors are reasonable, and some even post their prices out front.

SPORTS AND RECREATION
Ninh Kieu Park

Stretched along the waterfront, **Ninh Kieu Park** (Hai Ba Trung) is a popular local hang-out during the late afternoons and evenings. Much of Can Tho's population gathers along the riverbank to chat, watch the passing boats, and enjoy a few snacks. During the day, this narrow strip of greenery would be just as nice if it weren't for the heat, but with the sun high overhead there is little shade available, and groups of freelance boat drivers often gather here looking for a fare. A modern footbridge crosses the Cai Khe Canal, providing a popular backdrop for selfies and allowing pedestrians to wander a little farther away from the downtown bustle.

Swimming

Though it comes at a price, the **Victoria**

A boat travels along the river in the early morning.

Can Tho pool (Cai Khe, tel. 0292/381-0111, www.victoriahotels.asia, 6am-8pm daily, VND128,000) is a palm-fringed paradise with pleasant riverfront views, umbrellas, and comfy lounge chairs. Nonguests of the resort are able to use the riverside pool by purchasing a ticket at the reception desk.

FOOD

As the region's largest city, Can Tho is one of the only places in the Mekong Delta where you'll find Western food in addition to local fare. Dozens of restaurants are packed neatly along the riverfront, most catering to foreign tourists, while a handful of streets farther back from the water offer excellent street food and more local Vietnamese restaurants.

Vietnamese

Hop Pho (4-6 Ngo Gia Tu, tel. 0292/381-5208, 6:30am-10:30pm daily, VND30,000-125,000) is a typical Vietnamese *san vuon* (garden) café, but it also serves breakfast and lunch. With breezy outdoor seating and plenty of greenery to block out the passing traffic, patrons can enjoy the café-restaurant's extensive menu of Vietnamese dishes, as well as coffee, tea, smoothies, and ice cream in a mellow environment.

As the sun sets over Can Tho, the tables at **Mekong Restaurant** (38 Hai Ba Trung, tel. 0292/382-1646, 3pm-10pm daily, VND50,000-200,000) fill up with hungry tourists and people-watchers. One of the longest-running businesses along the waterfront, this jovial, family-run business serves up tasty Vietnamese dishes as well as cold beer. The staff is notably cheerful and always willing to dispense travel advice about the city.

Though more expensive than your average local eatery, **Nam Bo Restaurant** (1 Ngo Quyen, tel. 0292/381-9139, www.nambocantho.com, 6am-10:30pm daily, VND50,000-200,000) is located on the riverfront's best people-watching corner, directly opposite Ninh Kieu Park and the pier. Its menu offers a mixture of both Vietnamese and Western dishes served in the ground-floor dining room, with brown-and-white checked tablecloths and large bay windows opening onto Hai Ba Trung. A rotating collection of artwork enhances the restaurant's understated decor with Vietnamese-inspired paintings and photographs from local and foreign artists.

Equipped with a riverside location, a thatched roof, over-the-water dining huts, and a massive wedding hall, **Hoa Su** (Cai Khe Tourist Area, tel. 0292/382-0717, www.nhahanghoasu.com, 8am-10pm daily, VND50,000-300,000) is popular among the local crowd and serves up every type of river fish imaginable and then some, with snake, pigeon, and paddy rat also making an appearance on the menu. Tables are located in a vast outdoor area near the water, removed from the traffic noise by a short walk from the street to the entrance.

Street Food

To eat with the locals, your best bet is to head up to **De Tham street** (noon-late daily, VND15,000-80,000) near Xang Thoi Lake, a small street jam-packed with roadside restaurants serving rice and noodles, grilled meats, and dozens of other standard Vietnamese dishes, not to mention a well-placed *bia hoi* (Vietnamese beer) vendors here and there. While most meals include meat, you can also find a few *chay* (vegetarian) joints.

Droves of street carts gather in the clearing on **Phan Boi Chau and Phan Chu Trinh streets** (5pm-late daily, VND5,000-40,000) for the evening rush around Ninh Kieu Park. While most carts are dedicated strictly to snack foods like *ca vien* (fish paste balls) and grilled meats, you can also find a few more substantial meals like *xoi ga* (chicken and sticky rice). If you have trouble deciding, just look for the carts with a line out front.

Cafés and Bakeries

One of Can Tho's trendier cafés, **Hoa Cau Coffee** (4 Hai Ba Trung, tel. 0292/365-6999, 6am-11pm daily, VND20,000-80,000) is a modern version of your average Vietnamese garden coffee shop. Ample open-air seating is available and the management plays an ongoing selection of Western hits from decades past. Things really get going at night, when everyone in town is out and about around Ninh Kieu Park.

International

Just opposite Can Tho Market, **Cappuccino Pizza** (138 Hai Ba Trung, tel. 0292/246-1981, 11am-10pm daily, VND50,000-180,000) is a mostly Italian restaurant with a menu as thick as your thumb. Dishes include pasta, risotto, and several types of pizza, but the menu also veers off into Tex-Mex and vegetarian fare. The small corner building is a nice spot for watching the passing traffic and provides plenty to see in the evenings, when snack vendors set up in the square nearby.

Some of the only upmarket dining you'll find in Can Tho is at **L'Escale** (1 Ngo Quyen, tel. 0292/381-9139, www.nambocantho.com, 6am-10:30pm daily, VND75,000-500,000), a classy roof terrace restaurant located on the fourth floor of the Nam Bo Boutique Hotel.

Both Western and Vietnamese cuisine are served, but the former is most notable, with dishes like rabbit and steak on offer as well as European desserts. Both indoor and outdoor tables are available; try to grab a spot along the edge if you can for the best views of the river and the street below.

Vegetarian

A modest local joint on the shady side of the street, **Com Chay 14** (14 Dien Bien Phu, 6am-1pm daily, VND15,000-30,000) serves a meatless version of *hu tieu* noodle soup in the mornings before switching to a tasty pick-and-point selection of tofu, vegetables, and mock-meat with rice in the afternoons. Keep an eye out for the colorful hand-painted sign out front.

ACCOMMODATIONS

Downtown Can Tho is a fairly small place, despite being the largest city in the Delta. Most travelers prefer to base themselves closer to the riverfront and Ninh Kieu Pier, where boats to the floating market depart and the majority of the city's travel services are set up.

Under VND210,000

Bright and spacious, the **Hien Guesthouse 2** (106/3 Phan Dinh Phung, tel. 0292/381-2718, nhakhachhien@yahoo.com, VND185,000-275,000) combines large, clean rooms with a quiet alley location just a few blocks from the riverfront. Wi-Fi is included, TVs are standard, and you have your choice of fan or air-conditioning. Some rooms come with a balcony. The amiable owner speaks a bit of English and can help with motorbike rentals. Around the corner is the original **Hien Guesthouse** (118/10 Phan Dinh Phung, tel. 0292/381-2718, nhakhachhien@yahoo.com, VND160,000-230,000), another solid choice but smaller and without en suite baths.

VND210,000-525,000

Roomier than some of its budget counterparts, the **Tay Ho Hotel** (42 Hai Ba Trung, tel. 0292/382-3392, tayhohotel@canthotourist.

com.vn, VND330,000-630,000) boasts an excellent location on the riverfront, included Wi-Fi, TV, and toiletries. It's a nice, clean one-star joint.

Only a touch less fancy than the original, **Hau Giang 2 Hotel** (6-8 Hai Thuong Lan Ong, tel. 0292/382-4836, haugiang2hotel@ canthotourist.vn, VND380,000-450,000, breakfast included) is a steal for the price. Located close to Can Tho Market and the riverfront, this hotel features spacious modern rooms with standard amenities. Ask for a window, as not all rooms come with natural light. The staff doesn't speak much English but the value makes this hotel too good to pass up.

The tall, narrow **Mango Hotel (Hotel Xoai)** (93 Mau Than, tel. 0292/383-4283, www.hotelxoai.com, VND220,000-550,000, breakfast included) provides excellent value a short distance from Can Tho's main tourist area. Lodgings feature plush beds and large windows, Wi-Fi, TV, and air-conditioning. Solar-powered water heaters and energy-conserving light bulbs keep the building green. Opt for the double bed over the narrow twin. The friendly staff can assist with recommendations around town. The hotel also runs reliable tours to Cai Rang Floating Market as well as food tours through **Mekong Tours** (tel. 09/0785-2927, www.mekongtours.info).

A stone's throw from the waterfront, the skinny **Kim Lan Hotel** (138A Nguyen An Ninh, tel. 0292/381-7049, www.kimlanhotel-cantho.com, VND420,000-1,660,000, breakfast included) offers great value with spacious, clean rooms and friendly staff. Rooms feature modern decor and air-conditioning, hot water, TV, Wi-Fi, and a fridge. Kim Lan also arranges homestays in the nearby countryside. Costs are slightly higher but include meals and a trip to the floating market. These homestays are more like a rural guesthouse than a one-on-one overnight with a local family.

VND525,000-1,050,000

One of the nicer places in the city center, **Hau Giang Hotel** (34 Nam Ky Khoi Nghia,

tel. 0292/382-1851, VND735,000-1,890,000, breakfast included) showcases the best that Can Tho Tourist has to offer. Spacious rooms are well furnished and come with high-quality amenities as well as air-conditioning, Wi-Fi, TV, a minibar, and an array of toiletries.

VND1,050,000-2,100,000

The gargantuan **Ninh Kieu 2** (3 Hoa Binh, tel. 0292/378-9777, www.ninhkieuhotel.com, VND950,000-2,600,000) sits directly on the main drag not far from Can Tho Museum and the city post office. Rooms feature regal decor, with polished wood furniture and upholstered chairs. The hotel includes breakfast in its room rates and amenities such as TV, hot water, air-conditioning, and a minibar. Massage and spa services are available to guests, as well as a fitness center, a restaurant, and a bar.

A sizable building, the **Kim Tho Hotel** (1A Ngo Gia Tu, tel. 0292/381-7517, www.kimtho.com, VND990,000-3,000,000, breakfast included) has benefited from some good publicity over the last few years, as tour groups regularly turn up at this mid-range spot. Accommodations feature roomy low beds and large windows, some of which overlook the river, and there is also a 12th-floor roof terrace café, a restaurant, and a massage parlor in the building. Thanks to its popularity, the Kim Tho is often full, so book ahead.

The well-appointed **TTC Hotel** (2 Hai Ba Trung, tel. 0292/381-2210, www.cantho.ttchotels.com, VND1,300,000-6,000,000, breakfast included) is a bright, spacious, modern hotel in an excellent location at one end of the Ninh Kieu waterfront. In addition to comfy purple-hued rooms outfitted with the standard amenities, TTC also has a swimming pool, restaurant, and fitness center. Be sure to check out the eighth-floor café overlooking the river.

Over VND2,100,000

Housed in a 1930s colonial building, ★ **Nam Bo Boutique Hotel** (1 Ngo Quyen, tel. 0292/381-9139, www.nambo-cantho.com, VND2,900,000-3,400,000) manages to combine its classic colonial style with modern facilities. Perched on the corner of Ngo Quyen and Hai Ba Trung, this beautiful boutique hotel features seven individually designed corner suites, each with panoramic views of Ninh Kieu Pier and the river, as well as the street below. Rooms are spacious and feature both a bedroom, a living room, and, in some cases, a small in-room dining area.

Victoria Can Tho Resort (Cai Khe, tel. 0292/381-0111, www.victoriahotels.asia, VND3,065,000-6,784,000) is a four-star escape from the bustling Ninh Kieu district. This stunning riverfront retreat boasts gorgeous rooms complete with a bedroom and sitting area. Rooms come with peaceful river views or a view of the palm-lined pool. Downstairs is a spa, business center, a bar, and a restaurant. Guests can enjoy sunset cruises on the resort's beautiful converted rice barge as well as cycling and market tours.

Nam Bo Boutique Hotel

INFORMATION AND SERVICES

One of the more helpful government-run tourism branches, **Can Tho Tourist** (50 Hai Ba Trung, tel. 0292/382-1854, www.canthotourist.vn, 7am-6pm daily) assists travelers with everything from free maps of town to private boat and bicycle rentals to cooking tours, cycling tours, visits to the floating market, and homestays. Stop by the main office on Hai Ba Trung for advice, but not around lunchtime, as everyone steps out.

The most centrally located pair of ATMs is on Hai Ba Trung street just beside Can Tho Tourist. There are also several banks and cash machines along Nam Ky Khoi Nghia street near the corner of Phan Dinh Phung, as well as along Hoa Binh Boulevard. Most hotels are able to exchange currency, as is the local **Vietcombank** (3-7 Hoa Binh, tel. 0292/382-0445, www.vietcombank.com.vn, 7:30am-11:30am and 1pm-4:30pm Mon.-Fri.).

The mammoth **Can Tho post office** (2 Hoa Binh, tel. 0292/382-6653, 7:30am-11am and 1:30pm-5pm Mon.-Sat.) deals not only in letters but also provides Internet and phone services, as well as on-site cash payments for online bookings with Vietnam Airlines and Jetstar.

The **Can Tho General Hospital (Benh Vien Da Khoa Can Tho)** (4 Chau Van Liem, tel. 0292/372-1235) has both a clinic and 24-7 emergency services and can provide basic care for travelers. For more serious issues, a trip to Saigon is recommended.

GETTING THERE
Air
Ten kilometers northwest of the city is **Can Tho Airport (San Bay Quoc Te Can Tho)** (VCA), with direct flights from domestic destinations such as Phu Quoc (50 minutes) and Con Dao (55 minutes) as well as Danang (1.5 hours) and Hanoi (2 hours) via budget carriers like VietJet as well as national carrier Vietnam Airlines. Because Saigon is only a few hours' drive from Can Tho there are no flights between the cities.

The best way to get into town from the

airport is by taxi (around VND150,000) or, if you're traveling light, *xe om* (VND70,000-100,000). The airport is roughly 20 minutes (12 kilometers) from downtown Can Tho.

Bus

Can Tho's bus stations have moved around in the past couple years, so ask at your hotel first and confirm you're heading to the right station. Cushy air-conditioned **Phuong Trang** (tel. 0292/376-9768, www.futabuslines.com.vn, 24 hours daily) buses arrive at the city's **central bus station** (QL1A, 24 hours daily) daily from Saigon (3.5 hours, VND110,000), Chau Doc (3.5 hours, VND100,000), Ca Mau (4 hours, VND120,000), Rach Gia (3.5 hours, VND110,000), and Dalat (11 hours, VND325,000). Phuong Trang passengers need not worry about transportation from the bus station to their final destination, as the firm's transfer vehicles will take you from the bus station to any address downtown.

You can also hop on a local bus (smaller minibus-style vehicles) for nearby destinations like Vinh Long and Tra Vinh (1.5 hours). Fares on these vehicles tend to be cheaper, but things like air-conditioning and adequate space are not guaranteed. These buses tend

to leave from the old **91B bus station** (91B Hung Loi, 24 hours daily).

Stick to the official bus counter when buying tickets to avoid touts selling tickets at twice the price.

GETTING AROUND

Can Tho is a walkable city, with most land attractions within a three-kilometer radius of the waterfront. As long as you avoid midday, when the sun is high overhead and there is little shade, there should be no trouble walking around town.

Several cab companies operate in Can Tho, the most trusted being **Mailinh** (tel. 0292/382-8282) and **Khanh Cuong** (tel. 0292/386-8686). *Xe om* are ever-present along the waterfront and eager to take passengers. Chances are they'll spot you before you spot them.

Several hotels in town rent out bicycles, along with **Can Tho Tourist** (50 Hai Ba Trung, tel. 0292/382-1854, www.canthotourist.vn, 7am-6pm daily, VND40,000-70,000 per day). Beyond pedal power, motorbike rentals can be found at **Hotel Xoai** (93 Mau Than, tel. 0292/383-4283, www.hotelxoai.com, VND180,000).

Mekong River Islands

A collection of lush low-lying fields situated between the banks of the Tien River, My Tho and Ben Tre's fertile islands are considered the gateway to the Mekong Delta. Occupying a narrow bend just 72 kilometers south of Saigon, these four islands—Phoenix, Unicorn, Dragon, and Tortoise—offer a quick and easily accessible glimpse into the larger region with a variety of quintessential Delta scenery, from abundant fruit orchards and narrow canopied streams to wooden sampans and floating fish farms. Easily done in a day, these landscapes provide a crash course in life on the water for travelers who lack the time to explore the Delta in greater detail. Day trips

from Saigon set off early in the morning and tour each of the islands before turning back to the city by mid- to late afternoon. An overnight in either My Tho or Ben Tre can offer a satisfying escape from the buzzing southern city.

Most boat trips around the islands feature a whirlwind of lush gardens, small local factories, and winding canals, along with the occasional bike ride or horse-drawn cart. Those who overnight in either My Tho or Ben Tre will have the opportunity to explore the town up close, as far fewer travelers actually spend the night here. Half- and full-day excursions can be arranged from Ho Chi Minh City

Mekong River Cruises

As a traveler in the Mekong Delta, it is all but guaranteed that you will get on a boat at least once during your trip. Most people book day trips along the water, visiting a variety of river islands, floating markets, fruit orchards, and narrow canals. A handful of luxury cruises provide tours and transport from Saigon and Can Tho to other Delta destinations such as Cai Be, Sa Dec, and Chau Doc.

One of the more well-known outfits, **Mekong Eyes** (Van Phat 1 Hotel, 2 Nguyen Van Cu, tel. 0292/378-3586, www.mekongeyes.com, VND2,500,000-29,020,000) boasts a fleet of vessels ranging from a spacious, 16-cabin converted rice barge to a smaller 2-cabin houseboat. The company offers two- to four-day trips to places like Cai Be, Sa Dec, Chau Doc, and Can Tho. Travelers visit fruit orchards and countryside villages in much the same fashion as most day tours, with the added experience of an overnight on the river. Only the longer journeys come near the US$1,000 mark. Onward transportation to Phu Quoc and Cambodia can be arranged, though these connections usually include a speedboat, bus, or plane rather than slow-boat service.

TransMekong, the same company behind L'Escale Restaurant and Nam Bo Boutique Hotel, runs **Bassac Cruises** (144 Hai Ba Trung, tel. 0292/382-9540, www.transmekong.com, 8am-noon and 1:30pm-5:30pm Mon.-Fri., 8am-noon Sat.-Sun.). This outfitter runs a series of high-end overnight trips from Can Tho to Cai Be or vice versa; the cruise also plies the route from Can Tho up to Chau Doc and the Cambodian border. All vessels are traditional wooden rice barges that have been refurbished and equipped with modern conveniences such as air-conditioning and hot water. The company's rates fluctuate depending on the trip and the season; contact them for a quote.

(HCMC), My Tho, or Ben Tre. Given the fact that the main appeal of both towns is the islands, a day or two is really all you need before returning to Saigon or carrying on to other Delta destinations.

EXPLORING THE MEKONG RIVER ISLANDS

Unicorn Island

The largest of the four islands occupying the river between Ben Tre and Tien Giang provinces, **Unicorn Island (Cu Lao Thoi Son)** is home to several cottage industries, including local honey farms and orchards packed with ripe papayas, watermelon, pineapples, dragon fruit, and longans. Thanks to the Rach Mieu Bridge, the island's peaceful, verdant scenery can be reached over land, allowing travelers to explore the area on their own via bicycle or motorbike. Most local boat tours stop at Unicorn Island for the fresh fruit as well as the souvenir vendors. On account of its size and location, this is easily the most populated of the islands. A handful of small cafés set amid the greenery make for a nice spot to relax and take in the island's slower pace.

Phoenix Island

Just beyond Unicorn Island lies **Phoenix Island (Con Phung)**, the former residence of local religious figure Nguyen Thanh Nam, better known as the Coconut Monk. Born in 1909, Nam came from a wealthy family and studied in France for several years before returning to Vietnam, where he married and had a daughter. Later in life Nam found religion, joining a Buddhist monastery and, at one point, meditating day and night beneath a flagpole. The Coconut Monk earned his name by subsisting on a diet of fruits, vegetables, and coconut water, eating a single meal each day. In 1952 he took up residence in his home province of Ben Tre, building a colorful **sanctuary** (VND10,000), which still stands at the end of Phoenix Island, and gathering followers of his own syncretic religion, a mashup of Buddhism and Christianity called Tinh Do Cu Si, in which he insisted that man could live on nothing more than coconut water. The

Coconut Monk was also known for his clashes with the South Vietnamese authorities, who jailed him several times for spreading anti-government sentiment. Nguyen Thanh Nam died in 1990. The sanctuary is easy to spot from the boat docks. To visit the sanctuary, contact **Con Phung Tourist** (Hamlet 10, Tan Thach village, tel. 0275/382-2198, www.conphungtourist.com, 7:30am-5pm daily).

Nowadays, the sanctuary remains, looking like a rundown carnival with its maze of brightly hued columns and wiry statues, including a replica of an Apollo rocket. Tourists can also visit the nearby restaurant as well as a crocodile farm packed with sedate reptiles. It is possible to rent bicycles through **Con Phung Tourist** (Hamlet 10, Tan Thach village, tel. 0275/382-2198, www.conphungtourist.com, 7:30am-5pm daily), if you explore the island on your own. If you prefer to visit by land, a smaller connection past the long and narrow Rach Mieu Bridge leads to the opposite end of Phoenix Island, where the road then goes to the Con Phung Tourist area. Guests can stay overnight at the travel company's island **hotel** (VND300,000-450,000). There's not much point in basing yourself here, as the sights of Phoenix Island will take up no more than an hour or two.

Tortoise Island

Part of neighboring Ben Tre province, **Tortoise Island (Con Quy)** is less frequented than its larger counterparts, but several tours swing by here to get a look at the coconut candy factories, which churn out copious amounts of sticky sweet toffee every day. Visitors can watch the process as well as sample the candy, which comes in several varieties, including chocolate, coffee, and durian flavors.

Dragon Island

The least-visited of the four islands, **Dragon Island (Con Tan Long)** is a quieter, miniature version of My Tho town. Its narrow concrete paths slice through a sea of modest pastel-hued houses and over tiny creeks that cut deep into the land. Guided tours are less likely to visit Dragon Island, but visitors can take the **Tan Long ferry** (intersection of Trung Trac and Rach Gam, 5am-10pm daily, VND1,500-4,000) just a short walk up from the statue of Thu Khoa Huan. Once on Dragon Island, a right turn leads along the narrow road to a dead-end on the riverfront that looks back at My Tho town, while a left turn follows the concrete path farther into the neighborhoods of the island. This is an area best explored by bicycle. Due to the fact that very few foreigners make the trip out here, be prepared to draw some stares.

Boat Tours of the Islands
FROM HO CHI MINH CITY

As the gateway to the Delta, both My Tho and Ben Tre see frequent visitors from HCMC who are short on time but still want to experience the lush countryside and laid-back atmosphere of the Mekong. Scores of travel outfits in the city run day trips out to the area's river islands, hitting a few other mainland attractions along the way, and prices vary to suit a range of budgets. Companies like **Sinh Tourist** (246-248 De Tham, D1, tel. 028/3838-9593, www.thesinhtourist.vn, 6:30am-10:30pm daily) offer inexpensive mass tours, with upward of 30 or 40 fellow travelers on a trip, while **Vinaday goREISE** (230 De Tham, D1, tel. 028/3838-8382, www.goreise.com, 9am-8pm Mon.-Sat., 9am-noon Sun.) provides similar excursions with a higher level of service quality and fewer people per tour. For more personalized excursions, try outfits such as **Ho Chi Minh City Urban Adventures** (tel. 09/0990-4100, www.hochiminhcityurbanadventures.com) or **Tiger Tours** (109 Ly Van Phuc, tel. 028/3820-0682, www.mytigertour.com, 8am-5pm Mon.-Fri.), which run smaller public trips as well as private tours that can be tailored to your interests. Booking through an official travel company is recommended over a hotel, as the smaller outfits attached to budget accommodations can often be unpredictable.

FROM MY THO

Like life in any town in the Mekong Delta, life in My Tho revolves around the river, and so the main reason for a visit is its islands and the surrounding waterways. Hop on a boat from the **tourist pier** (8 30 Thang 4, tel. 0273/397-6697, 7am-7pm daily) and float alongside houseboats and fish farms, barges, and ferries. Both private and group tours are available from the several companies housed within the pier's main office, and whether you join a group or go it alone, prices are reasonable even for a solo traveler. Most tours are booked by the vessel, so the more people you have, the easier it will be on your wallet. The majority of tour providers leaving from My Tho visit the same places, making regular stops on three of the four principal islands between My Tho and Ben Tre, where you can sample local fruit and honey, drop in on a coconut candy workshop, visit the aging sanctuary of Phoenix Island's Coconut Monk, and listen to a group of *cai luong* singers; check with your chosen company for their exact itinerary. Most of the day trips coming from Saigon arrive at the pier around 10:30am-11am; if you'd like to avoid the rush, book a private boat and visit earlier in the morning.

FROM BEN TRE

Tours in Ben Tre focus on the two provinces' shared islands: Unicorn, Phoenix, Dragon, and Tortoise. While the town is only a short distance from the Tien River, many tours booked in Ben Tre actually set sail in My Tho, with travelers taking a 16-kilometer bus trip to the Tourist Pier in the other town, though some do depart directly from Ben Tre. Day tours featuring local fruit, honey, and coconut candy—Ben Tre's specialty—as well as southern music and a glimpse of country life can be arranged through most local hotels and at the offices of **Ben Tre Tourist** (16 Hai Ba Trung, tel. 0275/382-9618, www.bentretourist.vn, 7:30am-11am and 1pm-5pm daily). If you prefer more freedom, you can also hire a chartered boat from the tourism office or head down to the riverfront, where you may

be able to find a freelance driver who will take you around.

MY THO

Considered the Mekong Delta's gateway, this hyperactive little town lies 72 kilometers south of Saigon and welcomes dozens of day-trippers to its tourist pier every morning. Thanks to its proximity, My Tho has become the poster child for the Delta's lazy rivers and fertile green terrain, not to mention its numerous cottage industries. From local fish farms to fruit orchards, handicraft workshops, and candy factories, My Tho and its nearby river islands provide travelers with a glimpse into the life of the region and an escape from the smog and chaos of Ho Chi Minh City.

The majority of visitors prefer to tour My Tho for the day, returning to Saigon at night; however, it is also possible to base yourself in town. For budget travelers, the difference in cost between booking a day trip from the city and overnighting in My Tho is minimal, thus the decision to stay in Saigon or take a bus south is based on time. Those with an extra evening to spare can take in this friendly Delta town beyond the confines of a guided tour; but, if your schedule doesn't allow it, opting for a day tour is just as good.

Sights
VINH TRANG PAGODA

My Tho's **Vinh Trang Pagoda** (Nguyen Trung Truc, 6am-6pm daily) stands out among its contemporaries with a colorful exterior and several towering Buddha statues dotting its grounds. Before you reach the main gates, you'll be greeted by a pair of enormous figures: a somber, imposing Buddha followed by its hefty, happy seated counterpart. Several other sculptures around the area feature the Buddha in different poses, including a massive reclining version out back, and a cemetery off to the right marks the resting places of monks past.

To enter the pagoda, use the door on the right side of the building, where you'll pass through separate sections dedicated to the

Vicinity of My Tho

ancestors as well as to Buddha himself. A bright inner courtyard interrupts the pagoda roof, letting in some light, and the building's exterior is a rich mosaic of greens, blues, and yellows. Many tourist buses to My Tho make the rounds here, so you're likely to see a few foreign visitors wandering through. Though the pagoda doesn't have a specific number address, if you follow the Quay Bridge over Bao Dinh River and turn left onto Nguyen Huynh Duc, you'll see the mammoth Buddhas on your right as the road heads out of town.

CAO DAI TEMPLE

If the Cao Dai Holy See of Tay Ninh is not in your travel plans, My Tho's smaller **Cao Dai Temple** (85 Ly Thuong Kiet, 6am-6pm daily) is a worthy example of Cao Dai architecture. The temple rarely sees foreign visitors, but guests are welcome outside of prayer hours. Avoid showing up at noon, when the temple is in use and you'll have to stay outside.

Food

In the realm of cuisine, My Tho's claim to fame is a popular southern noodle soup called *hu tieu My Tho*. Featuring pork, fresh greens, and a unique version of rice noodles, this savory dish comes in several different varieties, including original, beef, and *sate,* which is served in a thicker, creamier broth. For other options, you'll find a handful of restaurants at some of the bigger hotels along the river, as well as dozens of small outdoor cafés lining the town's lake.

For an authentic bowl of the town specialty *hu tieu My Tho,* head to **Hu Tieu 44** (46 Nam Ky Khoi Nghia, tel. 0273/388-3044, 6am-noon and 1pm-9pm daily, VND25,000). This small hole-in-the-wall shop serves nothing but *hu tieu.*

Just beside the Tourist Pier on 30 Thang 4 street, **Phuoc Loc Tho Vegetarian Restaurant** (2A 30 Thang 4, tel. 0273/397-9467, 6am-10pm daily, VND15,000-30,000) serves a variety of vegetarian fare, including

My Tho

rice dishes and several noodle soups. Its signature meal is *hu tieu chay,* a meatless version of the town's namesake classic.

If you're craving street food but need a break from the ever-present *hu tieu* stalls, **Sau Bao Banh Xeo** (Le Loi, tel. 0273/387-9835, 3pm-7pm daily, VND50,000) is a nice local spot that does a delectable southern version of Vietnamese pancakes. The shop functions as a café in the mornings before transforming into a restaurant later in the afternoon.

Despite drawing a small crowd, the town's **night market** (8 30 Thang 4, 5pm-late daily, VND20,000-60,000) is open till the wee hours of the morning. A collection of different stalls serve rice-and-meat dishes as well as several types of noodles, from *bun* and pho to *hu tieu,* and a variety of soups. Smoothies and *che,* a local dessert, are also available. Some stalls are

better than others, so feel free to have a look around before deciding on a vendor.

Accommodations

Though you'll be hard-pressed to find anything above two-star accommodations in this town, most of the guest rooms are clean, tidy, and perfectly comfortable. The vast majority of My Tho's tourism focuses on its waterways, so the most strategic place to stay is 30 Thang 4 street or near it. There are several hotels along the waterfront, wrapping around to Trung Trac, as well as toward Rach Mieu Bridge on Le Thi Hong Gam. Wherever you stay, expect prices to be infinitely more affordable than HCMC and amenities to be fewer.

VND210,000-525,000

Rooms at the **Cong Doan Hotel** (61 30 Thang 4, tel. 0273/387-4324, congdoantravel@

Local Cuisine: Mekong Delta

The Mekong Delta is packed with local specialties. It seems as if every town in the south has a culinary claim to fame. Here are just a few of the Mekong's unique culinary contributions:

- *banh cong:* This fried rice cake is famous in Can Tho, though it's not as easily found as some other local specialties. Rice flour is combined with pork and shrimp, then fried, with the end result resembling a muffin. Use fresh greens to wrap up the cake, dip it in fish sauce, and enjoy.

- *bun nuoc leo:* Actually a Khmer meal, this cloudy noodle soup is often served with local greens, a combination of leafy vegetables from the countryside, and either grilled meat or congealed duck blood. You'll find *bun nuoc leo* heavily featured in Tra Vinh and Chau Doc.

- **coconut candy:** As Vietnam's coconut capital, Ben Tre province houses a boatload of coconuts. Here, sticky toffee-like coconut candy is a popular local treat. The fruit's flesh is pressed, extracting the juice, which is then combined with sugar, boiled, and turned into a thick paste. Once the concoction has cooled, sheets of the candy are cut into bite-size pieces and packaged.

- **fish sauce:** Though it's not a meal in itself, *nuoc mam* (fish sauce) is a fundamental part of Vietnamese cuisine. There is not a restaurant or street stall in the country where you won't find it. Made from a mixture of fish and salt, this pungent sauce requires at least 12 months of fermentation before it is bottled. Factories on Phu Quoc Island store the concoction in gigantic wooden barrels and are among the most renowned fish sauce producers in the country.

- **fruit:** From My Tho to Vinh Long, the Delta boasts an impressive variety of fruits, many of them foreign to Westerners. While you'll find tasty and familiar favorites like mango and papaya, other famed regional fruits include pomelo, dragon fruit (a juicy fruit hidden within a spiky, pink-and-green exterior), bite-size longans, rambutans, and jackfruit (the world's largest fruit).

- *hu tieu My Tho:* Originating in My Tho, the local version of this rice noodle soup is usually served with sliced pork, quail eggs, shrimp, and occasionally dumplings. There are several other equally delicious variations, including *hu tieu Nam Vang* and *hu tieu sa te.*

hcm.fpt.vn, VND250,000-300,000) are a little on the small side, but the beds are clean and the prices reasonable. You can choose from fan or air-conditioned accommodations, and each room comes with basic amenities such as a TV and bottled water. There is also a nice coffee shop just next door where you can get your morning caffeine fix.

The super-slender **Minh Quan Hotel** (69 30 Thang 4, tel. 0273/397-9979, VND450,000-800,000) sits near the statue of Thu Khoa Huan on the eastern end of 30 Thang 4 and has some exceptional river views. Rooms feature large beds and air-conditioning, TV, Wi-Fi, a minibar, and hot showers. Breakfast is served every morning at the rooftop café, another great spot to take in the surrounding scenery; beware that due to the café, the hotel's top floors can get noisy at night.

VND525,000-1,050,000

The spacious rooms at the **Song Tien Hotel** (101 Trung Trac, tel. 0273/387-2009, songtien. hotel@tiengiangtourist.com, VND550,000-850,000, breakfast included) are some of the few in town with modern decor and more luxury. Beds are generous, as are the baths. A small café is attached to the hotel, and there is karaoke on the first floor. If the Song Tien is full, you can also try the **Song Tien Annex** (33 Trung Trac, tel. 0273/397-7883, VND450,000-500,000), slightly cheaper, just down the street.

One of the grander hotels in My Tho, **Chuong Duong Hotel** (10 30 Thang 4, tel.

0273/387-0875, VND500,000-800,000) is a massive pale-yellow behemoth overlooking the river that features decent budget accommodations with a bit of outdated style. Downstairs, a large open-air restaurant caters to the odd tour group, and one of the town's larger travel outfits operates here.

Information and Services

The government-run **Tien Giang Tourist** (63 Trung Trac, tel. 0273/387-3184, www.tiengiangtourist.com, 7am-5pm daily) has a hand in most of the town's tourism offerings, from hotels and restaurants to river tours. They're worth consulting for further information on My Tho town and the surrounding area, including parts of Ben Tre province, and provide free maps upon request. From here, both single travelers and large groups can hire boats and book tours.

The friendly folks at **Viet Phong Mekong** (Thoi Thanh Hamlet, tel. 09/1828-5522, www.vietphongmekong.com.vn, 9am-9pm daily) provide not only day tours of My Tho's nearby islands but also homestays, bicycle and motorbike rentals, and general information on the Delta area. Maps of My Tho town are also available here.

The **Vietin Bank** (15B Nam Ky Khoi Nghia, tel. 0273/387-3025, www.vietinbank. vn, 7:30am-11:30am and 1:30pm-4:30pm Mon.-Fri.) exchanges currency and also has an ATM available. The massive **My Tho post office** (59 30 Thang 4, tel. 0273/387-3214, 7am-8pm daily) is located on the main drag. It also provides Internet services around the back on Truong Dinh street.

The large **My Tho Hospital (Benh Vien Da Khoa My Tho)** (2 Hung Vuong, tel. 0273/387-2363, benhviendktiengiang.vn) is as equipped as any hospital in southern Vietnam to treat minor illnesses and injuries. For serious emergencies, there are 24-hour services available, but you're far better heading to Saigon.

Transportation

Buses leave Ho Chi Minh City's Western bus station every half hour 7am-7pm daily (1.5 hours, VND35,000), arriving at My Tho's **Tien Giang bus station** (42 Ap Bac, tel. 0273/385-5404, 4am-10pm daily), roughly three kilometers from town. There are also several daily arrivals from neighboring Delta towns, including Ha Tien (5-6 hours, VND120,000), Can Tho (3 hours, VND75,000), and Chau Doc (4-4.5 hours, VND140,000).

Thanks to its size, My Tho town is easily accessible on foot. There are, however, a handful of *xe om* drivers that hang out along 30 Thang 4 street near the tourist pier and, should you need a cab, **Mailinh** (tel. 0273/387-8787) taxis are always available.

If you prefer your own set of wheels, **Viet Phong Mekong** (2 Le Loi, tel. 09/1828-5522, www.vietphongmekong.com.vn, 9am-9pm daily, VND100,000-150,000) rents out both bicycles and motorbikes. Fees are reasonable, but be prepared to put down some sort of collateral for your rental vehicle, usually either money or a passport, which will be returned to you once the rental is complete. A few hotels and guesthouses are also willing to hire out vehicles.

Dong Tam Snake Farm

If you're up for a bit of a trek, the **Dong Tam Snake Farm (Trai Ran Dong Tam)** (Cong 2 Trai Ran, tel. 0273/385-3204, www.trairandongtam.com.vn, 7am-4:30pm daily, VND30,000), about 10.5 kilometers from My Tho, offers an unusual break from the river. Located in Binh Duc, this massive complex was founded in 1977 and is wholly devoted to the care and study of various snakes found throughout the Southeast Asian region. In addition to providing the country with medical research into treating venomous snakebites and other ailments, the snake farm functions as something of a zoo for visitors and has expanded to include many more creatures, including ostriches, deer, monkeys, and birds of prey. These animals aren't kept in the finest of cages, which may turn off animal lovers. But, the serpents, particularly the trees full of bright-green snakes, are an interesting departure from your average menagerie. Check out the snake-feeding house to find the largest reptiles, or pose for a picture with a massive python. There is a small, eerie museum of preserved snakes as well as an informational video offered to visitors.

Beyond the animals themselves, finding the snake farm can be half the fun. The area is not well marked, but if you follow Le Thi Hong Gam west from My Tho past the Rach Mieu Bridge, you'll enter Binh Duc village. Continue along this road through Binh Duc market until you reach Binh Duc Primary School (Truong Tieu Hoc Binh Duc) on your right. Just beside the school is a small road topped with a sign reading "Ap Van Hoa Tan Thuan B." Take this pleasant, paved village road straight through to the end, bearing left at the fork, and you'll reach another large street. Dong Tam Snake Farm is on your left at the very end, just before the gargantuan military center. Budget about two hours for the trip, including travel time.

BEN TRE

Though it's only 16 kilometers from My Tho, the sleepy town of Ben Tre has managed to escape the same tourism hype as its northern neighbor and remains a placid, likable place with few specific attractions but plenty of pleasant scenery. A major agricultural contributor and the heart of the nation's coconut industry, this small island province is considered the birthplace of the National Liberation Front, the major guerrilla force that opposed southern Vietnamese soldiers during the American War. Having fought in the Tay Son rebellion in the 18th century and, later, taken on the French colonial government in the 1940s and 1950s, Ben Tre's fierce nationalism was already a local mainstay by the time American soldiers turned up, making the NLF a powerful adversary. U.S. soldiers proved to be equally ruthless: When an unnamed U.S. major uttered the now-famous line "It became necessary to destroy the village in order to save it," he was talking about Ben Tre.

Nowadays, you're more likely to find sleepy street corners and riverside cafés than any sort of aggression. Locals in Ben Tre embody the friendly, easygoing reputation of Delta hospitality, and life in this little corner of the country is wonderfully laid-back. While most visitors zip over to the My Tho-Ben Tre area on a day trip, it is also possible to spend the night in town. Like My Tho, two days is all you need in Ben Tre before it's time to move on.

Sights
RIVERFRONT
The most attractive feature of Ben Tre is its **riverfront.** A lively spot from morning to night, the street along the water is lined with fruit vendors and small cafés where you can sit and watch the world go by. Hung Vuong, the road along the water, extends all the way from Ben Tre Market to the nearby countryside, giving you plenty of space to stroll or cycle.

BEN TRE MUSEUM
The provincial **Ben Tre Museum** (146 Hung Vuong, tel. 0275/382-2735, 7:30am-10:30am and 1:30pm-4:30pm daily, free) is filled with the standard array of revolutionary exhibits and war artifacts. While the displays aren't exactly riveting, this museum is housed in yet another stately, aging colonial structure on the riverfront that is worth admiring from the outside.

VIEN MINH PAGODA AND AN HOI TEMPLE
If you're wandering around town, the generous **Vien Minh Pagoda** (near the corner of Nguyen Dinh Chieu and QL60, sunrise-sunset daily), near the central market and Ben Tre Bridge No. 1, is a nice place to visit. While it doesn't have the same exciting history as some other Vietnamese pagodas, the building is aesthetically pleasing and there are two massive white statues—one of Buddha, one of Quan Am—right out front that add to the atmosphere of the town's main roundabout. You'll also find **An Hoi Temple** next door, whose colorful dragons jump out of the front

Ben Tre

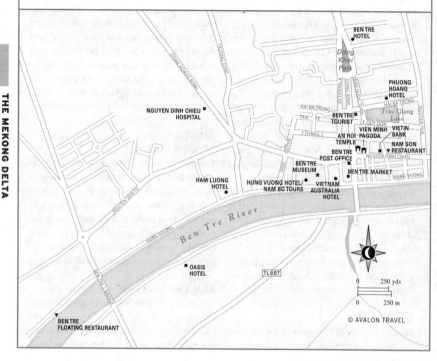

THE MEKONG DELTA
MEKONG RIVER ISLANDS

wall; depending upon the time of day, you may or may not be able to go inside.

Food

Due to its relative quiet as a tourist destination, Ben Tre has fewer restaurant options than its counterpart across the river. However, many hotels in town have restaurants attached in order to serve guests and there are plenty of street food options both in and around the central market.

Bustling with local clientele, **Nam Son Restaurant** (40 Phan Ngoc Tong, tel. 0275/382-2873, 9:30am-7:30pm daily, VND25,000-150,000) serves tasty Vietnamese fare, including *canh chua* (sour soup) and plenty of meat and fish dishes to accompany your rice. The place gets busy around lunch and again at dinner, so you may find yourself

sitting with strangers, but the restaurant is a nice place for a wide range of options.

The cool banquet-style ground-floor restaurant at **Hung Vuong** (148 Hung Vuong, tel. 0275/382-2408, www.hungvuonghotel-bentre.vn, 6am-11pm daily, VND35,000-90,000) serves simple meals from its English menu, including tofu, beef, shrimp, squid, and eel dishes. Though the decor isn't much, prices are reasonable and the food is decent.

The dining room at **Ham Luong** (200C Hung Vuong, tel. 0275/356-0560, www.hamluongtourist.com.vn, 6am-10pm daily, VND70,000-260,000) is one of Ben Tre's fancier setups, with a nice air-conditioned indoor seating area and more atmosphere than most places in town. A lengthy menu includes a host of Vietnamese favorites as well as beer and wine. The dining room often caters to large groups rather than individual travelers, so if you plan to eat here, be prepared to wait for your meal or order ahead of time to avoid the delay.

The **TTC Ben Tre Floating Restaurant** (Hung Vuong, tel. 0275/382-2492, 6am-10pm daily, VND35,000-400,000) may be out of commission as a boat but it manages to make for a nice, breezy dinner on the water. The multistory vehicle remains docked on Hung Vuong street just past Ben Tre Bridge No. 2 and serves everything under the sun, from pork and beef to crocodile, deer, and snails. If you prefer, you can also choose your dinner from a series of fish tanks in the restaurant's lobby.

Accommodations
VND210,000-525,000

A narrow building across from Truc Giang Lake, the family-run **Phuong Hoang Hotel (Khach San Phuong Hoang)** (28 Hai Ba Trung, tel. 0275/357-5377, VND200,000-300,000) is a worthy budget option. Rooms are small but comfortable and feature standard amenities, with your choice of fan or air-conditioned accommodations.

The most affordable riverfront option, **Hung Vuong Hotel** (148 Hung Vuong, tel. 0275/382-2408, www.hungvuonghotelben-tre.vn, VND450,000-505,000, breakfast included) offers great value for the price, with clean, modestly furnished rooms featuring air-conditioning, Wi-Fi, hot showers, a minibar, and a bathtub. The hotel runs a restaurant downstairs, as well as **Nam Bo Tours** (166 Hung Vuong, tel. 0275/351-1292, www.nambotours.com, 7:30am-4:30pm daily).

VND525,000-1,050,000

When it comes to ambience, the **Vietnam Australia Hotel (Khach San Viet Uc)** (144 Hung Vuong, tel. 0275/351-1888, www.hotel-vietuc.com, VND650,000-2,500,000) takes the cake. This stunning three-star hotel is the most modern in town, from its cavernous lobby and café to each of its well-appointed rooms. Accommodations at the front of the hotel offer excellent riverfront views, and the kind and professional staff make it well worth the price tag. Basic doubles range VND650,000-850,000 and TV, Wi-Fi, air-conditioning, hot water, and breakfast are included. Keep an eye out for the security guard's hut, which is designed to look like the Sydney Opera House.

Located across the river from the city center, **Oasis Hotel** (151 My Thanh An, tel. 0275/246-7799, www.bentrehoteloasis.com, VND685,000-1,050,000) lives up to its name. This quiet laid-back guesthouse is run by a Vietnamese-New Zealander couple who offer clean, comfortable rooms as well as a pool and bar right on the waterfront looking back at Ben Tre city. Staff can arrange private tours to the river islands and surrounding area as well as bicycle and motorbike hires. If you don't have your own set of wheels, this may not be the place for you, as it's a bit of a walk into town. Families with young kids may also want to find another location, as the management prefers not to have guests under age eight.

Popular with both tour groups and individual travelers, **Ham Luong Hotel** (200C Hung Vuong, tel. 0275/356-0560, www.hamluongtourist.com.vn, VND560,000-980,000) is one of Ben Tre's nicer lodgings. Its clean, modern rooms afford guests pleasant views of the river. Wi-Fi, air-conditioning, TV, and hot water are included in the rates, along with complimentary breakfast. The hotel runs an on-site restaurant as well as a travel agency, which can help you book boat tours to the river islands and around.

Information and Services
Ben Tre Tourist (16 Hai Ba Trung, tel. 0275/382-9618, 7:30am-11am and 1pm-5pm daily) offers tours of the surrounding islands and nearby rural areas, venturing more off the beaten path than its northern counterpart in Tien Giang. Cycling tours and homestays can also be arranged or, if you prefer to make your own itinerary, both slow and fast boats, as well as bicycles, are available for hire.

The local **Vietin Bank** (142A Nguyen Dinh Chieu, tel. 0275/382-4960, www.

vietinbank.vn, 7:30am-11:30am and 1:30pm-4:30pm Mon.-Fri.) has an ATM and can exchange currencies. The **Ben Tre post office** (corner of Dong Khoi and Cach Mang Thang 8, tel. 0275/382-2157, 6am-8pm daily) is located just behind the market and directly on the roundabout before Ben Tre Bridge No. 1.

The **Nguyen Dinh Chieu Hospital (Benh Vien Nguyen Dinh Chieu)** (109 Doan Hoang Minh, tel. 0275/382-2191, http://bvndc.vn) is the largest of several hospitals and medical facilities located on this busy street. While they may be able to help with minor ailments, for anything serious, return to Saigon.

Transportation

A mammoth, modern entity, the **Ben Tre** bus station **(Ben Xe Ben Tre)** (Quoc Lo 60, tel. 0275/382-2298, 3am-10pm daily) has arrivals from Saigon (2 hours, VND60,000-75,000) as well as several other destinations around the Mekong Delta, including Ha Tien (6 hours, VND130,000), Can Tho (2.5 hours, VND75,000), and Chau Doc (5 hours, VND130,000).

You'll find plenty of *xe om* hanging around Ben Tre's street corners, and **Mailinh** (tel. 0275/387-8787) taxis also make their way around town.

Bicycles are available for rent from **Ben Tre Tourist** (16 Hai Ba Trung, tel. 0275/382-9618, www.bentretourist.vn, 7:30am-11am and 1pm-5pm daily) and through several of the local hotels. Rates can be either hourly or daily, depending on the provider.

Vinh Long

Vinh Long is a city in two parts. As a provincial capital, the town sees its share of chaos and traffic, with the bustling central market bursting at its seams and running freely down 1 Thang 5 street. But step on a ferry across the Co Chien River and you'll be pleasantly surprised to find its peaceful, laid-back island antithesis on the other side. Flush with palm trees and fruit orchards, fishing boats, and more waterways than roads, the fertile lands of An Binh, Vinh Long's largest river island, are the very definition of this region, a plentiful oasis where houses hide under the lush cover of palms and the island's narrow dirt roads are lined with papaya trees.

For travelers looking to experience the unhurried pace and friendly demeanor of the Mekong Delta, An Binh is an ideal spot to fall in step with the locals. Even with plenty of day-trippers passing through to visit Cai Be floating market and make a quick tour of the island, Vinh Long has managed to remain an easygoing and welcoming place that still feels like an authentic part of the Mekong Delta. A number of homestay options have sprung up on the island, allowing visitors to spend a night or two in peaceful An Binh with a local family.

Vinh Long is best visited outside the rainy season (May-Oct.), as the shores of the low-lying island often recede around this time. Regardless of the season, it is a good idea to plan on at least one overnight here in order to get the full experience. Day trips are available from Saigon, but the drive to Cai Be can be time-consuming and An Binh's serene island feel is tricky to achieve in only a few hours.

SIGHTS
An Binh Island

Accessible by ferry, **An Binh Island** is a sleepy village community of pastel-hued bungalows and floating fish farms that represents life in the Delta at its finest. Lush, green landscapes take up most of the area, covering every inch of this massive river island with palm fronds and papaya trees, fruit orchards, and narrow meandering streams. While visitors come for the scenery, many wind up staying an extra day or two on account of the hospitable locals,

Vinh Long

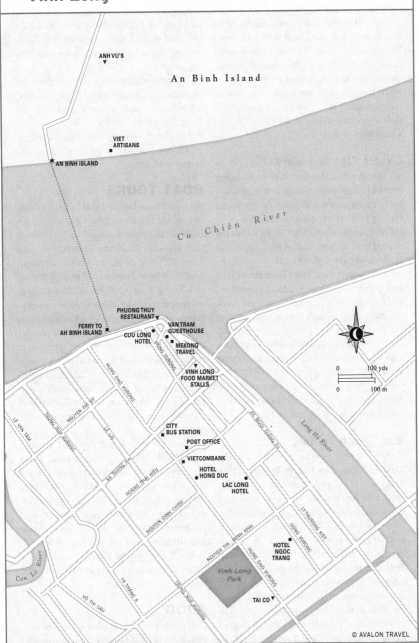

ANH VU'S

An Binh Island

VIET
ARTISANS

AN BINH ISLAND

Co Chiên River

PHUONG THUY
RESTAURANT

FERRY TO
AH BINH ISLAND

VAN TRAM
GUESTHOUSE

CUU LONG
HOTEL

MEKONG
TRAVEL

VINH LONG
FOOD MARKET
STALLS

HUNG VUONG

BA NGUYET HANG TU

Long Hồ River

HUNG DAO VUONG

NGUYEN THI UT

LE LAI

TRUNG NUU VUONG

LE VAN TAM

NGUYEN THI UT

BA THANG HAI

HOANG THAI HIEU

CITY
BUS STATION

POST OFFICE

VIETCOMBANK

HOTEL
HONG DUC

LAC LONG
HOTEL

LY THUONG KIET

HUNG VUONG

NGUYEN DINH CHIEU

Cau Lô River

19 THANG 8

VO THI SAU

TRUNG NUU VUONG

NGUYEN THI MINH KHAI

HUNG DAO VUONG

Vinh Long
Park

HOTEL
NGOC
TRANG

TAI CO

0   100 yds
0   100 m

© AVALON TRAVEL

who are quick to say hello or invite you for a chat over tea. An Binh can be reached via the local **ferry (Ben Pha An Binh)** (4am-10pm daily, VND500-2,500), which leaves from downtown Vinh Long, and is best explored by bicycle or by boat. Plenty of small wooden canoes ply the island's waterways, taking visitors to more hidden parts of An Binh. For cyclists, this is a sight that can be experienced independently, but many people supplement their own explorations with a guided tour or a local homestay.

Cai Be Floating Market

An hour north of An Binh, **Cai Be floating market** (5am-noon daily) is the Mekong Delta's second most popular on-the-water trading post. Though much smaller than its counterpart in Can Tho, Cai Be's floating market boasts a beautiful location, set before the towering spire of the local cathedral. As soon as the sun rises, boats from around the area gather to buy and sell fruit, vegetables, and fish, stringing up a sample of their product at the front of each boat to alert passing customers. Due to its distance from Vinh Long, a visit to Cai Be requires that you book a tour, which is easily done through **Cuu Long Tourist** (1 1 Thang 5, tel. 0270/382-3616, www.cuulongtourist.com, 7am-8pm daily). Arrive early in the morning, as the sun drives away many vendors around midday.

Van Thanh Temple

One of the only temples of its kind in the Mekong Delta, **Van Thanh Temple** (Tran Phu, 5am-11am and 1pm-7pm Mon.-Sat.) honors the intellect and scholarly pursuits of Confucius as well as several of his disciples. Completed in 1866, Van Thanh's long, rectangular grounds trace a tree-lined path up to the main building, where you'll find an altar dedicated to Confucius and, just before it, a large bust of 14th-century mandarin Chu Van An, considered to be Vietnam's first educator. Both of these men are often referred to in Vietnam as "the eternal teacher." Closer to the entrance, you'll find a smaller building honoring local hero Phan Thanh Gian, a 19th-century scholar who opposed colonial rule so vehemently that, in 1867, he took up a hunger strike against the French, which lasted a little over two weeks before, realizing that defeat was inevitable, he took his own life by drinking poison.

Though it appears deceptively far from the city center on a map, Van Thanh is a short 1.5-kilometer jaunt and sits just beside the Long Ho River. Despite its listed opening hours, the main temple is often locked, in which case you may have to find a grounds-keeper to let you in.

BOAT TOURS

Both private and group tours to Cai Be floating market and around the waterways of An Binh Island can be arranged, either through companies like **Cuu Long Tourist** (1 1 Thang 5, tel. 0270/382-3616, www.cuulongtourist. com, 7am-8pm daily) and **Mekong Travel** (8 1 Thang 5, tel. 0270/383-6252, vinhlong-mekongtravel@yahoo.com, www.mekong-travel.com.vn, 7am-5pm daily) or with most homestays on the island. Prices are reasonable (VND200,000-400,000 pp). These boat trips usually include a handful of brief stopovers at local handicraft workshops, fruit orchards, or flower gardens, as well as the odd *cai luong* performance, a traditional style of Vietnamese music that has its origins in the Mekong Delta.

There are also several day trips that run from Ho Chi Minh City to Vinh Long, which you can book through tour providers in the city. Since it's a bit of a drive to Cai Be, where the tours begin, you usually pass by the floating market a little later than is desirable. If you're pressed for time, this is a decent option and often preferred over day trips to My Tho or Ben Tre, but for the full experience, you're better off spending a night in Vinh Long and booking your trip locally.

FOOD

Despite its growing number of foreign visitors, much of Vinh Long's food scene remains local. While there are a handful of proper restaurants around town, the majority of residents opt for street food or eat at *binh dan*-style joints—the simple shops with plastic stools and metal tables you see around town. You can find plenty of snacks and street carts along 1 Thang 5 near the market as well as around **Vinh Long City Park** (Hung Dao Vuong and Nguyen Thi Minh Khai).

The sprawling, haphazard Vinh Long Market begins early, but its **food stalls** (7am-5pm daily, VND10,000-50,000) open later, around 7am. Find an assortment of local treats, snacks, and full-fledged meals under a covered area beside the main market.

Popular with the locals, **Tai Co** (corner of Hung Dao Vuong and 2 Thang 9, tel. 0270/382-4845, 8am-10pm daily, VND220,000-350,000) is a hot-pot restaurant located at the southern end of District 1 just before a small canal. Though it doesn't have a menu, its offerings are not hard to remember: the place serves only hot pot, with your choice of beef (*bo*), fish (*ca*), pork (*heo*), or vegetable (*rau*). There is also a *banh bao* (steamed pork dumpling) cart just outside the restaurant's entrance on 2 Thang 9 street that does decent business in the mornings.

A delicious option, **Phuong Thuy**

Restaurant (Phan Boi Chau, tel. 0270/382-4786, restaurant@cuulongtourist.com, 6am-10pm daily, VND30,000-150,000) features an English menu and plenty of delectable Vietnamese dishes, from fish to pork, chicken, beef, seafood, and vegetables. You also have your choice of eating street-side like a local or going for the upscale tablecloth seating by the water.

ACCOMMODATIONS

Though there are a handful of decent budget hotels in Vinh Long, one of the best and most popular ways to experience this river town and its scenery is by spending the night with a local family. Ever since tourists caught wind of the friendly residents and verdant greenery on An Binh, homestays have become all the rage, with many foreign visitors opting for a bed on the island rather than in town. If you base yourself on the mainland, your best bet is to stay near the market, as this area provides easy access to the city's restaurants and travel services, not to mention the ferry to An Binh Island.

VND210,000-525,000
Boasting the nicest accommodations among a trio of guesthouses around this intersection,

Storefronts line the banks of the Co Chien River in Vinh Long.

Homestays

When visiting Vinh Long, many travelers are keen to experience local life firsthand: floating around on a wooden fishing boat, sampling local cuisine, or wandering through the small village communities that make up An Binh Island. One of the best ways to get an authentic Delta experience is by organizing a homestay with a local family.

In Vinh Long, companies like **Cuu Long Tourist** (www.cuulongtourist.com) and **Mekong Travel** (www.mekongtravel.com.vn) orchestrate overnights on An Binh. For as little as VND210,000, local homestays cover your bed for the night as well as dinner, breakfast, and, in some cases, a bicycle rental for exploring the island.

Thanks to the growing popularity of homestays, many homestay spots are more like guesthouses than one-on-one overnights with a local family—so you may have to share your hosts with a few other foreign guests. These homestays are easily found on your own, either by checking online ahead of time or simply turning up on the island. Smaller tour operators and independent guides are your best bet for tracking down authentic homestays, as the government-run tourism companies do not have this information.

At a guesthouse-style homestay, even with a handful of other tourists around, getting off the mainland and into the peaceful environment of An Binh is a satisfying experience. Plenty of the larger homestays offer tours to Cai Be floating market and through the winding canals of An Binh.

Book a homestay in advance rather than just showing up; while there is a good chance that you'd be able to find a bed, planning ahead will guarantee that it is ready for you when you arrive.

Lac Long Hotel (2G Hung Vuong, tel. 0270/382-2099, VND200,000-300,000) offers your choice of fan or air-conditioned rooms with Wi-Fi, hot water, and a dizzying assortment of patterns in its decor. The hotel staff is friendly and speak some English. If you prefer a window, request one, as not all rooms have natural light.

The rooms at **Tin Khoa Hotel** (18 Hung Vuong, tel. 0270/383-2581, VND250,000-300,000) take the prize for the largest in town. Well-kept and tidy, each high-ceilinged room includes air-conditioning, a hot shower, and included Wi-Fi along with generous beds. Several rooms also come with a balcony with a view of the street below. The staff doesn't really speak English, but the beds are decent and the price is right. There is a small café downstairs with not much more than a few fold-out chairs.

Easily the best value in Vinh Long, **Van Tram Guesthouse** (4 1 Thang 5, tel. 0270/382-3820, VND200,000-350,000) boasts spacious rooms with TV, Wi-Fi, and one of the finest showers in the Mekong Delta. The balconies overlooking the street give guests a nice overhead view of the bustling market below, and there are bicycles for rent in the lobby. This guesthouse is in a central part of town, and it has been known to experience spontaneous karaoke outbursts in the early evenings, as well as some noise from the market in the wee hours of the morning.

One of the more modern in town, **Hotel Hong Duc** (3F-3G Hung Dao Vuong, tel. 0270/322-0121, VND300,000-500,000) is almost directly across from the post office and features hot water, clean beds, large windows, and, in some cases, balconies. Rooms are smartly decorated with new furnishings and include an in-room fridge as well as a TV and Wi-Fi. The hotel staff is friendly and speaks some English, and there is a café on the ground floor.

VND525,000-1,050,000

The state-run **Cuu Long Hotel** (1 1 Thang 5, tel. 0270/382-3656, www.cuulongtourist.com, VND420,000-870,000) is the busiest in town, with regular tour groups passing through its doors. Rooms are well appointed as far as Vinh Long goes, and several rooms offer nice views of the river as well as balconies. With plush beds and an unbeatable location, the Cuu Long is often full, so book ahead if you plan to stay here.

INFORMATION AND SERVICES

Sharing its space with the lobby of the Cuu Long Hotel, **Cuu Long Tourist** (1 1 Thang 5, tel. 0270/382-3616, www.cuulongtourist. com, 7am-8pm daily) arranges boat tours to Cai Be floating market and around An Binh Island as well as short cycling trips and homestays. There are also maps (VND20,000) of Vinh Long city and the entire province and the tour desk can help with onward travel to other Mekong Delta towns.

A much smaller, homegrown outfit, **Mekong Travel** (8 1 Thang 5, tel. 0270/383-6252, vinhlongmekongtravel@yahoo.com, www.mekongtravel.com.vn, 7am-5pm daily) organizes tours to An Binh Island and Cai Be floating market as well as homestays and assists in arranging bus tickets to other Delta destinations.

There are a handful of banks just opposite the post office. **Vietcombank** (1D-1E Hoang Thai Hieu, tel. 0270/383-7982, www. vietcombank.com.vn, 7am-11am and 1pm-5pm Mon.-Fri.) handles monetary needs. On the corner of Hung Dao Vuong and Hoang Thai Hieu, the **Vinh Long Post Office** (14 Hoang Thai Hieu, tel. 0270/382-3320, 7am-6pm daily) handles mail as well as Internet services.

The **Vinh Long General Hospital (Benh Vien Da Khoa Vinh Long)** (301 Tran Phu, tel. 0270/382-3520, bvdktinh.vinhlong.gov. vn) assists with minor illnesses and injuries, though services are basic. You'll have to head to Saigon for serious medical care.

TRANSPORTATION

Buses entering town stop at the **Vinh Long bus station** (Dinh Tien Hoang, tel. 0270/382-3458, 24 hours daily), roughly three kilometers from the city center. There are daily arrivals from Saigon (3 hours, VND105,000) via tourist bus company Phuong Trang. Local buses run the same routes but are cheaper: VND60,000-80,000 from Saigon. They also run from Can Tho (VND50,000). If you're arriving from a closer destination, like Sa Dec (30 minutes, VND15,000-30,000), public buses let off at the **city bus station** (3 Thang 2 and Hung Dao Vuong, 5am-5pm daily) right in the center of town.

Dozens of *xe om* drivers camp out near the An Binh ferry, as well as outside the local bus stations. There are also a couple of **Mailinh taxis** (tel. 0270/387-8878) roaming around that can take you where you need to go.

The best way to explore An Binh Island is via bicycle. Many hotels will rent out city bikes at reasonable rates and most homestays can provide two-wheeled transport as well—some even include it in the price. **Cuu Long Tourist** (1 1 Thang 5, tel. 0270/382-3616, www.cuulongtourist.com, 7am-8pm daily) and **Mekong Travel** (8 1 Thang 5, tel. 0270/383-6252, vinhlongmekongtravel@ yahoo.com, www.mekongtravel.com.vn, 7am-5pm daily) can also arrange rentals for those staying in the city.

Tra Vinh

Isolated by a pair of rivers that cut deep into the surrounding peninsula, Tra Vinh is a quiet stunning place off the beaten path. Hand-painted signs and angular 1970s-style facades give the town a retro feel, while the countless pagodas scattered between the storefronts offer a different side of the Mekong Delta.

The main reason for visiting Tra Vinh is its array of gold-drenched Theravada Buddhist pagodas. You'll be able to tell these apart from their Vietnamese counterparts, as their sharply peaked roofs and lavish or-namentation are often more in line with the type of pagoda you might find in Thailand or Cambodia. With the majority of these sights easily covered in a day, many people spend only a night or two in Tra Vinh, pagoda-hop-ping and enjoying the shaded streets of this quiet town.

SIGHTS

Barring a few exceptions, many of Tra Vinh's sights are not within the downtown area, but rather a few kilometers outside town. These sights are just too far to be walkable but are well within cycling distance. It is also possible to catch a cab or hire a *xe om*, but with the sights so close, you're better off putting in a little leg work and getting there on your own. Once you've had your fill of pagodas, the next best thing to do in Tra Vinh is pack a map, set off on your bicycle, and get lost on the small country roads surrounding town, as the aging colonial buildings, spiky, towering palm trees, and flooded fields make for some beautiful scenery.

Since Tra Vinh is a conservative town and Khmer pagodas are strict on respectful dress, wear long pants and cover your shoul-ders when visiting these religious sites, as you may not be permitted entry otherwise. While most pagodas have resident monks who live and study on-site, the buildings can appear empty from the outside. It is acceptable for you to wander in for a visit, but you may want to find someone first to let them know you're there. More often than not, you'll be free to wander the grounds on your own at this point.

Ong Pagoda

Proof of Tra Vinh's remaining ethnic Chinese community, one of the few in the Mekong Delta, **Ong Pagoda** (44 Dien Bien Phu, 7am-5pm daily) has occupied a corner of down-town Tra Vinh since 1556. Built by Chinese immigrants, this small building houses a statue of the red-faced, beard-twirling Quan Cong, a famous Chinese general and prom-inent figure in many pagodas throughout Vietnam. As is true of most Chinese pago-das, this one sports two guardians flanking the front door, a central celestial well where incense is burned, and a large main altar at the far end of the building. Around back, a small fish pond and a tribute to the Buddha are on display outdoors.

Ong Met Pagoda

Not to be confused with the Ong Pagoda, the **Ong Met Pagoda** (220 Le Loi, 7am-5pm daily) is farther down the street and is home to dozens of orange-clad resident monks. This Theravada Buddhist pagoda is the most centrally located of the bunch, sitting just a block away from the local post office. Enter through the front gates and you'll find three buildings inside; the one on the left houses dozens of Buddha statues and serves as the main prayer hall. At a few hundred years old, the main building is covered in faded murals and intricately carved ceilings. While the pa-goda shows its age in the crumbling rafters and chipped paint of its interior, this is part of its charm. The friendly monks are always around and happy to welcome visitors. If you fancy a walk, keep going past Ong Met and you'll come across the crisp, clean **Tra Vinh Church** (Le Loi). Its gates are usually closed,

Vicinity of Tra Vinh

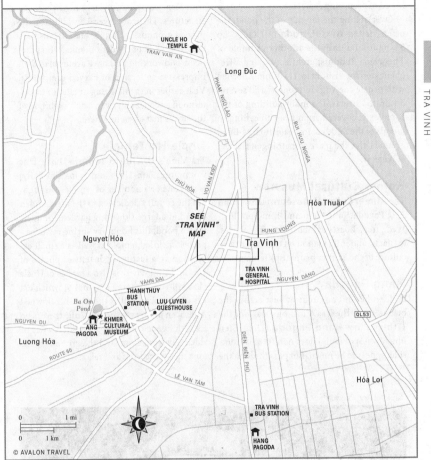

but the church itself, an all-white colonial-era structure nestled among the palms, is beautiful from outside.

Ba Om Pond and Ang Pagoda

A popular setting reserved for religious festivities and afternoon picnics, **Ba Om Pond** (off Quoc Lo 53) is surrounded by massive trees, each hundreds of years old. Also known as Square Pond, the legend goes that, many years ago, men and women could not agree on who should be responsible for proposing marriage.

Neither group wanted to ask for the other's hand, as this meant the person was obligated to foot the wedding bill. It was decided that the men and women of the village would have a pond-digging contest, in which each group had a single night, from sundown to sunrise, to dig the largest pond they could. A woman named Lady Om led the other females in entertaining the men after sundown and, once they were good and drunk, hung a lamp on a tree, which the men mistook for morning light. After their competition had gone home to sleep, Lady Om and her team dug the pond you see here and women were henceforth relieved of proposing marriage.

Overlooking the far side of the pond, the often-visited **Ang Pagoda** (off Quoc Lo 53, 8am-4pm daily) is another example of Theravada Buddhist architecture and a frequent stop for visitors to Tra Vinh. Adorned with ornate carvings of nymphs and several decorated stupas, the main building of the complex is covered from floor to ceiling in murals of the Buddha. Its beautiful tree-lined grounds give the place something of the feel of Angkor.

Khmer Cultural Museum

The **Khmer Cultural Museum** (across from Ang Pagoda, 7am-11am and 1pm-5pm Fri.-Wed., free), boasts exhibits featuring photos, artifacts, and information on the history and culture of the Khmer people in Vietnam.

Hang Pagoda

Hidden behind an archway just across the bridge from the Tra Vinh bus station, the 17th-century **Hang Pagoda** (Dien Bien Phu, 7am-5pm daily) does not, from the outside, appear to be much. But pass through the

tunnel-like entrance into the complex and you'll find a peaceful two-hectare garden with plenty of trees and large high-ceilinged structures. There are several buildings on the pagoda grounds, including one that displays the handiwork of resident monks, who practice woodworking and have accumulated an impressive collection of carved sculptures. Visit earlier in the morning or later in the afternoon and you may even catch a glimpse of the storks that often nest here.

Uncle Ho Temple

Tra Vinh's **Uncle Ho Temple** (Long Duc Commune, 7am-11am and 1pm-5pm daily) is just one of a number of temples throughout the country dedicated to the great leader. Set amid a large flowering garden complete with a pond, this honorary shrine includes a proper enclosed temple as well as a small exhibition area featuring dozens of photos of Ho Chi Minh. There is also a replica of Uncle Ho's stilted house, the original of which exists up north, as well as the requisite downed American military vehicles. While there is no English signage, the temple is a short cycle or ride away from town, and the grounds make for a nice place to sit and relax.

stupas at Ang Pagoda

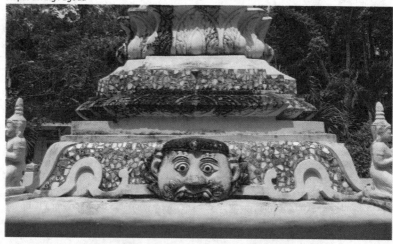

Tra Vinh

FESTIVALS AND EVENTS

The province's most famous and anticipated festival, **Ok Om Bok,** is a Khmer holiday in which locals give thanks to the moon for providing them with plentiful crops and fish. On the 15th day of the lunar calendar's 10th month (sometime in Nov.), festivities take place around the province and include cultural events, most notably a much-anticipated dragon boat race. Vessels as long as 24 meters speed along the river, competing for the top prize while spectators cheer them on. That evening, locals present offerings to the moon and traditional Khmer games and dances are held. In recent years, this has become a huge tourism event for the province, drawing many domestic visitors to the area.

FOOD

Tra Vinh is a city of street food. Though there are a few proper eateries, this tiny town does a much bigger turn in roadside fare. Starting around 6pm, head down to **Dien Bien Phu** street or around **Tra Vinh Market** and you'll see dozens of vendors selling everything from fresh fruit to boiled corn to tasty banh mi sandwiches. During the day, an abundance of cafés and bakery carts pop up throughout the city. Note, that beyond the odd baguette or pastry, there is no Western food to speak of. You might want to eat early, as many places begin to wind down by 8pm-9pm, some even earlier.

Though it's found on most street corners in Tra Vinh, the **bun nuoc leo** (in front of Long Khanh Pagoda, Bach Dang, from 2pm daily, VND10,000-15,000) in front of Long Khanh Pagoda is particularly nice. A traditional Khmer dish, this soup combines a murky-colored broth with local vegetables and rice noodles, plus your choice of roasted pork, fried shrimp cake, or congealed duck blood on the side. Extra helpings of meat or duck blood are allowed, but you'd better get there early, as the pot's usually empty by 5:30pm.

Right beside Duy Tung Hotel, **Tuy Huong** (8 Dien Bien Phu, tel. 0294/385-8312, 5am-6pm daily, VND10,000-50,000) is an old-school noodle shop with great eats but no English menu. Dishes and prices are listed on the wall: You can opt for wonton and egg noodle soup (*hoan thanh mi*), southern-style rice noodle soup (*hu tieu*), noodles and duck (*mi vit tiem*), or a handful of rice dishes, all of which are generous and satisfying.

A perfect spot to practice your pick-and-point ordering, the sidewalk around **Quan Bay Loan** (corner of Nguyen Thai Hoc and Tran Quoc Tuan, 10am-8pm daily, VND20,000-30,000) fills up with hungry locals around lunch time. Choose from an array of meats and vegetables to go with your plate of steamed rice and enjoy the people-watching on this shady street corner.

Hidden behind the Cuu Long Hotel, **La Trau Xanh** (999 Nguyen Thi Minh Khai, tel. 0294/386-2615, 6am-10pm daily, VND70,000-450,000) is the fanciest place in town. Featuring tablecloths, an English menu, and an array of meat, seafood, veggie, and hot pot dishes, this thatched-roof, open-air building is a bit of a hot spot for visiting tour groups and provides a nice escape from the noise of the street. Both family-style and single portions are available.

ACCOMMODATIONS

When it comes to lodgings in a town as sleepy as Tra Vinh, it's no surprise that you'll be hard-pressed to find much beyond your standard budget accommodations. Even the larger hotels in town are nothing to rave about, but there are definitely some nice corner buildings with balconies from which you can relax and enjoy the comings and goings of the street below. Hotels offer clean rooms at reasonable rates, though mattresses, as a rule, are firm. While some are farther from the city center, there's no need to worry, as Tra Vinh is small and, though the distance may seem larger on a map, most places are no more than a 10- or 15-minute walk from downtown.

VND210,000-525,000

Some of the best digs downtown, **Gia Hoa 2 Hotel** (50 Le Loi, tel. 0294/385-8008, VND320,000-480,000) sits on the corner of a shady side street not far from the park. Great balcony views and spacious rooms, friendly staff, and included Wi-Fi make this hotel a cut above many other Tra Vinh accommodations. Its original, the **Gia Hoa 1 Hotel** (75 Nguyen Thi Minh Khai, tel. 0294/386-4477, VND320,000-480,000), is equally well kept, but its location isn't as nice as Gia Hoa 2.

Just opposite the larger Cuu Long Hotel, **Hoan My Hotel** (105A Nguyen Thi Minh Khai, tel. 0294/386-2211, VND250,000-420,000) is a more affordable version, if a little smaller, of its competition across the street. Rooms are clean and include Wi-Fi, TV, and air-conditioning.

Adjacent to both the central market and the Duy Tung, **Tan Hang Hotel** (14 Dien Bien Phu, tel. 0294/626-6999, VND300,000-400,000) offers clean, reasonable rooms with Wi-Fi, air-conditioning, and TV. A handful of rooms also have balconies that look out over the town's main roundabout.

Directly on the town's main roundabout, **Duy Tung Hotel** (6 Dien Bien Phu, tel.

Tra Vinh's Cambodian Connection

Few provinces in the Mekong Delta boast such a deep connection to Cambodia as Tra Vinh, where nearly one-third of the population is made up of ethnic Khmer people. Before the Vietnamese took over this region in the late 17th and early 18th centuries, Tra Vinh and the surrounding provinces were known as Kampuchea Krom, or Lower Cambodia.

When ethnic Vietnamese began to move into the area, many of the Khmer towns were transformed. Ethnic Khmer have long maintained that the Vietnamese took their land without consent, making the Mekong Delta a tract of stolen property.

When the French later entered Indochina and began colonizing the area, they sealed the fate of Kampuchea Krom by incorporating it into Cochinchina, a territory that was later ceded to Vietnam when the country gained its independence. The Khmer still have their own names for most provinces and towns in the Delta, all the way from the Cambodian border across to Saigon, formerly Prey Nokor.

Once these southern provinces were incorporated into Vietnam, ethnic Khmer were forced to assimilate. The South Vietnam government assigned people Vietnamese names, giving the same last names to most ethnic Khmer in order to make the outsiders easier to identify. Many of this minority group, particularly monks, found themselves at odds with those in power as their outspoken disapproval of government policies and different religious beliefs often landed them in prison. Things worsened in the late 1970s when Vietnam took up arms against the Khmer Rouge along the southern border. Since then, countless Khmer Krom have fled the region, emigrating to other countries.

Tensions between the local Khmer population and the Vietnamese government remain to this day. The exact number of Khmer Krom in the Delta is unclear. Statistics from the Vietnamese government claim that 1.2 million ethnic Khmer live in the area, while rights groups such as Khmer Krom Federation and the Khmer Kampuchea Krom Community put the figure as high as 7 million.

Little to no tension between local Vietnamese and Khmer residents is visible on the surface. Instead, the ethnic Khmer of Tra Vinh continue to practice their own religion in addition to studying Khmer language, and residents of the town peacefully coexist.

0294/385-8959, VND250,000-400,000), also called Van Thanh Hotel, offers great value and clean rooms as well as TV and Wi-Fi. Opt for air-conditioning if possible, as the fans are a little weak. There is a small travel outfit attached to the hotel that can help plan your travels around Tra Vinh or rent a motorbike. Bicycles can be rented here for a small fee.

Boasting one of the best locations in the city, **Thanh Tra Hotel** (1 Pham Thai Buong, tel. 0294/625-0657, VND360,000-780,000, breakfast included) sits a stone's throw from Tra Vinh Market, the local park, and the riverfront. Rooms are aging but the beds and baths remain clean and well kept. There is a restaurant attached to the hotel. If possible, opt for a room with a view, as these are nicer and more spacious than their windowless counterparts.

VND525,000-1,050,000

Though it's an aging facility, the **Cuu Long Hotel** (999 Nguyen Thi Minh Khai, tel. 0294/386-2615, cuulonghoteltravinhcity@ yahoo.com.vn, VND400,000-1,100,000) serves as one of Tra Vinh's nicest accommodations, with more spacious and well-decorated rooms, not to mention comfier mattresses, than some of its budget competition. The hotel has Wi-Fi, TV, and air-conditioning, and a buffet breakfast is included in the rates.

INFORMATION AND SERVICES

While it's true that Tra Vinh is not exactly well trodden on the tourist trail, **Tra Vinh Tourist** (266-268 Le Loi, tel. 0294/374-4755, www.dulichtravinh.com.vn, 7:30am-11am and 1:30pm-5pm daily) manages to be a notably helpful place for visitors. In addition to organizing tours around the province, this outfit rents bicycles (VND80,000 per day or VND10,000 per hour) and provides one of the more useful tourist maps (VND20,000) in the Delta. Though the language barrier may be difficult, the staff is more than willing to dispense free travel information if prompted. Ask for a free copy of the tourist information booklet as well to get a full rundown of what to see and do in Tra Vinh.

The local **Vietin Bank** (15A Dien Bien Phu, tel. 0294/386-3827, www.vietinbank.vn, 7am-11am and 1pm-5pm Mon.-Fri., 7:30am-noon Sat.) exchanges currencies and has an ATM. The ultra-retro **Tra Vinh post office** (3 Phan Dinh Phung, tel. 0294/386-2233, 7am-11am and 1pm-5pm Mon.-Fri.) can take your postcards, letters, and packages.

For minor issues, the **Tra Vinh General Hospital (Benh Vien Da Khoa Tra Vinh)** (27 Dien Bien Phu, tel. 0294/386-2553, www.benhvientravinh.com.vn) assists travelers, although there are no English speakers on staff.

TRANSPORTATION

The **Tra Vinh bus station** (559 Quoc Lo 54, tel. 0294/384-0324) is located five kilometers (a 10-minute drive) from the city center, just before Hang Pagoda. Buses arrive daily from Can Tho (2.5 hours, VND65,000), Saigon (2.5-3 hours, VND130,000) and other Delta cities. These buses also drop passengers off on Nguyen Thi Minh Khai street, which is close to the center of town and the most convenient stop, as well as at the **Thanh Thuy bus station** (93 Tran Quoc Tuan, tel. 0294/385-8687, 7am-5pm daily, VND130,000), where coach buses from Saigon arrive on a regular basis. Every vehicle's final destination depends on the driver and the bus, but all three bus stops are close to town.

As you will quickly discover, getting around Tra Vinh town is easy on account of its size, but a bicycle may be necessary to access some sights, as they tend to be farther afield. **Tra Vinh Tourist** (266-268 Le Loi, tel. 0294/374-4755, www.dulichtravinh.com.vn, 7:30am-11am and 1:30pm-5pm daily) rents out bicycles (VND80,000 per day or VND10,000 per hour), as do most hotels.

This town is also one of the worst offenders when it comes to inconsistent addresses. All along Nguyen Thi Minh Khai and several other large streets, street addresses increase and decrease, change from even to odd, and sometimes even change to letters from numerals—all in the space of a single block. If you don't see your destination immediately, be patient and keep looking.

Xe om are readily available at the roundabout in front of Tra Vinh Market and they will no doubt be present whenever your bus arrives in Tra Vinh. You can also call **Mailinh Taxi** (tel. 0294/357-5757) or **Thanh Thuy Taxi** (tel. 0294/386-8686) for a ride.

The travel outfit located at **Duy Tung Hotel** (6 Dien Bien Phu, tel. 0294/385-8959) is one of the only places renting motorbikes to foreigners. Cars and larger vehicles can be hired from some of the larger hotels or through **Tra Vinh Tourist** (266-268 Le Loi, tel. 0294/374-4755, www.dulichtravinh.com.vn, 7:30am-11am and 1:30pm-5pm daily).

Tram Chim National Park and Vicinity

A serene landscape of flooded plains and cajuput trees, Tram Chim National Park is home to a quarter of all bird species found in Vietnam. Tram Chim's most famous resident, the sarus crane, is its main attraction and the reason most travelers visit the park. At 1.8 meters tall, sarus cranes are the world's tallest flying bird and an increasingly endangered species in Southeast Asia, with only a few thousand estimated to remain in the region. For birding and nature enthusiasts, these towering, majestic creatures are a must-see in Vietnam.

★ TRAM CHIM NATIONAL PARK

The stunning landscapes of **Tram Chim National Park (Vuon Quoc Gia Tram Chim)** (Hamlet 4, Tram Chim, tel. 0277/382-7436, www.vqgtc.dongthap.gov.vn, 7am-5pm daily, VND40,000) are awash with tall grass, flat, waterlogged land, and over 230 different aquatic birds swooping and wheeling across the park's 6,900 hectares. Visitors trace the watery avenues and flooded forests of this picturesque Delta scene by boat, spotting everything from an abundance of slender-necked storks to the vibrant yellow Asian golden weaver to towering sarus cranes, whose bright red feathers and jaw-dropping wingspan make them the stars of the park.

At the visitors center just inside the park's main gate, choose from three boat routes around the perimeter of the park. The shortest route (45 minutes, VND500,000 per boat) is a quick jaunt that affords travelers a brief glimpse of the park. Opt for one of the two longer routes to make your trip worthwhile, as these will take you deeper into bird-watching territory. A 25-kilometer loop (2 hours, VND800,000 per boat) through the park's main viewing area to its watchtower is the most popular option. There is also an 29-kilometer trip (2.5 hours, VND900,000 per boat), adding more sightseeing time. Each vessel seats 12, so the more passengers you have, the cheaper the cost per person.

Accompanying each group are a driver and a guide who carries binoculars or birding field guides. Some of the drivers and guides speak

Tram Chim National Park

English. The boats come within a few meters of the various species of birds. Views from the park watchtower are stunning, with sweeping panoramas of the park's greenery and birds in flight.

Traveling by car or by bus along the main road leading to the park, you'll see the offices of the park administration first and then a gate for the visitor center. Tram Chim is best visited in the early mornings and late afternoons, when the most birds are active. While the steady trickle of visitors Tram Chim receives have helped to put it on the map, you'll mostly have the place to yourself. Though the trip takes time and effort, it is worth it. When done by public bus, the trip can actually be affordable.

Food and Accommodations

Visitors to Tram Chim have the option of staying at one of the local guesthouses (VND 150,000-300,000) near the park, where services are limited, or back in Cao Lanh. Basic lodging can be found along the DT844 and DT843 roads along the perimeter of the park. While this allows you to rise early for the birds, it also limits dining options to the few simple noodle-soup eateries located on the main road near the park (a 5-minute walk). There is an on-site restaurant, but it only caters to groups of six or more and requires advance orders.

For more lodging and food options, not to mention more English menus, base yourself in Cao Lanh town, roughly 48 kilometers south of the park.

Transportation

Getting to Tram Chim requires some organization and prior planning. From Cao Lanh, **Dong Thap Tourist** (2 Doc Binh Kieu, Cao Lanh, tel. 0277/387-3026, www.dongthap-tourist.com, 7am-11:30am and 1:30pm-5pm daily) organizes private trips to the park, often combined with a stop at the Xeo Quyt Relic Area in a two-day, one-night. For a full-day tour to Tram Chim including an English-speaking guide, a private car, and lunch, Dong

Thap Tourist charges VND2,650,000 per person for a group of two. Similar itineraries are available from Saigon (VND2,500,000-3,000,000); however, these package tours are expensive and not worth the cost for small groups. Groups of three or more can hire a car to the park, roughly 48 kilometers north (a 45-minute drive); car rental rates are often negotiable, depending upon where you book. Dong Thap Tourist has private cars for rent; a four-seater costs VND1,600,000 for a full-day rental.

An alternative, provided you're up for a day of adventure, is to board a public bus to Tram Chim, which takes about 1.5 hours. From the **Cao Lanh bus station** (71/1 Ly Thuong Kiet, tel. 0277/385-1116, 5am-5pm daily), hop on one of the green buses bound for **Hong Ngu** (VND14,000). Let the fare collector know that you'd like to go to Tram Chim and the bus will stop at **Thanh Binh bus station** (Hwy. 30), where you'll switch to an orange bus bound for **Tan Hong** (VND13,000). Show the fare collector the park's name (Vuon Quoc Gia Tram Chim), and the bus will drop you right outside the visitor center.

Buses leave every 30 minutes from Cao Lanh, as early as 6am, and run through to the until about 5pm. Plan to leave Cao Lanh as early as possible to make the most of your day. The second leg of the trip—from Thanh Binh to Tram Chim—does not always run on schedule. These vehicles leave when full, but because there aren't many buses that drive this route, you may have no trouble finding one.

If you get stranded at either the Thanh Binh bus station or the park, it is possible to enlist the services of a *xe om* to ferry you to the next leg of your trip. It's about a 20-minute ride between the Thanh Binh bus station and Tram Chim's visitor center. Hiring a *xe om* between the main road (about 19 kilometers from the park entrance) and Tram Chim runs about VND50,000-60,000.

CAO LANH

Yet another Delta town built around the river, Cao Lanh is larger and more modern than many of its regional counterparts. As a result, it loses some of its charm. The town is more of a home base than an attraction, as most of its few visitors head out to Tram Chim National Park or into the forests of Xeo Quyt, but Cao Lanh does a fine job of accommodating its guests with decent hotels and restaurants, as well as a café or two. As the capital of Dong Thap province, this is also where the provincial tourism company is based; they assist in organizing services like guided tours or rental vehicles.

Dong Thap Museum

Housed in a former colonial residence, the **Dong Thap Museum** (226 Nguyen Thai Hoc, tel. 0277/385-1342, www.baotangdongthap.vn, 7am-11:30am and 1:30pm-5pm daily, free) is a well-organized provincial exhibition hall with the usual displays on ancient history, local fishing and farming, and, of course, revolutionary activities against both French and American forces. Though there is no English signage, the museum's layout is fairly straightforward and manages to be interesting even without the placards. There is also a small display on ancient Oc Eo sculpture as well as a collection of Vietnamese instruments, which are particularly pertinent to this region, as *cai luong*, a popular form of traditional Vietnamese music, hails from the Mekong Delta.

Nguyen Sinh Sac Memorial Park

Tucked behind Hoa Long Pagoda, the sprawling **Nguyen Sinh Sac Memorial Park (Khu Di Tich Mo Cu Nguyen Sinh Sac)** (137 Pham Huu Lau, tel. 0277/385-1259, www.ditichnguyensinhsac.vn, 7am-11:30am and 1:30pm-5pm daily) pays homage to a man credited with intelligence, a revolutionary spirit, and, most notably, a very famous son: President Ho Chi Minh. The father of Vietnam's most famous hero was buried behind Hoa Long Pagoda, where his grave remained for decades before the local government renovated it and turned the site into this park.

Born in 1862 in central Nghe An Province, Nguyen Sinh Sac rose from humble beginnings, losing his parents at a young age. He was taken in by a local scholar, and later entered the civil service, earning a job as a magistrate near the central city of Quy Nhon. As a government worker under French colonial rule, Sac often clashed with his employers, standing up for the marginalized of his community and setting free jailed protesters. The French did not react favorably to Sac's dissent. He was fired in 1910 and jailed. Upon release, Sac moved south, cultivating friendships with some of Vietnam's other famous movers and shakers, including the likes of Phan Chu Trinh and Phan Boi Chau. Toward the end of his life, Sac settled in Dong Thap, where he worked as a teacher and pharmacist. When he died in 1929 in Cao Lanh, Vietnam's fight for independence was far from over, but his son, Ho Chi Minh, saw victory in 1945.

Visiting the park is easy on your own, though it is not actually visible from Pham Huu Lau street. To reach the gates, take a left just before Hoa Long Pagoda—you'll see a sign with the Vietnamese name of the park—and follow the road around to the entrance. Inside, shaded pathways and plenty of park benches line a central pond. Few foreigners linger here, so you're sure to receive some friendly hellos on your visit as well as a few candid photo requests.

Farther along, a collection of wooden houses, including a replica of Ho Chi Minh's Hanoian stilt house, are grouped at the side of the property; visitors are not permitted to enter but only peek inside. The actual gravesite is located away from the entrance, right behind the pagoda grounds and protected by nine large dragons, a symbol of the Mekong Delta, which form a white pavilion over the site. Nguyen Sinh Sac's gravesite is a place that requires long pants and covered shoulders. There is also a temple dedicated to Nguyen Sinh Sac and a small exhibition hall. While the park area is open through midday, this area closes for a brief period at lunch.

Do Cong Tuong Temple

Amidst the bustle of the town's market, **Do Cong Tuong Temple (Den Tho Ong Ba Do Cung Tuong)** (Le Loi, 6am-5pm daily) commemorates a local couple credited with the founding of Cao Lanh's market. After moving to the area in 1817, Mr. and Mrs. Do Cong Tuong planted a garden of tangerine trees that fast grew into a meeting spot for local vendors and, in time, a busy trade center. The couple became known throughout the community for their kindness and their contributions. Three years later, a cholera outbreak decimated the population, leaving the market empty and the fate of the town looking very grim. Grief-stricken, Mr. and Mrs. Do Cong Tuong set up an altar in the middle of the market for people to come and pray. After three days of prayer, Mrs. Do Cong Tuong fell sick with cholera and died; her husband died early the next morning. After the couple was buried, the cholera epidemic broke and villagers believed that the pair had died so that the rest of the village could be spared. To honor their sacrifice, a temple was built for the couple.

Nowadays, the recently renovated building is full of beautiful gilded woodwork and Cao Dai-esque columns bedecked with serpentine dragons surrounded by wispy blue-and-white clouds. Framing many of the altars are statues depicting a crane atop a tortoise. This is a powerful symbol in Vietnamese culture, signifying longevity and happiness, and can be found at many local pagodas and temples. This particular one is unique in that Cao Lanh residents often come here to *xin xam* (ask for their fortune). Holding a container filled with wooden sticks, locals kneel before the altar and pray, submitting their queries to the ancestors, before drawing out a single stick. Each stick has a number on it with a corresponding fortune, which can be obtained by asking the temple's caretaker.

Food

There are only a handful of proper restaurants located in the downtown area, and they don't include prices on their menus. This sometimes means that restaurant owners will take liberties when it comes time to tally your bill. To avoid this issue, ask the price before ordering.

Right on the main drag up the street from the Song Tra Hotel, **Ngoc Lan** (210 Nguyen Hue, tel. 0277/385-1498, 9am-9pm daily, VND35,000-300,000) does some excellent renditions of Vietnamese dishes, including a mean fish sauce fried chicken (*ga chien nuoc mam*). While the eatery has an English menu, it seems to be the worst offender in creative pricing, and the going rate for a meal changes with the mood of the staff. Ask the cost of your meal before ordering.

A short walk from downtown and not far from the massive Hoa Binh Hotel, **Tan Nghia** (331 Le Duan, tel. 0277/387-1989, 8am-9pm daily, VND30,000-80,000) is a nice little place on the water with standard local dishes, including pork, chicken, beef, and several types of seafood. Though the decor is nothing much, its location beside the river makes it pleasantly quiet and the staff are notably cheerful.

Accommodations

Because it's the capital of Dong Thap, accommodations in Cao Lanh are more plentiful than other towns in the province. More plentiful doesn't necessarily mean more upscale; there are several clean, comfortable options that manage to do the job for a night or two.

VND210,000-525,000

Trung Hoang Hotel (96-98 Le Quy Don, tel. 0277/387-8787, kstrunghoang@yahoo.com. vn, VND250,000-350,000) is a nice family-run guesthouse with clean beds and notably large rooms. Though the rooms are bare, all the standard amenities are present, including TV, fridge, Wi-Fi, and air-conditioning. Most rooms accommodate two people comfortably, and some larger lodgings fit up to five or six.

Phuong Ngan Hotel (174 Hung Vuong, tel. 0277/385-2483, VND200,000-300,000) sits farther down Hung Vuong street and offers great value, with newer furnishings and comfortable rooms. Not all accommodations come with a window, but you will find both a fan and air-conditioning in your room, as well as TV, Wi-Fi, and a minibar. The staff doesn't speak English, but the rooms are worth their budget price.

VND525,000-1,050,000

One of the nicer government-owned offerings, **Dong Thap Hotel (Nha Khach Dong Thap)** (48 Ly Thuong Kiet, tel. 0277/387-2670, nhakhachtinhdt@yahoo.com.vn, VND800,000-1,200,000) has all the trimmings of a proper hotel, with bright well-kept rooms and a restaurant downstairs. Most rooms include bathtubs and balconies as well as Wi-Fi, TV, air-conditioning, and a minibar.

The best-known of Cao Lanh accommodations, **Song Tra Hotel** (178 Nguyen Hue, tel. 0277/385-2624, dtsongtrahotel@yahoo.com, VND480,000-1,500,000, breakfast included) appears to be more of a two- than a three-star joint. Its rooms are clean and comfortable, if a bit overpriced, and feature air-conditioning, Wi-Fi, TV, and a minibar. The hotel is also one of the few places in town with an English-speaking receptionist. The café out front gets lively at night and is a nice spot for a *ca phe sua da* (Vietnamese iced coffee with milk) and people-watching.

Information and Services

The offices of **Dong Thap Tourist** (2 Doc Binh Kieu, tel. 027/7387-3026, www.dongthaptourist.com, 7am-11:30am and 1:30pm-5pm daily) can supply you with a local map (VND20,000) of Cao Lanh and the entire province. Though they tend to deal more in private tours than group ones, this government-run outfit organizes trips and boats to destinations across Dong Thap, including Xeo Quyt and Tram Chim National Park, and can offer help to individual travelers as well.

The **Vietin Bank** (87 Nguyen Hue, tel. 0277/385-1224, www.vietinbank.vn, 7:30am-11:30am and 1:30pm-5:30pm Mon.-Fri., 7:30am-11:30am Sat.) exchanges currency and has an ATM. For postage and Internet needs, the **Dong Thap post office** (85 Nguyen

Hue, tel. 0277/385-1124, 6:30am-6pm Mon.-Fri., 7am-11:30am and 1pm-5pm Sat.-Sun.) is located right on the main drag.

For minor illnesses and injuries, the **Dong Thap People's Hospital (Benh Vien Nhan Dan Dong Thap)** (165 Ton Duc Thang, tel. 0277/385-1509) can be of help, though any serious incidents will require a trip to Saigon.

Transportation

Buses from Saigon (3 hours, VND110,000-135,000) and Can Tho (2-2.5 hours, VND90,000) to Cao Lanh stop at the conveniently located **Cao Lanh bus station** (71/1 Ly Thuong Kiet, tel. 0277/385-1116). **Phuong Trang** (17-19 Vo Thi Sau, tel. 0277/363-6636, www.futabus.vn, 5am-5pm daily) has offices across the street and runs to and from Saigon.

In Cao Lanh, *xe om* drivers are present in smaller numbers on some street corners and in full force at the bus station. You can also grab a **Mailinh** (tel. 0277/368-6868) taxi to get around.

Downtown Cao Lanh is fairly concentrated, so you should be able to get around on foot just fine. There are also **bicycle rentals** through several of the hotels. This is a town that really seems to enforce a "no motorbikes to foreigners" rule, so you will likely have a tough time finding your own set of motorized wheels.

XEO QUYT RELIC AREA

Hidden among 20 hectares of flooded forest, the **Xeo Quyt Relic Area** (Hamlet 4, My Hiep village, tel. 0277/391-0297, 8am-4:30pm daily, VND10,000) was once a secret base of local Dong Thap revolutionaries during the American War. From as early as 1960, members of the southern National Liberation Front, or NLF, and the local community began using the area as a base of operations for soldiers and higher-ups, planting hundreds of towering willowy cajuput trees to cover their location. Party offices and meeting halls were tucked away beneath the forest canopy, as was a medical tent and several underground barracks.

For most of the year, the circular path through the forest is underwater, necessitating a boat ride in a small sampan to view the sites. While the former offices are often nothing more than a canvas tent or a few small stilted buildings, Xeo Quyt is peacefully off the mass-tourist trail and is one of Dong Thap's nicer, more well-preserved natural areas. Beyond the historical zone, there is a small exhibition in a stilted house over the water, a restaurant, and some nice walking paths around the park's vast green fields.

Though most people visit Xeo Quyt on a day tour, it is also possible to reach the site yourself by public bus. From Cao Lanh bus station, take one of the bright orange buses heading for **An Thai Trung** (Nga 3 An Thai Trung, VND14,000). Make sure you tell the fare collector that you're headed to Xeo Quyt so that he or she can inform you when it's time to get off the bus; have the name of the place handy to show. Once you arrive at the Xeo Quyt intersection, you'll see a sign for the Sa Dec ferry (Ben Pha Sa Dec) on your right and a larger, albeit a bit hidden, sign for Xeo Quyt on your left. *Xe om* drivers hang out regularly at this intersection and will take you the remaining six kilometers to Xeo Quyt for roughly VND30,000-50,000. The return trip can be done until 4:30pm, when the park closes; make sure you arrange your *xe om* ride back beforehand, as drivers don't often hang around at Xeo Quyt. Many of these drivers—both in Cao Lanh and at the Xeo Quyt intersection—try to convince you to take a *xe om* all the way back into town for around VND100,000 or VND130,000. While this is doable, know that buses do run regularly along this road, even if some drivers insist that they do not; they're merely trying to drum up business.

Sa Dec

One of the prettiest towns in the Mekong Delta, Sa Dec is a cross-hatch of narrow bridges and winding canals lined with the faded, crumbling structures of a bygone era. Among the Vietnamese, this peaceful town is known for its plentiful flower gardens, which cultivate an array of blossoms and bonsai plants year-round. Beyond the border, Sa Dec's claim to fame is credited to French author Marguerite Duras, who was born in Saigon in 1914 and spent much of her childhood among the tree-lined avenues of this tiny town in what was then French Indochina. Though Duras left Vietnam for France at age 18, Sa Dec later became the backdrop for her semi-autobiographical novel *The Lover*, which garnered her a Prix Goncourt, France's highest literary honor, and has since been translated into over 40 languages. This makes Sa Dec an especially popular town for French visitors.

Being small as it is, Sa Dec doesn't see too much overnight tourist traffic, though several tour groups make the journey here from Cao Lanh, and a handful of Mekong River cruises pass through the town en route to Chau Doc. It is possible to book a one-day guided tour through the provincial tourism office in Cao Lanh, and there are also a few tours that run from Vinh Long. Travelers can hop on an inter-city bus from Vinh Long, which takes about an hour, and make a day trip of the town, or do a quick stopover en route to Cao Lanh.

Sa Dec Market (corner of Nguyen Sinh Sac and Lac Long Quan, sunrise-sunset daily) is located toward the southern edge of town near the river. There is an array of products available here, from household supplies to cookware, food, and clothes. The market is housed mostly under one long, narrow roof not far from the river and its stalls spill out onto the surrounding streets.

Sa Dec

Map labels:
- FLOWER GARDENS
- PHAM HUU LAM
- TRAN THI NHUONG
- TRAN HUNG DAO
- NGUYEN TAT THANH
- PHAM VAN VE
- HAI BA TRUNG
- CAO DAI TEMPLE
- NGUYEN TRAI
- HUNG VUONG
- NGUYEN DU
- DO CHIEU
- SA DEC CHURCH
- Tien River
- HUONG PAGODA
- HO XUAN HUONG
- HOANG DIEU
- TRAN HUNG DAO
- KIEN AN CUNG PAGODA
- HOUSE OF HUYNH THUY LE
- LY THUONG KIET
- TON DUC THANG
- TRAN PHU
- HUNG DAO
- HOLE THANH TON
- T CU TRINH
- FOOD STALLS
- THAO NGAN HOTEL
- SA DEC MARKET
- OUTDOOR MARKET
- SACOMBANK ATM
- TRAN VAN VOI
- NGUYEN SINH SAC
- CHANH KY
- ROUTE 80
- DINH HUU THUAT
- LE DUAN
- HUNG VUONG
- DINH TIEN HOANG
- SA DEC GENERAL HOSPITAL
- SA DEC BUS STATION
- © AVALON TRAVEL
- 0 300 yds / 0 300 m

SIGHTS

Kien An Cung Pagoda

A work of art both outside and in, the **Kien An Cung Pagoda** (corner of Tran Hung Dao and Phan Boi Chau, 7am-5pm daily, free) was completed in 1927 by Huynh Thuan, father of Huynh Thuy Le—the man with whom French author Marguerite Duras began an illicit affair at age 15—along with a group of other Chinese immigrants from Fujian province.

Also known as Chua Ong Quach, the pagoda pays homage to Ong Quach, a Buddhist from Fujian province who achieved enlightenment.

Outside, its roof boasts three layers of tiles and brick as well as some impressive mosaic ornamentation. Pass through the high hand-painted doors of the pagoda and you'll find black-and-white Chinese-style sketches on either side of the building and the open-roof incense-filled celestial well at the center. Beyond, the altar honors Ong Quach, and a small area off to the left is devoted to worship of both the ancestors and the Buddha. Every year, on the 22nd day of the second month of the lunar calendar (mid-Mar.-early Apr.), locals celebrate the birthday of Ong Quach, as well as the day he attained enlightenment, on the 22nd of the eighth month of the lunar calendar (late Sept.-early Oct).

Huong Pagoda

Adjacent to the much larger, more modern Buu Quang, **Huong Pagoda** (461 Hung Vuong, 6am-8pm daily, free), completed in 1838, is one of several Chinese-style Buddhist pagodas in Sa Dec. Weathered mosaics and crumbling enamel tiles show the building's age, while a pair of bright, vivid creatures appear to jump out of the wall below. Inside, the sturdy wooden columns that hold up the pagoda are lined with gilded woodwork and Chinese inscriptions. The altar is dedicated to Buddha, but there are also additional shrines to the ancestors as well as famed Chinese general Quan Cong. Visitors are welcome at the pagoda; enter through a smaller door off to the side rather than through the main entrance, as this is usually locked. One of the resident monks will accompany you around.

Flower Gardens

Sa Dec's famed **flower gardens** (Vuon Hong) are located across the bridge from the town center, about 1.5 kilometers away. Local gardeners use every inch of space they've got to pack in dozens upon dozens of plants, from flowers to cacti to bonsai trees, which are grown year-round, though these businesses often become bare just before Tet, when demand for ornamental plants is high. The most famous of these is the **Tu Ton Rose Garden** (Vuon Hong, 8am-11am and 1pm-5pm daily, free), which specializes in all variety of roses. While there are a few other flower gardens just beyond this road, Vuon Hong, literally "rose garden" street, is the ideal place for a stroll or cycle to take in the best of Sa Dec's flowers. Its houses are surrounded not only by the well-tended gardens of local residents but also

an altar at Kien An Cung Pagoda

plenty of natural foliage, and the road is split in two by a narrow canal.

To get to the gardens, follow Le Loi street along the water for river views and a couple of nice buildings en route, like the old **Sa Dec Church** or the twin spires of the town's **Cao Dai Temple**, both of which are on Le Loi.

House of Huynh Thuy Le

One of the few remaining colonial houses tucked between local shops and several newer, boxy residences, the **house of Huynh Thuy Le** (255A Nguyen Hue, tel. 0277/377-3937, nhaco_hthuyle@yahoo.com.vn, 8:30am-5pm daily, VND30,000) is noted for its blend of French and Chinese architecture as well as the romantic affairs of its owner. The son of a wealthy Chinese businessman, Huynh Thuy Le met the 15-year-old Marguerite Duras on a ferry crossing to Saigon in 1929. Not long after, the two began an affair that lasted until Duras left for France at 18. Though their romance was brief, the relationship inspired Duras' 1984 novel *The Lover*, which sold over three million copies and earned her wide acclaim. When the book was made into a movie in 1991, director Jean-Jacques Annaud chose to film parts of the story in Vietnam.

From the outside, the building looks every bit a French colonial house, with high archways and thick balustrades. However, step inside and everything turns to wood, with dozens of intricate carvings hanging from above and, on the ground, sturdy furniture inlaid with mother of pearl.

While preservation is an increasingly rare sight in Vietnam, Dong Thap Tourist, the government-run company that now owns the house, has gone a bit overboard with the souvenirs in the back room and is pushing to make this into a tourist attraction. Still, the house is a stunning example of turn-of-the-century colonial architecture, and your entry ticket includes a short spiel from one of the tour guides—though you may have to press them for it—as well as free lotus tea and candied ginger. It is even possible to spend a night in the house; but, at VND945,000 a room, it's not worth the price to sleep inside a museum.

FOOD

Housed in a covered pavilion behind the main market are dozens of **food stalls** (behind Sa Dec Market, Lac Long Quan, 6am-4:30pm daily, VND10,000-50,000) that cook up a variety of noodle soups, rice dishes, and other local fare. Vegetarian meals are also available—just look for the *chay* signs.

Opposite Sa Dec Market, **Chanh Ky** (193 Nguyen Sinh Sac, tel. 0277/386-4065, 5am-5pm daily, VND20,000-50,000) is run by a lovely bunch of Chinese-Vietnamese women and serves noodles, rice, and *hoan thanh mi* (wonton soup). There's a good chance that as soon as you enter the shop someone will go rooting around for the sole handwritten English menu to help you out.

Full of pick-and-point choices, **Com Thuy** (439 Hung Vuong, tel. 0277/386-1644, 9am-8pm daily, VND15,000-50,000) serves standard Vietnamese rice dishes and boasts more options than most of the other shops in town.

ACCOMMODATIONS

On account of its proximity to larger towns like Vinh Long and Cao Lanh, most people don't end up spending the night in Sa Dec. If you do, there are a couple of good value options.

Under VND210,000

The best of three small guesthouses on a charming little street across the canal from Kim Hue Pagoda, **Thanh Truc Guesthouse** (121 Phan Boi Chau, tel. 0277/386-8234, VND150,000-300,000) comes with clean beds, a TV, Wi-Fi, and a window in every room. Rates depend upon your choice of fan or air-conditioning as well as hot or cold showers.

VND210,000-525,000

The most centrally located option, **Thao Ngan Hotel** (6 An Duong Vuong, tel. 0277/377-4255, VND250,000-400,000) sits just beside Sa Dec Market and offers clean and comfortable digs for a one-star place. Baths are large, though the hot water comes and goes, and there is a minibar, TV, and Wi-Fi in every room.

Another excellent budget option, **Hotel Phuong Nam** (384A Nguyen Sinh Sac, tel. 0277/386-7867, khachsanphuongnam.com, VND300,000-400,000) is just a stone's throw from the town center and features Wi-Fi, TV, and hot showers, as well as a fan or air-conditioning. If you don't mind spending an extra US$3, splurge for the nicer rooms, as they are larger, and some include a balcony.

Sa Dec's finest accommodations, the **Bong Hong Hotel** (251A Nguyen Sinh Sac, tel. 0277/386-8288, bonghonghotelsadec@gmail.com, VND350,000-840,000) is run by Dong Thap Tourist and features charming views of the countryside as well as comfy beds, a minibar, Wi-Fi, TV, hot water, and modern decor. There is also a nice restaurant attached to the hotel and some tennis courts next door.

INFORMATION AND SERVICES

For withdrawals, you can visit the **Sacombank** (corner of Lac Long Quan and Nguyen Sinh Sac, tel. 0277/377-2355, www.sacombank.com.vn, 7:30am-11:30am and 1pm-5pm Mon.-Fri., 7:30am-11:30am Sat.) and its ATM near the central market. Don't expect to change currencies here, as this is a smaller town and banks are not equipped to do so. The **Sa Dec post office** (90 Hung Vuong, tel. 0277/386-1441, 6:30am-6pm Mon.-Fri., 7am-11:30am and 1pm-5pm Sat.-Sun.) is located at the corner of Nguyen Sinh Sac and Hung Vuong and also provides Internet services.

In the event of minor injuries or illnesses, the **Sa Dec General Hospital (Benh Vien Da Khoa Sa Dec)** (158 Nguyen Sinh Sac, tel. 0277/377-0263, www.bvdksadec.vn) can help, but don't expect anyone to speak English. For better care and a doctor who speaks your language, you'll have to head to Saigon.

TRANSPORTATION

Incoming local buses from Saigon (2.5 hours, VND105,000-135,000), Can Tho (1.5 hours, VND50,000), and nearby Vinh Long (30 minutes, VND15,000-30,000) stop either at the **Sa Dec bus station** (Nguyen Sinh Sac near Hung Vuong, tel. 0277/386-1436, 5:30am-6pm daily) or over the bridge at the bus stop just outside Sa Dec Market, slightly closer to town. The local **Phuong Trang** (149/8 Khom Hoa Khanh, tel. 0277/377-4993, www.futabus.vn, 5am-5pm daily) office is at the Sa Dec bus station.

Sa Dec is a small town and easily covered on foot. **Bicycles** are available for rent at some of the local hotels. For motorized transport, a group of *xe om* often gathers out front of Sa Dec Market near the bus stop. You can also call for a **Vinasa** (tel. 0277/386-6666) taxi, though don't expect to see them driving around.

Chau Doc

Less than three kilometers from the Cambodian border, Chau Doc is a pleasant, sleepy town often used by travelers as a convenient stopover between western Vietnam and its neighbor. Whether you're heading onward to Cambodia or not, the area's stunning scenery and rich diversity make this destination interesting in its own right, with verdant green mountains rising out of the surrounding rice paddies and entire floating villages settled along the Bassac River (Hau River). Beyond a series of photogenic landscapes, best viewed from the top of Sam Mountain or the surrounding countryside of Chau Doc, this patchwork town of sturdy colonial buildings and teetering clapboard houses boasts a uniquely diverse population, including Vietnamese, Khmer, and Chinese residents as well as a sizable ethnic Cham community, once the medieval rulers of much of south-central Vietnam. Farther afield, the natural beauty of Tra Su Forest, a peaceful, primitive grove of cajuput trees, hosts hundreds of storks as well as a variety of other birds.

Most travelers pass through Chau Doc for only a day or two before crossing the border or moving on to other destinations like Ha Tien, and later Phu Quoc, or back toward Can Tho and Saigon. For the full experience, it's best to stay for at least two days in order to visit Sam Mountain and Chau Doc's river attractions and still have enough time for a trip to Tra Su.

SIGHTS

Though none of them are very far, all of Chau Doc's prominent sights are located beyond the city limits. You'll find a handful of interesting temples and pagodas peppered throughout town, as well as an active central market. In order to experience the area's more intriguing elements, you'll have to either hit the water or hit the road—local guides are plentiful,

Chau Doc

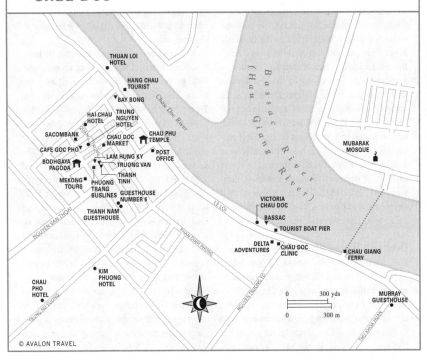

© AVALON TRAVEL

and several hotels arrange tours of nearby attractions.

Bodh Gaya

Unique for its outdoor setting, the **Bodh Gaya Pagoda** (Phan Van Vang and Chi Lang, sunrise-sunset daily) is in the middle of Chau Doc's only park, a large central square with few trees where street carts gather in the late afternoons and evenings. While it's not really a pagoda in the traditional sense, rather a collection of religious statues—most of which feature the Buddha in various poses, as well as a towering figure of Quan Am—this open-air spot is a popular gathering point for locals, who visit regularly to pray and burn incense. The pagoda's most notable feature is its large gnarled bodhi tree, which rises out of the middle of the clearing. Said to have originated from a seedling of the famous Indian bodhi

tree under which the Buddha sat and eventually attained enlightenment, this tree offers ample shade within the gated pagoda area.

Chau Phu Temple

Just opposite the river beside a bustling outdoor market, **Chau Phu Temple** (228 Tran Hung Dao, 8am-5pm daily) celebrates the accomplishments of Nguyen Huu Canh, one of several national heroes to shape the development of Vietnam's southern provinces. Born into a prominent noble family in 1650, Nguyen Huu Canh was a major player in fostering Vietnam's economy in the once untamed southern reaches of the country, fending off different opponents and establishing social order and administrative regions in these fledgling communities. By the time he reached Vietnam's southwestern border in 1700, the man was already a known figure among the Vietnamese. He fell ill shortly after arriving in Chau Doc and died that same year.

Today, he is remembered throughout the country, as his name features heavily on street signs and high schools from north to south. Several temples exist in Nguyen Huu Canh's honor, including one across the border in Phnom Penh. This is one of the best-known and the largest in the Mekong Delta. Its main altar features Nguyen Huu Canh himself, but you'll also find a smaller section of the building dedicated to Thoai Ngoc Hau, a local politician remembered for his contributions to southern development and who was in power during the time of the temple's original construction, 1820-1828. Though it was located elsewhere at the time, Chau Phu Temple relocated to its current residence in 1926.

Bassac River (Hau River)

Despite its name, the **Bassac River (Hau River)** is not so much a waterway hemmed in by riverbanks but rather a lake disrupted occasionally by bits of land. This wide unending stream leads northwest into Cambodia and southeast to Can Tho, fanning out across the flat landscape and, in the rainy season, devouring the nearby fields. In a region where water often takes precedence over land, entire communities are built on the river, with neighborhoods of floating houses bobbing along, supported by a few hollow floats and powered by a single electric line, strung up on a bamboo pole above the river. The effect is something like a miniature city, easily dismantled and always shifting with the current.

For Chau Doc's floating houses, real estate is tax-free, and residents may drop anchor wherever they please. For the ramshackle stilted houses that lean out precariously over the water, life is more challenging. From the river, you can get an idea of what the rainy season is like in Chau Doc, as the walls of these corrugated tin buildings note where water levels have surpassed the floors of some stationary houses. Each year, dwellings along the riverbank are subject to the unpredictable flooding of the river, and whole buildings

have collapsed into the water as a result of erosion. The problem is such that government offices are trying to relocate people inland in order to prevent these disasters from repeating themselves.

Visiting the river is only possible by boat. Check with one of the hotels in town, where local guides can be arranged as well as group tours. The local guides who coordinate with **Trung Nguyen** (86 Bach Dang, tel. 0296/356-1561) are honest, friendly, and reliable. Two-hour boat tours to Chau Doc's floating market, fish farms, and Cham villages can be booked through Trung Nguyen for around VND300,000-400,000 per boat. Another option is to arrange your boat ride with a freelance driver at the pier near Victoria Chau Doc, but be sure to agree on a price and an itinerary before you set off. Freelance boat tours are much more open to discussion, as you set the itinerary with your driver as well as the time frame and price. It's possible you could bargain a freelance driver down to VND200,000-250,000; however, the nature of your specific itinerary, the number of people, and the duration of the trip all factor into the cost.

★ FISH FARMS

As you travel along the Bassac, you're sure to see the colorful exteriors and flowering verandas of Chau Doc's floating houses. While many of these buoyant residences can easily pull up anchor and change address whenever they so choose, a number of locals keep their livelihoods beneath the floorboards in large stationary **fish farms.** Metal pens stretching across the area of the house and plunging several meters deep into the river can hold up to 100,000 fish at a time, which are caged within the river. When it's time to feed, a section of the floorboards is removed and a frenzy takes place, with hundreds of fish flapping around as soon as the food hits the water. On fishing day, farmers use a massive net attached to a bamboo pole and sweep the farm, catching hundreds of fish at a time to sell to large boats, which transport them to the market and beyond. Despite the hard work required of fish farmers, these businesses can be profitable, with some families owning several floating farms.

CHAM VILLAGE

Once a powerful empire that ruled much of Vietnam's south-central coast, the might of the Champa kingdom has long since faded, but several communities still remain in Vietnam. Chau Doc's ethnic Cham, who continue to practice Islam and follow their own traditions and culture, are one of the only communities in the Mekong Delta, with roughly 2,500 residents spread out on either side of the Bassac River. Many tourist boats stop at a local **Cham village** during their tour of the area's aquatic attractions. Visitors can catch a glimpse of a local workshop, where Cham women specialize in woven fabrics, crafting beautifully patterned materials with the help of a large wooden loom. In truth, the place is a bit of a tourist trap, as scores of fabric panels are on display for passing visitors to buy, but the locals are friendly and the pressure to make a purchase is not so great that you can't enjoy a quick look without interruption.

MUBARAK MOSQUE

Chau Doc's most frequented Cham landmark, the domed **Mubarak Mosque** (Provincial Hwy. TL953, sunrise-sunset daily) sits on the opposite side of the river in Chau Giang District. Completed in 1967, this pale-hued building serves not only as a place of worship for the local Cham community but also continues to teach the Quran as well as Arabic script. Passersby are able to catch a glimpse of the mosque's understated exterior on a quick stroll down the main street. While it is possible to enter the mosque, always ask permission first. Remember that appropriate dress rules apply (shorts and T-shirts are not acceptable). Prayer times are best avoided, as the place fills up with locals. This is also the only sight on the river that you can reach by boat as well as by land. If you prefer to see the mosque on your own, take the **Chau Giang ferry** (Le Loi between Nguyen Truong To and Truong Dinh, 24 hours daily, VND1,000 pp or VND5,000 per motorbike) just beyond the tourist boat pier and turn left at the main road once you reach Chau Giang District. A short walk will bring you to the mosque's main gates.

Mubarak Mosque

CHAU DOC FLOATING MARKET

Though it doesn't have the same hustle and bustle as the Delta's other floating markets, a spin around Chau Doc's **floating market** is a pleasant way to spend the morning. It is usually included in local boat tours and gives you the opportunity to see vendors on giant wooden boats buy and sell local produce along the water. Drinks and light meals, like the traditional Cambodian-style soup, *bun nuoc leo,* are available from little vessels motoring around the area.

★ Sam Mountain

Rising from the watery fields of An Giang province, **Sam Mountain** is Chau Doc's defining natural feature. This low, wide hill stands at 230 meters tall and, as the only elevation around for kilometers, its summit provides incredible views of the town and its watery surroundings. Take a fascinating (but exhausting) hike up the mountain, following a series of uneven stone steps past countless temples and pagodas, local houses, and vivid Buddhist cemeteries; it takes about an hour to hike to the summit. Or hop on a *xe om* from town and save your energy as you zip up to the clearing at the top, where an altar marks the original site of the locally famous Lady Xu statue. Some *xe om* drivers are only willing to transport downtown passengers out to the base of the mountain (VND50,000), but there are always drivers here who can take you the rest of the way for VND25,000. In future, visitors will have yet another way to reach the summit, as a cable car project is in the works.

TAY AN PAGODA

Standing before its colorful gates and a menagerie of plaster animals that guard the entrance, it doesn't take long to recognize that **Tay An Pagoda** (base of Sam Mountain, 4am-7pm daily) is unusual. The dome of its pastel-hued tower and arched doorways within the complex suggest a hint of Islamic influence that you won't find in most Buddhist pagodas. Along with a collection of nearly 200 statues—including several menacing soldiers

a tomb behind Tay An Pagoda in Chau Doc

that flank Buddha's usual altar and some impressively lifelike sculptures of deceased monks—the pagoda's grounds contain a vibrant cemetery that rambles up the mountainside in a flurry of pinks, yellows, and blues.

For locals, this pagoda is a holy site. You'll likely find groups of Vietnamese paying their respects not only at the altars inside but also at several of the more prominent gravesites. From within the cemetery area, you can ascend a staircase that begins the long but scenic walk up to the top of Sam Mountain. Just follow the "*len nui*" signs painted on rocks and signs. You'll likely get turned around a few times, but local residents can point you in the right direction up to the summit.

TEMPLE OF LADY XU

No one knows how the portly, colorful statue within the **Temple of Lady Xu** (Sam Mountain Rd., sunrise-sunset daily) came to exist on Sam Mountain. Lady Xu is considered a powerful figure and one of Chau Doc's most famous residents. The story goes that, roughly 200 years ago, a group of Siamese invaders happened upon the impressive sculpture at the top of Sam Mountain. The men attempted to take it but Lady Xu was immovable. Frustrated, they smashed the statue's left arm before heading down the mountain empty-handed.

Not long after the men left, villagers at the base of the mountain received a message from Lady Xu. Using a young girl as her medium, Lady Xu instructed the townspeople to carry her down from the summit. A group of strong men attempted to lift the statue but could not. Lady Xu appeared again, claiming she could only be moved down the mountain by a group of nine virgins. The villagers supplied such a team, and the young women transported Lady Xu downhill to her current residence, where she promptly became immovable again. Villagers took this as a message that Lady Xu preferred to stay put and built a bamboo temple to house the statue. In 1870, locals constructed a sturdier shelter out of brick.

Nowadays, people come in droves to pray to her and several festivals are held in Lady Xu's honor each year, including the bathing of the statue. The temple itself is less impressive than some of Sam Mountain's other buildings.

From the street, enter through the main gates. You will need to travel around the back of the main building in order to see the statue. The area in which Lady Xu resides is barren apart from the sculpture, and photos are strictly forbidden inside the temple. You can, however, pay your respects and then head into the room just beside Lady Xu's altar. Here, temple visitors often make a small donation and receive a piece of Lady Xu's clothing for good luck in return.

CAVE PAGODA

Boasting one of the best views on the hill, **Cave Pagoda** (Sam Mountain Rd., sunrise-sunset daily) is carved into the western side of Sam Mountain and features a stunning, newly renovated complex outfitted with lotus ponds and a blinding white statue of the Buddha.

Also known as Phuoc Dien Pagoda, this sight has undergone several renovations since its initial 19th-century completion. But you can still see the crumbling stupa, built in 1899, to honor a local woman called Ba Tho. Sometime in the middle of the 19th century, Ba Tho left her family to travel up Sam Mountain, where she lived for several decades in total isolation before locals discovered her there.

Today, the cave in which Ba Tho is said to have lived during these years is open to visitors, and the pagoda is home to several resident monks. Along with most of the buildings on Sam Mountain, this pagoda is a strictly religious place. Visitors should dress appropriately, covering their legs and shoulders, as those in shorts and tank tops won't be allowed inside. The exterior lookouts are especially worthwhile, as the pagoda overlooks nearby fields, making this an exceptional spot for photos. Inside, however, a growing display of Buddhist statues now lines the area's caves, complete with motion sensor-activated lights, music, and water features.

Travelers hoping to visit this pagoda should note that it can only be accessed from the ring road surrounding Sam Mountain. Those who travel up to the summit will have to head back down to the bottom before continuing on to Cave Pagoda.

Tours

Local tour guides coordinate with hotels like **Hai Chau** (63 Suong Nguyet Anh, tel. 0296/626-0066, www.haichauhotel.com) and **Trung Nguyen** (86 Bach Dang, tel. 0296/356-1561). They are honest, friendly, and reliable.

For trips packed with information, check out **Victoria Chau Doc** (1 Le Loi, tel. 0296/386-5010, www.victoriahotels.asia) for tailor-made, high-end tours. If you're on a budget, get in touch with **Mekong Tours** (14 Nguyen Huu Canh, tel. 0296/386-7817, longnguyen49@yahoo.com, 5am-6pm daily).

FOOD

The simple but satisfying meals at **Bay Bong** (22 Suong Nguyet Anh, tel. 0296/386-7271,

10am-9pm daily, VND40,000-80,000) draw a nightly crowd to its small sidewalk set-up along Suong Nguyet Anh. Rice and noodle dishes feature heavily on the menu, as do a few varieties of hot pot, and the staff is a cheerful bunch. There is also a **second location** (46 Trung Nu Vuong, tel. 0296/356-2747, 10am-9pm daily, VND40,000-80,000) closer to the road leading out to Sam Mountain.

For herbivorous diners, **Thanh Tinh** (13 Quang Trung, tel. 0296/386-5064, 6am-8pm daily, VND25,000-80,000) boasts not one but two large street carts sheltered within a clean storefront just beside the central market. Everything from noodles to rice to vegetarian hot pots is available.

Right beside Thanh Tinh, the vendors at **Truong Van** (15 Quang Trung, tel. 0296/386-6567, 7am-9pm daily, VND40,000-100,000) cook up the usual variety of noodles and rice as well as hot pots.

Dining at the **Bassac** (Victoria Chau Doc, 1 Le Loi, tel. 0296/386-5010, www.victoria-hotels.asia, 6am-10pm daily, VND80,000-325,000), Victoria Chau Doc's restaurant, is a departure from the city's rice-and-noodle joints. Perched on a deck overlooking the river, the restaurant and bar offer excellent views; be sure to have a sundown cocktail here. Indoors, white linen tablecloths and the opulent decor of the hotel add to its old-world ambience. The kitchen serves Western and Asian dishes, and a selection of wine, beer, and cocktails. While the dining room is only open for dinner, Bassac offers a snack menu throughout the day.

One of the fancier coffee shops in town, **Cafe Goc Pho** (86 Dong Da, tel. 0296/626-7888, 6am-10pm daily, VND20,000-80,000) serves a variety of smoothies, teas, and coffees in a bright, new air-conditioned building. The owner is a cycling enthusiast, and bicycle photos and other paraphernalia line the walls. There are also some snacks and small meals on the menu, including a pizza, though don't expect to be wowed by the pies—this is definitely a café first.

ACCOMMODATIONS

Hotels in Chau Doc range from dirt-cheap, basic *nha tro* (a step down from a guesthouse, *nha nghi*) to dapper modern accommodations. While there are plenty of options both in town and farther out around Sam Mountain, you're better off sticking close to the city center, as this is where you'll find most essentials.

Under VND210,000

Hotel Number 6 Thanh Mai (23-25 Phan Van Vang, tel. 0296/386-7622, VND120,000-400,000) provides reasonable lodging and has some of the lowest prices in town. TV, Wi-Fi, and optional air-conditioning and fans are available. Motorbikes are also available for rent.

VND210,000-525,000

For affordable and centrally located lodging, **Trung Nguyen Hotel** (86 Bach Dang, tel. 0296/356-1561, VND345,000-485,000) is one of the better options in town. Just a short walk from the Chau Doc Market, its rooms are fairly basic but clean and include air-conditioning, Wi-Fi, TV, hot water, and a mini-bar, as well as breakfast. The ground floor has a small restaurant, and the exceptionally friendly staff can help with everything from reliable local tours to onward transportation both in Vietnam and to Cambodia.

Another great corner hotel, the **Hai Chau Hotel** (63 Suong Nguyet Anh, tel. 0296/626-0066, VND350,000-550,000, breakfast included) offers tidy standard rooms, with hot water, air-conditioning, TV, and Wi-Fi, overlooking a quieter spot in the city center. Breakfast is served in the hotel's restaurant. Staff can assist in booking tours and transportation to other destinations. Note that the entrance to this hotel is around the corner on Quang Trung street rather than Suong Nguyet Anh.

Slightly beyond the city center, **Kim Phuong** (Trung Nu Vuong, tel. 0296/355-0585, VND270,000-320,000) is a decent option for those who can't get into the Chau Pho, though it is more basic. Complete with air-conditioning, Wi-Fi, TV, and hot water, the rooms are large, bare, and include soft beds.

VND525,000-1,050,000

The most inviting of Chau Doc's hotels, ★ **Murray Guesthouse** (11-15 Truong Dinh, tel. 0296/356-2108, www.murraymekong.com, VND720,000-1,012,000) puts you at ease from the moment you step inside. This clean and modern family-run guesthouse features finer amenities than most local hotels and, though a bit beyond the town center, also comes with a notably friendly and welcoming staff. Rooms are equipped with TV, Wi-Fi, air-conditioning, hot water, and a minibar. The common area boasts a pool table and dart board. For peace and quiet, head to the upstairs roof terrace for pleasant views of Chau Doc town. The guesthouse also provides bicycles free of charge and has a city guide in each room.

VND1,050,000-2,100,000

Though it's not on the most scenic of streets, **Chau Pho Hotel** (88 Trung Nu Vuong, tel. 0296/356-4139, www.chauphohotel.com, VND1,000,000-1,200,000) holds its own as one of the better mid-range places in Chau Doc, boasting nice private balconies as well as clean modern rooms with neatly made beds. Depending upon the room you choose, accommodations feature bathtubs or a spacious enclosed shower as well as the usual air-conditioning, hot water, a minibar, and TV. While standard rooms are nice, the superior and deluxe rooms offer great value and are worth the extra cash. There is a tennis court next door to the hotel as well as an in-house restaurant.

Over VND2,100,000

Set in a grand colonial building, **Victoria Chau Doc** (1 Le Loi, tel. 0296/386-5010, www.victoriahotels.asia, VND2,505,000-6,000,000) boasts a stunning location complete with a riverfront deck, swimming pool, and one of the nicest restaurants in town. Accommodations are spacious and modern, offering incredible views of the river or the town. The service-minded staff can arrange boat tours and other day trips with experienced local guides. The hotel also runs the **Victoria Nui Sam** (Sam Mountain, tel. 0296/357-5888, www.victoriahotels.asia, VND2,360,000-3,816,000), a breathtaking lodge tucked on the hillside of Sam Mountain that offers daily excursions around the area and a peaceful retreat.

INFORMATION AND SERVICES

The folks at **Mekong Tours** (14 Nguyen Huu Canh, tel. 0296/386-7817, longnguyen49@yahoo.com, 5am-6pm daily) can provide a few restaurant recommendations as well as tour and transportation services.

Sacombank (88 Dong Da, tel. 0296/326-0262, www.sacombank.com.vn, 7:30am-11:30am and 1pm-5pm Mon.-Fri., 7:30am-11:30am Sat.) has an ATM and a bank branch on the corner of Dong Da and Phan Van Vang that helps with currency exchange and other monetary needs. For mail and Internet, visit the local **post office** (2 Le Loi, tel. 0296/386-6416, 7am-6pm daily) on the riverfront.

Among the only medical facilities in town is **Nhat Tan Hospital** (14 Chau Long, tel. 0296/356-2357), which should handle minor ailments and has an emergency room open 24 hours daily, but anything major requires a trip to Saigon.

GETTING THERE
Bus

Cozy, air-conditioned **Phuong Trang buses** (89 Phan Van Vang, tel. 0296/356-5888, www.futabus.vn, 24 hours daily) arrive several times throughout the day from Saigon (6 hours, VND140,000) and Can Tho (3 hours, VND100,000). They make the return trip to both cities from Chau Doc's new **bus station** (QL91). A handful of vehicles, including minibuses run by **Hung Cuong** (96 Dong Da, tel. 0296/386-5116), also travel between the town's old **bus station** (Le Loi) and Ho Chi Minh City or Long Xuyen, though Phuong Trang is the more comfortable option. If you purchase a ticket from the downtown Phuong Trang office, you needn't worry about getting out to the station, as travelers can be picked up from the office or a nearby hotel.

Onward to Cambodia

While boat tickets to and from Cambodia do exist, organizing over-water transport is a mixed bag in Chau Doc. Several tour companies in town will sell you a boat ticket to Phnom Penh, but without enough passengers the boat does not usually run, and this information is often not relayed to travelers until the day of departure. Many local companies that book these tickets also have a reputation of overcharging travelers for just about everything, from a few extra dollars at the border for your Cambodian visa to additional bus fees when the boat "breaks down" or fails to depart. The only reliable provider is **Hang Chau Tourist** (Tran Hung Dao, tel. 0296/356-2771, www.hangchautourist.vn, 7am-11am and 1:30pm-5pm daily, VND570,000).

It's possible, though less popular, to reach Cambodia overland via bus. Speak with your hotel to arrange a bus ride to Phnom Penh, as buses that travel from Saigon to Phnom Penh pass through Chau Doc; your hotel can help you flag one down.

GETTING AROUND

Both *xe om* and *xe loi* (a cousin of the cyclo) are readily available throughout the downtown area, though this town is just as easily walkable on foot. **Mailinh** (tel. 0296/3838-3838) taxis also make their rounds. Most hotels and guesthouses rent out **bicycles** and **motorbikes** for a small fee.

TRA SU BIRD SANCTUARY

The **Tra Su Bird Sanctuary (Khu Du Lich Sinh Thai Rung Tram Tra Su)** (Van Giao Ward, Tinh Bien, tel. 0296/221-8025, 7:30am-4:30pm daily) is less visited than some other attractions in Chau Doc—perhaps because of its location 24 kilometers outside town—but

it is by far one of the area's most worthwhile sights. A flooded forest of narrow towering cajuput trees, Tra Su is home to a variety of bird species, including storks, herons, and egrets, all of which can be seen via the boats hired out through Tra Su's visitors center. Large motorized vessels ferry travelers from the forest's main gate, past lotus fields and down long canopied avenues to a smaller outpost, where wooden canoes are paddled around the forest itself, a maze of long spindly trees rising out of the water.

This spot is particularly good for birdwatching, as the quieter vehicles and the lack of apparent waterway allow birds to roam freely, swooping and soaring between the trees. The motorized boats will also make a trip out to Tra Su's watchtower, one of the taller and sturdier lookouts in Vietnam, from which you can see the rest of the forest as well as the distant mountains.

The entire trip lasts 1-2 hours, depending on how much time you spend at the lookout; costs begin at VND150,000 for a single traveler and get cheaper with more people. These trips don't include an English-speaking guide, but it is the scenery that really makes Tra Su.

To get to the forest, travelers can hire a *xe om* from Chau Doc or book a tour through one of the local hotels. For the more adventurous, it is also possible to rent a motorbike and find your own way, though expect to stop several times and ask to be pointed in the right direction—the only visible sign for the forest is in Vietnamese and just before the turnoff.

BA CHUC

It is possible to add a jaunt to **Ba Chuc** to your trip to Tra Su if you have the time. Thirty-nine kilometers outside Chau Doc and right near the edge of the Cambodian border, the small village of Ba Chuc is just one of several Vietnamese towns that suffered at the hands of the Khmer Rouge in the years immediately following the American War. As Pol Pot's reign of terror took the lives of millions of Cambodians across the border, a longstanding feud over land rights between the Vietnamese government and the Khmer Rouge regime boiled over, ultimately resulting in a two-year war.

While these land disputes may have sparked tension along the border, the senseless violence committed by the Khmer Rouge only solidified Vietnam's decision to retaliate. A series of random brutal massacres occurred at places like Ba Chuc, where, from April 18-30, 1978, Khmer Rouge forces crossed the border and slaughtered 3,157 people in this village alone, leaving behind only two survivors. Houses were burned, pagodas razed, and men, women, and children murdered. In the nearby **Phi Lai Tu Pagoda** (6am-6pm daily), the blood of local victims still stains the walls, while nearly all of the adjacent **Tam Buu Pagoda** (6am-6pm daily) was burned to the ground but for one altar, which is now revered as holy. Between these two buildings, a small **exhibit** (6am-6pm daily) shares the history of the tragedy, but only in Vietnamese, and includes several graphic photographs of the aftermath. Beyond that, the town itself is a hot and dusty place, but the drive out to Ba Chuc is nice, riding along an elevated road above infinite fields and past distant mountains.

Rach Gia and Ha Tien

A pair of port towns tucked along the westernmost edge of the country, Rach Gia and Ha Tien are among some of the Delta's more underappreciated destinations. Most often used as convenient stopovers en route to Phu Quoc or Cambodia, these two cities represent not only unique and stunning Delta scenery but also the final frontier of Vietnam's development.

Once part of a virtually uninhabited rainforest, the harsh environment of the country's western coast has been tamed somewhat, allowing for a full economic boom in both cities. Natural landscapes like the flooded forests of U Minh Thuong and Hon Chong's picturesque limestone islands, sometimes referred to as the Delta's miniature version of Ha Long Bay, hint at something more than simply a stopover destination.

RACH GIA

A southern boomtown crisscrossed with rivers and bustling avenues, Rach Gia usually serves as a stopover for tourists heading to Phu Quoc, as speedboats to the island depart daily from its harbor. Rach Gia is a pleasant town in its own right and has a handful of sights: a pair of vibrant pagodas with revolutionary histories, a well-decorated provincial museum, and a beautiful open temple devoted to a local hero, not to mention the lush greenery and still waters of a ravishing national park not far from town.

Along with Phu Quoc, the mainland's rainy season runs May-November, and thanks to the slump in island visitors at this time, Rach Gia gets even quieter. A day is all you need to explore this town. Birders and nature enthusiasts might tack on another day for a trip to the watery forest at U Minh Thuong National Park.

Sights

While passing the time in Rach Gia, visitors who didn't make it out to Tay Ninh can stop by the town's requisite **Cao Dai Temple** (189 Nguyen Trung Truc, 6am-6pm daily), as well as a handful of more unique pagodas and temples that are worth a look. On the way into town, look for the large three-door archway, called **Cong Tam Quan.** It's considered a symbol of Rach Gia and its silhouette can be found on local shops and businesses throughout Kien Giang province. The remainder of Rach Gia's sights make for a satisfying half-day outing.

Rach Gia

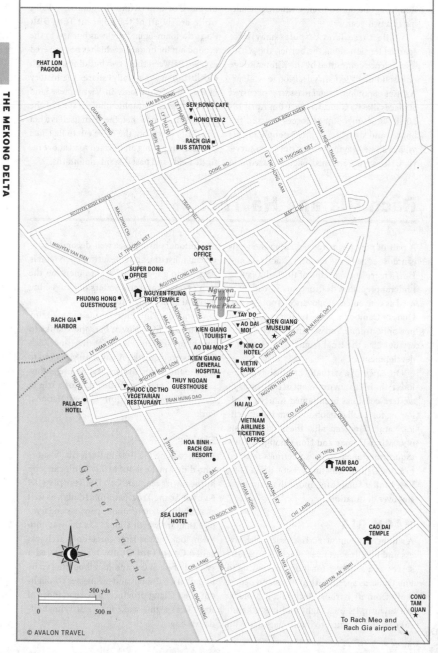

PHAT LON PAGODA

SEN HONG CAFE
HONG YEN 2

RACH GIA BUS STATION

HAI BA TRUNG
LE THANH TON
LY PHAT TO
DIEN BIEN PHU
QUANG TRUNG
NGUYEN BINH KHIEM
PHAM NGOC THACH
LY THUONG KIET
LE THI HONG GAM
DONG HO
TRAN PHU
MAC CUU

NGUYEN BINH KHIEM
MAC DINH CHI
LY THUONG KIET
NGUYEN VAN KIEN

POST OFFICE

SUPER DONG OFFICE
NGUYEN CONG TRU

NGUYEN TRUNG TRUC TEMPLE
THANH THAI

Nguyen Trung Truc Park

PHUONG HONG GUESTHOUSE
HUYNH TINH CUA

RACH GIA HARBOR

TAY DO
AO DAI MOI

KIEN GIANG MUSEUM

KIEN GIANG TOURIST
MAC DINH CHI
HOANG DIEU

AO DAI MOI 2
KIM CO HOTEL

NGUYEN VAN TROI
TRAN HUNG DAO

LY NHAN TONG
NGUYEN HUNG SON

KIEN GIANG GENERAL HOSPITAL
VIETIN BANK

THUY NGOAN GUESTHOUSE

PHUOC LOC THO VEGETARIAN RESTAURANT
TRAN HUNG DAO

TRAN PHU DO

PALACE HOTEL

HAI AU

NGUYEN THAI HOC

VIETNAM AIRLINES TICKETING OFFICE

CO GIANG
NGOC QUYEN

3 THANG 2
HOA BINH - RACH GIA RESORT

CO BAC
PHAM HUNG
LAN QUANG KY

NGUYEN TRUNG TRUC
SU THIEN AN

TAM BAO PAGODA

CHI LANG

SEA LIGHT HOTEL

TO NGOC VAN

CHI LANG
THANG

TON DUC THANG

CHAU VAN LIEM
NGUYEN AN NINH

CAO DAI TEMPLE

Gulf of Thailand

0   500 yds
0   500 m

CONG TAM QUAN

To Rach Meo and Rach Gia airport

© AVALON TRAVEL

KIEN GIANG MUSEUM

Housed in a beautiful colonial building over a century old, the **Kien Giang Museum** (21 Nguyen Van Troi, tel. 0297/386-3727, 7am-11am Mon.-Fri. and 1pm-5pm Wed.-Fri.) is a smaller version of a provincial museum that offers exhibits on local revolutionary history and the traditions, products, and ethnic diversity of the area. A handful of interesting displays on Oc Eo artifacts take up one section of the building, while there are also exhibits dedicated to some of Kien Giang's more famous heroes, such as Nguyen Trung Truc and Mac Cuu. Only parts of the signage are in English.

NGUYEN TRUNG TRUC TEMPLE

Just a block away from Rach Gia Harbor, the namesake **Nguyen Trung Truc Temple** (18 Nguyen Cong Tru, 5:30am-5pm daily) honors a southern revolutionary and national hero who took up arms against the French in the 1860s, most notably setting fire to the French naval ship *L'Esperance* and once taking over the colonial administration in Rach Gia for a few days. By the time he was finally arrested on Phu Quoc Island in 1868, the staunch anticolonial leader had made many enemies among the French. He was briefly imprisoned and later executed in Rach Gia by colonial authorities on October 27, 1868. Shortly before his death, Nguyen Trung Truc vowed that "only when all the grass in Vietnam is pulled up will there be no more Vietnamese people to fight against the French aggressors."

Today, the temple, completed in 1970, is a distinctly Vietnamese place, its gates adorned with golden dragons and swirling powder-blue clouds. Just inside the main entrance, a large bronze statue of the southern hero stands before the temple looking rather severe and poised to draw his sword. Inside the building, there are 13 separate altars to which you can offer incense and prayers, and most locals stop at each one when visiting. A handful of other revolutionary heroes are honored here with plaques and altars. While this temple is newer than many others in town, it is by far the most popular, with a constant stream of visitors.

PHAT LON PAGODA

A bit of a walk north of Rach Gia Harbor, **Phat Lon Pagoda** (151 Quang Trung, 7am-6pm daily) is one of 73 Theravada Buddhist pagodas in Kien Giang province. Like many of its counterparts, Phat Lon—literally, "Big Buddha" in Vietnamese—is not simply a house of worship but also a center of cultural study for the city's ethnic Khmer population and the residence of several monks.

This pagoda is famous for its involvement in the Soc Xoai battle, a fight between Vietnamese and French colonial forces. On August 11, 1948, the people of Kien Giang attacked their French oppressors at the small town of Soc Xoai, soundly defeating the Europeans in the second-largest battle between the French and Vietnamese of the Mekong Delta. Later in the day, stung by their loss, the French colonial forces returned, killing 32 Vietnamese revolutionaries. Monks at Phat Lon buried these fallen soldiers behind the pagoda, where a monument stands today.

From the street, a long sandy path leads up to the complex's central courtyard, where a fountain of dragons sits at the center. To the left is the actual pagoda, a large hall filled with neon-hued scenes from the life of the Buddha as well as intricately patterned ceilings. Out back, an assortment of stupas honor the deceased, while a large red- and gold-hued tower sits in the distance, close to the outer wall and fringed with lanterns. The place often appears empty, but you can explore on your own.

TAM BAO PAGODA

Small compared to some of the others in town, **Tam Bao Pagoda** (Su Thien An, 7am-7pm daily) is another site with historical significance. Built in 1802, it served as one of many centers of Communist activity during the late 1930s and early 1940s as the Vietnamese grew more resentful of colonial rule. At the pagoda, revolutionaries secretly held meetings and printed leaflets to distribute to the public in their campaign for independence from the French.

About halfway down Su Thien An lane is the colorful entrance to the pagoda. Though there is a door at the front of the building, this is usually gated. Instead, pass through to the open courtyard that divides Tam Bao into two parts. A statue of Quan Am housed in a blue gazebo presides over the central pond, while religious scripts penned in traditional Vietnamese calligraphy line the courtyard's outer wall. To the left, the main hall of the pagoda holds an altar dedicated to Buddha as well as several other shrines. The building on the right is dedicated to the ancestors. If you arrive on the 1st or 15th of the lunar month (religious days in Buddhism), you'll find the courtyard teeming with locals, who come to enjoy a vegetarian feast in honor of the religious day; you may be asked to join.

Festivals and Events

The annual **Nguyen Trung Truc Festival** takes place from the 26th to the 28th of the eighth lunar month (late Sept.-early Oct.). Celebrating the sacrifice of this national hero, who was executed by the French in Rach Gia in 1868, the festivities are held in Nguyen Trung Truc Park before a giant statue of the revolutionary, right at the center of town, and feature cultural performances and other events. Most foreigners don't bother with the event, but the festival draws hundreds of thousands of domestic tourists, who come to enjoy the celebration and to pay their respects to a famous fallen countryman.

Food

The breezy, inviting storefront of **Ao Dai Moi 2** (161 Nguyen Hung Son, tel. 0297/386-6272, 6am-midnight daily, VND20,000-50,000) boasts an English menu and an array of local dishes, including a particularly good *banh canh cua* (crab noodle soup), as well as *hu tieu* (southern-style rice noodle soup), egg noodles, rice, and a host of different smoothies. For breakfast, there is also the original **Ao Dai Moi** (26 Ly Tu Trong, tel. 0297/386-6295,

Buddha statues at Tam Bao Pagoda

5am-11pm daily, VND20,000-30,000) nearby, which has a bit less selection but is decked out with photos of the owner, a cycling enthusiast.

Though **Tay Do** (6 Nguyen Du, tel. 0297/391-5211, 10am-8pm daily, VND80,000-120,000) is a little overpriced for a rice shop, its dishes are tasty and an English menu is available for pick-and-point ordering. The narrow shop looks out over a quiet side street off Nguyen Trung Truc Park. Pork, beef, and chicken dishes are served, as well as seafood.

Not far from the bus station, **Sen Hong Cafe** (corner of Huynh Thuc Khang and Nguyen Tri Phuong, tel. 0297/860-1138, 6am-10pm daily, VND15,000-50,000) is a popular breakfast spot for locals, with quiet shaded seating. While the entire café is open-air, both sidewalk and covered seating is available, as is coffee, tea, and Vietnamese breakfast, though you'll have to arrive early if you want to eat, as the food is gone by 10am. The English-speaking owner can help you navigate your food choices, and the staff is pleasant.

Accommodations

There are several noteworthy budget accommodations in Rach Gia that offer great value for travelers. Bar a few exceptions, most of these hotels and guesthouses are centered around either the bus station or the harbor, while you'll find many of the town's restaurants and other services grouped near Le Loi and Nguyen Trung Truc streets.

VND210,000-525,000

For the rates, rooms at the ★ **Hong Yen 2** (G26-G27 Le Thanh Ton, tel. 0297/387-2655, VND200,000-300,000) are phenomenal. Snazzy black-and-white checked floors show off the impeccable cleanliness of the place and each spacious room comes with wooden furnishings, an enclosed shower, air-conditioning, TV, Wi-Fi, and a minibar. Several rooms have a nice view of the street, and the place is far enough from the main drag to miss most of the noise pollution. This hotel is a walk-up, so you'll have to haul your own baggage upstairs. You can also visit the original **Hong Yen** (259-261 Mac Cuu, tel. 0297/387-9095, VND200,000-400,000), though it is older and farther from town.

The centrally located **Kim Co Hotel** (141 Nguyen Hung Son, tel. 0297/387-9610, VND300,000-350,000) offers smart, clean rooms with Wi-Fi, air-conditioning, TV, a minibar, and a bathtub. Corner rooms have multiple windows and offer nice street views.

With clean, basic rooms right next to the harbor, **Phuong Hong Guesthouse** (5 Tu Do, tel. 0297/387-8777, VND250,000-400,000) is a popular spot for budget travelers. Accommodations come with a fan or air-conditioning as well as Wi-Fi, and the friendly owner can help with arranging boat and bus tickets.

VND525,000-1,050,000

Another place that seems almost too good to be true, the **Palace Hotel** (20 Lo L12 3 Thang 2, tel. 0297/386-6146, palacehotelkg@gmail. com, VND500,000-600,000) is stocked with modern furnishings and clean rooms, not to mention comfortable beds. TV, Wi-Fi, hot water, air-conditioning, and a minibar are included, and the English-speaking receptionist is friendly and outgoing. Both double and triple rooms are available. Breakfast is served at the hotel restaurant, though this is not included in the room rate.

VND1,050,000-2,100,000

Whether it's a precursor or an afterthought to your visit to Phu Quoc, the **Hoa Binh-Rach Gia Resort** (Lo A9, 3-7 Co Bac, tel. 0297/355-3355, www.hoabinhrachgiaresort. com.vn, VND1,050,000-2,400,000, breakfast included) is the city's only resort and a perfect place to extend your R&R time. The manicured grounds of this massive space boast two restaurants and an outdoor pool in addition to accommodations, which are spacious and well furnished. All rooms come with air-conditioning, Wi-Fi, TV, and a minibar, as well as your choice of garden or river views.

Information and Services

The staff at **Kien Giang Tourist** (5 Le Loi, tel. 0297/386-2081, 7:30am-11:30am and 1:30pm-5:30pm Mon.-Fri.) speak a little English if you're in need of restaurant recommendations. They aren't able to provide much else. Your hotel can probably help with restaurant recommendations as well.

Rach Gia's **Vietnam Airlines ticketing office** (16 Nguyen Trung Truc, tel. 0297/392-4320, 7:30am-11:30am and 1:30pm-5pm Mon.-Fri., 8am-11am and 2pm-4pm Sat.-Sun.) assists in purchasing flights to Phu Quoc or Ho Chi Minh City. If you're already in Rach Gia and planning to head to Phu Quoc, you're better off just taking the ferry and saving the extra cash.

The **Vietin Bank** (63 Le Loi, tel. 0297/386-3587, www.vietinbank.vn, 7am-11am and 1pm-5pm Mon.-Fri., 8am-11am Sat.), opposite the hospital, exchanges currency inside and has an ATM out front. The local **post office** (2 Mau Than, tel. 0297/386-6006, 7am-9pm daily) handles postage and Internet needs.

For medical services, the **Kien Giang**

General Hospital (Benh Vien Da Khoa Kien Giang) (46 Le Loi, tel. 0297/386-3328, www.bvdkkiengiang.vn) takes care of minor illnesses and injuries and has 24-hour emergency services.

Getting There

AIR

The **Rach Gia Airport (San Bay Rach Gia)** (VKG, 418 Cach Mang Thang Tam, tel. 0297/386-4326) receives daily Vietnam Airlines flights from Ho Chi Minh City (50 minutes, VND500,000-1,000,000 one-way).

BUS

Buses arrive and depart at the **Rach Gia bus station** (260A Nguyen Binh Khiem, tel. 0297/386-2274, 4am-midnight daily), near the city center, daily from Chau Doc (3 hours, VND70,000), Ha Tien (2 hours, VND85,000), and Saigon (5.5 hours, VND170,000). There are both cheaper local minibuses and large air-conditioned vehicles available. For the latter, try **Phuong Trang** (tel. 0297/369-1691, www.futabuslines. com.vn), which goes to both Can Tho (VND110,000) and Saigon (VND210,000), or **Mailinh Express** (tel. 0297/392-9292, www. mailinhexpress.vn), which runs minibuses to Ha Tien and Saigon.

BOAT

The speedboat from Ca Mau (morning and evening departures daily, 2-3 hours, VND120,000) drops passengers at **Rach Meo** (747 Ngo Quyen, 7am-4:30pm daily), roughly three kilometers from Rach Gia. From there, you can hop on a *xe om* into town for roughly VND40,000. Speedboats from Phu Quoc (2.5 hours, VND330,000) dock at the **Rach Gia harbor** (Nguyen Cong Tru) in town.

To travel onward to Phu Quoc, the boat transportation company **Super Dong** (14 Tu Do, tel. 0297/387-7742, www.superdong. com.vn, 6am-5pm daily, VND330,000), near the harbor, has five departures (8am-1pm daily) to the island. While there are other offices near the harbor that sell tickets, visit the Super Dong office directly to avoid any confusion. Reserve tickets about a day in advance, though it's sometimes possible to book a last-minute seat.

ONWARD TO PHU QUOC

There are two options for reaching Phu Quoc: Fly directly from Ho Chi Minh City to Phu Quoc (avoiding Rach Gia entirely), or, from the Delta area, make your way to Rach Gia or Ha Tien and take a speedboat to Phu Quoc from there.

Getting Around

Xe om are on every corner in Rach Gia, so you should have no trouble finding a ride, and **Mailinh** (tel. 0297/3838-3838) taxis run frequently throughout the downtown area. Most of the city center is walkable.

There is no official place to rent bicycles or motorbikes in Rach Gia. Check with your hotel, as they may have a motorbike or two to rent.

U Minh Thuong National Park

A stunning expanse of flooded forest, **U Minh Thuong National Park** (tel. 0297/380-9663, 7am-5pm daily, VND10,000) is home to a handful of rare feathered creatures, like the spot-billed pelican and the glossy ibis, as well as a few equally elusive mammals, including the hairy-nosed otter. One half of the U Minh forest parks—its counterpart, U Minh Ha, lies farther south near Ca Mau—U Minh Thuong is the more visited of the two and has more tourist services (though you'll still find these relatively limited). This park sees frequent weekend visitors, as groups will come from Saigon to Hoa Mai Lake to enjoy a fishing weekend. For birders, a small footpath circles the perimeter of the lake, from which you can spot storks and other large birds soaring from tree to tree.

Farther into the park, boats can be hired for bird-watching and fishing, with anglers taking the smaller, quieter vessels and other visitors hopping into a long narrow motorized canoe. Tickets are purchased per person and the cost depends upon the number of designated sightseeing spots you choose. Since the first watchtower is only located a short way from the boating docks, it's best to pay for at least two sightseeing spots, as this affords you the chance to float around the wider forest area where many birds congregate. On account of the larger boats' engines, most bird-watching will have to be done from afar, but the scenery and the bigger birds in flight make up for the noise.

From the lookout, visitors are able to see across the park, where a 2002 fire ripped through the forest, destroying much of the area. The canal you travel on to and from the boating docks was dug in order to save the remainder of U Minh from the fire, cutting the forest in half to protect the far bank as the fire became uncontrollable. Nowadays, the park closes for three months during the dry season to prevent the same disaster.

Travelers can visit U Minh Thuong on a day trip from Rach Gia, as the park is about a two-hour drive from town. **Kien Giang Tourist** (5 Le Loi, tel. 0297/386-2081, 7:30am-11:30am and 1:30pm-5:30pm Mon.-Fri.) offers private tours, though you will have to coordinate these ahead of time and costs can be steep (visit the office for a quote); otherwise, you'll need your own set of wheels, as local transportation can be unreliable and public tours to U Minh Thuong are not common. Tours and travel can be booked in Saigon as well, though you'll likely need to go through a private operator, as group tours to the forest are rare. The park shuts down briefly during dry season, so if you visit April-June, call ahead and confirm that it is open.

HA TIEN

Tucked away in the farthest reaches of the Mekong Delta, Ha Tien is poised to become a frequent tourist destination, as it lies just 6.5 kilometers from the Cambodian border and offers daily speedboat services to Phu Quoc. Already, the rapid pace of development in this lively little town shows no signs of stopping, with hotels cropping up along the riverfront and several bus companies setting up shop nearby.

The majority of travelers use Ha Tien as a stop en route to other destinations, usually sticking around for only a night. While the town doesn't have much in the way of scenery, its surrounding area is filled with some of the Delta's more unusual landscapes, featuring a coastline dotted with rocky islands; eerie bat-filled caves; and jagged limestone karsts rising from the flat expanse of paddy fields. This is also where you'll find the only mainland beaches in the Mekong Delta worth visiting.

Nowadays, a handful of travel outfits have come to town, most of whom focus on transportation rather than tours, but if you're up for independent exploring, Ha Tien can be a worthy destination in its own right.

Sights

In town, Ha Tien's sights are easily walkable from the riverside, where most hotels and services are located. You'll find several pagodas scattered around, as well as Ha Tien's massive fish market, which sits beside the river for easy boat access. Farther out, places like Thach Dong and Mui Nai Beach can be reached via bicycle or motor vehicle.

MAC CUU TOMBS

Sprawled along the western edge of town, the lush grounds of the **Mac Cuu Tombs** (Mac Cuu, 5am-6pm daily) are the final resting place of Ha Tien's most famous family. Born in 1655 in China, Mac Cuu was a wealthy explorer and merchant who traveled throughout much of Southeast Asia, fleeing his homeland in 1679 as the Qing dynasty rose to power. When he first reached southern Vietnam in 1700, much of the area in and around Ha Tien was uninhabited, covered by thick rainforest and teeming with wild animals. Only small isolated communities of Vietnamese, Chinese, and Khmer people existed along the coast but rarely interacted with one another. Mac Cuu recognized Ha Tien's economic potential as a settlement on the Gulf of Thailand. Over the next few years, he set about bringing together

Ha Tien

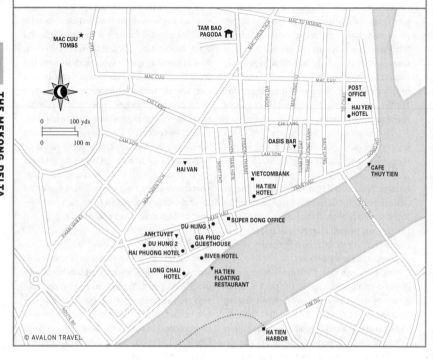

these disparate communities and developing the surrounding land into a successful port town. When the Thais began arriving in the area to loot and pillage Ha Tien in 1708, Mac Cuu sought the protection of the Nguyen Lords, officially bringing Ha Tien under Vietnamese control. After Mac Cuu's death in 1735, his son Mac Thien Tich carried on the family legacy.

Beyond the high stone walls of the entrance, visitors will find a small but elaborate temple dedicated to Mac Cuu's family. To the right of the building, a stone path leads the way up Binh San Mountain (more of a hill, really) to dozens of domed graves that line the hillside, their headstones in varying states of decay. While four generations of Mac Cuu's family reside here, including his mother, son, and grandson, the largest grave belongs to

Ha Tien's founder himself, a sweeping monument carved into the slope and guarded by shade trees. The path through this forested area carries on for a while and many other old gravesites exist nearby, leaving plenty for visitors to explore.

TAM BAO PAGODA

Built in 1730 by Mac Cuu in honor of his mother, **Tam Bao Pagoda** (near Mac Thien Tich and Phuong Thanh, 8am-4pm daily) is a small building but its immense courtyard is packed with dozens of statues, including a large reclining Buddha as well as a towering statue of Quan Am. These figures are surrounded by lush greenery, and you'll find a small lotus pond just beyond the main gates. A community of Buddhist nuns lives on the premises.

THACH DONG

Barely 1.5 kilometers from the Cambodian border, the massive limestone outcropping at **Thach Dong** (Hwy. 80, en route to the Xa Xia border gate, My Duc village, 7am-5pm daily, VND5,000) towers 93 meters above the surrounding rice paddies. Within its smooth vaulted interior, an 18th-century Buddhist pagoda doubles as a memorial for My Duc village, where Pol Pot's Khmer Rouge forces massacred 130 Vietnamese on March 14, 1978. During the lead-up to a two-year border war between the nations, acts of violence like this were not uncommon, causing many local residents to flee the frontier area for towns like Rach Gia and Ca Mau. Inside the cave pagoda, you can see photos of the victims alongside a Buddhist altar. There are also two lookouts from above that offer stunning views of the sea and nearby fields as well as a direct line of sight into Cambodia.

MUI NAI BEACH

One of a very small number of mainland beaches in the Mekong Delta, **Mui Nai Beach** is a nice sandy stretch about five kilometers from town where locals gather on weekends. Plenty of snack shops dot the shore. While it's not much of a swimming area—its sand is a bit coarse and, with Phu Quoc so close, most visitors prefer to just come for the scenery—this is a great spot from which to enjoy sunset and a cold drink. The **Mui Nai Tourist Area** (off Ba Ly, tel. 0297/385-1348, 6am-6pm daily, VND10,000) has plenty of beach chairs and vendors around.

Mui Nai can easily be accessed by bicycle or *xe om*. If you're making the trip solo, follow Highway 28 straight out of town. When you reach the fork in the road, a sign directs you to turn right toward Mui Nai (literally translated as Deer Cape); if you ignore the sign and turn left, you'll still come full circle to the beach, but with the added benefit of a nice drive along the coastline and around the edge of the cape, where you'll find views of both the sea and the small islands in the distance.

Food

There are scores of rice shops along Tran Hau street, as well as a few at the top of Mac Thien Tich, including some vegetarian options. You can also find plenty of food near the **Ha Tien Market** (beside bridge on Mac Thien Tich, sunrise-sunset daily), where snack and fruit vendors often hang out.

One of a number of small hole-in-the-wall shops on the block, **Anh Tuyet** (83 Tran Hau, tel. 0297/385-1575, 6am-8pm daily, VND20,000-50,000) is a typical pick-and-point rice cart with a steady flow of locals coming and going around lunchtime. There are plenty of options to choose from, including chicken, pork, fish, and veggies, and *tra da* (iced tea) is on the house. A second location sits just around the corner on Ly Chinh Thang street.

Meals at **Hai Van** (55 Lam Son, tel. 0297/385-0345, www.khachsanhaivan.com, 6am-evening daily, VND35,000-125,000) are standard Vietnamese fare but come with the added benefit of an English menu. Both individual and family-style dishes are served in this large banquet-hall environment, where chairs are decked out in delightfully gaudy pink seat coverings. Note that while the staff is friendly and willing to help, the kitchen does not always carry everything on its menu.

The only place you'll find Western food or any hint of nightlife is at **Oasis Bar** (42 Tuan Phu Dat, tel. 0297/370-1553, www.oasis-barhatien.com, 9am-late daily, VND20,000-120,000), a small bar and sometimes eatery located just off the main drag. In addition to alcoholic and other drinks, the bar serves breakfast and light meals—most notably, a full English breakfast—and also does the occasional special on bar snacks like hummus platters and a variety of soups and sandwiches. The owner, an Englishman called Andy, offers tourist maps and sound advice on travel to Cambodia or Phu Quoc.

Operated by the River Hotel, **Ha Tien Floating Restaurant** (in front of River Hotel, tel. 0297/395-5888, www.riverhotelvn.

com, 6:30am-10pm daily, VND35,000-400,000) is a permanently docked vessel that serves breakfast, lunch, and dinner in a nice breezy setting over the water. You may have to ask for additional menus, as the servers tend to equate a Western traveler with Western food and so will present only the more expensive Western menu. There is also Vietnamese food, both family-style and individual dishes.

On an otherwise shadeless sweltering block, **Cafe Thuy Tien** (Ben To Chau, tel. 0297/385-1828, 5am-10:30pm daily, VND10,000-45,000) sits directly over the water and provides a variety of drinks, including coffee, coconuts, tea, fruit shakes, and a much-needed escape from the heat. Though it looks like one good wave might take the place away, the location is unbeatable.

Accommodations

As Ha Tien sees more foreign visitors, hotels and guesthouses are cropping up along Tran Hau street and near the waterfront. Your best bet is to station yourself around the river area, as there are plenty of restaurants and other services nearby and it is close to the harbor for those catching a boat to Phu Quoc.

VND210,000-525,000

Surrounded by larger hotels with riverfront real estate, the **Gia Phuc** (48 Dang Thuy Tram, tel. 0297/385-1469, VND200,000-400,000) offers clean, comfortable budget accommodations in almost the same location as some of the more expensive offerings. Rooms are large and include air-conditioning, hot water, Wi-Fi, and TV. The owners can assist you in renting bicycles or motorbikes at reasonable rates.

Almost directly next door, the **Hai Phuong** (52 Dang Thuy Tram, tel. 0297/385-2240, VND400,000-800,000) is a larger enterprise that offers river views and nice, breezy balconies in addition to its large rooms, which come with air-conditioning, hot water, Wi-Fi, TV, and a minibar.

Even closer to the water, **Long Chau** (36-38 Lo 7 Trung Tam Thuong Mai, tel.

0297/395-9189, hotellongchau@yahoo.com, VND300,000-600,000) is a nice property that boasts some of the better views of the river as well as spotless rooms and balconies.

Tucked down a quieter street off the river, **Hai Yen** (15 To Chau, tel. 0297/385-1580, VND350,000-500,000) offers pleasant views on its higher floors and features spacious, bright rooms with comfy beds, hot water, air-conditioning, a minibar, TV, and Wi-Fi.

Rooms at the **Du Hung 2** (83 Tran Hau, tel. 0297/395-1555, VND300,000-450,000) are a good value and right on the main drag, surrounded by plenty of rice shops and convenience stores. Though the staff doesn't speak much English, everyone is helpful and welcoming. All rooms feature modern furnishings, air-conditioning, hot water, Wi-Fi, TV, and a fridge. Farther down the road, the slightly pricier **Du Hung 1** (27A Tran Hau, tel. 0297/395-1555, VND400,000-700,000) is also nice, if a little aged.

VND525,000-1,050,000

Though it's probably been usurped by the River Hotel, the **Ha Tien Hotel** (36 Tran Hau, tel. 0297/385-1563, hatienhotels@gmail.com, VND400,000-840,000, breakfast included) was likely this town's fanciest once upon a time, complete with small touches like carpeting and a series of framed paintings on the wall. Rooms are well furnished and include air-conditioning, hot water, Wi-Fi, TV, and a minibar. There is a restaurant attached to the hotel.

VND1,050,000-2,100,000

Hands down the town's finest lodging is **River Hotel** (Tran Hau Business Center, Dang Thuy Tram, tel. 0297/395-5888, www.riverhotelvn. com, VND890,000-2,100,000, breakfast included), formerly known as the Green Island, a modern and well-furnished building with sleek decor and a completely unobstructed view of the bridge and the river. Each room includes air-conditioning, hot water, Wi-Fi, TV, and a minibar. The hotel's restaurant serves both Vietnamese and Western meals, which can be enjoyed on land or at the floating restaurant across the street. There is a small triangular pool on the corner of the street for guests to use.

Information and Services
VISITOR INFORMATION
Despite the rise in tourist traffic around Ha Tien, the few novice travel outfits in the area are eager to sell overpriced boat or bus tickets but have little in the way of helpful information to hand out. Maps in Ha Tien are tough to come by, as are English speakers. If you have pressing inquiries, check in at **Oasis Bar** (42 Tuan Phu Dat, tel. 0297/370-1553, www.oasis-barhatien.com, 9am-8pm daily), where there is a small travel desk and Andy, the owner, can offer some tips on travel both in Ha Tien and beyond. You can also call the incredibly knowledgeable **Mr. The** (tel. 09/1857-4780), a lifelong local with nearly 20 years of experience as the only tour guide in town. In addition to offering reliable free advice, Mr. The rents motorbikes to foreigners and runs a lovely affordable day trip out to Hon Chong, the Moso Caves, Thach Dong, and Mui Nai.

BANKS, POSTAL SERVICES, AND INTERNET
The **Vietcombank** (4 Phuong Thanh, tel. 0297/395-1065, www.vietcombank.com.vn, 7am-11am and 1pm-4pm Mon.-Fri.) changes currencies and has an ATM out front. For mail and Internet, visit the **post office** (3 To Chau, tel. 0297/385-2190, 7am-5pm Mon.-Sat.), a short walk up from the riverfront.

MEDICAL SERVICES
Ha Tien's **general hospital (Benh Vien Da Khoa Ha Tien)** (Nguyen Van Troi, tel. 0297/385-2666) is located across the To Chau Bridge near the local harbor and assists with minor illnesses and injuries.

VISAS AND OFFICIALDOM
For those crossing into Cambodia at the Ha Tien border gate, visas are available through Cambodian immigration upon arrival at the border. Cambodian immigration offers both tourist (US$30) and ordinary visas (US$35). Many travelers make the mistake of opting for the ordinary visa and shelling out an extra US$5, which is unnecessary unless you plan to stay in Cambodia for an extended period of time. While both afford a 30-day stay, the ordinary visa can be extended indefinitely and are intended for those planning to work, study, or settle in the country. If you prefer to have your visa arranged prior to arrival at the border, Cambodia now offers e-visa processing (www.evisa.gov.kh) online, though you'll pay an extra US$6 for this service. Note that e-visas are not accepted at all border crossings so it's imperative that you check whether this service is available at your chosen point of entry.

It is possible to have the paperwork completed in advance in Ha Tien, but most travel outfits do this for an exorbitant fee, taking advantage of the fact that travelers don't realize they can complete the process on their own at the border. The application is very straightforward, and you're far better off doing it yourself. Regardless of how you get your visa, you will need to supply two passport photos (or a small extra fee instead) in order to complete the application.

Getting There
BUS
Most visitors to Ha Tien either come from Phu Quoc by speedboat or from the southern beach towns in Cambodia by bus. It's only 30 minutes from Kep, Cambodia, 1.5 hours from Kampot (US$9-11), and just over 2 hours from Sihanoukville. Buses arrive at either the **Ha Tien bus station** (Quoc Lo 80, tel. 0297/385-1830, 6am-10pm daily), 1.5 kilometers from the city center or right in town, where some vehicles pull up to the roadside on Highway 80 and let passengers off just over the bridge a short way from the top of Tran Hau street.

For departures from Ha Tien, book tickets through the bus station directly. There are some hotels and small travel outfits in town that offer transportation services, but they are overpriced.

BOAT

Boats from Phu Quoc (8am, 8:20am, 9:45am, and 1pm daily, 2 hours, VND230,000) arrive in Ha Tien at the **Ha Tien Harbor** (Kim Du, tel. 0297/385-0551). Several different companies offer speedboat services to and from the island, and tickets can be booked through some hotels as well as with the companies directly. You can find the local **Super Dong** (11 Tran Hau, tel. 0297/395-5933, www.super-dong.com.vn, 6am-8:30pm daily) office on the main drag near the riverfront.

Getting Around

If you're planning to sightsee only in Ha Tien town, then walking shouldn't be a problem, as even sights like the Mac Cuu Tombs are no more than a 10-minute walk from Tran Hau street. To visit sights farther afield, like Mui Nai Beach or Hon Chong, a set of wheels is necessary.

Xe om drivers are widely available and should be easy to find on the street. For larger vehicles, you may be out of luck: at the time of writing, Ha Tien's only taxi company was out of business.

If you're planning to go farther afield—to Mui Nai, for instance—most hotels can hire bicycles and motorbikes at reasonable rates, though this service is not always advertised. You can also contact **Mr. The** (tel. 09/1857-4780) for safe and affordable motorbike rentals.

MOSO CAVES

A bizarre sight so far south, the soaring limestone **Moso Caves** (off of National Hwy. QL80) are something of an alien landscape in the Mekong Delta, where you're more likely to find rivers and paddy fields than craggy mountains. Appearing from nowhere, this rocky outcropping sits in the middle of an open field and was, until a few years ago, solely accessible by boat. Nowadays, the water has receded and a road leads into the cave area where, over the course of roughly 30 years, Viet Minh and NLF supporters took cover in the 20-odd caves hidden within the mountain.

The dank confines of the caves became a haven for those fighting against the southern government and their American allies, with a makeshift hospital constructed in the hollows of the mountain. Several American bomb craters still surround the caves, now converted into small ponds.

During rainy season, visitors wade through ankle-deep waters and along the rickety wooden path that leads into the caves. Moso is far more deserted than some of its other historical counterparts and makes for a more authentic and eerie experience. The coffee carts and snack shops that hang around the area detract from the overall atmosphere, but Moso remains a mostly untouched piece of local war history. There's a small sign to indicate where the turnoff from the highway is, but it's probably best to go with a guide, as it's a bit tricky to find.

FATHER AND SON ISLAND

Thirty-five kilometers from Ha Tien town lies the **Hon Chong Peninsula,** an area sometimes touted as a miniature southern version of Ha Long Bay. The peninsula has beautiful natural scenery that is different from much of the Delta region: Rocky limestone cliffs soar above the unbroken landscape, many of them hollowed into caves, and several craggy escarpments dot the nearby coastline. The best-known of these landscapes is **Father and Son Island (Khu Du Lich Hon Phu Tu)** (tel. 0297/385-4584, 7am-5pm daily, VND5,000), a pair of limestone karsts that face one another and are said to resemble a father and son looking out over the sea. While the father island tumbled into the ocean after a storm in 2006, its other half still remains and is visible from the nearby beach, where snack and drink vendors abound.

Before you reach the shore, you travel through **Cave Pagoda** (Khu Du Lich Hon Phu Tu): Nestled within a massive rock, the pagoda's altar features a statue of the Buddha sitting beneath his famous bodhi tree, depicted in a mural on the cave wall, as well as several statues perched on various cliffs outside the entrance. Beyond the pagoda is a beach where visitors snap photos of the islands and take in the rest of Hon Chong's scenery. Tourist **boats** (tel. 0297/375-9028, VND10,000-35,000) make a short trip out to the islands and around a nearby cave; but, these boats don't run if not at full capacity. It's just as well, as the view is best admired from a distance.

Travelers can reach Hon Chong with a motorbike rental or hired guide. **Mr. The** (tel.

09/1857-4780) does a lovely day trip combining the drive to Father and Son Island with a visit to the Moso Caves, lunch at nearby **Duong Beach,** and a jaunt over to Mui Nai and Thach Dong to finish out the afternoon. It is also possible to stay at or around Duong Beach, where there are a handful of accommodations, though the mainland beaches of the Delta aren't nearly as nice and, with Phu Quoc only 34 kilometers away, it seems a waste to spend your beach time on this side of the water.

Phu Quoc Island

A world apart from the Mekong mainland, Phu Quoc has fast become one of Vietnam's most sought-after island escapes. In no time at all, the sleepy shores of the country's largest island have transformed into a bona fide tourist destination, complete with high-end resorts, an amusement park, and an ever-growing number of tour companies and restaurants, not to mention international visitors from all corners of the map. Blessed with pristine white-sand beaches, turquoise waters, shaggy palm trees, and an abundance of sunshine, the island's postcard-perfect coast sees droves of visitors during the high season, particularly December-January.

Phu Quoc's shoreline is its main attraction, but the island is also crisscrossed with dozens of winding red dirt roads and unspoiled landscapes waiting to be discovered. To the north, Phu Quoc's sprawling national park and deserted coast pack a full day's adventure, while the pepper farms and freshwater streams of the interior provide further opportunities for exploration. Avid divers will appreciate the island's underwater scenery. Though some of these untamed areas have been lost as more high-end resorts and chic beach bungalows crop up, the island still offers an exceptional combination of adventure and relaxation, allowing visitors to enjoy a lazy outing at the

beach one day and a backroads adventure along Phu Quoc's dusty forest trails the next.

Most visitors to Phu Quoc turn up November-April, outside the rainy season and when temperatures are at their best. Depending on how much you plan to explore, a trip here could last as long as three weeks, and you'd still have discovering left to do. Travelers get the gist of the island in 3-4 days, but many people tack on extra beach time. Due to its growing popularity, you'll find that Phu Quoc's prices—from food to accommodations to basic services—are more expensive than those on the mainland. These costs are easily split between two or more people; solo travelers might find themselves shelling out more, as the island tends to be a destination that sees more couples and families than individual visitors.

ORIENTATION

The majority of Phu Quoc's accommodations, restaurants, and other services are located along the western side of the island near the main town of **Duong Dong. Long Beach,** where many travelers base themselves, sits just south of Duong Dong on the western coast, while the area north of town, namely around **Ong Lang** and **Cua Can Beaches,** has grown exponentially in the last few years. There are smaller settlements in **An Thoi** on

Phu Quoc Island

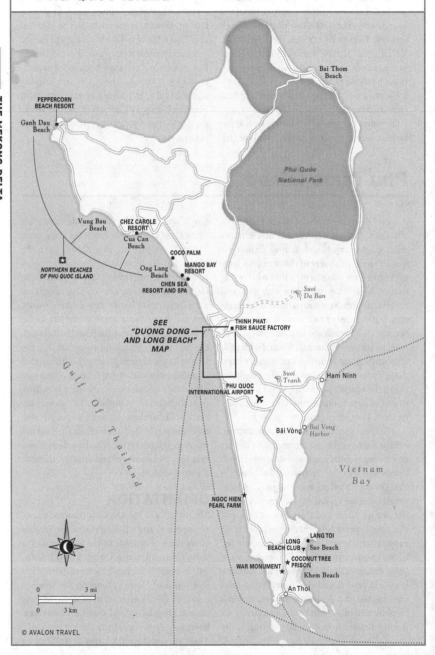

Bai Thom
Beach

Phú Quốc
National Park

PEPPERCORN
BEACH RESORT

Ganh Dau
Beach

Vung Bau
Beach

CHEZ CAROLE
RESORT

Cua Can
Beach

COCO PALM

NORTHERN BEACHES
OF PHU QUOC ISLAND

Ong Lang
Beach

MANGO BAY
RESORT

CHEN SEA
RESORT AND SPA

Suoi
Da Ban

SEE
"DUONG DONG
AND LONG BEACH"
MAP

THINH PHAT
FISH SAUCE FACTORY

Suoi
Tranh

Ham Ninh

PHU QUOC
INTERNATIONAL AIRPORT

Gulf Of Thailand

Bãi Vòng

Bai Vong
Harbor

Vietnam
Bay

NGOC HIEN
PEARL FARM

LANG TOI

LONG
BEACH CLUB

Sao Beach

COCONUT TREE
PRISON

WAR MONUMENT

Khem Beach

An Thoi

0   3 mi

0   3 km

© AVALON TRAVEL

The Dogs of Phu Quoc

Around the island you'll spot dogs trotting along the roadside or napping in the midday heat. This isn't particularly unusual for Vietnam, but take a closer look and you may notice that some of these animals have a long spiked ridge of hair running along their backs. The Phu Quoc ridgeback (*cho xoay* in Vietnamese) is one of only three species of dog in the world that has this backward-running ridge, not unlike a cowlick. Though its history isn't terribly well documented—some say the dogs were brought to the island by the French, while others believe that the Phu Quoc ridgeback is actually an offshoot of the Thai ridgeback—these canines have a local reputation for being intelligent and affable, and they make excellent hunters.

the southern tip of the island and east at Ham Ninh, a village near Bai Vong Harbor, where speedboats from Rach Gia and Ha Tien arrive. The areas outside of Duong Dong and Long Beach have fewer services and amenities, except for resorts.

SIGHTS

There is plenty to see in Phu Quoc beyond the beach, from the historical Phu Quoc prison near Ham Ninh town to the local fish sauce factories or the freshwater streams hidden deep within the island's interior. The best way to explore the island is by grabbing a map, renting a motorbike, and setting out on your own. If you're not a master of the motorbike, you may feel more at ease in the passenger's seat, as Phu Quoc's roads are constantly under construction—a smooth, paved highway can become a dirt path without warning. A handful of local tour companies provide trips to some of these places, but you may also be able to track down a local guide or *xe om* driver through your hotel who can take you around the island.

Duong Dong
DINH CAU
Perched on the edge of the harbor, **Dinh Cau** (end of Bach Dang street, 6am-9pm daily) is a small temple dedicated to the protection of all those who travel by sea. Its colorful red-and-gold doorway has looked out over the mouth of the town's narrow, meandering river since 1937 and sits just beside a miniature blue-and-white lighthouse. In the late afternoons,

this is a popular gathering spot for locals and it offers a nice view of the northern end of Long Beach.

FISH SAUCE FACTORIES
Something of an unusual attraction, the **Thinh Phat Fish Sauce Factory** (30 Thang 4, tel. 0297/398-0224, www.nuoc-mamthinhphat.com, 7am-7pm daily) and most other producers on the island are eager to share the finer details of the nation's favorite condiment: fish sauce. If you've eaten any local cuisine, chances are you've tasted this salty, reddish sauce, which is used in preparing everything from soups to noodle dishes to meat and veggies. On the island, fish sauce is something of a specialty. Each individual batch is unique in both strength and color. Heaps of anchovies are mixed with salt, piled into enormous wooden barrels that reach nearly as high as the ceiling, and left to sit for at least a year before the oily red sauce is dispensed from a tap at the bottom of the barrel, then bottled and sold. Though some batches can sit for longer, no less than 12 months is required, and each gargantuan container produces 800 gallons of fish sauce. If you pay a visit to any of the island's countless factories, you'll be allowed to look around and possibly even sample their product, but it may be difficult to ask questions, as factory employees rarely speak English. Whatever happens, one thing you'll remember is the scent. Thankfully, fish sauce tastes infinitely better than it smells.

SUOI TRANH

About 10 kilometers from Duong Dong town en route to Ham Ninh and Sao Beach, the freshwater stream at **Suoi Tranh (Khu Du Lich Suoi Tranh)** (Suoi May Hamlet, 7am-5pm daily, VND10,000 adults, VND5,000 children) runs during the rainy months of May-November. Hidden amid the lush cover of the forest, a growing number of tourists visit Suoi Tranh's rushing waters to take in the area's natural scenery and have a picnic or a swim. There is also **Suoi Da Ban** (Ap Ben Tram, 7am-5pm daily), another stream located farther into the island's interior. Suoi Tranh is the more scenic and more accessible of the two.

Long Beach

COI NGUON MUSEUM

The first privately owned museum in the Mekong Delta, the **Coi Nguon Museum** (149 Tran Hung Dao, tel. 0297/398-0206, www.coinguonphuquoc.com, 7am-9pm daily, VND20,000) is not unlike most provincial museums, featuring exhibits on the geography, history, and revolutionary activities of the island, but it restricts its scope solely to Phu Quoc. In an unusual building chock-full of small alcoves and religious shrines, the five-story exhibition hall includes English signage and an interesting collection of Oc Eo artifacts, natural souvenirs from the surrounding waters, and also a few displays dedicated to Phu Quoc's most famous visitors, including Mac Cuu, considered a major player in the island's development, and Nguyen Trung Truc, a revolutionary hero who was captured in the island's eastern town of Ham Ninh in 1868. From its many balconies Coi Nguon offers a nice view of Long Beach and the main drag along Tran Hung Dao.

PEARL FARMS

On the road from Long Beach south to An Thoi are a string of massive jewelry companies that harvest local pearls. While some bill these mega-centers as a tourist attraction, they are, for the most part, for serious shoppers only. Long, unending showrooms of pearls are tended to by eager sales assistants. A few times a day, someone will cut open an oyster from the small pool out front to show tourists how the pearls are collected. Many day tours make a stop at one of these places for a brief show and then leave ample time for shopping. There are several pearl farms located around the island, including Long Beach's **Ngoc Hien** (Duong Bao Hamlet en route to An Thoi, tel. 09/8809-7097, www.ngochienpearl.com, 8am-10pm daily), which has a showroom full of both high- and low-quality local pearls. Do your homework when purchasing jewelry on the island, as there are plenty of legitimate pearl companies but also several impostors.

An Thoi

COCONUT TREE PRISON

Hidden near the southern tip of the island, Phu Quoc's infamous **Coconut Tree Prison (Di Tich Lich Su Nha Tu Phu Quoc)** (tel. 0297/384-4578, 7:30am-11am and 1pm-5pm daily) is a faded, unassuming collection of iron stockades that is easily missed when following the road to Sao Beach. During the American War, this crumbling, shadeless complex claimed the lives of nearly 4,000 prisoners, as Communist supporters and prisoners of war were exiled to the confines of its high barbed-wire gates and subjected to harsh conditions, starvation, and torture.

Though the prison existed as early as the 1950s, its worst horrors came to pass between 1967 and 1973, when more than 40,000 men and women suffered the brutality of South Vietnamese soldiers. A variety of punishments were used, the worst being the tiger cages: low barbed-wire pens used to confine as many as five people in one small space near the main entrance of the prison. Left outdoors with no food or shelter and crammed into an area barely large enough to squat, inmates in the tiger cages often succumbed to the heat and dehydration and were unable to properly stand, sit, or lie down. Those who survived often remained permanently disabled,

Duong Dong and Long Beach

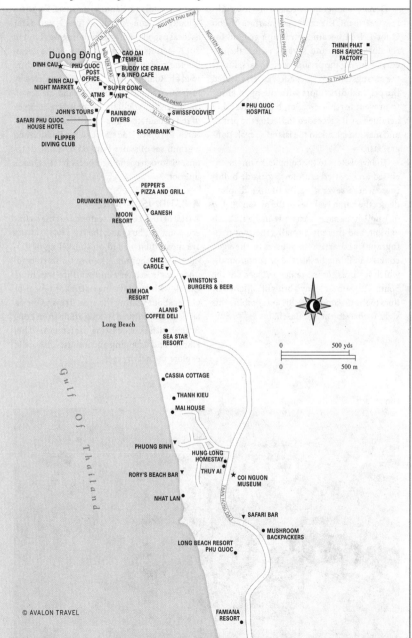

NGUYEN THAI BINH

NGUYEN PHUNG TRUC

PHAN DINH PHUNG

HUONG DUONG

NGUYEN HUE

Duong Đông

DINH CAU ★

CAO DAI TEMPLE

PHU QUOC POST OFFICE

BUDDY ICE CREAM & INFO CAFE

THINH PHAT FISH SAUCE FACTORY

30 THANG 4

DINH CAU NIGHT MARKET

SUPER DONG

VO THI SAU

ATMS

VNPT

BACH DANG

JOHN'S TOURS

SWISSFOODVIET

PHU QUOC HOSPITAL

RAINBOW DIVERS

30 THANG 4

SAFARI PHU QUOC HOUSE HOTEL

SACOMBANK

FLIPPER DIVING CLUB

PEPPER'S PIZZA AND GRILL

DRUNKEN MONKEY

MOON RESORT

GANESH

TRAN HUNG DAO

CHEZ CAROLE

WINSTON'S BURGERS & BEER

KIM HOA RESORT

ALANIS COFFEE DELI

Long Beach

SEA STAR RESORT

0   500 yds

0   500 m

CASSIA COTTAGE

THANH KIEU

MAI HOUSE

Gulf of Thailand

PHUONG BINH

HUNG LONG HOMESTAY

RORY'S BEACH BAR

THUY AI

COI NGUON MUSEUM

NHAT LAN

TRAN HUNG DAO

SAFARI BAR

MUSHROOM BACKPACKERS

LONG BEACH RESORT PHU QUOC

© AVALON TRAVEL

FAMIANA RESORT

unable to walk after extended periods of confinement.

Despite—or perhaps because of—this ruthless treatment, the cramped quarters of Phu Quoc Prison became a training ground for revolutionaries, and several jailbreaks occurred during the prison's worst years. Inside the corrugated iron stockades, jailers covered the original dirt floors with tile in an effort to prevent further escapes, but a handful of detainees still succeeded in fleeing the prison and making it back to the island's revolutionary base.

Today, visitors to the complex roam the enclosed area dotted with low stockade buildings, where several eerily lifelike displays depict the harsh realities of the prison. Plenty of English signage helps one navigate each exhibit, and there is a small gallery of photographs and artifacts housed in the aged colonial building beside the prison grounds, which features some graphic evidence of the South Vietnamese army's brutality. Many visitors to the Coconut Tree Prison combine this sight with a stop at Sao Beach.

HO QUOC PAGODA

Outside of An Thoi, about 10 kilometers north of the historic prison, **Ho Quoc Pagoda** (Duong To, 7am-7pm daily, free) is new as far as local pagodas go—the building was built in 2012—but its panoramic views of the ocean are the real attraction. Follow the winding road off Route 46 out to Ho Quoc, bordered by lush forested hills on one side and the sea on the other, and you'll find a sprawling complex of religious statues and larger-than-life structures. Beyond a jade statue of the Buddha and a grand set of stairs flanked by stone dragons, visitors pay their respects in Ho Quoc's interior.

AN THOI ISLANDS

A trail of rocky islands scattered off the southern point of Phu Quoc, the **An Thoi Islands** are most often visited on snorkeling or diving trips, as the area is known for its colorful underwater scenery and wildlife-watching. Check with local diving outfits or tour providers about visiting the area. Trips to the islands are usually a day-long affair from Long Beach, with boats casting off from An Thoi Harbor and dropping anchor just offshore to explore the nearby reefs.

Long Beach

Phu Quoc Bee Farm

Ong Lang and Cua Can Beaches
PHU QUOC BEE FARM

About five kilometers east of Cua Can Beach, the **Phu Quoc Bee Farm** (Cua Can, tel. 09/6666-3365, www.phuquocbeefarm. com, 9am-5pm, daily) is dedicated to saving its namesake insect. The farm, which was founded by a mainlander devoted to environmental responsibility, is home not only to bees but an array of local plants, flowers, and herbs. When you arrive, chances are one of the farm's eager young staff will give you a quick rundown of the place and introduce you to the bees before setting you free to stroll the garden on your own. Once you're done, grab a drink in the small café area, where every beverage contains at least some honey, or try any one of the farm's infused drinks, which include lemongrass, turmeric, ginger, cinnamon, and even garlic.

BEACHES

As tourism develops on Phu Quoc, the island's public beaches have begun to disappear. Though you'll still find several public access points along Long Beach, the most popular stretch of coast, Phu Quoc's other public beaches can be tricky to access and, at times, spoiled by rubbish. Find a good spot to lay your towel, however, and you can easily pass a few hours in the sand.

Long Beach

Long Beach is the island's most popular stretch of sand. Most of Long Beach has been chopped up by individual resorts and other businesses, but there are still a few bits left for the budget traveler, and it is walkable from any of the accommodations along Tran Hung Dao. Long Beach has dozens of bars and restaurants right on the shoreline, making it easy to grab a quick bite or a seaside drink. Though prices are steeper, it's worth it to buy a drink if only for the beach chairs offered. There are also several women advertising beach-side spa and massage services at low prices. For public beach access, your best bet is Tran Hung Dao's alleys 100 and 118.

Sao Beach

Tucked in a shallow cove on the southeastern coast, **Sao Beach (Bai Sao)** has earned enough attention from travelers to house a handful of seaside restaurants and a growing number of services, such as beach chairs and Jet Ski rentals. About 30 minutes' drive from Duong Dong town over mostly paved roads, development in the area has really begun to take off, making Sao Beach a relatively popular spot, though still not as busy as Long Beach.

You can gain access to the beach if your order food or drinks, or rent beach equipment, at certain facilities. Most people visit the beach park at the inaccurately named **Long Beach Club** (Hamlet 4, An Thoi, tel. 09/1242-0347, 8am-6pm daily), a tourist complex that rents out lounge chairs and other beach-going equipment in addition to housing a restaurant, bar, and small souvenir shop. Though this is the most expensive of the beach-side businesses, this venue also sports the cleanest shoreline. A quick wander down the shore brings you to **Lang Toi** (Bai Sao, tel. 0297/397-2123, 8am-8pm daily), a restaurant and guesthouse combo where the beach chairs are free for restaurant or overnight guests and prices are more reasonable. The folks at Lang Toi also rent out a series of small bungalows (VND1,200,000-1,400,000). Rooms are pretty minimal but comfortable. You will be bound to the place for breakfast, lunch, and dinner, as it is the only restaurant around for kilometers.

★ Northern Beaches

While Sao Beach is hailed as one of the most beautiful spots on the island and Long Beach is equipped with everything you could ever need, Phu Quoc's northern beaches give both spots a run for their money.

The more tranquil sands of these northern beaches have changed a great deal in the past few years, with large sections of the coast now occupied by various resorts, limiting public access.

But there are still such lovely spots to be found. The palm-fringed sands around Ganh Dau near Phu Quoc's northwestern point embody the best of the island's tropical scenery. And to the northeast, Bai Thom's rugged and rocky surroundings make a perfect rest stop for anyone exploring the island by motorbike.

Some of the more easygoing resort owners still allow beach access, provided you're a restaurant guest. This varies from place to place, so you may want to call ahead at specific resorts to check.

Navigating Phu Quoc's northern roads can be a bit tricky, as you'll be lucky to find a street sign of any kind north of Duong Dong. It's best to bring a map and remain patient, as you're likely to get lost a few times before reaching your destination.

ONG LANG BEACH

Not far from town, **Ong Lang Beach** is a quiet stretch of sand that is beginning to see more private resorts. Though its ocean-side real estate is hemmed in by a sea wall, the grassy field around the beach turns this area into something of a park where regular weekend visitors turn up for picnics and fresh air. The end of a narrow rutted path leads onto the beach's public access area, where visitors can

Ong Lang Beach

park and walk farther along the sand. You'll find a handful of snack and drink vendors here, and the restaurant at **Coco Palm Resort** (tel. 0297/398-7979, http://cocopalmphuquoc.vn) is open to nonguests. There's also plenty of space for visitors to camp out in the public area of Ong Lang, but with greater tourist numbers in the area over the past few years, the public beach sees its share of garbage. For the cleanest stretch of shoreline, you're better off grabbing a drink or a meal at Coco Palm.

CUA CAN BEACH

Separated from the main road by dense forest and local housing, **Cua Can Beach** is a charming, sleepy stretch of sand, with peaceful waters and a lack of foot traffic. Its outer edges are claimed by several resorts that, despite their proximity to Duong Dong, manage to feel off the beaten path, while the center of the beach remains untouched thanks to the presence of a fishing village that backs up onto its shores. Access here is pretty much entirely private, chopped up into different sections by a couple of resorts, but places like **Chez Carole** (tel. 0297/653-4679, http://chezcarol.com) allow beach access for restaurant guests.

VUNG BAU BEACH

A small cove protected by Fingernail Cape, **Vung Bau Beach** is pleasantly devoid of human interference—for now. Currently, there's nothing here but an endless expanse of white sand and turquoise seas. You'll catch a glimpse of passing fishermen or the odd motorbike. Most visitors appreciate the emptiness of the area. But the area is set to change as a number of resort construction projects gear up, though for now public access is still allowed. With its relative seclusion comes limited services; you won't find many restaurants or drink shops, so come prepared, and enjoy the isolated stretch of sand while you can.

GANH DAU BEACH

Perched on the northwestern edge of Phu Quoc and extending toward Cambodian shores, **Ganh Dau** is a small corner of the island that has fast become a destination for those hoping to escape the busier beaches down south. From this stunning pristine white-sand beach, you can see across the border to the southern coast of Cambodia. As one of the more remote parts of the island, the long road up to Ganh Dau eliminates all but resort guests and serious beach-goers. Getting to this area takes effort, so if you head this far north, make a day of it, and your efforts will be duly rewarded.

Public access is no longer allowed at this beach. A handful of resorts are around for food and drink, though not all facilities are open to nonguests. One of the nicer spots is **Gold Coast Resort** (tel. 0297/657-7878, www.goldcoastphuquoc.com), where you can buy a meal at its oceanfront Wooden House restaurant and gain access to the beach (call to confirm as policies can change).

BAI THOM

One of the most remote beaches on the island, **Bai Thom** hides on the northeastern edge of Phu Quoc just beyond the boundaries of the national park. Thanks to its location, this area sees few visitors; the small amount of usable coastline and a garbage problem may account for this. While the trip itself is a fun jaunt through the island's less-charted interior territory and a newly paved road makes access to the area relatively easy, Bai Thom is the kind of place to visit for a quick drink, a rest in the hammock, and a look at the waves rolling into shore. It's a nice publicly accessible spot to incorporate on a loop around the northern half of Phu Quoc, and the drive offers a brief respite from the sometimes bumpy roads that line most of the island's north.

TOURS

With so many tourists coming to the island, homegrown tour providers are springing up. Standard boat trips to the southern An Thoi islands for fishing, snorkeling, or sightseeing are popular and often include a quick stop at a pearl farm. In most cases, your hotel will be able to recommend a particular company or book a tour through their own outfit if this is what you're after. Ask the specifics of these tours first—from the itinerary to the number of people who will be joining you—as several different outfits band together and send their customers on the same mass ventures around the island.

Easily the largest and most well-represented company on the island is **John's Tours** (143 Tran Hung Dao, tel. 0297/399-9111, www. johnsislandtours.com, 8am-5pm daily), which offers affordable large-group excursions and is often featured in hotels and guesthouses across the island. These tours don't allow for much down time and visit very popular tourist spots. Other operators, such as **Jerry's Jungle & Beach Tours** (tel. 09/3822-6021, http://jerrystours.wix.com), arrange personalized trips around the island and run overland tours to snorkeling destinations as well as to the more uncharted parts of the island on the back of a motorbike.

NIGHTLIFE

As a destination that caters mostly to couples and families, there isn't much in the way of nightlife on Phu Quoc, but a handful of laid-back beach hangouts and bars advertising European sports channels exist along Tran Hung Dao. In truth, most restaurants and other businesses close their doors by 10pm or 11pm, but anyone who's out later than that can still find a place to relax, as bars stay open until the last patrons go home.

One of the only spots on the waterfront open late, **Rory's Beach Bar** (118/10 Tran Hung Dao, tel. 09/1933-3950, 9am-late daily, VND30,000-200,000) is an easygoing place that serves food and drinks during the day and rents out paddleboards before carrying on with its festivities at night. Up on deck, a long wraparound bar serves beer and cocktails as well as other beverages and still leaves some room for a dance floor. Down in the sand, low tables and chairs are lit by colorful overhead lanterns. The amiable and outgoing Rory is always around for a chat, too, and DJs are regularly featured.

The sign on the back wall of **Drunken Monkey** (85 Tran Hung Dao, tel. 09/0925-9605, 5pm-late daily, VND25,000-110,000) says it all: "Monkey to man: 1 million years. Man to monkey: 10 beers." Along with sports TV, a pool table, and several other cheeky slogans, the friendly bartenders at this roadside watering hole prepare a variety of cocktails and also serve beer. Grab a seat at the bar or at one of the tables around the interior.

The breezy terrace of **Chuon Chuon Sky Bar & Bistro** (alley between 69 and 71 Tran Hung Dao, tel. 0297/360-8883, www. chuonchuonbistro.com, 7am-11pm daily, VND35,000-155,000) is a must-visit for its sky-high panoramas of Duong Dong town and the ocean. Perched above the busy road parallel to Long Beach's main drag, the bar and restaurant serves inexpensive beer and a few basic cocktails as well as snacks and a few full meals. The staff is notably friendly and there is both indoor and outdoor seating available. Bear in mind, however, that a trip to Chuon Chuon involves a steep drive up—and, later, down—so you may want to leave your motorbike at home if you plan to visit at night.

On the rooftop of a trendy flash-packer hostel, the bar at **Q Hao** (122 Tran Hung Dao, tel. 0297/359-7999, www.q-hao.com, 4pm-11pm daily, VND20,000-90,000) is another charming spot for a sundowner. Its sea-facing balcony comes complete with a pool table, jetted pool, and an excellent view.

SPORTS AND RECREATION
Snorkeling and Diving

In the years before divers caught wind of Con Dao, Phu Quoc was known as home to the best underwater scenery in Vietnam. The ample reef surrounding the southern An Thois and a handful of smaller northern islands make them prime spots for snorkeling and diving, though the reef has taken a hit in recent years due to the high number of tourists visiting the island. Several outfits run day trips to each of these locations a few times a week, with the southern An Thois being the best of the bunch.

If you're interested in snorkeling and don't mind spending more cash, opt for a trip through one of the dive shops, as they are guaranteed to have less people on board as well as high-quality equipment, and the amount of time you spend in the water will be far greater than it is on cheaper excursions.

The longest-running PADI-certified dive center in the country, **Rainbow Divers** (11 Tran Hung Dao, tel. 09/1340-0964, www.divevietnam.com, 8am-9pm daily, VND680,000-9,668,000) is far and away the island's best-known brand. Like most outfits, Rainbow alternates day trips to the northern and southern islands of Phu Quoc each week, as well as offering night dives, snorkeling, and full-fledged diving certification for first-timers. All gear is included in the company's fees, and additional rental gear (such as GoPros and other underwater gadgets) can be rented from the shop.

One of the fastest-growing outfits on the island, **Flipper Diving Club** (60 Tran Hung Dao, tel. 09/3940-2872, www.flipperdiving.com, 8am-9pm daily, VND700,000-8,400,000) is also PADI-certified and organizes single- and multiple-day diving and snorkeling trips to both the northern islands and the An Thoi area. A variety of supplementary PADI courses are available.

Vinpearl Land Amusement Park

Take a drive up the northwestern coast and it's impossible to miss the behemoth that is **Vinpearl Land** (Ganh Dau, tel. 1/900-6677 ext. 2, www.phuquoc.vinpearlland.com, 9am-9pm daily, VND500,000-850,000). The sprawling complex includes an amusement park, an aquarium, a safari-style zoo, a water park, and a resort. Visitors can opt for park-only access (VND500,000) or spring for a combo ticket (VND850,000) into both the amusement park area and the zoo. Bear in mind that tickets are only valid for the day of

purchase, so you'll want to make this a full-day event.

Massages and Spas

Many of the island's resorts offer massage and other spa treatments in-house, though these are often expensive. For budget travelers, local masseuses set up shop on Long Beach, offering cheap spa services. There are one or two independent outfits on the waterfront that operate out of a proper shop, but these seem to provide a level of service that doesn't match the higher price.

FOOD

When it comes to dining on the island, Phu Quoc offers a much wider variety of cuisines than most destinations in the Mekong Delta. All along Tran Hung Dao, you'll find dozens of restaurants offering European and Asian dishes. These eateries are more expensive than their mainland counterparts, but their variety and the quality of the food usually make up for this increase. The cheapest option is local fare, with the Bach Dang Night Market being a popular spot to enjoy delicious local cuisine and fresh seafood. Thanks to the island's many foreign visitors, travelers will find plenty of vegetarian options available.

Vietnamese

For a taste of local fare, head to the **Bach Dang Night Market** (Bach Dang, 6pm-11pm daily), a bustling open-air affair where vendors roll out cartloads of fresh seafood—some of it still swimming—and diners are able to select their meal. With everything from fish and squid to prawns as big as your head, the market features mostly seafood but also offers a handful of other choices.

From morning to night, the beachside restaurant at **Phuong Binh** (Alley 118 Tran Hung Dao, tel. 0297/399-4101, www.phuongbinhhouse.com, 7:30am-10:30pm daily, VND30,000-150,000) offers a menu of mostly Vietnamese dishes with a few Western options and sees a steady crowd throughout the day.

It's located beside the public beach entrance off Alley 118, and is one of the more affordable spots right on the water.

The trendy black-and-white **Saigonese Eatery** (73 Tran Hung Dao, tel. 09/3805-9650, 7am-10pm daily, VND40,000-250,000) features a more contemporary menu and boasts a modern take on Vietnamese and Asian cuisine with dishes like roasted cauliflower with nori seaweed and spicy hollandaise sauce, or teriyaki pork skewers and brown rice. It also has a handful of bakery and café offerings. Both indoor and outdoor seating is available for breakfast, lunch, and dinner, and the staff is cheerful and attentive.

Overlooking Long Beach, **Xin Chao** (66 Tran Hung Dao, tel. 0297/399-9919, www. xinchaorestaurant.vn, 7am-11pm daily, VND60,000-375,000) presents a range of delectable seafood dishes in a sleek, swanky dining room. Upstairs, the lounge area serves beer, wine, and cocktails.

For tasty seafood in a more relaxed setting, the **Crab House** (21 Tran Hung Dao, tel. 0297/384-5067, 11am-10pm Tues.-Sun., VND175,000-3,150,000) is another solid option. Boasting a menu of fresh shrimp, squid and, of course, crab, you'll want to bring your appetite, as the combo meals are generous.

International

Located right on the main drag, with a narrow storefront that opens onto a long well-lit dining area, **Ganesh** (97 Tran Hung Dao, tel. 0297/399-4917, www.ganeshphuquoc.com, 10am-10pm daily, VND70,000-160,000) is the island's only Indian restaurant. Owned by the same folks responsible for Ganesh eateries in Saigon and other cities, the food here is just as good.

Now an island favorite, **Winston's Burgers & Beer** (121/1 Tran Hung Dao, tel. 012/6390-1093, 11am-11pm daily, VND155,000-385,000) serves a creative list of burger combinations. Its fixings include blue cheese and bacon, avocado, pineapple, and ham. The friendly owner is always around for a quick hello or a chat, giving the place a pleasant laid-back feel. Outdoor and indoor seating is available, and the place is surprisingly quiet given its proximity to the main road.

Pepper's Pizza and Grill (89 Tran Hung Dao, tel. 0297/384-8773, 10am-10pm daily, VND90,000-300,000) does a fair turn in pizza, pasta, and, inexplicably, German sausage. Its elevated open-front dining area looks out onto the traffic of Tran Hung Dao, a less scenic view than the ocean. The staff is friendly and the restaurant also does delivery.

Bach Dang Night Market

One of Long Beach's more upmarket restaurants, the Duong Dong extension of **Chez Carole** (127C Tran Hung Dao, tel. 0297/384-8884, 10am-11pm daily, VND80,000-380,000) is a high-end restaurant with plenty of palm trees and a peaceful setting. During dinner hours, a large wooden cart laden with the catch of the day greets visitors at the entrance, while the Filipino band keeps diners entertained 6:30pm-10pm. Chez Carole's menu features a variety of both Western and Vietnamese dishes, counting seafood among its specialties.

ACCOMMODATIONS

Like most services on Phu Quoc, accommodations are notably more expensive than the mainland. While several smaller dorms and other budget lodgings are available, local developers recognize Phu Quoc's immense potential as a tourism destination, and so prices will continue to climb. Most resorts are already charging upward of VND1,000,000 for a spot on Long Beach. High season for foreign tourists on the island is December-January. These months invariably bring higher rates and booked-up rooms, so reserve your place early and allot extra funds.

While there are dozens of beautiful, tranquil beach resorts stretched along the western side of the island, Phu Quoc is very much in development. Construction is a constant along Long Beach and up to Cua Can. For light sleepers and late risers, check with your hotel or resort before booking whether or not there is construction going on nearby, as workers begin at sunrise.

Resorts are scattered across the island, not only on Long Beach but as far away as Ganh Dau and Sao Beach. For budget travelers, Long Beach is the place to go, as you'll find a wider range of accommodations. The coast along Ong Lang Beach and up to Cua Can is filled with smaller boutique resorts that are more expensive but live up to their added value. Travelers can base themselves in more remote locations, but escaping the relative bustle of Long Beach means that you will be bound to the resort as, far from town, the on-site restaurant often becomes your only option.

Long Beach
UNDER VND210,000

The bright colors and open front of **Langchia Hostel** (84 Tran Hung Dao, tel. 09/1309-6766, VND114,000 dorm, VND340,000 d) are a welcoming sight for backpackers. This laid-back hostel boasts clean, affordable 10-bed dorms as well as a handful of private rooms and a swimming pool for guests. Up front, the restaurant and bar serves cheap beer and backpacker fare, a tour board keeps guests abreast of the day's activities, and the friendly staff is always willing to lend a hand.

At the top of alley 118, the modest **Antinho Hostel** (118/1 Tran Hung Dao, tel. 09/1933-6277, http://antinhohostel.com, VND120,000 dorm, VND340,000-420,000 d) is an easygoing backpacker spot close to the beach. Dorms have a shared bath as well as lockers. The cheerful crowd at reception is always ready to assist with travel advice, tours, and motorbike rentals, while the small café-restaurant up front serves local fare.

Though it's a bit farther along Tran Hung Dao, backpackers looking for a budget bed will appreciate **Mushroom Backpackers** (Tran Hung Dao, tel. 09/3794-2017, www.mushroomsphuquoc.com, VND136,000-273,000). With a large communal area and a constant flow of travelers hoping to do Phu Quoc on the cheap, this place draws a younger, livelier crowd and offers dirt-cheap, fan-only dorms, complete with individual lockers, Wi-Fi, and shared baths. The staff is easygoing, and someone is always hanging around the garden out front.

VND210,000-525,000

An excellent budget option, the **Phu Quoc An Guesthouse** (122 Tran Hung Dao, tel. 09/3962-2299, VND250,000-460,000) offers your choice of fan or air-conditioning as well as TV, hot water, and Wi-Fi. The guesthouse rents out motorbikes to guests and is just a short walk from Alley 118, which has public access to Long Beach.

VND525,000-1,050,000

Moon Resort (82 Tran Hung Dao, tel. 0297/399-4520, www.moonresort.vn, VND560,000-1,200,000) is a series of bungalows dotting a stone path to Long Beach. These are a decent value for the location. Rooms are basic but include hot water and your choice of fan or air-conditioning. A small restaurant and bar are set up right on the beach. Opt for the cheaper garden view rooms, as the beachside rooms can be up to double the price and don't provide much extra.

The lush, charming **Langchia Village Resort** (Tran Hung Dao, tel. 0297/399-2212, www.langchia-village.com, VND568,000-1,200,000) presents the best of both worlds. Nestled in dense rainforest foliage, the resort grounds offer a peaceful green escape with a generous swimming pool and sun chairs as well as great beach access at its sister hotel, Famiana Resort, along a pristine stretch of Long Beach. Rooms are on the small side, but amenities like air-conditioning, hot water, blow-dryers, and breakfast all make it into the mix.

VND1,050,000-2,100,000

One of the best values on Long Beach, **Thanh Kieu Resort** (100C/14 Tran Hung Dao, tel. 0297/384-8394, www.thanhkieuresort.com, VND1,600,000-2,100,000, breakfast included) is a collection of pleasant thatched-roof beach-side bungalows. Featuring a fridge, an in-room safe, a mosquito net, and a fan, the place is more rustic than some of its counterparts, but the private terraces and excellent sea views make up for it. Staff can assist guests with renting vehicles or booking tours to explore the island.

Near the north end of Tran Hung Dao, not far from Duong Dong town, the **Safari Phu Quoc House Hotel** (40 Tran Hung Dao, tel. 0297/399-9797, VND1,160,000-4,200,000, breakfast included) is a lovely little boutique hotel with pleasant views of Long Beach and the ocean. Decked out in an eco-chic decor, rooms feature tiled floors and wood accents as well as balconies in some. TV, air-conditioning, hot water, Wi-Fi, and a fridge are all standard amenities. The hotel staff is a friendly outgoing bunch who offer free travel advice. There is a café and bar downstairs.

One of the island's more popular accommodations, **Sea Star Resort** (98/2 Tran Hung Dao, tel. 0297/398-2161, www.seastarresort.com, VND1,580,000-2,500,000) offers resort-level accommodations at affordable prices. Private bungalows and double rooms are simple yet sophisticated in their decor and the staff assists with airport pickup as well as arranging day trips around the island. Sea Star has its own stretch of Long Beach, complete with lounge chairs as well as a restaurant on-site. Book ahead, as rooms fill up fast.

OVER VND2,100,000

Though its rates are higher than some, the exceptional service and top-notch accommodations at ★ **Cassia Cottage** (113/5 Tran Hung Dao, tel. 0297/384-8395, www.cassiacottage.com, VND3,500,000-9,200,000) are well worth the additional investment. From its stunning garden, featuring a variety of local foliage, to the pristine shoreline out front, the environment is a cut above the rest, made better by the friendliness and charm of its staff. Inside each room are beautiful wooden furnishings, and guests will appreciate the attention paid to detail, with added touches like tea sets and cinnamon-scented rooms. Both garden and sea view options are available, and breakfast at the resort's excellent beachside restaurant is included in the rates. There are also massage services on-site as well as a private beach and three swimming pools.

The ocean views from the top floor of the **Kim Hoa Resort** (88/2 Tran Hung Dao, tel. 09/0630-2916, www.kimhoaresort.com, VND1,125,000-3,155,000, breakfast included) would make for a good reason never to leave your room. This ocean-side property boasts private beach access, a restaurant, and a swimming pool in addition to a variety of room options, including beach and garden bungalows. All include air-conditioning, TV, Wi-Fi, hot water, and a minibar. The resort arranges tours around the island through their own outfit and offers airport pickup.

The wide-open grounds of **Mai House** (112/7/8 Tran Hung Dao, tel. 0297/384-7003, www.maihousephuquoc.com, VND2,300,000-2,852,000, breakfast included) offer a pleasant break from the close quarters that make up most Vietnamese accommodations. Set around the perimeter of a grassy lawn peppered with palm trees, these plush beach bungalows are minimally furnished but have generous baths, comfy beds, and modern decor. Amenities include hot water, air-conditioning, Wi-Fi, tea- and coffee-making facilities, and in-room safes. Staff can assist with motorbike rentals or in arranging tours around the island. Guests have easy access to Mai House's private beach.

Styled in the design of a traditional Vietnamese village, the impressive **Long Beach Resort** (Tran Hung Dao, tel. 0297/398-1818, www.longbeach-phuquoc.com, VND2,500,000-6,000,000, breakfast included) is lined with cobblestone pathways and towering palm trees. From deluxe rooms to semi-detached bungalows, all are furnished in beautiful, detailed solid wood and come with air-conditioning, hot water, TV, a DVD player, and a minibar. Overlooking the resort's private beach is a stunning lotus pond topped with a stone footbridge, which serves as the backdrop for its ocean-side restaurant. A swimming pool is located a few steps back from the water, and on-site spa services are available.

Famiana Resort (Tran Hung Dao, tel. 0297/398-3366, www.famianaresort.com, VND3,175,000-14,000,000) is a trendy modern retreat situated near the southern end of Long Beach. Its monochromatic Asian-inspired rooms boast plush beds and open-plan sitting rooms, as well as kitchenettes in the beachside villas. Guests can choose from garden or sea-view rooms, and both breakfast and dinner are included in the rates. Famiana

offers private beach access and a swimming pool as well as spa services, a fitness center, mini golf facilities, and a playground for young kids.

Ong Lang and Cua Can Beaches

VND1,050,000-2,100,000

The eco-friendly **Bo Resort** (Ong Lang, tel. 0297/370-2446, www.boresort-phuquoc.com, VND1,500,000-2,000,000) is a perfect spot for travelers hoping to get off the grid. Perched on a hillside rolling down toward Cua Can Beach, the grounds of this laid-back resort are awash with lush tropical forest and, at the shoreline, a stunning stretch of sand. Lodging is fairly basic: fan-only bungalows with mosquito nets, solar-powered hot water heaters, and a choice of sea or garden view. Bo Resort also has a modest restaurant on-site and can assist with travel advice and motorbike rentals.

Chez Carole (Hamlet 4, Cua Can, tel. 0297/653-4679, VND1,580,000-2,260,000, breakfast included) is an out-of-the-way boutique resort boasting a private beach and ocean-side pool. Each bungalow features rustic decor, baths with stone bathtubs, and a private sun terrace with views of unspoiled scenery. Snorkeling tours, Jet Ski rentals, and kayaking can be arranged through the resort. The on-site restaurant and bar is open to nonguests. Chez Carole has an additional restaurant near Duong Dong town on Long Beach that features fresh seafood and nightly live music.

OVER VND2,100,000

The rustic rooms at **Coco Palm Resort** (Ong Lang, tel. 0297/398-7979, http://cocopalmphuquoc.vn, VND2,200,000-3,300,000) are simple but offer a quiet, scenic location right on Ong Lang Beach. A collection of bungalows frame the resort's pleasant garden area, and you'll find air-conditioning, hot water, and a fridge in each room. Coco Palm's seaside restaurant serves the included breakfast as well as other meals, and the peaceful secluded beach is steps away.

One of Ong Lang's most upscale and exclusive accommodations, **Chen Sea Resort and Spa** (Bai Xep, Ong Lang, tel. 0297/399-5895, www.chensea-resort.com, VND5,175,000-19,895,000) is a sprawling, all-inclusive retreat nestled in a beautiful natural cove. Its sloping grounds boast private beach access, an infinity swimming pool, a restaurant, and a bar. Each spacious villa is constructed in the style of a traditional Vietnamese house but features modern touches such as flat-screen TVs, DVD players, an in-room safe, and a minibar. Depending upon your room, a private pool or whirlpool tub is also included, as well as a terrace overlooking the sweeping white-sand coastline. Water activities, such as kayaking, sailing, and windsurfing, are available, as are massage and spa services, a tennis court, and an open-air exercise area.

Bordered by lush wilderness and crystalline ocean, charming **Mango Bay Resort** (Ong Lang Beach, tel. 0297/398-1693, www.mangobayphuquoc.com, VND3,900,000-11,000,000, breakfast included) is an eco-friendly resort that emphasizes conservation and low-impact tourism. The thatched-roof bungalows feature fans and mosquito nets rather than air-conditioning. All rooms come with sturdy four-poster beds, an electricity-free icebox, and Wi-Fi. The resort's on-site restaurant serves appetizing fare throughout the day. Activities like snorkeling, kayaking, and tours around the island are available.

INFORMATION AND SERVICES
Visitor Information
Your go-to spot for a decent island map and sound travel advice, **Buddy Ice Cream & Info Cafe** (6 Bach Dang, tel. 0297/399-4181, www.visitphuquoc.info, 8am-10pm daily) is more or less Phu Quoc's unofficial tourist information spot. Beyond doling out useful tips about visiting the island, the amiable staff at Buddy provides proper New Zealand ice cream in a variety of flavors as well as coffee, smoothies, and some small meals. Both Wi-Fi and a wall of pamphlets, flyers, and general visitor information are available to guests.

Banks
For fast cash, there are several **ATMs** located at the intersection of Tran Hung Dao and Vo Thi Sau as well as a few near the top of Alley 118 on Tran Hung Dao. For currency exchange, many hotels offer this service, though check the rate against the local **Sacombank** (52B 30 Thang 4, tel. 0297/399-5118, www.sacombank.com.vn, 7:30am-11:30am and 1pm-5pm Mon.-Fri., 7:30am-11:30am Sat.), where you can also exchange currencies.

Postal Services and Internet
The island's **post office** (10 30 Thang 4, tel. 0297/384-6038, 7am-6pm daily) is located in the center of Duong Dong. For Internet, you can either grab a coffee at **Buddy Ice Cream & Info Cafe** (6 Bach Dang, tel. 0297/399-4181, www.visitphuquoc.info, 8am-10pm daily) and take advantage of their free Wi-Fi or visit **VNPT** (2 Tran Hung Dao, tel. 0297/399-4888, 7am-6pm daily), just around the corner from the post office.

Medical Services
For medical assistance, the **Vinmec Phu Quoc International Hospital** (Ganh Dau, tel. 0297/398-5522, www.vinmec.com/phuquoc/eng, 24 hours daily) is your best bet for sound expertise and reliable equipment. Should you require urgent care, dial the hospital's **emergency hotline** (tel. 09/8148-1924).

GETTING THERE
Air
Phu Quoc International Airport (San Bay Quoc Te Phu Quoc) (PQC) receives multiple daily flights from Saigon (1 hour, VND570,000-1,720,000 one-way), Can Tho (50 minutes, VND1,190,000 one-way), and Hanoi (2 hours, VND900,000-3,500,000). Both Vietnam Airlines and its budget competition—namely VietJet and Jetstar—fly between Saigon and Phu Quoc.

The airport is 10 kilometers northeast of Duong Dong. Taxis from the airport to Duong Dong and Long Beach cost VND150,000-170,000.

Boat

While there are high-speed boat services from two Mekong Delta towns—Rach Gia and Ha Tien—to Phu Quoc, catching a ferry to the island would require you to extricate yourself from Saigon's congested outer districts, a feat that winds up taking more time than it's worth. As such, it's recommended that short-term vacationers travel by air in order to maximize beach time.

If you should choose to go by boat, high-speed **Super Dong** (10 30 Thang 4, tel. 0297/398-0111, www.superdong.com.vn, 6am-8:30pm daily, VND230,000-330,000) vessels arriving from both Rach Gia (2.5 hours, VND330,000) and Ha Tien (2 hours, VND230,000), dock at the **Bai Vong harbor,** about 13 kilometers from Duong Dong, the largest town on the island. If you book ahead, many hotels and resorts will arrange pick up for you. You can also hop on a minibus (30 minutes, VND50,000) from the harbor. Be clear about where you want to go, as drivers will sometimes insist on bringing you to a particular guesthouse or hotel.

GETTING AROUND
Bike and Motorbike

For complete freedom, many travelers prefer to rent motorbikes to get around the island. The going rate for an automatic is around VND130,000-150,000. Driving yourself is the most cost-effective and efficient option. Some places will also rent out bicycles to travelers, though with little shade you may find yourself wilting before you make it to your destination.

Vehicles for Hire

Construction is everywhere, so novice drivers might want to stick to the passenger's seat. Both **Lang Chia Hostel** (84 Tran Hung Dao, tel. 09/1309-6766) and **Phu Quoc An Guesthouse** (122 Tran Hung Dao, tel. 09/3962-2299) can arrange reliable vehicle rentals. You can usually ask your hotel for driver recommendations, or chat up the drivers that hang around the harbor.

Taxi and *Xe Om*

At both the harbor and the airport, *xe om* are sure to find you before you find them. Throughout the rest of the island these drivers are harder to come by, as accommodations are fairly spread out. If you can't track anyone down, call a **Mailinh** (tel. 0297/397-9797) or **Vinasun** (tel. 0297/3827-2727) taxi.

Background

The Landscape

Covering a total area of 331,208 square kilometers, Vietnam is a skinny, S-shaped country that snakes its way from the southern border of China all the way down to the mouth of the mighty Mekong. While there is no official nickname for the country, its shape is sometimes likened to a dragon, a moniker that locals are happy to accept, as this mythical creature has ties to the origin story of the Vietnamese people. To the west, Vietnam shares a frontier with both Cambodia and Laos, while the north is bordered by China. Along the southern and eastern edges of the country is the East Sea, also known as the South China Sea.

GEOGRAPHY

While Vietnam's rice paddies seem to go on for kilometers across the Mekong and Red River Deltas, only about 20 percent of the country's land area is actually flat. The rest of Vietnam, from low rolling hills along the southern coast to the soaring peaks of the far north, spans a range of elevations. Near the sea, white-sand beaches are dotted with clusters of tropical foliage. The dense rainforest of Vietnam's mountainous regions, including the Central Highlands and much of the area north of Hanoi, is all but impenetrable.

Down south, the low-lying Mekong Delta is an unusual combination of water and land. This is largely a result of the region's namesake river, a mammoth waterway that begins in eastern Tibet and flows through several Southeast Asian nations before splintering into nine separate tributaries across the Vietnamese border. Moving along the coast, the shores east of Ho Chi Minh City bear an odd climate that lends itself to a coupling of tropical beaches and barren sand dunes.

The country's interior comprises undulating mountains and lush rainforest that extend all the way to the western border. Up north, the Red River Delta creates a similar effect to its southern counterpart, with an expanse of pancake-flat paddy fields around Hanoi extending toward the coast, punctuated only by limestone karsts, the same rocky outcroppings you'll see in Ha Long Bay and around Phong Nha-Ke Bang National Park, which rise unexpectedly out of these level landscapes. Along the northern border, the terrain becomes mountainous once again, rising and falling dramatically all the way from the East Sea west through Ha Giang and Lao Cai provinces to Laos. This region is also home to Vietnam's highest peak, Mount Fansipan (3,143 meters).

CLIMATE

While the majority of Vietnam never really gets cold, the northern and southern halves of the country experience two very different weather patterns. Residents in Hanoi and the surrounding region see four seasons throughout the year, though they are not as distinct as North American seasons. Up north, a cold, damp winter and a sweltering hot summer are separated by a few months of mild weather on either side. Temperatures in this part of the country fluctuate from a brisk 10°C in January to 38°C in July and August. Pack warm clothes if you plan to visit in winter, as Hanoi does not have heaters and the bone-chilling humidity can be deceptive. In the extreme north, some areas along the border even experience snow, though this is never more than a light dusting on mountain peaks and rooftops.

In the southern and central regions, temperatures remain more consistent, varying only a few degrees between the rainy and dry

Previous: Phong Nha-Ke Bang National Park; paper lanterns, used to celebrate special occasions.

seasons. Rainy season begins when temperatures are highest, breaking the heat with heavy rainfall for a few hours each day. These rains remain consistent until the end of the season, at which time a constant downpour ushers in slightly cooler weather. Dry season still sees some precipitation, though significantly less, as well as lower temperatures and occasional winds, with the heat building over time until rainy season returns. Depending on the location, these seasons come at different times of year, with the rains arriving in May down south and ending in late October, while the central region experiences rainy season from September to January. For southern Vietnam, temperatures usually change no more than a few degrees, holding steady around 32°C, with varying levels of humidity depending on the season. While central Vietnam's climate is more similar to the south than the north, this region experiences a wider range of temperatures, from a cool 18°C to around 29°C in the summer, as well as more intense storms. Danang, central Vietnam's most cosmopolitan city, is also the mainland's easternmost point. As a result, the surrounding area experiences yearly typhoons, which bring heavy rainfall and high winds, which have been known to destroy homes and farmland near the coast.

Vietnam's northwestern region is awash with soaring mountains and verdant river valleys.

ENVIRONMENTAL ISSUES

Vietnam has a poor track record on both conservation and clean-up efforts. A handful of NGOs and other independent organizations do their part to help protect the country's natural resources. Despite enacting laws to safeguard its forests and waterways, environmental regulations are only sometimes enforced, leading to issues such as water shortages and deforestation. In the Central Highlands, scores of hydroelectric plants harness the strength of the region's rivers for economic benefit, but the dams that come with these facilities often dry up riverbeds below, eliminating a valuable water source for downstream communities.

Industrial pollution has become a hot-button issue in recent years. In April 2016, a Taiwanese steel company dumped large amounts of toxic wastewater into the East Sea, killing an estimated 70 tons of fish and other marine life along a 200-kilometer stretch of central Vietnam's coast. The mass fish death affected the region's many fisherfolk and brought the country's seafood industry to a grinding halt. Though this incident was the largest and most publicized case, smaller instances of industrial pollution continue to take place elsewhere in the country, affecting local waterways and the people who rely on them to survive.

Along the coast, specifically in urban areas, air pollution is also a growing problem. Though Vietnamese cities are not as bad as some of their East Asian counterparts, rapid industrialization and expanding metropolitan areas are cause for future concern as nearby suburbs are devoured by modern development and increased pollution from traffic and factories leaves air quality diminished.

While none of the urban rivers, canals, or lakes you see may look like a nice place for a swim, officials in cities like HCMC and Hanoi have done a tremendous amount of work to rehabilitate these heavily polluted waterways. Garbage collection takes place on a daily basis, and younger generations are more conscious of how their individual actions can affect Vietnam's urban pollution.

Beyond these issues, the country's greatest challenge is bringing attention to the value of its natural resources and encouraging its citizens to clean up. More than a few breathtaking landscapes in Vietnam are clouded by reckless littering. While urban centers employ hundreds of street cleaners to remedy this, rural areas and smaller towns are often left to languish in their own garbage, and there is a general expectation that someone else will clean up the litter.

Plants and Animals

Stretching over 3,200 kilometers along the East Sea, Vietnam is home to countless varieties of flora and fauna. From the peaks of Sapa all the way down to the watery Mekong Delta, the country's range of climates and habitats lends itself to an equally diverse array of plant and wildlife. However, with an ever-growing population and a rapid pace of development, many of Vietnam's plant and animal species are in danger. Deforestation and the overuse of natural resources threaten to erase natural habitats, while several species, some of which are unique to Vietnam, have become critically endangered in recent years due to the illegal wildlife trade. Today, Vietnam is home to nine "death row" species, critically endangered and endemic to Vietnam, according to the International Union for Conservation of Nature (IUCN). High demand for animal parts, such as rhino horn, has also forced a handful of primates, turtles, and other creatures onto the IUCN Red List, which documents the world's most endangered flora and fauna. Vietnam is the leading market for the illegal rhino horn trade, but conservation efforts have improved in recent years, with nonprofit organizations launching education

The national flower of Vietnam is the lotus.

campaigns specifically geared toward young people in hopes of stemming demand.

While Vietnam boasts 30 protected national parks, not all are strictly supervised. Authorities have stepped up their punishment of poachers in recent years, but the wildlife trade continues to be a problem in Vietnam. In 2011, the World Wide Fund for Nature confirmed that the country's small population of Javan rhino, an extremely rare animal, was officially extinct after the last of its kind was likely killed by poachers. Additionally, nearly one-third of the country's protected lands are in and around the Mekong Delta, a region already straining under high population density. While the forests and rainforests of Vietnam contain countless fascinating creatures, the country still has a ways to go in protecting its natural resources and bringing endangered species back to healthy numbers.

PLANTS

According to the World Bank's World Development Indicators, over 45 percent of Vietnam's land area is covered by forest. These woodlands can be broken down into several categories, from the dry lowland forests of southern Vietnam, largely made up of tropical hardwood, to the flooded forests of mangroves and cajuput trees in that same region. Highland forests cover the northern region under a dense canopy of broad-leaved trees and moss. Inland, cooler climates like that of Lang Biang Plateau, are home to pine forests, which coexist alongside groves of bamboo. Fruit trees are common in the Mekong Delta, with jackfruit, durian, longans, rambutans, and papayas aplenty. Commercially prized woods like teak, rosewood, and ebony are raised here, as is bamboo. Rattan, an extremely durable wood used in basket-weaving, particularly by the minority communities of the north, is also prevalent.

ANIMALS

A growing number of people are flocking to the country's seaside areas, pushing many animals out of their natural habitats. Larger species like the Indochinese tiger, moon bear, and Asian elephant often take center stage thanks to their size and prominence around the world, but Vietnam is also home to a host of native species that are found only within its borders. Even today, scientists continue to discover rare creatures, like the thorny tree frog, an amphibian that lives only among the highest peaks of Vietnam in its remote northern region, and as late as the 1990s, large mammals were still being found in the dense forests of central and northern Vietnam. The most elusive of these is the *saola*, an ox-like creature with long horns that is sometimes called the Asian unicorn due to its rarity.

Chances are you won't get a glimpse of Vietnam's more exotic animals during your visit. Travelers are more likely to encounter domestic creatures during their trip: chickens are common even in urban centers like Ho Chi Minh City, where they are sometimes kept as pets; pigs and water buffalo are abundant in the countryside.

Those eager to see Vietnam's more exotic creatures, particularly its many varieties of primates, are encouraged to view these animals in the wild rather than at a zoo or tourist attraction, as the creatures in these centers tend to be mistreated. The majority of Vietnam's wildlife lives in national parks and nature reserves. National parks in Con Dao and Cat Ba have wild populations of different primates, including macaques, langurs, and gibbons, while Cuc Phuong National Park rehabilitates endangered primates, turtles, and other animals captured in the wildlife trade, providing a closer look at these creatures in an environment where they are safe and well looked after.

Mammals

Vietnam continues to boast incredible biodiversity, but today many of its mammal species exist only in protected wildlife areas. Fast-paced development and growing populations have encroached on the natural habitats of many species, including the country's array of primate species. Macaques are far and

water buffaloes

few geckos on the walls, even in urban areas. Several species of turtle, a revered animal in Vietnamese lore, exist throughout the country, from the massive Yangtze softshell turtle, of which just one remains in Vietnam, to several smaller varieties, such as the Chinese three-striped box turtle and the Indochinese box turtle, both of which appear on Vietnam's endangered species list. While the future of these animals is precarious, new species are still being discovered in some of Vietnam's more remote areas. As recently as 2014, scientists came upon a previously unknown variety of tree frog living in the mountainous central region. Along the coast, snakes are equally elusive thanks to the country's growing human population. There are over 200 different varieties of snakes in Vietnam, including 60 venomous species, many of which appear in the wilder interior regions.

Birds

Vietnam's wealth of feathered residents are a birder's dream. Over 850 different varieties of bird live within the country's borders, including the highest number of endemic species in mainland Southeast Asia. The rarest of these is the Edwards' pheasant, among the most endangered species in the world. There are also several varieties of laughingthrush that are endangered. Southern Vietnam, namely the Mekong Delta, is a prime location to catch a glimpse of the country's array of bird species. With endless flooded fields and high trees, sanctuaries such as Tra Su and Tram Chim National Park, home to the sarus crane, the world's largest flying bird, afford travelers a rare glimpse of local wildlife in its natural habitat.

away the most common and can be found in national parks and nature reserves from north to south. Endemic species like the Cat Ba, Ha Tinh, and douc langurs, also found in government-protected forests, are trickier to spot given their smaller numbers. Still, there's a chance you might catch a glimpse of these creatures in their respective habitats. Beyond primates, Vietnam's mammals include Asiatic black bears, banteng, gaur, deer, pangolins, and dugongs.

Reptiles and Amphibians

Reptiles are one of Vietnam's more visible categories of fauna, and you're likely to spot a

History

From the earliest days of the Dong Son to a 1,000-year occupation by the Chinese, centuries of dynastic rule, French colonialism, the rise of Communist revolutionaries, and a tragic war that captured the attention of the world, Vietnam's history has been one of struggle and resilience. The 20th century alone included wars against France, the United States, Cambodia, and China. As a result, nationalism runs deep in Vietnam. Regardless of age, gender, religion, or political opinion, Vietnamese take great pride in their cultural identity and in their perseverance against foreign invaders.

After years of postwar poverty followed by an incredible economic boom, Vietnam has transformed from a small war-stricken nation into one of Southeast Asia's most promising economies in little more than a few decades. As the country continues to prosper, the government struggles to reconcile its values with the rampant capitalism of Vietnam's urban centers, as well as the environmental impact of its fast-paced development.

ANCIENT CIVILIZATION

While most Western accounts of Vietnamese history tend to focus on more recent events, the earliest inhabitants of the S-shaped country arrived several thousand years ago. In the Mekong Delta, an ancient civilization known as Funan existed from around AD 100 up until the 6th century. The south-central coast was once occupied by Champa, a matriarchal Hindu civilization now remembered for its famous redbrick architecture. From the 2nd century AD to as late as the mid-1600s, the Cham held an ever-decreasing foothold in the region, farming rice, making pottery, trading with other civilizations, and often engaging in armed conflicts with their neighbors, a fact that led to their eventual demise at the hands of the Vietnamese.

Today's Vietnamese originated in the Red River Delta where, as far back as the first millennium BC, a highly evolved culture known as the Dong Son ran a thriving trade port, developed a complex irrigation system for rice farming, and is now remembered for its intricately patterned bronze drums. Hung Vuong, the first ruler of the Vietnamese people, is believed to have been a Dong Son ruler, though it is difficult to discern exactly when he lived, as the true origins of the Vietnamese people are intertwined with mythology. This dynasty reigned over northern Vietnam and parts of southern China for 18 generations before the throne was usurped by An Duong Vuong in the 3rd century BC.

1,000 YEARS UNDER THE CHINESE

In 208 BC, the Chinese invaded northern Vietnam, marking the start of a 1,000-year occupation that would deeply influence Vietnamese traditions and culture. At first, the Han dynasty was lax, allowing its colony to function in much the way it always had. But, once the Chinese began to impose high taxes and force the Vietnamese to adopt their traditions and style of dress, resentment flourished among the general population. Across the northern reaches of the country, rebellions were routinely suppressed. The most famous of these, an AD 39 insurrection led by the Trung sisters, drove the Chinese out of Vietnam for just over two years before the northern power returned to reclaim its colony. Following this semi-successful revolt, the Han dynasty gave up all pleasantries, removing Vietnamese lords from power and permitting local aristocrats to occupy only the lowest rungs of the political ladder.

Eventually, after centuries of rule, things began to come undone in China. Growing unrest along the border made it difficult for the northern empire to keep its colony in check. In the far north, minority hill tribes

The Trung Sisters

Two of Vietnam's most celebrated figures, the Trung sisters were a pair of aristocratic women born in Giao Chi, as the country was then called, in the 1st century AD. Like many at the time, Trung Trac and Trung Nhi opposed Chinese rule, but it wasn't until the husband of the elder sister, a Vietnamese nobleman named Thi Sach, was put to death by Giao Chi's Chinese ruler that the women took action.

In order to avenge Thi Sach's death, the Trung sisters launched a rebellion that unified anticolonialists against the Giao Chi administration, driving its Chinese ruler out of Vietnam in AD 39. Trung Trac became the nation's queen, her sister a high-ranking second, and the pair briefly held sovereignty over the kingdom until the Chinese returned in AD 42, armed to the teeth and with enough warriors to defeat their enemy. When it became clear that the fight was over and defeat inevitable for the Vietnamese, the sisters jumped into a river and committed suicide. To this day, their name, Hai Ba Trung, appears on street signs across the country and they are revered as an example of fierce nationalism and powerful Vietnamese women.

rebelled against Chinese rule, while several Vietnamese aristocrats began claiming a right to the throne. Ultimately, the Tang dynasty fell in China in 907, creating a weakened empire, and Vietnamese general Ngo Quyen swooped in to take independence for his country.

AN INDEPENDENT VIETNAM

Despite Ngo Quyen's victory over the Chinese, his own reign was brief. In less than three decades, the emperor was overthrown. A handful of other short-lived rulers took his place, but it wasn't until the Ly dynasty that the kingdom was able to grow. In 1075, royal officials in Vietnam wrote examinations for the first time, following in the footsteps of the Chinese empire. By 1089, the practice was required, creating a fixed hierarchy of public officials. At the same time, the Ly dynasty adopted Buddhism as its royal religion, which in turn encouraged Vietnamese subjects to convert.

Southward expansion also began, with the Dai Viet marching out to conquer the Cham kingdom of Vijaya in 1079. An arranged marriage in 1225 ended the Ly dynasty, transferring power from its last remaining princess to the Tran family, who carried on a similar tradition of success. During this time, Kublai Khan and his Mongol army began to eye northern Vietnam, thrice attempting to take over the empire. One of the Tran dynasty's most famous heroes is Tran Hung Dao, the celebrated general who thwarted the Mongols' final attempt at Bach Dang River by impaling his enemy's ships with wooden spikes during low tide.

Following the defeat of the Mongols, the Tran dynasty entered a steady decline. They managed to get in a few more victories over the Cham before a power shift came in 1400, when General Ho Quy Ly overthrew the king and claimed Dai Viet for himself. General Ho's policies proved unfavorable and local landowners appealed to the Chinese for help. China's Ming dynasty promptly returned and reasserted its authority in 1407. This second occupation lasted roughly two decades, with the Chinese exerting their unrestrained power over the Dai Viet. All local customs and traditions were banned, citizens were required to wear Chinese dress, and a particularly harsh forced labor policy came into effect, all of which had a significant impact on local culture for years to come. In 1428, colonization ended thanks to Le Loi, a scholar who had rejected the Ming dynasty's rule and amassed an army to defeat the Chinese. In an attempt to remain civil, he provided the losers with ships and supplies to sail home rather than putting them to death.

THE NGUYENS AND TRINHS

Throughout the 15th century, Vietnam's Le dynasty continued to move south, conquering any kingdom that stood in their way. However, as Vietnam's territory expanded, its rulers struggled to maintain control over the newer settlements, which were far removed from the capital. When a high-ranking official usurped the throne in 1527, two aristocratic families, the Trinh and Nguyen lords, backed the Le dynasty in hopes of sharing their power once the kingdom had been retaken. After 1545, Vietnam found itself divided: the Nguyens controlled the southern half of the country, while the Trinhs took charge of the north.

During this time, European missionaries began to appear in Vietnam, hoping to convert the local population to Christianity. One of the most famous was French priest Alexandre de Rhodes, who arrived in Indochina in 1619, picked up the local language, and promptly began espousing the benefits of Catholicism to the Vietnamese. By the time he was kicked out of the country in 1630, de Rhodes had converted over 6,000 Vietnamese. He is also credited with the development of the Romanized *quoc ngu* script used by the Vietnamese today.

Down south, the Nguyens ran an agricultural society, keeping uneducated peasants at bay, while the northern Trinh emphasized education and intellectual development. Neither gained a strong following among the masses, as ongoing war, natural disasters, and taxes left the general population frustrated and disillusioned. Rebellions were common, though they were often small and concentrated to a single area, making it easy for both ruling families to silence their opponents. That is, until a trio of brothers from Tay Son appeared on the scene.

TAY SON REBELLION

Nguyen Hue, Nguyen Nhac, and Nguyen Lu were three brothers from central Binh Dinh province whose ancestry actually traced back to the short-lived reign of General Ho Quy Ly in 1400. Like many subjects at the time, the brothers were thoroughly displeased with the Nguyen lords and unimpressed by imperial bureaucracy in general. Initially siding with the Trinhs of the north, the brothers launched a revolt in 1771, intending to overthrow the Nguyen lords on their own. By the following year, they had successfully taken Binh Dinh and Quang Nam provinces and, with growing support, managed to extend the takeover to all of southern Vietnam by 1778. Operating on a Robin Hood-style mantra, the brothers nixed taxes, set prisoners free, and gave out food to the peasant population. Their progressive policies later moved north, turning on the Trinh lords and once again fending off the Chinese to rule the entire country, with each brother presiding over a region of Vietnam.

In defeating the southern rulers, the Tay Son rebellion had failed to kill all heirs to the throne: Prince Nguyen Anh, the only remaining Nguyen lord, fled to Gia Dinh, now known as Ho Chi Minh City, and sought the assistance of Pigneau de Behaine, a French bishop. Shortly thereafter, Pigneau de Behaine sailed to Pondicherry in French India and, later, back to Europe to request the aid of the French king in restoring Nguyen Anh to the throne. Louis XVI agreed, so long as Vietnam would offer up the port of Danang and the Con Dao islands, then known as Poulo Condore, in exchange. But, on Pigneau de Behaine's return to Pondicherry, the French delegates refused to help. The bishop raised his own funds to hire ships and soldiers, returning to Vietnam in 1789 with enough ammunition to wipe out the Tay Son rebels by 1801, creating a unified Vietnam for the first time in 200 years.

Under newly crowned emperor Gia Long, the country returned to a more conservative imperial rule, with the king undoing many policies enacted by the Nguyen brothers in order to assert his authority. Opposition was strictly punished, and many of the previously erased taxes returned. Though there was occasional dissent, it wasn't until the death of emperor Gia Long that France's intention to invade solidified. Gia Long's son Minh Mang, an austere ruler and staunch believer in Confucianism, expelled all European missionaries from Vietnam and set about killing Vietnamese Catholics and any missionaries caught preaching the Bible.

FRENCH COLONIALISM

Convinced that invasion was the best course of action, the French stormed the shores of Danang in 1858, advancing south to take Gia Dinh the following year. Armed with a religious cause—to protect its missionaries—the French had hoped that Vietnamese Catholics would rush to their aid, but no one appeared. Instead, it became clear that the motives for this invasion had nothing to do with Catholicism and everything to do with business and military might. Over the next decade or so, the French managed to acquire all of Vietnam's territory, wresting power from then-emperor Tu Duc by 1874, although the country's colonization wasn't official until 1883.

The Vietnamese were caught between two evils: the French were unpopular for having taken the country by force, but the poor government of emperor Tu Duc and his failure to protect the people from harm had lost him a great deal of public support. In the beginning, some were open to the idea of a new governmental system. But as it became clear that economic exploitation was part of the plan, the French fell out of favor. Under colonial rule, most Vietnamese were overtaxed, overworked, and abused. While rice exports soared in the colonists' new open economy, all profits went to the European power. Many high-ranking Vietnamese scholars and officials refused to play a part in the colonial government for this reason.

By the turn of the 20th century, dissent sparked rebellions across the country. As World War I raged in Europe, Vietnamese troops were sent abroad in the name of France. Shortly thereafter, Ho Chi Minh arrived in Guangzhou, China, where he founded the Revolutionary Youth League in 1925, attempting to wrangle all of Vietnam's disparate Communist and anti-French parties together.

A 1930 conference solidified the main aims of the resistance from abroad, while in Vietnam, the people of Nghe An and Ha Tinh provinces rioted against colonial rule. As a response, the French bombed the area and sent many of its citizens to jail.

WORLD WAR II

Toward the end of the 1930s, trouble was brewing in Europe on the eve of World War II, and dissent in its Southeast Asian colonies had France on edge. In 1941, Ho Chi Minh returned to Vietnam after 30 years abroad and was welcomed with open arms. When France fell to the Nazis in 1940 and Japanese troops arrived in Vietnam, demanding safe passage of their military and weapons through the country, Ho Chi Minh's now-famous resistance army, the Viet Minh, took note of the colonial government's weakness.

By March 1945, Uncle Ho felt confident enough that he offered the French an ultimatum: relinquish power or face the consequences. Japan didn't wait for a response and wrested the country from European hands that same month, claiming it a free state under Japanese occupation. But while their Asian neighbors had removed authority from the Europeans, Vietnam recognized Japan's increasingly dire circumstances on the world stage and prepared to swoop into the anticipated power vacuum that would occur when they left. Sure enough, when Japan retreated from Vietnam in 1945, the Viet Minh launched its now-famous August Revolution across the country, stepping into power for the first time, just as Bao Dai, Vietnam's last emperor, relinquished his crown. Ho Chi Minh declared independence on September 2, 1945, in Hanoi.

FRANCO-VIETNAM WAR

The French refused to go quietly. Though Ho Chi Minh's declaration was met with an overwhelmingly positive response, the Europeans returned to Vietnam after World War II in hopes of regaining their colonial foothold. By 1946, it was clear that there would not be a peaceful resolution, and both sides prepared for war. Over nine years, the French and the Viet Minh duked it out across the country, the former well-armed, the latter boasting numerous soldiers. Though France had many Vietnamese cities within its grasp, the countryside belonged to the Viet Minh, who set up training camps and recruitment centers within its territory. After the People's Republic of China was officially established in 1949, the Viet Minh were able to source weapons from the north, a move that gave them the upper hand. As Vietnamese forces took back northern Vietnam, opening up supply lines and enabling them to attack the Red River Delta, the French began to lose heart.

Still, by the end of 1953, colonial forces took Dien Bien Phu, a far-off town in the mountainous northwest, hoping to turn the tide of war by interfering with their enemy's access to supplies. Instead, this was the move that sealed their fate. In March 1954, two months before diplomatic talks were set to begin in Geneva, the Viet Minh laid siege to Dien Bien Phu, bringing in ample artillery and over 100,000 troops to cut off all access to the outside world. By the time the Geneva talks began on May 8, France had surrendered and Ho Chi Minh's army was victorious.

In the resulting accords, which were signed by both Vietnam's Communist government and France, the country was divided in half at the 17th parallel with the promise of reuniting both sides in a 1956 election. While this agreement brought temporary peace and the exodus of Vietnam's colonizers, few—if any—of the parties present during the Geneva talks actually believed that Vietnam would be reunited so seamlessly.

With northern Vietnam now staunchly Communist and the southern Republic of Vietnam in limbo, the United States began to take a vested interest in the country's political situation. Hoping to keep the Communists out of power, they backed Ngo Dinh Diem, a Vietnamese Catholic with little political experience. Over the next two years, Diem

A statue commemorates the victory over French forces at Dien Bien Phu.

exercised strict control over religious groups in the Mekong Delta and quashed any dissent in Saigon. By 1955, Diem openly rejected the elections meant to reunify Vietnam and instead held his own rigged referendum, winning the presidency by a landslide.

Using his own family and connections, Diem fashioned himself a cabinet of leaders and began to rule, making little effort to win over public support. As the 1950s drew to a close, the southern government had become so careless with its power that many of the Communists who had opted to go north after the Geneva Accords returned in order to stage attacks against Diem's government. In the city, regular protests took place. Diem attempted to resettle all South Vietnamese into what he termed "strategic hamlets," an effort to separate average civilians from the NLF rebels fighting against him. These villages turned out to be a breeding ground for NLF converts, as South Vietnamese did not take kindly to leaving their homes and rebel fighters were able to tunnel beneath the

Long Hung Church, site of one of the bloodiest battles of the Vietnam War

receptiveness to a coup. They were hardly met with resistance.

By November, the generals of South Vietnam realized their plan, assassinating Diem and his brother, Nhu. The Americans remained neutral on the subject and, less than a month later, President John F. Kennedy met the same fate, shaking the stability of the American-backed south once more. Newly installed President Johnson took a different approach to his predecessor, sending increased military aid to Vietnam. In 1964, North Vietnamese forces exchanged fire with an American naval ship, prompting the Gulf of Tonkin Resolution, which granted President Johnson the power to take "necessary measures" against the Vietnamese Communists. Air strikes were ordered against the north, but American planes alone could not keep the enemy from advancing. Eventually, ground troops began to pour into Vietnam, their numbers swelling to 485,000 by the end of 1967. Defoliants like Agent Orange were used to destroy the dense rainforests where NLF and North Vietnamese forces hid, and heavy bombing ravaged the countryside. Americans at home, meanwhile, began to express their growing disapproval of the war, questioning the role of U.S. troops in the conflict and the increasing civilian casualties.

The 1968 Tet Offensive proved a turning point for the war. On January 31, the eve of the country's biggest holiday, North Vietnamese and NLF forces launched a coordinated attack. Five major cities, 36 provincial capitals, 64 district capitals, and over two dozen airfields were targeted and some taken over by Communist forces. Though U.S. soldiers ultimately regained the territory lost during these attacks, the event did major damage to public sentiment at home, where Americans were being told that victory was imminent. Instead, footage of the Tet battles broadcast around the world showed a far more dire situation.

In 1969, with troop numbers already exceeding 500,000, President Nixon began to withdraw American soldiers from Vietnam, a move that was met with approval at home

hamlets, establishing access to this increasingly disgruntled population.

VIETNAM WAR

By 1963, tensions in South Vietnam had reached a fever pitch: across Saigon, civilians routinely demonstrated against Diem's corrupt government. For his part, the president showed no interest in appeasing his public and carried on in the same disconnected fashion. When the Venerable Thich Quang Duc, senior monk of a Saigonese pagoda, lit himself on fire in the middle of a downtown intersection one morning in June, photos of the scene were splashed across front pages worldwide. In the face of an international outcry, Diem and his cronies remained flippant. Madame Nhu, the wife of Diem's brother and a powerful behind-the-scenes player, famously referred to the event as a "barbecue." However, the military arm of Diem's government saw the writing on the wall and discreetly approached the U.S. government in order to gauge their but only worsened the low morale of troops left behind. The new president pushed for "Vietnamization," handing over control to South Vietnamese forces. Peace talks were arranged in Paris. But, by 1971, little progress had been made. Meanwhile, news of the My Lai massacre, in which U.S. troops killed hundreds of unarmed Vietnamese in Quang Ngai province, was made public, as were Nixon's secret bombings of Communist bases in Cambodia, both of which fueled public outrage in the United States. Over the next two years, the United States and North Vietnam's Communist government went back and forth at the negotiating table, using military attacks to encourage their adversaries to bargain. On January 27, 1973, the Agreement on Ending the War and Restoring Peace in Vietnam was signed by North Vietnam, South Vietnam, and the United States and a cease-fire went into effect the following day.

By the end of March, the last American military units left Vietnam. Over the next two years, the country continued to suffer casualties as an ineffective South Vietnamese government aimed to win over civilians while its military, with a soaring number of deserters and the NLF hot on their heels, rapidly came undone. The following year, North Vietnamese forces made a push to reclaim the areas they had lost. On April 30, 1975, North Vietnamese tanks crashed through the gates of Saigon's Independence Palace, marking the end of the 30-year conflict.

AFTER 1975

At peace for the first time in 30 years, Vietnam's Communist government found itself faced with a new challenge: how to take a ravaged, war-stricken nation and bring it out of poverty. Still reeling from the after-effects of war and deeply paranoid about the possibility of any more foreign invaders, the country closed itself off from the world. This proved to be a justifiable concern, as brief border skirmishes with China and a two-year war with Cambodia followed; both conflicts were resolved by the end of 1979. Meanwhile, South Vietnam supporters were sent to study sessions and reeducation camps, essentially hard labor outfits, in order to restructure southern society to match the wishes of the northern government. Surveillance was heavy throughout the country, as the new government worked hard to squash any and all dissent. A central economy, built on austerity, steered people forward over the next decade or so, but it soon became clear that this government-run system was doing nothing to bring the average Vietnamese out of abject poverty.

For this reason, the government instituted *doi moi* in the mid-1980s, a series of economic reforms which eventually transitioned Vietnam to a market economy. As 1990 approached, the country began to open up again to the world. These reforms became the saving grace of Vietnam: in just two decades, *doi moi* took Vietnam's poverty rate from 60 percent of the population to 17 percent.

Today, Vietnam is a dynamic and fast-developing country. For better or worse, rapid economic growth has led to a host of environmental changes. In rural areas, the effects of climate change have weighed heavily on the country's agricultural sector, causing an influx of rural migrants to head for the city. In urban Vietnam, heavy traffic congestion, strained infrastructure, and increased air pollution have begun to affect local residents' quality of life. Still, in many ways Vietnam's strong growth and steady foreign investment have paid off: Thanks to rising incomes, the country is now home to a growing middle-class, and young people in Vietnam today have greater access to education and employment opportunities.

Government and Economy

GOVERNMENT

The Socialist Republic of Vietnam is a one-party Communist state. Its legislative body, the National Assembly, consists of 500 representatives who meet twice a year and are elected for five-year terms by popular vote. This organization has the power to both make and amend the country's laws, as well as its constitution, and is responsible for voting in the government's highest officials, including the president and prime minister. Both of these offices belong to the Politburo (executive branch) and are among the highest positions of power in the country. In addition to the president, the highest office in Vietnam, and the prime minister he appoints, several other ministers are proposed by the prime minister for specific areas such as finance, education and training, foreign affairs, and public security, and later approved by the National Assembly, rounding out the rest of the high-ranking cabinet. Both the president and the prime minister can serve up to two terms.

Elections for National Assembly delegates are held once every five years. This is the only governmental body to be selected by popular vote, but due to the fact that Vietnam is a one-party state, there is little difference from one candidate to another. Still, these elected officials—party members who have been chosen for the public to select—are responsible for voting in a president, who later has the power to select a prime minister.

ECONOMY

While Vietnam's economy took a rocky turn after the American War, stifled by strict centralized policies, the *doi moi* economic reforms of the mid-1980s opened the country to international trade and industrial development. Once a solely agricultural society, industry has made its way into the country, with plenty of foreign enterprises setting up offices in major cities, particularly Ho Chi Minh City. Vietnam has become an especially attractive destination for foreign firms to outsource work in garment and textile production, as well as electronics and food processing. Though growth has slowed somewhat

This colossal stone structure houses HCMC's branch of the State Bank of Vietnam.

in recent years, the country continues to make economic gains, albeit at a slower rate.

Today, much of Vietnam's wealth is concentrated in urban areas along the coast. The majority of Vietnam's rapidly growing middle class lives here, where greater work and educational opportunities are available. Rural areas remain at a disadvantage. Family members who move away from the countryside or overseas often remit part of their salary back to these rural communities as financial assistance—Vietnam is one of the top-10 remittance-receiving nations in the world. As economic growth slows in Vietnam, its poorest citizens remain in very remote areas where infrastructure is weak and access to education, job opportunities, and even basic necessities is limited. In the mountainous northern and interior regions, this lack of infrastructure and opportunity tends to affect minority communities more heavily than their ethnic Vietnamese counterparts. Meanwhile, a select group of urban Vietnamese are considered ultra-wealthy, boasting a net worth of US$30 million or more, highlighting the country's growing income disparity.

People and Culture

DEMOGRAPHY

Although Vietnam comprises 54 separate ethnic groups, the Kinh (ethnic Vietnamese) make up an overwhelming 87 percent of the population, which is now an estimated 93.7 million. Thanks to this rapid growth, a two-child rule is loosely in effect throughout Vietnam; while it is seldom enforced, you'll see signs across the country encouraging families to stop at two babies. Vietnam is an incredibly literate society, with over 90 percent of the country able to read and write.

The majority of Vietnam's population lives on or near the coast, leaving the more remote mountain areas for the country's ethnic minorities, once known to the French as *montagnards,* an array of small, tight-knit groups that still lead traditional farming lives and practice many of the same customs as their ancestors. In the Mekong Delta, a healthy Khmer community lives among the region's Kinh farmers, practicing their own brand of Buddhism, as do small isolated groups of Muslim Cham. The mountainous areas of the Central Highlands are inhabited by the Gia Rai, E De, and Churu, among other groups, while the soaring peaks around Sapa and the rest of the northwest are home to the Dao, Giay, Thai, and H'mong people, each with their own language, culture, and traditions. While these are some of the most diverse areas in the country, they are also the least developed and, in many cases, the poorest.

RELIGION

Vietnam is a largely Mahayana Buddhist country, with most people paying a visit to the local pagoda every few weeks. The country's religious beliefs are deeply influenced by Chinese beliefs, with traces of Taoism and Confucianism. Thanks to its former European ties, a strong Catholic following also exists, though their numbers are nowhere near as great as the Buddhist community. Several smaller, homegrown religions were invented in the 20th century in the Mekong Delta area, including Caodaism, a syncretic faith in which Victor Hugo and Elvis are considered saints, and Hoa Hao, which amassed a large following in the mid-1900s but later faded out after its military involvement in the Franco-Vietnam War.

Vietnamese culture includes a strong spiritual aspect, and most locals believe in worshipping their ancestors. In addition to the many pagodas and Roman Catholic churches throughout the country, the vibrant Caodaist temples, and even a small collection of local mosques, Vietnam boasts several temples in

Death Rituals

Vietnam's approach to death is different than that of the Western world. Regardless of religion, Vietnamese believe in ancestor worship. These include blood relatives as well as collective national ancestors like Ho Chi Minh or Tran Hung Dao. When a Vietnamese person dies, it is believed that one's life does not end but that the afterlife begins. The afterlife requires basic necessities, such as food, clothing, and money, all of which a family must provide for its deceased loved ones. In most homes, shops, and businesses, you'll find a small altar where local residents put food, beverages, and occasionally cigarettes for the dead. These offerings are often accompanied by prayers and incense. On holidays and certain Buddhist festivals, Vietnamese burn paper money and clothing for their ancestors to use in the afterlife. While it's bad luck for the living to keep these items, you'll likely spot stray hundred dollar bills on the sidewalk or in the streets. Though they're flimsier than the actual currency, these paper notes are surprisingly accurate—until you turn them over to find the phrase "Bank of the Dead" instead of "In God We Trust."

Beyond these ongoing rituals, Vietnamese funerals are a multiple-day affair meant to usher a loved one into the afterlife. When a Vietnamese person dies, his or her family will mourn for several days, inviting friends and family as well as a religious leader to say goodbye. Mourners often wear white headbands. The funeral, held at home, usually includes a large tent set up in front of the building for guests to visit. An altar, complete with offerings and portrait of the deceased, is set up inside. At the end of the mourning period, the body is placed in a coffin and carried to its final resting place in a large truck-like hearse, usually decorated with colorful symbols; some Vietnamese are cremated. This final procession begins before sunrise, sometimes as early as 4am-5am, and often involves a marching band. Don't be surprised if you wake up in the wee hours of the morning to trumpets and crashing cymbals—this is simply someone on their way to the afterlife.

Once the funeral is complete, Vietnamese carry on providing the essentials for their ancestors through offerings. The day of a person's death, rather than his or her birth, is remembered and celebrated as a holiday. This occasion, called *dam gio*, is a family event, in which members of that particular house come together and give offerings to their deceased relative, visit with family and friends, and often make trips to the local pagoda or church to commemorate the individual. Contrary to Western ideas of death, *dam gio* is not a somber occasion but rather a celebration of that individual and his or her life.

honor of national heroes and those considered collective ancestors of the Vietnamese people.

LANGUAGE

Vietnamese is the nation's official language and features a mind-boggling six tones and 11 vowel sounds. Though it was originally written in a modified version of Chinese characters, known as *chu nom,* European missionary Alexandre de Rhodes developed a Roman script for the language that is now used throughout the country, making Vietnam one of the only nations in mainland Southeast Asia to use the Roman alphabet. Throughout Vietnam, three major regional dialects are spoken, with the northern Hanoian dialect considered the most authentic Vietnamese thanks to its short, succinct tonal pronunciation. The southern and central regions of the country also have their own respective dialects: You'll find a slower, more fluid accent in Ho Chi Minh City and the Mekong Delta, while central Vietnam is known for its creative pronunciation and a slew of unique regional vocabulary. Among Vietnamese, the central accent is considered the most difficult to understand, with many native speakers straining to converse with those from cities like Hue or Hoi An.

Beyond Vietnamese, an array of languages is spoken among the country's ethnic minorities in their respective homelands. These languages are rarely heard on the coast, and all public transactions are conducted in

Vietnamese. Ethnic minority citizens must learn Vietnamese as a second language in order to participate fully in society.

VISUAL ARTS

Vietnamese visual art draws on an interesting variety of media and influences, thanks to its past relationships with China and France. Particularly over the last century, traditional handicrafts like lacquer painting and enamel have been combined with both Asian and European ideas to create uniquely Vietnamese artwork. While many of the masterpieces displayed in forums like the local fine arts museum are prime examples of traditional Vietnamese artwork, both Hanoi and Saigon have small but deep-rooted contemporary art scenes and plenty of up-and-coming artists whose work is shared in local cafés and smaller galleries.

MUSIC

Traditional Vietnamese music is often closely linked with theatrical performance: *Cheo,* a centuries-old satirical form of theater, uses music to communicate its messages, as does *cai luong,* a similarly operatic form of music from the south that had its heyday during the 20th century. For most locals today, famous revolutionary composers such as Trinh Cong Son, one of Vietnam's most prolific songwriters, and Pham Duy remain favorites among many Vietnamese, both old and young. Their songs are regular fixtures during karaoke sessions.

Beyond traditional music, the younger generation is following its Asian neighbors, eager to develop a V-Pop phenomenon similar to Japan or Korea, with plenty of doe-eyed young songstresses and flashy music videos making the rounds on the Internet. Music-related TV shows like *Vietnam Idol* and *The Voice of Vietnam,* knock-offs of their American counterparts, are also popular, as is the famed program *Paris by Night,* a much-loved musical revue filmed in France, Canada, and the United States. In recent years, alternative music scenes have also cropped up in both Hanoi and Saigon, showcasing the talents of young Western-influenced artists who write and perform music in their native language. Though these artists are less nationally recognized than their pop contemporaries, Vietnam boasts its own hip-hop, rock, and metal acts as well.

Essentials

Getting There

FROM NORTH AMERICA

Travelers may enter Vietnam by air through its three largest airports: **Tan Son Nhat International Airport** (SGN) in Ho Chi Minh City; **Noi Bai International Airport** (HAN) in Hanoi; and **Danang International Airport** (DAD) in Danang. From there, plenty of smaller regional airports serve the more remote areas of Vietnam.

The most expensive part of your trip to Vietnam will likely be the plane ticket. Even bargain fares across the Pacific are not cheap. Still, there are a couple of strategies to make your airfare as affordable as possible. Websites like **Kayak** (www.kayak.com), **Sky Scanner** (www.skyscanner.com), and **Expedia** (www.expedia.com) offer travelers a comprehensive range of airlines. When booking through these sites, monitor airfares 6-8 weeks in advance. While prices may fluctuate to some degree, US$100-200 either way, round-trip tickets hover at about US$1,000. Those leaving from the West Coast of the United States will find slightly cheaper fares.

It is sometimes possible to save money by flying into Los Angeles International Airport (LAX) or another West Coast airport via a budget airline and then heading for Asia from there. When traveling to Vietnam, most routes pass over the Pacific, connecting to Ho Chi Minh City or Hanoi in major hubs like Seoul, Hong Kong, Tokyo, or Taipei. A few airlines go the opposite direction, passing through Europe and the Middle East.

While dirt-cheap fares are offered by carriers like China Eastern and China Southern, these companies are not known for their service or safety ratings. Carriers like EVA, Japan Air, Emirates, Cathay Pacific, United, Singapore Airlines, and Qatar Airlines all serve Vietnam's major airports and, for a few extra dollars, are reliable, professional, and usually more comfortable (particularly important for a 14-hour flight).

If you're planning on making your way between Hanoi and Saigon, or adding on a trip to Siem Reap to visit the Angkor Archaeological Park, booking a multicity ticket is the most hassle-free, cost-effective option. While the cost is higher than a round-trip fare, it evens out when you factor in the price of additional flights/visas to return to a certain airport for a departure.

FROM NEIGHBORING COUNTRIES

Vietnam shares several foreigner-friendly overland border crossings with its neighbors: five with Cambodia, six with Laos, and three with China. These crossings are fairly straightforward but, like any point of entry into Vietnam, you are required to obtain a valid visa prior to arrival. With the exception of e-visa processing, which is only available at the country's three largest airports and requires you to secure a letter of approval beforehand, no crossing in Vietnam will supply you with a visa at the border gate. Regularly scheduled buses pass through the country's frontier areas on a daily basis and often provide service to major cities in neighboring countries. There are no international rail lines linking Vietnam to its neighbors.

Several budget airlines fly to and from Vietnam. Direct flights depart from major regional airports in Bangkok, Kuala Lumpur, Hong Kong, and Singapore, as well as Yangon and Taipei. For other destinations, connecting flights go through the aforementioned hubs from dozens of destinations within Southeast

---

Previous: Vietnamese visa; woman ladling *bun nuoc leo* into a bowl.

Asia. Airfare from neighboring countries is usually reasonable.

DISCOUNT TICKETS

Regional budget airlines such as **VietJet** (www.vietjetair.com), **Air Asia** (www.airasia.com), **Jetstar** (www.jetstar.com), and **Tiger Air** (www.tigerair.com) serve Southeast Asia's major airports, including those in Thailand, Cambodia, China, Laos, Malaysia, Myanmar, and Vietnam. VietJet, the country's only homegrown budget airline, covers even the most remote destinations in Vietnam as well as an ever-expanding network of international destinations throughout Asia. Air Asia's network is also extensive, providing connecting flights from across the region, while Tiger Air and Jetstar both fly to Australia and a handful of Southeast Asian nations. These are the most affordable of the bunch, but most budget airlines within the region tack on additional fees for just about everything; read the fine print when booking these fares.

ORGANIZED TOURS

In any given tourist destination, there are dozens of companies offering organized day trips and multiple-day tours. The majority of Vietnam's cheaper travel outfits follow the same tourist trail, offering cookie-cutter itineraries that present little in the way of authenticity or spontaneity. Larger companies have day trips for as little as VND100,000; these trips provide an easy way to meet other travelers, but the tours themselves are not groundbreaking. In most cases, if you're up for the challenge it's more worthwhile to make the trip on your own. For certain excursions (treks in Sapa, for example), hiring a guide and paying the extra cash is recommended to make the most of your time.

More independent tour outfits are popping up all the time. Many of these private companies have done great things for the country's tourism image, providing foreign travelers with exciting, worthwhile experiences that also benefit the local community. While prices are higher, these customized tour outfits are usually affordable when split between several people, and the level of service is a cut above what you would find in a larger corporate tour company.

Getting Around

AIR

Within Vietnam, there are three main airlines with domestic routes: the national carrier **Vietnam Airlines** (www.vietnamairlines.com); as well as two budget ventures, Australian company **Jetstar** (www.jetstar.com) and local outfit **VietJet** (www.vietjetair.com). For cheap fares, VietJet is more reliable than Jetstar. Vietnam Airlines, though more expensive, serves the widest range of destinations, including some of the more remote airports in Vietnam. The national carrier also has exclusive access to certain areas, such as the remote Con Dao Islands.

TRAIN

Vietnam's main rail line runs from Saigon to Hanoi along the coast, with major stops in Nha Trang and Danang. While some of these trains have seen better days, the sleeper cars are reasonably comfortable, though more expensive than sleeper buses, which, while slightly less safe, run more frequently. Trains are a great way to complete any long-distance journey, particularly with so many overnight routes offered, as you can spend a bit more money on train fare in exchange for saving on a hotel bill. There are a handful of destinations to which a train ride is even preferable over other options, particularly in the mountainous north, where winding roads make for a less-than-pleasant bus ride. The website **Man in Seat 61** (www.seat61.com) is an indispensable source of information on train travel within Vietnam and Southeast Asia. You can also check timetables and purchase tickets online at the website for **Vietnam Railways** (www.dsvn.vn).

BUS

The cheapest way to get around in-country is by bus. Vietnam has an extensive system of roadways and dozens of tourist bus companies featuring both seated and sleeper vehicles, which run regularly along the length of the coast, from Hanoi and its surrounding areas all the way south to the Mekong Delta and into neighboring countries. Many tourists get around on buses, though certain routes—from Hue to Hanoi, for instance, or the drive up to Sapa—are more dangerous than others. In these cases, it's better to travel via train, motorbike, or hired vehicle.

In most major cities there is a bus station serving both nearby and long-distance destinations. Safe and reliable tickets are available through many of the more well-known travel companies, like **Sinh Tourist** (www.thesinhtourist.com) and **Phuong Trang** (www.futabuslines.com.vn). When booking tickets, deal with the larger, more reputable bus lines rather than smaller, cheaper companies, as the few dollars you may save on a local bus could wind up costing you time as a result of breakdowns or other troubles.

While buses are an affordable and convenient way to travel within Vietnam, theft sometimes occurs, particularly on overnight buses. Take care when traveling to keep your belongings with you at all times, either in your lap or very close to your person. Sadly, more than a few travelers have taken an overnight bus only to wake up at their destination with one or more of their possessions missing.

TAXI

Even many of Vietnam's smaller cities are equipped with taxi services, and cabs are usually so abundant that it isn't necessary to call an operator or arrange a pickup unless you're in a remote area. Travelers should have no problem flagging down taxis in the street. The most reputable nationwide company is **Mailinh,** though there are dozens of smaller independent companies in various cities. While some of these cabs are more reliable than others, always check for a proper meter. Base rates for taxis in most major cities run VND10,000-15,000, with fares increasing incrementally based on the distance traveled. Never bargain with a driver for your fare, as this is not to your advantage.

RIDE-HAILING APPS

In recent years, transportation apps have come on the scene in urban Vietnam, upending the local taxi industry, not to mention the widespread use of traditional *xe om*. These services are mainly available in Hanoi, Saigon, and Danang, where you'll find Malaysian transportation app **Grab** (www.grab.com) in operation. Its services are safe and reliable, though few drivers speak English. Still, it's worth booking a Grab if you're trying to keep costs down: A motorbike ride can go for as little as VND10,000. You can hail either a private car or motorbike on the app.

XE OM

Xe om (motorbike taxis) are a popular and inexpensive means of transportation used throughout the country. Drivers—usually men—perch atop their vehicles on street corners near public parks or in busy tourist areas, waiting to ferry passengers around town. As a foreigner, you'll no doubt come into contact with at least a few of these, as *xe om* drivers often call out to passing pedestrians in order to drum up business. Don't be surprised if you hear a "You! Motorbi-i-ike!" or *"Xe om! Xe om!"* as you approach a street corner, even if you're not looking for a ride.

While *xe om* are an easy and affordable way to get around, most foreign visitors also find them to be a hair-raising experience. *Xe om* drivers move at their own pace, which is usually breakneck, and defy most of the laws of

motorbikes on the highway

honest hardworking men who make a living this way, but, like any profession, there are also a few bad apples. For this reason, it is strongly recommended that you opt for taxis over *xe om* when traveling at night, as it's not unheard of for passengers to be robbed or even thrown off a motorbike after dark, and the *xe om* driver is sometimes in on the deal. Be careful when heading back to your hotel after a night on the town, as it's also possible that your *xe om* driver has had as much to drink as you have. Never hop on a motorbike with someone who appears to be intoxicated—the streets of Vietnam can be dangerous enough as it is.

VEHICLES FOR HIRE

Cars and minibuses can be hired in Vietnam and are widely available. These rental vehicles come with a driver; while technically foreigners are allowed to operate a car or minivan with an International Driver's Permit, in reality you'll be hard-pressed to find an agency that will rent you one of these vehicles without a driver. The going rate for a hired car varies depending on the vehicle and its provider. Wherever you rent a car or minibus, be clear about the exact terms of the rental agreement, including which fees are included and which are not, before driving off.

MOTORBIKE

Vietnamese law requires all motorists to have a local license or an International Driver's License. Though enforcement of the law varies, it is illegal to drive without this licensure. In reality, most expats don't have a license and are able to rent and drive motorbikes without issue, and many Vietnamese people also operate a vehicle without one. Traveling in the countryside, you can see boys as young as 11 or 12 zipping by on a Honda Wave. It's worth noting, however, that if you're in a road accident, most travel insurance doesn't cover unlicensed drivers.

physics, not to mention traffic. *Xe om* are a good way to experience the true pulse of major cities like Saigon or Hanoi and a much faster alternative to cars, thanks to their ability to weave deftly through traffic. While the "helmets" provided by *xe om* drivers would probably prove useless in an accident, it's required by law to wear one. Even if you are advised otherwise, it's important to insist upon some headgear, at least when in the city. Voice your concern if you feel unsafe aboard a *xe om.*

When taking a *xe om,* have the address of your destination written down, as not every driver speaks English, and always agree upon a price before you set off. *Xe om* fares are open to negotiation. Feel free to haggle, but once you've settled on the price stand firm. Drivers will sometimes continue to negotiate their fee once you've already hopped on. If you stand your ground and stick to the original agreement then the driver will usually lay off.

With few qualifications required beyond a motorbike license and a full tank of gas, *xe om* drivers are a mixed bag: There are many

Affordable motorbike rentals are available in major tourist destinations throughout Vietnam. Rates usually hover around

VND80,000-200,000 per day, depending on the vehicle. All motorbike rentals should come with a helmet. Stick to recommended rental companies or ask around to find a reliable business. Rental companies often require some type of collateral—a down payment or, in some cases, a passport—before loaning out a bike in order to guarantee that their vehicle will be returned in good condition. This is usually not a problem, but beware that businesses have been known to tack on additional fees after they have your passport in their possession. To save yourself a headache, stick to recommended businesses only, check the brakes and gas gauge of your vehicle before you go, and, like any transaction in Vietnam, make sure that both you and the rental company are clear on the terms of your agreement before setting off.

In most cases, daily rentals are intended for use in or around the city. Barring certain exceptions, like the short trip between Hoi An and Danang or the drive from Nha Trang to Dai Lanh beach, you should not take a daily rental outside the city limits. If you plan to travel on the highway, inform the rental company of your intentions, as you may find yourself in hot water should anything happen to the bike while you're on the road.

When traveling long distances, such as the trip from Hanoi to Saigon, it's also possible to purchase a motorbike. Indeed, many travelers come to Vietnam, buy a heavy-duty vehicle, drive the length of the country, and then sell the motorbike once they've reached their destination. Particularly in Saigon and Hanoi, road-ready vehicles are often on sale in the backpacker neighborhoods, and you should have no trouble buying or selling a motorbike in these destinations.

Driving in Vietnam

Be aware that, while illegal, many people drive in Vietnam without a license. People also drive while texting, fail to use the correct turn signals (if they use them at all), routinely speed in the opposite direction down a one-way street, and generally disregard lane markings. Vehicles must drive on the right side of the road, with motorbikes staying in the far right lane at all times. Turning right on a red light is illegal—though it's a common practice in Saigon and seldom enforced by police in the southern hub. While the noise is unpleasant, honking is often a means of defensive driving, an announcement of the vehicle's presence. Beyond that, pay extra attention to larger vehicles when driving, as public buses, taxis, and transport trucks will not hesitate to play chicken with a motorbike.

While it is less likely for foreign drivers to be pulled over by law enforcement (except in large cities like Hanoi and HCMC), it does happen. Most traffic police don't usually go to the trouble of fining foreigners, though this has become more common in Saigon as local authorities become more fluent in English. If you are stopped by the police, remain calm and polite. The proper legal course of action for an unlicensed driver is to impound the motorbike and fine the individual, but this almost never happens. Instead, money often changes hands.

Visas and Officialdom

VISAS

All foreign visitors to Vietnam are required to obtain a visa prior to arrival, a process that can be completed up to six months in advance of your trip. Those applying for a tourist visa to Vietnam can do so in one of two ways: by applying through a Vietnamese embassy or consulate abroad or by applying through an online e-visa processing service. Whichever option you choose, all visa and visa-related fees must be paid in U.S. dollars.

In an effort to encourage foreign tourism to the country, the Vietnamese government provides 15-day visa exemptions to travelers from a handful of Western countries, but these regulations change frequently so it's best to check this information online prior to your trip.

U.S. Passport Holders

U.S. passport holders have one-month, three-month, six-month, and one-year tourist visas available to them. Depending on the duration of your visa and where you apply for it—whether through your local embassy or consulate, or via an online service—costs run US$43-180 for visas in one-, three- and six-month increments, while the yearlong visa will set you back US$170-220.

Other International Passport Holders

For all other international passport holders, tourist visas are available in one- and three-month increments and offer both single- and multiple-entry options. When applying through a Vietnamese embassy or consulate, 30-day visas cost around US$75-80 for a single-entry stamp and roughly US$120-135 for a multiple-entry stamp. For 90-day visas, expect to pay around US$100-110 for a single entry and US$145-160 for multiple entries. Check the official costs with your local embassy, as they change frequently. Those who opt to go the e-visa route will find costs much lower, with 30- and 90-day tourist visas ranging from US$25-50.

E-Visas

If you're entering the country by air, you can save time and money by applying for e-visa processing. This is the most cost-effective option for visitors coming to Vietnam via one of the country's three international airports; e-visas can only be used at Noi Bai International Airport, Danang International Airport, and Tan Son Nhat International Airport. You will not find information on e-visa processing through the country's official government websites. Vietnamese immigration does not openly advertise this service, but at each of the country's three international airports you will find an official e-visa kiosk through which plenty of travelers have safely and legitimately entered Vietnam.

E-visas can be obtained by contacting a travel agent within the country, many of which can provide e-visa services. You will be asked to supply an image of the identification page in your passport, and within 2-4 business days a letter of approval will be sent to your email. This letter should be two pages: one declaring that you are approved for a visa and the other bearing your name, nationality, and passport number. All travelers will have to pay a processing fee to the company providing this letter of approval, which varies depending upon the outfit that does your visa paperwork. This can cost anywhere from US$18-60.

While there are dozens of websites providing e-visa services, exercise caution when applying. There are many safe and reliable websites that provide travelers with legitimate letters of approval, but it is still wise to research reputable companies. Some outfits also offer "VIP" services upon arrival, which allow travelers to avoid waiting in line at the e-visa counter. These services are generally not worth the money; you're better off waiting your turn.

Despite the fact that many Vietnamese embassies and consulates discourage use of online visa processing services, in 2017 Vietnam launched its own e-visa processing website (https://evisa.xuatnhapcanh.gov.vn), which provides one-month, single-entry visas.

Upon arrival in Vietnam, you will be required to provide your letter along with a passport photo and tourist visa payment (called a stamping fee) in U.S. dollars. An immigration official will then supply you with a visa sticker and send you to the customs line.

Overland Visas

If you are entering the country by land, you can arrange a visa through one of Vietnam's many embassies or consulates in neighboring countries (there are several in Laos and Cambodia) in a matter of a few business days. Visa fees tend to vary depending upon the specific office providing the paperwork, so it's best to inquire about costs at your local embassy or consulate.

Extensions

Once in Vietnam, tourists may extend a 30-day visa for an additional 30 days by visiting any travel agency that provides visa services. Extensions are also available for 90-day visas, but they are more expensive and generally reserved for emergencies. Though the extension stamp officially costs about US$10, the going rate at local travel agencies is around US$40 for the 30-day visa extension and can reach as high as US$80 for a month-long extension of the 90-day visa. This is an unavoidable expense, as the extension process requires the assistance of a Vietnamese speaker, and attempting to complete the process on your own is all but impossible.

EMBASSIES AND CONSULATES

Within the United States, Vietnam has consular services in several cities, particularly near large communities of overseas Vietnamese. In addition to the **Vietnamese embassy** (1233 20th St. NW, Suite 400, tel. 202/861-0737, www.vietnamembassy-usa. org, 10am-noon and 2pm-5pm Mon.-Fri.) in Washington DC, there are also consulates in **San Francisco** (1700 California St., Suite 580, tel. 415/922-1707, www.vietnamconsulate-sf. org, 8:30am-noon and 2:30pm-4:30pm Mon.-Fri.), **Houston** (5251 Westheimer Rd., Suite 1100, tel. 713/850-1233, www.vietnamconsulateinhouston.org, 9am-noon Mon.-Fri., afternoon by appointment only), and **New York City** (866 UN Plaza, Suite 265, tel. 212/644-2535, www.vnconsul-ny.org, 9am-5:30pm Mon.-Fri.). Each of these offices provides visa services. The hours listed here are only for telephone inquiries; any in-person applications must take place in the morning, 9:30am-noon.

The United States has an **embassy in Hanoi** (170 Ngoc Khanh, 2nd Fl., D Ba Dinh, tel. 024/3850-5000, www.vn.usembassy. gov) and a **consulate in Ho Chi Minh City** (4 Le Duan, D1, tel. 028/3520-4200, www. vn.usembassy.gov), which are able to help American citizens in the event of an emergency. Any visa problems relating to your stay in Vietnam are better dealt with by a travel agent, as American consular services cannot assist citizens in arranging Vietnamese visas. Both the embassy and the consulate have separate hours for specific services; check their websites before paying either office a visit.

BORDER CROSSINGS

Border crossings in Vietnam are fairly straightforward. The only way to enter or exit overland is by bus, as there are no international trains connecting Vietnam to its neighbors. Frequent buses travel through Vietnam's many border gates, at which time you pass through two sets of border control: one for Vietnam and one for the country you are entering or exiting.

POLICE

The police in Vietnam do not have a stellar reputation. A large part of this stems from the fact that most police officers are underpaid and use traffic violations and other infractions as a way to line their pockets. Politicians have vowed to crack down on such behavior, even discussing a possible salary increase in order to deter both law enforcement and government officials from taking bribes; however, the practice remains common. Most cops steer clear of foreign visitors, in large part because of the language barrier. If you need to contact the police, have a Vietnamese speaker on hand, as few officers speak English.

BRIBES

It's rare for foreigners to have to deal with bribery during their trip. The only instance in which a traveler may be required to supply a bribe is at a police checkpoint, where traffic violations are meted out. Since it is illegal for anyone to drive in Vietnam without a local driver's license, if you are pulled over by a police officer, you will have to pay a "fine." In these instances, good manners and a little patience can help to minimize the dent in your wallet, but you will undoubtedly have to part with some cash. Refusing to pay the bribe is a bad idea. Legally, the police are allowed to impound your motorbike if you fail to provide a license. It is unlikely that the traffic authorities will actually do so, but don't call their bluff.

Food

Some of the freshest, most flavorful, and most varied dishes in Southeast Asia belong to Vietnam. From Hanoi's *bun cha* (grilled pork in fish sauce with noodles) to Hue's *bun bo* (spicy beef noodle soup) or the dozens of southern meals unique to each small village and town, Vietnamese cuisine's complex and irresistible flavors win over many a hungry traveler. Most meals consist of a rice or noodle base, a few fresh greens, and either meat or tofu. Portions tend to be smaller here than in Western countries. With the cost of meals so low, there's usually room for seconds in the budget.

STREET FOOD

You can't make it to the end of any city block in Vietnam without encountering a street food vendor. Meals are everywhere: in the park; on the sidewalk; outside government buildings and public meeting areas. Men and women push metal carts down the road or hustle along with a bamboo pole slung over one shoulder. At first glance, the setup appears to be nothing special, but take a closer look and you'll be amazed by what someone can do with a portable stove and a pair of chopsticks.

While you can buy anything from hot bowls of soup to quick sandwiches or smaller snacks for the road, there are a handful of dishes more commonly found on the street than in a restaurant. Sticky rice *(xoi),* for example, is a popular street-side snack; *xoi* is often cooked in different leaves or with certain ingredients that turn the rice green, purple, orange, or black. This snack can be served sweet with sugar, coconut, and mung bean, or savory, often accompanied by chicken. A handful of other sweets, including a hot tofu dessert with ginger and tapioca or fried rice cakes with mung bean, are also found on street carts or in a basket on someone's head.

There is something to be said for cooking your food out in the open: Street food kitchens, while simple, are almost always more transparent. You're able to tell which vendors are clean and which are not.

REGIONAL FOODS

While dishes like pho, Vietnam's national soup, and banh mi sandwiches come standard almost everywhere, local fare is divided into three main regions: the north, central, and south. Shaped in large part by its weather and surroundings, each region's cuisine relies upon both rice and fish sauce as main staples but also has its own distinguishing

The Stranger Side of Vietnamese Cuisine

In a nation as food-focused as Vietnam, it is all but impossible to come up with dozens of savory masterpieces without having created a few strange dishes along the way. While pho and banh mi have gained worldwide acclaim as delicious accessible cuisine, there are several specialties that manage to make some travelers wrinkle their noses.

Century eggs: A traditional Chinese delicacy that has carried over to Vietnam, century eggs are regular chicken or duck eggs that have been preserved in a combination of clay, ash, salt, lime, and rice for several weeks, during which time the pH of the egg elevates, changing the yolk to a dark-green creamy ball at the center of a gelatinous brown egg. The resulting dish is slightly off-putting in appearance. It's often included in local meals and is something of an acquired taste.

Dog: While foreign perceptions tend to suggest that Asia is far more into dog meat than it actually is, the majority of Vietnam's canine consumption occurs in the north, where dog is still considered a delicacy. Down south, you're less likely to find locals indulging in dog, but there are still people who enjoy it every now and again, and Saigon does have a small street dedicated to the sale of canine meat. Most meals are prepared in much the same way as chicken, beef, or other meats—roasted, steamed, boiled, or barbecued—and served with rice or added into a soup.

With a government ban on the sale of dog meat and growing concerns over its safety, this delicacy may be harder to come by over the next few years. The harsh reality of this dish is that most of the animals slaughtered and prepared are actually pets or strays that have been kidnapped. Given the persistence of rabies in Vietnam, contaminated meat is a risk. Many people also believe that canine meat is at its best when the animal has suffered, so the dogs are often killed in a brutal way. As demand increases throughout Southeast Asia, more and more dogs are being smuggled into Vietnam and killed, and the quality, safety, and humane treatment of these animals is fast decreasing.

Embryonic duck egg: Known locally as *hot vit lon* and more widely as *balut*, embryonic duck eggs are regularly consumed in Vietnam and several Southeast Asian countries, especially the Philippines. Larger and more dense than your average chicken egg, *hot vit lon* is consumed when the fetus is 19-21 days old—still too small to hatch but old enough that its wings, feet, beak, and eyes are visible. Like any egg, the yolk is thick and a little dry, while the tiny bird makes up the majority of the shell. *Hot vit lon* is commonly enjoyed on the street with salt, pepper, or lime and an ice-cold beer.

Pigeon: In the mountainous north where protein is scarce, small birds are often a part of local fare. Creatures like pigeons and other forest-dwelling birds are grilled and eaten with rice and rice wine or beer.

Rice paddy rat: In the Mekong Delta and parts of Cambodia, paddy field rats are a delicacy. Much cleaner than their city-dwelling counterparts, these countryside rodents are sold at the market on a seasonal basis and usually grilled, barbecued, or boiled. Dishes are best enjoyed with beer or rice wine.

Snake: Particularly in the north, snake meat is a delicacy. While some creatures are simply slaughtered and prepared like any other meal, eating snake is more often than not an almost ritualistic experience. First, the live animal is slit from neck to tail, slicing open the skin to reveal its flesh, before its blood and bile are drained into separate shot glasses and combined with rice wine. After the blood has been consumed, the snake's still-beating heart is removed and swallowed by the guest of honor.

characteristics. Furthermore, nearly every hamlet and every village across the country has its own unique recipes.

Northern fare is more meat-heavy, shying away from seafood in favor of chicken and beef, though fish sometimes makes an appearance. Hot dishes like *chao* (rice porridge) and what is officially considered the country's best pho are native to the north, as is *bun cha,* a simple but mouthwatering combination of cold rice noodles, fish sauce, pickled vegetables, and grilled meat.

Drinking in Vietnam

Though it is largely reserved for men, drinking is a large part of Vietnamese culture. As one of the world's top beer-drinking nations, this country takes its alcohol consumption seriously, as evidenced by the dozens of drinking slogans that can be heard during a weekend drinking session or at happy hour. Phrases like *mot tram phan tram* (100 percent, or bottoms up) and *khong say khong ve* (you can't go home until you're drunk) spell out the Vietnamese attitude toward imbibing. Drinking is a social event and is often accompanied by *do nhau* (drinking food), such as snails, grilled meat, or other savory snacks. Beer is often enjoyed with ice and shared among the group. If you go out drinking with a local crowd, be prepared to clink glasses a lot: *Mot, hai, ba, dzo!* (One, two, three, cheers!) is a phrase commonly repeated throughout the night.

Drinking in Vietnam can be an enjoyable experience but it can also be a dangerous one. Drinking and driving is a common practice in a country where road safety is already dismal at best. Exercise the same good judgment you would when going out at home: Never get on the back of a motorbike with someone who has been drinking or appears to be drunk, and always opt for an alternative means of transportation in the event that someone in your party is not able to drive.

While it is not a widespread problem, methanol poisoning can occur as a result of poorly produced homemade alcohol or counterfeit spirits. This is a very serious condition that can result in permanent disability or life-threatening complications.

Things heat up in the central region, where spicier dishes like *bun bo Hue* (spicy beef noodle soup) are all the rage, not to mention the dozens of tiny bite-size foods found in the Nguyen dynasty's former capital, including *banh beo* (steamed rice cake with shrimp paste), *banh duc* (sticky steamed rice cake), *banh loc* (steamed shrimp and pork fat dumplings), and *banh hoi* (bundles of rice vermicelli).

By the time you reach Saigon and the rest of the south, foods are sweeter, with more sugar in local dishes. Whether it be the massive river fish of the Delta or the tasty grilled octopus of the southern coast, seafood features heavily in southern cuisine, and many dishes are fried, including all varieties of *banh xeo* (savory pancakes), as well as a handful of local specialties like *banh khot* (Vung Tau's delicious bite-size rice cakes).

BEER AND RICE WINE

Along with local favorites like southern Saigon Red or Huda, a brew from the central region, freshly made beer is a popular fixture during local happy hours. *Bia tuoi* (fresh beer) is a locally produced lager sold in 100-liter barrels to small shops across town (also called *bia hoi*), particularly in Hanoi. Often going for as little as VND10,000 a glass on the street, this watered-down beverage is incredibly popular up north and must be drunk the day it is made, as its shelf life is very short. Men regularly gather at *bia hoi* after close of business to enjoy a few drinks and catch up. While fresh beer would not under most circumstances be considered a fine beer, the cultural experience of hanging out at a *bia hoi* in the city is well worth the dirt-cheap price tag.

Much stronger than fresh beer, rice wine is a high-octane spirit that is often enjoyed in the countryside and becomes a major fixture during Tet, the Vietnamese lunar new year. Across Vietnam, locals make their own alcohol, storing it in massive plastic jugs for the coming festivities. Glutinous rice is steamed and left to sit for several days, adding yeast to the mixture, to produce a spirit that can carry a concentration of up to 22 percent alcohol. While you won't often find rice wine in local shops, it is everywhere in the countryside. In many cases, making local friends off the beaten path is likely to earn you at least a shot or two.

Accommodations

Throughout Vietnam, accommodations run the gamut from dingy budget hostels to luxurious high-end resorts, sometimes even within the same neighborhood. While there are plenty of good beds available at any price, certain rules hold true for most accommodations. Thanks to the size of many of Vietnam's coastal cities, for instance, noise levels should always be considered when booking, as rooms closer to the ground floor tend to be much louder than rooms higher up, and the same goes for street-facing accommodations versus those in the back of the building. Windows are not a given; it's customary for travelers to ask to see a hotel room before committing to stay the night. A few other amenities, such as elevators, are not always included, but hot water and air-conditioning typically come standard with a room.

Furthermore, though public double-occupancy rates are listed in this book, it is often possible to secure a discount from hotels or guesthouses depending on the season, the length of your stay, and the number of rooms available. Many hotels and guesthouses in larger cities use online reservation sites like Agoda or Booking.com, which can sometimes work to the traveler's advantage by providing cheaper rates, though there are a handful of accommodations that cost more when booking online. For the best price, consult both the hotel directly and their online booking site when available.

When you check in to a hotel in Vietnam you will often be asked to hand over your passport. This can be a source of worry among travelers, but holding one's passport is common practice in Vietnam. Since hotels are required by law to register their guests with the police, many will hold your passport at the front desk during your stay, partly for the authorities and partly for insurance that you don't walk out on your bill (these things occasionally happen). It is acceptable to request that your passport is returned to you after the receptionist has filled out your registration form, though you may be asked to pay in advance.

MAKING RESERVATIONS

Depending on the location and the time of year, the need for booking accommodations may vary. Most major cities in Vietnam do not require a reservation. With such an abundance of hotels and guesthouses in places like Ho Chi Minh City's Pham Ngu Lao area and the Old Quarter of Hanoi, travelers will never find themselves out in the cold. If you prefer to stay in nicer accommodations and would rather not do the door-to-door legwork, then booking a room is recommended. Be sure when making a reservation that you ask the price up front, as rates may change, and take care to confirm your reservation at least once before arriving at the hotel. Even online sites like Agoda and Booking.com, while reliable, can sometimes make mistakes or lose reservations.

HOTELS

You'll find all manner of accommodations that refer to themselves as *khach san* (hotels). These tend to be larger buildings with more rooms. There is a star rating issued by the Vietnamese government each year, but the criteria for the rating seems to focus on the size of the building rather than the quality of the accommodations. Two- to four-star accommodations are a mixed bag, with plenty of outstanding rooms as well as deteriorating facilities. Boutique and privately owned hotels are usually more impressive, though these are often more expensive, too. Depending on the rates and quality of the hotel, amenities vary from as little as a bed, air-conditioning, and a hot shower to safety deposit boxes, in-room computers, and fresh fruit or complimentary breakfast.

GUESTHOUSES

Almost interchangeable with budget hotels, Vietnam's guesthouses *(nha nghi)* are smaller versions of the same lodgings, often providing 5-6 rooms where a budget hotel might have 10-12. In general, amenities at a guesthouse include air-conditioning, hot water, and sometimes a fridge or TV. These places tend to be the most bare-bones and often the most affordable.

HOSTELS

Hostels and dormitory accommodations are only popular in Vietnam's major cities. While there are a handful of these lodgings in Saigon, Hanoi, and a couple other coastal cities, only one or two hostels actually stand out. All dormitory lodgings should come with proper bedding and a secure locker for each guest, and many also include en suite baths, which limits the number of people sharing a shower.

HOMESTAYS

While there are still plenty of authentic homestays throughout Vietnam, particularly in the Mekong Delta, this is an interesting term nowadays, as "homestay" is often conflated with "guesthouse." Bar a few exceptions, most homestay accommodations are akin to a remote guesthouse, offering the added benefit of home-cooked meals and a bit of interaction with locals, though not as much as you might expect. A growing number of high-end "homestays" are cropping up in more heavily touristed areas—Hoi An, for example; these take on the feel of a bed-and-breakfast, offering more of a local connection along with fancier accommodations.

SHORT-TERM RENTALS

In recent years, the popularity of short-term rental sites like AirBNB (www.airbnb.com) has exploded. Travelers can find everything from trendy downtown apartments to cozy countryside houses available for rent, often with a more personal touch than you would find in the standard hotel. While some other sites, such as VRBO, also advertise short-term rentals in Vietnam, AirBNB is by far the most trusted of these services. Prices for these rentals tend to be comparable to a stay in a boutique hotel, and while some accommodations are on the basic side, travelers can also find beautiful, well-designed apartments through AirBNB.

CAMPING

Camping in Vietnam can have a few different meanings. You may find yourself in a one-room beachside bungalow, a log cabin in the woods, or a tent on the ground. While the lodgings vary, most of these accommodations are located either in national parks or on beaches across the country. Pitching a tent just anywhere is not accepted. In more remote areas, travelers may be able to get away with overnighting in their own accommodations, but along the coast you'll be hard-pressed to find a place to set up camp. In designated areas, camping fees tend to be inexpensive.

Conduct and Customs

GENERAL ETIQUETTE

Vietnam is a very polite country. Though Western-style customer service is not always observed in restaurants or hotels, you'll be hard-pressed to find people who are intentionally rude. Locals rarely raise their voices out of anger or show intense emotions in public. Daily interactions are handled calmly and politely. When problems arise, the typical Vietnamese reaction is often awkward laughter. This can be a frustrating and seemingly inappropriate response. In Vietnamese culture, showing anger is considered a lack of self-control and will likely cause the person you're dealing with to shut down, leaving you no better off than when you started.

As much as the average person is polite and respectful, the rules of etiquette, like most rules in Vietnam, are sometimes overlooked. Lining up, it seems, is the worst: people push, shove, and openly cut in front while waiting for a bus or at the supermarket checkout counter. If this happens, politely ask the person to move and you'll usually get a feigned surprise or even an apology, and most of the time that individual will get out of line. Acts like these are rarely meant to be rude; it's just that they were hoping you wouldn't say anything.

APPROPRIATE DRESS

Though you wouldn't know it in larger cities, Vietnam's sense of style tends to be rather conservative, with most people opting for long pants and shirts that cover their shoulders. Women in particular are usually more reserved, though sheer shirts are in fashion. In professional or religious settings, outfits that hit below the knee are appropriate for women and long pants are a must for men. At night all rules go out the window, as you'll see young Vietnamese women flying by on the back of a motorbike in sky-high stilettos and a miniskirt. For the most part, the same rules apply in Vietnam as in the United States: you wouldn't show up to work in your party dress or shorts and flip-flops; if you visit a pagoda or an office building, the same holds true.

Offering objects with two hands is considered a sign of respect.

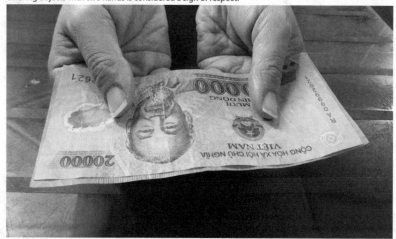

BODY LANGUAGE

Unlike Cambodia or Thailand, bowing in Vietnam, while still respectful, does not carry the same significance. Instead, when handing something to an elder or a stranger, for instance, it is polite to give the item with both hands as a sign of respect, or to offer the item with the right hand while placing the left hand on the right elbow. Certain gestures are inappropriate here where they would not be at home. Crossing your forefinger and middle finger over one another, for instance, is a rude gesture in Vietnam. When beckoning someone, it's better to use an underhand motion.

Vietnamese culture dictates that the top of a person's head is the most sacred part of his or her body (because it is closest to God), while the soles of one's feet are the lowest. Touching the top of a person's head is considered impolite, particularly with children, as is showing a person the soles of your feet. In pagodas especially, directing the soles of your feet at the Buddha is considered an offensive gesture.

TABLE MANNERS

There are several Vietnamese dining habits that break with Western ideas of what is polite. Slurping your soup, talking with a full mouth, and shouting for the waiter are all acceptable practices at a local restaurant. You can shout *em oi!* to beckon a waiter over to your table. While it may seem odd at first, you'll want to get the hang of it, as servers don't check up on quiet tables and only bring the bill when you've asked for it. If you're visiting a street food stall or a more local restaurant, throwing rubbish like napkins and used toothpicks on the floor is also acceptable.

This may seem unsanitary, but a restaurant employee will come by and sweep up any garbage that gets left on the floor. Occasionally, wastebaskets are positioned at the end of each table. If you're in doubt, take a look around: if you can see squeezed limes, napkins, and other rubbish strewn across the floor, then you're allowed to do the same.

When eating with a local family, Vietnamese hospitality dictates that no guest go hungry: in a Vietnamese house, you will eat until you're full and then some. Be warned that any time you empty your bowl it will be filled again before you have the chance to decline. Dining family-style means that anyone can pick at the assortment of meats and veggies on offer and drop some into your bowl, and people often do when guests are around. In situations like these, rice is served in a small *chen* (bowl) for each person, while the main dishes are set out in the middle. When eating, it is acceptable to pick up your *chen* and bring it closer to your mouth; as you reach the bottom of the bowl, you may lift it to your mouth and use your chopsticks to shovel the rice in. Take what is closest to you, as any piece you touch is yours, and always put the food in your *chen* first before bringing it to your mouth.

There are a long list of dos and don'ts regarding chopstick etiquette. For most transgressions, foreigners will likely be forgiven. Always lay your chopsticks parallel to one another, never crossed, and do not point them at other people, as these gestures are considered rude. It is also inappropriate to leave your utensils in the shape of a "V," and chopsticks should never be stuck upright into a bowl of rice, as this resembles incense sticks and is viewed as an omen of death.

Travel Tips

LANGUAGE AND COMMUNICATION

While English-speakers are likely to find communication easy in major cities like Hanoi and Saigon, if you head outside these hubs the language barrier becomes more apparent. In part due to the complexities of their own language, the Vietnamese have a great deal of trouble with English (and, it's safe to say, English-speakers face the same challenges with Vietnamese). Staying patient and simplifying your requests will go a long way to helping make yourself understood. In English, we often make requests more polite by adding extra words. For instance, at home you might say, "I was wondering if you could tell me where the restroom is?" For a weaker English speaker these extra words add confusion. Instead, "Excuse me, where is the toilet?" will make you more easily understood and locals will not take offense to the shorter sentences.

Whenever you arrange a service—whether it be a motorbike rental, a *xe om* ride, a day tour, or a cooking course—always be clear on the cost and the expectations of both parties before setting out, as this will help to prevent disagreements. Patience goes a long way. Expressing anger or being short with someone will keep you from gaining that person's respect.

WHAT TO PACK

Thanks to a steady influx of foreign visitors, Vietnam offers plenty of Western amenities, but some items are still hard to come by. Sunscreen, for instance, is almost never used among the local population and so can be difficult to track down. When you do find it, it's overpriced, and the locally produced version is not particularly effective. You're better off bringing your own from abroad. The same goes for insect repellent. For women, feminine care pads are available at most pharmacies and drugstores, but tampons are less common, so bring your own.

Given the humidity, lightweight, breathable clothing and sturdy shoes are a wise choice for any traveler. Anyone planning to go pagoda-hopping should opt for at least one long-sleeved shirt and pants or shorts that reach the knee. A hat is a good idea as certain destinations like the Mekong Delta and Nha Trang are notably devoid of shade. While backpacking through Vietnam is a dirty business and your standard shorts-and-T-shirt attire is perfectly acceptable, pack one or two nice outfits if you plan to go out in the bigger cities like Hanoi or Saigon. You will likely need a raincoat at one time or another while in Vietnam, but bringing your own is optional, as cheap, plastic cover-ups are widely available.

OPPORTUNITIES FOR STUDY AND EMPLOYMENT

As Southeast Asia becomes more visible on the international stage, a growing number of Western travelers are choosing to make a home in Asia, if only for a year or two. A combination of increasing tourism and growing demand for English-language education in Vietnam have created ample opportunities for foreigners looking to experience another part of the world and earn money at the same time. Short-term employment can be found at hostels and guesthouses around the country, where simple housework or other odd jobs are sometimes traded for room and board. For more permanent employment, most companies require you to make connections once you've already arrived in Vietnam. Websites like **VietnamWorks** (www.vietnamworks. com) provide insight into what's available from abroad, though the best way to learn about job opportunities in Vietnam is by visiting the country.

If you plan to be in Asia for six months or

more, ESL teaching is an excellent option. Jobs teaching English in Vietnam are widely available in Saigon and Hanoi, while employment in smaller cities like Danang is growing. Most English-teaching contracts range between six months and one year, and several schools within Vietnam offer ESL teaching certification courses, like the CELTA or TESOL, both of which are recognized internationally. **Apollo English** (www.apollo.edu.vn), **ILA** (www.ilavietnam.com), and **VUS** (www.vus.edu.vn) are reputable English teaching centers that employ foreign instructors. You can work under-the-table gigs with a tax-free hourly wage, but these businesses are far less reliable. In order to get a legitimate job with a reasonable salary, you'll need a bachelor's degree in any field, a TESOL or CELTA certificate, a police background check from your home country or state, and a medical check to confirm that you are in good health. If you decide to teach in Vietnam, it is infinitely easier to apply for a work permit and a legitimate visa if you have an original copy of your bachelor's degree notarized at home and your police check completed before you arrive rather than coordinating these documents from Vietnam, as the red tape can be exhausting.

Beyond teaching English, a variety of other opportunities are available but often require you to make connections within Vietnam first, which is why a teaching job is often the way foreigners get started in Vietnam. Once you've met some of your fellow expats and gotten to know the lay of the land, you can find jobs in anything from marketing and sales to graphic design, business, science, and even the food and beverage industry.

ACCESS FOR TRAVELERS WITH DISABILITIES

Vietnam is not easily accessible for travelers with physical disabilities, particularly anyone who uses a wheelchair. Elevators are seldom available outside of major cities, streets and sidewalks are often crumbled and aging, and many of Vietnam's tourist attractions require some mobility. Major cities are better equipped to accommodate travelers with disabilities, including Ho Chi Minh City, Danang, and Hanoi. Particularly around Danang and Hoi An, a popular area for many older travelers, businesses and accommodations will likely be more equipped to serve tourists with disabilities.

WOMEN TRAVELING ALONE

Vietnam is safe for female tourists. Women are able to travel freely without much harassment. Solo women will receive their fair share of lighthearted marriage proposals and occasional pestering from local men, but this rarely results in any serious issues. Always be polite but firm when encountering unwanted attention and, once you have made your point, ignore the other party. This is more effective than continuing to respond.

GAY AND LESBIAN TRAVELERS

Gay and lesbian travelers will find that Vietnam is an accepting place. The speed with which Vietnam has come to accept its own LGBTQ citizens is incredibly heartening. In little more than a few years, large swaths of the urban population have come to understand, albeit tentatively, the presence of homosexuality in local society. In 2015, the Vietnamese government legalized same-sex weddings, with one high-ranking official even publicly supporting same-sex marriage. (Note the difference here between a wedding and a marriage.) Since 2012, Hanoi has held an annual **VietPride festival** (www.vietpride.info) and continues to push for greater recognition of LGBTQ Vietnamese throughout the country. For the most part, many locals are happy to live and let live, though public displays of affection from any couple—gay or straight—are usually discouraged. More and more young Vietnamese are empowered to come out and a handful of great organizations in the major cities are improving social perceptions of LGBTQ people in Vietnam. The countryside is still a conservative place where tolerance may be less forthcoming.

RACE AND DIVERSITY

As more and more foreigners head to Vietnam for work or travel, Vietnamese people are gaining more exposure to people of different ethnicities, races, and cultures from around the world. International travelers will find that being in Vietnam is not without its cross-cultural frustrations, but by and large Vietnamese people are welcoming, and most negative attitudes stem more from ignorance and lack of exposure. In some cities and many rural areas, local people have a tendency to view foreigners as exotic. Travelers of African, Middle Eastern, or Latin descent may find themselves subject to higher levels of curiosity. As a result, you may receive a bit more attention—sometimes unwanted. For the most part, offering a smile or a hello can help to break the ice and either prompt a conversation or deter further staring, pointing, or touching. As Vietnamese culture is notably more direct than its Western counterparts in regards to physical appearance in general—manifesting in matter-of-fact remarks that might be considered insensitive or rude by Western culture standards—international travelers may find themselves being asked to address questions pertaining to ethnicity or race quite bluntly, though this is generally out of curiosity, not confrontation.

Local perceptions of other people and places are also often based upon Western popular culture, which can lead to stereotypes. The flip side of this is that Vietnamese people of all ages tend to view Western tourists in a positive light, Americans included despite the history between the respective countries. Part of this is due to the attitudes of young Vietnamese, who have no personal memory of the Vietnam War and have instead grown up with access to U.S. pop culture. Another reason for this openness comes from the country's approach to the aftermath of the conflict: While Vietnamese people certainly suffered during and after the war, their general attitude has been to get on with things and move past that period in time.

Health and Safety

VACCINATIONS

As per **Centers for Disease Control and Prevention** (CDC, www.cdc.gov/travel) guidelines, all travelers to Vietnam should be up-to-date on routine vaccinations before going abroad for hepatitis A and typhoid, both of which can be spread through contaminated food or water. For more adventurous travelers and anyone planning to visit remote areas in Vietnam or to stay for a long time, vaccinations against hepatitis B and Japanese encephalitis are encouraged, as well as preemptive rabies prophylaxis.

Malaria

Though malaria is less common in Vietnam than other parts of Southeast Asia, this flu-like potentially fatal illness still exists in some parts of the country. CDC guidelines recommend that travelers to rural areas in the south and central interior take malaria prophylaxis. Check with your doctor to find out which prophylaxis is best for you, as Vietnam's particular strain of malaria is resistant to certain drugs. There are many side effects associated with malaria prophylaxis, including minor annoyances like upset stomach, nausea, and sensitivity to sunlight but also more serious issues such as anxiety, hallucinations, and even seizures. Many travelers forgo using malaria drugs and instead take extra precautions in covering up and preventing mosquito bites. While DEET repellents are not intended for long-term use, a couple of days of strong insect repellent should be fine. If you believe that you have contracted malaria, seek medical attention immediately. When caught early, malaria is very treatable.

Rabies

For anyone traveling to remote areas, spending a lot of time outdoors, or planning to travel by bicycle, the rabies vaccination is recommended, as people continue to die from the disease in Vietnam each year. Almost always fatal, rabies can be transmitted to humans through a bite or scratch from monkeys, cats, dogs, and bats. Avoid touching animals in Vietnam, even pets, as they are often left to their own devices and not cared for in the same way as Western pets. If you are bitten or scratched by a wild animal, wash the wound immediately with soap and water before seeking medical attention. Typically, an unvaccinated person requires a series of five shots following rabies exposure; those who have had preemptive prophylaxis need only two shots as soon as possible following the encounter. Due to the number of wild animals in Vietnam, rabies vaccines are widely available in the country and can be administered almost anywhere, including remote areas.

HEALTH
Allergies

Travelers with severe allergies may have trouble in Vietnam, especially those allergic to shellfish and peanuts, as these are frequent ingredients in Vietnamese cuisine. Cross-contamination is difficult to manage at street carts or in local restaurants, and even if you explain your dilemma to a local server there is no guarantee that the message will be understood. Take care to read all packaged foods and bring your own means of treatment, such as an EpiPen, to counter an allergic reaction. In the event of a severe allergic reaction, seek medical attention immediately.

Traveler's Diarrhea

One of the less glamorous facets of traveling, traveler's diarrhea is common among visitors to Vietnam, particularly those who enjoy street food. Some guidelines urge visitors to avoid roadside food carts as well as ice and fresh vegetables, but this may make your stay more expensive, not to mention detract from the overall experience. Avoiding specific street vendors or restaurants whose kitchens appear unclean or have food that has been sitting out for some time will help to decrease your risk of traveler's diarrhea and other foodborne illnesses. Dishes that are served hot and meat and veggies that have been fried, grilled, or otherwise prepared with high heat should be fine. In many cases, a good street food restaurant will prepare their meals in plain sight, giving you the ability to see the kitchen for yourself. When it comes to dishes like pho, *bun bo* (spicy beef noodle soup), and *banh xeo* (savory Vietnamese pancakes), fresh greens are usually served on the side, so you are able to easily avoid them if you so choose.

Regarding beverages, the ice at most restaurants in backpacker areas and higher-end eateries is safe to consume. Tap water is not meant for anything beyond showers and brushing your teeth. Though water can be boiled, nearly everyone in the country drinks bottled water or *tra da,* a light tea served at local restaurants.

In the event that you find yourself with traveler's diarrhea, it's best to stick to bland foods and proper restaurants for a day or two until your symptoms subside. Over-the-counter antidiarrheal drugs like Imodium are available both in Vietnam and at home. If the issue persists, visit a doctor, who will prescribe something stronger. If you visit a physician in the United States prior to your trip abroad, ask about antidiarrheal medicines, as procuring medications at home is generally safer than doing so in Vietnam.

Dengue

One of the few more serious illnesses that exists in Vietnam's cities as well as in rural areas is dengue. Passed through mosquito bites, the disease causes fever, headaches, and muscle and joint pain along with flu-like symptoms. There is no vaccination for dengue. Anyone who believes to be suffering from the disease should seek medical attention, as dengue is highly treatable but can become fatal if left unchecked. Should you become ill, avoid mosquitoes, rest, stay hydrated, and, of course, see a doctor. Acetaminophen-based pain killers can be used to relieve muscle and joint aches, but you should avoid any medications with aspirin, ibuprofen, or naproxen. Take extra care to monitor your health as the symptoms recede; in rare cases, dengue can turn into a fatal condition just as the initial symptoms appear to subside. If you experience difficulty breathing, pale or clammy skin, persistent vomiting, bleeding from your nose or gums, or red spots on your skin, go to a hospital immediately, as these may be signs of a more serious condition.

Zika Virus

In April 2016, Vietnam's Ministry of Health confirmed the country's first Zika cases. Since then, the southern half of Vietnam has seen a marked increase in the spread of the illness, with dozens of reported cases in Ho Chi Minh City alone. Popular tourist destinations like Nha Trang and the Mekong Delta region have also been affected. A handful of international travelers have returned home after a trip to Vietnam and begun showing symptoms of the virus. Vietnam has also reported one case of Zika-linked microcephaly in the Central Highlands.

The virus is currently considered endemic in Vietnam, meaning occasional cases may follow. It's unlikely that the rate of Zika infection will be so high as to cause an epidemic. As of the time of writing, Vietnam had recorded Zika cases in Saigon, Binh Duong, Nha Trang, and Phu Yen; it's expected the virus will also spread to northern Vietnam.

While there is no vaccination to prevent Zika infection, travelers can limit their risk by wearing long sleeves and mosquito repellent during the day and opting for air-conditioned accommodations at night. Check the CDC website (www.cdc.gov) for the most up-to-date information.

Methanol Poisoning

Though this is still a rare problem among travelers, a handful of cases in recent years have raised the need for awareness regarding methanol poisoning. More commonly known as wood alcohol, methanol is the cousin of ethanol, the type of alcohol found in spirits like vodka, whiskey, or rum. Where ethanol can leave you with a regular hangover, methanol is much worse, with even small doses causing serious side effects or even death.

As a means of cutting costs, some local businesses attempt to create their own homemade versions of alcoholic spirits using this substance, which they then sell to local bars, some of whom don't even know they're purchasing counterfeit booze. Regardless, unsafe amounts of methanol, which can be undetectable in a mixed drink, have found their way into the hands of locals and travelers. Symptoms of methanol poisoning may not show up until as late as 72 hours after initial exposure and can often mirror the predictable symptoms of a hangover, including confusion, dizziness, headaches, nausea, vomiting, and inability to coordinate muscle movements. In more serious cases, it can cause loss of vision; kidney, heart, and respiratory failure; gastrointestinal bleeding; and seizures, the combination of which can prove fatal.

It is extremely important to exercise caution when going out on the town, particularly in backpacker areas and in certain cities like Saigon and Nha Trang. Cheap drinks are available everywhere, but if a price seems too good to be true, then it probably is. Purchasing your own spirits from a supermarket or chain convenience store is safer than opting for the local corner store. At the bar, if you order a drink and something doesn't seem right—the taste is particularly sweet or harsh, or the beverage is discolored—don't bother finishing it. For the most part, higher-end bars and lounges are safer than local watering holes or cheap backpacker spots. If all else fails, stick to beer and wine. Should you or a friend become a victim of methanol poisoning, go to a hospital immediately.

INSECTS

The local mosquito population continues to pester everyone in Vietnam. When traveling both in the city and throughout the countryside, take care to cover up at dawn and dusk, when insects are out in the greatest numbers, and use insect repellent. While it is possible to find repellent sprays in Vietnam, it's better to purchase them at home or in neighboring countries like Thailand, as these products can be more difficult to come by in-country and are usually more expensive. Avoid leaving your hotel room windows open at night and, if possible, sleep with the air-conditioning on or use a mosquito net around your bed. While rare, bed bugs are also an occasional problem in Vietnam, particularly if you are staying in dormitory-style accommodations. Check thoroughly for the critters before climbing into bed.

WILD ANIMALS

Vietnam's largest animal problems tend to stem from dogs and cats, many of which are technically pets but whose owners let them roam freely outside. In more remote areas, locals keep dogs for protection. Cyclists in particular will want to steer clear of these animals, as they've been known to chase bikes. Avoid touching animals, even if they appear to be pets. If you come into contact with an animal, wash your hands thoroughly.

MEDICAL SERVICES

Medical services in Vietnamese hospitals are dismal at best, with major overcrowding and sanitation problems. In larger cities, international facilities provide a reasonable level of quality and will usually suffice in the event of illness or minor emergencies. More serious cases may require airlifting to Singapore or Bangkok; all of this should be covered by adequate travel insurance.

INSURANCE

Travel insurance is a must for visitors to Vietnam, as even a healthy tourist can become the victim of an accident, and while local hospitals may be significantly cheaper than their American counterparts, the cost of quality medical care can add up. Check with your current insurance provider to see if you are covered outside of your home country and what exactly falls within your plan. Travel insurance can be purchased through providers such as **Travel Guard** (www.travelguard. com). For most minor illnesses and injuries, health care in Vietnam is inexpensive enough that you may be able to cover the costs on your own, but at the very least be sure that your insurance plan covers major accidents and injuries. Confirm your plan's payment policy, as some hospitals in Vietnam require cash up front in order to perform medical services, and emergency evacuations can run in the hundreds of thousands of dollars. For those keen on hiring a motorbike, most travel insurance does not cover road accidents if the driver is unlicensed.

CRIME

The vast majority of crime in Vietnam involves bending the rules in business. While violent crimes occur, these incidents rarely involve foreigners. The most common trouble you'll encounter is petty theft, which, while frustrating, seldom turns dangerous or violent. The second greatest concern for foreign visitors is drugs, which are illegal in Vietnam: Possession in large amounts can garner the death penalty or a protracted sentence for offenders.

Pickpocketing and Petty Theft

Though it's a minor offense compared to more violent crimes, petty theft is a problem in Vietnam, especially in urban areas. Foreigners just getting the hang of a new country are often the victims. Particularly at night and around backpacker areas, tourists stand out as easy targets. Bag snatching, pickpocketing, and burglary are frequent occurrences, even in broad daylight.

There are steps you can take to minimize vulnerability. When walking around town, opt for pockets that close and keep your belongings in sight at all times. When paying for purchases, avoid showing large amounts of money, as this makes you a target. Anyone carrying a backpack should wear both straps; shoulder bags are best worn across the body and on the side furthest from the street. Avoid walking near the sidewalk's edge, as thieves on motorbikes have been known to snatch purses, phones, and wallets, sometimes dragging the person along with them. The same rules apply when you're on a motorbike: place your bag or backpack in front of you, hugging it to your chest, and tuck any necklaces into your shirt, as they can be snatched, too. Whether you're on foot or on a motorbike, use caution when taking out your belongings in public; even if you're just answering a text message or finding directions on your cell phone, duck into a local shop and out of view. These tips may sound extreme, but the number of tourists who have been robbed multiple times on a single trip suggests that, while slightly over-the-top, such practices are necessary. At night, common sense should be exercised. Male or female, don't walk alone around town, avoid alleyways, and always take taxis rather than *xe om* after dark.

If you are robbed, especially at night, it's best to go along with it. The majority of these criminals are after your monetary goods, not your life. Your first priority should always be your own safety; remember that goods are replaceable, your life is not. Not everyone is out to steal your money. Locals are incredibly

a busy city street

kind, and if you follow precautions, you are less likely to encounter trouble.

Drugs

Recreational drugs like marijuana, heroin, and synthetic tablets are both widely available and illegal in Vietnam. There is a harsh zero-tolerance policy for drug trafficking and possession.

Information and Services

MONEY
Currency
The official currency of Vietnam is known as the dong. Bills come in denominations of VND500, VND1,000, VND2,000, VND5,000, VND10,000, VND20,000, VND50,000, VND100,000, VND200,000, and VND500,000. Refuse ripped or torn bills, particularly those with denominations

of VND10,000 or higher, as they are often rejected by shops and local businesses and you may find yourself stuck with money you cannot spend.

Exchange Rates
At the time of writing, the exchange rate for the Vietnam dong is roughly VND22,700 to one U.S. dollar. Current rates can be found

online at **Oanda** (www.oanda.com) and **XE** (www.xe.com). Businesses within Vietnam operate on a rate that fluctuates between VND20,000 and VND23,000.

Changing Money

Most major tourist destinations have proper currency exchange kiosks, in addition to the countless hotels, restaurants, travel agencies, and gold shops that offer exchange services at various rates. While exchange kiosks are usually not affiliated with a bank, they are safe to use, as counterfeit currency is not a major problem in Vietnam. Ripped or torn bills are not accepted by many local businesses. If you receive any bills in this state, or if they are noticeably worn or faded, ask to have them switched out.

ATMs

ATMs are everywhere in Vietnam, with even the most remote destinations having at least one or two machines. Major cities often have ATMs from international banks such as ANZ, HSBC, Citibank, and Commonwealth Bank, as well as domestic institutions like Sacombank, Techcombank, and Vietcombank. Most domestic ATMs charge minimal fees for using their machines. International institutions

sometimes charge more, though the cost rarely exceeds VND10,000 per withdrawal.

Bank Hours

For international banks, business hours are 8am-5pm; domestic institutions follow the same schedule but sometimes close earlier, at 4pm or 4:30pm, and almost always break for lunch, closing at 11am or 11:30am and re-opening at 1pm or 1:30pm. All banks are open Monday-Friday, with some open on Saturday mornings as well.

Traveler's Checks

While it is possible to cash traveler's checks in certain banks in major cities, these are often far more trouble than they're worth. Not every financial institution will cash them and, when they do, many banks include fees and surcharges that eat away at the value of the check. **Vietcombank** (tel. 024/3824-3524, www.vietcombank.com.vn) is one of the few institutions that accepts traveler's checks, though the service is only provided in larger cities and not nationwide. With the availability of ATMs all over the country and the lack of places in which a stolen bank card could be used, you're better off bringing plastic and withdrawing money from a machine.

ESSENTIALS
INFORMATION AND SERVICES

fruits, teas, and other dry goods on sale in Sapa Market

Costs

In Vietnam, the price of many items, from food and accommodations to shopping, is up for negotiation. In major cities, a good local meal can go for as little as VND15,000-20,000 at a street stall to as much as VND500,000 in a restaurant. In these instances, what you pay for is the atmosphere—more often than not, the food at a small hole-in-the-wall shop or street cart is just as good, if not better, than what you'll find at a high-end restaurant in the trendier part of town. When eating street-side it is a good idea to ask the price beforehand, as vendors occasionally try to rip off tourists by doubling or tripling the bill at the end. You can avoid being had by knowing the cost from the beginning.

Other goods and services are trickier to gauge in terms of cost. Prices fluctuate depending upon location. More tourist-heavy areas like Phu Quoc or Hoi An are often more expensive, while less-visited areas like the Mekong Delta and the Central Highlands tend to be a fraction of the cost. With prices changing all the time, it's difficult to say what an appropriate amount is for any given good or service.

Bargaining

In markets and shops across the country, bargaining is a common practice. Prices for everything from fresh produce to clothing to motorbike rides are up for negotiation. It is often expected that you'll haggle for goods and services if a price tag is not affixed to them. While it can be difficult to discern what a fair price is, your best bet is to ask around, gauge the average asking price of a few vendors, and then cut that number by 20-40 percent. In some cases this will be too much, in other cases too little. Take care not to enter into negotiations with a vendor unless you actually want the product. It's perfectly acceptable to ask the price of an item out of curiosity, but once you begin haggling it's assumed that you actually intend to buy the item.

Tipping

Outside of high-end restaurants, tipping is not required, nor is it a common practice. Some businesses tack on a service charge for their employees, but you are not obligated to include something extra unless you feel inclined to do so. The only exception is in spas and massage parlors, where tips are usually expected and you may even be asked to fill out a gratuity form after your massage. In this case, VND40,000 and up is usually acceptable. If you decide to leave a gratuity elsewhere, the amount really is up to you: In a country where one U.S. dollar can buy a meal, a motorbike ride, or even a pair of shoes, any extra cash you leave will be appreciated.

MAPS AND VISITOR INFORMATION

Vietnam is not great at providing accurate or detailed plans of the national road system. Cheap walking maps can be found in many towns. For anyone on a serious navigational mission, the only decent Vietnamese atlas is called *Tap Ban Do Giao Thong Duong Bo Viet Nam* and runs about VND300,000 in local bookshops.

The efficacy of local tourism offices varies depending upon the location. Places like Hanoi and Hoi An are packed with tour companies and travel agents who are willing to help, while a place like Con Dao, one of Vietnam's most remote islands, has maybe one or two English-speaking businesses.

COMMUNICATIONS AND MEDIA
Postal Services

Postage in Vietnam is cheap, with postcards traveling halfway around the world for VND10,000-20,000. The same goes for mail, but once you ship larger packages abroad the costs skyrocket, and in many cases there is no guarantee that the item will arrive at all. Most mail arrives at its destination within 2-3 weeks.

Area Codes

The country code for Vietnam is +84. Each city or province has its own area code, which is included in all phone numbers listed in this book. When calling locally, phone numbers can be dialed as they are listed here. International calls require 1, followed by the country code, but without the zero that appears at the beginning of each number in this book.

Cell Phones

Cell phones in Vietnam run on a pay-as-you-go basis and can be purchased new or used in most cities. For travelers, dirt-cheap brands like Nokia are useful and cost-effective; SIM cards are usually sold with the cell phone.

Internet Access

With the exception of the most remote corners of the country, Internet access in Vietnam is widespread. You can easily find Wi-Fi in local cafés and restaurants, while a smaller number of Internet and gaming cafés with computers are also available. Most hotels in major cities keep a desktop computer in the lobby for guests to use.

Local Newspapers and Magazines

A handful of national publications come out daily, weekly, or monthly in English, namely **Tuoi Tre** (www.tuoitrenews.vn), the online English-language version of the Vietnamese paper of the same name, and **VnExpress** (www.e.vnexpress.net), an online newswire.

Saigoneer (www.saigoneer.com) is a good source of news as well as information on local history, social issues, arts and culture, and food. **Hanoi Grapevine** (www.hanoigrapevine.com) provides up-to-date event listings for Hanoi, while Saigoneer does the same for HCMC.

Monthly magazines geared toward expats are available for free in the country's two main hubs, Hanoi and Saigon, namely *AsiaLIFE* (www.asialifemagazine.com), *The Word* (www.wordhanoi.com, www.wordhcmc.com), and *Oi* (www.oivietnam.com).

Local Television

Local television leaves much to be desired, especially because only a few channels play programs in English. Popular foreign channels like National Geographic and Animal Planet broadcast English-language programming, while Star World and AXN are filled with dated prime time American sitcoms and reruns of *CSI*. All of these channels can be found on basic cable, along with at least one English-language news station. Hotels and restaurants with specific television packages carry European sports channels, the international version of ESPN, sometimes HBO, Star Movies, a regional channel featuring Western films, and Cinemax.

WEIGHTS AND MEASURES

Vietnam uses the metric system. Temperatures are recorded in Celsius, distances in kilometers, and weight in kilograms.

Resources

Glossary

ao dai: traditional Vietnamese garment

banh bao: steamed pork dumpling

banh beo: steamed rice flour cake

banh mi: Vietnamese bread, or a sandwich made out of this bread

banh trung thu: moon cake, a round, dense pastry whose reputation is not unlike fruitcake at Christmas—pretty, ornamental, and not nearly as delicious as it looks

banh xeo: savory Vietnamese pancakes

bia hoi: locally brewed beer (a variant is called *bia tuoi*); also the name for the shops that sell this beer

bun bo Hue: soup with beef and rice noodles, a specialty of Hue

bun cha: grilled meat and rice noodles in fish sauce, a Hanoian specialty

bun nem vit: soup with rice noodles, fresh greens, and duck spring rolls

bun thit nuong: rice noodles and grilled pork

cai luong: a popular form of traditional Vietnamese music

ca phe sua da: iced coffee with milk

cà phe trung: egg coffee

ca tru: ancient chamber music

cha ca: pan-fried fish

chao: rice porridge

com chay: vegetarian food

com cháy: a Ninh Binh specialty made from rice that is sun-dried, then fried

com ga: Hoi An-style chicken and rice

dan nhi: a musical instrument, resembling a two-stringed violin

doi moi: series of economic reforms instituted in the mid-1980s that transitioned Vietnam to a market economy

do nhau: drinking food

giay: paper

hu tieu: a southern-style rice noodle soup

khach san: hotel

linga-yoni statue: a statue representing male and female energies

mam tom: fermented shrimp paste

mua roi: water puppet

nem cua be: square-shaped seafood spring rolls

nha hang: restaurant

nha nghi: guesthouse

nha thuoc tay: pharmacies

nha tro: very basic hotel, a step down from a guesthouse, *nha nghi*

nuoc cham: a diluted fish sauce

phap lam: handicraft of enamel on metal, native to Hue

quat: paper fan

roi nuoc: water puppet theater

tap hoa: convenience store

xe om: motorbike taxi

xoi: sticky rice; popular street food

yen sao: edible bird's nests sold as souvenirs in Nha Trang

Vietnamese Phrasebook

The Vietnamese language consists of six tones. The rising, falling, flat, low, broken, and question tones can morph a single group of letters into any number of different words. Take *ma*, for instance, which can mean ghost (*ma*), horse (*mã*), grave (*mả*), mother (*má*), rice seedling (*mạ*), or which (*mà*), depending on the tone. It is for this reason that most newcomers to the language have difficulty. Even the slightest change in tone can render a word contextually incomprehensible.

To make matters more challenging, most consonant sounds in Vietnamese are enunciated farther back in the speaker's mouth. When you make the "d" sound in English, for example, your tongue strikes the top of your mouth behind the teeth. In Vietnamese, the same letter is pronounced by striking near the center of the roof of your mouth, producing a duller version of the "d" sound, as in *đi* (to go) or *đỏ* (red). Add to that extra vowel sounds like *ơ* (pronounced "uh") and *ư* (pronounced like the "ou" in could) and you've got your work cut out for you.

On paper, Vietnamese is an easier language. Verbs require no conjugation and can be used without the past or future tense. Pronouns are not always necessary. In informal conversation, sentences can be shortened to nothing more than a few words and still retain their meaning. Vietnamese is also one of the only languages in the region to use the Roman alphabet, which makes navigating most cities and towns infinitely simpler, even for someone who doesn't speak the language.

PRONUNCIATION

A handful of letters are pronounced differently in Vietnamese than in English.

Vowels

a   like ah, as in "ant"
ă   like uh, as in "cut"
â   like uh, as in "an"
e   like eh, as in "echo"
ê   like ay, as in "say"
i   like ee, as in "see"
o   like aw, as in "cot"
ô   like oh, as in "broke"
ơ   like uh, as in "fun"
u   like oo, as in "food"
ư   like ouh, as in "could"
y   like ee, as in "bee"

Consonants

c   a muted "c" sound, like a half-step between "c" and "g"
d   like y, as in "you"
đ   like d, as in "dog"
gi   like y, as in "you"
nh   like ny, as in "canyon"
ph   like f, as in "phone"
qu   like kw, as in "question" (northern) or like w, as in "wood"
x   like s, as in "sink"

BASIC EXPRESSIONS

Hello./Goodbye. *Xin chào.*
How are you? *(Bạn) có khỏe không?*
I'm fine, thanks. And you? *Tôi khỏe. Còn bạn?*
Thank you. *Cảm ơn.*
You're welcome./No problem. *Không có gì./Không sao.*
yes *có*
no *không*
I don't know. *Tôi không biết.*
Please wait a minute. *Xin (bạn) chờ một phút.*
Excuse me./I'm sorry. *Xin lỗi.*
Pleased to meet you. *Rất vui gặp bạn.*
What is your name? *(Bạn) tên gì?*
Do you speak English? *(Bạn) biết tiếng Anh không? or (Bạn) nói tiếng Anh được không?*
I don't speak Vietnamese. *Tôi không biết tiếng Việt. or Tôi không nói tiếng Việt được.*
I don't understand. *Tôi không hiểu.*
How do you say . . . in Vietnamese? *. . . tiếng Việt là gì?*

My name is . . . *Tôi tên là . . .*
Would you like . . . ? *(Bạn) có muốn . . .*
  không?
Let's go to . . . *Chúng ta hãy đi . . .*

TERMS OF ADDRESS

Vietnamese terms of address vary depending on the relationship between the speaker and the person to whom he or she is speaking. There are dozens of pronouns to signify the gender and age of a person as well as the level of intimacy between two people. A mother and her child, for instance, would always refer to one another as *mẹ* (mother) and *con* (child), while a teacher and a young student would use *cô* (female teacher) or *thầy* (male teacher) and *con* (in this context, student).

For most travelers, these terms won't be necessary. On the road, most of your interactions will only require you to use pronouns of age and gender. It's simplest to use the neutral pronoun *tôi* when referring to yourself.

When visiting a restaurant or shop, a waiter or shop assistant will likely refer to you as *anh* (slightly older male) or *chị* (slightly older female) and themselves as *em* (a younger person), not necessarily because you are older, but because it shows respect.

If you happen to choose the incorrect pronoun, the other party will politely set you straight before continuing the conversation. In most cases, locals will be appreciative of your efforts and willing to let an error or two slide. Note that appreciation in Vietnamese culture is not always communicated in a way you might expect. Upon hearing a foreigner speak Vietnamese, locals are often quick to laugh. This is borne more out of surprise than anything and is not meant to offend.

In the chart below, the English pronouns "he" and "she" are not listed. With the exception of *tôi* and *bạn,* each of the pronouns below can be modified into "he" or "she" by tacking on the word *ấy* at the end. This means that *anh* (you, male) becomes *anh ấy* (he) or *cô* (you, female) turns into *cô ấy* (she).

I (neutral) *tôi*
person of equivalent age *bạn*
slightly older male *anh*
slightly older female *chị*
younger person, male or female *em*
**female old enough to be your
  mother** *cô*
male old enough to be your father *chú*
**male slightly older than your
  father** *bắc*
**female old enough to be your
  grandmother** *bà*
**male old enough to be your
  grandfather** *ông*
**niece/nephew (self-referential; used
  when speaking to someone old
  enough to be your parent)** *cháu*
**child (self-referential; used when
  speaking to someone old enough to
  be your grandparent)** *con*
we (listener not included) *chúng tôi*
we (listener included) *chúng ta*
you (plural) *các anh/chị/em/bạn*
they *họ*

TRANSPORTATION

Where is . . . ? *. . . ở đâu?*
How far is it to . . . ? *. . . cách đây mấy cây số?*
How far is it from . . . to . . . ? *Từ . . . đến . . .
  cách mấy cây số?*
Do you know the way to . . . ? *(Bạn) có biết
  đường đi . . . không?*
bus station *bến xe*
bus stop *trạm xe búyt*
Where is this bus going? *Xe búyt này đi
  đâu?*
taxi cab *xe taxi*
train station *ga xe lửa* (south), *ga tàu*
  (north)
boat *chiếc tàu*
airport *sân bay*
I'd like a ticket to . . . *Tôi muốn mua vé đi . . .*
one way *một chiều*
round-trip *khứ hồi*
reservation *đặt vé*
Stop here, please. *Xin (bạn) dừng lại ở đây.*
entrance *lối vào*
exit *lối ra*
ticket office *phòng vé*
near *gần*

far *xa*
Turn left. *queo trái (south), rẽ trái (north)*
Turn right. *queo phải (south), rẽ phải (north)*
right side *bên phải*
left side *bên trái*
Go straight. *đi thẳng*
in front of *trước*
beside *bên cạnh*
behind *sau*
corner *góc*
stoplight *đèn đỏ*
here *ở đây*
street *đường phố*
bridge *cây câu*
address *địa chỉ*
north *bác*
south *nam*
east *đồng*
west *tây*

FOOD

I'm hungry. *(Tôi) đói bụng.*
I'm thirsty. *(Tôi) khát nước.*
menu *thức đơn*
to order *gọi*
glass *ly*
fork *nĩa*
knife *dao*
spoon *muỗng*
chopsticks *đôi đũa*
napkin *khăn giấy*
soft drink *nước ngọt*
coffee/hot coffee/iced coffee *cà phê/cà phê sữa nóng/cà phê sữa đá*
coffee with milk *cà phê sữa*
tea/hot tea/iced tea *trà/trà nóng/trà đá*
bottled water *chai nước suối*
beer *bia*
juice *nước ép*
smoothie *sinh tố*
sugar *đường*
breakfast *ăn sáng*
lunch *ăn trưa*
dinner *ăn tối*
check, please *tính tiền*
eggs *trứng*
fruit *trái cây*
pineapple *trái thơm*

mango *trái xoài*
watermelon *dừa hấu*
papaya *đu đủ*
coconut *trái dừa*
lime *chánh*
durian *sầu riêng*
jackfruit *trái mít*
fish *cá*
shrimp *tôm*
chicken *thịt gà*
beef *thịt bò*
pork *thịt heo (south), thịt lợn (north)*
tofu *đậu hủ*
fried *chiên (south), rán (north)*
grilled *nướng*
boiled *luộc*
spicy *cay*

ACCOMMODATIONS

hotel *khách sạn*
guesthouse *nhà nghỉ*
Is there a room available? *Ở đây có phòng không?*
May I see it? *Tôi có thể coi phòng được không?*
What is the rate? *Giá phòng là bao nhiêu?*
Is there something cheaper? *(Bạn) có phòng rẻ hơn không?*
single room *phòng đơn*
double room *phòng đôi*
double bed *giường đôi*
dormitory *phòng tập thể*
key *chìa khóa*
reception *tiếp tân*
hot water *nước nóng*
shower *phòng tắm*
towel *khăn*
soap *sa bông*
toilet paper *giấy vệ sinh*
blanket *mền*
air-conditioning *máy lạnh (south), máy điều hòa (north)*
fan *quạt máy*
mosquito net *màng*
laundry *giặt ủi*

SHOPPING

money *tiền*

bank *ngân hàng*
Do you accept credit cards? *Ở đây có nhận thẻ tín dụng không?*
How much does it cost? *Cái này là bao nhiêu tiền?*
expensive *mắc tiền (south), đắt tiền (north)*
too expensive *mắc qúa (south), đắt quá (north)*
cheap *rẻ*
more *nhiều hơn*
less *ít hơn*
a little *một ít*
too much *quá nhiều*

HEALTH

Help me, please. *Xin (bạn) giúp tôi đi.*
I am sick. *(Tôi) bị bệnh.*
Call a doctor. *Gọi cho bác sĩ đi.*
Please take me to… *Xin (bạn) đưa tôi đến…*
hospital *bệnh viện*
drugstore/pharmacy *nhà thuốc tây*
I'm allergic to… *Tôi bị dị ứng với…*
bees *con ong*
peanuts *đậu phộng*
seafood *hải sản*
I'm asthmatic. *Tôi bị suyễn.*
I'm diabetic. *Tôi bị bệnh đái đường.*
I'm epileptic. *Tôi bị động kinh.*
pain *đau*
fever *bệnh sốt*
headache *đau đầu*
stomachache *đau bụng*
burn *vết bỏng*
nausea *buồn nôn*
vomiting *bị mửa*
diarrhea *tiêu chảy*
antibiotics *thuốc kháng sinh*
aspirin *thuốc giảm đau*
penicillin *thuốc pênicilin*
pill, tablet *viên thuốc*
cream *kem*
contraceptive *cách ngừa thai*
condoms *bao cao su*
insect repellent *thuốc chống muỗi*
sunscreen *kem chống nắng*
sanitary pads *băng vệ sinh*
tampons *ống băng vệ sinh*

toothbrush *bàn chải đánh răng*
toothpaste *kem đánh răng*
dentist *nhà sĩ*
toothache *nhức răng*

COMMON SIGNS

entrance *lối vào*
exit *lối ra*
men *đàn ông*
women *phụ nữ*
toilet *nhà vệ sinh/WC*
information *hướng dẫn/thông tin*
open *mở cửa*
closed *đóng cửa*
prohibited *cấm*

POST OFFICE AND COMMUNICATIONS

I would like to call… *(Tôi) muốn gọi cho…*
collect/collect call *thu thập gọi*
credit card *thẻ tín dụng*
post office *bưu điện*
airmail *thư gửi bằng máy bay*
letter *thư*
stamp *tem*
postcard *bưu thiếp*
registered/certified *thư bảo đảm*
box, package *hộp, gói*

AT THE BORDER

border *biên giới*
customs *hải quan*
immigration *nhập cư*
inspection *sự thanh tra*
passport *hộ chiếu*
profession *nghề nghiệp*
insurance *bảo hiểm*
driver's license *giấy phép lái xe, bằng lái*

AT THE GAS STATION

gas station *trạm xăng*
gasoline *xăng*
full *hết bình*
tire *bánh*
air *bơm xe*
water *nước*
oil change *thay dầu*
my…doesn't work *…của tôi bị hư*

battery *pin*
repair shop *tiệm sửa xe*

VERBS

to buy *mua*
to eat *ăn*
to climb *leo*
to make *làm*
to go, to leave *đi*
to walk *đi bộ*
to like *thích*
to love *yêu*
to work *làm việc*
to want *muốn*
to need *cần*
to read *đọc*
to write *viết*
to repair *sửa*
to stop *dừng lại*
to get off (the bus) *xuống xe*
to arrive, to come *đến*
to stay *ở lại*
to sleep *ngủ*
to look at *xem*
to look for *tìm*
to give *đưa*
to carry *mang*
to have *có*

NUMBERS

one *một*
two *hai*
three *ba*
four *bốn*
five *năm*
six *sáu*
seven *bảy*
eight *tám*
nine *chín*
10 *mười*
11 *mười một*
12 *mười hai*
13 *mười ba*
14 *mười bốn*
15 *mười lăm*
16 *mười sáu*
17 *mười bảy*
18 *mười tám*

19 *mười chín*
20 *hai mười*
30 *ba mười*
100 *một trăm*
101 *một trăm lẻ một*
200 *hai trăm*
1,000 *một ngàn* (south), *một nghìn* (north)
10,000 *mười ngàn* (south), *mười nghìn* (north)
100,000 *một trăm ngàn* (south), *một trăm nghìn* (north)
1,000,000 *một triệu*
one-half *nửa phần*

TIME

What time is it? *Bây giờ là mấy giờ rồi?*
It's one o'clock. *Bây giờ là một giờ.*
It's four in the afternoon. *Bây giờ là bốn giờ chiều.*
It's noon. *Bây giờ là mười hai giờ trưa.*
It's midnight. *Bây giờ là mười hai giờ khuya.*
morning *sáng*
afternoon *chiều*
evening *tối*
one minute *một phút*
one hour *một giờ, một tiếng*

DAYS AND MONTHS

Monday *thứ hai*
Tuesday *thứ ba*
Wednesday *thứ tư*
Thursday *thứ năm*
Friday *thứ sáu*
Saturday *thứ bảy*
Sunday *chủ nhật*
January *tháng giêng*
February *tháng hai*
March *tháng ba*
April *tháng tư*
May *tháng năm*
June *tháng sáu*
July *tháng bảy*
August *tháng tám*
September *tháng chín*
October *tháng mười*
November *tháng mười một*
December *tháng mười hai*
today *hôm nay*

yesterday *hôm qua*	**rainy season** *mùa mưa*
tomorrow *ngày mai*	**dry season** *mùa khô*
a day *một ngày*	**spring** *mùa xuân*
a week *một tuần*	**summer** *mùa hè*
a month *một tháng*	**winter** *mùa đông*
after *sau đây*	**fall** *mùa thu*
before *trước đây*	

Suggested Reading

HISTORY

Bartimus, Tad, Ed. *War Torn: Stories of War from the Women Reporters Who Covered Vietnam.* New York: Random House, 2002. Written by a group of women ranging from veteran journalists to 20-something novices, this collection of memoirs presents a different side of Vietnam through the eyes of some of the first female reporters to cover a conflict from the front lines.

Goscha, Christopher. *The Penguin History of Modern Vietnam.* London: Penguin UK, 2017. A comprehensive look at the country's more recent history in all its complexity.

Herr, Michael. *Dispatches.* New York: Vintage, 1977. Lauded as one of America's most famous firsthand accounts of the Vietnam War, *Dispatches* is the product of Michael Herr's years as a journalist covering the conflict for *Esquire* magazine. The author went on to cowrite *Apocalypse Now* and *Full Metal Jacket.*

Karnow, Stanley. *Vietnam: A History.* New York: Viking, 1983. The best-selling masterpiece of Stanley Karnow, a veteran journalist and historian who covered the Vietnam War and its aftermath both at home and abroad.

Mangold, Tom. *The Tunnels of Cu Chi.* New York: Ballantine, 1985. The fascinating story of the citizens of Cu Chi and the intricate system of tunnels they dug by hand

to protect their homes. This book is a must-read for anyone interested in war history, with firsthand accounts of the harsh and unforgiving conditions of life underground and the struggles of NLF rebel fighters, as well as the stories of the U.S. Army's "tunnel rats": a group of men who descended into the pitch-black tunnels to combat the enemy.

BIOGRAPHY AND MEMOIR

Bui, Thanh. *The Best We Could Do.* New York: Abrams ComicArts, 2017. A stunning graphic memoir illustrating Bui's journey as a first-generation American to understand and connect with her refugee parents.

Duiker, William J. *Ho Chi Minh: A Life.* New York: Hyperion, 2000. A comprehensive biography of Vietnam's greatest leader and one of the 20th century's most influential politicians.

Pham, Andrew X. *Catfish and Mandala.* New York: Picador, 1999. In his early 30s, uncertain of his future and curious about his past, Andrew Pham set out from Saigon on a bicycle, heading up the coast of a Vietnam newly opened to the outside world, encountering the country's people, its problems, and its unbreakable spirit.

Sachs, Dana. *The House on Dream Street: Memoir of an American Woman in Vietnam.* Chapel Hill, NC: Algonquin Books,

2000. The memoir of a woman in her late 20s bound for Vietnam just as the country is beginning to open up after years of war and poverty.

FICTION

Butler, Robert Olen. *A Good Scent from a Strange Mountain*. New York: Grove Press, 2001. A Pulitzer Prize-winning collection of short stories that peers into the lives of Vietnamese immigrants living in the United States as they navigate the cultural differences and war wounds of a turbulent history between the two nations.

Greene, Graham. *The Quiet American*. London: Vintage, 1955. An ominous and controversial novel twice adapted to film, Graham Greene's opus is set in early 1950s Saigon, a time and place rife with political tension and deception. This is perhaps one of the most famous English-language novels set in Vietnam.

Nguyen, Viet Thanh. *The Refugees*. New York: Grove Press, 2017. Told mainly through the lens of Vietnamese characters, this short story collection explores the lives of displaced people and what it means to be a refugee in the modern world.

Nguyen, Viet Thanh. *The Sympathizer*. New York: Grove Press, 2016. A Pulitzer Prize winner, Nguyen's highly acclaimed first novel follows a conflicted communist sympathizer whose political ideals are often at odds with his personal loyalties, in the aftermath of the American War.

O'Brien, Tim. *The Things They Carried*. New York: Mariner, 1990. A semiautobiographical collection of short stories, Tim O'Brien's fictional masterpiece follows a platoon of American soldiers in the rainforest of Vietnam as they fight their way through the war.

Internet Resources

TRAVEL INFORMATION

Rusty Compass
www.rustycompass.com
This outstanding, well-researched independent travel guide covers a wide range of Vietnamese destinations, providing travelers with helpful tips and recommendations as well as dozens of photos and videos. Run by Aussie expat Mark Bowyer, who has been based in Vietnam since the early 1990s, Rusty Compass is a great resource when planning your trip.

Travelfish
www.travelfish.org
A handy resource for anyone traveling in Southeast Asia, Travelfish offers independent reviews, practical information, and sound advice on countries throughout the region. The site's Vietnam section covers both major tourist destinations and several less visited towns.

Vietnam Coracle
www.vietnamcoracle.com
Those who aren't afraid of a little adventure will appreciate Vietnam Coracle's frank independent travel guides, which cover DIY visits to all corners of the country. Penned by Tom, a Vietnam resident, the website includes food recommendations and hotel reviews as well as several handy itineraries for those who plan to venture off to more remote parts of Vietnam by motorbike.

Vietnam Tourism
http://vietnamtourism.vn
A joint effort between the Vietnamese government and a tourism advisory board made up

of local businesses, this site features suggestions on what to see and where to go throughout Vietnam.

PRACTICALITIES

Centers for Disease Control
www.cdc.gov

Before traveling to Vietnam, check the CDC website for more country-specific information on vaccinations, malaria prophylaxis, and other preventive measures.

U.S. State Department
www.travel.state.gov

Providing up-to-date information on all things Vietnam, the State Department's website stays abreast of current situations within the country and also offers useful information on practicalities such as border crossings, visas, and health and safety tips.

CULTURE

Saigoneer
www.saigoneer.com

A comprehensive English-language website covering local news, events, development, history, food, and arts and culture, Saigoneer is a great resource for up-to-date information on what's happening in the country's southern hub.

Vietcetera
www.vietcetera.com

Geared toward bringing stories of Vietnam to a wider audience, this website profiles Vietnam-based entrepreneurs as well as dabbles in a bit of travel, opinion, and lifestyle content.

Index

WXYZ

List of Maps

Photo Credits

All interior photos © Dana Filek-Gibson except: page 10 © Eldelik | Dreamstime.com; page 11 (top) © Salajean | Dreamstime.com, (bottom) © Catalina Zaharescu Tiensuu | Dreamstime.com; page 13 © Grace5648 | Dreamstime.com; page 14 © Tatyana Chekrygina | Dreamstime.com; page 17 © Aidman | Dreamstime.com; page 83 © Kapyos | Dreamstime.com; page 377 © ePhotocorp | Dreamstime.com; page 380 © Rafał Cichawa | Dreamstime.com

ARUBA

BELIZE

BERMUDA

COASTAL CALIFORNIA

COASTAL CAROLINAS

Outer Banks, Myrtle Beach, Charleston & Hilton Head

JIM MORELKIS

DOMINICAN REPUBLIC

FLORIDA

HAWAII

JAMAICA

SAN DIEGO

TULUM

YUCATÁN PENINSULA

Beachy Getaways

MOON ROAD TRIP GUIDES

Road Trip USA

Criss-cross the country on America's classic two-lane highways with the newest edition of *Road Trip USA!*

Packed with over 125 detailed driving maps (covering more than 35,000 miles), colorful photos and illustrations of America both then and now, and mile-by-mile highlights

MAP SYMBOLS

≡≡≡	Expressway	○	City/Town	✈	Airport	⌂	Golf Course
≡≡≡	Primary Road	◉	State Capital	✗	Airfield	P	Parking Area
═══	Secondary Road	◈	National Capital	▲	Mountain	≜	Archaeological Site
- - -	Unpaved Road	★	Point of Interest	✦	Unique Natural Feature	♦	Church
———	Feature Trail	•	Accommodation			▯	Gas Station
- - - -	Other Trail	▾	Restaurant/Bar	⚲	Waterfall	⬭	Glacier
··········	Ferry	▪	Other Location	⚑	Park	▨	Mangrove
Pedestrian Walkway		▲	Campground	⊞	Trailhead	▱	Reef
▥▥▥	Stairs			⛷	Skiing Area	▤	Swamp

CONVERSION TABLES

$°C = (°F - 32) / 1.8$
$°F = (°C \times 1.8) + 32$
1 inch = 2.54 centimeters (cm)
1 foot = 0.304 meters (m)
1 yard = 0.914 meters
1 mile = 1.6093 kilometers (km)
1 km = 0.6214 miles
1 fathom = 1.8288 m
1 chain = 20.1168 m
1 furlong = 201.168 m
1 acre = 0.4047 hectares
1 sq km = 100 hectares
1 sq mile = 2.59 square km
1 ounce = 28.35 grams
1 pound = 0.4536 kilograms
1 short ton = 0.90718 metric ton
1 short ton = 2,000 pounds
1 long ton = 1.016 metric tons
1 long ton = 2,240 pounds
1 metric ton = 1,000 kilograms
1 quart = 0.94635 liters
1 US gallon = 3.7854 liters
1 Imperial gallon = 4.5459 liters
1 nautical mile = 1.852 km

MOON VIETNAM
Avalon Travel
Hachette Book Group
1700 Fourth Street
Berkeley, CA 94710, USA
www.moon.com

Editor: Kristi Mitsuda
Series Manager: Kathryn Ettinger
Copy Editor: Christopher Church
Graphics and Production Coordinator:
 Suzanne Albertson
Cover Design: Faceout Studios, Charles Brock
Interior Design: Domini Dragoone
Moon Logo: Tim McGrath
Map Editor: Albert Angulo
Cartographers: Albert Angulo, Brian Shotwell
Indexer: Greg Jewett

ISBN-13: 9781640492639

Printing History
1st Edition — 2015
2nd Edition — November 2018
5 4 3 2 1

Front cover photo: Linh Ung Pagoda © Dana Filek-
 Gibson

Back cover photo: gold and red lacquer door at
 Hanoi's Temple of Literature © Dana Filek-Gibson

Printed in Canada by Friesens

Avalon Travel is a division of Hachette Book Group,
 Inc. Moon and the Moon logo are trademarks of
 Hachette Book Group, Inc. All other marks and
 logos depicted are the property of the original
 owners.